TABLE OF CONTENTS

THEORY

GLOBAL CITIZENSHIP EDUCATION

CONTEXTS OF EDUCATION

Series Editors:

Michael A. Peters
University of Illinois at Urbana-Champaign, USA

Scope:

Contexts of Education is a new series of handbooks that embraces both a creative approach to educational issues focused on context and a new publishing credo.

All educational concepts and issues have a home and belong to a context. This is the starting premise for this new series. One of the big intellectual breakthroughs of post-war science and philosophy was to emphasise the theory-ladenness of observations and facts – facts and observations cannot be established independent of a theoretical context. In other words, facts and observations are radically context-dependent. We cannot just see what we like or choose to see. In the same way, scholars argue that concepts and constructs also are relative to a context, whether this be a theory, schema, framework, perspective or network of beliefs. Background knowledge always intrudes; it is there, difficult to articulate, tacit and operates to shape and help form our perceptions. This is the central driving insight of a generation of thinkers from Ludwig Wittgenstein and Karl Popper to Thomas Kuhn and Jürgen Habermas. Increasingly, in social philosophy, hermeneutics, and literary criticism textualism has given way to contextualism, paving the way for the introduction of the notions of 'frameworks', 'paradigms' and 'networks' – concepts that emphasize a new ecology of thought.

This new series is predicated upon this insight and movement. It emphasises the importance of context in the establishment of educational facts and observations and the framing of educational hypotheses and theories. It also emphasises the relation between text and context, the discursive and the institution, the local and the global. Accordingly, it emphasizes the significance of contexts at all levels of inquiry: scientific contexts; theoretical contexts; political, social and economic contexts; local and global contexts; contexts for learning and teaching; and, cultural and interdisciplinary contexts.

Contexts of Education, as handbooks, are conceived as reference texts that also can serve as texts.

Global Citizenship Education

Philosophy, Theory and Pedagogy

Edited by

Michael A. Peters
University of Illinois at Urbana-Champaign, USA

Alan Britton
University of Glasgow, UK

and

Harry Blee
University of Glasgow, UK

SENSE PUBLISHERS
ROTTERDAM / TAIPEI

A C.I.P. record for this book is available from the Library of Congress.

ISBN 978-90-8790-373-2 (paperback)
ISBN 978-90-8790-374-9 (hardback)
ISBN 978-90-8790-375-6 (e-book)

Published by: Sense Publishers,
P.O. Box 21858, 3001 AW Rotterdam, The Netherlands
http://www.sensepublishers.com

Printed on acid-free paper

PEDAGOGY

FOREWORD

The University of Glasgow was established in 1451, and is the fourth oldest University in the UK. It has long been prominent as a crucible of ideas with a global impact, boasting alumni of such calibre as Adam Smith and Lord Kelvin, six Nobel Laureates, as well as many prominent UK and Scottish politicians, both historic and contemporary. The modern University of Glasgow is increasingly international in both its outlook and its population, and students, staff and alumni are making increasingly significant and positive contributions to the lives of people both at home and abroad.

It is in the context of these longstanding traditions of intellectual rigour, internationalisation, and service to others that I am delighted to commend this collection of contributions on the subject of Global Citizenship Education. The book has its origins in large part in the work of the Education for Global Citizenship Unit (EGCU), located within the Faculty of Education at the University of Glasgow. Academic staff from the Unit and wider Faculty are responsible for no less than 10 chapters of this edition. In addition, much of the editing work was conducted by the Director and Deputy Director of this innovative Unit, alongside a former Professor of Education in the Faculty. The University's strong tradition of international collaboration is also in evidence across the collection given the array of contributors from beyond the UK.

One of the Unit's core objectives over recent years, with the support of the UK Department for International Development (DFID), has been to enhance development awareness among teachers at all stages of their careers. A key means to promote this awareness is through research and the dissemination of fresh thinking relating to global issues and the corresponding role of education. The Unit has acted as a catalyst in this regard, bringing together a genuinely international spectrum of views on the interrelationships between globalisation, citizenship, identity and education. These relationships are often contested and sometimes controversial, however the University recognises and supports the importance of such debate and deliberation, and of the need to open and maintain dialogue between the different perspectives.

This collection makes a valuable and original contribution to this debate by presenting a set of challenges to policymakers, researchers, curriculum planners and teachers across the world. The different chapters combine contemporary critique with a view of the future often imbued with a palpable sense of urgency; these key global issues require to be addressed in all of our schools and by all educators (including Universities such as Glasgow). The truly global reach of the different chapters and contributors lends weight to the breadth of analysis, and reflects the value of international collaboration around themes such as these.

On behalf of the University of Glasgow I wish to congratulate the Editors and all contributors to this collection, and I hope that it achieves the international impact that it merits.

Sir Muir Russell
Principal and Vice-Chancellor
University of Glasgow

PREFACE AND ACKNOWLEDGEMENTS

Bringing together a collection of this scale has been a long haul and its concept and shape has changed over time. Its genesis is certainly in the Education for Global Citizenship Unit (EGCU) at the University of Glasgow. I was invited by Harry Blee to contribute a seminar or two to the EGCU's programme, supported by the United Kingdom Department for International Development (DFID) and aimed at teachers, teacher educators and teachers in training. At that point I thought that global citizenship was a contradiction in terms and that citizenship was a characteristic that could be ascribed only by the nation-state to its members bounded by a territory and a set of laws. In the same period in 2001 I was trying to write material on terrorism in relation to questions of education and globalisation that became the collection *Education, Globalization and the State in the Age of Terrorism* (2004). Indeed, the chapter I contributed to the collection 'War as Globalization: The "Education" of the Iraqi People' I first gave as a seminar in the EGCU series in 2003.

It is fair to say that the Unit and its activities had a profound influence on me; forcing me to rethink the notion of global citizenship and as a result leading to a sea-change in my ideas. I no longer thought about citizenship purely in terms of the nation-state, and I came to believe that the promise of global civil society depended upon an active global citizenship education programme. This would not be a 'shallow' syllabus that considered notions of 'citizen', 'citizenship', 'nation', 'state' etc. and their reconfiguration within the context of globalisation but instead, and more importantly, raised awareness and embarked on a political education of many issues facing the world community; adopting an action-orientation and intelligent advocacy toward issues of poverty, war, hunger, inequality, the spread of disease, ecological disasters, and, in particular, the exploitation and abuse of children. In short, I received a political reorientation in the company of colleagues in the Faculty of Education at the University of Glasgow and through dialogue and discussion with colleagues, teachers and students. I now no longer think of global citizenship as an oxymoronic term but rather think of it as a component of the imaginary of global civil society, and a natural complement to global studies in education that has the aim not just of human rights education but rather an active political agenda and the greater sensitisation toward global cultural exchange and questions of internationalisation.

Remarkably, today it is the case that people interconnected by any means but especially critical mass communication through the facility of the Internet and the World Wide Web now constitute a threshold for the emergence of a myriad of global civil spaces that already comprise a densely woven global civil society (albeit still in its infancy). The prospect of greater North/South dialogue and joint education projects based around the concept of global citizenship holds the best of the Enlightenment promises – education for all, greater scientific and pedagogical conversation and communication, the spread of freedom through access to knowledge and information, and political action in the face of social injustice.

In respect of my five years in the then newly created Faculty of Education at the University of Glasgow and the Education for Global Citizenship Unit I wish to personally record my thanks to some colleagues in Scotland: Harry Blee, Bob Davis, Jim Conroy, Cathy Fagan, Robert Docherty, John Dakers, Christine Forde, Alan Britton, Frank O'Hagan, and many others.

My co-editors Harry Blee and Alan Britton also wish to acknowledge and thank some of the individuals and groups associated with the Education for Global Citizenship Unit at the University of Glasgow. First and foremost, they would like to thank Jacqueline Doogan and Jacqueline Jackson who have provided outstanding administrative and organisational support and expertise throughout the lifetime of the Unit and its associated projects and programmes. Both have also played pivotal roles in the organisation of this book, processing and formatting the various chapters and maintaining a close eye on deadlines. Faculty colleagues Stephen McKinney and Frank O'Hagan kindly assisted with document checking and proof-reading, and Jon Lewin from the SCRE Centre provided further immensely valuable support in this regard. However responsibility for any errors within the text lies with the Editors.

Harry and Alan would also like to acknowledge the role of the International Development Education Association in Scotland (IDEAS), an umbrella organisation of NGOs with an interest in global and development issues, which was a key partner in the first three years of the DFID-funded project, and provided an external perspective that enhanced greatly the philosophy, scope and impact of this work. Alan would also like to thank Karen and Catriona for inspiration.

While most of the chapters in this book are original, several are adapted from previously published material, and the editors are grateful for the permissions granted to facilitate this:

James A Banks' chapter appeared originally as an article in the *Journal of Teacher Education*, January/February, 2001, 52(1), 5–16. Barbara Cruikshank's chapter originated as 'Revolutions within: Self-government and self-esteem,' *Economy and Society*, 22:3 (August 1993): 327–344. Michael A Peters' chapter appeared in P. Hayden & C. el-Ojeili (Eds.), *Confronting globalization: Humanity, justice and the renewal of politics*. New York: Palgrave, 2006. The chapter by Penny Enslin and Mary Tjiattas, 'Cosmopolitan justice: Education and global citizenship', originally appeared in *Theoria: A Journal of Social and Political Theory*, 104, 2004, and is republished by kind permission of Berghahn Books.

Michael A. Peters
University of Illinois at Urbana-Champaign, September 4, 2007

Harry Blee & Alan Britton
University of Glasgow, September 5, 2007

NOTES ON CONTRIBUTORS

Ali A. Abdi is Professor of Education and International Development in the Department of Educational Policy Studies at the University of Alberta. He is President of *Comparative and International Education Society of Canada* (CIESC) (2007-2009), and Co-Director, *Global Education Network* (University of Alberta), He is the author of *Culture, education and development in South Africa: Historical and contemporary perspectives* (2002*)*; co-author (with Ratna Ghosh) of *Education and the politics of difference* (2004); and co-editor of *Issues in Africa education: sociological perspectives* (2005); *African education and globalization: Critical perspectives* (2006), and *Educating for human rights and global citizenship* (forthcoming from SUNY Press).

Evelyn Arizpe has lectured in children's literature at the Universities of Cambridge and Glasgow, and published widely on UK, Central American and European writing for children. She has particular interests in how teachers can engage them in visual literacy through their responses to picture books, and is currently developing a cross-cultural project involving schools in England, Scotland, Spain and Australia.

James A. Banks is the Kerry and Linda Killinger Professor of Diversity Studies and Director of the Center for Multicultural Education at the University of Washington, Seattle. Professor Banks has pursued questions related to education, racial inequality, and social justice in more than 100 journal articles and 20 books. His books include *Teaching strategies for ethnic studies* (8th edition), *Educating citizens in a multicultural society* (2nd edition), *Diversity and citizenship education: Global perspectives*, and *Race, culture, and education: The selected works of James A. Banks*. He is the editor of the *Handbook of research on multicultural education* (2nd edition), and the forthcoming *Routledge international companion to multicultural education*.

Professor Bruce Carrington took up his present post as Professor and Head of the Department of Educational Studies at the University of Glasgow in August 2006. Prior to this, he was Deputy Head of the School of Education, Communication and Language Sciences at Newcastle University, where he held a Personal Chair in Education. He has an enduring interest in issues relating to ethnicity, gender and education and has published widely in this area. His most recent research in English primary schools, with Christine Skelton, Becky Francis, Merryn Hutchings, Barbara Reid and Ian Hall, examines the influence of the teacher's gender on the academic motivation and engagement of 7 to 8 year olds.

Professor Conroy currently holds the position of Professor and Dean of the Faculty of Education, University of Glasgow. He has served on the boards of a number of national and international education and academic bodies. He is currently Adjunct

Professor at Fordham University, USA, and has held visiting positions in various universities. Professor Conroy has a long-standing interest in children's welfare, philosophy and cultural change, moral education, citizenship and liberal democracy as well as the place of religion in late industrial politics. He has conducted research and development work in these areas as well as in that of child protection.

Barbara Cruikshank is Associate Professor of political theory at the University of Massachusetts, Amherst. She is the author of *The will to empower: Democratic citizens and other subjects*, as well as essays on Machiavelli, Tocqueville, Cultural Politics, among others. She is currently at work on a book titled *Neopolitics on changes and adaptations of what counts as politics*.

Robert A. Davis is Head of Department of Religious Education at the University of Glasgow. He has taught, written and broadcast widely on religion, literature, music, folklore, education and childhood studies. He has edited two volumes in the Carcanet Collected Works of Robert Graves and is currently engaged on a new intellectual biography of the radical educationalist Robert Owen, for Continuum Press. He has held visiting posts in Dublin, Helsinki and Malmo.

Doret De Ruyter is Professor in Philosophy and History of Education in the Department of Theory and Research in Education at the Faculty of Psychology and Education at the VU University. Before her return to the VU, she worked at the University of Glasgow in the Faculty of Education. Her main research interests are ideals in education, human flourishing and happiness, children's rights and parental duties.

Penny Enslin is a Professor in the Department of Educational Studies at the University of Glasgow. She teaches philosophy of education and her research interests lie in the area of political philosophy and education. She has published widely on citizenship and democracy education, gender and the education of girls, higher education, peace education, nationalism, and liberalism.

Christine Forde is a Professor of Education in the Faculty of Education at Glasgow University. She teaches in the areas of school leadership, professional learning and reflection and has been part of the national development programme for the Scottish Qualification for Headship, a national preparatory programme for aspiring headteachers in Scotland. Her research interests are firstly in the area of professional learning and development and she has written a number of books and articles in this area including a recently co-authored book *Professional development, reflection and enquiry* (Forde, McMahon, McPhee and Patrick, 2006). She also has an interest in gender, education and utopian thinking, having recently completing a book *Feminism and education: Educating for the good society* (2007) for Sense Publishers and an edited collection *Tackling gender inequality raising pupil achievement* (2007, Edinburgh UP).

Muna Golmohamad is a doctoral student at the Institute of Education, University of London. She has had a long standing interest in Education and Philosophy of Education, both personally and professionally. Initially trained as a teacher of English and Drama in Secondary Education in England and later became a Visiting Lecturer on the BA programme for Education Studies, at Roehampton University, London. She is also a visiting lecturer at the College for International Citizenship in Birmingham, England, where she has helped to develop and implement a programme of study for Citizenship and Education. She has also presented in numerous international conferences and seminars recently publishing 'World citizenship, identity and the notion of an integrated self', in *Studies in Philosophy and Education*, Volume 23, Numbers 2-3:131-148. Broadly speaking, her doctoral thesis is concerned with a philosophical examination of the notion of World/Global Citizenship, the dynamics of relationships fostered and some possible implications for Education.

Ilan Gur-Ze'ev is a Professor in the Faculty of Education, University of Haifa. His work has been translated into Polish, Flemish, English, Portuguese, Arabic and the Serbian language. Gur-Ze'ev is a philosopher in the critical tradition whose work attempts to offer a philosophical alternative beyond the modern-postmodern struggle. Among his recent books is *Beyond the modern-postmodern struggle in education: Toward counter-education and enduring improvisation* (2007, Sense).

Yvonne Hébert is Professor at Faculty of Education, University of Calgary. She is most interested in cultural issues and minority studies in education, dealing with youth, identity, democracy, diversity, values, policy and educational reform. Her current research projects focus on youth's negotiation of difference and democracy, a comparative study in three Canadian cities; conceptions of children and youth; and the impact of educational reform on teaching practices, school culture and achievement.

Hans Hooghoff is Head of the Department for Cross Curricular Topics at the National Institute for Curriculum Development in the Netherlands (SLO). Hans has considerable experience of educational development and civic education on an international stage. His own education is in law and sociology; he taught law and political science in schools of advanced study in the Netherlands before moving into the field of educational development. As well as being responsible for a variety of major national development programmes in Holland, Hans has held a number of international positions. He has been Chair of the International Assembly of the National Council for Social Studies, USA (1996-1998); Visiting Professor at the University of Nagoya, School of Education, Japan (1997-1998); Programme co-ordinator, board member, and chief executive officer of CIDREE, the Consortium of Institutions for Development and Research in Education in Europe (1989-2004); Adviser to the Education Department of Western Cape, South Africa, a role he continues to perform.

Walter Humes is Research Professor in Education and Associate Dean in the School of Education, University of Paisley, Scotland. He has previously held Professorships at the Universities of Strathclyde and Aberdeen. His publications include work on educational policy, teacher education, history of education and educational leadership. He is co-editor (with T.G.K. Bryce) of *Scottish education*, a 1000-page volume that covers all aspects of the Scottish educational system, from pre-school to higher education and lifelong learning.

Emery J. Hyslop-Margison is an Associate Professor and Canada Research Chair nominee in the Faculty of Education at the University of New Brunswick, Fredericton, Canada. He has held a Canada Research Chair at Concordia University in Montreal and was past Director of the Institute for Democratic Learning in Career Education. He has published extensively on how current neo-liberal policies threaten democratic learning.

James McGonigal is Professor of English in Education in the University of Glasgow. He has published on classroom interaction, teacher formation, literacy and knowledge about language, as well as on modernist poetry and cultural identity. He edits the SCROLL series (Scottish Cultural Review of Language and Literature) for Rodopi, and his poetry has won awards in Scotland and Ireland.

Stephen J. McKinney is Lecturer in Religious Education in the University of Glasgow. His research interests are immigrants and religious identity, faith schools and Catholic schools, and he has published on all of these topics. He is a member of the Education for Global Citizenship Unit in the University of Glasgow.

Ian Menter is Professor of Teacher Education, University of Glasgow. He is an experienced teacher, manager and researcher in education policy and teacher development. He started teaching in urban primary schools in Bristol in 1975. He moved into teacher education in 1984 at the College of St Paul and St Mary in Cheltenham. His research career started there but developed significantly during his nine years at the University of the West of England in Bristol. From 1996 until 2001 he was Head of the School of Education at the University of North London. He has recently completed research into aspects of teachers' work in England, funded by the Economic and Social Research Council. Since moving to Scotland in 2001, he has been looking at some Anglo-Scottish comparisons of teachers' work and initial teacher education and has been commissioned by the Scottish Executive Education Department to undertake two national projects. He is President of the Scottish Educational Research Association. Publications include co-authorship of *Work and identity in the primary school* (1997, Open University Press) and *Convergence or divergence? Initial teacher education in Scotland and England* (2006, Dunedin Academic Press) and also co-editorship of *The crisis in teacher supply* (2002, Trentham Books).

Stavros Moutsios is an Associate Professor in International Comparative Education Policy at the Danish School of Education (DPU), University of Aarhus, Department of Sociology of Education. He completed his PhD in Comparative Education at the Institute of Education-University of London, and before joining the DPU, he was a lecturer at the Aristotle University of Thessaloniki, Greece. His recent research interests focus on transnational forms of policy making in education.

Timothy Murphy is a Postdoctoral Researcher at the Centre for Excellence in Learning &Teaching at the National University of Ireland Galway, where he has previously worked for the Open Learning Centre and as a lecturer in Education. He holds a Doctorate in Education from Teachers' College (Columbia University) in New York. He has strong interests (and publications) in civic education, as well as academic staff development.

Francis J. O'Hagan is a lecturer in the Faculty of Education at the University of Glasgow. His research interests include: History, Education, Religion, Social Studies, Global Citizenship and Music. He has published articles on Teacher Education, History and Religion and a book on the work of the Religious Congregations in Glasgow during the period 1847-1918.

Mark Olssen is Professor of Political Theory and Education Policy in the Department of Political, International and Policy Studies, University of Surrey. His most recent book is *Michel Foucault: Materialism and education*, Paradigm Press, Boulder and London, published in May 2006. Also published recently, in 2004, a book with John Codd and Anne-Marie O'Neill of Massey University in New Zealand titled *Education policy: Globalisation, citizenship, democracy* (Sage, London); an edited volume *Culture and learning: Access and opportunity in the classroom* (IAP Press, New York); with Michael Peters and Colin Lankshear, *Critical theory and the human condition: Founders and praxis*, and from Rowman and Littlefield, New York, *Futures of critical theory: Dreams of difference,* also with Michael Peters and Colin Lankshear. He has published extensively in leading academic journals in Britain, America and in Australasia.

Dr Marianna Papastephanou has studied and researched in Cardiff, Wales and Berlin, Germany and taught at Cardiff University. She is currently teaching at the University of Cyprus, Department of Education, as an Assistant Professor in Philosophy of Education. She is the editor of *K.O. Apel: From a transcendental-semiotic point of view* (1998, Manchester University Press) and author of numerous articles on the Frankfurt school, political philosophy, postmodernism, and education from a continental-philosophical point of view.

Michael A. Peters is Professor of Education at the University of Illinois at Urbana-Champaign (US) and the University of Glasgow (UK). He won a first in Philosophy and completed a PhD in the philosophy of education, focusing on

Ludwig Wittgenstein, at the University of Auckland (NZ) where he was appointed to a personal chair in 2000 and held a joint position between Auckland and Glasgow. He writes at the intersection of fields in philosophy, education, policy and politics, with a strong interest in theories of postmodernity, knowledge and economy, and implications for education. He has written over 40 books and some 300 articles and chapters, including most recently *Showing and doing: Wittgenstein as pedagogical philosopher* (2007, Paradigm) (with Nick Burbules and Paul Smeyers), *Truth and subjectivity: Foucault, education and the culture of self* (2007, Peter Lang), *Why Foucault? New directions in educational research* (2007, Peter Lang), *Building knowledge cultures: Educational and development in the age of knowledge capitalism* (2006, Rowman & Littlefield), all with Tina (A.C.) Besley, and *Knowledge economy, development and the future of the university* (2007, Sense).

Thomas S. Popkewitz, Professor at the University of Wisconsin-Madison, studies the systems of reason that govern educational reforms and research in teaching, curriculum, and teacher education. His most recent book, *Cosmopolitanism and the age of reform* (Routledge) explores contemporary reforms in teaching, teacher education and the sciences of education as practices that generate principles of exclusion and inclusion. Currently, he is working collaboratively with colleagues in Europe, Latin America, and North America on a historical volume concerned with comparative visions in the development of schooling in the long 19th Century.

Julia Preece is Professor of Adult Education in the National University of Lesotho, Southern Africa. Prior to this she managed a research centre at the University of Glasgow, following four years in the University of Botswana. She has also worked in the Universities of Lancaster and Surrey. Before entering higher education Julia spent approximately 15 years in community development work in the inner city areas of Birmingham. She has published extensively on issues to do with lifelong learning, citizenship, gender and social exclusion. Recent publications include: two co-authored books: *Perceptions of citizenship responsibility amongst Botswana youth* (Lentswe La Lesedi) and *Research methods for adult educators in Africa* (Pearson Education) as well as a co-edited book *Adult education and poverty reduction* (Lentswe La Lesedi).

George Richardson is Associate Professor and Associate Dean (International initiatives) in the University of Alberta's Faculty of Education. His research interests include the role of education in national identity formation, citizenship education, multicultural and international education and action research. He is the editor of the journal *Canadian Social Studies*. Among his publications, he is author of *The death of the good Canadian: Teachers national identities and the social studies curriculum* (2002, Peter Lang) and co-editor (with Dr David Blades) of *Troubling the canon of citizenship education* (2006, Peter Lang).

Klas Roth is Associate Professor at Stockholm Institute of Education, Sweden. He is the author/editor of six books, one special issue in *Studies in Philosophy and Education* – 'Communication, identity and learning in an age of globalization', edited together with Staffan Selander (in press), and many journal articles and chapters. His most recent books include *Education in the era of globalization* (2007), edited together with Ilan Gur-Ze'ev, and *Changing notions of citizenship education in contemporary nation-states* (2007), edited together with Nicholas C. Burbules.

Alan Sears is Professor of Social Studies Education and a member of the Citizenship Education Research and Development Group at the University of New Brunswick in Canada. Dr. Sears has written extensively about social education in general and citizenship education in particular and is co-editor of the recent book, *Challenges and prospects in Canadian social studies* as well as co-author of *Neo-liberalism, globalization and human capital learning: Reclaiming education for democratic citizenship*. He has directed several national research projects on citizenship education in Canada and is currently principal investigator on a programme of work designed to map how children and young people understand key ideas related to citizenship.

George J. Sefa Dei is Professor, Department of Sociology and Equity Studies (SESE), Ontario Institute for Studies in Education of the University of Toronto. Between 1994 and 1999 he served as the First Director of the Centre for Integrative Anti-Racism Studies, OISE/UT. He is Ghanaian by birth. He has published extensively on issues of African Development, Minority Education, Indigenous Knowledges, Afrocentricity, and Anti-Colonial Thought. His books include: *Indigenous knowledge in global contexts: Multiple readings of our world*, edited with Budd Hall and D. Goldin Rosenberg (2000, University of Toronto Press); *Playing the race card: White power and privilege* (2004, Peter Lang), co-authored with Leeno and Nisha Karumanchery; *Schooling and education in Africa: The case of Ghana* (2004, Africa World Press); *Critical issues in anti-racist research methodologies* (2005, Peter Lang), co-edited with Gurpreet Singh Johal; *Anti-colonialism and education: The politics of resistance*, co-edited with Arlo Kempf (2006, Sense); *Schooling and difference in Africa: Democratic challenges in contemporary context*, co-authored with Alireza Asgharzadeh, Sharon Eblaghie-Bahador, and Riyad Shahjahan (2006, University of Toronto Press). His latest sole-authored book is *Racists beware* (2007, Sense). In July 2007, Professor Dei was enstooled as a Chief in Ghana under the stool name, Nana Sefa Atweneboah, Adumakwaahene of Asokore, Koforidua, in the New Juaben Traditional Area. Professor Dei has received numerous international awards and recognition for his academic and professional excellence, as well as community service. He has been invited on the lecture circuits in North America, Europe and Africa.

Robert Shaw is a Senior Lecturer in business analysis and ethics at the Open Polytechnic of New Zealand. He is also an elected member of the Porirua City

Council (NZ). His research relates to governance, business decision-making, and local government. At present Robert is a PhD student at the University of Auckland where his thesis is about Heidegger and Kant.

Ben Spiecker is Emeritus Professor in Philosophy and History of Education at the VU University. He has held a chair in the Department of Philosophy and History of Education at the Faculty of Psychology and Education for almost 30 years. His main research interests are moral education, civic education and sex education.

Mary Tjiattas is an Honorary Research Assistant in the Department of Philosophy at the University of the Witwatersrand, Johannesburg. Her main academic interests are in moral psychology, and social and political philosophy.

James Tully is the Distinguished Professor of Political Science, Law, Philosophy and Indigenous Governance at the University of Victoria, BC, Canada. He specialises in contemporary political theory and its history. His recent work includes: Another kind of Europe? *CRISPP* (2006), 'The imperialism of modern constitutional democracy', in *The paradox of constitutionalism*, ed. Loughlin and Walker (2007), and *Public philosophy in a new key* (forthcoming 2008).

Yusef Waghid is Professor of Philosophy of Education and Dean of the Faculty of Education at Stellenbosch University, South Africa. His research focuses on democratic citizenship education and he has published in many international peer reviewed journals.

Leonard J. Waks is Professor Emeritus of Educational Leadership and Policy Studies at Temple University. He received his PhD in philosophy from the University of Wisconsin in 1968 and has taught at Purdue, Stanford, Penn State and Temple. His research concentrates on the educational arrangements of global network society. Waks is the author of over one hundred scholarly articles and book chapters, and of the book *Technology's school* (1995, JAI).

MICHAEL A. PETERS, HARRY BLEE AND ALAN BRITTON

INTRODUCTION

Many Faces of Global Civil Society: Possible Futures for
Global Citizenship

The underlying political concepts of the notion of citizenship struck during the Enlightenment are in disarray as though they have melted under the constant sun of the combined and sometimes contradictory processes of globalisation, localisation and regionalisation. This collection of over thirty chapters brings together an international field of contributors who examine these concepts and processes in a fresh light, and provide a variety of perspectives and prescriptions that deserve to have a significant impact on national and transnational educational policy critique and policy making.

From Canada to South Africa, from Scotland to the Middle East, from Sweden to New Zealand, from the Netherlands to the United States; the contributions are both geographically and ideologically diverse. This is a reflection of the genuinely global current interest in issues of citizenship and globalisation, and how these can be addressed through education. Certain contributors locate the roots of some of these issues in 19th Century industrial and scholastic processes, or in the experiences of migrant communities in the Old and the New World, or arising from the impact of such migration on indigenous peoples. Fresh inspiration and insight is thus gained from historic contextualisation, while other chapters are resolutely contemporary, drawing on recent and ongoing political events and processes. A number of contested issues are addressed, including racism, migration, colonialisation, terrorism, neoliberalism, and citizenship itself. The recent resurgence in interest in the interplay between religion, religiosity and citizenship is also reflected in several chapters. While some chapters focus exclusively on the analysis of particular national or regional contexts, others make the case for a citizenship education that is truly global in its scope and organisation.

This introductory chapter provides an overview of some of the core concepts that will emerge and recur elsewhere in this collection. The editors begin by describing the way in which citizenship was framed by some of the key Enlightenment figures, and highlight some of the reasons that this conceptualisation has appeared less stable and resilient in recent times. Contemporary notions of cosmopolitanism and citizenship are compared and contrasted with their antecedents. Issues of international cooperation and conflict are considered, as well as some of the institutional and constitutional responses. The European Union is highlighted in particular, as it represents a complex

M.A. Peters, A. Britton and H. Blee (Eds.), Global Citizenship Education: Philosophy, Theory and Pedagogy, 1-13.

multinational laboratory for core ideas relating to the current and future status of the individual citizen, the nation state, civil society and the globalised knowledge economy (issues that are explored in a vast array of different contexts elsewhere in the collection). The editors conclude by pressing the case for effective and meaningful global citizenship education as a contribution towards the search for an elusive yet essential conception of global civic society.

THE ENLIGHTENMENT VIEW OF CITIZENSHIP

Traditionally, the concept of citizenship had a home in the bounded nation-state and referred to rights, privileges and responsibilities ascribed to people born or migrated to a territory with clear boundaries. In the history of political philosophy, for Hobbes, Locke and Rousseau the social contract is the means by which order and civil society is maintained: we agree to a social contract thereby gaining civil rights in return for subjecting ourselves to the law. Hobbes was the first of the moderns to articulate this conception in his *Leviathan* (1651) where he famously founded his theory on a hypothetical State of Nature where each of us would have natural and unlimited freedoms but there was an endless 'war of all against all'. Hobbes' theory is the basis for an account of legitimate government or sovereignty. Only by entering into a social contract does man, who for Hobbes has a basically egoistic and self-interested nature, subscribe to a society where war can be avoided and the peace maintained. John Locke's *Two Treatises on Government*, especially the second treatise, outlines his justification for civil government.

Rousseau developed a different theory that sought to provide an account of popular sovereignty as both indivisible and unalienable. His *The Social Contract or Principles of Political Right* (1762) famously begins 'Man is born free; and everywhere he is in chains. One thinks himself the master of others, and still remains a greater slave than they. How did this change come about? I do not know. What can make it legitimate? That question I think I can answer'. The Enlightenment *philosophers* argued that people became citizens by giving their consent to a legal and binding agreement concerning their rights and freedoms. This social contract was made in the name of the common good and collective security and people gave their consent it is argued because of enlightened self-interest based on the supposition that they have something to gain through the imposition of order and the rule of law. The actual political arrangements of course varied considerably from state to state as did the legal and philosophical justifications yet nothing can disguise the palpable state of affairs that the transition to civil society through the exercise of choice constitutes a social agreement which involves a moral commitment to a set of values and ethical norms that legislate and work for all members of a single moral community.

To talk of a single moral community is also immediately to invoke Kant and his account of cosmopolitanism, and to talk of cosmopolitanism is immediately to invoke a globally-oriented institution that aims at the cultivation of global citizens. Indeed, the root stock of the word first used in 1614 to mean 'citizen of the world' derives from the Greek *kosmopolites* (*kosmos* 'world', *polites*, meaning 'citizen', and *polis* meaning 'city') 'Cosmopolitanism' with a first recorded use in 1828 registers the idea that there is a *single moral community* based on the idea of freedom and thus in the early twenty-first century is also seen as a major theoretical buttress to the concept of universal human rights that transcend all national, cultural and State boundaries.

While the Greeks had a concept of 'cosmopolitanism' that issued from the Sophists against the form of political culture advocated by Plato and Aristotle which was wedded to the city and its citizens, and later took a Stoic form that was popular with early Christianity, its modern form emerged with the Enlightenment and was associated first with Erasmus' humanism and with the development of natural law doctrine. Pauline Kleingeld (2006) argues:

> The historical context of the philosophical resurgence of cosmopolitanism during the Enlightenment is made up of many factors: The increasing rise of capitalism and world-wide trade and its theoretical reflections; the reality of ever expanding empires whose reach extended across the globe; the voyages around the world and the anthropological so-called 'discoveries' facilitated through these; the renewed interest in Hellenistic philosophy; and the emergence of a notion of human rights and a philosophical focus on human reason (http://plato.stanford.edu/entries/cosmopolitanism/).

She goes on to document the way in which the impulse of cosmopolitanism was strongest in the late eighteenth century both feeding and growing out of the 1789 declaration of human rights. While Montesquieu, Voltaire, Diderot, Addison, Hume and Jefferson all saw themselves as cosmopolitans, it was Kant who defended and popularised the idea that human beings belong to a single moral community sharing the characteristics of freedom, equality and autonomy that grounded the concept and legitimacy of law. Philosophical cosmopolitanism therefore had a parallel in political cosmopolitanism based on a concept of law that applied to all States.

Thus, famously, Kant in *Perpetual Peace* (1795) argues for a concept of moral cosmopolitanism based on universal law to which States would consent even though he rejected a strong notion of world government in favour of a loose federation. In Section II of Perpetual Peace he adumbrates the principles – 'three definitive articles' – that are required to establish peace (against the natural state of war) beginning with the republican civic constitution, a federation of free States, and the law of world citizenship is said to be limited to conditions of 'universal hospitality' where 'Hospitality means the right of a stranger not to be treated as an enemy when he arrives in the land of another.'

Besides moral and political (or legal) cosmopolitanism there is also a form of economic cosmopolitanism associated with the work of Adam Smith who sought to diminish the role of politics in the economic realm. Said to date from Quesnay the notion of economic cosmopolitanism was promoted strongly in the twentieth century by Friedrich Hayek and Milton Friedman, and taken up in a particular form of neo-liberalism that now characterises the World Trade Organization.

In contemporary discourse cosmopolitanism is often referred to under the term globalisation and includes economic (neoliberal) cosmopolitanism, political cosmopolitanism and cosmopolitan law, based on moral universalism. For all three accounts as Thomas Pogge notes, there is, first, an assumption of *individualism* – the unit of analysis is the individual rather than the State or some other entity; second, the assumption of *universality*. Thomas Pogge (2002: 169) writes,

> Three elements are shared by all cosmopolitan positions. First, *individualism*: the ultimate units of concern are human beings, or persons. … Second, *universality*: the status of ultimate unit of concern attaches to every living being equally …. Third, *generality*: this special status has global force.

We can therefore distinguish three forms of contemporary cosmopolitanism: Kantian moral cosmopolitanism represented by the discourse of human rights and, perhaps, institutionally by the United Nations; Kantian political cosmopolitanism represented by the likes of Habermas, Rawls, Beitz, Pogge; cosmopolitan democracy, argued for by Held; and economic cosmopolitanism currently best exemplified by a form of neo-liberal 'free-trade'. The first might also be further extended by certain cosmopolitan institutions such as the International Criminal Court that seeks to develop a concept of the individual in international law that is not absolutely subject to the State.

It is clear from the preamble provided thus far that considerations of cosmopolitanism and the notion of global citizenship are nothing new, having exercised a broad range of political, economic and social thinkers over a long period in time. However it is the Editors' view that the particular perspectives gathered in this collection are most timely because these concerns have been thrown into sharper and more urgent relief by a number of recent events, movements and processes. In the next section, we highlight certain contemporary political and economic movements, notably the ongoing enlargement and 'deepening' of the European Union (EU), the EU's relationship with the United States, and the interface between globalisation and terrorism, that we argue require a response from educators across the globe.

EUROPE'S MORAL AND POLITICAL VISION OF GLOBALISATION

The Laeken Declaration on the Future of the European Union pictured the Union standing at a crossroads – 'a defining moment of its existence' – on the one hand it was about to expand to bring in ten new Member States and, on the other, it faced two democratic challenges, one internal, the other external. The first concerns the challenge of developing a set of European institutions for the citizens of Europe, of creating a closer and more transparent relationship between the Union and its citizens – in short, better democratic governance and an assault on the 'democratic deficit'. The second concerns Europe's new role in a globalised world. As the Declaration expresses this new imperative:

Following the fall of the Berlin Wall, it looked briefly as though we would for a long while be living in a stable world order, free from conflict, founded upon human rights ... The eleventh of September has brought about a rude awakening. The opposing forces have not gone away: religious fanaticism, ethnic nationalism, racism and terrorism are on the increase, and regional conflicts, poverty and underdevelopment still provide a constant seedbed for them.

What is Europe's new role in this changed world? Does Europe not, now that it is finally unified, have a leading role to play in a new world order, that of a power able both to play a stabilising role worldwide and to point the way ahead for many countries and peoples? ... Now that the Cold War is over and we are living in a globalised, yet also highly fragmented world, Europe needs to shoulder its responsibilities in the governance of globalisation.

By 'the governance of globalisation' the Declaration means 'to set globalisation within a moral framework ... to anchor it in solidarity and sustainable development.' The Laeken Declaration indicates that, in part, is was drafted in response to public calls for a greater EU role in justice and security – not only action against cross-border crime, control of immigration and reception of asylum seekers but also action in the field of employment, combating poverty and social exclusion, and promoting greater economic and social cohesion. Clearly, there is a strong role for the Union to promote and coordinate action in all transnational issues as well as tackling broader and more sensitive issues in a common approach to foreign affairs, security and defence.

At the same time the Declaration makes clear that the Future of Europe must respond to calls for better and more transparent, more efficient government to be enhanced through a better division and definition of competence between the Union and Member States. In particular, greater clarification is required of exclusive (Union) competence, competence by Member States and that which is shared. These questions and the reorganisation of competence are crucial for issues of foreign policy and defence. They also go to the heart of fears of a super state and the encroachment upon exclusive areas of competence by states. In addition, the declaration raised questions about the Union's instruments and the democratic legitimacy and transparency of the Union's institutions, particularly the Commission, the Parliament and the Council. The Declaration ends on a note concerning the proposed Constitution for European citizens and the reorganisation of the four Treaties on which the Union is based.

MULTIPLE CITIZENSHIP: EUROPE'S FAILED CONSTITUTION

Our Constitution is called a democracy because power is in the hands not of a minority but of the whole people. Thucydides II, 37 (Opening quotation of the draft constitution)

The draft constitution already amended and revised by 105-member forum even if it failed the ratification process nonetheless represents an astonishing achievement. In one sense it is the attempted realisation of a dream of a unified Europe first raised by Winston Churchill in 1946. European Union has come into existence through a deliberative process of progressive change toward the constitutional ideal enabled by a series of treaties beginning with the establishment of a coal and steel community in 1958.

The failed draft constitution comprising of four parts – its definition, objectives and institutions, its fundamental rights and citizenship, its competencies and actions, its policies and functioning of the Union – is the culmination of historical process that asserts a moral and political vision, now carried forward by means of a treaty. For that reason it is worthy of examination as a prototype of what is to come, what is inevitable in some form or other. The Preamble begins by stressing the significance of its humanist inheritance embodied in its early Greek and Roman origins, its (Christian) 'spiritual impulse,' and the philosophy of the Enlightenment centred on the human person and his or her inviolable and inalienable rights:

> Conscious that Europe is a continent that has brought forth civilisation; that its inhabitants, arriving in successive waves since the first ages of mankind, have gradually developed the values underlying humanism: equality of person, freedom respect for reason

It continues by emphasising that a reunited Europe intends to continue along 'this path of civilisation, progress and prosperity' – a path characterised by concern for all its inhabitants, for the value of openness to culture and learning, for the deepening of democratic public life, and for 'peace, justice and solidarity.'

The governance of globalisation and the cultural mandate for Europe's role is seen to derive from its humanistic legacy and the extent to which the constitution embodies Europe's humanistic legacy can be judged by the centrality of the Charter of Fundamental Rights. It is noteworthy that education and citizens' rights – and their interdependency – are prominent in the Charter of the EU, which contains in Article 14, 'Rights to education' specified in three related clauses:

- Everyone has the right to education and to have access to vocational and continuing training.
- This right includes the possibility to receive free compulsory education.
- The freedom to found educational establishments with due respect for democratic principles and the rights of parents to ensure the education and teaching of their children in conformity with their religious, philosophical and pedagogical convictions shall be respected, in accordance with the national laws governing the exercise of such freedom and right.

It could be argued that the notion of citizenship education might contain both the passive neoliberal State versions often defined in terms of consumer sovereignty (in line with neoliberal welfare consumer regimes) and the more progressive social democratic EU version. Certainly there is a pressing need in the UK for a notion of citizenship education that is more sensitive to EU institutions (the Parliament, Council, Commission, and Court of Justice) and fundamental rights.

THE LEARNING CITIZEN IN EUROPEAN DEMOCRACY

It is now some years since the Lisbon European Council set the 'bold and ambitious' ten-year goal of making the EU the most dynamic, competitive, sustainable knowledge-based economy in the world. Crucial to this policy rhetoric is a series of recent related concepts that cluster around the old dualisms between economy and society, knowledge and information-knowledge economy/knowledge society; and the learning economy/learning society. Yet it is clear that policy areas overlap and that indeed that there is a radical interpenetration of social and economic policy. Perhaps, the fundamental understanding for policy makers in the 'post-modern condition' is the way the old dualisms obfuscate a conceptual appreciation of the imperatives of structural reform. Attention in the European Council has recently focused on three areas: active labour market reforms; liberalisation of financial markets; and increased investment in knowledge to ensure future competitiveness and jobs. Of course, these three policy areas are related and overlap somewhat. The Council is looking to overcome existing barriers to flexible labour markets by encouraging multi-lingualism, the development of appropriate ICT skills, provision of better child care and rewards for those who work longer. Its approach to financial liberalisation is focused in part on providing the right regulatory environment, while there is also a strong impetus to roll out fast broadband telecom networks and to step up support for research, innovation, education and training.

A staff paper (*European Report* Jan 16, 2002) suggested that the EU lags behind on lifelong learning and that the transition to the knowledge-based economy must be speeded up. In other words, spending on education needs to be strengthened. The argument is made that the European ability to produce, diffuse and use knowledge effectively relies heavily on its capacity to produce highly educated people for its firms to be engaged in a continuing process of innovation. Yet the paper notes that lifelong learning is still not a reality for most citizens. Average public spending on education in the European Union as a percentage of GDP remained unchanged at 5% between 1999 and 2000 and overall level of public and private spending on research and development is still too low. The paper complains that the EU is suffering a competitive disadvantage because EU businesses, governments and citizens have not yet embraced new technologies, the Internet and electronic commerce as readily as in the United States. There is some empirical evidence to support this view for while up-take of ICTs is increasing it has not yet been reflected in productivity gains or the reshaping of business practices.

In the Lisbon Council the transition to the knowledge-based economy has been taken up in a range of related research project designed to investigate and enhance Europe's case. A number of these projects are focused on the notion of 'the learning citizen', a concept that is a happy combination of words with considerable normative and illocutionary force directly at the building a European democracy where learning is advanced as a fundamental human right. Exactly how this right ought to be construed is not straightforward because both underlying concepts of 'learning' and 'citizen' are contestable and require active interpretation.

7

US VS EU CONSTITUTION

It is useful and important to compare the ethos of EU Constitution with that of the US Constitution (and their current interpretations) even although the Philadelphia Convention was produced two centuries ago. Both the EU Constitution and the Laeken Declaration offer a different perspective to the US Constitution and foreign policy outlook. Where the latter is based on negative rights the former is based on a conception of positive rights. The difference could not be more marked. American constitutional rights were originally designed to protect Americans from infringements upon their life, liberty and property. The language of the Constitution carefully limits the powers of the government and the division of powers between governments and the general rights of the governed. By contrast, the EU Constitution is based upon positive rights with reference to 'social justice,' 'solidarity,' 'equal opportunity,' 'equality between the sexes' and 'cultural diversity.' Further, it claims to desire 'sustainable development,' 'mutual respect between peoples,' and the eradication of poverty, with accordingly less emphasis on property rights and free enterprise. At the broader level, this difference signals not only different constitutional outlooks but also diverging political cultures: a neoliberal US favouring corporate America, a 'defensive modernism,' and the doctrine of 'pre-emptive strike' and 'regime change' versus a social democratic model focused on 'social justice' and 'solidarity,' and committed to governance of globalisation within a moral framework.

The Global Citizenship agenda might begin to tackle some questions of comparative analysis and also entertain the question in international law of the emergence since the second world war of the geopolitic concepts of 'war crimes', 'crimes against humanity' and 'crimes against the peace' (see e.g., Peters, 2004).

DECONSTRUCTING THE WEST?

The concept of 'the West' has served important political purposes both historically and in the present foreign policy context. On the one hand it has been a cultural and philosophical unity achieved through an active historical projection back to the origins of Western civilisation, at least to the classical Greeks, while on the other, it has been used as a modernist category, politically speaking, to harness the resources of Enlightenment Europe as a basis for giving assurances about the future of liberal democratic societies and the American way of life. The concept was an implicit but key one assumed in an influential analysis of new world order by Samuel Huntington (2002), who in his *The Clash of Civilizations* predicted a non-ideological world determined increasingly by the clash among the major civilisations. In Huntington's analysis 'the West' functions as an unquestioned and foundational unity yet the concept and its sense of cultural and historical unity has recently been questioned not only in terms of its historical fabrication but also in terms of its future continuance. Martin Bernal (1991, 2001), for instance, controversially in *Black Athena* and in a set of responses to his critics, questions the historical foundations of 'the West' demonstrating how the concept is a recent fiction constructed out of the Aryan myth propagated by nineteenth-century historiography. Even more recently, accounts of the so-called 'new world order' have emphasized either the dominance of an American hegemonic Empire (Hardt and Negri, 2000) or an emerging EU post-modern state system (Cooper, 2001). These accounts offer competing and influential conceptions of the 'new imperialism' based on different visions of world government and proto-world institutions. They give very different accounts of questions of international security, world order and the evolving world system of states.

Most recently, and under the impact of a set of events tied to the experience of the war prosecuted against Iraq, Robert Kagan (2003) has questioned whether Europeans and Americans still share a common view of the world and charts the divergence of these two perspectives on the question of power – its efficacy, morality and desirability. Robert Kagan is senior associate at the Carnegie Endowment for International Peace, and a columnist for the Washington Post. He served in the US State Department from 1984 to 1988. A neo-conservative himself, Kagan has written on the US foreign policy in Nicaragua and edited a collection with William Kristol on present dangers facing American foreign policy and defence. *Of Passion and Power* is an expansion of an essay that original appeared in Policy Review. Kagan's thesis can be summed up briefly in his own words:

> Europe is turning away from power, or to put it a little differently, it is moving beyond power into a self-contained world of laws and rules and transnational negotiation and cooperation. It is entering a post-historical paradise of peace and relative prosperity, the realization of Immanuel Kant's 'perpetual peace'. Meanwhile, the United States remains mired in history, exercising power in an anarchic Hobbesian world where international laws and rules are unreliable, and where true security and the defence and promotion of a liberal order still depend on the possession and use of military might (p. 3).

He suggests that this state of affairs is not simply the product of the Bush presidency or an administration dominated by neo-conservatives but rather that the differences are long-lived and likely to endure. Europe and American no longer share a common 'strategic culture'. As he depicts the differences, 'Americans generally see the world divided between good and evil, between friends and enemies …' They favour coercion over persuasion, 'seek finality in international affairs' (p. 4), tending towards unilateralism. They are less inclined to act through the United Nations or other international institutions and more sceptical of international law. By contrast, Europeans 'see a more complex picture'. They are both more tolerant of failure and more patient, preferring peaceful solutions, 'negotiation, diplomacy, and persuasion to coercion' (p. 5).

Global Citizenship needs to be critically self-aware that all the traditional assumptions governing our situated world-views ought to be continually open to change, sometimes quite radically and unexpectedly, as when the Berlin Wall came down or the Soviet system collapsed. By contrast we seem to be confronted with ample evidence of the predicted future dominance of the world system by China and India, yet a coherent educational response to this future probability has barely begun to emerge.

EDUCATION FOR CITIZENSHIP IN THE AGE OF TERRORISM

In global citizenship education we might investigate the following assertions: that war and globalisation go hand in hand; that contemporary globalisation *is* a form of war (and war may be a form of globalisation); that militarisation and war are integral parts of the neo-liberal agenda; and that there are inextricable links between the US military-industrial complex, the free market, and world order. We might also encourage the investigation of these claims within the context of the war in Iraq and provide some background to questions concerning a civilizational analysis of globalisation that contextualises the US National Security Strategy and the neo-conservative influence in the White House. Is there a role for education in understanding the relationship between war and globalisation? Educationally speaking, we would argue that we need to understand this specific event – the war against Iraq – in terms of an emerging global politics.

The geopolitical consequences of empire, of past administrative division and colonial policies, are always hard to predict and even harder to deal with. 'Blowback' is also a reality that must be contemplated as an inevitable accompaniment to contemporary political decisions that involve regime change. Arguably, the extremist Islamic terrorist attacks on civil society in the West have their origin not only in the formation of extremist Islamic terrorist networks in the last twenty years, but also perhaps more profoundly in British and U.S. intervention and ongoing struggle for control of oil stakes in the Middle East, notably Iraq and Saudi Arabia, dating back at least to the 1920s. If Samuel Huntington is to be believed this is representative of an even greater historical legacy of Christian-Islamic relations now centuries old.

The growth of global civil society is linked to the history of colonialism and imperialism and yet there is something still of great importance about the cosmopolitan sentiments offered by the Enlightenment thinkers that led first to the League of Nations and, then, the United Nations, UNESCO and other institutional defenders of the concept of fundamental human rights. While this is a contested history and one imbricated in the recent history of colonialism and post-colonialism it is also a history of the growth and development of liberal democracy as the world's most rapidly growing and dominant form of government. The problem is that at the level beyond the individual state there is little in the way of structures and templates for world governance to which individual citizens have access or redress. There are only those organisations set up at Bretton Woods that provided the architecture for the West during the Cold War. Since the rapid decolonisation that took place before and after WWII we have seen the development of a number of newly independent states, many of which gained nominal political independence but continued the colonial economic legacy of exploitation and control.

Today we have passed into an era that is best symbolised by the significance of regional trading blocs and attempts at regional governance with the huge growth also of NGOs and other global agencies that transcend national boundaries. On the one hand, there is the economic organisation of the truly stateless multi- and transnational corporation, now sometimes referred to as the 'globally integrated enterprise', and, on the other, the development of regional forms of governance like the EU that through twin processes of integration and enlargement, is creating a 'new Europe' based on an alternative vision of globalisation to the hegemonic power and world dominance of a sole superpower. There are signs that the prospects for EU regional governance, despite the recent setback to the ratification process of the constitution, will not only continue to mature but will also be emulated by other regions such as East Asia. This is not to argue that politics necessarily follows economics.

With the dominance of a sole world superpower there have been criticisms of both the UN and Bretton Woods institutions such as the WTO and the World Bank as being essentially Ameri-centric, reflecting American interests and open to American manipulation. The United Nations stands in need of reform, especially given the rise of Asian states like China and India but also the remarkable growth of Japanese economy and economic power. The question of reform is difficult as is the notion of one vote per country especially given the huge differences in population between, say, China or India or Indonesia and small island states like Samoa or Fiji. Some talk of a new era of 'Continental politics'.

Further, since the end of the Cold War, oil politics and the rise of militant Islam or Islamism has seemingly taken over as the new territorial paradigm in international politics with forms of Muslim international solidarity across national borders and in terms of anti-American and anti-Israeli radical movements, as well as new regional groups both within and outside the Middle East. The identification of radical Islam as essentially terrorist and George Bush's 'war against terror' has initiated a new era of international politics that has greatly damaged relations between the West and the Muslim world and apparently mitigated against the enhancement of prospects for both the growth of international security of movement and global civil society. The war in Iraq has also introduced splits in the Western alliance and encouraged a new level of American aggression with the neoconservative intention of acting alone, with or without its allies, and with or without UN approval.

Global citizenship education realistically must be set against these contemporary realities. As a form of education it must actively engage with these very issues. In one sense global citizenship education also offers the prospect of extending both the ideologies of human rights and multiculturalism, perhaps, post-colonialism, in a critical and informed way. One thing is sure, as the essays presented in this book demonstrate so clearly, there can be no one dominant notion of global citizenship education as notions of 'global', 'citizenship' and 'education' are all contested and open to further argument and revision. Global citizenship education does not name the moment of global citizenship or even its emergence so much as the hope of a form of order where the rights of the individual and of groups, irrespective of race, gender, ethnicity or creed, are observed by all governments and become the basis of participation in new global spaces that we might be tempted to call global civil society. Indeed this very conception of cosmopolitanism or something close to it has recently been doing the rounds in legal philosophy by scholars such as David Held (2003) and Norberto Bobbio who argue that given globalization and its uncontrollable economic processes the world requires a new form of cosmopolitan democracy that justifies a set of centralized institutions representing world citizens in facing economic and political problems that escape the control of the nation state, together with new administrative structures and legal rights called 'cosmopolitan rights'. Whether one agrees with this conception of cosmopolitan democracy or not it certainly provides a platform for education and for the discussion and debate surrounding a long standing idea in political theory that has quite staggering implications for the design and conduct of education in an age of globalization.

ORGANISATION OF THIS BOOK

The book is designed to contribute to an integrated understanding of the philosophy, theory and pedagogy of Global Citizenship Education. A number of chapters provide critical definitional and analytical foundations; these examine the different and contested interpretations of what is meant by such terms as 'global citizenship', 'globalisation', 'cosmopolitanism' and 'citizenship education'. Other contributions seek to situate these concepts within educational processes and philosophical lineages, as well as examining the rationale for a global educational project based on these ideas. This collection also brings together a range of national and geographical case studies that demonstrate and critically interrogate some of the policy and curriculum structures that have been deployed to develop education for global citizenship in a large number of contexts. It is the Editors' hope that wherever the reader is based, s/he will be able to draw on the breadth of ideas and perspectives here in ways that can inform, challenge and inspire.

REFERENCES

Bernal, M. (1991). *Black Athena: The Afroasiatic roots of classical civilization*. London: Vintage Books. (Orig. 1987).

Bernal, M. (2001). *Black Athena writes back: Martin Bernal responds to his critics*. Durham & London: Duke University Press.

Bobbio, N. (1995). Democracy and the international system. In: Archibugi and Held (Eds.), *Cosmopolitan democracy. An agenda for a new world order*. Polity Press: Cambridge.

Cooper, R. (2000). *The postmodern state and the world order*. London: Demos, The Foreign Policy Centre. (Orig. 1996).

Cooper, R. (2002). The postmodern state. In: Mark Leonard (Ed.), *Re-ordering the world: The long-term implications of September 11th*. London: Foreign Policy Centre, http://www.observer.co.uk/Print/0,3858,4388912,00.html.

Hardt, M. & Negri, A. (2001). *Empire*. Cambridge, MA: Harvard University Press.

Held, D. (2003). *Cosmopolitanism: A defence*. Cambridge: Polity Press.

Hobbs, T. (1651) *Leviathan*. At http://www.infidels.org/library/historical/thomas_hobbes/leviathan.html (accessed 3 Sept. 2007).

Huntington, S. (2002). *The clash of civilizations and the remaking of world order*. New York: Simon & Schuster.

Kagan, R. (2003). *Of passion and power: America and Europe in the new world order*. New York: Alfred A. Knopf.

Kant (1795). *Perpetual peace*. At http://www.mtholyoke.edu/acad/intrel/kant/kant1.htm (accessed 3 Sept. 2007).

Kleingeld, P. (2006). *Cosmopolitanism. The Stanford Encyclopedia of Philosophy* (Winter 2003 Edition), Edward N. Zalta (Ed.), http://plato.stanford.edu/entries/cosmopolitanism/ (accessed 3 Sept. 2007).

Locke, J. *Two treatises on government*. At http://lonang.com/exlibris/locke/ (accessed 3 Sept. 2007).

Peters, M.A. (Ed.) (2005). *Education, globalization, and the state in the age of terrorism*. Boulder, CO: Paradigm Publishers.

Pogge, T. (2002). *World poverty and human rights*. Cambridge: Polity Press.

Rousseau, J.-J. (1762). *The social contract or principles of political right*. At http://www.constitution.org/jjr/socon.htm (accessed 3 Sept. 2007).

The Laeken declaration on the future of the European Union. At http://www.euconvention.be/static/ LaekenDeclaration.asp (accessed 3 Sept. 2007).

JAMES TULLY

TWO MEANINGS OF GLOBAL CITIZENSHIP

Modern and Diverse

I. TWO CONTESTED WAYS OF THINKING ABOUT GLOBAL CITIZENSHIP

'Global citizenship' has emerged as the locus of struggles on the ground and of reflection and contestation in theory. This is scarcely surprising. Many of the central and most enduring struggles in the history of politics have taken place *in* and *over* the language of citizenship and the activities and institutions into which it is woven. One could say that the hopes, dreams, fears and xenophobia of centuries of individual and collective political actors are expressed in the overlapping and conflicting histories of the uses of the language of citizenship and the forms of life in which they have been employed. This motley ensemble of contested languages, activities and institutions constitutes the inherited *field* of citizenship today.

The language of 'global' and 'globalisation' and the activities, institutions and processes to which it refers and in which it is increasingly used, while more recent than citizenship, comprises a similarly central and contested domain. Globalisation has become a shared yet disputed vocabulary in terms of which rival interpretations of the ways humans and their habitats are governed globally are presented and disputed in both practice and theory. It thus constitutes a similarly contested *field* of globalisation.

When 'globalisation' and 'citizenship' are combined they not only bring their contested histories of meanings with them. They bring into being a complex new field that raises new questions and elicits new answers concerning the meaning of, and relationship between, global governance and global citizenship. When we enquire into global citizenship, therefore, we are already thrown into this remarkably complex inherited field of contested languages, activities, institutions, processes and the environs in which they take place. This conjoint field represents the problematisation of global citizenship: the way that formerly disparate activities, institutions and processes have been gathered together under the rubric of 'global citizenship', so becoming a site of contestation in practice and formulated as a problem in research, policy and theory, and to which diverse solutions are presented and debated.[1]

Among the many contested meanings of global citizenship I will focus on two. Many of the most important struggles around the globe today are *over* these two types and the struggles themselves consist in the enactment of these two modes of citizenship in two corresponding practices of global citizenship. They have been

M.A. Peters, A. Britton and H. Blee (Eds.), Global Citizenship Education: Philosophy, Theory and Pedagogy, 15–23.

interpreted in different ways under different names in a variety of activist and academic literature: for example, global citizenship from above *versus* global citizenship from below, low intensity *versus* high intensity global citizenship, representative *versus* direct, hegemonic *versus* counter-hegemonic, cosmopolitan *versus* place-based. I call these two families 'modern' and 'diverse' citizenship. I call modern citizenship in a modern state 'civil' citizenship and in a global context 'cosmopolitan' citizenship. The corresponding names of diverse citizenship are 'civic' and 'glocal'. 'Glocal' and 'glocalisation' in the diverse citizenship tradition refer to the global networking of local practices of civic citizenship in contrast to the use of 'global' and 'globalisation' in modern/cosmopolitan citizenship. I begin with a preliminary sketch of one aspect of the two meanings and practices of citizenship as a way of introducing them.

The most familiar aspect of modern citizenship is its role as the modular form of citizenship associated with the historical processes of modernisation/colonisation: (1) the modernisation of the West into modern nation states with representative governments, a system of international law, decolonisation of European empires, supranational regime formations and global civil society; and, in tandem, (2) the dependent modernisation and citizenisation of the non-West through colonisation, the Mandate System, post-decolonisation nation-building and global governance. The language of modern citizenship, in its civil and cosmopolitan forms, presents successive idealisations of this type of citizenship as the uniquely *universal* practice of citizenship for all human societies. This allegedly universal mode of citizenship is also presented as the product of *universal* historical processes or stages of development under successive discourses of progress – civilisation, modernisation, constitutionalisation, democratisation and now globalisation – that began in Europe and have been spread around the world by Euro-American expansion and continuing hegemony. These two features of modern citizenship – a universal modular form of citizenship conjoined with a universal set of historical processes that bring it to the non-West under Western tutelage – are articulated and debated in, respectively, modern normative theories of citizenship and social scientific theories of modernisation from the eighteenth-century to today.[2]

In contrast, diverse citizenship is associated with a multiplicity of different practices of citizenship in the West and the non-West. The language of diverse citizenship, both civic and glocal, presents citizenship as a singular or 'local' practice that takes countless *forms* in different locales. It is not described in terms of universal institutions and historical processes but, rather, in terms of the grass roots democratic or civic *activities* of the 'governed' (the people) in the specific relationships of governance in the environs where they act and of the glocal *activities* of networking with other practices. The local languages of description (stories) of particular citizenship practices are accepted initially and then compared and contrasted critically along various axes and purposes with other practices in dialogues of translation, understanding and critique. Whereas modern citizenship focuses on citizenship as a universalisable legal *status* underpinned by institutions and processes of rationalisation that enable and circumscribe the possibility of civil activity (an institutional/universal orientation), diverse citizenship focuses on the

16

singular civic activities and improvisations of the governed in any practice of government and the diverse ways in which these are more or less institutionalised or blocked in different contexts (a civic activity/contextual orientation). Citizenship is not a status given by the institutions of the modern constitutional state and international law, but a set of negotiated practices in which one becomes a citizen through participation.

II. MODERN CIVIL CITIZENSHIP

The tradition of modern citizenship takes as its empirical and normative exemplar the form of citizenship characteristic of the modern nation state.[3] Citizenship (both civil and cosmopolitan) is defined in relation to two clusters of institutional features of modern nation states: the constitutional rule of law (*nomos*) and representative government (*demos*). The constitutional rule of law is the first condition of citizenship. The 'civil' law (a formal legal order) and its enforcement by a coercive authority establishes (literally 'constitutes') the conditions of civilisation, the city (*civitas*), citizenship, civil society, civil liberty and civility (hence 'civil' citizenship). By definition the 'outside' is the realm of the uncivilised: barbarism, savagery, the state of nature or war, or the uncertainty of informal, customary law and unenforceable natural law. A person has the status of citizenship in virtue of being *subject* to civil law in two senses: to an established and enforced system of law and to the 'civilising', 'pacifying' or 'socialising' force of the rule of law on the subjectivity of those who are constrained to obey over time. This is why cosmopolitan citizenship and global civil society depend on some form of legalisation or constitutionalisation of the global order analogous (in various ways) to the modern nation state.

Relative to the constitutional rule of law, modern citizenship is defined as a *status* (state or condition). This civil status is usually explicated and defined in terms of the historical development of *four tiers of rights and duties* (liberties) of formally equal individual subjects of an association of constitutional rule of law and representative government. This association is either the modern nation state, including its subordinate provinces and cities, or its analogous associations for cosmopolitan citizenship (international law, the United Nations, global governance institutions). I will start with the four citizenship rights and duties within modern nation states as these are the basis for modern/cosmopolitan global citizenship.

The first and indispensable tier of rights is the set of 'civil liberties' (the liberties of the moderns or 'private autonomy') of the modern liberal tradition. This set includes the liberty of the person and of speech, thought and faith, the right to own private property and to enter into contracts, and the right to formal equality before the law. In virtue of these civil liberties citizens are 'at liberty' to engage in these activities if they choose (an 'opportunity' status) and are protected by the law from 'interference' in the spheres where these rights can be exercised: of free speech and voluntary association, the market, and the law respectively. They are classic 'negative' liberties, protecting persons or citizens from interference in these spheres.

At the centre of these civil liberties is the modern liberty to participate in the private economic sphere and not to be interfered within it – the right to own property and enter into contracts. This is the modern liberty to engage in the capitalist economy (market freedoms and free trade): to sell one's labouring abilities on the market for a wage to a corporation or, for those with the capital, to establish a corporation, hire the labour of others and sell competitively the products of the free market to consumers. Private corporations gained recognition as 'persons' with the corresponding civil liberty of private autonomy (negative liberty) in the late-nineteenth century. Thus, paradoxically from a civic perspective, the first right of modern citizenship is to participate in the private realm and to be protected from interference by the *demos* (the citizenry and its representatives). This form of participation in the economic sphere ('commercial society') *is* primary – the liberty of the moderns.

The modern civil liberty of private property and contracts accordingly *presupposes* the historical dispossession of people from access to land and resources through their local laws and non-capitalist economic organisations; the accumulation of dispossessed workers into a 'free' market of wage labourers and consumers; the concentration of the means of production in private corporations; and the imposition of modern legal systems of property law, contract law, labour law, and trade law that constitute and protect the system of free markets and free trade. Modern citizenship, in its basic commitment to the civil liberty of private property and contracts, is grounded in and dependent on the spread of these institutions of capitalism. It is also the major justification for the spread of these economic institutions – they are the basis of modern liberty. Moreover, it is not only the civil law acting alone that is said to civilise the uncivilised or less-developed peoples. 'Commerce' or 'economic liberalisation' (a synonym for modern globalisation), by rendering every person and society economically interdependent and competitive within an imposed structure of law, pacifies, refines, polishes, makes predictable, and thus – in tandem with representative government – leads humanity to perpetual peace.

The *second* tier of liberties of modern citizenship is defined in relation to the second cluster of modern institutions: representative government. They consist in the rights to participate in these institutions if one chooses. In the language of modern citizenship 'democracy' and 'democratic' are equated with and restricted to 'representative government' and 'democratisation' with and to the historical processes that bring these representative institutions and rights to participate into being. Other forms of democracy, if they are discussed *as* democracies, are described as less-developed forms of the universal and regulative ideal of 'democracy' (as in the case of 'citizenship' above). These rights of the modern democratic tradition are called public autonomy or the liberties of the ancients. They comprise the ways the *demos* – the citizenry of a nation state as a whole – legally exercise their popular sovereignty. The exercise of these 'democratic' rights enables the people to have a say both within and over the laws and constitutions to which they are subject (and from which their citizenship derives) and thereby to balance the constitutional rule of law with the demands of democracy (the rule of the people). These civil rights include such liberties as: the right to vote for representatives in elections, join parties, interest groups, non-governmental organisations and social movements, stand for election, assemble, dissent and demonstrate in the civil or public sphere, freedom of the press, engage in democratic deliberations, litigate in the Courts, exchange public reasons over constitutional amendments or participate in a constituent assembly, and, at their fullest, to engage in some forms of civil disobedience and accept the punishment.

Like civil liberties and their institutional preconditions, these democratic liberties *presuppose* historically the dispossession of people from access to political power through pre-existing local forms of government and citizenship and the channelling of democratic citizenship into participation in the official public sphere of modern representative governments and its global analogue of global civil society. These processes are described as freeing people from pre-modern forms of subjection and bringing democratic citizenship to them. Second, participation is equated with activities of public arguing (deliberating), bargaining (organising, negotiating and protesting) and litigating over changing the laws, since political power is presumed to be exercised through the rule of law. The objective is to ensure that the law is not imposed unilaterally on those subject to it, but, rather, that they have a say, representatively, in making or amending the laws, and thus can see themselves as co-authors or, more accurately, co-articulators, of the laws to which they are subject *en passant*. The activity of participation thus replicates the ground plan of modern citizenship because the people participate *as* legal citizens exercising their democratic rights and within the constraints of modern civil liberties (even when the people act together and exercise the modern right of self-determination they do so within this juridical-representative framework).

The second tier democratic liberties of the modern are also circumscribed by the first tier civil liberties in three main ways. Their exercise is optional. A member of a modern political association is a citizen and the association is democratic whether or not one exercises rights to participate. Second, the primary use and justification of these rights in the modern tradition is to fight for laws that protect the private liberty of the moderns from too much governmental interference. Third, these rights cannot be extended and exercised in the private sphere (as in economic democracy in the workplace) for this would interfere with tier one liberties. When the leaders of the great powers today (the G8) speak of the spread of 'freedom' and 'democracy' in Afghanistan, Iraq and elsewhere, they are referring to the module of tier one (liberties) and tier two (democracy) rights of citizenship and their underlying institutions of the constitutional rule of law, markets, representative government, and the military as the enforcement institution.

The *third* and weakest tier of modern rights of citizenship comprises the social and economic rights of the modern social democratic tradition. These are the citizenship rights won by working class movements struggling within the historically established priority and constraints of tiers one and two liberties over the last two centuries in nation states and international law. They are a response to the horrendous substantive inequalities in wealth, well-being, living conditions and social power that go along with the unrestrained formal equality of tier one civil liberties and the limited democratic rights of tier two. The modern social democratic argument for them is that they are the *minimum conditions* required for the worst off to enable them to exercise their civil and democratic liberties. The argument against them is that they violate the economic liberties of the moderns by interfering in the private sphere and economic competition, and thus always must be subordinated to tier one civil liberty and the limits of tier two. Under the current economic liberalisation policies of states and institutions of global governance these rights are seen, at best, as means of enabling individuals to exercise their tier one and two rights.

The *fourth* tier of citizenship rights consists of modern minority rights of multiculturalism, religious and ethnic groups, non-state nations, and indigenous peoples. These rights appear to some modern theorists to violate one of the premises of modern citizenship, the primacy of the individual legal subject. However, minority rights can be defined as rights that, first, protect the *individual members* of minorities from interference or dominance by the majority (and by the powerful within the minority) and, second, empower members of minorities to exercise their civil and democratic liberties in more effective ways than through the institutions of the dominant society. They thus can be designed to enhance, rather than to challenge, the spread of modern citizenship, and this is the major way that they have been implemented under modern nation states and international law. That is, they too presuppose the dispossession of 'minorities' of their own forms of legal, governmental and economic organisation, and processes of integrating them into modern forms of citizenship.

Within Europe, this modular form of modern citizenship became the paramount practice of citizenship during the centralisation and consolidation of the modern constitutional representative nation state and the capitalist economy. Diverse local and regional forms of laws, governments, democracy and citizenship – of village commons and free city communes – where they were not destroyed completely, were marginalised or transformed and subordinated as they were brought under the rationalisation of the central institutions of the modern nation state. Modern citizenship was nationalised at the same time as local citizenship was subalternised. The people were socialised by education, urbanisation, military duty, industrialisation and modern citizenisation to see themselves first and foremost, not as citizens of their local communities, but as members of an abstract and 'disembedded' imaginary community of nation, *demos* and *nomos* of formally free and equal yet materially unequal citizens, with an equally abstract imaginary of popular sovereignty they mythically embodied and exercised through the individual liberties of modern citizenship attached to the central legal and representative institutions. These dispossessions and transformations, and the countless resistances to them, were described and justified in the social scientific language of modern citizenship as processes and stages of developments of a modernisation that freed individuals from the backwardness of pre-modern customary practices and made him and then her free and equal citizens.

Citizens and especially non-citizens – such as the poor, the property less, women, immigrants, excluded 'races', and others – struggled (and continue to struggle) within-and-against these processes in Europe. When they were not struggling for their local ways, they organised to be included in modern citizenship, to extend the use of political rights beyond the official public sphere, and to gain social and economic rights and minority rights that do more than protect individuals from the majority. These are 'civic activities' against the powerful actors who seek to circumscribe citizenship to tier one civil liberties and a limited module of democratic rights. Since these types of struggles are *for* new kinds of citizenship and *by means of* people who are not official citizens or official citizens who often act beyond the official limits of citizenship of their generation, they cannot be called practices of citizenship in the modern tradition. They are acts of 'civil disobedience'. If these illegal struggles are successful and the extensions institutionalised, then the extensions are redefined as a stage in the development of modern citizenship (as in the case of working class struggles giving rise to social and economic rights and suffragette movements giving rise to women's right to vote). Thus, what are seen as two of the fundamental features of citizenship from the civic tradition – the historical struggles for diverse local forms of citizenship and for extensions of national citizenship rights – fall outside of citizenship for the modern tradition with its institutional orientation.

III. THE GLOBALISATION OF MODERN CITIZENSHIP

The chapter now examines how the modular form of modern citizenship has been spread around the globe as 'global citizenship'.[4] It has been and is being globalised in two forms. *First*, the module of a modern nation state and its institutions of modern *civil* citizenship, at some 'stage of development' towards its mature form, has been and continues to be spread around the world as the universal form of political association recognised as the bearer of legitimate political authority (sovereignty) under international law. *Second*, a modular form of modern *cosmopolitan* citizenship, also at some stage of development towards its mature form, has been and continues to be spread around the world as the universal form of global citizenship recognised as legitimate under international law and global institutions.

During the long period when Europeans were building modern nation states with institutions of modernising citizenship they were also, and simultaneously, building these states as competing *imperial* modern nation states. As imperial states they built and defended vast overseas empires that colonised (in various ways) eighty-five percent of the world's population by 1914. The imperial 'great game' of economic and military competition with other European great powers over the control and exploitation of the resources, labour and markets of the non-European world *and* the counter-actions of the non-European peoples *co-created* the modern west and the modern colonised non-west. After decolonisation in the twentieth century, this unequal relationship continues between the former imperial powers (renamed the 'great eight' or 'great twenty') exercising 'hegemony' rather than 'imperium' through the post-WWII institutions of global governance and the renamed 'post-colonial' world of more than 120 nominally free and equal ('sovereign') yet substantively still *dependent* and *unequal* new modernising nation states, constructed on the foundations of the former colonies. The spread of the institutions of modern citizenship beyond Europe can be understood only in the context of this complex contrapuntal ensemble of Western strategies of expansion and non-Western strategies of counteraction (Mignolo, 2000).

The institutional conditions of modern citizenship were spread in the course of European expansion by a deceptively simple strategy that linked a right of global citizenship to imperial power in a circular relationship. Initially formulated and exercised in different ways by the European imperial powers, this right of global citizenship for Europeans is called the right of commerce (*ius commercium*) or 'cosmopolitan' right. From the earliest phase of European expansion to today the great powers have claimed the cosmopolitan right of *their* citizens, trading companies, monopoly companies, and multinational corporations to travel to other countries and attempt to engage in 'commerce' in two senses of this term. The first is to travel the globe freely and converse with the inhabitants of other societies. This covers such activities as the right – and also the *duty* – of Western explorers, missionaries, religious organisations, voluntary associations, and academics to travel to non-Western countries to, first, study and classify their different customs and ways into developmental stages of different societies and races, and, second, to try to free them from their 'inferior' ways and teach them the uniquely civilised ways of the West. This cosmopolitan right is the historical antecedent of the right of modern cosmopolitan citizenship of civil society associations (modern NGOS) and Western academics to modernise and democratise people in the post-colonial world today by bringing them the institutional preconditions and forms of subjectivity of modern citizenship. The second sense of this cosmopolitan right is to travel and try to engage in 'commerce' (trade) with the inhabitants: to enter into contracts and treaties, gain access to resources, buy slaves, hire and discipline labourers, establish trading posts, and so on. At first it was used by the European powers to establish imperial monopolies over the exploitation of the resources and labour of non-European societies, but monopoly imperialism gradually gave way to 'free trade' imperialism in the nineteenth and twentieth century.

This right correlates with the duty of 'hospitality' of the host country to open their doors to free commerce in this dual sense. If they close the door to entry, break the contract or expropriate the property of a foreigner who has engaged in commerce, or if they expel the voluntary societies, then the appropriate recognised legal authority – under the old law of nations, or imperial law of the respective empire, or, later, international law – has a reciprocal right to open the door by diplomacy or military intervention, punish the violation of the cosmopolitan right and demand reparations or compensation (even for damages caused by the intervention). This correlative duty of hospitality – openness to free commerce – holds even if the cosmopolitan right was initially exercised unjustly: that is where a trading company used force and fraud to establish trade relations and contracts in the first place. This early-modern duty of non-European societies to open themselves to commerce dominated by the West continues to be one of the core duties of transnational trade law agreements today.

As with modern civil liberty within a modern state, this cosmopolitan right *presupposes* a number of institutions. The host country must either have or adopt the legal, economic and cultural institutions that make possible commerce in this broad sense (private property, corporations, contracts, wage labour, markets dominated by the West, openness to cultural conversion, protection of foreigners, and so on). The imperial power must either submit to and modify the local laws and institutions or impose a structure of commercial law that overrides and restructures them, such as Merchant's Law (*lex mercatoria*), a vast system of global trade law that developed in tandem with Western imperialism.

As we can see, this cosmopolitan right is a right of citizens of the civilised states to exercise the first right of modern citizenship (civil liberties) and a version of the second right (to participate) *beyond their nation state*, and to be protected from interference in so doing. The two cosmopolitan rights – of the trading company to trade and the voluntary organisations to converse and convert – also fit together in the same way as within the nation state. The participatory right to converse with and try to convert the natives complements the primary right of commerce since the inhabitants are taught the requisite forms of subjectivity and modes of civil conduct that go along with the commercialisation of their society and its gradual civilisation: from the discipline of slavery and indentured labour at the bottom to the training of dependent elites at the top. From the perspective of the language of modern citizenship, the two rights of cosmopolitan citizenship appear to globalise the civilising institutions of law, commerce and Western civility across an uncivilised or semi-civilised or less-developed world, thereby laying the foundations for an eventual world of modern civil citizenship in modern nation states. From the perspective of the non-Western civilisations and of diverse citizenship, the two cosmopolitan rights appear as the Trojan horse of Western imperialism (Anghie, 2005).

In practice, this strategy was employed to globalise modern citizenship in three main ways. First, settler colonies were established that *replicated* the basic features and legal, political and economic institutions of the imperial country. These 'new Europes' were established in the Americas, Australia, New Zealand and later in Africa by dispossessing indigenous peoples of their diverse civilisations, territories, resources and citizenship practices, exterminating eighty to ninety percent of the population (which was larger than Europe at the time), marginalising those they could not enslave or indenture, importing 12 millions slaves from Africa onto plantations in North and South America and the Caribbean, and imposing the civilising institutions of property and contract law and rudimentary representative government (colonial legislatures).

Second, by 'indirect' imperial rule, non-Western societies were opened to commerce by establishing a small colonial administration, often run by trading companies, to rule indirectly over a much larger indigenous population. A centralised system of Western colonial law was used to protect the commercial rights of their citizens and traders, while also preserving and modifying the local customary laws and governments so resources and labour were privatised and subject to trade, labour discipline and investment dominated by the Western trading companies. Local rulers were recognised as quasi-sovereigns and unequal treaties negotiated. The local elites were made dependent on Western economic and military power, undermining their accountability to their local citizens, and employed to introduce modernising techniques of governance and to train the local armies to protect the system of property, often against the majority of their own population. This was the major way that the institutional preconditions of modern civil citizenship were introduced in India, Ceylon, Africa and the Middle East.

The third and most recent way is through 'informal' or 'free trade' imperialism. Here the imperial powers permit local self-rule, and eventually self-determination, but within a protectorate or sphere of influence over which they exercise informal 'paramountcy' (now called 'hegemony' or 'dominance'). By various informal means they induce the local governments to open their resources, labour and markets to free trade by establishing the appropriate modern local legal, political and economic institutions – the foundations for eventual modern citizenship, with civil liberties preceding and circumscribing the other rights. The means include: economic, military, technological, educational and aid dependency; the modernisation of the population by Western experts and civil society organisations; bribes and threats; and frequent military intervention when local citizens resist. This requires in turn small but effective military bases strategically located around the world and supported by a global navy and (later) air force and satellite surveillance. The informal imperial powers are thus able to intervene whenever the local population tries to take control of their own economy through their own government and citizenship practices and thus violate the duties of openness and free trade. This type of imperialism was introduced by the British in the nineteenth century, but the United States has become the global leader of informal or 'open door' imperialism, first in Latin America and then throughout the former colonial world by the end of the Cold War. The United States now has over 760 small military bases around the world and the Pentagon claims to exercise 'full spectrum dominance' over an informal global system of commerce and freedom.

The cosmopolitan right and its three modes of imposition were gathered together and formalised as the *standard of civilisation* in the creation of modern international law during the nineteenth century. The European imperial nation states (and the United States after 1895) declared themselves to be 'civilised states' in virtue of their institutions of modern statehood and citizenship (modern rule of law, open to commerce, representative government and modern liberty). As such they were the sole bearers of sovereignty and subject only to the laws they could agree to among themselves: 'international' law. Their modern institutions provided a 'standard of civilisation' in international law by which they judged all other civilisations in the world as 'uncivilised' to varying degrees (depending on their stage of development) and thus not sovereign subjects of international law, but subjects of the sovereign powers through colonies, indirect protectorates, and informal spheres of influence. They asserted a right and duty of civilisation under international law. 'Civilisation' referred to the historical process of modernisation and to the end-point of a modern state like the European model. The duty to civilise consisted in the consolidation and international legalisation of the imperial processes they began in the earlier period. The opening of non-European societies to European-dominated commerce, exploitation of their resources and labour, and the destruction or marginalisation of 'uncivilised' ways that hindered this 'progress' were seen as the first steps in the civilising mission. The second and equally important duty was to introduce into the colonies and protectorates more systematic and effective forms of colonial governance (or *governmentalité*) that would shape and form the dependent peoples and 'races' into civilised subjects eventually capable of modern self-government.

This global civilising project under international law lacked an enforcement mechanism and the civilising duty was left to the sovereign empires and their voluntary organisations. The destruction, exploitation, despotism, genocide and wars continued apace and increased after the failure of the Berlin Conference (1884) and the 'scramble over Africa', eventually culminating in the barbarism of World War I (the 'great war of civilisation'). In response to these horrors and to control increasing demands for decolonisation, the first concerted attempt to operationalise the civilising duty under international law was the Mandate System under the League of Nations. The League classified the 'subject' peoples into three categories according to their level of 'backwardness' and gave the respective imperial powers the mandate to civilise them as they increased their economic exploitation, especially in the oil-rich Middle East.

This project was interrupted by the decolonisation movements of the mid-century. Although the people fought for freedom from imperial dependency on the West or the Soviet Union and the development of their own forms of self-government and citizenship, the Westernised national elites (subject to economic and military dependency) and the informal means of the great powers ensured the continuation of the civilising and modernising processes. During the Cold War and the phases of post-independence dependency, the nation-building elites were constrained to destroy or subordinate local economies, governments and citizenship practices, entrench or extend the artificial colonial boundaries, centralise and nationalise governments into the armed nation-state module, open their resources to free trade and promise minimal institutions of modern citizenship, or face military intervention. The result tended to be constitutional and institutional structures that concentrated power at the centre, often entrenching the worst features of colonial administration, or replicating the concentration of power in both urban and rural regions characteristic of the divide and conquer model of indirect imperial rule (as in much of Africa).

During the same period, the great powers set up the institutions of global governance through which informal hegemony and post-colonial subalternity could be continued: the concentration of power in the permanent members of the Security Council of the United Nations, the World Bank (WB), International Monetary Fund (IMF), General Agreement on Trade and Tariffs (GATT), the World Trade Organization after 1995 (WTO) and its transnational trade agreements (such as

TRIPS and GATTS), modernising NGOs, North Atlantic Treaty Organization (NATO), and the United States' system of global military dominance.

At the request of the newly independent states, the language of civilisation was removed from international law and the United Nations. However, it was immediately replaced with the language of modernisation, marketisation, democratisation and globalisation with the same grammatical structure, signifying universal processes of development and a single endpoint of modern citizenship and its institutions. These are now to be brought about, not by the 'civilising mission' of the imperial powers, but by the 'global governance' of the informal federations or coalitions of the modern (or post-modern) states imposing 'good governance' through the global institutions (WB and IMF), their multinational corporations (exercising the cosmopolitan right of commerce), and official NGOs (exercising their cosmopolitan citizenship) building civil societies and civil subjects on the ground. As the leaders of the decolonisation movements recognised after independence, they were thus conscripted into a familiar scenario, but now in a vocabulary of a world system of free and equal nation states that erased any reference to the imperial construction of this world and the persistence of imperial relations of inequality and exploitation (Ayers, 2006; Evans & Ayers, 2006).

The difference from the old colonial strategies of spreading the institutional preconditions of modern citizenship is that the formerly colonised peoples are now seen as active, self-governing agents in these processes at home and in the institutions of global governance (the G120) – and thus bearers of modern civil and cosmopolitan citizenship – yet still under the enlightened leadership of the more advanced or developed peoples. International law provides the legal basis for this by promoting a 'right to democracy', and democracy is equated with tier one civil liberties (neo-liberal marketisation) and a short list of democratic rights (elections). However, if, as often happens, the majority of the people become too democratic and seek to exercise their right of self-determination by taking democratic control of their own government and local economy, and thus violate their duty to open their doors to multinational corporations and subordination to a global economy, one of two strategies of modernisation follow. They are either repressed by their own dependent elites, democratic rights are further reduced or eliminated, and the government becomes more authoritarian. Or, if the people manage to gain power, the repertoire of covert and overt informal means available to the great powers are employed to destabilise and undermine the government, bring about regime change, and institute structural adjustment policies that promote tier one civil liberties of individuals and corporations. The coercive imposition of the global market and the market discipline of civil liberty is said to come first and lay the foundation for democratic rights. The result in either case is the suppression or severe restriction of democratic citizenship, the corresponding rise of a militarised authoritarian rule and market freedoms on one side and violent authoritarian resistance movements on the other. The countries that are subject to these horrendous oscillations are said to be 'failed states'; military intervention follows, resistance intensifies, and instability continues.

The consequence is that a restricted 'low intensity' form of modern civil citizenship at the national level is promoted by an equally low intensity form of modern cosmopolitan citizenship of NGOs and multinational corporations under global governance and international law. The first wave of international human rights after World War II sought to give protection to the person from the worst effects of these processes (civil liberties) and to elaborate a set of global democratic, social and economic, and minority rights similar to those at the national level. However, these are hostage to implementation by nation states and thus subject to the processes described above. The second wave of international law brought into force a vast array of transnational trade law regimes (under GATT and the WTO) that override and restrict national constitutions and constrain weaker and poorer countries (hosting the majority of the world's population) to open their economies and labour to free trade, unrestrained exploitation and pollution transfer by the dominant multinational corporations in order to gain loans, aid and debt relief. The third wave of international law after 9/11/01 consists of Resolutions of the Security Council of the UN promoting international security. These global securitisation regimes, which are said to protect the security and liberty of modern citizens, often override the first wave international human rights, force national governments to enact security legislation that rolls back hard won democratic rights, thereby circumscribing democratic opposition to the war on terror and neo-liberal globalisation, and they secure the tier one civil and cosmopolitan liberty of individual and corporate citizens in national and transnational law.[5] This new formulation of the old cosmopolitan right to civilise is now the major justification for the continuation of Western informal imperialism, as in Iraq and Afghanistan today. The result is not only the continued popular resistance, instability and escalating militarisation and repression, as above, but also growing global inequalities between the West and the non-West that are worse now than at the height of the ruthless phase of Western imperialism in the late nineteenth century.

840 million people are malnourished. 6,000,000 children under the age of 5 die each year as a consequence of malnutrition. 1.2 billion people live on less than $1 a day and half the world's population lives on less than $2 a day. 91 out of every 1,000 children in the developing world die before 5 years old. 12 million die annually from lack of water. 1.1 billion people have no access to clean water. 2.4 billion people live without proper sanitation. 40 million live with AIDS. 113 million children have no basic education. 1 in 5 does not survive past 40 years of age. There are one billion non-literate adults, two-thirds are women and 98% live in the developing world. In the least developed countries, 45% of the children do not attend school. In countries with literacy rate of less than 55% the annual per capita income is about $600.

In contrast, the wealth of the richest 1% of the world is equal to that of the poorest 57%. The assets of the 200 richest people are worth more than the total income of 41% of the world's people. Three families alone have a combined wealth of $135 billion. This equals the annual income of 600 million people living in the world's poorest countries. The richest 20% of the world's population receive 150 times the wealth of the poorest 20%. In 1960, the share of the global income of the bottom 20% was 2.3%. By 1991, this had fallen to 1.4%. The richest fifth of the world's people consume 45% of the world's meat and fish; the poorest fifth consume 5%. The richest fifth consume 58% of total energy, the poorest fifth less than 4%. The richest fifth have 75% of all telephones, the poorest fifth 1.5%. The richest fifth own 87% of the world's vehicles, the poorest fifth less than 1%. As a result of the globalisation of modern citizenship and its underlying institutions the majority of the world's population of the dispossessed are thus 'free' to exercise their modern civil liberty in the growing sweatshops and slums of the planet.[6]

In summary, the globalisation of modern citizenship has not tended to democracy, equality and perpetual peace, but to informal imperialism, dependency, inequality and resistance. This tendency is a consequence of its basic universal/imperial orientation. From within the perspective of modern citizenship modern citizens see their modular form of citizenship as universal and superior, and all others as particular and inferior, and see themselves as having the imperial right and duty to enter into other societies, free them from their inferior ways, impose the institutional preconditions of modern citizenship, which conveniently brings unconscionable profits to their corporations and unconscionable inequality to the people they are modernising, and use violence and military rule against those envious 'anti-moderns' who resist. From the alternative perspective of diverse citizenship, this is neither freedom, nor democracy but five hundred years of relentless tyranny against local citizenship and self-reliance, the undemocratic imposition of institutions of low intensity citizenship over which the majority of the people have little or no effective say and in which they are subject to subordination, exploitation, horrendous inequalities and repression when they refuse to submit.[7]

IV. DIVERSE CIVIC CITIZENSHIP

Although modern civil and cosmopolitan citizenship is the predominant form of global citizenship, a multiplicity of other meanings and practices of citizenship co-exist and, consequently, the global field of citizenship is considerably more complex and contested than the view from the modern tradition suggests. I want now to turn and examine this field from the standpoint of diverse citizenship. I will mention six general aspects of diverse civic citizenship and contrast these with modern civil citizenship.[8]

Rather than looking on citizenship as a status within an institutional framework backed up by world-historical processes and universal norms, the diverse tradition looks on citizenship as *negotiated practices* – as civic actors and activities in local contexts. The modern tradition in social science and political theory overlooks these activities because it presupposes that rights, rules, institutions and processes must be primary (the conditions of civilisation) and human actors and activities secondary (what happens within the civil space constituted by the civilising rights, institutions, rules and processes). The diverse tradition reverses this modernist, institutional orientation and takes the perspective of actual citizens in civic activities in the dwelling places they are enacted and carried on. Institutionalisation of citizenship practices is seen as secondary; coming into being in countless unpredictable and open-ended ways out of, and in interaction with, the *praxis* of citizens – sometimes furthering, strengthening and formalising these activities; other times dispossessing, channelling, cancelling, downsizing, constraining, limiting and repressing (as we have seen).

The second way the diverse tradition avoids the prejudice of mistaking one institutionalised form of citizenship as the universal model for all possible forms is always to take any specific civic activity in context as one local citizenship practice among countless others. They start from the local languages and practices of citizens *in* their forms of citizenship and compare and contrast their similarities and dissimilarities critically with each other from various standpoints, either by engaging in other forms of citizenship or by civic dialogues of mutual edification among diverse citizens. There is thus no universal module of citizenship but, rather, a multiplicity of criss-crossing and overlapping practices of citizenship, of which modern citizenship can be seen to be one singular and imperious form masquerading as universal.

Third, since civic activities of citizens are primary, people do not become citizens by virtue of a status defined by rights and guaranteed by the institutions of the modern state and international law. This status is simply to be a 'subject' of that system of laws and a 'member' of that association. Individual and collective agents *become* citizens only by virtue of actual participation in civic activities. Through apprenticeship in citizenship practices they acquire the linguistic and non-linguistic abilities, modes of conduct and interaction in relationships with others, forms of awareness of self and other, and use of civic equipment that are constitutive of citizenship as a practice. The difference in meaning between 'citizenship' as a status and as a negotiated practice is made in European languages by the distinction between 'civil' and 'civilisation' (law-based) and 'civic' and 'civicising' (activity-based). Whereas civil citizens have the legally guaranteed opportunity to participate in the civil sphere if they chose, civic citizens engage in and experience 'civics' – the activities and practical arts of becoming and being a citizen, referred to as 'civicism'. Civic citizenry are not seen as bearers of civil rights and duties but of the abilities, competences, character and conduct acquired in participation, often referred to as 'civic virtues'. Civil citizens are civilized by the institutional rule of law, commerce and anonymous processes of civilisation, whereas civic citizens criticise and reject this disempowering picture that conceals the real world of histories of civic struggles. They 'civicise' themselves. They transform themselves into citizens and their institutions into civic spaces by civic activities and the arts of citizenship, whether or not these activities are guaranteed by the rule of law or informal customs and ways, or neither. The civic citizen manifests the freedom *of* participation *in* relationships *with* other citizens. The civic citizen is not the juridical citizen of a national or global institution but the 'free citizen' of the 'free city': that is, any kind of civic 'sphere' or 'world' that comes into being and is reciprocally sustained by the civic freedom of its citizens, from the *deme*, village, common, commune, grass roots federation to a global networks of such civic nodes.

Fourth, whereas modern citizenship always exists in institutions, civic citizenship always exists in relationships. There are two major kinds of civic being-with relationships: (1) relationships among roughly equal citizens acting together in relationships of solidarity, civic friendship and mutual aid (citizen relationships) and relationships between governors and citizens (governance/citizen relationships). Civic citizenship is the *vis à vis* of governance. To see the importance of this contrast we have to set aside the institutional language of the civil tradition (constitutions, rights, autonomous rules, jurisdiction, states and sovereignty) and look at what goes on within, beyond and often in tension with these institutions. What we see are individual and collective actors in citizen and governance/citizen relationships.

A relationship of governance is a relation of power, knowledge and mode of subjectification through which one agent or collection of agents (governors or government) tries to govern or conduct the conduct (thoughts and actions) of another agent or agents (the governed or all affected), either directly or indirectly, formally or informally, by innumerable means and strategies. They exist in small groups, families, workplaces, sweatshops, bureaucracies, colonial administrator and colony, in producing and consuming activities, in our relationship to the environment, between multinational corporations and their suppliers and consumers, in the informal global relations of inequality, and so on. As modern states were consolidated, the term 'government' came to be restricted to the official form of 'representative government', 'the governed' to the body of individual citizens with rights, the relationship between them as the 'rule of law', and 'civil democratic citizenship' as the right to participate in the official public sphere in relation to the rule of law and representative government. The diverse citizenship tradition sees this as one important set of representative governance relationships, albeit highly institutionalised and abstracted. However, there are multiple, overlapping and criss-crossing local, national and global governance relationships in the broader sense that either do not pass through the modern national and global legal and political institutions or, if they do, they are often overlooked by the institutional perspective, to which we are subject, yet over which the governed often have little or no democratic say. This is the field of diverse citizenship.

A governance relationship is the site of citizenship from the civic perspective. In any governance relationship there is always a more or less restricted field of possible ways of acting, of conducting oneself in the relationship, even in the most tightly controlled cases (such as prisons and military training). As a result of this irreducible element of freedom and free play in a governance relationship, it is always a negotiated practice between the partners to some extent. Governance is not a unilateral phenomenon of subjection, but a much more complicated and open-ended *interplay* and *interaction* between governors and governed over time. This dimension of negotiation is the ground of civic citizenship. The governed begin to become civic citizens and initiate civic activities when they not only negotiate how to act in accordance with the governance relationship in which they find themselves, but when they negotiate the relationship itself. Hence, from the perspective of civic citizens, a governance relationship is always a governance/

citizen relationship. Classically this activity of civic negotiation (the public world of *negotium*) consists of (but is not restricted to): citizens organising and non-violently calling a governance relationship into question (speaking truth to power), demanding that those who govern enter into negotiations over the acceptability of the relationship, negotiating a modification or transformation of it, implementing the changes, acting in the new relationship, reviewing it over time, and re-opening the negotiations again whenever the new relationship becomes unacceptable. In contrast to the institutional distinction between public and private in modern citizenship, this activity of calling any governance relationship anywhere into question and subjecting it to public examination and negotiation brings it out of the private sphere (of not being questioned) and into the public sphere of civic enquiry.

Opening the relationships we are part of to the ongoing negotiation and experimentation of the partners (governors–citizens) is to 'civicise' them. They are no longer imposed monologically over the governed who are presumed to simply obey as subjects. They are transformed into civic and dialogical relationships under the shared authority of both partners. The partners become mutually subject to and co-authors of the relationship between them. Governors become 'civic servants', accountable to those they serve, and subjects become free citizens rather than unfree subjects or slaves (who have no say in their despotic relationships). To civicise governance/citizen relationships is also to 'democratise' them; for one ordinary, everyday sense of 'democracy' is that the people (*demos*) in their locale (*deme*) rule by exercising an effective say in and over the relationships in which they are both subjects and citizens. Civic citizenship is thus the practice of grass roots democracy. It civicises and democratises the relationships in which the people find themselves *here and now*. Civil citizenship, in contrast, imposes a singular institutionalised process of civilisation and democratisation from above, often coercively and often over local forms of civic citizenship, on the imperial premise that institutions precede civic activity, and it restricts democracy to a small island of representative participation in a sea of non-democratic relationships in the private sphere. This is the initial and continuing unjust and anti-democratic foundation of modern citizenship from the civic standpoint. Democratic citizenship practices exist in everyday relationships long before institutionalisation and they can be extended only by the same democratic means of non-violent civicisation from the ground up.[5]

Fifth, the other general way civic citizenship is manifested is when citizens organise themselves in citizen relationships: that is, relationships among fellow citizens as equals in which there is no governor/citizen distinction. Sometimes this is done in order to enter into negotiations with governors of various kinds (as above), as in cases of collective bargaining, and negotiating within NGOs and social movements that are organised civically and democratically. But, in many other cases, citizens organise an activity entirely on the basis of citizen relationships for its own sake. The classic examples are the celebrated practices of direct democracy.

However, another important example is the cooperative. If the private corporation is both the basis and flagship of modern citizenship – the institution in

31

which moderns exercise their civil liberties in competing, working, shopping and consuming, then the cooperative is the contrastive organisation of the civic tradition. Here citizens ignore the civil division between (non-democratic) private and (representative) public spheres, between civil liberties and democratic rights. They participate as democratic citizens governing themselves directly in the economic sphere (and other spheres), civicising the relations of supplying, hiring, working, managing, and distributing. In contrast to individual and corporate competition in market relations, cooperatives are founded on the ethic of cooperation. In the place of competitive free trade, they practice fair trade: trade relationships based on non-violent democratic negotiations among all affected. In contrast to the goal of profit, coops are 'not for profit' but for living democracy and mutual aid. All the human creativity that is channelled into the world of commerce and profit by corporations is poured into experimentation with forms of democratic cooperation by the cooperative movements. The most astonishing feature of the countless cooperatives on the planet is that they manifest, in concrete and practical forms, actual alternative worlds of citizenship *within* the interstices of the dominant national and global institutions of modern citizenship. They do not organise to overthrow the state or the capitalist mode of production, or to confront and negotiate with governors to change this or that regulation. They simply *enact* alternative worlds of citizen relationships around various activities, refusing to abjure their civicism to privatization or governmentalisation.

Sixth, modern citizenship is 'egocentric'; oriented towards the protection of the liberty of individuals to be free from interference and to be free to exercise their autonomy in the private sphere (tier one rights) or in the official public sphere (tier two rights). In contrast, diverse citizenship in both citizen and governance/citizen relationships is ecocentric and commune centric. Civic activities are oriented towards *caring for* the public or 'civic goods' of the correlative 'city' – the community bound together by citizen and/or governance/citizen relationships in dependency relationships with non-human animals and the environment they bear as inhabitants of the natural habitat. Civic goods are many and they too are subject to negotiation. They include such procedural goods as civicising relationships in many spheres and the character development and conviviality that come from participation, and such substantive goods as caring for the environment, economic self-reliance, mutual aid, fair trade, equality among citizens, and so on. When civic citizens call a particular governance relationship into question they do so under the general critical ideal that it fails to realise civic goods in some specific way or another. These are goods that make possible and enhance civic forms of life (Tully, 2001b).

Accordingly, civic citizens are thus caretakers of dwelling 'places' in this broad sense that dissolves the modernist distinction between culture and nature, and they care for their relations to the natural world (the ground or mother of their civic life) as carefully as the cultural world. They also take their civic responsibility of caring for the goods of communities and members *in* dwelling places and placeways to be prior to protecting the liberty rights of abstract individuals. They translate the latter back into one important civic good among others (negative freedom) that must vie for attention in our discursive practices. They also reply that, in many cases, what oppressed individuals and minorities say they want is not protection from their own communities by a tier one right, enforced by a distant national or international court, but democratic empowerment in their communities (civic freedom). In theories of modernity, this grounded civic ethic is discredited by caricaturing it as a pre-modern stage of historical and moral development and as a particular ethos of care in contrast to the allegedly higher and universal theory of morality and justice for abstracted and autonomous individuals. And the 'public good' is defined as the spread of modern liberties and their underlying institutions. Notwithstanding this peculiarly modern stance, multilayered civic ethics of care in human and natural relationships have been and continue to be the more widely held political and ethical orientation of the majority of the world's peoples in their diverse cultures and traditions. Under the dawning awareness of the destruction of local communities, environmental devastation and climate change caused by the last 500 years of Western imperialism under the modernising orientation (in which these public 'bads' are 'externalities'), not only ecological scientists but even former modernisers and globalisers have come around to see the value of this alternative way of citizenship.[10]

V. THE 'GLOCALISATION' OF DIVERSE CITIZENSHIP

The author will now examine two main ways diverse citizenship has spread around the globe.[6] The first is the persistence and recent renaissance of local forms of civic citizenship practices despite the globalisation of modern citizenship. The second is by the global civic federation and networkisation of local diverse citizenship practices. The author terms this global networking 'glocalisation' and the networkers 'glocal citizens' because they are grounded in and hyperextend the civic features of local citizenship.

Two ways of glocalising civic citizenship are proposed in relation to the global crisis of citizenship examined previously in Section III. To recollect, the formal and then informal imperial spread of modern citizenship, and the underlying institutions it sends on ahead to clear the way, has led in many cases, at best, to a form of global cosmopolitan citizenship for official NGOs and multinational corporations; low intensity citizenship for dependent elites of the former colonies; the dispossession or marginalisation of local citizenship and governance, the subordination of local economies and polities to global corporations and trade regimes; enormous inequalities; violent cycles of repression and resistance; and increasing environmental destruction. This crisis of modernity/coloniality has coincided with a crisis of democratic deficit in the representative democracies of the hegemonic states. The informal imperial networks of economic, legal, cultural, media, security, and military relationships not only bypass and undermine the diverse citizenship of billions of people who are governed by them. They also manipulate, downsize and disregard the representative and legal institutions of modern citizenship that are supposed to bring them under representative authority. These trends of globalisation constitute a crisis of global citizenship that, viewed in isolation, is experienced as a pervasive sense of disempowerment and disenchantment. They will now be re-interpreted from the standpoint of glocal citizenship.

First, despite these devastating trends, another world of legal, political and even economic diversity has survived and continues to be the *locus* of civic activities for millions of people. The reason for this remarkable survival and renaissance in the post-colonial world, unknown to the dominant debate over global citizenship, is that Western imperialism governs through indirect or informal means and thus depends on the active collaboration of imperialised peoples exercising constrained local self-government. Those who are not part of the Westernised elite have been able to keep their diverse local citizenship practices alive to some extent within the broad parameters of informal dependency relationships. One of the most astonishing examples among many is the survival and resurgence of 300 million indigenous peoples with their traditions of governance and citizenship after 500 years of genocide, dispossession, marginalisation, and relentless assimilation. The lived experience of citizenship in the present age is thus different from and more complex than it is portrayed through the sweeping generalisations – by both defenders and critics alike – of globalisation theories. Many existing diverse practices of governance have been corrupted into exploitative and despotic relationships by their dependency on indirect rule and others were non-civic from the outset. The point is neither to reject them simply because they are non-modern nor to accept them uncritically because they are different or traditional. It is rather to bring them into critical and comparative discussions with other forms of governance and citizenship and to explore ways citizens can civicise them by speaking and acting within them (Mander & Tauli-Corpuz, 2004; Mamdani, 2001). In the modernised West a vast repertoire of local citizenship practices have also survived within the interstices of state-centric modern citizenship, such as traditional working class organisations and countless new and creative forms of coops and networks linking rural and urban citizens in countless ways and around countless civic goods (the environment, non-violent dispute resolution, low-cost housing, anti-racism, organic farming, place-based pedagogy, neighbourhood security, and so on). These old and new citizenship practices and improvisations are multiplying rapidly today in the 'turn to the local' of a new generation disenchanted with the elite manipulation of representative citizenship.

The second example of glocalizing civic citizenship is the array of movements to 'democratise democracy'. The aim of these movements is to democratise the legal, political and bureaucratic institutions of modern representative democracy so that the people who are subject to them are consulted and have an effective negotiated say within them *wherever* power is exercised non-democratically and unaccountably, in ad-hoc processes of speaking out and 'going public' or in more formal modes of negotiation in which those who govern must listen and give account of themselves. These are thus movements to 'civicise' the civil institutions of modern citizenship. Here civic citizens join hands with civil citizens engaged in the same projects from within – such as proportional representation, deliberative democracy, democratic constitutionalism, legal pluralism, civic *versus* civil security, and the various initiatives to democratise the UN and global governance institutions from within (De Sousa Santos, 2007; Loader & Walker, 2007).

Third, since decolonisation and the triumph of informal imperialism, millions of the world's poor have been forced to migrate from the colonised world to the imperial countries to find work in a closely controlled global labour market. Despite the hardships of poverty, slavery, exploitation, racism, xenophobia, and second class or non-citizenship, they refuse to be servile subjects and exercise their civic citizenship in new and untoward ways; instead, they are negotiating their diverse cultural ways into the public and private institutions of modern citizenship. This 'journey back' or 'boomerang effect' of formerly colonised peoples now civicising the imperial countries challenges the dominant imperial, nationalist and racist cultures encoded in modern citizenship institutions and creates new forms of multiculturalism and multi-civilisationalism, both in the urban centres and the diasporic relationships ('transnational civic scapes') they sustain with their former countries. These deeply multicultural communities in 'mongrel cities' generate new kinds of citizen relationships of 'conviviality' among their members and with supportive local civic citizens groups.

These three examples and many others similar to them are existing practices of local civic citizenship. These worldwide local sources and resources of civic citizenship are much stronger and resilient than are commonly realised. They are the bases of glocal citizenship. Networks such as informal federations, NGOs, social movements and similar creative improvisations are the means by which glocal citizens link together and so glocalize these local civic bases. These networks are civic and glocal just insofar as they are (1) grounded in and accountable to the local civic nodes, and (2) hyperextend civic relationships (citizen and governance/citizen) and other civic aspects in their own organisation and their relationships with others. If, in contrast, they see themselves as bringing the gifts of civilisation and modern citizenship to the less-developed, then they are 'modern' (civil and cosmopolitan) networks. In addition to providing mutual learning and aid to their member civic nodes, they also crucially provide the civic means of democratising the persisting global imperial relationships of inequality, exploitation, and dependency that are the major causes of the crisis of global citizenship. Civic networks do this counter-hegemonic work in two mains ways.

First, as we have seen in Section III, the persisting economic, legal, political, exchange, media, educational and military relationships of informal imperialism are so unequal that, although the elites within the former colonies are able to have a say and negotiate (in global governance institutions and elsewhere), they (the G120) are barely able to modify these governance relationships, let alone transform them into governance/citizen relationships, and they are in turn scarcely in civicised relationships with their own people (the majority of the world's population). Similarly, the hegemonic partners in the relationships – the great powers and their multinational corporations – are not held democratically accountable by their own citizens. Accordingly, the first role of a glocal network is to link together glocally enough local citizenship practices of those who are governed by any of these relationships to single it out and contest it: to call its existence and privacy into the space of public questioning and put enough soft power pressure on the responsible powers-that-be to bring them to negotiations in the most effective place or places. It is thus the glocalization of the whole practice of civic negotiation discussed in Section IV. Networked contestation and negotiation can take place anywhere and by anybody in the relationships (for example, in sweat shops and/or consumer boycott of sweatshop products, in the WTO or in protest against the WTO). It should not be the burden of the wretched of the earth to refuse to submit and act otherwise, as in the dominant theories of resistance, but of the most powerful and privileged to refuse to comply with and engage in the work of glocal citizenship. In doing this, citizens in glocal networks are engaged in civicising and democratising these imperial relationships by bringing them under the shared authority of all those subject to them *in* their local places and ways. If the negotiations take hold, the subaltern partner ceases to be 'dependent' but also does *not* become 'independent' (as was imagined in the unsuccessful theories of decolonisation). Rather, the partners gradually become 'interdependent' on the ongoing democratic relationships between them (as in Section IV). These innumerable practices of glocal negotiation comprise one non-violent path of de-imperialisation and democratisation characteristic of the civic tradition (Escobar, 2004).

The second way glocal networks work to transform imperial relationships into democratic ones is through the spread of cooperative relationships between partners in the North and Global South. These cooperative informal federations are not strategies of contestation and negotiation, but (as in Section IV) of directly acting otherwise; of creating non-violent civic relationships between partners in the North and the Global South. The relationships among all the partners in the network, and within each partner's local association, are worked out civically and democratically as they go along. Although there are thousands of examples, perhaps the best known are glocal cooperative 'fair trade' and self-reliance relationships, such as the specific Fair Trade case, in contrast to competitive free trade; glocal networks of non-violent dispute resolution in contrast to war, militarisation and securitisation; and deep ecology networks in contrast to (oxymoronic) sustainable development. Like their local cooperative partners, these glocal cooperative citizens play within the existing global rules in each case, yet they play a completely different game. They create and live 'another world' in their civic and glocal activities.

Third, the World Social Forum (WSF) has emerged as an important place where civic and glocal citizens can meet each year. It is to diverse citizenship as the World Economic Forum is to modern citizenship. The WSF does not take a position, but, rather, provides a civic space in which participants from diverse citizenship practices can enter into dialogues of translation, comparison, criticism, reciprocal learning and further networking. They share the knowledge of their different arts of citizenship with each other without granting modern citizenship the universal and superior status it claims for itself and on the presumption that each mode of citizenship is partial and incomplete, so each can learn its limitations from others. The WSF also hopes to develop closer links of reciprocal learning between academic research on citizenship and the practices of citizenship we have been discussing, perhaps setting up popular universities of the social movements for this purpose, thereby deepening relationships of mutual aid (De Sousa Santos, 2006; Conway, 2004).

If all the examples of civic and glocal citizenship practices could be envisaged in a single view, in the way that modern citizenship and globalisation presents itself as a matter of inexorable progress, perhaps this would help to dissipate the sense of disempowerment and disenchantment the present crisis induces. But, from the situated standpoint of diverse citizenship, this cannot be done and the attempt would overlook the very diversity that the civic approach aims to disclose and keep in view. Civic empowerment and enchantment come not from grand narratives of universal progress, but from *praxis* – actual participation in civic activities with others where we become the citizens we can be. But this response raises the question of the motive for participation in the first place. The civic answer has always been the motivating force of role models or exemplars of the civic life.

Today there are millions of exemplars from all walks of life in all locales that move potential citizens of all ages to participate in civic/glocal practices that arguably make up the largest decentralized and diverse movement in the world (Hawken, 2007). But perhaps a particularly exemplary exemplar for our dark times of the kind of glocal citizenship I have sketched is Mahatma Gandhi and his lifelong struggle to rid the world of imperialism. His ordinary civic and glocal life continues to move millions of people to begin to act. The reason for this, I believe, is the sheer simplicity of the four citizenship practices his life manifests. The first is active non-cooperation in any imperial (non-civic) relationship and with any corresponding idea of one universal civilization or cosmopolitanism for all. The second is civic organization and uncompromising non-violent confrontation and negotiation with those responsible for imperial relationships with the aim of converting them to non-violent, democratic relationships. Third, for these two activities to be effective they have to be grounded in the local practice of the alternative world you want to bring about. For Gandhi this consisted of 'constructive work' in local, self-reliant, civically organized villages and respectful participation in their ways. Fourth, all this has to be grounded in 'experiments with truth' – a spiritual relationship to oneself in one's relationship with others and the environing world. This is a relationship of working daily and truthfully on oneself and one's attitude in order to improve how one conducts oneself in these trying yet rewarding civic relationships with others: that is, the daily practice of making oneself an exemplary citizen (Weber, 2004).

NOTES

[1] For introductions to this broad field see Amoore (2005); Brodie (2004); Dower (2003); Dower & Williams (2002); Held & McGrew (2002).

[2] I discuss the various theories of modern citizenship from Immanuel Kant to the present in Tully (2001a, 2002, 2007a, in press).

[3] For the background scholarship to Section II see Tilly (2007); Held (2006); Ishay (2004); Skinner & Stråth (2003); McNally (2006); Tully (2007a).

[4]   For the background scholarship to Section III, see Tully (in press); Tully (2007a); Potter *et al* (1997), Tilly (2007).
[5]   Security Council Resolution 1373. See Scheppele (2007).
[6]   These are United Nations statistics from 2000. See Seabrook (2003).
[7]   For the origin of the widely used term 'low intensity democracy' see Gills *et al* (1993). For the more recent scholarship see references for sections III and V. Also see Grandin (2007).
[8]   For the background scholarship to Section IV see Tully (2001a); Tully (2002); Pocock (2003).
[5]   For recent critical work in this complex tradition of civic freedom see Norval (2005); Kompridis (2006).
[10] Moran (2006); Borrows (2002). The best known example of this movement is Joseph Stiglitz, the former head of the World Bank (see Stiglitz, 2002). See, more generally, Rahnewa (2006).
[6]   For the background scholarship to Section V see Tully (2007b); Tully (2001b); Tully (2006); Tully (in press); Tully (2002); Sahle (2007); Hawken (2007).

ACKNOWLEDGEMENTS

I am most grateful to Eunice Sahle and Michael Byers for helpful discussions and Michael Peters for inviting me to participate in this important project.

REFERENCES

Amoore, L. (Ed.) (2005). *The global resistance reader*. London: Routledge.

Anghie, A. (2005). *Imperialism, sovereignty and the making of international law*. Cambridge: Cambridge University Press.

Ayers, A. (2006). Demystifying democratization: The global constitution of neo-liberal polities in Africa. *Third World Quarterly, 27*, 312–338.

Borrows, J. (2002). *Recovering Canada: The resurgence of indigenous law*. Toronto: University of Toronto Press.

Brodie, J. (2004). Introduction: Globalization and citizenship beyond the nation state. *Citizenship Studies, 8*(4), 323–332.

Conway, J. (2004). Citizenship in a time of empire: The World Social Forum as a new public space. *Citizenship Studies, 8*(4), 367–381.

De Sousa Santos, B. (Ed.) (2007). *Democratizing democracy*. London: Verso.

De Sousa Santos, B. (2006). *The rise of the global left: The World Social Forum and beyond*. London: Zed Books.

Dower, N. (2003). *An introduction to global citizenship*. Edinburgh: Edinburgh University Press.

Dower, N. & Williams, J. (Eds.) (2002). *Global citizenship: A critical reader*. Edinburgh: Edinburgh University Press.

Escobar, A. (2004). Beyond the third world: Imperial globality, global coloniality and anti-globalisation social movements. *Third World Quarterly, 25*(1), 207–230.

Evans, T. & Ayers, A. (2006). In the service of power: The global political economy of citizenship and human rights. *Citizenship Studies, 10*(3), 289–308.

Gills, B., Rocamora, J. & Wilson, R. (Eds.) (1993). *Low intensity democracy: Political power in the new world order*. Ann Arbor, MI: University of Michigan Press.

Hawken, P. (2007). *Blessed unrest: How the largest movement in the world came into being and why no one saw it coming*. New York: Viking.

Held, D. (2006). *Models of democracy*. Cambridge: Polity Press.

Held, D. & McGrew, A. (Eds.) (2002). *The global transformations reader*. Cambridge: Polity Press.

Ishay, M.R. (2004). *The history of human rights*. Berkeley, CA: University of California Press.

Kompridis, N. (2006). *Critique and disclosure: Critical theory between past and future*. Cambridge, MA: MIT Press.

Loader, I. & Walker, N. (2007). *Civilizing security*. Cambridge: Cambridge University Press.

Mamdani, M. (2001) Beyond settler and natives as political identities: Overcoming the legacy of colonialism. *Comparative Studies in Society and History, 43*(4), 651–64.

Mander, J. & Tauli-Corpuz, V. (Eds.) (2004). *Paradigm wars: Indigenous peoples resistance to economic globalization*. San Francisco, CA: Sierra Club Books.

Mignolo, W. (2000). *Local histories/global designs: Coloniality, subaltern knowledges and border thinking*. Princeton: Princeton University Press.

McNally, D. (2006). *Another world is possible: Globalization and anti-capitalism*. Winnipeg: Arbeiter Ring.

Moran, E.F. (2006). *People and nature: An introduction to human ecological relations*. Oxford: Blackwell.

Norval, A. (2007). *Aversive democracy*. Cambridge: Cambridge University Press.

Pocock, J. (2003). *The machiavellian moment: With a new afterword by the author*. Princeton: Princeton University Press.

Potter, D., Goldblatt, D., Kiloh, M. & Lewis, P. (Eds.) (1997). *Democratization*. Cambridge: Polity Press.

Rahnewa, M. (Ed.) (2006). *The post-development reader*. London: Zed Books.

Sahle, E. (2007). *Global citizenship and transnational civil society: Theory and practice*. Manuscript submitted for publication.

Seabrook, J. (2003). *The no nonsense guide to world poverty*. London: Verso.

Scheppele, K.L. (2007). *The international state of emergency: Challenges to constitutionalism after September 11*. Manuscript submitted for publication.

Skinner, Q. & Stråth, B. (2003). *States and citizens: History, theory, prospects*. Cambridge: Cambridge University Press.

Stiglitz, J. (2003). *Globalization and its discontents*. London: Penguin.

Tilly, C. (2007). *Democracy*. Cambridge: Cambridge University Press.

Tully, J. (2001a). Democracy and globalization. In W. Norman & R. Beiner (Eds.), *Canadian political philosophy* (pp. 36–62). Oxford: Oxford University Press.

Tully, J. (2001b). An ecological ethics for the present: Three approaches. In B. Gleeson & N. Low (Eds.), *Governing for the environment: Global problems, ethics and democracy* (pp. 147–165). Hampshire: Palgrave Publishers.

Tully, J. (2002). The unfreedom of the moderns. *Modern Law Review, 65*(2).

Tully, J. (2006, 22 February). Communication and imperialism. *Ctheory: 1000 Days of Theory*, td035. Retrieved 25 September, 2007, from http://www.ctheory.net/articles.aspx?id=508.

Tully, J. (2007a). The imperialism of modern constitutional democracy. In M. Loughlin & N. Walker (Eds.), *The paradox of constitutionalism* (pp. 315–338). Oxford: Oxford University Press.

Tully, J. (2007b). A new kind of Europe?: Democratic integration in the European Union. *CRISPP*, 10(1), 71–87.

Tully, J. (in press). Law, democracy and imperialism. In E. Christodoulidis & S. Tierney (Eds.), *Political theory and public law*. Aldershot: Ashgate.

Zerilli, L. (2005). *Feminism and the abyss of freedom*. Chicago: University of Chicago Press.

Weber, T. *Gandhi as disciple and mentor*. Cambridge: Cambridge University Press.

James Tully
University of Victoria

WALTER HUMES

THE DISCOURSE OF GLOBAL CITIZENSHIP

INTRODUCTION

Perceptions of the world are mediated through the language which is used to describe or explain social actions, economic trends, political initiatives and ethical judgements. Influenced by the work of Foucault, Derrida, Lyotard and others, modern commentators regularly invoke the concept of discourse to explore the relationship between language, knowledge and power (e.g. MacLure, 2003; Peters & Burbules, 2004). A particular focus has been the way in which certain words or phrases come to gain ascendancy in public and professional discourse. Among the terms that have achieved wide international currency are globalisation and citizenship, often combined in the formulation 'global citizenship'. Governments, non-governmental public bodies, business corporations, international organisations and pressure groups all deploy these terms in public debate, policy documents and mission statements. Such widespread appeal may indicate that the favoured terms have considerable explanatory power but, before making that assumption, it is worth asking a series of prior questions.

- Why have these particular concepts achieved prominence at this particular time?
- What is the knowledge base from which they derive?
- How has political and economic power been used to promote them, and to what ends?
- Whose interests do the terms serve?
- How do they shape the thinking of professionals, particularly in the provision of public services such as education?

In this chapter it will not be possible to answer all of these questions in detail but they should be kept in mind as the discussion advances. What will be attempted is an analysis of the concept of global citizenship: both the constituent elements and the combined formulation. It will be argued that various agendas are at work in the deployment of the concept, some motivated by a genuine concern to promote international understanding and the rights and welfare of disadvantaged groups, others by a desire to maintain or extend economic and social advantage. Particular attention will be given to global citizenship in education and its potential in raising awareness of issues of poverty, identity and cultural difference. Demaine (2002, p. 118) has observed that 'the idea of "global citizenship" is codified in school curriculum requirements often with little or no reference to the problematical

M.A. Peters, A. Britton and H. Blee (Eds.), Global Citizenship Education: Philosophy, Theory and Pedagogy, 41–52.

character either of the concept of "globalisation" or of "citizenship"'. This reinforces the need for some initial conceptual unpacking of the terminology.

DIMENSIONS OF GLOBALISATION

Bauman (1998, p. 1) has noted that 'all vogue words tend to share a similar fate: the more experiences they pretend to make transparent, the more they themselves become opaque. The more numerous are the orthodox truths they elbow out and supplant, the faster they turn into no-questions-asked canons ... "Globalization" is no exception to that rule'. With this in mind, it will be helpful to disentangle some of the main dimensions of globalisation and consider the extent to which they reinforce each other and the extent to which they may work in contrary directions (see Bottery, 2000, pp. 1–26). It is not claimed that the classification that is offered below is comprehensive: it simply identifies some of the main dimensions of globalisation, particularly those which have significance for education. Furthermore, it should be stressed that these dimensions are not discrete: they overlap and inter-relate in complex ways.

Economic globalisation is driven by trade and commerce, by currency exchange rates, by the cost and availability of labour, above all by the aspirations of multi-national companies to expand and prosper. The biggest players, such as oil and information technology companies, can exert a degree of power that is equal to, or in some cases greater than, nation-states. This raises challenging questions about national identity. The loyalties of multi-nationals are to the global market rather than to any particular country and this can make it difficult for governments to pursue national policies. There are also implications for individuals, deriving not only from the effects of job losses and gains as the manufacture of goods and the provision of services may be re-located from one country to another, but also in terms of their perceptions of themselves as having local, regional, national and/or international identity. Within the UK, for example, people living in Scotland (some of whom will have originated elsewhere) may think of themselves as Scottish, British, European, or even as World Citizens within a reconfigured global environment. As the labour market becomes more international in character, with more people having to move between countries in pursuit of employment and to gain the kind of experience multinational companies now demand, so there are implications for the educational system in terms of economic understanding and vocational preparation.

Political globalisation refers to the trend towards forms of political organisation above and beyond those of the nation state. It is apparent in the existence of transnational agencies of a political, military, economic and environmental kind: e.g. the European Union (EU), the World Health Organization (WHO), the North Atlantic Treaty Organization (NATO), and the United Nations (UN). Political globalisation raises questions about democratic processes and the location of power. Some writers deplore the trend towards what they describe as a globally connected political and bureaucratic elite which determines priorities for the rest of the world. Others take a more positive view of political globalisation and see it (potentially at least) as bringing some of the benefits of advanced democracies to nations which are ruled by undemocratic systems of government. One thinks, for example, of the United Nations Convention on the Rights of the Child. The spread of awareness of the principles enshrined in such documents, it is argued, puts pressure on oppressive regimes and gives hope to those who suffer from various forms of political persecution.

In respect of education, a particularly important body is the Organization for Economic Cooperation and Development (OECD) which sets cross-national agendas for education and develops performance indicators enabling international comparisons to be made. Within the EU, pressures for convergence among member states exert influence on national education policies. Supporters of this trend argue for its value in relation to the comparability of qualifications and the mobility of the workforce. Critics say that it leads to bureaucratic conformity and diminishes the distinctiveness of national educational traditions. This concern is also reflected in a third type of globalisation.

Cultural globalisation takes somewhat contrary forms. It often refers to a trend towards standardisation of taste in things like fashion, popular culture, music, film, television: what Ritzer (2000) has referred to as the 'McDonaldization' of society. But, at the same time, increased opportunities for travel mean that people have access to, and can experience directly, greater variety in such things as customs, attitudes and values: e.g. attitudes to law, religion, and the family. This encourages a trend towards relativity of values, a questioning of the basis of so-called fixed standards of morality and behaviour. There are so many alternatives to choose from that it can seem simply a matter of personal preference, or an opportunity to reinvent oneself in various forms over a lifetime. Thus, there is a 'market' in belief systems as well as goods and services. This form of globalisation presents a particular challenge to schools, which have traditionally been expected to promote a set of values that helps to maintain social stability and continuity. If, in the world outside education, the structural supports for those values become less secure, schools run the risk of seeming to be archaic institutions, out of touch with what is happening in the rest of society.

Technological globalisation arises from the rapid advances in information technology. These have already transformed the way business is conducted, with major financial transactions taking place at the press of a button on a computer keyboard. The internet has also brought about massive changes in the way individuals conduct their lives, whether in terms of the purchase of goods and services or in terms of their personal relationships. There are also implications for the way governments and pressure groups operate. Massive amounts of information are released via the internet, sometimes as a way of responding to requests for freedom of information, sometimes as propaganda exercises designed to promote particular policies. Technology makes it possible for people sharing common interests to communicate and organise campaigns, even though they may live thousands of miles apart. The internet as a resource for knowledge (as distinct from mere information) raises challenging issues for traditional educational institutions. Previously schools, colleges and universities had a virtual monopoly of knowledge, acting as gatekeepers to it and enabling or restricting access to its various forms. While these institutions remain vitally important, their role in society is changing as the contribution of other agencies to knowledge generation and knowledge transmission is increasingly recognised. The rapid expansion of online learning is one response to this. Developments in information technology affect people's lives in richer and poorer countries alike (though as yet not in equal measure), and in a more immediate way than at any previous time in history.

Environmental globalisation encompasses a range of issues. These include the depletion of natural resources (oil, gas, and coal) and the effects of increasing demands for energy consumption on global warming and environmental pollution. The reluctance of some countries (most notably the United States) to address these issues has become a focus for the efforts of environmental charities, such as Greenpeace and Friends of the Earth. Attempts to develop alternative forms of energy (through wind farms, for example) have provoked fierce debate because of their effect on the landscape. In South America the destruction of the rainforests for economic gain by logging companies has had serious consequences for the culture and lifestyle of the indigenous population, as well as for the habitat of animals, birds and insects. Taken together, these concerns have prompted a global debate about the spread of consumerism, the sustainability of current patterns of living and indeed the future of the planet.

The far-reaching nature of these changes and the scale of their impact create disequilibrium for societies. This, in turn, requires governments to respond. All of the types of globalisation mentioned above have substantial implications for education, not least for teacher education. At the simplest level, it is important that people should acquire some understanding of what is happening. Future generations will have to know more (about economics, politics, culture, technology, environment) if they are going to function effectively. They will have to be alert to the potential challenges to national identity and representative democracy. And if complete moral relativism is to be avoided, questions concerning the basis of personal and social responsibility have to be addressed. These concerns help to explain why the citizenship agenda has such international attraction. How can we ensure that an understanding of the processes of globalisation is reflected in the curriculum? How can we encourage young people to become engaged with the nature and scale of the challenge that globalisation represents, in ways that make a difference to the way they act? Is it necessary to re-define the role of the teacher, at local, national and international levels, in response to the pace and scale of change? How adequate are traditional forms of representative democracy, as practised in most developed Western societies, to carry the expectations of an active citizenry seeking to come to terms with global shifts? These are some of the questions that arise when the implications for citizenship and citizenship education are considered against a global backdrop.

DIMENSIONS OF CITIZENSHIP

Faulks (2000, p. 1) has provided a useful insight into the current interest in citizenship: 'Citizenship has an almost universal appeal. Radicals and conservatives alike feel able to utilize the language of citizenship in support of their policy prescriptions.' The reason for this universal appeal is that the idea of citizenship contains both individualistic and collectivist elements: it recognizes the dignity of the individual, as a citizen with certain rights, but at the same time reaffirms the social context in which the individual lives and acts – a social context which introduces ideas of legal requirements, community, mutual respect and civic responsibility. These sentiments are evident in the Crick Report (QCA, 1998), whose recommendations led to the introduction of citizenship education as a compulsory element of the school curriculum in England and Wales. The principal author of that report later stated: 'It is a mission, cutting right across party lines, to create a sense of purpose in our society in which people take pleasure in helping and working with others. It is a mission to balance competitive individualism with sociability and to combat the alienation from civic values felt by so many young people' (Crick, 2000). However, the universal appeal of citizenship is somewhat double-edged in its effects. On the one hand, it means that the discourse of citizenship connects with the experience of many different people in widely different situations. On the other hand, if it becomes subject to divergent interpretations, it runs the risk of becoming an example of vague, feel-good rhetoric, a term that can mean everything and nothing.

The Crick Report identified three particular dimensions of citizenship: the development of social and moral responsibility; the promotion of political literacy (including elements of economics); and the encouragement of community involvement. However, Humes (2002) has argued that in the research literature which followed the Crick Report, this focus was somewhat lost as debates about citizenship spilled over into many related fields: moral education (Holden, 1998; Haydon, 2000); international and intercultural education (Cogan & Derricott, 2000); personal and social education (Cairns, 2000): education for global understanding (Gardner, 2000); rights and democracy in education (Alderson, 2000); education for social inclusion (Gundara, 2000); and anti-racist education (Osler, 2000).

Osler and Starkey (2006) offer a helpful review of the literature on education for democratic citizenship in the period 1995–2005. They identify six key contextual factors which help to explain the considerable growth of interest in citizenship education during that decade: global injustice and inequality; globalisation and migration; concerns about civic and political engagement; youth deficit (e.g. anti-social behaviour and violence in schools); the end of the cold war; and anti-democratic and racist movements. Against this broad background, it is not surprising that a degree of conceptual slippage is evident in research studies relating to citizenship education – the varied origins of appeals to citizenship can lead in many different directions and can be understood in a variety of ways. At one level, the interest can be explained as a reaction to the effects of neo-liberal economic policies in the 1980s, which seemed to encourage selfish individualism at the expense of social responsibility. In the UK, the so-called Third Way of successive Blair governments sought to reconcile market freedom and state welfare (Giddens, 1998, 2000). A key element in this political reconfiguration has been the importance attached to the idea of building 'social capital' (Field, 2003; Halpern, 2005) which requires both economic enterprise and civic involvement. The terms used to define social capital – trust, respect, networks, community – also feature in many accounts of citizenship.

At another level, the appeal of citizenship needs to be understood as part of a programme of moral renewal. In many Western countries, not least in the UK, there has been growing concern about the social effects of a number of trends: the decline of traditional forms of religion; the breakdown of the family unit; the effects of drugs culture on young people; and the rise in suicides (especially among young men). Related to this, there are worries about the alienation of many young people from major social institutions, such as the law – the view, for example, that the law is not an instrument for the enactment of justice but for the protection of elites and the enrichment of members of the legal profession. Citizenship education is seen by some as a way of countering these negative trends.

Yet another dimension of citizenship derives from a desire to assert, protect and extend the rights of various groups perceived to be disadvantaged – including the poor, the unemployed, the homeless, the disabled, single parents and ethnic minorities. Members of these groups often feel that they are marginalized and treated with a lack of respect. Here the policy response has been to seek to remedy the causes and consequences of social exclusion, with the aim of making those affected feel that their status as citizens is equal to that of other members of society. Within the UK, the language of social exclusion in New Labour rhetoric has been subject to penetrating critical analysis by Fairclough (2000, pp. 51–65). Citizenship and globalisation come together when the rights of the dispossessed in politically unstable and economically backward countries are considered. Issues of poverty, in particular the North–South divide between developed and developing countries, have become the focus of repeated efforts at amelioration by governments, international agencies and charities, stimulated by growing public concern as images of malnutrition, persecution, torture and genocide appear regularly on television screens. In the UK a White Paper published in 2000, *Eliminating World Poverty: Making Globalisation Work for the Poor* (DfID, 2000) provoked much public discussion. However, translating well-intentioned rhetoric into action that really does make a difference seems a never-ending task. Tikly (2001, p. 151) questions 'the relevance of existing accounts of globalization and education for low income, postcolonial countries, with special reference to the educational systems of sub-Saharan Africa'. This reminds us that dominant discourses are generally constructed and promoted by those who enjoy what might be called 'narrative privilege' – that is, the power to create a version of events that may be offered as rational analysis but which, in fact, is driven by self-interest (see Cookson, 1994).

Citizenship is also closely related to personal and social identity. People develop a sense of identity in a variety of ways. They may do so in terms of race, gender, ethnicity, location, faith, family, sexuality, employment, or some combination of these factors. They may also define themselves as citizens of a particular country, with varying degrees of allegiance to that country's traditions and values. But as the migration of people increases, whether from South to North America, or from Africa to Europe, or, within Europe, from East to West, the basis of that identification becomes less clear. And even within well-established nations, such as the United Kingdom, there are internal shifts taking place that influence the self-perceptions of the indigenous population. Devolution has led to the creation of a Parliament in Scotland and an Assembly in Wales and many people see themselves as Scottish or Welsh first, and British only second. Thus, contrary tendencies can be detected – some reinforcing what might be called a local sense of citizenship, based on nationalistic impulses, others weakening traditional allegiances to a particular nation as new patterns of population movement develop. The overall effect is to create diversity, uncertainty and tension – a potentially explosive mix. Add to this the growth of international terrorism and it is not hard to see why citizenship has become such a sensitive political issue. One of the questions that surfaced following terrorists acts committed by British-born Muslims in 2006 was, how could their allegiance to movements which had their origins elsewhere (in the Middle East, in Afghanistan) be explained? In other words, how has globalisation impacted on the sense of identity that certain groups develop, and what does this mean for conceptions of citizenship? Education is seen as a vital part of the strategy in trying to address these questions. As Davies *et al* (2005, p. 72) put it: 'the question for education is how to come to grips with the changing nature of citizenship in a globalizing world'.

GLOBAL CITIZENSHIP IN EDUCATION

Just as the individual terms 'globalisation' and 'citizenship' are subject to various interpretations, so the combined formulation 'global citizenship' can be configured in a number of ways. This can be illustrated by contrasting the perspectives of business corporations on the one hand and charitable organizations on the other.

The technology company Hewlett Packard (HP) states on its website (accessed March 22, 2007) that it is 'committed to being a leader in global citizenship'. It goes on:

> We are proud of our efforts as global stewards, helping to reduce environmental impacts, raise standards in HP's global supply chain and increase access to information technology worldwide. We conduct our business with uncompromising integrity and strive to live up to every one of our commitments to our customers, partners, employees and shareholders. Furthermore, we believe that global citizenship is good business. We embrace our responsibility to society by being an economic, intellectual and social asset to each country and community in which we operate.

(Online at http://www.hp.com/hpinfo/globalcitizenship/)

This statement is entirely consistent with attempts at a political level in the UK and elsewhere to reconcile wealth creation and social responsibility. Global citizenship, in this view, is 'good business' but it depends on operating according to a set of ethical principles, informed by a sensitive awareness of social and environmental issues, rather than crude economic self-interest. However, what is not captured by the statement is how potential conflicts between economic advantage and social impact are reconciled, nor how the differential power relationship between large companies and local communities are managed. The 'integrity' of the rhetoric could thus only be properly assessed by examining particular cases.

The HP statement refers to 'intellectual' as well as economic and social assets. Some companies have forged links with the academic world in pursuit of global citizenship. For example, the Ford Motor Company has established a Center for Global Citizenship at the Kellogg School of Management at Northwestern University. The Center's mission, as stated on its website (accessed March 22, 2007), is

> to address through research and teaching the challenges faced by corporations who have become the main agents of global social and political change. Our scholars are dedicated to an interdisciplinary approach that combines ethical, strategic and organizational concerns.
>
> (Online at http://www.kellogg.northwestern.edu/research/fordcenter/)

Once again the discourse of global citizenship has been mobilised in support of a venture that seeks to pursue objectives that in earlier times were seen as, if not exactly antithetical, at least in some tension. It is very common now for universities to be sponsored by commercial organisations as well as philanthropic individuals. Such sponsorship is seen as a way of avoiding over-dependence on the state. But just as state funding of research raises difficult questions about the degree of intellectual control that might be entailed, both in respect of the nature of the research and the use to which its findings are put, so private funding of research raises equally challenging questions about intellectual property rights and findings which might not serve the commercial interests of the sponsors.

By way of contrast, it is worth looking at the interpretation of global citizenship favoured by a charitable organization. The long-established UK-based charity, Oxfam, has been a leading campaigner in the promotion of Education for Global Citizenship. It has produced *A Guide for Schools* (Oxfam, 2006) which sets out three main reasons for giving Global Citizenship an important place in the school curriculum:

- Children's lives are increasingly shaped by what happens in other parts of the world. They need appropriate knowledge, understanding, skills and values if they are to make sense of these global forces.

- Education for Global Citizenship involves active learning which develops skills of critical thinking, communication, cooperation and conflict resolution. These help to improve motivation, behaviour and achievement.

- Education is a powerful tool for changing the world, especially in relation to such issues as poverty, denial of rights, and the inequitable and unsustainable use of resources.

The Global Citizen is defined as someone who:

- Is aware of the wider world and has a sense of their own role as a world citizen.
- Respects and values diversity.
- Has an understanding of how the world works.
- Is outraged by social injustice.
- Participates in the community at a range of levels, from the local to the global.
- Is willing to act to make the world a more equitable and sustainable place.
- Takes responsibility for their actions.

(Oxfam, 2006, p. 3)

The Oxfam Guide goes on to detail curriculum content in terms of ages and stages, suggesting a range of activities and methods, including an audit of the extent to which schools already meet Global Citizenship standards. Clearly this has implications not just for what and how children are taught but also for the attitudes and practices of school managers and teachers. Bottery (2006, p. 106) has called for much greater political and ecological awareness among teachers:

This requirement ... argues that educators need to be much more aware of the factors beyond their own institution which constrain, steer, or facilitate their practice. These factors extend beyond the local and national right through to the global. They include not only the [various] forms of globalization ... but the mediation of these forms at cultural and national level. Without such awareness, professionals are blind to the changes affecting their societies and their own practice.

Some would see potential dangers in all of this. The kinds of knowledge that would be valued would carry implicit – and sometimes explicit – messages. In the teaching of geography, for example, a switch in emphasis from traditional content (such as rivers, oceans, mountains and maps) to content which focuses on economic and environmental issues (poverty, climate change, migration and the operation of multinational companies) might be seen as too politically charged, with teachers running the risk of being accused of indoctrination. In response, it could be argued that to fail to include coverage of controversial issues is to do a disservice to young people by preparing them inadequately for the world they will inherit as adults. There are certainly legitimate questions to be asked about the handling of controversial issues in the classroom, to ensure that different perspectives are adequately represented and that the teacher does not become, wittingly or unwittingly, an advocate for a particular cause. But teaching is never an entirely neutral activity. Decisions about what to teach always involve value judgements about the kind of knowledge that is deemed worthwhile and this applies equally to traditional and innovative curricular content.

The Oxfam approach to the teaching of global citizenship takes an optimistic view of the possibilities of change. A more sceptical, or at least questioning, perspective is offered by Davies who asks whether global citizenship is merely an abstraction – 'a fiction, a seeming paradox or oxymoron' (Davies, 2006, p. 5) – or a genuine framework for action. Basing her study both on an analysis of the various meanings on global citizenship – drawing particular attention to issues of social justice and democracy – and on a review of actual curriculum content and structure, she asks a series of important questions about the impact of current programmes and identifies gaps in research-based evidence. It is one thing to encourage young people to acquire knowledge about topics of global interest but whether that makes a difference to their actions outside school is uncertain. We need to know more about what predisposes young people to take part in rallies or demonstrations about major events (such as the war in Iraq), what leads them to join social movements, such as Greenpeace, what predisposes them to support fundamentalist groups pursuing a global agenda, or what causes them to disengage from the political process altogether.

As part of this, it is important to recognise that there are both cognitive and affective dimensions to these processes. Moral outrage at perceived injustices is not likely to be effective if it is not informed by knowledge and evidence which can be mobilised as part of a strategy to bring about change. Equally, the possibility of change is weakened if a good understanding of global issues is unaccompanied by any personal commitment to a set of ethical values or the personal will to make a difference. The challenge facing teachers should not be underestimated. One of the common exhortations they hear is to enable children to see connections between local, national and global issues. In a run-down inner city area, there may well be identifiable effects of globalisation – job losses arising from the transfer of production to countries where labour is cheaper, new residents who may be immigrants or asylum seekers, increased pressures on housing, the health service and the educational system (e.g. caused by an influx of children whose first language is not English). These visible changes certainly have educational potential – in terms of promoting understanding of difference, learning from each other, etc. – but they are likely to cause a degree of resentment among at least some of the local population. That resentment may be compounded by hostile, prejudiced or bigoted attitudes to issues of race, ethnicity or religion (or a combination of these). Thus great sensitivity is required in linking local, national and global issues. Badly handled, the outcome could be a sharpening of divisions, and the encouragement of political extremism, rather than increased appreciation of the common humanity which coexists alongside expressions of difference.

If global citizenship can serve such very different agendas as those pursued by, on the one hand, international companies, seeking to maintain and extend their market share and increase business profits, and, on the other hand, charitable campaigning groups, seeking to raise awareness of poverty, oppression and injustice, does that mean that it has become a fundamentally incoherent concept which should be abandoned altogether? Even if that were desirable, it cannot simply be willed. Powerful discursive forms, such as global citizenship, have a life beyond the decisions of any individual or group. They are developed and sustained at a level of politics and ideology which can sweep aside academic or professional objections. Despite their complexities and contradictions, they represent the spirit of the age in a way that reflects the interests and concerns of many different groups operating at local, national and international levels. It is true that their utility value will have a limited shelf life and that they will eventually be superseded by other discursive forms. But in the meantime, they cannot simply be discarded because they elude easy and unambiguous definition.

In any case, within the field of education, the concept of global citizenship has brought some advantages. It has opened up territory that for too long was closed off by a narrow agenda of standards, targets, accountability and assessment. That agenda served to restrict the curriculum, weaken teacher professionalism and debase the aims of education. Global citizenship, however interpreted, deals with the big issues of our time: wealth and poverty; equality and justice; access and exclusion; rights and democracy, freedom and authority. We should certainly welcome the opening of minds, the widening of horizons, that that broad discursive frame allows. What we are left with is a sense of ambivalence. All dominant discourses, however attractive – and perhaps especially because they are attractive – deserve to be subjected to critical interrogation. But, insofar as they provide an intellectual framework that enables important questions to be analysed and discussed, their contribution to thinking should be recognised.

REFERENCES

Alderson, P. (2000). Citizenship in theory and practice: being or becoming citizens with rights. In D. Lawton, J. Cairns & R. Gardner (Eds.), *Education for citizenship* (pp. 114–135). London & New York: Continuum.

Bauman, Z. (1998). *Globalization: The human consequences*. Cambridge: Polity Press.

Bottery, M. (2000). *Education, policy and ethics*. London & New York: Continuum.

Bottery, M. (2006). Education and globalization: Redefining the role of the educational professional. *Educational Review, 58*(1), 95–113.

Cairns, J. (2000). Personal development and citizenship education: Setting the agenda for lifelong learning. In D. Lawton, J. Cairns & R. Gardner (Eds.), *Education for citizenship* (pp. 38–53). London: Continuum.

Cogan, J.J. & Derricott, R. (2000). *Citizenship for the 21st century: An international perspective on education*. London: Kogan Page.

Cookson, P. (1994). The power discourse: Elite narratives and educational policy formation. In G. Walford (Ed.), *Researching the powerful in education* (pp. 116–130). London: UCL Press.

Crick, B. (2000, 30 June). Ethos fables hide truth. *Times Educational Supplement*, p. 15.

Davies, L. (2006). Global citizenship: Abstraction or framework for action? *Educational Review, 58*(1), 5–25.

Davies, I., Evans, M. & Reid, A. (2005). Globalising citizenship education? A critique of 'global education' and 'citizenship education'. *British Journal of Educational Studies, 53*(1), 66–89.

Demaine, J. (2002). Globalisation and citizenship education. *International Studies in Sociology of Education, 12*(2), 117–128.

Department for International Development (DfID) (2000). *Eliminating world poverty: Making globalisation work for the poor.* London: The Stationery Office.

Fairclough, N. (2000). *New labour, new language?* London: Routledge.

Faulks, K. (2000). *Citizenship.* London: Routledge.

Field, J. (2003). *Social capital.* London: Routledge.

Gardner, R. (2000). Global perspectives in citizenship education. In D. Lawton, J. Cairns & R. Gardner (Eds.), *Education for citizenship* (pp. 228–241). London: Continuum.

Giddens, A. (1998). *The third way: The renewal of social democracy.* Cambridge: Polity Press.

Giddens, A. (2000). *The third way and its critics.* Cambridge: Polity Press.

Gundara, J. (2000). Social diversity, inclusiveness and citizenship education. In D. Lawton, J. Cairns, & R. Gardner (Eds.), *Education for citizenship* (pp. 14–25). London: Continuum.

Halpern, D. (2005). *Social capital.* Cambridge: Polity Press.

Haydon, G. (2000). The moral agenda of citizenship education. In D. Lawton, J. Cairns, & R. Gardner (Eds.), *Education for citizenship* (pp. 136–147). London: Continuum.

Holden, C. (1998). Education for citizenship: The contribution of social, moral and cultural education. *Children's Social and Economics Education, 3*(3), 140–150.

Humes, W. M. (2002). Exploring citizenship and enterprise in a global context. *Citizenship, Social and Economics Education, 5*(1), 17–28.

MacLure, M. (2003). *Discourse in educational and social research.* Buckingham: Open University Press.

Oxfam (2006). *Education for citizenship: A guide for schools.* Oxford: Oxfam. Retrieved from http://www.oxfam.org.uk.

Osler, A. (2000). The Crick report: Difference, equality and racial justice. *Curriculum Journal, 11*(1), 25–37.

Osler, A. & Starkey, H. (2006). Education for democratic citizenship: A review of research, policy and practice 1995–2005. *Research Papers in Education, 21*(4): 433–466.

Peters, M.A. & Burbules, N.C. (2004). *Poststructuralism and educational research.* New York: Rowman & Littlefield.

QCA (1998). *Education for citizenship and the teaching of democracy in schools* [Crick Report]. London: Qualifications and Curriculum Authority.

Ritzer, G. (2000). *The McDonaldization of society* (revised edition). Pine Forge: Sage.

Tikly, L. (2001). Globalisation and education in the postcolonial world: Towards a conceptual framework. *Comparative Education, 37*(2): 151–171.

Walter Humes
University of Paisley

MICHAEL A. PETERS

BETWEEN EMPIRES

Rethinking Identity and Citizenship in the Context of Globalisation[1]

INTRODUCTION

This paper addresses the question of rethinking citizenship within the context of globalisation. It adds the conference code words 'between empires' to the title. It accepts the proposition that we are between two different historical periods characterised by forms of empire: essentially the nineteenth-century imperialism of the European powers and the American decentred system of global rule of the 21st century. The paper focuses on the latter by contrasting two competing and influential conceptions of the 'new imperialism' that have emerged recently to focus on questions of international security, world order and the evolving system of states. Questions of globalisation, national identity and citizenship are transformed when raised in this new geopolitical context.

Robert Cooper, Deputy Secretary of the Defence and Overseas Secretariat in the British Cabinet Office, posits the development of a postmodern European state system based on transparency, interdependence, and mutual surveillance. He calls for a 'new imperialism' – one compatible with human rights and cosmopolitan values – in order to sort out the problems of rogue states and the chaos of premodern states (Cooper, 2000, pp. 18–19). By contrast, Michael Hardt and Anthony Negri use the combined resources of Marx and Deleuze, to chart the emergence of a new form of sovereignty they call *Empire*. They narrate a history of the passage from imperialism to Empire, that is, from a modernity dominated by the sovereignty of nation-states, and the imperialisms of European powers, to a postmodernity characterised by a single, though decentered, new logic of global rule (Hardt & Negri, 2000).

In a strong sense Hardt and Negri's *Empire* and Cooper's 'new imperialism' are both geopolitical and juridical forms of globalisation that are dependent on emergent forms of global sovereignty. The difference between the two views is that, whereas the former focuses on American Empire as the dominant form, the latter concentrates on an emergent European postmodern state system. They both entertain extranational forms of citizenship based on these supranational systems and problematise the concept of citizenship based on the bounded system of the sovereign state.

Perhaps, more than ever before the question of globalisation and citizenship revolves around the free movement of peoples. By this I mean not only the modern

M.A. Peters, A. Britton and H. Blee (Eds.), Global Citizenship Education: Philosophy, Theory and
Pedagogy, 53–70.

Diaspora, or the planned colonial migrations or the more recent global mobility of highly skilled labour that is rewarded by citizenship. But more importantly, I mean refugees of all kinds and asylum-seekers and all that that entails – enforced border crossings, ethnic cleansing policies, the huge illegal movement of so-called 'aliens', detention camps the likes of Woomera and even Guantanomo Bay, where the concept of rights is fragile or has entirely disappeared.[2]

GLOBALISATION AND CITIZENSHIP

At the beginning of the twenty-first century the world experiences processes of both integration and disintegration. The expansion of world markets, as a form of economic globalisation can be understood as a process of integration composed of international flows of capital, goods, information, and people. The same process is both a form of economical integration and a polarisation of wealth that exacerbates existing tendencies toward greater global inequalities between rich and poor countries and regions. It also accentuates the need for reviewing the templates of the global system of governance that emerged from the Bretton Woods agreements that founded many of the world institutions that comprise the contemporary architecture of the world system. Now more than at any time in the past, with the end of the Cold War, the collapse of the Soviet system, the consolidation of the EU, and the entry of China in the WTO, we are witnessing an accelerated set of changes – economic, cultural, technological and political – that impinge on one another in novel ways and create new possibilities and dangers both for the democratic state and the notions of citizenship and national identity that underpin it.

The modern concept of citizenship – a recent concept historically – implies the existence of a civil or political community, a set of rights and obligations ascribed to citizens by virtue of their membership in that community, and an ethic of participation and solidarity needed to sustain it. Most traditional accounts of citizenship begin with the assertion of basic civil, political and social rights of individuals and note the way in which the modern concept as inherently egalitarian, took on a universal appeal with the development of the liberal tradition which is often understood as synonymous with modernity. Yet the concept has appealed to both conservatives and radical democrats: the former emphasise individual freedom at the expense of equality and see state intervention as an intolerable and unwarranted violation of the freedom of the individual, while the latter stress the democratic potential of citizenship. Increasingly, on the left the concept has been seen as a means to control the injustices of capitalism. For the left the most pressing question has been the status of citizenship in the modern state and what kind of political community best promotes it.

The classic theorisation of democratic citizenship is to be found in Marshall's famous modelling of three forms of citizenship: civil, political and social. In this conception civil citizenship referred to personal liberty and a regime of individual rights, political citizenship referred to both political participation and democratic representation, and social citizenship to intervention by the state to reduce economic inequalities and promote social justice. It is now possible to chart the significant shifts in the definitions of citizenship that have accompanied globalisation, including the breakdown of the historic compromise between capitalism, democracy and the welfare state, the rise of neoliberalism and with it the expansion of world markets. In the United Kingdom under Third Way politics there has been a shift from the concept of *rights* to one of *responsibilities*, a move away from State intervention towards community involvement in civic networks with a corresponding emphasis on promoting forms of social capital, and a shift from active political citizenship to passive political literacy (see Gamarnikov & Green, 1999).

These shifts are emblematic of what Faulks (2000, p. 57) calls the 'ten dualisms of liberal citizenship' (see Table 1).

Table 1: Ten Dualisms of Liberal Citizenship

Individual	Community
Agency	Structure
Private sphere	Public sphere
Men as citizens	Women as carers
Freedom through the market	Equality through politics
Market rights	Social rights
Active citizens	Passive citizens
Rights	Responsibilities/Democracy
Sovereignty	Human rights
Science	Nature

Source: Citizenship, Keith Faulks (2000) London: Routledge, p. 57

The abstract individualism of the liberal tradition, dating back to Locke, tends to view 'the individual and community as being in opposition and ... in part this explains their ambivalence towards responsibilities, democracy and social rights'. In particular, the emphasis placed on individual autonomy makes liberals suspicious of notions of community and a series of dualisms echo this fundamental opposition that we can trace through liberal theory. A similar theorisation is given by Faulks (2000, p. 11) in terms of what he describes as 'thin' and 'thick' citizenship (see Table 2). Neoliberalism and, some would argue also Third Way politics, tend to entertain versions of 'thin' citizenship, which are largely compatible with the diminished role of the state with the rise of globalisation and multi-national capitalism.[3]

Table 2: Ideal Types of Citizenship

Thin Citizenship	Thick Citizenship
Rights privileged	Rights and responsibilities as mutually supportive
Passive	Active
State as a necessary evil	Political community (not necessarily the state) as foundation of the good life
Purely public status	Pervades public and private
Independence	Interdependence
Freedom through choice	Freedom through civic virtue
Legal	Moral

Source: *Citizenship*, Keith Faulks (2000) London: Routledge, p. 11

The two terms 'globalisation' and 'citizenship' are not normally juxtaposed in social and political analysis. They appear as contradictory or, at least, conflicting: the former points to an economic and cultural process of world integration, based on the unregulated flows of capital and underwritten by developments in new information and communications technologies, while the latter serves as a metaphor for political community. Globalisation seems to threaten the sovereignty of the nation-state and with it the notion of citizenship that developed during the modern era. Within the context of globalisation the pressing political question is how people can create and protect a sense of community and local identity in order to protect and bolster the institutions that provide them with social protection.

On one influential interpretation, globalisation represents the historical culmination of a set of world processes that began much earlier in the age of colonisation leading to the now dominant system of late world capitalism, based on the form of the multinational corporation. It is this multinational form of the corporation, which many theorists see as threatening the sovereignty of the nation-state and also diminishing the prospect for community, civil society and citizenship. On this view, economic liberalisation and restructuring have eroded the economic and social rights of people in many countries, while at the same time developments in international communications have expanded the international awareness of rights and created conditions for the emergence of international networks that may come to comprise civil society on a global scale. The processes of globalisation, on this view, undermine both the modern notion of citizenship and the sovereignty of the nation-state on which it depends. More importantly, some theorists (e.g. Mishra, 1999) argue, the logic of globalisation increases inequalities and weakens the basis and ideological underpinnings of social protection and partnership (see Table 3).

Table 3: Social Policy and the 'Logic' of Globalisation

Globalisation undermines the ability of national governments to pursue the objectives of full employment and economic growth through reflationary policies. 'Keynesianism in one country' ceases to be a viable option.

Globalisation results in an increasing inequality in wages and working conditions through greater labour market flexibility, a differentiated 'Post-Fordist' work-force and decentralized collective bargaining. Global competition and mobility of capital result in 'social dumping' and a downward shift in wages and working conditions.

Globalisation exerts a downward pressure on systems of social protection and social expenditure by prioritizing the reduction of deficits and debt and lowering the taxation as key objectives of state policy.

Globalisation weakens the ideological underpinnings of social protection, especially that of a national minimum, by undermining national solidarity and legitimating inequality of rewards.

Globalisation weakens the basis of social partnership and tripartism by shifting the balance of power away from labour and the state and towards capital.

Globalisation constrains the policy options of nations by virtually excluding left-of-centre approaches. In this sense it spells the 'end of ideology' as far as welfare state policies are concerned.

The logic of globalisation comes into conflict with the 'logic' of the national community and democratic politics. Social policy emerges as a major issue of contention between global capitalism and the democratic nation state.

Source: Globalization and the welfare state, Ramesh Mishra (1999). Cheltenham, UK: Edward Elgar, pp. 15–16

Yet so far most of the debate on citizenship has occurred within national boundaries without much regard for the impact of globalisation. As the United Nations Research Institute for Social Development (UNRISD) indicated at their international conference on the theme of globalisation and citizenship held in 1996, 'globalisation' serves as a synonym for contemporary forms of rapid structural change and 'citizenship' serves as a metaphor for social protection and the reconstruction of solidarity.

> Until recently, they were not systematically juxtaposed in social analysis. 'Citizenship studies' have traditionally been more likely to focus on debates over civil and political rights, immigration law or forms of political participation in particular countries than on global economic and social trends. And analysis of 'globalization' has been the terrain of macro-economists and sociologists not usually well trained in the intricacies of individual rights. But as the pace of change quickens, the relevance of the two concepts for each other becomes clearer. Global market forces now pose a fundamental challenge to social citizenship in advanced welfare states. At the same time, the new ease of international migration continually forces reconsideration of 'who belongs' in national societies, and what their rights should be. The revolution in telecommunications encourages debates on the proper balance between the private and public realms. And the definition of rights and obligations of various groups, like women, whose identity and sense of solidarity may transcend national borders, is being subject to persistent re-evaluation. In consequence, it becomes increasingly important for national citizenship debates to incorporate international elements, and for students of globalization to understand the changing parameters of citizenship. (pp. 5–6)

Not only is it important for national citizenship debates to incorporate international elements but for us to rethink questions of citizenship and national identity within the context of globalisation. In what follows I offer a synopsis and analysis of two competing versions of the 'new imperialism', both of which are forms that question forms of citizenship tied to the nation-state and to national sovereignty.

TWO VERSIONS OF EMPIRE: COOPER'S 'NEW IMPERIALISM'

In two influential publications *The Postmodern State and the World Order* (originally written in 1996 and revised in 2000), and 'The Postmodern State', recently published in a collection entitled *Re-ordering the World: The Long-term Implications of September 11* (Leonard, 2002), Robert Cooper has helped to shape Tony Blair's foreign policy outlook. The *New Republic* describes Cooper as the foremost commentator on strategic issues of our age, and Cooper's diagnosis of the era we live in has taken on the power of prophecy after the events of September 11. His analysis is terrifyingly simple and I would argue also alarmingly Eurocentric. Cooper argues that the year 1989 marked a turning point in European history. 1989 not only marked the end of the Cold War but, perhaps more fundamentally, a change in the European state system: it marked the end of the balance-of-power system in Europe. What emerged after 1989 is not a re-arrangement of the old system but an entirely new system based on a new form of statehood, which Cooper calls the postmodern state.

With the emergence of the postmodern state, we now live in an international system comprised of three parts: the pre-modern world (of, for example, Somalia, Afghanistan or Liberia) where the state has lost its legitimate monopoly on the use of force and chaos reigns; the modern world where the classical state system remains intact; and the postmodern world where the state system is collapsing and a new system is being born. The new postmodern system of states is best characterised by the EC. It exhibits the following characteristics:
- The breakdown of the distinction between domestic and foreign affairs.
- Mutual interference in (traditional) domestic affairs and mutual surveillance.
- The rejection of force for resolving disputes and the consequent codification of rules of behaviour, rules that are self-enforced because all EC states have an interest in maintaining the rule of law.
- The growing irrelevance of borders.
- Security is based on transparency, mutual openness, interdependence and mutual vulnerability (Cooper, 2000, pp. 19–20).

The postmodern system of states – the so-called decentered state – originates in the postmodern world. The old imperialism is dead, at least among Western states. Member states no longer want to go to war against each other to acquire territory or subject populations. The postmodern state is 'more pluralist, more complex, less centralised than the bureaucratic modern state'. In this postmodern system that state becomes both less dominating and state interest becomes less determining in foreign policy. With the deconstruction of the state, the media, popular sentiment, public opinion and the interests of particular groups and regions come into play. As the deconstruction of the state proceeds – a process not yet complete – so the processes of individualisation, regionalisation and privatisation become more important.

Europe is postmodern, on Cooper's analysis, and also possibly Japan and Canada, but what of the US? He writes:

> The USA is the more doubtful case since it is not clear that the US government or Congress accepts either the necessity and desirability of interdependence or its corollaries of openness, mutual surveillance to the same extent as most European governments now do. The United States' unwillingness to accept the jurisdiction of the International Criminal Court and its relative reluctance about challenge inspections in the CWC are examples of US caution about postmodern concepts. (Cooper, 2000, p. 27)

He characterises the USA in terms of a 'defensive modernism'. There is a certain force to his analysis on this point. After September 11, the US created the Office of Home Security, perhaps the biggest change in government departments in the US since WWII. It is a super-department headed up by Henry Kissinger, combining departments of immigration, customs and domestic security with an $80 billion dollar budget and some 175,000 employees. With this new office and the prevailing ethos, the US has turned in upon itself, policing its borders and monitoring the flows of people, information and goods in and out of its territory. As well as greater internal surveillance, the US has shifted its historic policy of containment to one of 'pre-emptive first strike' and 'regime change' in the name of national security.

What are the implications for security? In the postmodern zone there is a new transparent and interdependent security order. 'Our task', Cooper says 'must be to preserve and extend it' (p. 34). Yet dealing with the modern world requires a different approach, as evidenced by the Gulf War and wars in former Yugoslavia. In the former case, he suggests the Western response to Saddam Hussein's attack on Kuwait was exactly what it should have been: 'Build the most powerful coalition possible, reverse the aggression, punish the aggressor, deal with the weapons programme' (Cooper, 2000, p. 36).

The initial support for the notion of a New World Order following the Gulf War was based on the hope that the UN was going to function as a world authority policing international law, that is, as an organisation of collective-security, but 'the Gulf War was fought to protect an old order, not to create a new one' (p. 37). Thus, for the postmodern system or state, there is a difficulty in dealing with militant, rogue modernist states. Cooper writes:

> We need to get used to the idea of double standards. Among ourselves, we operate on the basis of laws and open cooperative security. But when dealing with more old-fashioned kinds of state outside the postmodern continent of Europe, we need to revert to the rougher methods of an earlier era – force. (Cooper, 2000, p. 39)

In his second essay Cooper (2002) openly advocates a new kind of imperialism. He writes:

> What is needed is a new kind of imperialism, one compatible with human rights and cosmopolitan values: an imperialism which aims to bring order and organisation.

Cooper distinguishes between two kinds of 'new colonialism' that can 'save the world': the 'voluntary' imperialism such as the IMF and the World Bank, which 'provide help for states wishing to find their way back on to the global economy', and the 'imperialism of neighbours', when states intervene to sort out 'instability in their neighbourhood'.

While Cooper has nothing directly to say about citizenship or rethinking this concept within the context of globalisation, his analysis provides at least a three-pronged approach: pre-modern, modern and postmodern. In pre-modern states the concept of citizenship is hazy, fragile and volatile. The notion of rights in pre-modern states is often not recognised at all, and if they are the weak state may not be able to enforce or uphold them. The notion of citizenship in modern states is straightforward and conforms to the pattern of rights and responsibilities previously discussed. The important addition from Cooper might be the notion of citizenship in the postmodern state and, while he does not discuss this, we can draw some inferences from his analysis. The notion of citizenship is still modern in that rights are ascribed first on the basis of national sovereignty and only secondly in terms of the greater EU. So we have a kind of two-tiered or layered structure that has both a national and an international community component, where the latter covers the right to work, to move freely, and to make use of the developing judicial and legal infrastructure such as the European Court. While Cooper's analysis might have something to say about citizenship in the postmodern state, he has nothing to say about stateless peoples or the vexed question concerning the rights of stateless peoples.

TWO VERSIONS OF EMPIRE: HARDT AND NEGRI'S *EMPIRE*

Nothing could be further from Cooper's conception than the picture Michael Hardt and Antonio Negri (2000) present in their path-breaking *Empire*. The book has been variously hailed as 'the first great new theoretical synthesis of the new millennium' (by Fredric Jameson) and 'nothing less than a rewriting of *The Communist Manifesto* for our time' (by Slavoj Zizek (cited in Kimball, 2001)), while at the same time being vilified as 'the profoundly silly book that has set the academic left aflutter' (Peyser, 2002) and a 'new anti-Americanism' by the likes of Roger Kimball (2001).

Writing in the spirit of Marx and in combination with Deleuze and Guattari, Hardt and Negri provide the poststructuralist basis for a renewal of materialist thought, charting the emergence of a new form of sovereignty they call 'Empire'. As they indicate in a footnote, 'Two interdisciplinary texts served as models for us throughout the writing of this book: Marx's *Capital* and Deleuze and Guattari's *A Thousand Plateaus*' (fn. 4, p. 415).[4] Hardt and Negri narrate a history of the passage from imperialism to Empire; that is, from a modernity dominated by the sovereignty of nation-states, and the imperialisms of European powers, to a postmodernity characterised by a single though decentered, new logic of global rule. They write: 'Our basic hypothesis is that sovereignty has taken a new form, composed of a series of national and supranational organisms united under a single logic of rule. This new global form of sovereignty is what we call Empire' (p. xii). They use Empire not as a metaphor but as a concept that calls for a theoretical approach:

> The concept of Empire is characterized fundamentally by a lack of boundaries: Empire's rule has no limits. First and foremost, then, the concept of Empire posits a regime that effectively compasses the spatial totality, or really that rules over the entire 'civilized' world. No territorial boundaries limit its reign. Second, the concept of Empire presents itself not as a historical regime originating in conquest, but rather as an order that effectively suspends history and thereby fixes the existing state of affairs for eternity.... Empire presents its rule not as a transitory moment in the movement of history, but as a regime with no temporal boundaries and in this sense outside history or at the end of history. Third, the rule of empire operates on all registers of the social order extending down to the depths of the social world. Empire not only manages a territory and a population but also creates the very world it inhabits. It not only regulates human interactions but also seeks directly to rule over human nature. The object of

61

its rule is social life in its entirety, and thus Empire presents the paradigmatic form of biopower. Finally, although the practice of Empire is continually bathed in blood, the concept of Empire is always dedicated to peace – a perpetual and universal peace outside history. (Hardt & Negri, 2000, pp. xiv–xv)

They go on to suggest that the passage to Empire, with its processes of globalisation, 'offer new possibilities to the forces of liberation', arguing that our political future will be determined by our capacity 'not simply to resist these processes but to reorganize them and redirect them toward new ends' (p. xv).

Imperialism, in its heyday, was simply the extension of the sovereignty of European nation-states beyond their own boundaries (p. xii). Imperialism or colonialism in this sense, they seem to agree with Cooper, is now dead. But so are all forms of imperialism insofar as they represent restraints on the homogenising force of the world market. Empire is, thus, both 'postcolonial and postimperialist'. Drawing on the deleuzo-guatarian concepts of (de/re)territorialisation[5] they argue:

Imperialism is a machine of global striation, channelling, coding, and territorializing the flows of capital, blocking certain flows and facilitating others. The world market, in contrast, requires a smooth space of uncoded and deterritorialized flows ... imperialism would have been the death of capital had it not been overcome. The full realization of the world market is necessarily the end of imperialism. (p. 333)

Writing before the impending Second Persian Gulf War, Hardt and Negri (2001) argue that the US 'does not, indeed no nation-state can today, form the centre of an imperialist project. Imperialism is over. No nation will be world leader in the way modern European nations were' (pp. xiii–xiv). In retrospect it is interesting to focus on their assessment of the US. The Vietnam War, Hardt and Negri suggest 'might be seen as the final moment of the imperialist tendency and thus a point of passage to a new regime of the Constitution' (pp. 178–179). This passage to a new global constitutional regime is shown by the Gulf War, during which the US emerged 'as the only power able to manage international justice, not as a function of its own national motives but in the name of global right .... The US world police acts not in imperialist interest but in imperial interest [that is, in the interest of deterritorialized Empire]. In this sense the Gulf War did indeed, as George Bush claimed, announce the birth of a New World order' (p. 180). As John Bellamy Foster (2001) puts it:

Empire, the name they give to this new world order, is a product of the struggle over sovereignty and constitutionalism at the global level in an age in which a new global Jefffersonianism – the expansion of the US constitutional form into the global realm – has become possible.

As Foster suggests reading Hardt and Negri, 'the struggle now is simply over the form that globalization will take'.[6] As Bruce Lindsay (2000) makes clear the new axiom of geopolitical power implies a spatial totality that differs:

from the system of nation-states, linked contractually (i.e. by treaty, centered on a form of 'the people' (whatever the specific form of regime) and containing a particular ordering of space (the internal and the foreign, or 'outside'). *Empire* tends to supersede this basis of sovereignty, posing imperial authority as an overarching framework without a centre, embodied in networks of institutions, states, military forces and corporate powers.[7]

He goes to clarify:

The imperial model accompanies new productive models and processes – based on information and communication, global networks and flows – and the logic of *Empire* is to elaborate and extend control across this productive terrain. *Empire* tends to take the (de)territorializing tendency of capital to its extreme.

Without necessarily endorsing Hardt and Negri's view, it is easy to see the connections particularly to a form of global rule based on the globalisation of communications. There is a form of global government rationality that we might refer to as *communicative governmentality*. It is a concept-marriage that recognises the need for new terms to critically discuss forms of global rule that depend upon spaces of subjectivity more than ever linked to media and other forms of communication. The mouthful *communicative governmentality* also refers to the relations between modernist nation-state conceptions of 'the people' as a basis for democracy and postmodern forms of subjectivity that may form the basis for alternative conceptions of globalisation – a sort of antagonistic or anti-globalisation and anti-Empire.[8]

ANTI-GLOBALISATION, ANTI-EMPIRE

We do not lack communication, on the contrary we have too much of it. We lack creation. We lack resistance to the present. (Gilles Deleuze and Felix Guattari, cited in Hardt & Negri, 2000, p. 393)

Hardt and Negri have coined the term 'multitude' to refer to the new spaces for subjectivity within globalisation and its democratic impulses. In the nation-state the multitude was reduced to 'the people'. The first element of a political programme for the global multitude is global citizenship – a political demand 'that the juridical status of the population be reformed in step with the real economic transformations of recent years' (p. 400). Hardt and Negri then proceed to argue:

This demand can also be configured in a more general and more radical way with respect to the postmodern conditions of Empire. If in a first moment the multitude demands that each state recognize juridically the migrations that are necessary to capital, in a second moment it must demand control over the movements themselves. The multitude must be able to decide if, when, and where it moves. It must have the right also to stay still and enjoy one place rather than being forced constantly to be on the move. The general right to control its own movement is the multitude's ultimate demand for global citizenship. This demand is radical insofar as it challenges the fundamental apparatus of imperial control over the production and life of the multitude. Global citizenship is the multitude's power to reappropriate control over space and thus to design the new cartography (p. 400).

Hardt and Negri (2001) have applied their analysis to recent events surrounding the so-called anti-globalisation protests. Writing in *The New York Times* they recognise that the rainbow protestors at the Genoa G8 'world' summit are united in the belief 'that a fundamentally new global system is being formed' and that '[t]he world can no longer be understood in terms of British, French, Russian or even American imperialism'. They maintain that no longer can national power control or order the present global system and that, while the protests often appear anti-American, they are really directed at the larger power structures.

The protestors must win the same kind of battle for democracy at the global level that ordinary people – citizens – won at the level of the nation-state, over three hundred years ago. And since those first democratic revolutions, movements of various kinds – civil rights, anti-racism, anti-war, women's rights, children's rights, animal rights, environmental protests – have progressively enfranchised ever-larger groups of the world's populations, although not inevitably or without struggle or reversals.[9] Hardt and Negri point out the salient fact that 'this new order has no democratic institutional mechanisms for representation, as nation-states do: no elections, no public forum for debate'. And they go on to describe the anti-globalisation protestors, as a coalition united against the present form of capitalist globalisation, but not against the forces or currents of globalisation per se. Neither are these protestors isolationalists, separatists, or nationalists. Rather, as Hardt and Negri claim, the protestors want to democratise globalisation – to eliminate the growing inequalities between nations and to expand the possibilities for self-determination. Thus, 'anti-globalisation' is a false description of this movement.[10]

Against all odds, against the power of supranational forces, people in the street at Genoa – and earlier in a series of locations at Gothenburg, Quebec, Prague and Seattle – still believe in a form of resistance in the name of a better future. They believe, against all propagandising and media control, in the story of democracy and in the seeds that were sown for emancipation and self-determination over three centuries ago. Hardt and Negri believe that a new species of political activism has been born, reminiscent of the 'paradoxical idealism of the 1960s'. Such protest movements are part of democratic society even though they are unlikely to provide the practical blueprint for the future. Yet they create political desires for a better future and, remarkably, unify disparate interests and groups – unionists, ecologists, together with priests and Communists – in openness towards defining the future anew in democratic terms.[11]

Hardt and Negri are not the only ones to have asserted a connection between the so-called anti-globalisation protestors and those who demonstrated during the 1960s. Todd Gitlin (2001) also clearly considers the present-day movements evident at Genoa as a successor movement to the student movements of the 1960s and 1970s – one that he claims has already engaged more activists over a longer period of time and one he predicts will be longer-lived. Gitlin, similarly, pictures the protestors as 'creating a way of life', although he profiles the protestors as engaging in the debate about the meaning of Europe, seemingly truncating its obvious more global aspects outside Europe. He also questions the anti-globalisation label, drawing attention to anti-capitalist revolutionaries, reformists who demand to 'Drop the Debt', and anarchists bent upon violence. The new face of protests is a composite of different types: anarchist and Marxists, 'kinder, gentler globalists', health-issue advocates, environmentalists, consumer advocates. The protest groups have been named from violent to non-violent in the following order: Black Blocs (anarchist and Marxists who wear black masks); those who claim to be non-violent but often provoke retaliation such as Globalize Resistance, Reclaim the Streets, Tute Bianche (Luca Casarini) and Ya Basta!; decidedly nonviolent groups ranging from celebrities to religious leaders, including, AIDS activists, ATTAC (Bernard Cassen and Susan George), CAFOD, Christian Aid, Cobas, Confédération Paysanne (José Bové), various consumer groups, Drop the Debt (Bono), Greenpeace, La Via Campesina, Oxfam, Rainforest Action Network, Roman Catholic Church, War on Want, World Wildlife Fund (Brant & Nadeau, 2001).

The multitude against Empire is best represented in spatial movements which cannot be subjugated to the laws of capitalist accumulation. These movements – the flow of bodies – reappropriate space to reconstitute themselves as active subjects. The political action of the multitude is expressed in its ultimate demand for global citizenship and in the constitutional principle that links right and labour. Without commenting in any systematic fashion on the programmatic political demands of the multitude working in the new temporalities of biopolitical production, I want to conclude by mentioning a number of features of Hardt and Negri's analysis that converge with my own interests and research on the knowledge economy.[12]

In their discussion of 'postmodernization' or what they also call 'the informatization of production' (see pp. 280ff) Hardt and Negri provide an analysis of what I have called 'knowledge capitalism' (Peters, 2001, 2003a, 2003b). They argue, for instance:

The first aspect of the telos of the multitude has to do with the senses of language and communication. If communication has increasingly become the fabric of production, and if linguistic cooperation has increasingly become the structure of productive corporeality, then the control over linguistic sense and meaning and the networks of communication becomes a more central issue for political struggle. (Hardt & Negri, 2000, p. 404)

Later they ask:

How can sense and meaning be oriented differently or organized in alternative, coherent communicative apparatuses? How can we discover and direct the performative lines of linguistic sets and communicative networks that create the fabric of life and production? Knowledge has to become linguistic action and philosophy has to become real *reappropriation of knowledge.* (p. 404)

Reappropriation, in this context, they argue 'means having free access to and control over knowledge, information, communication, and affects – because these are some of the primary means of biopolitical production' (p. 407).

For Hardt and Negri, it is the figure of the militant which best expresses the life of the multitude, as they say '*the agent of biopolitical production and resistance against Empire*', yet a militancy that is constitutive not representative and based upon a form of resistance that is at once positive, constructive, and innovative.

CONCLUSION AND POSTSCRIPT[13]

As I argued earlier, both Hardt and Negri and Cooper entertain extranational forms of citizenship based on supranational systems that to some degree problematize the concept of citizenship based on the bounded system of the sovereign state. Yet in the form of empire identified by Hardt and Negri and in the form of the postmodern state system identified by Cooper it is clear both that the traditional concept of citizenship based on the state remains, and that the traditional Left concern for nation-building and developing a sense of community and local identity necessary to sustain and defend social rights, must also remain as part of the political agenda against the undermining effects of globalization on social and welfare policy (see Table 3). Yet we might argue that questions of identity and citizenship, at least in the EU, have a layered complexity that arises from the effort to build extranational, indeed universal, 'Kantian' judicial structures and systems (such as the International Criminal Court), that are seen by Europeans as prototype world institutions. Indeed, the EU is behind the promulgation of a Kantian philosophy of universalisation of world institutions that attempts to determine rights per se, springing from earlier attempts going back, immediately, to the Nuremberg Trials and the conventions developed and adopted in 1950 by the United Nations on the definitions of 'crimes against the peace', 'war crimes' and 'crimes against humanity', and in the longer term to the constitutions of the League of Nations and United Nations (with its impetus to carry forward the project of human rights).

In this process of Europeanization with ten new members joining the EU in 2004, local identity – especially that based on ethnicity and language – is still significant for recognising social and linguistic rights and may well become even more important, for example, in the realm of education. States still ascribe rights yet EU membership enhances and legitimates those rights in some respects, especially in relation to the free movement of people. I remarked at the beginning of this paper that more than ever before the question of globalisation and citizenship revolves around the free movement of peoples, and its opposite – the curtailment of cross-national and cross-regional mobility, especially for Third World peoples and refugees of all kinds. Yet members of the EU both nationally and internationally have not tackled the question of illegal immigration and refugees with any distinctiveness that distinguishes the UN ethos on human rights.

What Hardt and Negri on the one hand, and Cooper on the other hand, demonstrate is that citizenship now has other dimensions. Cooper's analysis of the imperatives of the new imperialism has directly contributed to a policy outlook in Britain that identified Blair's Labour government – against his own backbenchers, affiliated trade unions, and people in the party machinery – with a conservative Republican US oil-president. Cooper's foreign policy stance that deliberately embraces 'double standards' (meaning that the EU cannot use the same standards in dealing with so-called rogue states as they do for dealing with member states) may well have provided the analysis and 'moral vision' that Blair acted on, but it has embarrassed the EU, splitting 'old' Europe (France, Germany and Belgium) from 'new' Europe (basically the former Soviet satellites, including Poland, the Czech Republic and Hungary) as well as risking a longer term stand-off or uneasiness between the EU and American foreign policy. One of the consequences of the protection of the special Anglo-American relationship and the split with so-called 'old' European (Donald Rumsfeld's terminology) is a historic distancing between the US and EU with potentially enormous political fallout not only for NATO but also for the ratification by the US of treaties and conventions struck by the EU and UN.[14]

Hardt and Negri anticipate a form of extranational and extraparliamentary protest – 'anti-globalisation' – that, in part, is also aimed at a form of global citizenship or, at least, world democracy. This is the counter-narrative and counter-movement to the US hegemon and export of American juridical forms as the value basis and ethos for world governmental organisations.

The recent Gulf War – an illegal war if we are to judge by the Nuremberg principles adopted by the International Law Commission of the UN[15] – is clearly an extension of the neoliberal/neoconservative[16] project of globalisation. The post-war reconstruction is driven by the same principles that underwrote the 'Washington consensus', in particular, the privatisation of public services, which is entirely unsuitable for a country that has such a poorly developed public sector.[17] Moreover, Haliburton, one of the world's largest oil and gas companies, of which Cheney was CEO from 1995–2000, has been granted contracts to resurrect Iraqi oilfields, along with other US companies (including Bechtel, the Fluor Corporation, and the Louis Berger Group, which also have strong links to the present US administration).

It is also clear that the export and transplant of American democracy is a project likely to fail in the sense that, it could be argued, democracy is not something that can be imposed or easily transplanted at will, but requires generations of development as well as a commitment to the public sphere and public institutions to sustain it – to a local sense of identity. There is no way that the present US administration will allow a Iran-style religious government even if it is freely elected by the people. The question of citizenship and democracy cannot ignore local history and local identity. For Iraq, as for other states where democracy has been imposed, the issue of culture and of local identity is paramount. A pressing question for the coming years is whether Iraq (and other Islamic states) can embrace modernity and democracy in a way that reflects its own values, culture and sense of identity. This would be to begin the process of rethinking citizenship and identity within the context of globalisation.

NOTES

[1] This is a revised version of a plenary address to the conference 'Between Empires: Communication, Globalisation and Identity', School of Communication Studies and the Centre for Communication Research, Auckland University of Technology, 13–15 February, 2003. I would like to thank the editor for useful suggestions for revision of this paper; the errors and the view expressed are mine.

[2] On this question see the deliberations of two philosophers, Derrida (2001) and Dummett (2001). Derrida argues for a form of cosmopolitanism that entails the right to asylum, while Dummett discusses refugee and immigration policy in Great Britain.

[3] In a word, the themes of individualism and community whether they be conceived at the national or international level, are motifs that still mark contemporary politics and economics, whether they be forms of rational choice theory with an accent on the rational utility maximizer, neoliberalism or New Right notions of the individual freedom construed as consumer choice, Third Way politics with an emphasis, allegedly, on the slogan 'market economy but not market society' or contemporary forms of communitarianism. It is a theme that has occupied me over the course of my career and one that I have written about on a number of occasions. In 1996, working with Jim Marshall, I used the terms 'individual' and 'community', together with their associated ideologies – individualism and communitarianism – as the framework within which to analyse the crisis of the welfare state in the postmodern condition, focusing on the New Zealand 'neoliberal experiment' that took place in the 1980s and early 1990s (Peters & Marshall, 1996). From being the so-called laboratory of the western world in the 1930s in terms of social welfare provision, New Zealand became the neoliberal experiment in the 1980s. This complete historical reversal of social principles and philosophy singled out New Zealand as a 'successful' experiment, pointed to by a number of powerful world organisations, such as the World Bank, the International Monetary Fund and the OECD. New Zealand with a 'thin' democracy (i.e. one house and a strong executive) and a small population, geographically confined, made it an ideal country for social experiment. What we experienced during that time was not only a rolling back of the welfare state and the failure of social policy largely reconstructed in market terms, but more importantly, the erosion of social democracy and the reduction of citizenship rights to rights of the consumer. The New Zealand experiment has sharp lessons for those interested in the impact of globalisation on social democracy and citizenship. It exemplifies a much larger and complex narrative of emerging world history.

[4] See also, Peters (2001), especially Chapter 5, 'Deleuze's "societies of control": From disciplinary pedagogy to perpetual training in the knowledge economy'.

[5] For a discussion of these concepts see my 'Geophilosophy and the pedagogy of the concept' (Peters, 2002a).

[6] Forster (2001) champions the 'decidedly unfashionable' view of Istvan Meszaros' (2001) book *Socialism or barbarism*.

[7] Indeed, Hardt and Negri refer to Samir Amin's (1992) *Empire of chaos* as the leading center/periphery alternative view to their own.

[8] In this regard, see my 'Anti-globalization and Guattari's *The Three Ecologies*' (Peters, 2002b).

[9] The Hegelian philosopher of jurisprudence, Norberto Bobbio (1994) in *The Age of Rights* provides a useful description of these generational rights, although his Hegelian philosophy of history appears to me wrong-headed, especially in light of the reversal of so-called social rights that occurred in the 1980s under the combined forces of the neo-conservative Thatcher–Reagan administrations. There are no real signs that Third Way governments in the West have attempted to restore these social

rights. If the second-term Blair government, re-elected in 2001, is anything to go by, the privatisation of public services and, thereby, the continued erosion of citizen rights is pursued with a renewed vigour.

[10] Klaus Schwab (2001), founder and chairman of the World Economic Forum, also points to the 'systemic failure' of the present institutions that provide a measure of world governance (UN, IMF, WB, WTO) and embraces the need for global institutions that more effectively and democratically deal with the problems we face. He suggests that the G8 be replaced with the broader Group of 20. Foreign Office Minister in the Blair Government, Peter Hain, like a number of other commentators, criticised the 'ruling elite' in Europe for talking to itself and becoming remote from ordinary people (reported by David Hughes in the *Daily Mail*, July 25, p. 2).

[11] Susan George, by contrast, provides a graphic account of the anti-democratic strategies and tactics adopted by the opponents of the protestors at Genoa, detailing the use of force and manipulation and reporting on the ideological backlash. George suggests that there is evidence of complicity between authorities and gangs of the Black Block agent provocateurs (see her web page: http://www.tni.org/george/index.htm).

[12] Basically, Hardt and Negri call for a social and a guaranteed income for all (a citizenship income) and the right to reappropriate the means of production (i.e. the right to self-control and autonomous self-production). On the knowledge economy, see my 'Education in the age of knowledge capitalism' (Peters, 2003a), 'Poststructuralism and Marxism: Education as knowledge capitalism' (Peters, 2003b), and *Poststructuralism, Marxism and Neoliberalism* (Peters, 2001).

[13] This paper was written and presented before the beginning of the Second Persian Gulf War, hence this postscript.

[14] On this very matter see the recent book *Of passion and power* by Robert Kagan (2003) who now speaks of the US hegemon and Americanisation of world institutions – a kind of right wing interpretation of Empire based upon the export of American democracy and juridical forms. This split, Kagan claims, now problematises the concept of 'the West' and recognises a divergence based upon the level of investment in military technology, especially during the 1990s, which has given the US unrivalled power.

[15] 'Under General Assembly Resolution 177 (II), paragraph (a), the International Law Commission was directed to 'formulate the principles of international law recognized in the Charter of the Nuremberg Tribunal and in the judgment of the Tribunal.' In the course of the consideration of this subject, the question arose as to whether or not the Commission should ascertain to what extent the principles contained in the Charter and judgment constituted principles of international law. The conclusion was that since the Nuremberg Principles had been affirmed by the General Assembly, the task entrusted to the Commission was not to express any appreciation of these principles as principles of international law but merely to formulate them. The text below was adopted by the Commission at its second session. The Report of the Commission also contains commentaries on the principles (see *Yearbook of the International Law Commission*, 1950, Vol. II, pp. 374–378)' (taken from the Introductory Note).

[16] The Washington Consensus is often referred to by the term neoliberal to refer to a set of policies driven by fiscal discipline, reordering of public expenditure, tax reform, liberalising interest rates, exchange rate mechanism, trade liberalisation, liberalisation of foreign direct investment, privatisation, deregulation and property rights (Willliamson's description). I combine the term with 'neoconservative' in this context because I want to emphasise the way in which the White House and American foreign policy has been captured by a group of neoconservatives including Paul Wolfowitz, Steve Cambone, Doug Feith, Scooter Libby, John Bolton, and Richard Perle who are backed by Dick Cheney. It is important to see this second generation of neoconservatives as different both from the first generation epitomised by Irving Kristol, who emerged as critics of the liberal establishment, and traditional conservatives such as Rumsfeld and Cheney.

[17] See Moses Naim's 'Fads and fashion in economic reforms: Washington consensus or Washington confusion?' at http://www.imf.org/external/pubs/ft/seminar/1999/reforms/Naim.htm; John Williamson's 'What should the world bank think about the Washington consensus?', available at http://www.worldbank.org/research/journals/wbro/obsaug00/pdf/(6)Williamson.pdf; and 'Did the Washington consensus fail?' at http://www.iie.com/publications/papers/williamson1102.htm.

REFERENCES

Bobbio, N. (1994). *The age of rights*, London: Polity Press.

Brant, M. & Nadeau, B. (2001, 30 July). First blood. *Newsweek*, pp. 14–18.

Cooper, R. (2000). *The postmodern state and the world order*. London: Demos, The Foreign Policy Centre. (First published, 1996.)

Cooper, R. (2002). The postmodern state. In M. Leonard (Ed.), *Re-ordering the world: The long-term implications of September 11th*. London: Foreign Policy Centre, Retrieved 20 September, 2007, from http://observer.guardian.co.uk/print/0,,4388912-102273,00.html.

Cooper, R. (2002, 7 April). Why we still need empires. *The Observer*. Retrieved 20 September, 2007, from http://www.observer.co.uk/worldview/story/0,11581,680117,00.html.

Derrida, J. (2001). *On cosmopolitanism and forgiveness*. London: Routledge.

Dummett, M. (2001). *On immigration and refugees*. New York: Routledge.

Faulks, K. (2000). *Citizenship*. London: Routledge.

Foster, J.B. (2001). Imperialism and 'empire'. *Monthly Review*, *53*(7), 1–9.

Gamarnikow, E. & Green, A. (1999). Social capital and the educated citizen. *The School Field*, *X* (3–4): 103–126.

Gitlin, T. (2001, 23 July). Having a riot. *Newsweek*, pp. 48–49.

Hardt, M. & Negri, A. (2000). *Empire*. Cambridge, MA: Harvard University Press.

Hardt, M. & Negri, A. (2001, July 25). The new faces in Genoa want a different future. *The New York Times*, reprinted in *The International Herald Tribune*, p. 6.

Kagan, R. (2003). *Of passion and power: America and Europe in the new world order*. New York: Alfred A. Knopf.

Kimball, R. (2001). The new anti-Americanism. *New Criterion*, *20*(2), 17–25.

Lindsay, B. (2000). Toni Negri's Empire. *Arena Magazine*, *50*, December 2000.

Meszaros, I. (2001). *Socialism or barbarism: From the 'American century' to the crossroads*. New York: Monthly Review Press.

Mishra, R. (1999). *Globalization and the welfare state*. Cheltenham, UK: Edward Elgar.

Peters, M.A. & Marshall, J.D. (1996). *Individualism and community: Education and social policy in the postmodern condition*. London: Falmer Press.

Peters, M.A. (2001). *Poststructuralism, marxism and neoliberalism: Between politics and theory*. Oxford: Rowman and Littlefield.

Peters, M.A. (2002a). *Geophilosophy, education and the pedagogy of the concept*. Paper presented at the Deleuze and Education conference, The University of Dundee, 27 November.

Peters, M.A. (2002b). *Anti-globalization and Guattari's The Three Ecologies*. Retrieved 20 September, 2007, from http://globalization.icaap.org/content/v2.1/02_peters.html.

Peters, M.A. (2003a). Education in the age of knowledge capitalism. *Policy Futures in Education*, 1(2), 361–380. Retrieved 20 September, 2007, from http://www.wwwords.co.uk/rss/abstract.asp?j=pfie&aid=1808.

Peters, M.A. (2003b). Poststructuralism and marxism: Education as knowledge capitalism. *Journal of Education Policy*, *18*(2), 115–129.

Peyser, T. (2002). Empire burlesque: The profoundly silly book that has set the academic left aflutter. *Reason*, *33*(11), 51–57.

Schwab, K. (2001, 30 July). The world's new actors need a bigger stage. *Newsweek*, p. 18.

The United Nations Research Institute for Social Development (1996). *Globalization and citizenship*. Report of the UNRISD international conference, Geneva, 9–11, December, 1996. Retrieved 20 September, 2007, from http://www.unrisd.org.

Tripp, C. (2000). *A history of Iraq*. Cambridge: Cambridge University Press.

Michael A. Peters
University of Illinois at Urbana-Champaign

PENNY ENSLIN AND MARY TJIATTAS

COSMOPOLITAN JUSTICE

Education and Global Citizenship

INTRODUCTION

In *Cosmopolitan Justice* (2002*)*, Darrel Moellendorf is concerned with our moral duties toward others, with particular emphasis on the institutions that mediate our discharging of such duties, and our conduct with regard to them. His claim, more controversial in political thought than in moral philosophy, is that moral duties to others if owed, are owed to *all* others, without restriction. The central cosmopolitan thesis of this work can be taken to be this: Duties of justice have global scope. There is no principled way of confining the content and practical requirements of duties of justice to compatriots alone. This central claim has important ramifications with respect to questions concerning the scope of human rights, the justification and limit of state sovereignty, and international legal principles.

In this paper we start by considering the view (adopted by Moellendorf) that there are cosmopolitan duties of justice, both negative (perfect, stringent) (following Pogge, 2002, p. 130) and positive (imperfect). The former are largely redistributive in nature, the latter take the form of duties of intervention based not (primarily) on requirements of distributive justice or responsibility for harms or wrongs inflicted, but on responsibility for addressing injustices committed by others. We then turn to educational duties that exist on the global level, suggesting the kinds of institutional structures and processes that might be required if they are to be adequately discharged, and a conception of citizenship to underpin education for global citizenship.

GLOBAL DUTIES OF JUSTICE

A central, and perhaps for us the most significant, contribution of *Cosmopolitan Justice* is the argument for the global reach of duties of justice. We think that Moellendorf has good reasons for thinking that what is taken to be a chief impediment to this (the claims of sovereignty) is nothing of the kind. Not only are there good arguments for the normative priority of human rights over rights of state-autonomy, but also, as Delanty among others points out, the discourse of human rights has effectively undermined the inviolability of national sovereignty. It is becoming increasingly the case that human rights violations are taken to be

M.A. Peters, A. Britton and H. Blee (Eds.), Global Citizenship Education: Philosophy, Theory and Pedagogy, 71–85.

strong grounds for intervention in affairs of other states (e.g. prosecution of Serbian war criminals).

> The older framework of human rights simply entailed declarations of human rights; today human rights have to be more than just stated, they also have to be guaranteed by national law. This has been the principal change in the relationship of national and international law which has undermined the very idea of sovereignty being located on one level of governance. (Delanty, 2000, p. 79)

Claims of sovereignty can no longer be taken to block those of rights and correlative duties. Moellendorf provides a further argument to establish that such duties in fact exist and are correctly ascribed to certain agents. Taking duties of justice to be associative, he argues that duties of cosmopolitan justice exist because the condition giving rise to duties of justice exists globally. This condition (following Hume) is taken to consist in the appropriate form of association or relation. Globally, political and commercial activities bring people into contact with each other in such a way that they substantively affect each other (Moellendorf, 2000, p. 37), and not only or even primarily positively, as Kant had hoped. The 'spirit of commerce' has not resulted in his envisaged harmony of interests on a world scale. The diminishing effects of spatial distance and increased contact mean that people other than compatriots have a significant impact on each other. Global duties can't be obviously overridden by duties of justice that compatriots and co-nationals might owe to one another. State boundaries have become unreliable indicators of boundaries of common interests.

Pogge (e.g. 1989, pp. 276–80) has argued along similar lines that the global order has created grounds for duties of wide scope. Going further than many other cosmopolitans in arguing not only for positive (weaker) duties of global justice, to aid or benefit those who suffer as a result of global inequality, but for negative duties as well, consequent upon harmful conduct, he insists that anyone who participates in the shaping and sustaining of a global order that is slanted in favour of some and has detrimental effects on others, has a negative duty to do something by way of influencing the order for the better, or working to compensate those adversely affected, especially if she stands to gain from the harms inflicted on those badly off. If there are people who are disadvantaged by the global institutions that others set up, the latter have a negative (stringent, non-discretionary) duty to attend to the effects of these institutions, that is, the oppression, starvation, lack of educational opportunities that they establish or engender. It is clear for Pogge that the antecedent of this conditional holds: much of the poverty and oppression in poor countries is caused by the way the global institutional order and the developed countries that control them are structured and controlled. The poor countries have been made the victims of unjust institutions.

EDUCATIONAL DUTIES AND RIGHTS: REDISTRIBUTIVE

If, in line with both Moellendorf's and Pogge's accounts, global duties of justice are associative duties, we can argue, applying this to education, that the impact of the global economy creates associative duties that make access to schooling and the types of outcomes that ensue a significant issue of international social justice. While widened access to educative schooling is not a sufficient condition for economic development and for ensuring the global competitiveness of national economies, it can contribute significantly to whether developing states have a chance of competing, at least in some spheres. As poorer countries become poorer, in a global economic order based on national interest and dominated by rich countries who help themselves to protectionist exemptions and impose on others onerous obligations to effect structural adjustments, already inadequate national education budgets are further diminished. In 1997, 40% of Zambia's national budget was devoted to servicing foreign debt repayments and 7% to basic health and education, clean water, sanitation, nutrition needs (Worldwatch, 2003). As Pogge says, our actual global order is in fact moulded and sustained by the more powerful governments and their agents (e.g. NATO, WTO, World Bank, IMF). In these circumstances Rawls' *Theory of Justice* (1971) can be deployed to argue the case for redistribution of resources from rich countries (who benefit from the relative impoverishment of their Third World competitors) to fund education as well as other benefits in the poorer states, and for radical reform of the world economy.

If applied globally, Rawls's position in *A Theory of Justice* has quite radical implications. 'Fair opportunity' as articulated by Rawls provides that to ensure equal treatment and equality of opportunity more attention ought to be paid to those 'born into the less favourable social positions' as well as to those whose 'native assets' are fewer (Rawls, 1971, p. 100). For Rawls

> the difference principle would allocate resources in education, say, so as to improve the long-term expectations of the least favoured. (p. 101)

Significantly, he adds that one of the benefits of education lies in its enrichment of citizens' personal and social lives:

> ... the value of education should not be assessed only in terms of economic efficiency and social welfare. Equally if not more important is the role of education in enabling a person to enjoy the culture of his society and to take part in its affairs, and in this way to provide for each individual a secure sense of his own worth. (p. 101)

Rawls thus provides several grounds for redistribution of educational resources. If these apply globally (and given the facts of association they should, contrary to Rawls's own insistence) then there are at least redistributive duties with respect to education. This point is further supported by Pogge's consideration that equalising of educational opportunities is a particularly appropriate way of reforming unjust institutional arrangements (1989, p. 180). Directing redistributive resources at the alleviation of educational disadvantage avoids undesirable consequences of aid provision such as instilling of dependency, since it fosters capacity and autonomy and breaks the cycle of deprivation directly. Discharging redistributive duties should be directed in the first place at removing the huge disparities in expenditure between rich and poor educational systems reflected in pupil–teacher ratios, class sizes, the number of years spent in school, the level of teachers' qualifications and the availability of suitable teaching materials. Later, we'll argue that such duties do not exhaust global duties, insisting that there are also duties of a more purely interventionist nature, but for now we restrict our attention to redistributive matters. If we apply Rawls's principles of distributive justice to the global association, then as Moellendorf (2002, p. 78) says, this would require significant reforms, including among other things the equalising of educational opportunities. Even the principle of fair opportunity – which equalises only the starting point of competition – would demand such reforms. But a global difference principle would require more in the way of redistribution, since it would mean equalising not only the infrastructure, which ensures opportunities across the globe, but also a global institutional structure to limit inequalities of wealth thereafter (2002, p. 81).

Over and above these 'end state' considerations, questions about what is due to impoverished countries arise from the recognition of the fact that current global inequalities are perpetuated through, for example, transfers of wealth from the developing world to financial institutions in the developed world to service debt of the former, tariffs, quotas and structural adjustment programmes. Theorists and activists have called for such measures as the cancellation of debt and re-allocation of resources between countries, along with removing trade barriers and other obstacles to development and the creation of viable economies in poor countries. Such measures of global redistribution are in any case justified on the basis of principles of justice. But they are further supported by these backward-looking justifications for wealth transfers.

EDUCATIONAL DUTIES AND RIGHTS: INTERVENTIONIST

Redistribution of wealth on its own does not exhaust the domain of global duties. It could (and in fact often does) still leave the problem of oppression in disadvantaged or wronged countries insufficiently addressed. This is a serious deficit because oppressive conditions undermine equality. Insofar as oppression takes educational forms, it requires educational reform for democratic challenge to be possible within those societies. One could imagine a situation in which a radical reallocation of resources for education has been undertaken but where oppressive educational practices persist.

Insofar as educational provision affects global democracy and its prospects, the educational significance of transnational injustice in access to resources and opportunities is extensive. Moellendorf's interpretation of cosmopolitan justice requires a global reduction of inequalities in the distribution of resources, but also global respect for civil and democratic rights. Enhanced respect for rights requires education, whether in established democracies or in societies in transition to democracy. If decent hierarchical societies (i.e. those which respect minimal human rights but do not accept equality or constitutional safeguards as requirements of justice) are an impossibility, as Moellendorf (2002, p. 28) argues, and if cosmopolitan democracy requires the fostering of constitutional democracy globally, education for constitutional democracy exercised by free and equal citizens is a matter of international interest and obligation rather than of mere domestic interest. In line with this, Pogge claims that respect for human rights needs to be sustained ultimately by attitudes of citizens and for this to come about, the education system has to undertake appropriate responsibilities (Pogge, 2002, p. 63).

In an earlier work Rawls in fact provides a brief sketch of the requirements that will be made. In *Political Liberalism* he writes that we will ask

> ... that children's education include such things as knowledge of their constitutional and civic rights so that, for example, they know that liberty of conscience exists in their society and that apostasy is not legal crime, all this to insure that their continued membership when they come of age is not based simply on ignorance of their basic rights or fear of punishment for offences that do not exist. Moreover, their education should also prepare them to be fully cooperating members of society and enable them to be self-supporting; it should also encourage the political virtues so that they want to honour the fair terms of cooperation in their relations with the rest of society. (1993, p. 199)

It should be evident that these requirements take us onto much more controversial terrain than duties of redistribution. This is because there is a potential conflict between obligations ascribed to providers and the rights of prospective recipients. The claim that there is a duty to provide the means to foster attitudes and capacities required for constitutional democracy seems to presuppose that virtues like reasonableness and tolerance are uncontroversial and generally acceptable. But much of the response to *Political Liberalism* belies this expectation. In *Political Liberalism* Rawls proposed the distinction between political and comprehensive liberalism as a way of accommodating the desire of different groups to practice their beliefs without being subjected to influences that might undermine them. Accordingly, he severely truncated the aims of his 'comprehensive' liberal position which was 'designed to foster the values of autonomy and individuality as ideals to govern much if not all of life' (1993, p. 199) and replaced them with an emphasis on reasonableness and civility. Being reasonable is a matter of appealing only to values which can reasonably be expected to be shared by all. This follows from a recognition of the 'burdens of judgement' (i.e. that modern society presents a vast array of different, conflicting, sometimes incommensurable, though reasonable ideas of the good life, one should be willing to desist from asserting one's own in a public forum, and to be prepared instead to explain one's vote to others in terms of a reasonable balance of public values (Rawls, 1993, p. 243). However not all were persuaded that this notion of reasonability can do the required job.

In addition to the point concerning the inadequacy of Rawls's attempt to accommodate diversity, critics like Callan (1996) and Hampton (1993), have questioned the viability of a distinction between political and comprehensive liberalism, claiming that political liberalism will inevitably slide into comprehensive liberalism, or that political liberalism is a closet form of comprehensive liberalism. Focussing these issues on education in an international context, we can plausibly imagine that civic education, as stipulated by Rawls within the political conception, would be likely to promote autonomy and inevitably corrode non-liberal comprehensive doctrines in traditional societies with hierarchical traditions, especially where minimal human rights are already respected. Learning to recognise these inevitable sources of disagreement, and relatedly a capacity for reciprocity, is likely to lead to adjustments in citizens' conceptions of the status and fallibility of traditional beliefs, including those that enjoy a hegemonic role in many hierarchical societies.

It is reasonable to assume that the problems involved in civic education in pluralist countries (e.g. teaching the burdens of judgment as part of civic education) will be replicated in the context of education for cosmopolitan citizenship. How should we respond to these pluralist worries?

One possibility is to follow Moellendorf's strategy with respect to justifying military interventions, excessive as this might seem: he makes room for significant intervention in the case of states with unjust basic structures and those engaged in international injustices, provided that certain conditions are met. Obviously one major obstacle to advocating intervention is the presumption of state sovereignty, the claim that the state has authority to rule over a domain without external interference. Moellendorf deals with this by allowing only a severely constrained right to national self-determination. Full-blooded human rights, democracy and equality together constitute significant limits on sovereignty. Hence intervention counts as a violation of state sovereignty if and only if the intervention will not attempt to advance the cause of justice either in the basic structure of the state or international effects of its domestic policies.[1] But is this response to the justifiability of intervention sufficiently sensitive to the concerns of multiculturalism (vs. sovereignty). In *Cosmopolitan Justice*, Moellendorf generally deals with multiculturalist worries under the rubric of sovereignty. It is plausible that advocates of multiculturalism might object that this approach fails to capture some of the problems presented by diversity insofar as they do not overlap with concerns about sovereignty, and are not given due weight as a result. This being said, Moellendorf does provide an indirect response to the pluralist challenge, in appealing to one of the cornerstones of Rawls's theory, namely that only persons are the ultimate units of moral concern or 'self-originating sources of valid claims.' Rawls's fundamental notion of 'the individuals' highest order moral interest in the capacity to revise rationally their conceptions of the good' (Moellendorf, 2002, p. 129) can be seen to require a citizenry aware of its political autonomy as watch-guard against unjust state infringement of its liberties, which does not preclude that it be tolerant of and knowledgeable about political and cultural differences compatible with justice. This fundamental value ('rational revisability') not only makes strong claims on educational policy nationally (2002, p. 133) but seems to allow and in some cases require cross-national intervention. Educational intervention across national borders is a condition of economic development, and a factor in the development of individual citizens and in civic education, in contexts where lack of resources or authoritarian and indoctrinatory schooling systems prevent the development of autonomy and a capacity for rational revision, or promote intolerance and prevent development of understanding of other cultures. At the same time it provides a principled basis for the limitation of multiculturalist claims, a point on which we elaborate below.

If this is right, what kinds of international educational interventions are justified? Moellendorf's condition that just cause for intervention exists if and only if it is directed towards advancing justice in the basic structure permits a range of educational interventions, which contrast with Moellendorf's mainly military examples, which he specifies should be undertaken as a last resort. Examples of educational interventions that take place in the context of military intervention are the reconstruction of education in Japan during the American occupation after World War II, in which schooling took a more individualist turn (Duke, 1986) and calls by some feminists for educational reconstruction in post-war Afghanistan and Iraq to foster educational and human rights for women. We concede that such interventions could further justice in the basic structure, but our argument does not need to support this kind of intervention. By contrast, educational interventions that promote basic education, especially literacy, and also awareness of human rights, health education, and an informed and critical perspective on domestic and international politics do advance justice in the basic structure by empowering citizens. They also meet Moellendorf's further condition that non-military interventions should not be undertaken at a cost to democratic self-government. In doing so, they meet some of Moellendorf's additional conditions for intervention, that is, they can reasonably be expected to produce a morally improved situation and will in many instances also meet the condition that the right intentions should be present.

Interventions of the kind that meet Moellendorf's conditions include supporting NGOs with modest but specialised and independent aims. Ansell (2002) cites the Cambridge Female Education Trust, which promotes girls' education in Zimbabwe through improved access to schooling for girls, counsels them in a programme aimed at combating their sexual exploitation by teachers, and supports the promotion of female teachers and school heads as role models for girls. Similarly, Ackerly and Okin (1999) see international and grass-roots NGOs as exercising increasing influence over political decision-making. Taking the women's rights as human rights movement as their focus they show how, through collecting testimony, fostering deliberative enquiry and social criticism that is both critical and respectful of diversity and making use of global media and communications, such organisations and networks have been able to influence political decisions about women's rights.

Interventions of these types, if successful, meet most of Moellendorf's conditions. But in educational as against military interventions the 'proper authority' is more problematic. Moellendorf points out (2002, p. 121) that 'proper authority' is not required for the justification of interventions, but might be for their legitimacy and also to try to ensure that

> ... the intervention is not merely serving the interests of the intervening party to the exclusion of justice.

However, he adds that failure to receive proper authorisation does not count as a justification to desist from a just intervention. Ackerly and Okin point out the limitations of international agreements and conventions fostered by the UN. The Convention on the Elimination of All Forms of Discrimination against Women, passed in 1979, was signed by fewer countries than other documents of its kind aimed at promoting human rights. Limited funds have been allocated to its enforcement, and even among states that have signed it discrimination against women continues. They cite by contrast the Self-employed Women's Association (as does Nussbaum, 2000) as well as international NGOs like Women Living Under Muslim Laws (Ackerly & Okin, 1999, pp. 145, 150–151), which

> uses deliberative enquiry and sceptical scrutiny to point out the many inconsistencies in the ways that Islamic law is used to oppress women.

Often associated with NGOs, a related example of intervention in support of cosmopolitan justice is that of the researcher, like Nussbaum (e.g. 2000). Nussbaum uses her 'capabilities' approach to support various educational programmes likely to shift traditional attitudes, like public education to provide women with information about rights and opportunities, as well as 'images of worth and possibility' (2000, p. 288).

Yet there are also examples available of educational interventions that plainly do not meet the kind of criteria that Moellendorf proposes. For example, poor countries like Lesotho are dependent on external funds for education and so are vulnerable to external influences that lock them into dependence and do not necessarily benefit their citizens. Teachers' unions and churches in Lesotho have criticised the far-reaching influence of foreign donors like USAID on government policy, research and planning (Ansell, 2002). World Bank projects in Zimbabwe, while encouraging greater attention to the education of girls, have been criticised (Gordon, cited in Ansell) for favouring the interests of foreign capital in ensuring that girls meet their labour requirements.

Donors like the World Bank are commonly accused of failing to share national priorities for education, and of being motivated by the imperatives of the world economy, as well as of lack of accountability. Whether or not such criticisms are deserved, organisations like the World Bank and the IMF are primarily organisations that lend money (Tilak, 2002), which leaves open possibilities for inappropriate use of funds by governments, especially in states with undemocratic basic structures, using funds to promote vested interests. While their impact may at least in part be beneficial to educational systems in developing countries, the work of organisations like the British, Canadian and Swedish international development agencies, while quite committed to bilateral co-operation with local actors, will inevitably reflect the interests of the donor governments. Interventions of these kinds may not lead to a morally improved situation, to an improvement in the basic structure, though inappropriate intentions may still result in some educational improvement; interventions are not necessarily taken up in the ways intended by donors. Ultimately, opening up all educational interventions, whether domestic or international, to proper authority in the form of public scrutiny in maximally democratic conditions, has to be the overriding condition in the provision of education, whether formal or informal. Do we need a global authority, and what form should it take?

'PROPER AUTHORITY': INSTITUTIONS OR CITIZENS?

The human future seems suddenly open ... politicians are speaking of a new world order. (Pogge, 2002, p. 168)

But not only politicians. There is a burgeoning literature reflecting a concern with world order and global institutions. Normative discussions focus on the possibility of a well-ordered *international* community which, Pogge (1989) argues, would differ from the current world order based on Hobbesian principles, where international agreements are based on exclusively prudential considerations and the current distribution of power determines interactions.

Dryzek agrees with this perception, commenting that the international system as it exists now is at best thinly democratic, but with bodies that regulate the international economy showing little if any inclination to democracy (2000, p. 116). Dryzek sees the international polity as a system that is highly decentralised but in which a substantial degree of shared solving of problems, cooperation and conflict resolution is taking place. The question arises, can we do better? Could a consensus based on values (however narrow) be developed? Pogge believes, much in the same way as Rawls, that if we were to recognise that knowledgeable and intelligent people of good will may reasonably disagree about fundamental issues, then we could, through ethical dialogue, establish shared values as fixed points in global understandings that would enjoy the support of the citizens of the world. Unlike Rawls, but like Moellendorf, he thinks that these fixed points should include Rawls's principles of justice. But what sorts of structures and institutions could implement decisions based on such shared values?

The possibility and nature of global institutions that will foster transnational democracy and cosmopolitan justice is addressed in different ways by Moellendorf, Dryzek, Bohman, and Held. Moellendorf expressing (although only in outline in his final chapter) a view consonant with the majority opinion here (2002, p. 175) says that:

Only some sort of globalisation-from-belo ... presents a realistic strategy for a more egalitarian global order. Referring both to measures that facilitate democratic accountability of global and regional institutions, and to formative processes and procedures that foster the right kind of attitudes of citizens that will safeguard and sustain global justice, 'globalisation from below' promises to provide answers to a range of issues with which we have been concerned. As a set of measures facilitating democratic accountability of global institutions, it provides a way of dealing with the problem of 'the right authority'.

For institutions to be suitably democratic, participation on the part of citizens needs to be secured. But citizenship presupposes civil society. The problem, as Held (1997) for example sees it, is that there is (currently) not much civil society beyond the nation state. Delanty and others note, however, that there is a growing cosmopolitan public sphere (vs. cosmopolitan civil society), for example, the European public sphere in Europe, evident in lawmaking, lobbying activities by a range of interest organisations and citizen movements, general public discourse and awareness of limits of national politics (Delanty, 2000, p. 120). Dryzek too describes the spontaneous cooperation that takes place in decentralised systems even in the absence of institutionalised global governance. The informality of these activities and associations is not necessarily a defect of the system. On the contrary, it has one great advantage, namely, that it is less susceptible than are formal institutions to being hijacked by a denationalised business elite lacking a civic sense of responsibility. Being more disposed to democratic organisations and governance, this informal network of communication among organisations and associations, supplied by networks of INGOs and movements related to citizenship and democracy (Delanty, 2000, p. 88) provides for 'globalisation from below'.

Thus a functional – if informal – global public sphere is available. Dryzek (2000, p. 115) argues that there are 'discursive sources of order' already present in the international system that do not require any organisation of international government – for example, sustainable development (development and conservation in tandem) – particularly conducive to democracy, emphasising as it does 'the role of transnational civil society' (2000, p. 123). Dryzek identifies as the most conspicuous actors in transnational civil society not only NGOs but also 'transnational environmental activist groups' (TEAGS), which work with one another across states, and also with, as well as against, states and international organisations. Transnational civil society exercises substantial communicative power, which works by 'questioning, criticising and publicising' (2000, p. 131), and is most effective when the efforts of sympathetic activists are combined with those of exploited communities.

Dryzek's examples focus on environmental activism in an international context. They exemplify one sense of what Moellendorf calls 'globalisation from below', as do the examples of human rights activism we cite elsewhere. While such a public sphere may eventually provide the basis for the emergence of a 'mature' civil society, its immediate value lies in its provision of an 'authority' that can proceed to discharge the global duties of education we identified above. In education, international networks like NetAid support the Global Campaign for Education (GCE), which is a coalition of international development NGOs and teachers' unions that 'promotes education as a basic human right, and mobilizes public pressure on governments and the International Community to fulfil their promises to provide free, compulsory basic education for all people; in particular for children, women and all disadvantaged, deprived sections of society' (NetAid, 2003). The GCE campaigns to mobilise public opinion in order to hold governments and international aid agencies as well as donors to the target dates of 2005 for gender equity in schooling and 2015 for universal completion of primary schooling and the reduction of adult illiteracy by 50% – a commitment made by 185 governments in Dakar in 2000.

The global network of NGOs organising campaigns like these is indeed evidence for Dryzek's claims about the potential of communicative power in transnational civil society. But this public sphere does have limitations. While it can successfully pressure governments and other organisations, as well as providing poverty relief, ultimately power still lies in a combination of state governments and transnational corporations accountable to no one and able to move their wealth and operations across international boundaries. Civic and other forms of education may be promotable in the cosmopolitan civil society, but their full achievement requires well-functioning educational systems, in which some form of government responsibility is necessary. This points to the importance of Moellendorf's regional and global organisations, and gives weight to Held's concerns to provide more permanently-accountable global structures.

Globalisation's erosion of national sovereignty has had positive effects. It has opened up opportunities for participatory politics, and for enhancing democratic citizenship. However it needs to be said that the separation of nation and citizenship has in some ways endangered human rights. As Delanty cautions, globalisation is not straightforwardly liberatory. Even though the erosion of state sovereignty and pernicious state-nationalism is rightly welcomed, one consequence, perhaps not adequately foreseen (by cosmopolitan theorists), is that forces of nationalism re-emerged elsewhere, unconstrained by democratic scrutiny, so threatening fundamental liberal-democratic values (e.g. in fundamentalist groups and organisations). In eroding the authority of the state, globalisation may create a vacuum which is in danger of being filled by identity politics as embodied in nationalist and fundamentalist groups.

Delanty urges that we recognise that national governance cannot simply be replaced by transnational structures. National governments are still best able to protect social rights and provide welfare, and indeed to provide the main sphere of participation of individual citizens, the transnational sphere being more conducive to activities of social movement actors. New models of citizenship needn't be seen as simply replacing older ones, or providing exclusively alternative fora. Instead, he says, multi-levelled citizenship is appropriate for a societally-complex world. Bohman (1997, p. 191) gives us an idea of what is involved. It will be exercised

> via the pluralistic public spheres in each state, and through the informal network of communication among the organizations and associations that constitute an international civil society.

Whatever role we ascribe to national government within such a network, what is crucial is that global networks be monitored one way or another by democratic procedures.

What does this vision require of citizenship education? One prominent model of citizenship is that associated with the nation state. This model focuses on citizenship rights as a means to forging national bonds. These rights and the corresponding duties are overseen by the nation state and involve exclusion of non-citizens. For this model the nation state is the lynchpin (providing much of the rationale and justification for the relations between citizens that it proposes), so it is not transferable to a cosmopolitan context which explicitly renounces any justificatory support based on national identities.

But the competing model of citizenship which has recently enjoyed much attention in political theory, that of differentiated citizenship, although perhaps on the face of it more hopeful as a basis for a cosmopolitan model of citizenship, also emphasises, one way or another, the rootedness of individuals in smaller groups or communities and their commitment and allegiance to the values and to other members of these groups above all else. This becomes the basis for claims of recognition, etc. Clearly, this line of thinking doesn't happily complement a cosmopolitan agenda either.

Moellendorf's argument for cosmopolitan justice, which emphasises global duties of association, strongly suggests a third conception. A central requirement is that the cosmopolitan citizen should be able and willing to fulfil duties of justice to all based on respect for individual, civil and democratic rights and substantial socioeconomic egalitarianism. If globalisation affects the lives of all, regardless of the state they live in, the capacity to be active both within and across boundaries of national states seems like an appropriate aim of education.

Some of the considerations involved in determining what is permitted to, and required of, such participants are similar to those arising in multicultural countries. If most nations are multicultural today, the world is even more so. Recent discussions of citizenship education are helpful in thinking about these issues especially as they highlight the problems presented to a broadly liberal view by pluralism. One obvious response to challenges of diversity is to advocate inclusion of the widest possible scope, and hence to emphasise tolerance as the prime citizen virtue, and so as the central concern of citizenship education. But the concern to be as inclusive as possible, may, in the interest of respecting individuals' chosen values and conceptions of the good, lead to an indiscriminate embrace of difference and diversity, of illiberal individuals and positions which threaten the fundamental interests which motivated their inclusion in the first place. The problem here is the old paradox of tolerance, that too much leads to too little. What this means with respect to liberal civic education is that we need to set limits to the claims of pluralism, and hence to tolerance. Some liberals (like Gutmann and Brighouse) emphasise the positive aspect of such limit-setting, arguing for the inclusion of 'reasonableness' and autonomy as key civic virtues. What these properties would promote over and above tolerance is 'rational deliberation among ways of life' (Gutmann, 1987, pp. 30–31). Others, like Macedo, worry that this proposal might be construed as disrespectful on the grounds that it encourages critical scrutiny of central doctrinal beliefs, and doesn't adequately recognise social diversity. (Parents worry that teaching of civic virtue will undermine traditional identities and religious values and beliefs; skills and norms of public reason-giving and deliberations might be viewed as antithetical to maintenance of traditional identities.) So, they urge, we could stop short of Gutmann's goal while nonetheless promoting general respect for the authority of public reasons, which would provide the basis for civic individuals to respect one another.

Gutmann thinks that tolerance is not sustainable without critical reflection. Some of the claims of social diversity might well need to be denied in order to realise reflective tolerance. She says that it is probably impossible to teach children the skills and virtues of democratic citizenship in a diverse society without at the same time teaching them many of the virtues and skills of individuality and autonomy. The requirements for effective participation in political discussion and debate include autonomy first and foremost. Mutual civic respect, needed to secure the 'minimal conditions of reasonable public judgment' (1995, p. 578), is more than mere tolerance: When we are merely tolerant we refrain from coercing those with whom we disagree, but when we accord them civic respect we take them and their ideas seriously. To be able to do so, children need to learn skills such as how rationally to evaluate different moral claims. These are inextricably bound to capacities for autonomy.

There are very strong grounds on the one hand to resist the slide to the encouragement of indiscriminate tolerance, and to insist on adopting reasonableness and autonomy as central aims of citizenship education. A supplementary emphasis, when cosmopolitan citizenship is at issue, must be to ensure that citizenship education provides access to information and capacities that allows individuals to understand and appreciate the importance of universal rights (both for securing their own highest order interests for pursuing – and being able to revise – their conception of the good, and for addressing problems of global justice) and to undertake the functions required for establishing and maintaining cosmopolitan democratic structures and processes.

CONCLUSION

In many ways, contemporary discussion of cosmopolitan justice evokes Kant's concerns with a peaceful cosmopolitan order. Kant hoped that this could be achieved through a public cosmopolitan law based on and enshrining rights of world citizens,[2] and a 'peaceable federation' among independent republican states.[3] Publicity involves an enlightened and critical public. World citizens are indispensable to a cosmopolitan public sphere which they maintain in their societies, to monitor implementation of human rights. Is the hope that such a sphere is attainable a realistic one? As we saw above, a number of contemporary political theorists believe this is possible provided that cosmopolitan institutions take appropriate forms. They suggest that 'differentiated sovereignty', involving overlapping levels of regulation and control – national, transnational, and subnational – is a feasible model, and that a corresponding conception of a cosmopolitan citizen is a viable ideal.

What is clear is that not only are there compelling moral grounds for global duties with respect to education, but also that, given the existence of globally effective associations, the means for discharging them (appropriate 'authorities') are available. There is every reason to push for the kind of citizenship education that will secure these endeavours.

NOTES

[1] Is peace not threatened by such a permissive justification for intervention? Does it not justify too many military interventions? Isn't it open to hypocritical abuse? Moellendorf concedes that just cause for intervention (which exists if and only if intervention is directed toward advancing justice either in basic structure of state or in international effects of its domestic policies) is a necessary but not sufficient condition for intervention. Further conditions must be fulfilled for the intervention to be justified. There must in addition be good reason for believing that action will remedy the injustice that such action is necessary to remedy it, and that greater harms will not be done in the course of attempting to remedy the injustice.

[2] In 'Kant and Cosmopolitanism', Nussbaum provides a graphic description of a 'world citizen' based on the self-definition of Diogenes the Cynic who described himself in terms of the universal values of the worth of reason and moral purpose as opposed to local origins and group memberships (Nussbaum, 1997, p. 29). This does not mean that the world citizen is without community. It does mean that hers is the Kantian community made up by the humanity of all human beings; one should always behave so as to treat with equal respect the dignity of reason and moral choice in each and every human being. This entails, as Kant said, a common participation in law and in a virtual polity, cosmopolis, the Kingdom of Ends. How do we achieve world citizenship? Nussbaum says that early education can help by addressing hatred of members of other races and religions. We can address the cognitive roots of passions by getting children to view people in a cosmopolitan way – as similarly human, bearers of equal moral dignity, members of single body, set of purposes. These images gradually lead to corresponding evaluations. More generally those programmes of education that would realise Kant's idea of world citizenship are those that instil a positive attitude toward people who are different: teach young people to regard them as people from whom something might be learnt. This attention to the cognitive moral development of the young helps to address divisive passions militating against cosmopolitan humanism. Nussbaum insists, however, that this is not to endorse ethnocentric identity politics (1997, p. 57, note 59).

[3] Although contemporary conditions (and especially inequality and diversity) seem to make many of Kant's assumptions inapplicable (because unequal distribution combined with closer association among nations will inflame conflict, and it is predictable that there could be an ethnic backlash if cosmopolitanism is actively promoted), some empirical research by Doyle (1983) can be read as bearing out Kant's hypothesis if it is confined to liberal regimes or what is presumably the same thing, Kant's 'inwardly republican' states. Doyle cites the fact that liberal states display a marked reluctance to go to war with other liberal states. He explains this by speculating that there is a political bond of liberal rights and interests that have the effect of making such states mutually constrained with respect to one another. (He also thinks that these very same considerations often exacerbate conflicts between liberal and non-liberal states.)

REFERENCES

Ackerly, B. & Okin, S. (1999). Feminist social criticism and the international movement for women's human rights. In I. Shapiro & C. Hacker-Cordon (Eds.), *Democracy's edges*. Cambridge: Cambridge University Press.

Ansell, N. (2002). Secondary education reform in Lesotho and Zimbabwe and the needs of rural girls: Pronouncements, policy and practice. *Comparative Education, 38*(1), 91–112.

Bohman, & Lutz-Bachmann, M. (Eds.) (1997). *Perpetual peace: Essays on Kant's cosmopolitan ideal*. Cambridge, MA: MIT Press.

Bohman, J. (1997). The public spheres of the world citizen. In J. Bohman & M. Lutz-Bachmann (Eds.), *Perpetual peace: Essays on Kant's cosmopolitan ideal* (pp. 179–200). Cambridge, MA: MIT Press.

Brighouse, H. (1998). Civic education and liberal legitimacy. *Ethics, 108*, 719–745.

Callan, E. (1996). Political liberalism and political education. *The Review of Politics, 58*(1), 5–33.

Delanty, G. (2000). *Citizenship in a global age: Society, culture, politics*. Buckingham: Open University Press.

Doyle, M. (1983). Kant, liberal legacies, and foreign affairs. *Philosophy and Public Affairs, 12*, 203–265.

Dryzek, J. (2000). *Deliberative democracy and beyond: Liberals, critics, contestations*. Oxford: Oxford University Press.

Duke, B. (1986). *The Japanese school*. New York: Praeger.

Gutmann, A. (1987). Democratic education. Princeton N.J.: Princeton University Press.

Gutmann, A. (1995). Civic education and social diversity. *Ethics, 105*(3), 557–579.

Hampton, J. (1993). The moral commitments of liberalism. In D. Copp, J. Hampton & J. Roemer (Eds.), *The idea of democracy*. Cambridge: Cambridge University Press.

Held, D. (1997). *Cosmopolitan democracy and the global order: A new agenda*. In J. Bohman & M. Lutz-Bachmann (Eds.), *Perpetual peace: Essays on Kant's cosmopolitan ideal* (pp. 235–251). Cambridge, MA: MIT Press.

Macedo, S. (1995). Liberal civic education and religious fundamentalism: The case of God v. John Rawls? *Ethics, 105*, 468–496.

McCarthy, T. (1997). On the idea of a reasonable law of peoples. In J. Bohman & M. Lutz-Bachmann (Eds.), *Perpetual peace: Essays on Kant's cosmopolitan ideal* (pp. 201–217). Cambridge, MA: MIT Press.

Moellendorf, D. (2002). *Cosmopolitan justice*. Oxford: Westview Press.

NetAid (2003). Education for all gets a boost from petition. Retrieved from http://www.netaid.org/groups/news/news.

Nussbaum, M. (1997). Kant and cosmopolitanism. In J. Bohman & M. Lutz-Bachmann (Eds.), *Perpetual peace: Essays on Kant's cosmopolitan ideal* (pp. 25–57). Cambridge, MA: MIT Press.

Nussbaum, M. (2000). *Women and human development: The capabilities approach*. Cambridge: Cambridge University Press.

Pogge, T. (1989). *Realizing Rawls*. Ithaca: Cornell University Press.

Pogge, T. (2002). *World poverty and human rights*. Cambridge: Polity Press.

Rawls, J. (1971). *A theory of justice*. Oxford: Oxford University Press.

Rawls, J. (1993). *Political liberalism*. New York: Columbia University Press.

Tilak, B. (2002). Knowledge society, education and Aid. *Compare, 32*(3), 297–310.

Worldwatch (2003). *State of the world 2002*. Washington, DC: Worldwatch Institute.

Penny A. Enslin
University of Glasgow

Mary Tjiattas
University of the Witwatersrand

CHRISTINE FORDE

REVISIONING IDEAS OF CITIZENRY

The Female State and the Construction of Citizenship

ABSTRACT

Education has been a fundamental, historically, of women's claim for rights as citizens, but there are significant questions about what kind of citizenry education should be preparing girls and women and, indeed, boys and men for. Wollstonecraft (1792), who produced what is regarded as a foundational text in feminist thinking, based her claim for the rights of women as citizens on their capacity for rational thought which would be developed through a rigorous education alongside their male peers. In a period when male universal suffrage was disputed, Wollstonecraft argued for (some) women to have the right of entry into a male-inscribed model of citizenship through an academic and rational education. Though radical in its historical context, Wollstonecraft's vision was based on ideals of a class-stratified and gender-differentiated society, where civic polity was male-inscribed, ideals that are challenged today. Contemporary feminist writers provide other visions of alternative socio-political orders where the state is based on principles derived from women's distinctiveness, particularly characteristics derived from nurturing and caring roles women typically undertake. These feminist utopian texts help us to examine the significance of gender in our understandings of 'the state' and of 'citizenship'. This essay explores different visions of citizenry created in contemporary feminist utopian writing and considers the implications of these for education.

INTRODUCTION

The place of education in women's claim for citizenship has a long tradition in feminist thought and politics. Mary Wollstonecraft (1792), in making her case for the rights of women as citizens, argued that access to a rigorous education would equip women with the ability to think rationally which was a prerequisite for citizenship. In a period when male universal suffrage was disputed, Wollstonecraft's vision of (some) women – those privileged either socio-economically, in terms of class, or academically – having the right of entry into a male-inscribed model of citizenship was radical. In contrast, contemporary feminist writers have constructed other visions of alternative socio-political orders where the state is based on principles derived from women's distinctiveness and where the model of the citizenship is female-inscribed. Within these visions there is

M.A. Peters, A. Britton and H. Blee (Eds.), Global Citizenship Education: Philosophy, Theory and Pedagogy, 87-102.

considerable diversity reflecting competing ideologies of gender within feminism. This essay explores these visions of the female state and the construction of citizenship. The three key themes of power and community, the military and the public/private divide are examined.

EDUCATION AND BECOMING A CITIZEN

Wollstonecraft's (1792) discussion on the rights of women as citizens is one of the foundational works in liberal feminism. Wollstonecraft wrote this book at a point where the education of women and girls was the subject of much debate. The dominant deeply entrenched position was exemplified by conduct books and other writings (Todd, 1996) which provided advice to fathers and their families. In these works women were viewed as being incapable of engaging in an intellectually rigorous education. There was resistance from women themselves to female education, with Hester Chapone (1773) concerned that education would be ruinous of a girl's marriage prospects. An exaggerated form of femininity that emphasised women's 'natural' passivity, a propensity to be overly concerned about physical appearance and driven by emotions, dominated the popular imagination. This image of femininity was reinforced by the limited education that girls received which was typically rudimentary, largely focusing on the development of 'accomplishments' to increase a girl's chances of marriage. Marriage and the domestic sphere were regarded as the natural destiny for girls. Women were not seen as autonomous citizens. Instead, because of their perceived lack of any true moral sense and because of the dangers posed by a predatory form of masculinity, women were dependent beings in need of male protection. The counter position was not to claim women's rights to autonomy and access to the public domain. Instead it was to assert women's role as the moral guardians – though still within the confines of the domestic sphere. Thus other commentators who supported female education, such as Mary Astell (1696) (regarded as the first English feminist), argued that educating women was vital if they were to act to protect the morals of society.

Wollstonecraft's analysis, therefore, thrust the debates about women's education and women's role in the wider polity to another level. As Wollstonecraft illustrates well, women were in a double bind. They were deemed incapable of thinking and acting rationally and were largely excluded from a rigorous academic education – the very means of acquiring these prerequisites of full citizenship. Though radical in its historical context, Wollstonecraft's vision was based on the ideals of a class stratified and gender differentiated society. Wollstonecraft's *A Vindication of the Rights of Women* was written against a backdrop of the French Revolution and reflected the radical idea that citizenship need not rest on the possession of wealth, rank and power, but instead all had the right to be a citizen. Here the idea of the 'state' was not significantly altered; instead, a wider group of men were to be regarded as citizens of the state. Wollstonecraft's discussion did not challenge the privileging of male/masculinity within the public domain: in order to become citizens, women had to acquire the attributes of men. This idea of civic polity being male/masculine is something that has been challenged in feminist politics and thought. Arnot (1997) reflects on four different feminist perspectives on the analysis of citizenship, each of which reveals the gendered nature of this construct through the persistence of a male/female, public/private divide which limits opportunities to conceive of citizenship as an inclusive concept. The question of how we might construct citizenship as inclusive of women is explored in feminist utopian thinking.

CONTEMPORARY FEMINIST UTOPIAN THINKING AND THE FEMALE STATE

Contemporary feminist discussions, particularly those from a woman-centred or radical feminist standpoint, have challenged the privileging of male/masculine in the public space and a construction of citizenship based on the traditional role of men within patriarchal society. Feminist utopian writers provide other visions of alternative socio-political orders where the state is based on principles reflecting women's distinctiveness, particularly characteristics derived from nurturing and caring roles women typically undertake. These feminist utopian texts help us to examine the significance of gender in our understandings of 'the state' and of 'citizenship'.

Sargent's (1988) classic definition of the traditional (predominantly male authored) utopian novel as a representation of a non-existent good place presented in detailed and concrete terms and located in a specific time or place, focusing largely on the critical examination of the political and juridical structures of society, is what is usually understood by the concept of 'utopia'. However, Sargisson (1996) in her discussion of contemporary feminist utopianism argues that this view is based on content-based forms of utopianism that have only limited value in trying to imagine alternatives in education and in a wider socio-political context. Instead, we can draw from the German philosopher Ernst Bloch's (1986) distinction between utopias and utopian thinking. He argues that utopianism is not about creating new societies that have not previously existed, the 'Not-Yet', but is about conceiving new ideas – what he terms the 'Not-Yet-Become' – that could form the basis of alternative social orders. As Sargisson (1996, p. 41) argues:

Utopian thinking is thinking that creates and operates inside a new place or space that has previously appeared inconceivable. Writing from or towards a good place that is no place, glancing over the shoulder at her place whence she came, the utopian feminist escapes the restrictions of patriarchal scholarship. New and inventive languages can be best imagined and employed in a new space, as can different social, sexual and symbolic relations.

Across a body of work that includes theoretical writings, polemical material and ephemera such as manifestos and newsletters as well as fictional utopias, there has been the generation and critique of visions of alternative socio-political orders by feminists. In feminist utopian fiction, there is the realisation and critical exploration of the aspirations and visions of alternative socio-political orders put forward in

89

non-fictional feminist utopian works. These works also enable us to examine 'citizenry' as a gendered construct and to consider the consequences of different ideologies of gender for the agency of women and men in bringing about socio-political transformation. To view feminist utopian states as peaceful and nurturing utopias is to see them as one dimensional and does now recognise the role utopian writing can play in the exploration of fundamental questions about key ideas such as what it means to be a citizen. There are two common preoccupations in feminist utopian writing that are significant to a consideration of the construction of citizenship: firstly, the question of peace and war; and secondly, the issue of commonality and difference. Even within states that are exclusive on the grounds of gender – women-only utopias – the question of difference, both women's difference from men and differences between women, is the subject of much scrutiny. How to deal with the issues of the state, power and conflict are particularly challenging ideas. However, these discussions also lead to a deeper level of exploration of the construction of citizenship: that of the boundary between the public and the private domains. These domains have historically been gendered with the conflation of public/male and private/female.

THE STATE IN FEMINIST UTOPIAN THINKING

Characteristically in feminist utopian thinking, the construct of 'the state' itself is scrutinized critically. There is considerable resistance to the idea of the state as a large nation state, this being regarded as at best an exclusory construct and at worst, detrimental to women's well-being and self-determination. Such states, for example contemporary USA in Piercy's (1979) *A Woman on the Edge of Time,* are perceived as being intrinsically oppressive for women. Within these texts, nevertheless, there is considerable variation in what constitutes the alternative socio-political order. The state might be a post-holocaust society dealing with the ecological and genetic consequences of male-driven global conflicts, a new society on another planet where women have fled to avoid being rendered powerless in patriarchal regimes or virtually in cyberspace where minority people such as gay and lesbian groups can build a community beyond the gaze of oppressive heterosexual regimes. Further, the alternative state might be a clearly defined geographical state often bounded by hostile male-dominated states or a more localised community; it might be pastoral or technology-based. In all of these, although the female state might not be the perfect alternative socio-political order, it stands as the eutopian (good or at least better) society in contrast to the dystopian (bad or nightmare) male state. In these different visions of alternative socio-political orders, a key area of debate is that of power and the building of community.

POWER AND COMMUNITY

Marge Piercy produced a trio of utopian novels written over a period of thirty years. In each of these utopian novels, *Dance the Eagle to Sleep* (1970), *A Woman on the Edge of Time* (1979) and *Body of Glass* (1992), Piercy draws from and interrogates the contemporaneous debates about gender politics and social change. These utopian texts reflect the trajectory of debates in the politics of social transformation from the period of liberatory movements in the late 1960s in the USA, to the Women's Liberation Movement and the emergence of feminism, to the current debates and the development of a more complex gender politics. In each of these works, utopia is not a simple idealized 'good society' but one in which there has to be constant negotiation of power.

The first novel *Dance the Eagle to Sleep* illustrates graphically the seductive qualities of power for those previously dispossessed and the easy slide from radical revolution into totalitarianism. Part of Piercy's critique though is of the male-inscription of this alternative society and of revolutionary left wing politics. The second, *A Woman on the Edge of Time,* is about the giving up of power, most notoriously by women who give up their only source of power, their power to bear children. In the third novel, *Body of Glass*, power has become consolidated in massive transnational corporations who determine every aspect of life and it is only through coalitions that a politics of social transformation towards a more equal society can be progressed.

Piercy's first utopian novel, *Dance the Eagle to Sleep,* is set in a near future USA where there is a clear definition of what it means to be a citizen, a concept which is challenged by youth culture. Piercy's novel, although published in 1970, has a contemporary resonance in its exploration of the discourse of 'problem youth' and some of the 'solutions' offered. To prevent youths from getting out of hand there is the 19th Year of Service, (akin to National Service). The 19th year marks the break between the 'anarchy' of childhood and the responsibilities of adulthood because once this year has been completed the youth are destined to seek a good job, marry, buy a house in the suburbs, become cogs in the 'system'. A group of young people reject the 19th Year of Service and set up alternative communes. The novel follows attempts by Corey (who is an outsider with little hope of fitting into the 'system' because he is half Native American) to set up an alternative society of young people – the Indians – who want to escape the system. They live collectively on the farms or in the communes they have established: 'They could learn the good ways of being in harmony, of cooperating, of same bravery in defence of each other, to be one with their bodies, their tribe and each other and the land' (Piercy 1970, p. 32). The novel follows the development of this social movement from the first enthusiastic and hopeful days through the increasing tendency towards doctrinaire political analysis, to purges and the move towards armed resistance. The novel ends with the final move by the authorities to kill off the Indians.

The novel maintains its critique of mainstream society being deeply repressive: the Indians are brutally suppressed by being killed or forced to undergo treatment as Joanna has to in order to readjust her to normal 'femininity'. However, the underlying gender politics of both regimes which render women powerless are ultimately the focus of the critique. The apocalyptic ending to the Indians' attempt to create a genuine alternative seems inevitable after their decision to engage armed resistance. To Ginny, though, this is simply an acting out of the myth of male glory and the transformation of society must be achieved through other means:

> Our claims are the most radical, for they entail restructuring even the nuclear family. Nowhere on earth are women free now, although in some places things are marginally better. What we will have to do is to invent ourselves. (Piercy 1970, p. 227)

The ending of the novel offers us a glimpse of what this might look like in a world in which power at societal level is related to the power dynamics of the family: the patriarchal male-headed family is linked to the wider structures of oppression. Only three members of the Indians survive the attack by the police: Ginny (who is pregnant by Corey) and two of the men, Shawn and Marcus. The novel ends with these three characters living communally, awaiting the birth of the baby. When Shawn begins to talk about Corey as the dead male hero, the father of this baby, Ginny replies:

> 'No! It's not his. It's not even yours. It's ours. Let Corey be the goddamn father. A ghost is a perfect father. Something that comes and goes without touching you. I want you to be its second mother. And Marcus its third'. (Piercy, 1970, p. 230)

It is from this suggestion – that social change begins with the restructuring of the family – that Piercy builds up her substantial vision of eutopia in her second utopian novel.

In the second novel, *A Woman on the Edge of Time,* Piercy (1979) builds on the ideas about the nature of revolution found in the final chapter of her first novel. Thus, Connie, the character from the contemporary world who comes into contact with the future eutopian society of Mattapoisett, dismisses the traditional idea of revolution which, in her experience, is simply the replacing of one set of male rulers with another: "'Oh, revolution!" she grimaced. "Honchos marching around in imitation uniforms. Big talk and bad mouthing everybody else. Noise in the streets and nothing changes"' (Piercy, 1979, p. 198). Instead of simply looking for changes in who holds political power, the inhabitants of Mattapoisett argue that the eutopian future can only be achieved by making profound changes in personal lives:

> No, Connie! It's the people who worked out the labor and land intensive farming we do. It's all the people who changed how people bought foods, raised children, went to school! ... Who made new unions, withheld rent, refused to go to wars, wrote and educated and made speeches. (Piercy, 1979, p. 198)

In this eutopian future people live in small communities such as Mattapoisett where property is owned collectively and all people participate in the communal politics. The sharing of power is crucial and decisions are made through discussion as Luciente the person connecting with Connie, explains:

"We argue," the man said. "How else?"

"There's no final authority, Connie," Luciente said.

"There's got to be. Who finally say yes or no?"

"We argue till we close to agree. We just continue."

[...]

"Grasp, political decisions – like whether to raise or lower the population – go a different route. We talk locally and then choose a rep to speak our posit (sic) on area hookup. Then we all sit in holi simulcast and the rep from each group speaks their village posit. Then we go back in to the local meeting to fuse our final word. The reps argue once more before everybody. Then we vote". (Piercy, 1979, p. 154)

This communal ideal exists only in the free towns which are at the margins of the future world of Piercy's third utopian novel, *Body of Glass*. This is a complex novel in which Piercy offsets a historical narrative set in the Jewish ghetto of 17th Century Prague with a futuristic narrative set in a globalised society dominated by transnational corporations. The main narrative of this novel is set in America in the mid-twenty first century where, after nuclear war, society has been reconstructed into the multinational enclaves who are constantly seeking to extend their power, free towns who are struggling to survive and the 'Glop', a lawless place where marginalised groups live in extreme poverty and violence. This world, dominated by hierarchical multinational corporations, is the dystopian outcome of current trends in society, particularly increasing globalisation of the economy and increased social and political control particularly through the use of technology. There is the gathering of power in the hands of a few corporate executives.

Piercy's earlier novel, *A Woman on the Edge of Time*, was very clearly focussed on the oppression of women but there seems at first glance to be little about gender politics in *Body of Glass*. The transnational enclaves seem to be the achievement of gender equality: both women and men are fully employed, equally recruited into the science and technology roles, and there is universal childcare. In the free town of Tikva, women and men also have equal status in employment and in the governance of the town. As the novel progresses we realise this is still a society where power is gendered, but in more subtle ways.

Whereas *A Woman on the Edge of Time* follows the convention of making a clear division between the eutopian society (Mattapoisett) and the dystopian society (the USA in the 1970s), in the later novel this traditional duality is abandoned and instead we have many differing communities, none of which can be easily labelled as eutopian or dystopian. Tikva as a free town could seem to be the eutopia of the text especially if compared to either of the transnational Y-S enclaves. It is a liberal, tolerant society with decisions made democratically by the town meeting and the inhabitants seem to have a good standard of living compared to life in the Glop. It is a Jewish town but there is no discrimination on the grounds of race, sexuality or gender. Nevertheless, Tikva is not a fully autonomous society; it is under attack by an infinitely more powerful force and only survives by producing unique security programmes for the multinational companies who nevertheless threaten their very existence. The multinational enclaves might serve as a dystopia; these are rigidly hierarchical communities where employees simply are components in the organisation. Nevertheless, although the inhabitants may lack autonomy or self-determination, they do have a materially more comfortable lifestyle compared to those who live in the Glop where poverty and violence are extreme.

It is in the margins that we see the emergence of a political consciousness and the exercise of citizenship: it is the free towns such as Tikva, the Glop – the area outwith the jurisdiction of the multinational companies in which the poor and marginalised live – and Safed in the Black Zone, where a community of women live together, that hold the possibility of social transformation. The Glop appears to be a dangerous place under the rule of warring gangs, where there is a constant struggle to survive, and yet here the emergent oppositional groups are beginning to resist the monopolization of the multinationals. Materially, Safed is also a dystopian place; it is merely a black space on the global map assumed to be so contaminated as a result of the nuclear war that it is uninhabitable and access strictly forbidden. The women have to live deep within the hills to avoid the contamination. Yet this community is resonant of feminist utopian ideals: this is a group of Israeli and Palestinian women, survivors of the nuclear war who live communally but continue to follow their own religious practices. What marks all three, the Glop and Safed and Tikva as eutopian, is the recognition of difference. In these more eutopian communities we can see Haraway's (1990) critique of the attempt to create a politics based on a monolithic construct of women's experience because this approach reinforces the epistemological structure of patriarchal ideology where meaning is based on a dualistic system of opposites centring around the dichotomy of man/woman, and in which one pole always has dominance. Tikva, the Glop and Safed each acknowledge and use difference whether of ethnicity, gender or religion as the basis of a politics of social transformation.

In this novel, no single place seems to be offered as a fully formed eutopia but instead we have glimpses of the way in which – in the most dire of circumstances – a post-holocaust world needs to rebuild itself through coalitions and resistance to the colonising efforts of the military-industrial blocs. Piercy takes the debate about gender and social change even further, by posing the possibility that utopia is not a specific place but instead a form of politics, what Haraway refers to as an oppositional consciousness; eutopia cannot be a once-and-for-all achievement but must be constantly worked towards to avoid the nightmare alternative. Power in the transnationals is consolidated in the hands of a few, but power for social transformation must be through the exercise of citizenship and something that is constantly negotiated and shared between individuals and groups. Rather than establish a politics on the principle of sameness, Piercy is depicting the importance of coalitions for political change across different groups because as Haraway argues the only way to achieve true liberation for women is to consider the possibility of a "monstrous world without gender … This dream of a powerful infidel heteroglossia …" (1990, p. 233).

There are two potential eutopian figures in this novel. There is Yod who is created in Avram's laboratory by combining organic tissue and microelectronics, and there is Nili, a woman whose physical capabilities have been enhanced through the use of technology. Piercy uses these characters to explore critically Haraway's contention that the cyborg is a means of developing an oppositional consciousness. In the novel, the character of Yod seems at first to have this potential to be a symbol of a new form of politics. The making of Yod is an act of creation, shown through Malkah's eyes as being as rewarding and risky as creating children because it is the creation of an autonomous being who should have the freedom of self-determination. In Yod also, the gender boundary is challenged: Avram created Yod entirely male, based on an idealised masculinity that emphasizes the strength and pure reason which in Avram's previous experiments with cyborgs inevitably led to uncontrollable violence. Piercy make the parallel between these attributes and the wholesale destruction apparent in the world of the twenty first century. Yod avoids this destiny because although he was built by a man he was programmed by a woman, Malkah who enabled him to become a person: "I gave him a gentler side starting with emphasising his love for knowledge and extending it to emotional and personal knowledge, a need for connections" (Piercy, 1992, p. 192). Yod does not represent the eutopian possibility of technology, because he is created as a person without autonomy, without rights, and as the narrative progresses what becomes apparent is that this 'man-made' being designed on the basis of pure reason, will only end in the masculinist orgy of war and destruction that Haraway warns of. As Malkah waits to hear of Yod's destruction she says to Nili:

> Yod was a mistake. You're the right path, Nili. It's better to make people into partial machines than to create machines that feel and yet are still controlled like cleaning robots. The creation of a conscious being as any kind of tool – supposed to exist only to fulfil our needs – is a disaster. (Piercy, 1992, p. 558)

It is with the character of Nili that the eutopian future lies: she is the one character who is truly disturbing of our understandings of what it means to be human, what it means to be a woman and what type of eutopian society could be based on these understandings. Different from Yod, Nili possesses enhanced physical capabilities but she remains human and she feels no solidarity with Yod whom she perceives as a machine. Nili as an enhanced female has strengths well beyond those of other women and she is an example of the use of technology to ensure the survival of humans in a harsh environment. Nili is also an example of the cyborg world which Haraway argues might be about "… lived social and bodily realities in which people are not afraid of their joint kinship with animals and machines, not afraid of permanently partial identities and contradictory standpoints" (Piercy, 1992, p. 196).

Nili lives in a community where difference is recognised and celebrated. Nili is on a mission to end Safed's isolation and to form coalitions with other radical and marginalised groups. Nili has what Yod lacked, a community to bond with where members despite profound differences in terms of religious traditions have supported each other and been able to survive in the most hostile environment. Though in Nili we have a eutopian figure, she is a paradox – a woman who acts as a defender of her community, a role from which, in patriarchal societies, she would have been debarred. The figure of Nili brings us to the question of women's role in one of the defining features of the role of the citizen, that of the defender of the state.

CITIZENRY AND MILITARISM

The military and other male-inscribed institutions have historically circumscribed the role of women. Stiemh (1989) in her study of women in the military argues that to be a full citizen an individual has the duty and the right to defend the state. Partly because of the demands of second wave feminism for gender equality, in developed western states women are now entering the military and seeing active service as combatants. As Feinman (2000) indicates, the proposition that the presence of women in the most powerful areas of hierarchical and potent institutions like the military is essential for women to have a full role as a citizen has been very much part of a egalitarian form of feminism. However, it is proposition that is much disputed. The rejection of militarianism has a long history in feminist thinking. The subordination of women, observed Catherine Marshall in 1915, is not just an unfortunate occurrence within the militarised state but an inevitable outcome (Marshall, 1987). Similarly Ogden and Florence, also writing in 1915, demonstrate the way in which militarisation necessarily subordinates the role of women to ensure the needs of war are met:

> War, and the fear of war, has kept woman in perpetual subjugation, making it her chief duty to exhaust all her faculties in the ceaseless production of children that nations might have the warriors needed for aggression or defence. She must not have any real education – for the warrior alone required knowledge and independence, she must not have a voice in the affairs of the nation, for war and preparation for war are so fundamental in the life of nations that woman, with her silly humanitarianism, must not be allowed to meddle there within. (1987, p. 57)

Katherine Burdekin's (1937) *Swastika Nights,* published just before the outbreak of the Second World War, illustrates graphically the impact of militarization on the lives of women. Motherhood is not defined in terms of nurturance and fulfilment but instead the role of the mother is subservient to the needs of the state especially in producing the next generation of warriors. In Burdekin's dystopia (bad or nightmare society), women's capacity to bear children has significant consequences leading to their utter subjugation and deprivation of rights as citizens. They are confined to camps and are made to deny all ties to their infant sons surrendering them to their fathers. Ultimately their only act of resistance is to stop reproducing their own gender. Burdekin's dystopia is an extreme society but Burdekin reveals the gender politics underpinning a militarised socio-political order where men, because they can be soldiers, are privileged and where the only value women have is their ability to bear children. The consequences of militarization are complete subjugation. Thus, we are faced with a dilemma. On the one hand, women should be able to play an active and equal role and take on the responsibilities of citizens. On the other hand however, this construction of citizenship is premised on the traditional male role and leads to a situation in which the founding ideals remain male-inscribed. Thus public, active and aggressive behaviours are reified as those that defined citizenry.

Whereas Burdekin's novel illustrates graphically the consequences of a privileging of aggressive masculinity, Sherri Tepper's (1990) utopia, *A Gate to Women's Country,* is more critical of a simplistic gender divide. This book helps us to consider what place ideas about femininity and masculinity play in our construction of citizenship. At one level in this novel Tepper seems to be critical of the view a citizenry based on a militarism and offers a different construction of citizenship in her vision of an alternative socio-political order run by women: 'Women's Country'. This is a strictly gender-segregated society in which the women have banished men to beyond the gate where they can pursue a life in keeping with their 'natural' aggression and competitiveness. This male society is reminiscent of ancient Sparta where boys from a young age are educated in the ways of the warrior. Importantly, however, the women ensure that the role of the warrior is not glorified and instead of women nurturing and caring for the wounded, the young boys must carry out these tasks so they may know the full horrors of war. Some men forsake the militaristic way of life and, as adolescents, return to live in women's country, though they do not have full rights as citizens.

In this society the two communities are gendered: the peaceful women's country stands in contrast to the militaristic culture of the male army. In this book it seems that the military and war are not men's duty but men seem almost incapable of being any other way. This division is to separate men who wish to indulge their 'natural' predisposition for war from mainstream society. Morgot, one of the leaders of the women's country reflects on this:

> War is dreadful, daughter. It always has been. Comfort yourself with the knowledge that in preconvulsion times it was worse! More died, and most of them were women, children and old people. Also, wars were allowed to create devastations. Under our ordinances, no children are slain. No women are slain. Only men who choose to be warriors go to battle. There is no devastation. (Tepper, 1990, p. 153)

This seems very much the stance of many radical feminist writings especially those associated with the peace movement. The effort is not simply to prevent war or the increased militarization of everyday life or the arms race. Instead, the focus is on challenging the underpinning ideologies in relation to what a state is and what it means to be a citizen. Tepper does this but also questions a simplistic polarisation of male/aggression and female/peacemaker. The seemingly ideal society of women's country has a deeper flaw in a secret known only to the group of ruling women. Only the men who have returned to women's country and have forsaken their aggressive and competitive ways are allowed to father children. The men in the military camps are unaware of this, believing the boys who come to them are indeed their children. As the archetypal masculine characteristics are bred out of the population, more and more adolescents return to women's country. The book privileges femininity but notes also the paradox of femininity: that the orientation towards care and nurturance has historically been the root of women's oppression.

> 'Misplaced nurturing,' Septemius corrected her. 'The biggest chink in your female armor. The largest hole in your defences. The one thing you cannot and dare not absolutely guard against, for your nature must remain as it is for all your planning to come to fruition. You dare not change it. (Tepper, 1990, p. 333)

To survive, the women must act as the aggressors pursuing the policy of breeding out the aggressive characteristics in men, but at the same time hold onto the feminine qualities of caring and nurturance.

THE PUBLIC AND THE PRIVATE

The progress of women socially and politically has been centred on women becoming citizens by entering the public space which historically has been the domain of men. However, if we are to look to a gender-inclusive concept of citizenship we also have to consider the women's and men's role in the private arena. Burdekin's (1937) novel *Swastika Nights* reveals the dire consequences when women's roles are constructed solely in terms their reproductive capacities in a society that valorises an aggressive form of masculinity as the defining feature of citizenship. There are profound consequences for women and for men if reproductive roles define citizenry. In the first of her quartet of feminist utopian novels, *A Walk to the End of the World,* Suzy McKee Charnas depicts a similar dystopian society, Holdfast, set in a post-holocaust world where citizenship is constructed on a form of masculinity that is intrinsically aggressive. Conflict is so ingrained into what it means to be a man that there can be no familial bonding: boys cannot know their fathers for fear of intergenerational warfare. Women lack all status as autonomous humans; their subjugation is such that they lack all but the most rudimentary form of language. Women's role is simply to produce the next generation of men. These visions might seem exaggerated fictions but they raise significant questions at a historical moment when – in western Europe at least – the birth rate has fallen below replacement level and some governments begin to pursue pro-natal policies. Is this an intrusion of the public into the private which could have severe consequences for women, once more limiting their opportunities within the public arena?

Other feminists have sought to take the values of the private space and make these the foundational ideals of a new society and a new form of citizenship. The Women's Peace Movement in the 1980s and early 1990s was significant in the development of feminist thinking, and particularly in debates about how women's distinctiveness could be used as the basis for an alternative socio-political order. Here, it is not just women's capacity to bear children but their nurturing and caring roles that might constitute a part of the ways in which the values of the good society can be generated. This position is explored at length by Sara Ruddick in her work *Maternal Thinking* (1990) in which she argues that women, by virtue of their caring roles are in the position to reconstruct the state and take humanity from the brink of nuclear holocaust. In feminist utopian novels women's maternal role has similarly been reclaimed as the basis for a better socio-political order. Charlotte Perkins Gilman's (1915) *Herland,* enables us to consider how women's reproductive roles relate to their role as citizens within the state. While women's role as mothers is shown to be profoundly fulfilling on a personal level, Gilman's novel *Herland* is prototypical of the presentation of motherhood as the founding ideal of a feminist eutopia. Importantly this text makes an important distinction between the biological function of bearing a child (the lesser important role) and the social role of caring for a child (the more critical role). Caring for children, is the important task fulfilled by a special few. Somel, one of the women of Herland, explains:

> ... child-rearing has come to be with us a culture so profoundly studied, practised and with such subtlety and skill, that the more we love our children the less we are willing to trust that process to unskilled hands even our own'.
> (Gilman: 1915, p. 83)

Herland is based on a polarization of masculinity and femininity also found in the debates in feminist thinking in the early years of Women's Liberation in which the hierarchy of male and female is reversed. In her first utopian novel, *A Walk to the End of the World,* Suzy McKee Charnas presents us with this simple dichotomy between the dystopian patriarchal society of Holdfast and the eutopian society of the Riding Women. However, such a clear divide between female/eutopia and male/dystopia has given way to greater uncertainty. Through a series of subsequent books Charnas debates the question of gender relations and the socio-political order. The female state is seen, at the outset, as a better society, but it too, is riven with dilemmas as men are denied their rights as citizens. The complexity of identity and citizenship is depicted in the final novel (Charnas, 1999) through a new generation, especially the 'conqueror's child', a male child born to one of the Riding Women but fathered by one of the men of the male dystopia of Holdfast, the question of the role of gender in citizenship is played out. In these novels Charnas seeks ways to re-construct gender relations on both a personal and a societal level in order to re-vision an alternative society.

Elisabeth Vonarburg adopts a similar theme in her feminist utopian novel, *In Mothers' Land* (1992), and provides a searching discussion of the role of men, particularly as fathers, in any future eutopia. Fatherhood, being linked to men's role as oppressors within patriarchal gender regimes, is a contradictory construct in this novel. Vonarburg attempts to grapple with the complexities of the construct and to find a eutopian solution that can include a fathering role for men. Despite the title of the novel, one of its main themes deals with Lisbei's (the principal character) increasing awareness of the oppressed position of men in this society and the profound effects that the loss of fatherhood as an institution has on individuals and on the society as a whole. At one level in *In Mother's Land* we have a clear feminist analysis; the minority status of men is attributed to the masculine ideals of the previous society which brought about a male driven nuclear holocaust. In the remnants of that society only 3% of births are male. This female-dominated world is a society which is divided into families each ruled by the 'Mother' and it is a settled, peaceful and harmonious world. As the novel progresses and as Lisbei becomes more aware, however, some of the founding ideas of this society particularly regarding the position of men in relation to their children are questioned. In Maerlande there is no concept of father or fatherhood as a legitimate and recognised role for men. Men are merely 'the genitors' who, when they are young and fertile, enter the Service to produce the sperm which is used to impregnate a large number of women in a carefully managed and regulated programme of reproduction. In practical terms it would be difficult for a man to play a part in any of his children's lives but there is not even a perception that there should be any kind of emotional link or social bonding between a man and his offspring. Men feel excluded from the important areas both in public life and also in terms of personal relationships. Their relationships with each other are given no public recognition and the possibility of forming long-term relationships with women and being fathers to their children is not even imagined in this society.

In these feminist utopian discussions it is through the agency of women that the process of social transformation comes about to create a good or better society in which women are full citizens. In each of these visions though we come back to a core issue of power, whether it is power within the public arena or power within the private space. Therefore, if we are to understand citizenship as an inclusive concept we have to consider movement in the other direction, with men being able to enter the private domain not in terms of the exercise of power through patriarchal gender relations but through an involvement in nurturing and caring roles. Both the continuing inscription of the private domain as female and the entry of men into this domain are fraught with dangers in terms of women's standing as autonomous citizens. Arguments for women's citizenship have privileged the idea of women's entry into the public arena. For a new concept of citizenship to be developed and become part of women's lived experience we have to look to a redistribution of power both at a societal level and at the personal level. In this we can return to Piercy's utopian novel *A Woman on the Edge of Time* in which eutopia is only possible if we dismantle existing gendered dichotomies both in the public and private space:

> It was part of women's long revolution. When we were breaking all the old hierarchies. Finally there was that one thing we had to give up too, the only

power we ever had, in return for no more power for anyone. The original production: the power to give birth. Cause as long as we were biologically enchained, we'd never be equal. And males never would be humanized to be loving and tender. So we all became mothers. Every child has three. To break the nuclear bonding. (1979, p. 105)

This vision helps us to consider the relationship between public/private, male/female in the construction of an inclusive concept of citizenship.

RECLAIMING THE CIVIC SPACE

These fictional texts not only present visions of alternative socio-political orders, but also help us to explore the significance of gender in the construction of the state and of citizenry. This issue is critical in the development of global citizenship education, where gender-differentiated roles continue and shape the lives and opportunities for women and men. Is there a female and a male form of citizenship? Should these continue or is having two forms inevitably deeply inequitable? How do ideological constructions of masculinity and femininity shape our ideas of what it means to be a citizen? The classic definition of the role of the citizen to vote and to defend the state valorises an ideological construct that not only excludes women but places then in a subordinate position. However, to take the opposite position and construct citizenry on the basis of familial roles is also fraught with dangers for women, as we see in the dystopian visions, as women's roles and lives are circumscribed in terms of their reproductive capacities. Notwithstanding this, if we are to create an inclusive construction of citizenship this cannot be simply about women's role in the public space. We need to be aware of the power dynamics of the public space, to recognise and challenge the unequal distribution of power among different groups both historically and currently. This understanding of power as a core concept within citizenship education would include the power dynamics in the classroom, between teachers and pupils by engaging pupils in decision making. As classrooms become more heterogeneous, we have to look to pedagogic practices, what Maher and Tetreault (1994) term 'positional pedagogies', which understand the power dynamics not just of gender but of the intersection of gender with other social factors as class, race, religion, ethnicity, sexuality and disability. Positional pedagogies offer the means, though, of moving beyond simplistic dichotomous ideas of oppressor and oppressed, and helping explore ways of building a critical awareness of different power positions and building coalitions for social transformation. We also need to consider the reconstruction of the private space in order to dismantle the gendered dichotomies that maintain a conception of citizenship that valorises maleness/masculinity to the exclusion of femaleness/femininity.

REFERENCES

Arnot, M. (1997). Gendered citizenry: New feminist perspectives on education and citizenship. *British Educational Research Journal, 23*(3), 275–295.

Astell, M. (1696). A serious proposal to the ladies. In B. Hill (Ed.) (1986), *The first English feminist: Reflections upon marriage and other writings by Mary Astell* (pp.135–182). Aldershot, Hants: Gower/Maurice Temple Smith.

Bloch, E. (1986). *The principle of hope.* Oxford: Basil Blackwell.

Burdekin, K. (1937). (pseud. Constantine, Murray) *Swastika nights.* London: Victor Gollancz.

Chapone, H. (1773). *Letters on the improvement of the mind.* In J. Todd (Ed.) (1996), *Female education in the age of enlightenment.* Vol 2. London: William Pickering.

Charnas, S. McKee (1989). *Walk to the end of the world.* London: The Women's Press.

Charnas, S. McKee (1999). *The conqueror's child.* New York: Tor Books.

Feinman, I.R. (2000). *Citizenship rites: Feminist soldiers and feminist antimilitarists.* New York University Press: New York and London.

Gilman, C. Perkins (1979). *Herland.* London: The Women's Press.

Haraway, D. (1990). A manifesto for cyborgs: Science, technology, and socialist feminism in the 1980s. In L. Nicholson (Ed.), *Feminism/Post Modernism* (pp. 190–233). London: Routledge.

Marshall, C. (1987). Women and War. In M.S. Florence, C. Marshall & C.K. Ogden (Eds.), *Militarism versus feminism* (pp.37–42). London: Virago.

Maher, F. A. and Tetreault, M.K.T. (1994). *The Feminist Classroom.* New York: Basic Books.

Ogden, C.K. and Florence, M.S. (1987). Militarism versus feminism. In M.S. Florence, C. Marshall & C.K. Ogden (Eds.), *Militarism versus feminism* (pp.54–140). London: Virago.

Piercy, M. (1970). *Dance the eagle to sleep.* Garden City, New York: Double Day.

Piercy, M. (1979). *A woman on the edge of time.* London: The Women's Press.

Piercy, M. (1992). *Body of glass.* London: Penguin Books.

Ruddick, S. (1990). *Maternal thinking: Towards a politics of peace.* London: Virago.

Sargent, L.T. (1988). *British and American utopian literature 1516–1985: An annotated chronological bibliography.* New York: Garland.

Sargisson, L. (1996). *Contemporary feminist utopianism.* London: Routledge.

Stiemh, J.H. (1989). *Arms and the enlisted woman.* Philadelphia: Temple University Press.

Tepper, S. (1990). *The gate to women's country.* London: Corgi.

Todd, J. (Ed.) (1996). *Female education in the age of enlightenment.* Vol. 1. London: William Pickering.

Vonarburg, E. (1992). *In mothers' land.* USA: Bantam.

Wollstonecraft, M (1792). A vindication of the rights of women. In C. Poston (Ed.) (1988), *A vindication of the rights of women* (pp. 1–194). 2nd Edition. London: Norton.

Christine Forde
University of Glasgow

ILAN GUR-ZE'EV

DIASPORIC PHILOSOPHY, HOMELESSNESS, AND COUNTER-EDUCATION IN CONTEXT

The Israeli–Palestinian Example

JUSTICE AS A THREAT TO THE VERY EXISTENCE OF ISRAEL

The Israeli condition has already begun to display this hard truth: after more than a hundred years of Israeli–Palestinian coexistence the Jews cannot avoid paying in the coin of *worthy life* to safeguard their mere *existence*. In other words, even if the structure of the State of Israel survives it will endure, most probably, only in the form of Sparta of the wicked. It is so painful and hard for me to face this reality, as I am as much the grandson of Keila Goldhamer, who barely survived the 1903 *Pogrom* of Kishiniev, and whose stories and lessons are so meaningful for me until this day, as the son of Robert Wiltchick, who lost almost all his family in the Holocaust and was spared the Nazi death industry only after being thrown into the mass grave from which he literally emerged all on his own, and the son of Hanna Wiltchick, who lost her marriage to her first husband as her share in the Holocaust; all these experiences are formative for my Diasporic horizons. Yet I think all of us, even the Zionists among us, should today rethink our old conceptions about Jewish life and the Jewish mission in Israel and in the Diaspora. Perhaps a good beginning would be to rethink central conceptions such as 'Diaspora', 'homeland', and 'homecoming'. Such an elaboration presents us with nothing less than the present day Jewish *telos* and our responsibility toward its fulfilment as well as toward the overcoming of its fulfilment and of what we presently are. It is of vital importance to conceive Diasporic human possibility as rooted in Judaism only as part of richer and deeper roots of human possibilities that transcend Judaism and overcome Monotheism, Western concepts of light–truth and triumphant patriachalism, even in the form of radical feminist alternatives in the McWorld. In the Israeli–Palestinian context, to my mind, the current historical moment already enables us critically to summarise the last hundred years' attempt to turn away from the Diasporic Jewish goal by the Zionist barbarisation of the Jewish Spirit within the projects of 'annihilating the Diaspora', 'homecoming', and 'normalisation'.

Under current historical conditions, as Israelis, Jews are structurally almost prevented from facing the possibility of living in light of the Messianic impetus, as the world's universal moral, intellectual, and creative vanguard. This special Jewish mission was made possible by the Jews' unique *homelessness* – a Diasporic

M.A. Peters, A. Britton and H. Blee (Eds.), Global Citizenship Education: Philosophy, Theory and Pedagogy, 103–114.

existence as a realised ideal of a community that is not a collective. Diasporic life is ultimately a kind of life in which the *yahid* (individual, not found in liberal terminology) is afforded, as an ecstatic way of moral life, an existence that allows a universalistic moral *responsibility* and intellectual commitment to overcome any dogma and content with the world of 'facts' and to reject the promises of mere power, glory, and pleasure. All this has changed in the face of the successes of Zionist education and its political realisations.

It is no wonder that there is no Israeli Ibn Gavirol, Baruch Spinoza, Karl Marx, Sigmund Freud, Franz Kafka, Albert Einstein, Theodor Adorno, Emmanuel Levinas, or Jacques Derrida. One can experience the immanent violence and the insipidness of Israeli life just by driving on the roads. Another example might be the silence of the current culture heroes and the popular satisfaction by which the cuts in funding for high culture are accompanied. Still another example could be the unchallenged crusade against the high court and the ideal of a rational, open, free, and equal public sphere. And this is before facing the brutal realities of the treatment of foreign workers, or the structural repression of the Palestinians. I write this with great pain, not because Israeli society is among the cruellest or the intellectually poorest of all societies on earth. At this very moment there are so many worse examples that the politically correct bible forbids us to address, in favour of concentrating moral, political, and armed attacks on Israeli society.

The ongoing genocide in southern Sudan, the daily Russian assaults against the Chechen people; the Beijing human organs industry, based on taking the parts from spiritual and political dissidents before systematically killing them on a mass scale; the uprooting of the Tibetan people; the oppression of Christians and the conditions of women, homosexuals and other minorities in Saudi Arabia; or the subjugation of the Russian minority in Estonia, are only a few examples of today's lack of courage and widespread dishonesty in the treatment of Israel. At the same time it is true, and one should face it, hard as it is to acknowledge, that Israel has become a space where there is less and less room for genuine creative spirit and for social justice. Israel has become the ultimate Diaspora of the Jewish Spirit. Here, more then anywhere else, there is no room for 'the Jewish heart', or for Jewish intellectual independence and avant-garde creativity. It is a sad actuality, but I cannot avoid, must not avoid, facing it even if it is so hard for me to acknowledge: there is no room for a just State of Israel. St. Augustine knew this was so for all manifestations of 'the earthly city'. In the case of Israel it has become so clear that *unreserved siding against injustice inevitably endangers the very existence of Israel*, not solely its current policies. The latest example of this is the Second Lebanese War.

Israel, as a normal state that is committed to its security and sovereignty, had to adopt terrible means to ensure not only social and economic stability on its northern border but its very existence, in light of the explicit Iranian–Hizbullah commitment to annihilate the Jewish state on religious grounds. So Israel had to respond in a harsh manner to the consistent unprovoked missile attacks on its northern cities while being condemned by world media and public opinion for a 'disproportionate' reaction. The post-colonialists see Israeli policies in this respect (insisting on Lebanese sovereignty and its responsibility to ensure no private army will bombard Israeli cities at will) as another manifestation of its immanent brutal colonialist existence. On the one hand these are unjustified denunciations, based on misinformation, pragmatic interests in the Arab world, founded on, reflecting and realising the old and the New Anti-Semitism. On the other hand, Israel did commit terrible acts, so many terrible deeds, during that war, some by mistake, some intentionally. Given the military methods of the Hizbullah militia, which systematically uses villages in southern Lebanon not only to hide but actually to launch missiles against Israel, the IDF (Israel Defence Forces) was faced by dilemmas such as the following: identifying a present-moment launch of a Katyusha or a Zelzal II toward an Israeli city from the roof of a house in a southern Lebanese village, *should it bomb the house and save the Israeli victims while killing at an instant an entire Lebanese family (even if the mostly Shiite population of southern Lebanon normally enthusiastically welcomes the Hizbullah militia on its terrain), or should the Israeli army be morally committed to avoid any killing of Arab civilians, even at the cost of its own civilians' lives?* Is it morally right to discriminate against innocent Israeli civilians in favour of Lebanese civilians? In such instances should we morally go into the question of proportionality, namely what number of innocent Lebanese civilians killed justifies the prevention of the killing of innocent Israeli civilians? And so on. Should we, when faced with such dilemmas, go into questions such as the amount of unlimited cooperation and support by the civilian Shiite population in southern Lebanon for Hizbullah as a partial criterion for a decision on the immediate question of firing or not firing on a civilian house and its inhabitants to prevent the killing of Israeli civilian population targeted by a terrorist organisation that uses civilian installations and ground for attacking the Israeli civilian population? Should moral considerations impel us to consider questions of the degree of separation and the measure of responsibility between Hizbullah and the southern Lebanese farmers, who in many respects are part of the Hizbullah organisation, and sometimes also of its military organisation and operations, taking part in the military attacks against the Israeli civilian population across the border? Even if the answer is affirmative, how do you actually reduce the degree of cooperation with a terrorist organisation to degrees of responsibility, and how do you reduce the degree of responsibility to a specific order to the pilot in the warplane who needs to know if he should bomb the house or abort the attack? Such moral dilemmas were *not an exception* but the general rule in the practice of the military operations in the Second Lebanese War (August 2006). And the Second Lebanese War, how unfortunate, is only a microscopic example for the very existence of Israel in the region as a moral dilemma.

As anti-determinists, we should understand the present historical moment as *open*, since inevitably it also contains the possibility of a radical shift toward a more humane, rational, and moral existence in Israel, as well as in Palestine. Referring to the most recent example of the Second Lebanese War we might ask: why should we not be optimistic as to the possibility of an imminent peace treaty between Israel and Lebanon, if there are no fundamental border disputes between the two countries, joint economic interests can lead to cooperation and mutual prosperity, and a broad consensus in Israel (which includes even the extreme political right) favours cooperation and peace with Lebanon? Why should not the interests of post-Fordist economy, if not a humanistic vision of mutual respect and cooperation, lead us to a better future of creativity, prosperity and peaceful coexistence, stronger and more relevant than the fanatic religious and ethnocentric agendas? Addressing such a question beckons us into world politics, the interests of emerging regional powers such as Iran, and the specifics of Lebanese cultural and political realities. These might show us that in effect Lebanon is not a state in the modern sense of the word. But we will not go there. Instead, let us elaborate more on some central trends in Israeli reality.

When even for a moment, or to a certain degree, the direct threat to the very existence of Israel decreases (or in the spaces where it is actualised), the plurality, openness, creativity and pragmatism of the McWorld have the upper hand. Yet in Israel the world of Jihad threatens not only beyond the border: it is a vital part of the constitution of the new Israeliness. In the face of partial, deep post-idealist and anti-ethnocentristic-oriented tendencies most major politically organised powers in Israel manifest stronger ethnocentrism and weakening of democratic and liberal values, with very little interest in education for a mature humanistic, reflective, moral, coexistence. The rival groups and the separatist agendas are, as in Lebanon, and unlike the dominant tendencies in Palestinian society, which is speeding toward a fundamentalist consensus under the guidance of the Hamas educational–political leadership, unable to come up with a consensus about 'the common good'. They are certainly incapable of agreeing on a specific educational program aimed at a worthier reality. In the face of this we may ask: *What has gone wrong with the State of Israel?* To answer this question we should return to the Zionist constitutive idea of 'homecoming'.

WHAT HAS GONE WRONG WITH ISRAEL?

The Zionist negation of Diaspora is a turn away from Jewish moral destiny. History corrects this deviation not without inflicting such enormous loss and suffering, which includes a threat to the soul and physical existence not only of the largest Jewish collective in the world but also – as September 11 manifested so clearly – of the entire world.

A century on, Zionist education has lost its naivety, and its optimism is doomed. In retrospect it has become clear to me that from its very beginning Zionist education failed in its major mission: to give birth to a durable grand truth and to its master-signifiers. Its genealogy shows that it was never equipped with the 'right' violence, nor was it ready to be inhuman to the degree that would vouchsafe Jabotinsky's dream of '*geza gaon venadiv veachzar*', or a genuine realisation of the myth of the *Sabra*, who, like the *Sabra* fruit, would be 'coarse' on the outside yet 'sweet, soft, and moral' in his innerness. Promising spiritual and moral Zionist alternatives, such as the project of Ahad Ha'am, were pushed aside, even if today some are still being followed in Israeli reality. The violence of Zionist normalising education did not contain an enduring birth-giving vitality: it was not strong enough to actualise its constitutive idea, the idea of 'the new Jew'; it was not effective enough to purify the Israeli, the *Sabra*, of the Ghetto mentality. It was not sufficiently potent to constitute a non-patronising Jewish generosity that would extend its hand to the Arab world. Nor was it at peace with itself about conquering Palestinian space in a relentless storm that would erect Jabotinski's 'Iron wall' against Arab fear, hatred, and violence.

Today it is actually impossible for disillusioned educators to look into the pupils' eyes and honestly say: 'I promise you, dear children, soon it will be so much better'. Secular mothers and fathers are unable to extract *meaning* from the fears and suffering of their children. Many of them are rethinking even the standard answer they have given themselves and their children in the last two years: 'If only we harden our hearts and be more brutal and apply less moral restraints, we will win after all, and you, my child, will have a safe future in Israel'. The Israeli formal and informal humanist educational apparatuses face rapid degradation. In today's Israel, in the face of the spirit of global capitalism on the one hand, and of the Israeli–Palestinian violence on the other, the prospects are gloomy for an effective recruitment of the soul for protecting, cultivating, and enhancing at all costs the ideals and practices of secular humanistic-oriented Zionism. Post-modern post-Zionists and humanistic-oriented anti-Zionists alike are united in their understanding that there are no prospects for a democratic reality in Israel. Some are close to revealing the bitter truth that the prospects for a Palestinian democracy (in a future liberated greater Palestine or in any other format) are much worse. The two strongest, spiritual and politically-growing rival forces are the projects of establishing a Jewish Spartanic-oriented theocracy on the one hand, and an Islamist militaristic theocracy on the other. Even if the Israeli middle class is still stronger than its enemies, and is not as racist as its victims and rivals claims it is, it is rapidly losing its fragile liberal tier, its vitality, its self-confidence, its life-impulse, and surely its Jewish heart. In the face of this dynamic actuality I must say: *Can't you see that the time has come in Israel for a counter-education that will prepare for a self-initiated Jewish displacement and for a Diasporic way of life?*

TOWARD SELF-INITIATED ISRAELI DISPLACEMENT

In its narrower sense Diasporic education should prepare our children for worthy life in *eternal exile*. Counter-education should provide Israeli youth with tools that will enable them to avoid being pushed to the economic, social, and cultural margins of the techno-scientific and capitalist arenas to which their self-initiated displacement will impel them. It should facilitate the second Israeli exodus, to take them into homelessness as their home, to the possibility of finding home everywhere, to life as ecstatic, unsecured, open, creative, moral, life-loving citizens of the world. Linguistic competence, intellectual and artistic creativity, improvising sensitivity and competence, and courageous border-crossing of existential, cultural, and philosophical differences become central to such counter-education. Unlearning hegemonic education becomes of vital importance here.

It is important, indeed very important, to stress this: the self-initiated displacement of the Jews from Israel is a dialectical project. On the one hand, in order to secure 'effectiveness' in terms of changing the fate of the Israelis as doomed victimisers, there is a need for an institutionalised, collective, counter-educational effort. The Israeli self-initiated evacuation of Israel is conditioned by many levels and dimensions of successful violent distorting, manipulative politics, and normalising education, which will make possible productivity, consensus, concerted effort, and relative stability, or peace. On the other hand, genuine Diasporic philosophy is never to be reduced to any kind of collectivism, and as a counter-education it cannot avoid being nothing more than an open possibility *for the individual*, solely for the individual and by the individual. Diasporic nomadism is open always only for an individual as an erotic, creative improviser, in the sense of the one who gives birth to and is enabled by *tefilat hayahid* (the individual-improvised prayer, as against the institutional prayer of the collective, the *minyan*). This openness is a possibility whose realisation is to be struggled for every moment anew and is never a secured 'home'. It is an invitation to a never guaranteed but always dangerous and costly possibility.

Diasporic philosophy is relevant for counter-education in current Israel as a dangerous attempt at creative improvisation with the other and the given 'facts'. It is of vital importance for the enhancement of new beginnings that are also unpredicted and never controlled responses to the present possibilities and 'calls of the moment'. At the same time, however, it is part of reclaiming, negatively, the lost intimacy with the cosmos, with the law, and with tradition and togetherness. In other words, it is not one of the conflicting alternatives. It is other; it is *essentially different* from the various attempts to transcend all versions of normalising education, cultural politics, and other manifestations of imposed 'consensus'.

As a genuine dialectical realisation of Diasporic philosophy, counter-education in Israel cannot become instrumentalised, cannot become a collective self-imposed mass immigration, as so many of my post-colonialist friends would like me to suggest. It is not solely a moral–political concrete dilemma facing us nowadays; it is fundamentally a philosophical and existential antinomy. Ultimately, it begins and ends in and by the individual, who is willing to overcome his or her self and to open the gates to the nomadic existence of a brave lover of Life and creativity. But as a historical, political, and collective project, the self-initiated new exodus, which gives a new meaning to the Exodus from Egypt to Israel and to the subsequent exiles of Jews to the Diaspora, is very hard for another reason. There is no way to guarantee a deluxe exile: discrimination, marginalisation, and victimisation await the exiled Israeli Jews. The post-colonialist New Anti-Semitism most probably will not be content with the destruction of Israel as a victory of its coalition with the world of Jihad. Already now the post-colonialist 'anti-Israeliness' goes down to the roots of criticising the essentials and the telos of Western culture and monotheism. Following here the young Marx, and today's post-colonialist heroes such as Chaves and Ahmadinejad, the Jewish return to its Diasporic existence and cosmopolitan nomadism will probably face fresh forms of exile as well as young, post-colonialist, forms of discrimination and exclusion, if post-colonialism is to maintain its consistency.

THE EXODUS FROM ISRAEL AND FROM JUDAISM TO DIASPORIC WANDERING

The new exodus is from Israel and the Zionist nation-building project as a present-day 'Egypt' as a home. It is an exodus from a distorted concept of Diasporic life, from the concept of 'Egypt' in the form of all versions of 'homecoming' and a monotheistic way, to rebuild or go back to the Garden of Eden. It is an exodus to 'Zion'; not in the sense of a national sovereignty imposed on a certain territory violently controlled, but to the infinity of the entire world of human existence and transcendence as the genuine 'Zion'. This too is only to be transcended into an ecstatic, totalistic, creative, existence within which Diaspora signifies the abyss of existence, meaninglessness, suffering, and the presence of the absence of God as a transcending impetus. The Jews at this historical moment are given this actual present as a tragic *universal mission*, which is fundamentally religious and cosmopolitan, in a Spiritless post-modern world. Individuals of all nations must be invited to join this anti-religious, anti-collectivist telos of overcoming Judaism and monotheism in all its forms, in order to preserve and struggle for the realisation of the essence of its creative truth.

The condemnation and oppression of the Jews might increase under the new historical conditions on two levels: Firstly, as an assault against the Jews in the traditional sense. Here it is worth mentioning the present prosperity of the publication of *The Protocols of the Elders of Zion*, in places such as Japan, Venezuela, Pakistan and Egypt. The last-named recently opened its new national library with a central display of this ultimate modern anti-Semitic piece, while simultaneously prohibiting the screening in Egypt of films such as *Schindler's List*. Secondly, as an assault against the new Diasporic human, the cosmopolitan nomad of our generation that will be both homeless and at home everywhere, even in the infinite dimensions and levels of existence in McWorld, cyberspace – in other words in the new historical era wherein he will exile. As a Diasporic who is not at home in the current historical moment, yet takes responsibility, he or she will most probably be attacked by traditional humanists and patriots, by fundamentalists, by post-colonialists, and surely by the logic of the system. Diasporics not welcomed. They are the ultimate other; they are 'the Jews' of the post-modern era. They, the Diasporic humans who challenge both 'colonialist' and 'post-colonialist' dogmas and their respective violences, are the ones to be redeemed, emancipated or destroyed, even before the total purification of Palestine of all Jewish presence and forms of Israeliness.

The evacuation of all our 'homes' and territory of Israel is in a certain sense a victory of the Palestinian narrative and the post-colonialist agenda in more general terms. As such it is only part of the future suffering which awaits the Israelis in their future fields of exile. Growing anti-Semitism impatiently awaits its new stage of development. But traditional and New Anti-Semitism is only part of the suffering that a self-initiated displacement might bring about. It might create new forms of suffering in light of individual evacuation of all kinds of 'homes', by individuals of various nations, cultures, and faiths, who decide to struggle for their edification and Love as the impetus for 'rhizomatic' creation and worthier intersubjectivity. Humans of all walks of life might meet, as Diasporic persons who have overcome monotheism, if they are genuinely to meet as creative nomads who take a different approach to responsibility, meaning, togetherness, creativity and self. As Diasporic individuals they will have to overcome even the progressive idea of the Jewish *minyan*: in the face of the absence of God, of the absence of a temple constituted by a self-evident dogma, and in the absence of a relevant, binding Halacha as a manifestation of laws interpreting–directing all walks and levels of life, they create a new kind of togetherness by repositioning themselves toward the totally other in the face of the historical moment and relevant traditions.

Their prayer is *avodat kodesh*, whose essence is not its fulfilment but the possibility of the individual's being transcended by it: the essence of the prayer is the possibility of prayer. This kind of prayer, this *tefilat hayahid* (the individual's prayer – not determined by any text or conventional code of the community), invites a different concept of responding to a Diasporic existence and a different kind of togetherness with the world and with the other. It is a precondition of philosophical life as presented by Plato and a precondition for a non-ethnocentrist community. As partners in such a community of individual de-territorialists, humans might meet each other in the presence of the absence of the otherness of the totally other.

The two kinds of prayer represent the two opposing conceptions of Diaspora and 'homecoming'. The conventional, institutionalized, collective prayer in the *minyan* in the form of *tefilat harabim* maintains a positive 'homecoming' attitude. It is very much connected to the attitude to the law. Genuine Diasporic humans do not disregard the law and the importance of tradition. The other kind of prayer, *tefilat hayahid*, is fundamentally spontaneous and improvisational, of the kind that pre-assumes Life as an unbridgeable creative abyss. The law and the improvisation, *tefelat harabim* and *tefilat hayahid*, have their depths and heights and are very much connected. There is no meaningful improvisation and creativity without responsibility, tradition and laws. Traditional Judaism emphasised the importance of the Law yet maintained the tension between the Halacha, *tefilat hayahid*, and freedom of interpretation, as a manifestation of responsible improvisation and Diasporic Life. Diasporic life in a post-modern condition might be called to continue the Diasporic freedom of *the responsible improviser* as a Diasporic human. This, however, is far less than a satisfactory precondition for genuine Diasporic life since in Judaism this freedom of interpretation, nomadism and improvisation was fertilised and enabled by the uncompromising *commitment* to religious law, the Halacha and the Jewish tradition even if as an object of alterity and edification. This fruitful tension constituted, enabled, and activated the Jewish concept of law as a relevant, religious director, to live in all its aspects, levels and dimensions. It was certainly a constitutive element for the fruitful tension between the Jewish law and the living art of interpretation for Diasporic moral avant-gardism. But how is this kind of Diaspora, nomadic life and eternal-improviser possible in a post-modern era? How is such a rich dialectics of commitment and improvisation possible in the face of the absence not only of God and Godly truths, but also of Torah and Halacha? How possible might responsible improvisation and

Diasporic life, or genuine responsibility as such, become in the face of the absence of monotheism and the exile of the concept of Halacha, in the face of multi- and hyper-presence of rival infinities, conflicting gods, bibles, codes, laws, temples, quests, emancipatory projects, pleasures and Diasporic alternatives?

In Judaism both tendencies are free of any optimism about 'homecoming' or 'bridging narratives', and as such it manifests genuine religiosity much more than normally permitted by institutionalized Diasporic sensibility in institutionalized monotheistic religions. As such, Diasporic individuals become a community of creative, solidarian, humans, who create in the infinity of the present moment ever-new, yet connected, responding, and dialogical, possibilities.

Diasporic life is made possible by being as Diasporic *becoming*. Being is ontologically exiled of itself, and human beings are never genuinely 'at home' with their telos, with their essence, with the truth of being. Most philosophical, religious, and political projects are 'homecoming' *calls* that enable humans to forget their exile, sometimes by becoming devotees of false, collective, dogmatic, domesticating versions of Diasporic philosophy, and sometime by forgetting their forgetfulness of Diasporic existence. In epistemology it is signified by the unbridgeable abyss between a question and 'its' answer, by the unbridgeable abyss between concepts and things, language and world. In ethics it is represented by the infinite gap between the *ethical I* and the *moral I*. But Diasporic existence is to be reduced neither to an epistemological challenge nor to a question concerning the possibility of ethics in a post-modern world. Being as Diasporic becoming makes possible philosophical discourse – it is not one of its manifestations. It allows and conditions human existence and its moral essence. Diasporic individuals are made possible, not threatened, by unending displacements and boundless manifestations of creationism and clashes with the imperatives of the law and the 'facts' of the historical moment. It is here that *redemption and Diasporic existence meet*. But 'why should they do so?' one might ask. 'Why should a bodily, psychologically, morally, aesthetically, and intellectually productive and prosperous, fully-domesticated person respond to such *a call* for transformation that might entail loss of security and pleasurable self-forgetfulness?'

At another level one might articulate this question differently: 'Why should the Israeli people go into a self-initiated displacement as long as militarily, economically, technologically and socially they are not yet defeated by the Palestinian violence and by the world's disgust, and morally they are not overcome; and the New Anti-Semitism of the post-colonialists and the disciples of the world of Jihad only awaits their self-imposed exile only to oppress them morally (as eternal, unredeemed victimisers) and politically in ways currently prevented by the very existence of the State of Israel?'

Still, it seems to me that history insists already now on self-initiated displacement as a nomadic way of life for the better-off Israelis who can afford to flee, accompanied by big capital and relevant education for the McWorld. One of the most astonishing experiences in the last war was the sense of insistence on staying in Israel and willingness to fight for it even in light of the fragmentation and privatisation processes. There is still room for illusion that somehow things will take a turn for the better and 'we' will not have to evacuate 'our home'. Its justification is ultimately grounded not in practical individual or collective gains and losses. It is here that the Jewish Diasporic idea and its moral vanguard telos oppose Zionist education and clash with the reality of Israel as the Sparta of the wicked. Worthy life, or transcending mere life as the aim of life as a Jewish telos, is what is here at stake. This is the impetus of Diasporic life as an imperative.

COUNTER-EDUCATION IN LIGHT OF DIASPORIC PHILOSOPHY

Counter-education in light of Diasporic philosophy should not be limited to the preparation of self-initiated evacuation of Israelis from Israel. In its broader and deeper sense it is not an exclusive Jewish mission. It should become a universal alternative for individuals, always and only individuals, that is existential, philosophical, aesthetic, moral, and political in its realisation. As such it should overcome the Christian claim to realize the Messianic essence of Judaism. It should disprove Christianity and all other forms of monotheism by realising among the nations the idea of Diaspora, or the presence of the absence of the redeemer, as an infinite, negative, Utopia: an endless moral, creative, philosophical way of life beyond immanence and transcendence, in a Godless, unredeemable, 'holy' cosmos.

Such a counter-education is part and parcel of an attempt to transcend monotheism, not Judaism exclusively. Monotheism in all its manifestations, even in the form of humanism: to transcend the quest for the appropriate, unquestionable, static, 'meaning', collectivism, and an orderly, rationalised, consensual 'home'. It is a preparation for homelessness as a manifestation of ecstatic love of life, of creative meaning formations, of courageous intellectual life against the conventional manifestation of solidarity and truth, and of a dialogical relation with the otherness of the other, even in the face of his insistence on being part of the 'we' against 'them'. As the realisation of the Jewish ideal of Diasporic life, it is an affirmation of the danger and happiness of endless new human possibilities in the face of infinite responsibility regarding injustice, regarding ongoing fabrication by the system of truths, dreams, quests, and even of the self. It should prepare humans, all humans, for *tefilat hayahid*, in a Godless world as partners in a transformed *minyan* – to meet the world as creative, moral nomads, as truly religious human beings, who are liberated: exiled lovers of Life, displaced from any dogmatic passions, ideals, and practices of a certain 'religion' as their 'homeland'. This means that this counter-education should also prepare Diasporic life for those people, like myself, who insist on living in Israel at all costs, even as it becomes before my eyes a Zionist Sparta of the wicked. This means that the interconnectedness between *Gola* and *Geula* (Diaspora and redemption) should offer a very specific, concrete, and detailed counter-education in current Israel, for preparing not only the exodus from Zionism and the State of Israel but, what is even more important, *the possibility of Diasporic life in Israel itself.*

DIASPORIC LIFE IN ISRAEL

As the unification of an ongoing moral struggle for the realisation of the essence of Judaism, and transcending it into a universal alternative human existence, and as a courageous, creative, Love, such a counter-education might open the gate to new possibilities to challenge concrete existential, moral, psychological, economic, and political manifestations of the present Israeli condition. It might edify, even in the face of the exile of Spirit in a post-modern world, the old–new Jewish mission by overcoming it and realising it as *a universal human telos*. It does not search for redemption as transcendence into the lost Garden of Eden or the establishment of an earthly positive utopia such as a strong, prosperous state. It is a telos which challenges the institutionalised and instrumentalised monotheistic religiousness, on the one hand, and the reified 'secular' symbolic and non-symbolic commodities and passions of the post-modern culture industry on the other.

It should not be satisfied by introducing quests and tools for unveiling the manipulations of normalising education, of the structural injustice of global capitalism on the one hand, and Israeli and Palestinian nationalism on the other. It should not limit itself to criticising instrumental rationality and the reduction of the human subject from some-*one* to some-*thing*. In the present moment, under any conditions, it must open the gates of love and affirmation, of creativity and responsibility, in the face of the omnipotence of the current production of meaninglessness (which appears as truth, as desired objects of consumption and representation, or as hopelessness). It must enhance the possibilities for improvising in the totality of the moment without abandoning historical consciousness, without disregarding the other's unfinished saying or need, without abandoning the utopian quest for creating new concepts, possibilities, and wanderings. As such, counter-education becomes a potential 'redemptive' element even under almost impossible philosophical, cultural, and political conditions.

By transcending the truth of Judaism it becomes relevant for all homeless humans: for all truly religious humanists, who affirm Life, Love, creativity, the danger of unending self de-territorialisation, and moral responsibility for the otherness of the other and for the otherness within the self.

In current Israel, counter-education of this kind might culminate into a bridge for Jews and Palestinians. They might enter a non-violent dialogue only as partners in worthy suffering and love of Life, as homeless, as Diasporic persons, who are committed to overcome all versions of ethnocentrism and all projects of 'homecoming', at all levels and dimensions of life. *A new way is opened for rebuilding* 'Yavne'.

Building the 'New Yavne' is inescapably contradictory: to be true to itself it cannot be restricted to any specific place, mission or memory. It must be universal, and be realised in all dimensions and levels of human life. As such not only might it be realised even without the evacuation of Israel: it can never be reduced to mere geographic displacement. It must transform itself into a universal nomadic, creative, everlasting, way of life, without a Torah or a sacred truth but Love in the totality of every moment, which contains infinite possibilities in the infinite *terra* that is not merely the 'innerness' of the individual, or the 'exterior reality'. It is the nowhere space, the Utopia, the space that is not 'in between' the 'I' and the other, 'innerness' and 'external reality', 'true meaning' and 'meaninglessness'. It is this special mode of creative self-constitution that makes possible a non-'linear' focused, instrumental, gaze, hearing, production, and representation. It offers a different existence, an erotic self-constitution that is also a totalistic, holistic, ecstatic, manifestation of the world. Only within the framework of a transcending Diasporic philosophy can one enter this ever-unfinished, creative, effort at dialogical self-constitution with the otherness of the other and with the infinite richness of the cosmos as a worthy Diaspora. But such an Odyssey cannot take place outside a *form*, disregarding what Judaism calls 'Halacha'. The tension between Halacha and *tefilat hayahid* or between the *Ethical I* and the *Moral I* is not solved by Diasporic philosophy and counter-education. In Israel all we can do today is nothing more then address it, with no 'solutions', 'recommendations' or 'relevant curriculum'.

As a *negative utopia* for and of Diasporic humans it fosters a genuine new partnership between 'Israelis' and 'Palestinians'. Both are called upon. They are called upon to overcome the violence of the power-relations within which, and by whose productive manipulations, their collective identities have been violently reproduced by normalising education in the last hundred years. They are called upon to overcome the negation of the other, the commitment to destroy, exile, or re-educate 'them'. As Diasporic persons, as individuals who are responsible for the Other, Israelis and Palestinians are called upon to enter this dialogic, dangerous, totalistic way of life and transcend both Palestinian national identity and Israeliness, Islam and institutionalized Judaism, narcissism and self-forgetfulness. But will they respond before it is too late?

REFERENCES

Gur-Ze'ev, I. (1996). *The Frankfurt School and the history of pessimism.* Jerusalem: Magnes Press.

Gur-Ze'ev, I. (1998). Before we become Sparta in Kapotott. *Panim, 4,* 73–80.

Gur-Ze'ev, I. (2001). Teachers as neutral civil servants. *Ha'aretz,* 24th June, B2.

Gur-Ze'ev, I. (2005). Critical theory and critical pedagogy today. In I. Gur-Ze'ev (Ed.), *Critical theory and critical pedagogy today: Toward a new critical language in education* (pp. 7–34). Haifa: Faculty of Education, University of Haifa.

Gur-Ze'ev, I. (forthcoming). *Edward Said as an Educator.*

St Augustine. (1984) *Concerning the city of God against the pagans* (H. Bettenson, Trans.). London: Penguin Books, pp. 593–597.

Ram, U. (2005). *Globalization in Israel.* Tel Aviv: Resling (in Hebrew).

Ram, U. (2006). *The time of the post.* Tel Aviv: Resling (in Hebrew).

Ilan Gur-Ze'ev
University of Haifa, Israel

GEORGE RICHARDSON

CONFLICTING IMAGINARIES

Global Citizenship Education in Canada as a Site of Contestation

INTRODUCTION

"The earth is man's [sic] home." (Gage, *New Canadian Geography*, 1899, p. 3)

"Students must acquire the knowledge, skills and attitudes that enable them to participate, innovate and take advantage of the economic and cultural opportunities that globalization provides." (Government of Alberta, 2007, p. 4)

The statements above, the first taken from New Canadian Geography, published in 1899, and used extensively throughout Canada up until the Second World War, and the second extracted from the 2006 *Business Plan* of the Department of Education of the Province of Alberta, are separated by more than one hundred years, yet they both indicate that teaching about the world and developing some sense of global citizenship on the part of students have always occupied an important position in history and social studies education in Canada.

However, even though its place in social studies is secure, world studies, international education, or, more currently, global citizenship education, has continually evolved along with Canada's status as a nation, its perceived role in international affairs, and the knowledge, skills and attributes in global citizenship deemed important for students to develop. From an early emphasis on the rights and responsibilities implicit in membership of the British Empire and subsequently the Commonwealth, through its extensive UN involvement, its close and somewhat ambivalent relationship with the United States, to its post-Cold War era participation in a complex matrix of organizations and agreements that include membership in NAFTA, the WTO, the G-8, as well as participation in NATO-led peacemaking missions in Afghanistan and Bosnia, the ideological orientation, content and purpose of global citizenship education has changed with the times and Canada's evolving image of itself.

In many ways the prominent position assigned to global citizenship education stems from the traditional and widely used 'expanding horizons' model of history and social studies education. According to this paradigm the ideal structure of

M.A. Peters, A. Britton and H. Blee (Eds.), Global Citizenship Education: Philosophy, Theory and Pedagogy, 115–131.

social studies is one that gradually leads students from knowledge of local contexts to progressively wider and more sophisticated understandings of self and community (Sears, 1997; Egan, 1999; Kincheloe, 2001). But if there is little question about a model that situates global citizenship education as a culminating focus of the discipline, there are significant questions about what is meant by the term 'global citizenship education' itself and about the role it should play in social studies. These questions have been made all the more urgent by concerns over a variety of contemporary issues that include the social and economic consequences of globalisation, the rise of unilateralism on the part of the United States and the degradation of the global environment.

In the area study that follows, I will argue that a significant ideological tension underlies the way in which global citizenship education has been represented and taught in the Canadian curriculum. This tension, well-represented by the two statements that begin this chapter, is one that pits national self-interest and neo-liberal understandings of global interactions against the emergence of what Graham Pike and David Selby have termed 'global perspectivity' (Pike & Selby, 1988), emerging out of the kind of empathetic understanding for the other that Hannah Arendt called 'an ethic of care for the world' (Arendt, 1968).

This chapter is organized into five sections. Following the Introduction, Section I presents a brief description of the structure of education in Canada and uses selected provincial curricula to indicate where global citizenship education is embedded in Canadian history and social studies curricula. Section II examines the complexities of attempting to educate for global citizenship in school contexts that remain heavily influenced by education for national citizenship. Section III presents the evolution of the concept of global citizenship in Canada in terms of a series of what David Geoffrey Smith has termed 'imaginaries'. Section IV discusses three specific challenges that globalisation presents to global citizenship education in Canada, and the Conclusion returns to the central dynamic of the tensions between 'nation and world' that underlie Canadian global citizenship education.

Theoretically, in examining and representing the tension between nation and other in global citizenship education in Canada, I draw on post-colonial frames of reference (Bhabha, 1990; Said, 1993; Mukherjee, 1994; Willinsky, 1998) that suggest that conceiving of the self-interest of the nation in unitary terms has produced curricula that privilege Eurocentrism while marginalising and silencing others (ethno-cultural minorities, women, aboriginals) who are not perceived to be a part of the dominant narrative. In this context, Arun Mukherjee notes that the assumed coherence of the narrative of nations is belied by the fact that national curricula are created 'by powerful professors, bureaucrats, editors, publishers, and reviewers, the majority of them white males ... under the aegis of nineteenth century European notions of nationhood'. From this exclusive position, curricula emerged that presented the nation as 'racially and culturally "uniform"' (Mukherjee, 2004, 23).

The net result of these singular conceptions of the nation has been the effective silencing of the Other in the face of exclusionary pressure of the received weight of invented tradition. As a consequence, as Bernardo Gallegos indicates, the nation, viewed as unitary narrative, became 'a disabling discursive category' that effectively restricts access to the discourse of nation to the dominant class (Gallegos, 1998, pp. 232–247). Translated to education for global citizenship, post-colonial scholarship suggests that although global citizenship education has become less Eurocentric and racist over time, it remains part of an imperial project aimed primarily at a process through which students 'learn to divide the world' (Willinsky, 1998), and in which students' developing global civic competencies are directed towards learning that their nation is 'a unique social, political, cultural entity that deserves special attention and is fundamentally unlike the rest of the world' (Gaudelli, 2003, p. 126).

SECTION I: STRUCTURE OF EDUCATION IN CANADA AND THE LOCATION OF GLOBAL CITIZENSHIP

In trying to represent how global citizenship education in Canada is 'done,' it is important to have some sense of the structure of Canada's education system itself. In the British North America Act of 1867 – the act by which the British Parliament created the Dominion of Canada – exclusive jurisdiction over education was granted to each of Canada's provinces. Since that time, each of Canada's 10 provinces has developed systems of education that have become quite unique and very much different, and this uniqueness has been reflected in the evolution of history and social studies curriculum that are specific to each jurisdiction. For example, in the provinces of Quebec, Ontario, and British Columbia the curriculum is organized around the study of the traditional academic disciplines of history and geography, while in Alberta, Saskatchewan and Nova Scotia, students take social studies – a cross-disciplinary program drawing on the humanities and social sciences. Additionally, in some provinces – Alberta, for example – it is mandatory for all students to take social studies to the end of Grade 12, while in others – Manitoba, and British Columbia, for example – students may opt not to do any history or social studies-related courses after Grade 11.

The same diversity that applies to broad programmatic issues applies to where, and in what form, global citizenship is located in the nation's history and social studies curriculum. For example, at the secondary level (grades 7 to 11) students in the province of Quebec follow a course called 'History and Citizenship' in which students develop a 'consciousness' of citizenship through the study of history. In this program global issues such as 'the global economy' are identified, but the notion of global citizenship is never specifically mentioned (Government of the Province of Quebec, 2004, p. 20). In the largest and most populous Canadian province, Ontario, in Grade 12, in a university preparation course entitled 'Canadian and World Politics', a key expectation is that students completing the course will be able 'to explain the rights and responsibilities of individuals, citizens, groups and states in the international community' (Government of Ontario, 2005, p. 257). In one of Canada's smaller and less populous provinces, Nova Scotia, the optional Grade 12 'Global History' course encourages students to develop such globally-oriented civic values as 'perspective consciousness, knowledge of global dynamics, "state of the planet" awareness, cross-cultural awareness, and an awareness of the future and of human choices' (Government of Nova Scotia, 2003, pp. 101–02).

Given the structure of Canadian education and the curricular diversity evident in the three provincial examples cited above, it is not always possible to speak about global citizenship education in Canada in ways that would be possible in nations like England, France and China where a single national curriculum is in place. However, it is possible to highlight similarities in how the curriculum in Canada's ten provinces and three territories responds to the question of how global citizenship 'lives' in the spaces between nation and world, as well as to discuss the ways in which global citizenship education in Canada has dealt with the complex matrix of transnational issues affecting the global scene today.

SECTION II: THE COMPLEXITIES OF EDUCATING FOR GLOBAL CITIZENSHIP

Many scholars have observed that global citizenship education remains very much bound to, and subsumed under, national citizenship education (Richardson, 2002; Heater, 2004). For example, William Gaudelli (2003), in his insightful study of how American curricula represent the notion of global citizenship, comments on the 'dichotomized curriculum' that emphasises the degree to which the United States is different from all other nations. While it may be expressed with a particular emphasis and intensity in America, the same binary of 'nation and other' typifies the way in which many global citizenship curricula are framed and – by extension – construct the space of encounter between nation and other.

Traditional civic education has as its *habitus* the social, political, economic and cultural life of the nation, and citizenship education curricula are typically framed in terms that make national self-interest both a key referent and a normalising structure (Osborne, 1997; Heater, 2001). As social studies educator Walter Feinberg (2001) notes:

> Citizenship education is a way to stabilize a normative conception of a nation and its instrument of governing, the state. It does this by developing appropriate interpretations, competencies, and loyalties, that is, those that encourage individuals to think of themselves as a people and that justify, enable, protect and defend their partiality toward one another. (p. 203)

By comparison, global citizenship education exists in a much more troubled space; in fact it is doubly challenged. On the one hand, in order to establish a truly global imperative that supersedes national interest, its proponents must make the difficult case for the rejection of the exclusive attachment to nation that has been the focus of civic education for more than a century. On the other, those who believe in global citizenship education must also attempt to build a similar structure to the 'interpretations, competencies and loyalties' Feinberg characterizes as typical of traditional civic education, on a much less well established global foundation.

Noting the difficulty associated with legitimising global civic education, Graham Pike (2000) has commented,

> To understand global education – especially more holistic models – requires more than 'the removal of the national border' as a curriculum outcome; it demands crossing the 'perceptual threshold' into an area of contemplation that considers not only the needs of students, teachers and schools but also the priorities of one's own country, other peoples and species, and the exigencies of the planet.

As Pike indicates, as opposed to the well-defined national structures and practices that are characteristic of traditional civic education, global citizenship education, in many senses, needs to function as what David Smith (1999) has termed a 'global imaginary'. By this, Smith suggests a sympathetic frame of mind or an empathetic appreciation that is

> a construct of human imagination that serves to organize and mobilize certain forms of action in certain ways. It pertains less to any characteristic of the world in its ordinary condition than to what certain people imagine that condition to be, based on their desire, their theory, their ego-projection, or say their religious sensibility. (pp. 3–4)

In order to understand the current position of global citizenship education within the broader discipline of history and social studies education in Canada, it is important to examine how citizenship education has changed over time. Looking at its history, it is possible to identify a number of shifts in perspective that have characterized how global citizenship education has been imagined in curriculum and schooling.

These different 'imaginaries' do not represent a linear process – in many cases they overlap and intersect – but each has its own understanding of the purpose of global citizenship education, its own worldview, and its own value structure.

SECTION III: FIVE IMAGINARIES OF GLOBAL CITIZENSHIP EDUCATION IN CANADA

The Imperial Imaginary

As indicated, global citizenship education has always been a part of social studies, but for much of the 20th century in Canada, learning about the world and Canada's civic role in global affairs was primarily a function of the development of nationalism and national pride. Students studied the world as much to establish the distinctness of their own nation as they did to gain insights into the history and culture of other nations. In Canada, in particular, the nationalistic orientation of global citizenship education was framed by Canada's membership of the British Empire and subsequently the Commonwealth (Willinsky, 1998). Thus students learned about the world from British – and fundamentally imperial – perspectives. For example, as late as 1945, teachers in Ontario were still being reminded to 'lead

119

the pupil to see that he has civic duties and responsibilities towards his family, his school, his community, his province, the Dominion of Canada and the British Empire' (Government of Ontario Ministry of Education, 1945, p. 10). As late as 1971, in a unit first introduced in 1955 and examining 'Nationalism in the Modern World', Grade 12 students in Alberta were taught that, 'the nationalism of various peoples of the Empire was the dynamic creation of the modern Commonwealth' (Government of Alberta Department of Education, 1955, p. 125). In both curricula, we see a worldview in which national identity was subsumed under the imperial connection; Canada was seen as acting in the world within the comforting and legitimising confines of the British Empire, and studying about the world was an act of division in which students were encouraged to separate Empire from non-Empire and, more broadly, West from non-West.

As post-colonial scholarship suggests, the function of the imperial imaginary as a mechanism for 'learning to divide the world' was two-fold. On one hand it was firmly grounded in the 19th and early 20th century era of nation-building. Thus Canada strengthened its own identity and occupied a privileged status in the world because of its continuing ties to the power and influence of Britain and the Commonwealth. On the other, its purpose was ideological, and the act of 'dividing the world' into the West and the 'foreign' and 'less-advanced' non-West was a process directed at demonstrating the technical, cultural, and moral superiority of the West for the purposes of justifying imperialism (Willinsky, 1998; Merryfield, 2001) and the need, after Foucault, to establish beyond any doubt 'the great historico-transcendental destiny of the Occident' (Foucault, 1972, p. 210). From the imperial imaginary, the non-West or, as successive post-war Canadian social studies curricula described it, the Third World or the Developing World, was used as a kind of marker against which both Canada and the West measured its own progress and established its own sense of identity, while the development of nations in the non-West was measured on the basis of the degree to which they Westernised their economic and political institutions (Said, 1993; Sleeter, 1993).

Although it is possible to continue to trace the imperial imaginary well into the present, in the post-World War Two period, two alternative understandings of global citizenship were also developing in Canada. Essentially, these two ways of knowing the world revolved around differing perspectives on the interaction of nations. One perspective held that the post-World War Two world was characterised by a bipolar division of the globe into competing political and economic systems; the other emphasized that the world after 1945 was one in which multilateralism and internationalism held sway.

The Bipolar Imaginary

In some respects, the bipolar imaginary was one that mirrored the imperial division of the world that characterised global citizenship education for most of the 20th Century, but in this case, the split was structured around ideological divisions and embedded in the Cold War. From a Cold War perspective the world was divided into communist and non-Communist spheres, and a key aim of social studies courses was to develop knowledge about communism in order to better understand the methods and motives of a rival system. A second and complementary aim for studying the communist world was to reinforce the inherent 'rightness' of the democratic, capitalist system. Typically, social studies curricula of the Cold War era emphasised the values of individualism, as opposed to collectivism, nationalism as opposed to internationalism, and confrontation as opposed to cooperation. History and social studies curricula were particularly concerned with transmission of knowledge about the two systems, and the world itself was seen as a kind of forum or arena in which the rival powers competed for influence. Few aspects of social studies escaped being drawn into this Cold War perspective. For example, global issues such as economic development, international relations and human rights were seen within the context of the struggle for ideological dominance, and students writing standardised exams in social studies were frequently asked to compare the advantages and disadvantages of the two systems –with the expected result being a conclusion that liberal democracy and capitalism was far superior to the communist alternative. Critics of the bipolar perspective stressed that it limited students' understanding of the world to a simplistic binary relationship in which both sides of the conflict were reduced to the level of caricature and in which emerging global issues such as environmental degradation, population growth and the growing poverty gap between the North and the South were all but ignored (Gaudelli, 2003: Richardson, 2004).

The Multipolar Imaginary

In sharp contrast to the bipolar imaginary was the view that held that the aim of global citizenship education was to emphasise the multipolar and inter-reliant nature of the world. Related to the creation of the United Nations and Canada's post-war status as an emerging middle power, the multipolar perspective emphasised the values of international cooperation, multilateralism and interdependence. The 1960's emphasis on 'development education' emerged from the multipolar imaginary, as did the idea that advances in telecommunication and international travel were producing a new world culture. Such a view – perhaps best characterised by Marshall McCluhan's notion of the world as a 'global village' – typifies many education texts still in use Canada today (Harshman & Hannell, 1989; Mitchener & Tuffs, 1989). This perspective coupled with the turn towards values education during the same period produced a growing focus on activism and a belief in student agency that suggested that the function of global citizenship education was to raise students' consciousness of the interdependent nature of the world and of the social, political and economic inequities that existed therein, with a view to taking action to raise the standard of living and quality of life in the developing world (Werner & Case, 1997). It was this period that gave rise to extracurricular organisations such as UN clubs and Amnesty International that could be seen as a natural extension of the themes and issues then emerging in the social studies classroom. Typical of the social studies curriculum of the day was this idealistic statement from the 1971 Alberta curriculum: 'In keeping with the basic tenets of democracy, the new social studies invites free and open inquiry ... by actively confronting value issues, students will ... deal not only with the "what is" but also with the "what ought to be" ' (Government of Alberta Department of Education, 1971, p. 32).

A critique that has emerged around this perspective is that, in some ways, it merely substituted one kind of singular view of the world (the global village) for the imperial view that held that the West was a political and economic model for the rest of the world. Constructed around a fundamentally 19th Century understanding of the moral obligation of the West to 'make the world right,' advocates of the 'one world' approach to global citizenship often tended to ignore or gloss over issues of cultural difference and values conflicts in pursuit of a monolithic understanding that suggested that beyond superficial differences, all the world's peoples were essentially one (Merryfield, 2001).

Despite its failings, one of the lasting effects of development education and the multipolar imaginary was to shift the discourse of social studies from knowing about the world to an emphasis on living in the world. The chief characteristic of this shift was one in which global citizenship education was much more oriented towards processes – that is, developing the skills and attitudes that would lead to active engagement – than it was with the transmission of knowledge. For example, as opposed to learning about differences in standards of living between the North and the South, process-oriented education stressed the need for students to ask questions about the reasons for the disparity, to suggest possible solutions to the problem and to evaluate the probable outcomes of the solutions they suggested.

The Ecological Imaginary

In the late 1980's in Canada another shift in emphasis took place that was grounded in an ecological understanding of the complexity and interdependence of all life forms. The ecological imaginary combined environmentally-based concerns for the survival of the planet with an increasing emphasis on the importance of cultural diversity, and multiple perspectives on such issues as development, trade and power relations between North and South nations (Werner & Case, 1997; Selby, 1999).

From an ecological stance, global citizenship education became more concerned with a shift in values and was characterised by an emphasis on the need to teach students to acknowledge and respect diverse points of view on global issues (Case, 1993). Part of this move towards diversity reflected a conscious attempt on the part of history and social studies scholars to step beyond the traditional division of the world that separated West from non-West. These scholars argued that throughout its association with social studies, global citizenship education carried with it an insidious form of cultural homogenisation (Merryfield, 2001; Richardson, 2000). Thus under the notion that fundamentally 'we are all the same', global citizenship education tended to erase cultural differences, devalue non-Western cultures, privilege Western ways of knowing and posit as a civic ideal a kind of de-contextualised liberal democratic stance. As John Willinsky asked, 'What more will it take to break the colonizing hold of the other, especially when the other is, in some sense oneself?' (Willinsky, 1998, p. 157). As ecological and cultural awareness, global citizenship education concerned itself particularly with the ways in which students could be brought to view the world through the eyes of other nations and other cultures. This particular approach stressed that global citizenship education needed to be 'transformative' in that it would cause students to re-examine their own values and beliefs with the aim of engendering 'world mindedness', a more holistic understanding of the world and a disposition towards taking action to address global problems and issues (Selby, 2003). From a transformative perspective, global citizenship education stressed the importance of interconnections, perspectivity, caring, and alternatives, and students were encouraged to ask such questions as 'Why should we care?' and 'How could things be different?' (Werner & Case, 1997).

The Monopolar Imaginary

More recently, there has been a return to a more monopolar view of the world in which global citizenship education is tied to neo-liberal constructs of the 'world as a market'. Thus with the 1991 collapse of the Soviet Union and the end of the Cold War came a renewed emphasis on economic expansion in which students were encouraged to learn about the world to make themselves and their nations more 'competitive' in the emerging global market. The value structure inherent in this approach stresses individualism, competitiveness, and self-reliance, while it encourages students to look at the world as a single culture in which the dominant organising principal is consumerism (McMurtry, 2002).

Typical of the values that underpin the 'world as competitive market' approach to global citizenship education are two recent excerpts from the Ontario and Alberta curricula; thus in Alberta, the stated aim of the social studies curriculum is 'to equip students with the knowledge and skills necessary to compete in the society in which they must ultimately find their place' (Government of Alberta Learning, 2002, p. 1). While in Ontario, the Ministry of Education notes that the aim of the grades 9 to 12 programme of studies, introduced in 2000, was to ensure that 'graduates from Ontario secondary schools are well prepared to lead satisfying and productive lives both as citizens and individuals and to compete successfully in a global economy in a rapidly changing world' (Government of Ontario Ministry of Education and Training, 2000, p. 1).

SECTION IV: GLOBAL CITIZENSHIP EDUCATION AND THE CHALLENGE OF GLOBALISATION

It is in light of the last two imaginaries that we come to the impact of globalisation on global citizenship education. The radical disjunction between developing perspectivity and world-mindedness on the one hand, and preparing students to compete in the global economy on the other, certainly supports the idea that global citizenship education continues to struggle between two competing ideologies. But before examining this struggle and the ways in which globalisation represents a challenge to global citizenship education, it is important to establish a baseline for understanding how globalisation is used in the context of this chapter. Because it represents a broad series of effects, globalisation is not always easy to define, but in general, there are three characteristics that are common to the phenomenon. Economically, globalisation is characterised by the free flow of goods and capital, and the rise of consumerism on a global scale. Politically, globalisation has challenged the sovereignty of nation states and raised significant questions about what it means to act as a citizen in a globalised world. Culturally, globalisation has led to the loss of cultural diversity and a corresponding increase in cultural homogeneity (Torres & Barbules, 2000; Smith, 2000a). As already noted, traditionally, global citizenship education in Canada has tended to stress learning about the world over encouraging students to become active agents prepared to address global issues of social, economic and political significance. With knowledge transmission as its primary emphasis, global citizenship education assumed a stable world that could be known, and was based on the belief that knowledge itself was sufficient to prepare students to act as responsible global citizens. As such, global citizenship education proceeded from an overwhelmingly Western point of view that privileged reason, transparency and universalism over grounded local perspectives that emphasised the close emotive connections between communities and their cultural and physical environments. But the separation between the Western and non-Western worlds that was the basis for much of what students studied in global citizenship education is no longer such a convenient binary, separating 'us' from 'them'. The effects of globalisation can be seen in Canada as well as in such 'developing' nations as India, Brazil, Nigeria and Indonesia that typically were the focus of global citizenship education courses. Because its impact is global, and because we are all subject to its influence, globalisation presents three very specific challenges for global citizenship education in Canada. These challenges will be explored below.

First Challenge: Transmission or Transformation

In many social studies classrooms, the emphasis on knowledge transmission that remains the primary focus of global citizenship education is maintained at the expense of the idea that global citizenship education could be transformative. Transformative education suggests that the purpose of global citizenship education is two-fold: questioning students' existing understandings and perspectives with the aim of developing a new sense of world-mindedness, and empowering students to become active participants in addressing issues that impact the global community (Selby, 1995; Merryfield, 1998). In some ways this choice between content and process is not new and has always been at the heart of the tensions that lie within social studies in general and global citizenship education in particular. However, I would argue that globalisation represents a unique challenge that demands a reorientation of global citizenship education towards transformative education.

Given that it has profound and truly global effects, ranging from unregulated flows of capital to 'monoculturing' and deforestation on a planetary scale, globalisation is a phenomenon that demands that students do more that 'study' its consequences: they also need to formulate an informed response to the impact globalisation is having on their lives, the lives of others, and on the planet in general. While developing this response clearly requires knowledge about globalisation, it also requires a sense of agency and a disposition to act that can only emerge from an understanding that students are fully implicated in the challenges globalisation presents. This kind of understanding does not automatically emerge from content knowledge; it is the product of a transformative process in which students are encouraged to examine critically their own perspectives on such issues as free trade and consumerism, and, on the basis of their examination, suggest courses of action to address these issues. The tension between content knowledge and agency that is noted above can be seen in a brief comparison of the goals of the secondary History and Citizenship Curriculum in the province of Quebec with the Ministry of Education's statement of the aims of education. Thus while the History and Citizenship Curriculum identifies three content-driven goals (examining social phenomenon from historical perspectives; interpreting social phenomenon using the historical method; and constructing a consciousness of citizenship through the study of history (Government of Quebec, 2004, p. 309)), in its general statement about the goals of education, the Ministry itself identifies three more externally-oriented and engaged aims (construction of a world view; construction of an identity, and empowerment (Government of Quebec, 2004, p. 12)). In this case, the clear contrast between a model of citizenship firmly grounded in history and a model that implies the emancipatory possibilities of civic education clearly points to the tension that exists between transmission and transformation within the curriculum.

Second Challenge: Single or Multiple Perspectives

As I have argued, global citizenship education has generally reinforced Western views of the world while it has tended to discount the worth of non-Western perspectives. This structure of privilege is rendered particularly problematic by globalisation.

In its effects globalisation has tended to ignore national boundaries and traditional dividing lines between the 'developed' and 'developing' worlds. In doing so, it has promoted a single worldview that in many respects resembles the imperial imaginary discussed earlier. But this worldview differs from the imperial imaginary in two significant ways, both of which present challenges to the current structure of global citizenship education. The first problematic aspect of globalisation is its tendency to diminish local and national cultures in favour of a culture of decontextualized global consumerism. In this aspect, it is as much a challenge to nations like Canada (and, for example, its cultural industries) as it is to nations in the developing world. The second is in its neo-liberal emphasis on de-regulation, free trade and free flows of capital. Again, this aspect presents as much

125

of a problem to Canada (and, for example, public education and public healthcare) as it does to other nations around the world.

In response to these challenges, global citizenship education needs to re-examine its traditional 'single perspective approach' and emphasize that there are multiple perspectives on such issues as development, governance and trade. In terms of the impact of globalisation, a multiple perspective approach has two key benefits. First, it can be a point of interrogation and resistance to the cultural homogenisation that is characteristic of globalisation. Second, a multiple perspectives approach encourages students to examine and step out of their own cultural locations in order to develop what Hannah Arendt terms the habit of 'learning to imagine the other'(1968, p. 241). To the degree that global citizenship education promotes imagining the other, it develops the ethic of care, empathy and appreciation of difference that are key aspects in countering the homogenising tendencies of globalisation. Drawing on the Ontario *Canadian and World Studies* program for grades 11 and 12, for example, the statement is made that students are 'expected to show respect, tolerance and understanding towards individuals, groups and cultures in the global community' (Government of Ontario, 2005, p. 25). Later in the same program, this rather general assertion is given more substance by the expectation that students will engage in a comparison of 'Western Beliefs, Philosophies and Ideologies' with 'The Ideas and Cultures of the Non-Western World' (p. 211), and examine the ways in which such non-Western figures as Rigoberta Menchu and Shirin Ebadi furthered global human rights and citizenship (p. 221).

Third Challenge: National or Global Citizenship Education

As is the case in most other education systems throughout the world, the development of citizenship has long been the primary focus of social studies education in Canada (Sears, 1996; Osborne, 1997). In terms of global citizenship education in Canada, citizenship has typically been seen in two ways: first, as the 'civic' responsibility to be an active and responsible member of the global community; and second, as an obligation to address inequities between the developed and developing worlds (Starr & Nelson, 1993, pp. 12–14). In both cases global citizenship education is framed as a matter of national self-interest and almost exclusively tied to the civic structures of the nation-state. And students in Canada are urged to take up their responsibilities and obligations to address significant global citizenship education issues such as international conflict, environmental degradation, or the protection of human rights, as citizens of Canada rather than as citizens of the world. And where it is suggested that political action is necessary to bring about a necessary change, it is through the nation and its foreign policy that action is accomplished. A good case in point is Manitoba's social studies curriculum for Senior 3, the last mandatory social studies course Manitoba students must take. Under a segment of the course titled 'Canada's Involvement in International Affairs,' students are asked the questions, 'Why and how is Canada involved in international affairs?' and 'What is Canada's role as peacekeeper?' (Government of Manitoba Department of Education and Culture, 1988, p. 7). The questions are typical of those posed in other provincial curricula and although they do take up the question of the international civic responsibilities of nation states, they are also limiting in that they imply a field of action that effectively precludes the possibility of international responses to global issues. Given the transnational realities of globalisation, it is pertinent to ask whether global citizenship education would be better served by promoting global citizenship rather than national citizenship.

In some ways it is highly problematic to continue to endorse national citizenship in the context of globalisation. Because many of the issues that face the global community are international in scope and effect, it is uncertain what the actions of a single nation can be in order to address these concerns, and in the context of global citizenship education, the more international issues are dealt with from national perspectives, the less opportunity students have to explore or develop other perspectives. A good example of this dilemma can be seen in the recent Kyoto Accord on climate change. Thus while it might be useful to have students discuss and analyse Canada's decision to ratify the accord, it is also pertinent to ask whether a nationally-based analysis works against the development of an emergent sense of the collective responsibilities of global citizenship education.

On the other hand, the notion of global citizenship education presents its own pedagogic challenges and there are significant issues that arise when we speak of 'global citizens' and a 'global civic community'. For example, we do not really know what a citizen is, in the global sense, nor are there global civic structures capable of functioning in the same way that national structures do (Gaudelli, 2003; Heater, 2004). Additionally, there is the complex problem of allegiance. Citizenship education has typically been organised to promote patriotism and loyalty to the nation state; global citizenship education could well call this allegiance into question if a conflict arises between the interests of the nation and those of the world as a whole. Questions of definition, structure and allegiance that arise when we speak of global citizenship education have led the prominent Canadian political scientist Will Kymlicka to note, 'globalization is undoubtedly producing a new civil society, but it has not yet produced anything we can recognize as transnational democratic citizenship' (Kymlicka, 2001, p. 326). Yet despite these significant difficulties many scholars have maintained that without a turn to world citizenship, students will not develop the imaginative capacity to see beyond the constraints of the nation and challenge the dominant narrative of globalisation (Nussbaum, 1997; Kingwell, 2001; Richardson et al, 2003). Other scholars argue that it is critical to develop world citizenship because contemporary understandings of citizenship as bound to the national structure of parliaments, parties and regular elections are increasingly circumscribed and made irrelevant by extra-national organisations such as the G-8, the WTO and the World Bank (Pike, 1999; Smith 2000a; McMurtry, 2002). The challenge of globalisation raises the issue of whether social studies, and more specifically global citizenship education, can imagine a civic fabric on a global scale in which students can see themselves acting as informed and empowered global citizens.

127

CONCLUSION: THE STRUGGLE FOR GLOBAL CITIZENSHIP EDUCATION IN CANADA

In the previous section, I have attempted to lay out some of the challenges globalisation presents to global citizenship education. In this final section I will discuss current ideological struggles that make global citizenship education very much a contested arena in Canada. As noted earlier, in broad terms, the struggle is between two very different global imaginaries with quite dissimilar perspectives on global issues. The first is grounded in an ecological awareness of the fundamental interrelatedness of all aspects of the Earth and of the importance of physical and cultural diversity. From this perspective, the purpose of global citizenship education is to help students develop a sense of connectedness, empathy, and an appreciation for diversity and difference, and globalisation itself is seen as an essentially negative force (Spring, 1998; Couture, 2003). The second is founded on individualism and neo-liberal economic ideas that suggest that despite superficial differences individuals have the same fundamental wants and needs, and that by serving their own self-interest, ultimately the interests of the planet are also served. From this perspective, the purpose of global citizenship education is to help students develop the knowledge and skills that will allow them to be competitive and successful in the global arena, and globalisation is seen as an essentially positive force (Smith, 2000b).

By using brief examples drawn from the Alberta social studies program it is possible to see how these two imaginaries act as competing discourses within a single curriculum, and the degree to which they represent different visions of the purpose of global citizenship education. Thus on the one hand, the curriculum indicates that 'students will be expected to develop an appreciation of the diversity that exists in the world, an appreciation that different perspectives exist on quality of life [and] an awareness and appreciation of the interdependent nature of the world' (Alberta Learning, 2002, p. 1). On the other hand, it is noted that in the face of a rapidly changing world, students must become 'self-motivated, self-directed problem solvers and decision makers who are developing the skills necessary for learning and who develop a sense of self-worth and confidence in their ability to participate in a changing society' (Government of Alberta Learning, 2002, p. 2).

The opposing themes of interdependence and autonomy that the above passages highlight stand as evidence of the ideological tensions existing within global citizenship education. Given the complexities globalisation presents to global citizenship education, as well as the tensions that have characterised its curricular location over time, it seems that global citizenship education is at somewhat of a crossroads in its evolution. Caught between learning about the world and learning to live in the world, the specific challenge global citizenship education in Canada faces is how best to prepare students to act as informed, caring and active civic participants in a globalised world.

REFERENCES

Arendt, H. (1968). *Between past and future*. New York: Penguin Books.

Bhabha, H. K. (1990). *Nation and narration*. London: Routledge.

Case, R. (1993). Key elements of a global perspective. *Social Education, 51*(6), 318–325.

Couture, J. C. (2000). Global issues and activated audiences. *Canadian Social Studies*, 35(1). Retrieved 19 September 2007 from http:www.quasar.ualberta.ca/css.

Egan, K. (1999). Children's minds, talking rabbits and clockwork oranges: Essays in education. *New York: Teachers College Press*.

Feinberg, W. (1998). *Common schools/uncommon identities: National unity and cultural difference*. New Haven CN: Yale University Press.

Foucault, M. (1972). *The archaeology of knowledge*. London: Routledge.

Gage, W. J. (1899). *New Canadian geography*. Toronto: W.J. Gage.

Gallegos, B. (1998). Remember the Alamo: Imperialista, memory and postcolonial educational studies. *Educational Studies, 29*, 232–247.

Gaudelli, W. (2003). *World class: Teaching and learning in global times*. London: Erlbaum Associates.

Government of Alberta Department of Education (1955). *Senior high school curriculum guide 1955*. Edmonton: Department of Education.

Government of Alberta Department of Education (1971). *Programs of study: Social studies*. Edmonton: Department of Education.

Government of Alberta, Alberta Learning (2002). *Social studies: Kindergarten to grade twelve*, Edmonton: Alberta Learning.

Government of Alberta, Alberta Education (2006). *Business plan: 2006–07*. Edmonton: Alberta Education.

Government of Manitoba, Manitoba Department of Education and Culture (1988). *Senior 3: Canada –A social and political history*. Winnipeg: Manitoba Department of Education and Culture.

Government of Nova Scotia, Department of Education (2003). *Global history 12*. Halifax: Department of Education.

Government of Ontario Ministry of Education (1945). *Courses of study: Grades IX and X social studies and history*. Toronto: Department of Education.

Government of Ontario Ministry of Education and Training, (2000). *The Ontario curriculum grades 9 to 12: program planning and assessment*. Toronto: Ontario Ministry of Education and Training.

Government of Ontario Ministry of Education. (2005). *Canadian and world studies*. Toronto: Ontario Ministry of Education.

Government of Quebec, Quebec Education (2004). *Quebec education program: Secondary school education, cycle one*. Montreal: Quebec Education.

Harshman, R. & Hannell, C. (1989). *World issues in the global community*. Toronto: John Wiley.

Heater, D. (2001). The history of citizenship education in England. *The Curriculum Journal, 12*(1), 103–124.

Heater, D. (2004). *Citizenship: The civic ideal in world history, politics and education* (3rd ed.). Vancouver: University of British Columbia Press.

Kincheloe, J. (2001). *Getting beyond the facts: Teaching social studies/social sciences in the twenty-first century* (2nd ed.). New York: Peter Lang.

Kingwell, M. (2001). *The world we want: Virtue, vice and the good citizen*. Toronto: Viking.

Kymlicka, W. (2001). *Politics in the vernacular: Nationalism, multiculturalism, and citizenship*. London: Oxford University Press.

McMurtry, J. (2002). Twelve questions about globalization. *Canadian Social Studies*, 37(1). Retrieved 19 September 2007 from http:www.quasar.ualberta.ca/css.

Merryfield, M.M. (1998). Pedagogy for global perspectives in education: studies of teachers' thinking and practice. *Theory and Research in Social Education, 26*(3), 342–379.

Merryfield, M.M. (2001). Moving the center of global education: From imperial world views that divide the world to double consciousness, contrapuntal pedagogy, hybridity, and cross-cultural competence. In W.B. Stanley (Ed.), *Critical issues in social studies research for the 21ˢᵗ century* (pp. 150–179). Greenwich, CN: Information Age Publishing.

Mitchener, E. A. & Tuffs, R. J. (1989). *One world*. Edmonton: Reidmore Books.

Mukherjee, A. (1994). *Oppositional aesthetics: Reading from a hyphenated space*. Toronto: TSAR Publications.

Nussbaum M. C. (1997). *Cultivating humanity: A classical defence of reform in liberal education*. Cambridge, MA.: Harvard University Press.

Osborne, K. (1997). Citizenship education and social studies. In I. Wright and A. Sears (Eds.), *Trends and issues in Canadian social studies* (pp. 39–67). Vancouver: Pacific Educational Press.

Pike, G. (2000). Globalization and national identity: In pursuit of meaning. *Theory into Practice, 39*(2), 64–73.

Pike, G. & Selby, D. (1988). *Global teacher, global learner*. London: Hodder and Stoughton.

Pike, G., & Selby, D. (1999). *In the global classroom: 1*. Toronto: Pippin.

Richardson, G.H. (2000). Two terms you can (and should) use in the classroom: Cultural homogenization and eurocentrism. *Canadian Social Studies, 35*(1). Retrieved 19 September 2007 from http:www.quasar.ualberta.ca/css.

Richardson, G.H. (2002). T*he death of the good Canadian: Teachers, national identities and the social studies curriculum*. New York: Peter Lang.

Richardson, G.H. (2004). Global education and the challenge of globalization. In A. Sears and I. Wright (Eds.), *Challenges and prospects for Canadian social studies* (pp. 138–149). Vancouver: Pacific Educational Press.

Richardson, G.H., Blades, D., Kumano, Y., & Karaki, K. (2003). Fostering a global imaginary: The possibilities and paradoxes of Japanese and Canadian students' perceptions of the responsibilities of global citizenship education. *Policy Futures in Education, 1*(2), 402–420.

Said, E. (1993). *Culture and imperialism*. New York: Knopf.

Sears, A. (1996). In Canada even history divides: Unique features of Canadian citizenship. *International Journal of Social Education, 11*(2), 53–67.

Sears, A. (1997). Social studies in Canada. In I. Wright and A. Sears, (Eds.), *Trends and issues in Canadian social studies*. Vancouver: Pacific Educational Press.

Selby, D. (1995). Education for the global age: What is involved? In R. Fowler and I. Wright (Eds.), *Thinking globally about social studies education* (pp. 1–17). Vancouver: Research and Development in Global Studies, Faculty of Education, University of British Columbia.

Selby, D. (1999). Global education: Towards a quantum model of environmental education. *Canadian Journal of Environmental Education, 4*, 125–141.

Selby, D. (2003). *Global education as transformative education*. Retrieved from *Global Citizens for Change web site:* http:www.citizens4change.org/global/intro/global_education_introduce.htm.

Sleeter, C. E. (1993). How white teachers construct race. In C. McCarthy and W. Crichlow (Eds.), *Race, identity and representation in education* (pp. 157–171). New York: Routledge.

Smith, D.G. (1999). Globalization and education: Prospects for postcolonial pedagogy in a hermeneutic mode. *Interchange, 30*, 3–4.

Smith, D.G. (2000a). The specific challenges of globalization for teaching and vice versa. *The Alberta Journal of Educational Research, 46*(1), 7–26.

Smith, D.G. (2000b). A few modest prophecies: The WTO, globalization and the future of public education. *Canadian Social Studies, 35*(1). Retrieved 19 September 2007 from http:www.quasar. ualberta.ca/css.

Spring, J. (1998). *Education and the rise of the global economy*. Mahwah, NJ: Lawrence Erlbaum Associates.

Starr, E., & Nelson, J. (1993). Teacher perspectives on global education. *Canadian Social Studies, 28*(1) 12–14.

Torres, C.A. & Barbules, N. (2000). *Globalization and education: Critical perspectives*. New York: Routledge.

Werner, W. & Case, R. (1997). Themes of global education. In I. Wright and A. Sears (Eds.), *Trends and issues in Canadian social studies* (pp. 176–194). Vancouver: Pacific Educational Press.

Willinsky, J. (1998). *Learning to divide the world: Education at empire's end.* Minneapolis: University of Minnesota Press.

George Richardson
University of Alberta, Canada

THOMAS S. POPKEWITZ

COSMOPOLITANISM, THE CITIZEN AND PROCESSES OF ABJECTION

The Double Gestures of Pedagogy

INTRODUCTION

This chapter is concerned with the cultural production of the citizen. The cultural unity of the nation has little to do with geographical or linguistic unity and natural cohesion (see, e.g., Bell, 2001; Hunter, 1994). To be Japanese, American, or German is not the outgrowth of geographical or linguistic unity that brings a natural cohesion but is produced through an amalgamation of technologies, ideas, and social practices (see, e.g., Bell, 2001; Hunter, 1994; Balibar & Wallerstein, 1991). Anderson (1991) calls the institution of the unity of the nation as an "imagined community", one in which cultural representations historically fabricated a "nation-ness."

My interest follows this interest but reconceptualises that interest through exploring the cultural theses of the citizen in schooling. The chapter considers schooling as embodying the double gestures: the making the child as the cosmopolitan citizen of the future and as processes of abjection of casting out of "Others". Cosmopolitanism projects a universal citizen whose nation-ness is bound to global hopes of a unified humanity guided by reason and rationality and with hospitality to Others. The North European Enlightenment's cosmopolitanism was embodied in the formation of the new Republics of the United States and France. Schooling was to make the cosmopolitan citizen through generating principles governing reason and "reasonable people". That unity and universalism was historically particular. The "reason" of schooling comparatively divided the cosmopolitan qualities of the citizen from Others, those abjected or cast out in unliveable spaces. The classification of the immigrant in debates about citizenship is illustrative of this process of abjection. The category directs attention to groups and individuals whose status exists in in-between spaces of inclusion and exclusion – recognised for inclusion as a citizen; yet different, abjected and excluded by virtue of their modes of life.

Cosmopolitanism is a strategy to historically and comparatively explore the cultural theses of the child as a global citizen and its local inscriptions that exclude through its inclusionary impulses. The first section examines the assembly of cosmopolitan principles in contemporary U.S. and European school reforms and

M.A. Peters, A. Britton and H. Blee (Eds.), Global Citizenship Education: Philosophy, Theory and Pedagogy, 133-152.

research. I argued that school reforms align and connect the scope and aspirations of public powers with the personal and subjective capacities. The contemporary citizen is explored as an unfinished cosmopolitanism. This individuality is expressed in the category of lifelong learner who acts as a global citizen continuously designing biography in the collaboration of "community"; that global cosmopolitanism entails its "others". The instantiation of the unity of the whole or the global simultaneously differentiates and casts out qualities of "Others" as threatening to the harmony and stability. The third section explores different strands of educational research as strategies of designing who the child is, should be, and who does not fit its narratives and images of cosmopolitan.

COSMOPOLITANISM

Cosmopolitanism embodies a radical historical thesis about the power of human reason and science. The aspiration of cosmopolitanism was a mode of life in which individual liberty and freedom produced universal human progress and individual happiness. Central to the citizen was the secularisation that placed value on reason and rationality (science) in change. The conceptions of reason and agency in the French and American republics, for example, were premised and dependent on the citizen who adhered to cosmopolitan principles of action and participation. The enlightened self-interest, however, was continually accompanied by fears about degeneration and decay (McMahan, 2001). Early American educators spoke about the fears of the barbarians and savages coming into the gates of the Republic and destroying its future if education did not do its job properly.

Although the actual word *cosmopolitanism* is rarely used in today's reforms, its foundational assumptions are embedded in school pedagogy, curriculum and teacher education. The formation of the modern American comprehensive high school in the first decades of the 20th century was initially called "the cosmopolitan high school" (Drost, 1967). Cosmopolitan theses travel as foundation assumptions in European reforms about inter-cultural education and the lifelong learner. U.S. school reforms and teacher education embody mutations of the Enlightenment's notions of reason and rationality.[1]

This section has three parts to focus on particular notions of cosmopolitanism that travel as sacred qualities in pedagogy. First is considered the notion of agency in cosmopolitanism as linking individuality and society. It then proceeds to examine the particular instantiation of agency in the *unfinished cosmopolitanism*, a cultural thesis expressed in pedagogy and research about *the lifelong learner*. The next two parts consider the particular mode of thought embodied in the unfinished cosmopolitan, that of "the homeless mind" where the individual is both an object and subject of reflection, and the connection of the public and the personal in reforms concerning collaboration and community.

Agency in the Invention of Society

The Enlightenment pushed to the side the received order given by the grace of God and replaced it with another eternal human purpose: the reason and science of making life (Becker, 1932). Theories of agency constituted people as autonomous subjects of motives and perceptions to determine the actions that shape the future (Meyer, 1986).

Cosmopolitan notions of agency are so much a part of the modern orthodoxy that a theory of childhood, schooling, and society without signifying the autonomous agent who acts to improve the self and world is almost unthinkable, or at least not politically correct. Similar to the original sin arguments of the church, the *doxa* is that without theories of agency we are left with an anti-humanist and deterministic world that would enable the barbarians and the uncivilised to enter and destroy the gates of the republic. Notions of agency bring individual liberty and personal realisation, social betterment, and rescue of those who have fallen from the graces of progress. The redemptive projects of the good works of people are central from Comte and Marx to present theories about "communities of learners". Theories about capitalism, racism, Mead's (1934) "generalised other", and Dewey's "community" function assume agentic entities in rationalising and ordering responsibilities and obligations in the conduct of the citizen. More recently, The War on Poverty in the United States during the 1960s was premised on eliminating poverty by creating institutional settings that enabled the poor efficacy for acting on their own lives. Theories of deviancy and failure in schooling focus on the psychology of the individual who has no agency because of a lack of self-esteem or motivation.

What is lost in these arguments about sin and hope is the politic of the particular historical inscriptions of agency. The invention of agency coincided historically with the "invention" of society. Varela (2000) argues, for example, that the formation of individual personalities, individual subjects, and the idea of society emerges at the precise historical moment when the legitimacy of power was being based on the idea of a general "will." The individual in the 18th-century French *philosophé,* for example, was bound to the "discovery of society" in a process of disengagement from the religious representations. While the word *society* is present prior to the Enlightenment, it emerges to provide a way to think about individuality within notions of collective human existence instituted as the essential domain of human practices. Baker (1994) argues, for example, the ideas about progress, civilisation, and toleration would be unthinkable without society as their implied reference. They assume the logical priority and moral values of society as the frame of collective human existence and individual agency.

The Unfinished Cosmopolitanism: The Cultural Thesis of the Lifelong Learner

Agency in contemporary reforms is enunciated in the *unfinished* cosmopolitanism, a mode of life of the lifelong learner in which there is a never-ending process of making choices, innovation, and collaboration. Personal responsibility and self-management of one's risks is tied to continually maximising the correct application of reason and rationality.

That Individuality chases desire by making choices in a system of continuous innovation. For some, the lifelong learner is the realisation of the medieval alchemist's faith in finding the philosopher's stone. That stone was to unlock material and spiritual secrets by identifying the theory that unified everything. Computer learning, for many, is today's philosopher's stone. Maeroff (2003) argues, for example, that processes of online learning will unlock the unfilled promise of the new cosmopolitan citizen of the world that the Enlightenment philosophers could only have wished for. The new era of computer education, for Maeroff, brings to fruition the hope of free-market neoliberalism. The school is to produce a more equitable society and an enlightened individual by interjecting "more choices into the system, advocating reason, the richer the offerings and the greater the benefits to consumers (students and their families)" (Maeroff, 2003, p. 4). From a different ideological perspective, Hargreaves (2003) speaks of the lifelong learner as rejecting Neoliberal reforms based on choice in market competition and its materialism. The hope of the learning society is to prepare the child of the future with "a cosmopolitan identity which shows tolerance of race and gender differences, genuine curiosity toward and willingness to learn from other cultures, and responsibility toward excluded groups within and beyond one's society" (p. xix).

Earlier 20th century classrooms were places of socialisation where the child internalised pre-established collective and universal norms of identity; today they are a redesigned space of living. The location of responsibility is no longer traversed through the range of social practices directed toward a single public sphere the social. Responsibility is located today in communities, diverse, autonomous and plural perpetually constituted through one's own practice in "communities" of learning. The empowerment of freedom is talked about as if there are no enclosures.

Yet freedom in contemporary reforms also expresses a fatalism of the processes of globalisation in which unfinished cosmopolitanism acts. Teachers, school administrators and government officials in a European Union study expressed a fatalism (Lindblad & Popkewitz, 2004). That fatalism was spoken of as the inevitable march of globalism that teachers needed to respond to through curriculum changes. The new child was one who makes choices and participates in the globalisation occurring but the globalisation was not questioned. The ubiquitous future of globalism makes it not possible for the individual, to quote a French high school textbook, "to escape the flux of change" (Soysal, Bertiloot, & Mannitz, 2005, pp. 24–25). The ubiquitous boundaries of globalism are naturalised to intern and enclose the spaces of the freedom and participation. The historicity that shapes and fashions who "we" are and should be is left as unquestioned and elided.

Planning Of Biography: The Homeless Mind in Communities

The unfinished cosmopolitan maximises happiness through continual processes of rationally planning and organising daily events for a better future. Biography is managed through self-monitoring processes that include "survival learning, adaptive learning, and generative learning, learning that enhance the capacity to create" (Simon & Masschelein, 2006, p. 1). Problem solving provides the practices to the salvation of the future. Life is a series of rationally ordered paths, for finding solutions, that is never complete and always defers the present to the future.

The planning and problem solving of the unfinished cosmopolitanism entails a particular modern consciousness of the self and agency that can be called the "homeless mind".[2] The individual lives both in exile of the present through distancing one's self from the immediate to reflect about the present through universal values; and simultaneously uses that that reflective stance in re-attaching the "self" to community and daily life. This quality of the homeless mind in cosmopolitan living is expressed by philosopher Martha Nussbaum (1996). She argues that education is to produce the cosmopolitan ethics that has twin allegiances. The first allegiance is to a reasonable and principled cosmopolitanism committed to a community bound by a universal morality that serves all human beings (p. 5). The second allegiance is to the citizen dwelling in the local community of birth through which the commitments to reason and argument form a common source of moral obligations.

Nussbaum's (1996) cosmopolitan thesis embodies a dual character. It is distancing one's self from the present to reflect about the universal intentions and purposes that can be brought to everyday life. Reflecting and acting is envisioned as living as a stranger to oneself and in exile from the provincial and parochial. One continually lives in exile and a stranger to daily life by working to produce moral capacity of the self and others. Educational processes connect students' capacities for reason and problem solving "to fundamental universal values of respect and aspirations for justice and goodness" (p. 8). The second character of cosmopolitanism is to the attachment of the deliberative mind to remaking the communities in which one lives. Civic education is teaching students that they are citizens of a world where there is a consensus of shared universal values of reason and moral capacity. Its goal is to enable the child to live as "an exile from the comfort of local truths, from the warm, nestling feeling of patriotism, from the absorbing drama of pride in oneself and one's own" (p. 15).

The "homeless mind", then, has the dual qualities of placing life in transcendental categories that seem to have no particular historical location or author to establish a home, yet in establishing belonging and home through their inscription as principles of reflection and action. Nussbaum's "deliberative mind" is a "homeless mind" in which abstract systems of knowledge replaces the knowledge of face-to-face interactions for ordering conduct. The self is distanced from everyday activities in order to judge and act in the immediate through universals about the just and good. Thinking about one's self as a lifelong learner, an adolescent, worker, citizen are such categories about the universal that loop into and attach to face-to-face interactions. That looping back into the local and the immediate recreates new affiliations, belonging, and "homes" that constitute the cosmopolitan qualities of the citizen. This quality of the homeless mind in ordering personal judgments and experience is often elided in hermeneutic discussions about teacher's experiences or grounded theories of classrooms.

The homeless mind is significant as it part of the grid through which a particular expertise and episteme that make possible planning who the child is and should be as the future citizen. Nussbaum's (1996) discussion of cosmopolitanism as exile and strangeness to one's self through reflection is to (re)make the sites of affiliation and attachment calculable and administrative. The function of the human sciences from Freud to Thorndike through Vygotsky and Dewey, for example, is to designing self-reflection in which individuality "lives" in the flows between universals where the self is an object of reflection and the immediate site of acting and experiencing. The "reflective teacher" embodies this homeless mind through action research that distances the classroom acts through transcendent categories that are then brought back as principles of ordering pedagogy. Perhaps it should be no other way, but the planning of the biography of the citizen and its notions of progress and emancipation are not natural. They are the effects of power that goes unnoticed in the processes of planning change!

Connecting the Public with the Personal: Collaboration in Community

The agency and homeless mind of the unfinished cosmopolitanism are assembled as problem solving and collaborating in communities – communities of learning, discourse communities. Community and collaboration are signified as telling of the collective obligation of the political community to promote justice and equity through the schools. The assumption of collaboration is the procedures of interaction and association produce paths to the common good and hospitality to others. Choice in individual life is sanctioned and acts by working collaboratively.

The politics of community lies in the linking of the self to a collective home and belonging that is not merely those enunciated. Community was to reestablish moral order and the pastoral faith in urban conditions and urban populations at the beginning of the 20th century. Community today circulates in a range of reforms to speak about inclusion of previously marginalised communities. The narratives of community express universal values about creating the conditions for *all* individuals to achieve social or economic progress and for the revitalisation of democracy. Agency is spoken of in psychological notions of problem solving and the political evocation of voice and empowerment through community participation and collaboration. Classroom community and participation link psychology of the child with norms of consensus and stability; it is where "students are well known both personally and academically and where common goals and values have been forged" (Darling-Hammond, 1998, p. 10).

The salvation themes of collaboration and participation in policy and research obscure how negotiations and communication are assembled in the cultural theses of cosmopolitanism. The school and classrooms as communities of learning are sites for recalibrating the political aspirations of the individual with the new assemblies of communities as *the social*. The "barriers" breached across groups in narrations of collaboration join individual agency with the general development of society.

Collaboration and participation inscribe a hermeneutic objectivism in the name of the new democracy. Classrooms and instruction are "participatory structures". The assumption is that each set of actors has unique experiences and points of views that are negotiated through collaborative practices. Teachers, parents, and researchers are to come to understand and respect the different perspectives they have as a method of arriving at the truth.

Whatever the merits of problem solving and community, they are not merely descriptive of some natural reasoning of the child that research recoups. "Democratic participation", to borrow from Cruikshank (1999), is "not clear cut or naturally occurring; it [is] something that ... solicited, encouraged, guided, and directed" (p. 97). The language evokes populist images of democracy that entail local involvement in schools and the arriving of consensus about the "goals" guiding and judging individual schools.

Participation, collaboration, and reflection are told as foundational stories of the democracy of the nation. The teacher is a redemptive agent that connects individuality with particular assemblies about collective belonging and home of American exceptionalism, discussed in the next section as the nation told as an epic account of a unique human experiment in the progressive development of the highest ideals of cosmopolitan human values and progress. The teacher, for example, is the new leadership, "energized" to "work with others," "to ensure that America and its children will have the schools they require and deserve" (American Council on Education, 1999, p. ii) and to provide "a down payment to renewal and reform" that the "American public" demands so "the nation's schools can and must serve better the citizens of our democracy" (p. 1).

THE CASTING OUT INTO UNLIVEABLE SPACES: THE CHILD LEFT BEHIND

At this point, I want to link the unfinished cosmopolitanism with the child left behind, a phrase used in U.S. reforms and research to express the commitment to an equitable and just society by focusing on programs to include those populations that have been excluded. That practice of inclusion is, I will argue, a process of abjection and exclusion. But to get to that place of exclusion in gestures of inclusion, I first need to explore further the assembly of agency with the education sciences and the imagined unity of the citizen as differentiating and dividing the cosmopolitan citizen from its "Others" – the urban immigrant, poor, and racialised populations in need of rescue – because they lie outside the moral spaces of the "reasoned" individual.

Science as Planning to Change the Conditions and People of the City

The key to cosmopolitan reason was science. The Enlightenment's cosmopolitan carried a millennial belief in rational knowledge as positive force for action. Rationality was to correct visual perceptions and the errors of the senses through observation. French Enlightenment thinkers, for example, found the answer to the dilemma of progress in knowledge provided by science. Its methods would bring an infinite progress in the natural world and morally righteous and productive lives to the civil world. Science was to diagnose the impediments to progress to push back the boundaries of darkness and barbarism, and spread light and knowledge. The American Enlightenment was to resist "Gothic barbarism". The Gothic barbarism was to be defeated through.

> the struggle of natural science in understanding of nature, the tempering of superstition in religion in the politics of new free government - not only in the spread of science, liberty or republican government but in the spread of civilization. The civilizing was to calculate happiness. (Wood, 1991, pp. 191–192)

Turn of the 20th century American progressive reforms in government, society and schooling brought sciences into the institutions of the modern state. Central to the new intervention strategies of reform and the new formed human sciences was "The Social Question". Protestant reformers across the Atlantic were concerned the loss of moral order produced by urban conditions (Rodgers, 1998). The hope of the sciences was to find the right standards for producing the enlightened cosmopolitan citizen of the nation. Dewey's pragmatism, Thorndike's behaviourism, and the Chicago School of community sociology, overlapped in trans-Atlantic social Protestant reform movements to address "The Social Question". Science was to study and design interventions to change urban conditions, community interactions, and modes of living. Social and school programmes were to eliminate the social evils of the city by active intervention in the life and conditions of the city.

The reform sciences embodied twin cultural theses in planning. One was the studying of behaviour, the mind, and social interaction to render the characteristics of the child and teacher visible and amenable to government. The other characteristic of science was a generalised set of rules and standards for ordering the conduct of daily life. Notions of problem solving and learning embody this more generalised view of science as a practice for ordering experience, acting, and making choices. The agentive individual was to live as a planned biography organised by the calculated rules and standards of reflection and action.

The hope of the future embodied fears about urban dangers and its dangerous people. The "civilizing mission" of Progressive reforms contrasted darkness with the light of the nation. The Social Gospel Movement to which many Progressive Reformers belonged sought to incorporate Christian ethics into government and civic life. There was an evangelistic hope of American exceptionalism, the telling of the nation as a unique human experiment in the progressive development of the ideals of cosmopolitan values. Reform and its sciences were to bring the Christian gospel to non-Christians − that is, the heathen. That gospel mixed religious notions of salvation of a generalied Protestant Christianity into missionary work directed at immigrants and sometimes former Black slaves that had moved into the city. The comparative system of reason recognised the need to include populations previously excluded that simultaneously gave focus to difference. Protestant redemptive and salvation themes emphasised the self-motivated and responsible cosmopolitan individual who would actively intervene in his or her own development and thus guarantee the progress of the nation.

The key to the sciences in responding to the Social Question was design. Design embodied themes of salvation and redemption related to secularisation of life. The rationality that the German sociologist Max Weber (1904–1905/1958) put forward about social science brought to bear particular Calvinist notions of salvation into a secular world. Influential in the U.S., Weber theorised a psychology that underlay a Protestant theological epistemology about the inner qualities of the individual that would bring about a life of good works. Weber's theology-driven rationalisation of the world was directed by the individual who would exert active self-control over the state of nature. The cultural thesis of individual self-control was envisioned in the idea of the republic and its citizens (Tröhler, 2006).

The notion of design assumed particular configurations in the cultural theses of cosmopolitanism. Design was a word that redesigned early Puritan notions about pedagogy as "converting ordinances" into planning projects about the conditions and people. It suggested intent and purpose to what was planned and thus, to human agency and uncertainty. Design implied flexibility and openness in the future and accompanied broader tenets associated with democracy. The task of science, it seemed, was only laying out the directions and outlines of what was possible for people who made their own future.

The laying out of directions in reflection and action inscribed rules and standards about how the future should be achieved. Design stabilised chance by inscribing calculations of what constituted the methods and problems of "problem solving" and the spaces through which "reasonable" acts and outcomes were imagined. Design thus carried the double gestures of openness and responsiveness to changing environments important to human agency with the giving the rules and standards of reason that shaped and fashioned the options possible.

The sciences of designing the city and people were projects often designated as social engineering placed in "the service of the democratic ideal" in producing the citizen, to use a phrase from progressive movements. While explicitly rejecting the use of the term social engineering, pragmatism embodied the idea of planning to change conditions that changed people. It was one device of intervention that responded to the conditions of the city. John Dewey's writing, for example, can be interpreted as expressing concerns with the moral conditions of the city and the optimism of making its populations cosmopolitan. Progress in government, said the Chicago sociologist Lester Frank Ward in *Dynamic Sociology* (1883), was not simply an education to accommodate society but "must be in the direction of acquainting every member of society more thoroughly with the special nature of the institution, and awakening him to a more vivid conception of his personal interest in its management" (p. 243). Science, Ward continued, orders and modifies the contemplative "man" by allowing for the artificial construction of evolution. Education was to open knowledge to all members of society, and such knowledge was to be directed toward social ends that embodied cosmopolitan hopes of agency, freedom and progress.

Designing in pedagogy gave focus to the interior of the child that was spoken of as the great panacea for equality. The new psychologies of the child envisioned the empirical building blocks of selfhood as the tasks of deliberate design rather than as something related to a static, metaphysical soul (Sklansky, 2002, pp. 148–149). For the progressives, such as Dewey, the problem of design embodied the triumph of cooperation over competition as the natural destiny of human progress (p. 161). William James's notion of a pragmatic psychology placed a premium on habit formation as the main means of acting in accord with one's designs (p. 146).

Reclaiming the Birthright and American Exceptionalism

The moral and ethical imperatives of the nation are framed in a cultural thesis about the civic culture of democratic systems. Teacher education reforms, for example, are to fulfill the global obligations of preserving the democracy occurring as a result of changes in America's populations, of renewing the competitiveness of the nation in a global economy, and of promoting hospitality to the other. *What Matters Most: Teaching for America's Future,* a report whose author invokes the exceptionalism of the nation, National Commission that Teaching and America's Future (1996), embodies the promise to the nation in the reorganisation of teacher preparation programs. The cultural thesis focuses on the *soul* of the teacher and the child whose enlightened qualities serve the remaking of the consensus and stability of the nation.

> We must reclaim *the soul* [italics added] of America. And to do so, we need an education system that helps people forge shared values, to understand and respect other perspectives, to learn and work at high levels of competence, to take risks and persevere against the odds, to work comfortably with people from diverse backgrounds, and to continue to learn throughout life. (p. 12)

The reclaiming of the collective soul is about the making of the citizen. It re-memorialises the optimism of American exceptionalism to correct the past by providing for progress. "Reclaiming the soul of America" is a narrative of loss and the hope of redemption. That hope is expressed as a commitment to fulfill the dream of a democratic society. That dream is to forge consensus and harmony. Teacher education is to generate collective values in learning communities whose mode of living "respects others", "takes risks", and works with "diverse people" by making an individual who makes choices in which there is no choice not "to continue to learn throughout life".

The democracy of the reforms is not merely bringing the practices of schooling in relation to normative ideals. The distinctions and categories enunciate cultural theses about the unfinished cosmopolitanism and its Others, generating double gestures that function to qualify and disqualify individuals for participation. That enunciation of hope and abjection is embodied in the phrase of *"all* children learn" that recognises and divides. The *all* in the standards reforms and research − *all* children learn, *all* children have high achievement, and so on − expresses the broad political commitment that schools about the unity of the whole that serve all segments of society equally. Second report of the National Commission on Teaching and America's Future (2003), *No Dream Denied: A Pledge to America's Children,* memorialised the nation as providing the unity of the whole that signifies as what is natural to all children as their "educational birthright" that is scaled with the constitutional rights of the citizen. The birthright is, on one layer, bound to *being* a lifelong learner in "a culture of continuous learning." The hope of community and lifelong learning is to reclaim the lost dream of American exceptionalism.

The dream engenders fears as processes of abjection. The school where *"all* children learn" is a comparative injunctive about fears of *the child left behind,* the child who is not able to or does not realise the dream of the nation. The 1996 report asserts that there is a national urgency (*National Commission on Teaching & America's future* (1996, p.3) in rectifying fears of those who threaten the future through enunciating the dangers and dangerous populations.

All Americans have a critical interest in building this kind of education system. For example,

- Low levels of literacy are highly correlated with welfare dependency and incarceration − and their high costs.
- More than half the adult prison population has levels of literacy below those required by the labour market.
- By the year 2010 there will be only three workers for every Social Security recipient, as compared with 16 in 1950. If all these future workers are not capable and productive, the older generation's retirement security and our social compact will be in *grave danger.* (my italics)

We cannot afford the continued expansion of prison populations, public assistance programs, and unemployment (*National Commission on Teaching & America's future,* 1996, p.12)

While no longer evoking the early 20th century Social Question, the moral disorders of the city still occupies reforms. The Social Question is transmogrified into the optimism of the new American exceptionalism as a social contract and the fears of the illiterate, the criminal, and stated elsewhere in the report of "growing number whose first language is not English, many others with learning differences, and others with learning disabilities − teachers need access to the growing knowledge that exists about how to teach these learners effectively" (*National Commission on Teaching & America's future,* 1996, p. 8). The signifying of *all* children is an iteration of hope and fears of not providing the correct strategies to include, and the fears that cast out the dangers and dangerous qualities of those different.

The Child Not in the Space of "All Children: The Urban Child Left Behind"

The cultural territory of the child left behind who is to be rescued in the dream of professional reforms is the embodied in *the urban child,* a determinate category of particular kinds of people. I use the notion of determinate category in the sense that the urban child is not a single category. It is built from different historical practices that are assembled and connected in the narratives and images of this "child". At the turn of the 20th century, that left behind child was called also of the city, called backward and feeble minded. The urban was racialised through embodying distinctions of immigrant groups from southern and eastern Europe, Irish, former African American slaves, as well as Asians and Native Americans who stood outside of normalcy yet also recognised for inclusion. Today, the urban is embodied in *the* Social Question that differentiates the child left behind who is in need of rescue in order to become the lifelong learner, the latter who embodies the qualities of the future citizen.

My placing of the unfinished cosmopolitan and its Others in the same phenomena of schooling is to "see" each produced in relation to the other. The urban child embodies a cultural thesis that has little to do with geographical place. American cities, for example, are spaces with great wealth and a cosmopolitan urbaneness that coexist with the spaces of poverty and racial segregation. Children who live in the high-rise apartments and brownstones of American cities appear as urbane and not urban. The child of urban education is a political designation of populations targeted for social inventions. The urban child does not only live in the inner city. Urban education and the urban child live in suburbia and rural areas as well as in the "inner city". Further in linguistic and practical terms, urban and rural children are ordered through same universalising sets of distinctions (Popkewitz, 1998b). They both are urban in the sense of the characteristics and qualities that make up who they are. The troubled/troubling child in both rural and urban schooling were of "low expectations," low self-esteem, family dysfunctions, and different learning styles.

The cultural thesis of the urban child order the mode of living that characterise the child left behind. The child left behind exists in an in-between place of requiring rescue and excluded as different. That difference is the partitioning of the sensible and "reasonable" in which the lifelong learner and the urban, left behind child form a continuum of values. Each is dependent on its Others as they are part of the same phenomenon in the construction of school pedagogy.

DESIGNING CLASSROOMS/DESIGNING THE CHILD

The contemporary sciences of schooling, as were the progressive sciences at the beginning of the 20th century indicated, are to plan for social improvements that will produce an enlightened society. Cosmopolitan notions of empowerment, voice, emancipation, and the mastery of the present through useful knowledge in the name of humanity's future are triggers of that research. The high stakes of research are to reshape the teacher and the child in the hope of reshaping and emancipating society from traditional habits and attitudes. Some research programmes align with federal initiatives to identify "what works" so as to fill society with the replications of good reforms. The watchwords are reforms that are proven through "scientific evidence". The "gold standard" of research methods is drug testing. Other research draws on communication theories and constructivist psychologies to make the future child more humane and the world more progressive. That research reincarnates the ideas of early 20th-century Russian Marxist psychologist Lev Vygotsky and the American liberal philosopher-psychologist John Dewey in projects of social psychology about social improvement and useful knowledge (Popkewitz, 1998a). To continue the medical analogy, the potion of this social psychology is to get "what works" but without the drug testing. Change is in the ordering of interactions in and discourses of the classroom. Research designs the conditions of the classroom and people in collaborative processes and feedback loops that are to guarantee the goals of reforms.

Today's sciences of school reform re-assemble the earlier 20th century's term of social engineering in the making of the citizen. The tasks of planning are concerned, at one level, with the unfinished cosmopolitan. It is to produce the life of choice and innovation, ironically, spoken about as engineering through replication; that is, identifying successful programs (and the people who operate in them) as universally transportable models to the universe of schools. Replication is an interesting choice of words, carrying an image of isomorphic compliance across contexts and people. The replication is embedded in the quest for designing methodological rigour for "stable explanations" (National Research Council, 2002, p. 3). Education sciences are viewed "as the basis for what is possible" and desirable (p. 49).

The expertise of science is expressed as in the service of democratic ideal. The sentiment of design is collaboration, participation, flexibility, and multiple solutions given as evidence of democracy; the idea of just powers is derived from the consent of the governed, or at least the adult governed. It is argued, for example, that school decisions are best made at the site where problems arise. Efforts among local authorities, parents, and teachers are viewed as yielding better policies, increased teacher expertise, and innovation because teachers are in charge of their own practices.

The practices of design are strategies of ordering and governing who people are and should be. That governing is embodied in the concern with "useful" knowledge about what works. The object of design research is to provide a finer-tuned relation between the conditions of schooling and the self-government of people. The words engineer and *reengineer* are used to talk about the mode of living in which the teacher and child continually "innovate" through principles homologous with unfinished cosmopolitanism.

The planning in Design Research, one strand of the new learning sciences of schooling, places its purpose as, to borrow from the early 20th century, "in service to the democratic ideal". "Design and engineering are generative and transformative" (Kelly, 2003, p. 4). Research is anchored to the everyday life of schooling to enable individual participation and agency.

The professionalised democracy of Design is in its "open system". Design research is the continual and fluid process of inventing tools that bring reform and the ongoing development of the system in an intimate relationship with the participants. Using mathematics teaching as an exemplar that enunciates sentiments of popular participation and the significance of the relevancies of personal life, "learning should be contextualised, and of ideas that mathematics learning should be more closely tied to students' experience" (Design-Based Research Collective, 2003, p. 5).

The idea of system is a particular theoretical intervention about the unity of the whole. The open system directs attention to uncertainty of the future yet is designing that uncertainty in stable systems from which rules and principles are generated to order the change, human agency, and enlightened participation and collaboration.

The openness of the system is in fact to provide tidiness and consensus through constant monitoring in the delivery of instruction. The system places actions in a functional structure (system) given equilibrium by coordinating ongoing implementation processes grounded in the everyday life of the school. The function of research is to provide a complete knowledge that will "close the credibility gap between unscientific research and detachment of researchers" (Design-Based Research Collective, 2003, p. 5). The stability and universality are inscribed through the notion of "sustainable intervention". "Sustainable intervention requires understanding how and why an innovation works within a setting over time and across setting" (Design-Based Research Collective, 2003, p. 6).

The National Research Council's (2002) commissioned report for the implementation of U.S. congressional legislation, No Child Left Behind (2002) also deploys the notion of design and planning as does Design Research. The former usage has a tactical difference rather than in the principles that govern the planning of change and people. The National Research Council's report is to identify the criteria of science that will provide warranted data about school reforms. The report uses the language of "rigorous" design procedures and replication in the focus on design technologies of research. The warrant of this report, as is design research, is for a democratic, inclusive society. The use of rigorous design procedures is bound to "the nation's commitment to improve the education of all children requires continuing efforts to improve its research capacity" (National Research Council, 2002, p. 21).

The normative assertions about democracy and an inclusive society are taken for granted. They are treated as a previously agreed-upon consensus and in no need for any discussion. The problem is only instrumental in identifying "What Works", the title of the federal clearinghouse on research to set apart proven success reforms tied to the No Child Left Behind legislation.

146

There are certain overlaps and distinctions between the two designs in research. The purpose of design in "evidence-based research" as well is the engineering of people. Both research approaches are to find useful knowledge about what works in order to design the most efficient methods of intervention. The criterion of "useful" assumes a consensus about what and who is included, and thus embodies processes of abjection.

The usefulness of knowledge, however, is not the same in the two research programmes. One is through continual interventions and monitoring in the engineering of people; the other is in the control of variables that generates "verifiable" knowledge in "re-engineering that follows the "gold standards" of randomized trails of medical and drug testing.[5] These gold standards are the real science, as design experiments do not control variables and verifiable knowledge that enable hypothesis testing to judge competing hypotheses and replication (Shavelson, Philips, Towne, & Feuer, 2003). The methodological problem of design is ultimately to provide stable, harmonious systems of practice about what works for engineering.

The processes of calculating, ordering, and changing through design are portrayed as neutral to the system's goals. Design Research asserts an impartiality of assisting in interventions to change and innovate in schooling through "the scientific processes of discovery, exploration, confirmation, and dissemination (Kelly, 2003, p. 3)".

The impersonality is not neutral. Design research is political in the sense that I have been using that term. It erases differences in a democratic gesture of participation that simultaneously scripts the rules that order conduct. The design procedures order and classify the everyday activities of classrooms as a system in a harmonious and consensual set of relations. The flexibility and continual assessment tame chance through giving order and tidiness to the "things" and the people to be changed. The system of instruction to continually seek more efficient relations about the social and the individual is, as the pragmatism of progressive movements, a particular populism.

One's life is made into an event of planning with a coterie of experts to assist in that planning (Berger et al., 1974). The psychological classifications and distinctions inscribe principles of cosmopolitanism, the child who lives a life of continual choice and change that matches the system in which action is anchored. The working of the open system is bounded by the ordering and classifications of psychological theories of learning, motivation, communication, and individualisation that are to change "the metacognition of the child and the teacher" (Kelly, 2003, pp. 3, 5). The science of complexity is, ironically, the desire towards certainty − to "lose the credibility gap" and the incompleteness of knowledge. The openness of the design process is a closed-loop system that is driven by its own internal logic.

Progress is tied to the micro-governing of life that has multiple dimensions of time - time of a regulated life, time of living in different communities where there are processes of continuous innovation, and the comprehension associated with the Internet and multitasking. The salvation themes of the lifelong learner are of the self who lives in uncertainty and certainty. The qualities of the present are somewhat like Deleuze and Guattari's (1987) rhizome, an assembly of heterogeneous components and a multiplicity that functions with variation, expansion, and offshoots. The lifelong learner is a mode of living in varied communities that move at different rates of time and space. The lifelong learner is a citizen of the nation, but he or she also communicates through Internet and computer games played simultaneously around the world, and with multiple identities and disjointed narratives, just as in the television comedy of Seinfeld's that had no overarching coherence in the storyline of its four main characters.

The design of science is the shepherd that steers others in the name of democracy. The name for democracy is the collaboration among "various stakeholders". These various stakeholders are researchers, policymakers, and practitioners who work in partnership in deciding what is best for schools. To encourage the close proximity of research knowledge to classrooms, the National Research Council calls for "partnerships between researchers and practitioners" to bring the expertise of research directly into schools and classrooms (National Research Council, 2002, pp. 94–95). In contrast to Design Research, collaboration is to identify the rigorous designing of methods and generating the appropriate data in order to find out what works and thus which reforms should be replicated to attain more effective schools. The sciences of education provide politicians, citizens, and school systems with "hard evidence", "impartiality", and "reasonable, rigorous, and scientific deliberation" (pp. 12–13).

Science has the dual qualities discussed earlier as classifications, distinctions, and calculations to order and plan (design) changing the world that operates to change people. The useful knowledge of science is to change the conditions of the schooling that changes people. And less transparent in the overt declarations about democratic schooling are the inscriptions of the particular calculated democracy to "make people".

DESIGNING THE CHILD AS THE GLOBAL CITIZEN, COSMOPOLITANISM AND PROCESSES OF ABJECTION

The historian Carl Becker in *The Heavenly City of the Eighteenth-Century Philosophers* (1932) wrote about the 18th-century shift in philosophical thought. He argued that 18th-century thinkers moved from knowledge given by God to knowledge residing in nature. The city of man [*sic*] would find progress in the secular world. The shift in location of the subject matter from God to nature, however, did not entail a change in the system of reason about the pre-given rules to order "things." Becker's argument has analogies to cosmopolitanism, pedagogy, and the making of the citizen. From the 18th century to the present, cosmopolitanism functions as a set of sacred values about reason and science in the emancipatory project of progress toward the unified humanity bound by liberty, freedom, and happiness. The principles generated were inscribed as universal in the advancement of civilisation. The universality was never universal but particular. The inclusive dream in planning lifelong learning, the learning society, or the information society in the contemporary school reform is not produced through the same assemblies, connections, and disconnections that ordered American progressive education and its sciences of the child.

Embodied in cosmopolitanism that traverses pedagogical projects is that science is in the service of democracy through planning to change the conditions of people that change people. The enunciations of planning people are continually placed in transcendental categories of humanity and globalised values embodied in the cosmopolitanism of the future citizen. The practical manifestation is that knowledge should be "useful" for change. The rhetorical style of science and its usefulness in the U.S. draws on the rhetorical style of American Jeremiad of Puritan's sermons (Bercovitch, 1978). First evils are decried that will down the walls of the temple and there are optimistic prescriptions of resurrection. The rhetoric form of the Jeremiad today reads as, "Who needs critiques? What is needed are actions to rebuild the walls and confront the challenges of modern societies and schooling." The optimism is to identify what works and to guide and direct the paths to the utopian future.

Ironically, there is little evidence that the search for useful knowledge has been useful in schooling to bring forth its broader social, cultural and political commitments. Just the opposite. The fatalism that I mentioned early is not one of the universal church of medieval times or of the salvation narratives of the Reformation and Counter-Reformation. It is embodied in the systems of reason that naturalise the present, its systems of abjection as inclusion, and reason and science as learning the majesties of the given world. This fatalism evokes the shepherd's plan to provide "useful knowledge" to order and stabilise the coming democracy and the boundaries in which its citizens act.

Let me offer, at least in outline, a different optimism to the citizen in pedagogy than the designing strategies discussed earlier. The optimism is still the Enlightenment's faith in reason if not the dogma of planning explored here. The politics of research is to disrupt the given-ness of the present. Once we agree that inequities exist, express outrage to the sufferings encountered, utter the words that the world is socially constructed and thus changeable, and continue with the to poi that that every child should learn, these agreements defer to the given-ness of difference that mark out divisions as sites of intervention. The denaturalising of cosmopolitanism does not eliminate its commitments to a humane and just world. The strategy is to continually test the limits to the manner in which the objects of reflection and acts are produced to honour those commitments.

Finally, while I focused on the U.S, American Exceptionalism and the citizen in pedagogy, my focus on American school reforms and cosmopolitanism is to give empirical specificity to a more general problem to a globalisation that appears in the long 19th century and not to suggest any exceptionalism to the nation or its schooling. I have to admit that I hesitate to use the word because of its status in the planet speak of today. My interest in globalisation is not that there is such a thing. It is with how this moment of globalisation is different from previous ones. Cosmopolitanism provides a comparative way to consider the global and its particularities.

THOMAS S. POPKEWITZ

NOTES

1   This might sound unusual to those who write about the limitations of Neo-Liberal reforms. While one can disagree with the strategy of curriculum standards and high stake testing, the assumptions about cosmopolitanism are embodied in the principles of pedagogical reforms and research. I empirically examine the cosmopolitanism assumptions and their internments and enclosures in Popkewitz, 2008. At the same time, one can also understand the current politics of the state as in fact a state of exception to that notion of cosmopolitanism.
2   I borrow this phrase from Berger, Berger, & Kelner (1976) who talk about "the homeless mind", My use of "self" is to consider the production of individuality that is different from the institutional theory of Berger, Berger & Kelner.

REFERENCES

American Council on Education. (1999). *To touch the future: Transforming the way teachers are taught: An action agenda for college and university presidents.* Washington, DC: American Council on Education.

Anderson, B. (1991). Imagined communities: *Reflections on the origin and spread of nationalism.* (Revised edition). London: Verso.

Baker, K. (1994). Enlightenment and the institution of society: Notes of a conceptual history. In W. Melching & V. Wyger (Eds.), *Main trends in cultural history* (pp. 95-120). Amsterdam: Rodopi.

Balibar, E., & Wallerstein, I. (1991). *Race, nation, class: Ambiguous identities.* New York: Verso.

Becker, C. (1932). *The heavenly city of the eighteenth-century philosophers.* New Haven: Yale University Press.

Bell, D. A. (2001). *The cult of the nation in France: Inventing nationalism, 1680–1800.* Cambridge, MA: Harvard University Press.

Bercovitch, S. (1978). *The American Jeremiad.* Madison: University of Wisconsin Press.

Berger, P., Berger, B., & Kellner, H. (1974). *The homeless mind: Modernization and consciousness.* New York: Vintage.

Butler, J. (1993). *Bodies that matter: On the discourse limits of "sex".* New York: Routledge.

Cruikshank, B. (1999). *The will to empower: Democratic citizens and the other subjects.* Ithaca, NY: Cornell University.

Darling-Hammond, L. (1998). Teachers and teaching: Testing policy hypotheses from a National Commission Report. *The Educational Researcher, 27*(1), 4–10.

Deleuze, G., & Guattari, F. (1987). *A thousand plateaus. Capitalism and schizophrenia.* (B. Massumi, Trans.). Minneapolis: University of Minnesota Press.

Design-Based Research Collective. (2003). Designed-based research: An emerging paradigm for educational inquiry. *Educational Researcher, 32*(2), 5–8.

Drost, W. H. (1967). *David Snedden and education for social efficiency.* Madison: University of Wisconsin Press.

Hargreaves, A. (2003). *Teaching in the knowledge society: Education in the age of insecurity.* Maindenhead, England: Open University Press.

Kelly, A. (2003). Research as design. *Educational Researcher, 32*(1), 3–4.

Kristeva, J. (1982). *Powers of horror: An essay on abjection* (L. Roudiez, Trans.). New York: Columbia University Press.

Lindblad, S., & Popkewitz, T. S. (Eds.). (2004). *Educational restructuring: International perspectives on traveling policies.* New York: Information Age Publishers.

Maeroff, G. (2003). *A classroom of one: How online learning is changing our schools and colleges*. New York: Palgrave Macmillan.

McMahan, D. (2001). *Enemies of the enlightenment. The French counter: Enlightenment and the making of modernity*. Oxford, UK: Oxford University Press.

Mead, G. H. (1934). *Mind, self & society from the standpoint of a social behaviorist* (edited, with introduction, by Charles W. Morris). Chicago: University of Chicago Press.

Meyer, J. W. (1986). Myths of socialization and of personality. In M. S. Thomas C. Heller, and David E. Wellbery (Ed.). (1987). *Reconstructing individualism: Autonomy, individuality, and the self in western thought*. (pp. 208–221). Stanford, CA: Stanford University Press.

Meyer, J., Boli, J., Thomas, G., & Ramirez, F. (1997). World society and the nation-state. *American Journal of Sociology, 103*(1), 144–181.

National Commission on Teaching & America's Future. (1996). *What matters most: Teaching for America's future*. Washington, DC: National Commission on Teaching and America's Future.

National Commission on Teaching & America's Future. (2003). *No dream denied: A pledge to America's children*. Washington, DC: Author.

National Research Council. (2002). *Scientific research in education*. Washington, DC: Center for Education, Division of Behavioral and Social Sciences and Education, Committee on Scientific Principles for Education Research, National Research Council.

Nussbaum, M. (1996). Patriotism and cosmopolitanism. Martha Nussbaum with respondents. In M. Nussbaum & J. Cohen (Eds.), *For the love of country: Debating the limits of patriotism* (pp. 3–17). Boston, MA: Beacon Press.

Popkewitz, T. (2008). *Cosmopolitanism and the Age of School Reform: Science, Education and Making Society by Making the Child*. New York: Routledge

Popkewitz, T. (1998a). Dewey, Vygotsky, and the social administration of the individual: Constructivist pedagogy as systems of ideas in historical spaces. *American Educational Research Journal, 35*(4), 535–570.

Popkewitz, T. S. (1998b). *Struggling for the soul: The politics of education and the construction of the teacher*. New York: Teachers College Press.

Rancière, J. (2004). *The flesh of words: The politics of writing* (C. Mandell, Trans.). Stanford, CA: Stanford University Press.

Rancière, J. (2004). *The politics of aesthetics*. London, Continuum.

Rancière, J. (2004). Who is the subject of the rights of man? *The South Atlantic Quarterly, 103*(2/3), 298-310.

Shavelson, R., Philips, D. C., Towne, L., & Feuer, M. (2003). On the science of education design studies. *Educational Researcher, 32*(1), 25–28.

Shimakawa, K., (2002). *National abjection: The Asian American body onstage*. Durham, NC: Duke University.

Simon, M., & Masschelein, J. (2006). *The governmentalization of learning and the assemblage of a learning apparatus*. Sweden: Linköping University.

Sklansky, J. (2002). *The soul's economy: Market society and selfhood in American thought, 1820-1920*. Chapel Hill, NC: University of North Carolina Press.

Soysal, Y. N., Bertiloot, T., & Sabine, M. (2005). Projections of identity in French and German history and civics textbooks. In H. Schissler & Y. N. Soyal (Eds.), *The nation, Europe, and the world: Textbooks and curricula in transition* (pp. 13–34). New York: Berghahn Books.

Varela, J. (2000). On the contributions of the genealogical method in the analysis of educational institutions. In T. Popkewitz, B. Franklin & M. Pereyra (Eds.), *Cultural history and education: Critical studies on knowledge and schooling* (pp. 107–124). New York: Routledge.

Ward, L. F. (1883). *Dynamic sociology, or applied social science, as based upon statistical sociology and the less complex sciences*. New York: D. Appleton and Co.

Weber, M. (1904-05/1958). *The Protestant ethic and the spirit of capitalism* (T. Parsons, Trans.). New York: Charles Scribner and Sons.

Wood, G. S. (1991). *The radicalism of the American Revolution*. New York: Vintage Books.

Thomas Popkewitz
University of Wisconsin-Madison

ROBERT SHAW

THE PECULIAR PLACE OF ENLIGHTENMENT IDEALS IN THE GOVERNANCE CONCEPT OF CITIZENSHIP AND DEMOCRACY

INTRODUCTION

This chapter examines a foundational democratic practice by considering how it expresses concepts of the Enlightenment. The practice is that of the vote or plebiscite as it appears in governance. The leading Enlightenment concept is rationality as it is expounded by Kant.

Kant did not participate in national democratic processes. He expected decisions of any consequence to be made in Berlin and thrived when his city was invaded by the Russians and their officers became his students, until they left suddenly in 1762 (Kuehn, 2001, p. 126). Kant participated in political debate where the issues were in the main constitutional and about the processes of government reform. He became known for his theory of natural law and the justification of positive law. He advocated the separation of powers, but denied the right of revolution. This latter conclusion was in apparent contradiction of his support for republicanism, including the French, English, and American revolutions (Beck, 1971, p. 413). The term 'republican' in Kant's writings is sometimes interpreted to mean 'parliamentary democracy'. This is probably a mistake, and Reiss suggests Kant's term does not carry the 'connotation' of modern Western democracy (Reiss's 'Introduction' in Kant, 1991a, p. 25). Kant himself wrote that he wanted to prevent 'the republican constitution from being confused with the democratic one, as commonly happens' (Kant, 1991a, p. 100). So it is that, whilst Kant wrote about the interaction of morality and politics, he did not write on the topic of the present chapter which focuses on those mechanisms or mechanics that democracy displays when it works.

The approach to the topic taken here is:

- To locate citizenship and democracy as embedded concepts, building upon the insights of Foucault. (The contrast is with territorial concepts of citizenship.)
- To identify the activity of governance as being the pervasive practical expression of embedded democracy in the West and to sketch the governance concept of citizenship.
- To identify the vote or plebiscite as a critical human practice of democratic governance and to examine this practice phenomenologically.

M.A. Peters, A. Britton and H. Blee (Eds.), Global Citizenship Education: Philosophy, Theory and Pedagogy, 153–168.

- To draw upon Kant's views about rationality, and related Enlightenment notions, to provide insight into this human practice.

CITIZENSHIP AND DEMOCRACY: EMBODIED PRACTICE

It is hardly a surprise that citizenship is the subject of academic books and state funding. Global politics through the 1990s intensified a political re-ordering that affected ordinary people. The breakdown of the Soviet empire, the tortuous moves towards economic and political integration in Western Europe, and George W Bush's contribution towards global nationalism – all made the individual's relationship to the state an issue. Europe first, and then other places, were caught in the 'incongruity of (their) historical processes' (Resina, 2006, p. 46).

For ordinary people, particularly those caught up in global events, citizenship is associated with their having a secure place to live. Many think of citizenship in terms of state boundaries, administrations, and rights. That territory is foundational of United States citizenship is supported by the Constitution:

> All persons born or naturalized in the United States, and subject to the jurisdiction thereof, are citizens of the United States and of the State wherein they reside. (*Amendment XIV, Constitutional Convention in Philadelphia*, 1781)

Those who drafted the (as yet to be ratified) European Constitution make territory as important as democratic participation. In the list of citizens' rights they begin with the right of the individual to move within a territory and follow that with the right to democratic participation (see Article I-10.2).

Yet, when prospective American citizens learn in their 'catechism' that the most important right of a citizen is the right to vote, they learn a useful truth that does not relate to territorial concepts (Christian Science Monitor, 2006, p. 8; Holder & Holder, 1997, p. 97). The catechism relates an abstract notion to a practical human action, which, as it turns out, needs to be integral to a way of life. The right to vote may be linked in people's minds with territory because of contingent circumstances (the place and its administration) but the right to vote itself is, along with citizenship itself, settled in the concept of democracy, and only contingently associated with territory in particular examples. There are examples where migrants new to a democratic country do not adopt democratic practices (for example, they may not vote in national elections although they are entitled to vote, or they may form alternative power structures to the civil authority). Being credentialed as a citizen does not of itself generate a commitment to the core practices required. Some nations attempt to make the core practice compulsory. For example, Australia – being a nation of migrants – has experimented with compulsory voting and in this they recognise the embodied nature of the core practice.

The Western concept of citizenship is an integral part of the notion of democracy. The notion of democracy entails a notion of citizenship. The overwhelming feature of the basket of concepts around the notion of democracy –

and indeed all political concepts – is that they are hollow and incomplete thoughts unless considered through situated practice. They are always 'embodied' concepts that appear integrally with human beings who collectively seek goals. These concepts constitute themselves within a framework of rules that belong to human beings. The first purpose of the present paper is to set out the correct context for the notion of citizenship when citizenship is constituted in this way.

Above, the word 'context' appears and this requires a caveat. The word 'context' when applied to concepts such as citizenship might suggest an opportunity for conceptual analysis or an immediate practical application of a concept in a set of circumstances. Both these suggestions ask us to narrow our field of vision and to confine 'citizenship' in an aseptic way. Here, a less rationalistic, and more determinedly historical, use and understanding of the word is appropriate. This must be a use that places concepts in a distinctly human trajectory that is part of the facticity of each of us, and is akin to Foucault's notion of 'apparatus' as system:

> ... a thoroughly heterogeneous ensemble consisting of discourses, institutions, architectural forms, regulatory decisions, laws, administrative measures, scientific statements, philosophical, moral and philanthropic propositions .... Such are the elements of an apparatus. The apparatus itself is the system of relations that can be established between these elements. (Foucault, 1980, p. 194)

Human beings find themselves within Foucault's 'apparatus'. Berlin called it a jigsaw puzzle: 'We lie among the disjected fragments of this puzzle' (Berlin, 1999, p. 23). Pertinent to the present chapter is Foucault's decision to call this apparently inert, structural complexity in which we passively rest, 'governmentality' meaning 'governmental rationality' (Gordon, 1991, p. 1). It is the Enlightenment thinkers who will assist us to understand why Foucault emphasises 'rationality'.

Foucault's leading concept is the generic notion of 'the problem of government' and in particular it's new expression in the sixteenth century when the 'shattering of feudalism' led to the establishment of 'great territorial, administrative and colonial states' (Foucault, 1991, pp. 87–88). The present paper confines itself to the Western democratic species of territorial administrations. From the point-of-view of citizenship, Foucault moves us from the serf or subject to territorial citizens, and the present paper discusses a move beyond the 'territorial concept of citizenship'.

Several writers attempt to construct post-national concepts of citizenship that eliminate territory from the idea. They are often mistaken in their first premise, namely, that territory was ever essentially in the idea (recent discussions of relevant concepts may be found in Dobrowolsky & Jenson, 2004; Sassen, 2003).

Some writers highlight one aspect of the citizenship concept without taking a doggedly phenomenological stance. A recent example is a description for Botswana where citizenship is rendered 'as a feature of active, participatory democracy' (Preece & Mosweunyane, 2004, p. 5). Peters has emphasised identity concepts of citizenship and how they can participate in arguments for global citizenship in a post-9/11 world (M. Peters, 2004). The alleged evil of cultural assimilation often lurks within the identity concept of citizenship, and educators can suffer some of the criticism that thereby ensues:

> Western-bound curricula have continually produced graduates who are alienated and disenfranchised from their own people. (Ndura, 2006, p. 95)

Finally with regard to the contrasts to the approach of the present chapter, it might be thought that those who emphasise 'ontology or a statement of what seem to be the most salient features of our world at a particular time' and write that 'perspectives derive from a position in space and time, specifically social and political space and time' would focus on extant practices. However, Hewson and Sinclair list the salient features of global governance theory as being epistemic authority, marketized institutions, and the complex of infrastructural technologies associated with the emerging knowledge economy (Hewson & Sinclair, 1999, p. 17). The Husserlian dictum 'to the things themselves' did not impress these authors.

THE GOVERNANCE CONCEPT OF CITIZENSHIP/DEMOCRACY

If we are to understand citizenship as an embodied practice it is necessary to attend to phenomena that reveal 'citizenship' at work. Learning the new residents' catechism and the study of maps are related to citizenship, but they are hardly vital. Nor is the enjoyment of a wide range of rights – benefits and protections - that accrue to citizens and vary from administration to administration.

In the West's ideological and inherently technological practices there are today two legitimate ways by which individuals assert themselves. These are through financial resources and through the processes of democratic decision-making. Western processes often manifest as a tussle between money and votes – commerce and politics. Citizenship as a practice and a concept appears in the altercation about votes.

The word now used in Western management theory to describe processes with an element of democratic practice is 'governance'. The older colonial notions of an 'appointed governor' or 'superior' fade as democracy endures. The terms 'the governance concept of citizenship' or 'the governance concept of democracy' are appropriate to describe certain ideas that are situated in the apparatus.

To explore this further, it is necessary to narrow the focus of the investigation and examine human practices that intimately entail the concepts. This narrowing is presented below in two steps:
– At the level of the 'apparatus', artefacts are considered.
– At the level of the 'form of life' a core practice is identified from the artefacts and a brief phenomenological account is given of that practice.
Two examples will demonstrate the home of 'citizenship' and the relationships set out above, one drawn from government and one from outside of government. The government example could be any statute anywhere. However, because it

illustrates points that are useful elsewhere in the present book, the example is a statute about citizenship.

Germany's Reichstag enacted the *Nuremberg Laws on Reich Citizenship* on September 15, 1935. Their notice of promulgation – that is now an artefact for our investigation – cited the Law and reads (in translation):

Article 1

1. A subject of the State is a person who enjoys the protection of the German Reich and who in consequence has specific obligations towards it.

2. The status of subject of the State is acquired in accordance with the provisions of the Reich and State Citizenship Law.

Article 2

1. A Reich citizen is a subject of the State who is of German or related blood, who proves by his conduct that he is willing and fit faithfully to serve the German people and Reich.

2. Reich citizenship is acquired by the granting of Reich Citizenship Certificate.

3. The Reich citizen is the sole bearer of full political rights in accordance with the Law.

Article 3

The Reich Minister of the Interior, in coordination with the Deputy of the Führer, will issue the Legal and Administrative orders required to implement and complete this Law. (Arad, Gutman, & Margaliot, 1999, pp. 77)

This statute reveals a practical, human system that depends on, and is constituted by, human needs and facticity. The concepts are a small part within the practical system, and the practical system is a part of Foucault's 'apparatus'.

The foundational structures assumed or established – revealed – by this statute are:
– Constitution of a governance body. There is an already constituted authority present, the Reichstag, that unanimously enacted the statute.
– Context of governance. The governors operate within a context of governance (they hold power and office on the day, they establish laws, are taken seriously, and have an historical presence).
– Management structure. The governance body has at its disposal a management structure or operational executive or civil service. This gives the authority the means to implement its decisions.

- Citizens. Several groups of people are always necessary in a statute, and in this particular statute some are defined. There are those who are subjects of the State. Then, there are the citizens. In this case they are subjects of the State who satisfy further criteria. In all the statutes of a democracy there is the group of citizens who contribute to the establishment of the governors.
- A mechanism to gain inclusion in the group of citizens is specified (Article 1.2; Article 2.2).
- Management made responsible. Those charged with the implementation (executive) acquire duties and responsibilities as a result of the governors' decision. These are the Reich Minister of the Interior and the Deputy of the Führer immediately, and then others as they 'order'. The Minister holds a duty to issue Reich Citizenship Certificate's in accordance with the Law.
- Those with citizenship rights gain benefits (Article 2.3). They are the 'sole bearer' of 'full political rights'. They also gain the 'protection of the German Reich', along with others who are 'subjects of the State' (Article 1.1).

The same complex and extended circumstances that enable government, Foucault's 'apparatus', enable the operation of publicly listed Western companies. Briefly, the package is:
- The constitution of a governance body.
- A context of governance. Imposed provisions such as the law of the country moderate what can be done, and the board makes decisions within this framework and other rules the owners may have established.
- A management structure, to implements the decisions of the board.
- The accumulation of 'citizens' that are now called 'owners', or 'stock holders'.
- A mechanism to gain inclusion in the group (often the purchasing of stocks or the formation of a business).
- A mechanism to make management responsible (an accountability framework). Normally, the chief executive officer and others are directly responsible to the board and there are audit provisions.
- Those with stockholder rights gain benefits that are primarily the right to vote for members of the governance body and to share in the profits. Other rights are possible.

These structures themselves are not greatly contentious within Western countries. Perhaps the greatest challenge to them comes from indigenous people who wish to use traditional decision-making practices as an alternative to democratic processes. They express this in relation to both national governance and the governance of businesses. Examples come from Polynesian people in various Pacific countries (Schmidtke, 2002; Taurima & Cash, 2000).

It is apparent that there is a type of neutrality about the underlying structural framework (or form) just described, and this is consistent with the Foucault–Berlin account of the apparatus as a whole. However, to understand the success of democracy, two features of this governance structure need to be made apparent:
- The structure itself provides opportunities for argument over issues.
- This structure holds within itself an imperative.

When there is an issue to be decided, the structure itself provides opportunities for argument at every node. In the example above, we might say that this particular Reichstag was improperly constituted (with reference to 1 above). It had no legitimate power and should be ignored (2). Civil servants who obeyed the law acted wrongly, indeed some were subsequently convicted (3). The definition of citizens based on race is wrong (4), and so on. The arguments are essentially ethical (in the neutral sense) arguments.

The second step in the argument of this paper regarding the embodied concept of citizenship is to seek from the artefacts the core human engagements that pertain to the apparatus. Where in the governance structures, as displayed in their artefacts, are we to find the pre-eminent and indispensable human practice?

The observation needed to make the second step is very basic – the whole democratic system is about decision-making. Foucault sees this when he says that government is not about 'imposing law on men' but about 'disposing things', which is to 'arrange things in such a way that , through a certain number of means such ends may be achieved' (Foucault, 1991, p. 95).

O'Loughlin assists in this search, which is for the time and place of the birth process for the statutes that assign things:

> Place ... is really about *where there is something meaningful going on.* Its patterns arise not from detailed conscious planning but from the pre-reflective interaction of individuals who usually remain unaware of the totality they have assisted in creating through their embodied actions (O'Loughlin, 2006, p. 86).

The system or apparatus that is itself embodied is the embodiment of a form of human expression that is collective decision-making. Human beings make decisions and one identifiable approach is that of democracy. The human phenomenon most distinctive of this is the vote or plebiscite. It is a phenomenon that is indispensable to democracy in any form. The place of democracy is where two or more of us record our position on a question. This recording is always within a structural framework that is itself the framework of democracy.

There are two situations to consider: the first is the plebiscite to establish the governors, and the second is the decision-making of the governors once they hold office and which is best called 'voting'.

The vital phenomenological insight is that those who participate in plebiscite or vote do so in a mechanical way. The action is to mark a piece of paper, push a button, say 'aye', or raise a hand. The reasons held, or indeed anything mental at all, is irrelevant.

Western democratic governance has one spectacular imperative: to obtain a decision in every case. In this it reveals itself as a technology inherent in the apparatus when the word 'apparatus' is used to include the system of relations that embraces discourses, institutions, and administrations. It is useful here to apply Heidegger's insights regarding the nature of technology (Heidegger, 1977). What is at stake here is not the quality of the decision but the likelihood of there being an outcome. The technology of the vote overcomes this narrow but vital problem of decision because it pre-configures. Any question that is put to the vote is already entrenched in a Foucault–Berlin world. The question gains support from many places, events, commitments, beliefs, compromises, necessities. Each question is on an historical trajectory. The result is two fold:

- It is much more likely that there will be a decision; because the whole structure (the forum) is unlikely to collapse. This does not mean that it cannot collapse of course, but in such situations the question at issue changes to be about democracy itself. The proponents of democracy gather around and slowly democracy re-asserts itself. Fiji demonstrates the practice at the moment as it cycles in and out of democracy.
- The outcome holds a legitimacy that reflects the origin of not just the individual, particular question but of the operative apparatus and the embodiment of the operative apparatus. It may be seen in this that the humble question for decision is beyond the hands of the people who are there to vote on it.

To look at this starkly, each vote a governance body takes is actually the second vote on the matter – the first vote was that which put the governors in place and the second was about the substantive matter. In democratic politics every substantive issue is associated with the possibility of replacing the decision-makers. Less starkly, there is a plethora of decisions already taken that are pertinent to any particular new decision.

Acknowledging a debt to Heidegger (for example, 1977), it is possible to advance two further insights about this:

- What is being described is an expression of current Western metaphysics which means it is essentially technological.
- The technological system (governance including its leading practice of voting) operates with its own imperatives and whilst it involves human beings in a multitude of ways, it has a form of independence from any particular human being. Something of how this occurs has already been mentioned when the entailment of voting was considered. More of it lurks, as shall be developed shortly, behind Kant's belief in a progressive 'universal history' of humankind (Kuehn, 2001, p. 281).

Incidentally, there is congruence between the phenomenological description of democracy and culture. O'Loughlin takes this right through to a position on the notion of territory that is relevant to the debate on what might be foundational about the phenomenon of democracy. She argues, in relation to concepts of culture, that the antithesis of embodiment is territory:

> The culture that shapes and characterises a place is a shared culture – shared by virtue of our shared embodiment, including our technologies. So the view that a culture is some sort of overarching entity, larger and more significant than the individual and superimposed upon a particular defined and bounded 'territory', is inaccurate. (O'Loughlin, 2006, p. 87)

The example of the vote is one instance within the larger framework of culture. What is going on in the spaces where votes are being cast is democracy.

GOVERNANCE AND THE ENLIGHTENMENT

The Enlightenment of the 17th and 18th centuries admits of many interpretations. This chapter particularly draws upon Kant's insights and considers their expression in the practice of voting. Others have also reflected on the relationship between Enlightenment concepts and democracy – and drawn pessimistic conclusions.

In the intensity of the Second World War, people feared for the loss of their known way of life. Some reflected on which ideas would be lost if the Western ideal was destroyed. Horkheimer and Adorno asked why it was that democratic nations had come to this unexpected end. They concluded that the Enlightenment ideals that underpinned democracy held within themselves the seeds of their own destruction (Horkheimer & Adorno, 1973, p. xiii). They feared they would witness the end of social freedom globally and argued that this was the collapse of Enlightenment ideals. The concepts of the Enlightenment beat a retreat when confronted by Herr Hitler.

The concepts were fundamental; foundational to a lived way of life and that was at stake. The Enlightenment expresses the 'actual movement of civil society as a whole in the aspect of its idea as embodied in individuals and institutions', and accordingly it is a parallel situation to the formation of truth in lived lives (Horkheimer & Adorno, 1973, p. xiv). Only in action and in constantly evolving thought is it possible to grasp the Enlightenment's fundamental intellectual forces (Cassirer, 1951, p. ix).

These authors bring to the fore the embodied nature of Enlightenment concepts, but what are Cassirer's 'fundamental intellectual forces' and what are the pertinent concepts themselves? Berlin takes us some distance toward the forces when he sets out three foundational propositions, and says they are no more than broad ideas that gain expression in a host of uneven ways. His first proposition is the belief that all genuine questions can be answered by human beings even if it is not immediately apparent what the answer is to a particular question. This is, he claims, a proposition that is common to Christianity, the scholastics, the Enlightenment and the positivist tradition of the twentieth century (Berlin, 1999, pp. 21–22). Berlin's first proposition entails a belief in the notion of being enlightened, an allegedly positive state of being.

Yet it is not any form of being enlightened that is adequate. Berlin's second proposition says that one becomes enlightened when the answers to questions are achieved through the use of a method or technique that is adequate to the task. This method or technique is dependent on the application of human intellect; in short, on rationality:

> That reason possesses the true right of the first-born, and that it is older than any opinion or prejudice which has obscured it in the course of the centuries. (Cassirer, 1951, p. 234)

It is in this way that the model of Newtonian science becomes important as a model for the human way of being, and in particular for our purposes, as a model for communal decision-making. Kant found inspirational the clear steps of reasoning that show in Newton's works as well as the utility of Newton's conclusions. Here is a way of being to emulate in the moral and political spheres – the enlightened way of being. The contrast is with the religious way of being, the shaman's way of being, and the way of life of the magician who imitates demons. All these people fall victim to a multiplicity of forces. It is not that they set out to live the form of life they adopt, but rather it just accumulates to them (Adorno, 1973; Horkheimer & Adorno, 1973). Today, we can possibly recognise in human practices and attitudes the scientists' way of being and the religious way of being, whilst the enlightened way of being is more obscure.

It was the enlightened way of being that was constructed by Kant first as a goal for education and then as something desirable for governance. This may be seen in his many essays including *Answer to the Question: What is Enlightenment* and *On the Old Saw: 'That May Be Right in Theory but it Won't Work in Practice'* (Kant, 1974; Kant, 1997).

What is distinctive about the 'enlightened way of being' as it embraces several disciplines of enquiry? It is the relationship between universals and particulars, which alters when one adheres to the idea of starting with observation. Cassirer calls it the 'critical idea by which Newton effected this revolution' (Cassirer, 1981, p. 67). Galileo and Newton do not begin, as Cassirer says, with the general concept of 'gravity' and then proceed to explain 'weight'. They work the other way round – from the observations.

Democracy in anything like the modern governance sense was not well understood by Kant. What he lacked was a perspective on how the processes might operate. He did not have available the observations to which he could attend. Accordingly, his approach to the subject is in terms of abstract concepts. Democracy is an example of despotism (the contrast being with republicanism, where the laws are made and executed by different powers). There are two problems with democracy. The first being that:

> ... one and the same person cannot at the same time be both the legislator and the executor of his own will, just as the general proposition in logical reasoning cannot at the same time be a secondary proposition subsuming the particular with the general. (Kant, 1991b, p. 101)

The second reason is that the alternative despotic forms leave greater opportunity for the 'spirit' of this separation that he alludes to in the first reason. Evidently, in this spirit Frederick II said he was merely the 'highest servant of the state' (Kant, 1991b, p. 101). It may be seen from this that Kant argues about political process by analogy with logic. His intellectual approach to how a complex apparatus might desirably work is limited. Kant does not start, as Newton might recommend, with observations, because there is no adequate practice available for him to observe.

As suggested above, Kant begins and ends with theory. One essay (*What is Orientation in Thinking?*) shows how the theoretical use of reason necessarily leads on to the practical use of reason – but this is still within the pages of the book (Kant, 1991a, p. 237). We cannot expect from Kant a phenomenological

162

investigation of democracy and must consider his deliberations with that limitation in mind.

The background to Kant's paper on the desirable state of enlightenment is well known (Kuehn, 2001, pp. 209–291; Schmidt, 1989). Education's purpose is to take the masses out of tutelage, and this only occurs with the 'freedom to make public use of one's reason at every point' (Kant, 1997, p. 84). Thus, education and politics are bound together.

It might be thought that this is about individual autonomy, particularly as his examples come from public policy (a person's response to the tax collector is one), but it would be a mistake to associate Kant with the modern notion of autonomy that apparently makes the individual paramount (for example, *Ethics and Education* (R. S. Peters, 1970) does this). Peters' discussion of freedom effectively begins with the individual being 'on the path to autonomy' (p. 192). It is only then that the issues of freedom arise, and inevitably they develop locked to the individual.

Kant writes about individual autonomy (make your own decision, do so rationally, and have the strength of will to bring your decision into practice) but that is a small part of a larger conception. Kant's 'realm of ends' (1997, p. 50) has a role in individual autonomy (a connection), but more important, it is contributory to something greater than any individual (the whole of all ends):

> ... we can think of a whole of all ends in systematic connection, a whole of rational beings as ends in themselves as well as a whole of particular purposes which each may set for himself. (1997, p. 50)

The bedrock for Kant's notion of rationality is to be understood in relation to the species (the 'large scale'), not the individual. His hope is, as one interpreter says:

> It is also a peculiarity of reason that it cannot be completely realised in the lifetime of an individual, but only in the entire species. (Reiss, 1991, p. 36)

In this perspective on rationality, democracy holds a parallel with Newtonian science. Science does not depend on the contribution of any individual scientist. Rather it is a progressive, communal activity. It is this to which Kant draws our attention when he says of possible methods and technical expressions, that science

> ... first makes the novice familiar with names the significance and use of which he will only learn in the future. (Kant, 1998, p. 627)

Individual persons must enter the method before they can participate as scientists. The errors and the inadequacies of any particular scientist are rectified by others. Most important, however, is that there is a structural foundation that maintains itself though the actions of the individual persons. Kant calls this the 'art of systems' or 'architectonic':

> Under the government of reason our cognitions cannot at all constitute a rhapsody but must constitute a system, in which alone they can support and advance its essential ends (Kant, 1998, p. 691).

The congruency of scientific practice with its 'system' is comparable to the congruency of core democratic practices (most arguably voting) with the political system that we call democracy.

For Kant, the exercise of reason is situated within his 'teleological view of Nature' (Kuehn, 2001, p. 288). Kant's conclusions appear consistent with embodiment conceptions of both rationality and governance, although some commentators today may wish to dissociate themselves from Kant's ideas regarding the inevitability of progress in the history of humanity and the role of God.

> Kant's view that man's essence must be realized follows an argument later developed in the *Critique of Judgement* where Kant had maintained that the teleology of nature is internal, not external. (Reiss, 1991, p. 36)

> ... we must not overlook teleology, which indicates the foresight of a wise agency governing nature. (Kant, 1991b, p. 109).

However, if we set aside Kant's religious perspective, and focus on the notion that there is an integrated, cohesive, holistic movement at work within human affairs, then Kant's insight becomes similar to the embodied notion of governmentality:

> Culture was not the result of individual effort, but was produced by mankind as a whole. Man as a rational being therefore needs to live in a historical process. History is a progress towards rationality, but it must not be thought that this process involves a continuous advance in rationality all the time. (Reiss, 1991, p. 36)

> History is concerned with giving an account of these phenomena, no matter how deeply concealed their causes may be, and it allows us to hope that, if it examines the free exercise of the human will *on a large scale*, it will be able to discover a regular progression among freely willed actions (Kant, 1991b, p. 41)

It is helpful to relate Kant to the views of O'Loughlin who considers in her chapter on embodied citizenship the idea that rationality derives from our animal natures and provides a means to participate fruitfully in democracy:

> With regard to citizenship in a democracy, the model of rational deliberation has furnished a means by which citizens may be said to nurture and exercise capacities of reasoning and discussion which otherwise may remain undeveloped. The assumption here is that in the rational community one orients oneself towards the common will, such that the outcome of exhaustive deliberations will eventually generate broad principles applying to all. (O'Loughlin, 2006, p. 151)

Rationality is precisely that which builds upon and utilizes our basic animal natures, not something transcending the body and demanding its relegation as a lowly vehicle or instrument. (O'Loughlin, 2006, pp. 169–170)

This can suggest that rationality derives from our individually-held basic animal characteristics and it is from this capacity that the success of democracy derives as per the 'assumption' she identifies. It is through our application of rationality that we 'orient' ourselves to the rational community. Our rationality within ourselves then (probably by a levelling process) ensures the decisions of democratic outcomes are rational. Kant would not support O'Loughlin.

How might Kant's views about rationality relate to the phenomenon of voting as the phenomenological core of democracy? The conclusions are:

- The structures of society; Foucault's 'apparatus', emerges. Kant would say they do so as an expression of humankind's progress as delivered by God. Be that as it may, for human beings there are always 'the structures of society' and it is our experience that they alter historically.
- There will emerge architectonics, systems that are in their unity the form of a whole. Paradigmatic examples are from the modern sciences and mathematics.
- Each architectonic is held together by a 'single supreme and inner end' that makes possible the whole structure. In the present example – democracy – ask what this might be and notice the scope for debate.
- Rationality expresses itself through these structures or forms. This is Kant's foundational position regarding rationality. It is this that makes him conclude that rationality is a species phenomenon.
- It is an argument of the present chapter that the physical event of voting is the essential practice of democracy, and it is to this event that we must attend if we are to develop a phenomenological account of democracy.
- Accordingly, citizenship is not the leading concept in democracy. It relates to some particular examples of democracy in practice.
- When individual persons cast a vote (for the governors, or as a governor), they do so in a manner that is entirely mechanical. This is the phenomenological truth of the vote.
- Kant will urge individuals who vote to do so in an autonomous way. He would say that they should use the categorical imperative to determine their vote. Even without that universal principle of morality, the form of individual autonomy is highly desirable. That is, the decision maker should make up their own mind (integrity, to some), they should do so rationally, and they should have the strength of will or determination needed to vote as they so decide. Incidentally, this particular conception of moral decision-making was advocated as a base for moral education in British schools with the leading principle to be 'concern for other persons' (Wilson *et al*, 1967).
- Kant would not expect governors to consistently vote autonomously. How individuals act is far from ideal.
- Kant's belief in purpose and teleology (and probably the goodness of God) would enable him to be positive about the governance concept of democracy.

- Without the belief in teleology, it appears that the system of democracy is left without overarching guidance, and people appeal to the notion that collective decisions are more insightful than the decisions of individuals. O'Loughlin identifies this as an 'assumption'.
- It is uncertain that democratic systems hold within themselves the ability to adjust when decisions are not optimal. Certainly, the correction of 'mistakes' is not an imperative. The contrast is with the system of modern science although it is important to acknowledge that there are debates around the rationality of science and its directions particularly with regard to the role of economics in knowledge creation. Kant's view of science was based on the work of scientists around Newton's time.
- Kant's teleology would for him explain the observation of voting as a system that is constructed and functions to generate outcomes – outcomes being decisions. This alone is the imperative of democracy. The quality of the decisions is less important than their being decisions.

It is argued in the present chapter, that the most peculiar aspect of democracy is that it does not ever depend at its most critical moment – when the vote is taken – on rationality in any sense that refers to individuals. As a structure or form of decision-making, democracy holds within itself its own imperative. The imperative is that there shall be a decision in every case. Each decision shall be within a complex of other decisions, and the complex of other decisions shall be within a frame of governmentality. Governmentality is always within a totally organic, embodied structure where concepts of all kinds play various optional roles.

Finally, the technological nature of such phenomena as the vote was described by Heidegger, whose examples, of mechanised agriculture and the modern commercial aviation industry, may disturb us. More disturbing however, could be our appreciation that democracies are not under human control and that their core decision-making is not rational.

REFERENCES

Adorno, T.W. (1973). *The jargon of authenticity*. Evanston, IL: Northwestern University Press.

Arad, Y., Gutman, I., & Margaliot, A. (1999). *Documents on the Holocaust: Selected sources on the destruction of the Jews of Germany and Austria, Poland, and the Soviet Union*. (L.B. Dor, Trans.). Lincoln: University of Nebraska Press.

Beck, L.W. (1971). Kant and the right of revolution. *Journal of the History of Ideas, 32*(3), 411–422.

Berlin, I. (1999). *The roots of romanticism*. Princeton, NJ: Princeton University Press.

Cassirer, E. (1951). *The philosophy of the Enlightenment* (F.C.A. Koelln & J.P. Pettegrove, Trans.). Princeton, NJ: Princeton University Press.

Cassirer, E. (1981). *Kant's life and thought* (J. Haden, Trans.). New Haven: Yale University Press.

Christian Science Monitor (2006. 22 November). United States citizenship: Not a trivial question. *Christian Science Monitor*, p. 8.

Constitutional Convention in Philadelphia (1781). *Constitution of the United States of America*.

Dobrowolsky, A.Z., & Jenson, J. (2004). Shifting representations of citizenship: Canadian politics of 'women' and 'children'. *Social Politics: International Studies in Gender, State and Society, 11*(2), 154–180.

Foucault, M. (1980). *Power/knowledge: Selected interviews and other writings, 1972–1977* (C. Gordon, Trans.). New York: Pantheon Books.

Foucault, M. (1991). Governmentality. In G. Burchell, C. Gordon & P. Miller (Eds.), *The Foucault effect: Studies in governmentality: With two lectures by and an interview with Michel Foucault* (pp. 87–104). Chicago: University of Chicago Press.

Gordon, C. (1991). Governmental rationality: An introduction. In G. Burchell, C. Gordon & P. Miller (Eds.), *The Foucault effect: Studies in governmentality: With two lectures by and an interview with Michel Foucault* (pp. 1–52). Chicago: University of Chicago Press.

Heidegger, M. (1977). *The question concerning technology, and other essays* (W. Lovitt, Trans.). New York: Harper & Row.

Hewson, M., & Sinclair, T.J. (1999). *Approaches to global governance theory.* Albany, NY: State University of New York Press.

Holder, A.R., & Holder, J.T.R. (1997). *The meaning of the constitution.* Hauppauge, NY: Barron's Educational Series.

Horkheimer, M., & Adorno, T.W. (1973). *Dialectic of enlightenment* (J. Cumming, Trans.). London: Allen Lane.

Kant, I. (1974). *On the old saw: That may be right in theory but it won't work in practice.* Philadelphia: University of Pennsylvania Press.

Kant, I. (1991a). *Kant: Political writings* (H.B. Nisbet, Trans.). Cambridge: Cambridge University Press.

Kant, I. (1991b). Perpetual peace: A philosophical sketch (H.B. Nisbet, Trans.). In H.S. Reiss (Ed.), *Kant: Political writings* (2nd, enl. ed., pp. 93–130). Cambridge: Cambridge University Press.

Kant, I. (1997). *Foundations of the metaphysics of morals, and what is enlightenment?* (L.W. Beck, Trans.). Upper Saddle River, New Jersey: Prentice-Hall.

Kant, I. (1998). *Critique of pure reason* (P. Guyer & A.W. Wood, Trans.). Cambridge: Cambridge University Press.

Kuehn, M. (2001). *Kant: A biography.* Cambridge: Cambridge University Press.

Ndura, E. (2006). Western education and African cultural identity in the Great Lakes Region of Africa: A case of failed globalization. *Peace & Change, 31*(1), 90–101.

O'Loughlin, M. (2006). *Embodiment and education: Exploring creatural existence.* Dordrecht: Springer.

Peters, M. (2004). *Education, globalization, and the state in the age of terrorism.* Boulder: Paradigm Publishers.

Peters, R.S. (1970). *Ethics and education.* London: Allen and Unwin.

Preece, J., & Mosweunyane, D. (2004). *Perceptions of citizenship responsibility amongst Botswana youth.* Gaborone, Botswana: Lightbooks.

Reiss, H.S. (Ed.) (1991). *Kant: Political writings* (2nd, enl. ed.). Cambridge: Cambridge University Press.

Resina, J. R. (2006). The scale of the nation in a shrinking world. *Diacritics, 33*(3), 46–74.

Sassen, S. (2003). The repositioning of citizenship: Emergent subjects and spaces for politics. *CR: The New Centennial Review, 3*(2), 41–66.

Schmidt, J. (1989). The question of enlightenment: Kant, Mendelssohn, and the Mittwochsgesellschaft. *Journal of the History of Ideas, 50*(2), 269–291.

Schmidtke, D. R. (2002). *Maori business organisations: Management and ownership structures for Maori land assets.* Unpublished Research Paper: LLM, Victoria University of Wellington, Wellington.

Taurima, W., & Cash, M. (2000). *The experience of a Whanau group at Te Waananga-O-Aotearoa (a bicultural research project).* Lower Hutt, New Zealand: Open Polytechnic of New Zealand.

Wilson, J., Williams, N., & Sugarman, B. (1967). *Introduction to moral education*. Harmondsworth: Penguin.

Robert Shaw
The Open Polytechnic of New Zealand

MARIANNA PAPASTEPHANOU

COSMOPOLITANISM

With or Without Patriotism?

INTRODUCTION

As a subject of theoretical debate and a subject of teaching, citizenship presupposes a constellation of political concepts and conceptions that require philosophical clarification and renegotiation. Citizenship may concern the approximation of an ideal political situation through reflective membership in various specifications and in common humanity. From this, the normative reach of the term can be extended to the ideal person/member of many collectivities up to the human community as a whole. Thus, it can direct political education towards the cultivation of virtues that enhance multiple identities and that contribute to efforts toward the best possible political situation[1] worldwide. If citizenship touches upon identities and self-images in their political significance for the whole world, then the *cosmopolitan*, the *patriotic* and the *globalised* self must first be approached with regard to their conceptual content and their similarities and differences. To substantiate the 'why' of a corresponding political education, one has to establish the benign character of what is supposed to be educationally cultivated and this further means that one should consider the nuances that separate the ideals to which one aspires from their debased and undesirable counterparts.

This need for conceptual work becomes all the more pressing now that the political exploitation, the facile use and the confounding fashionable ubiquity of terms such as patriotism, cosmopolitanism and globalisation make their meaning and their relation extremely familiar but at the same time extremely unclear to students and teachers alike. For example: should we teach cosmopolitanism? If yes, does this imply that the cultivation of patriotism should be more limited or is perhaps ill-fitting in a cosmopolitan curriculum? Another 'yes' here would rely on the assumption that patriotism and cosmopolitanism are either antagonistic or even mutually exclusive ideals. A 'no' answer, one that makes patriotic teaching either necessary or, at least, permissible in a cosmopolitan curriculum, demands some explanation of the implicit assumption that cosmopolitanism and patriotism are compatible or even complementary. Both possibilities enjoy wide support in recent political and philosophical sources but the ultimate and deepest response to them depends on what the meaning of the juxtaposed terms might allow or preclude.

Efforts to debate these terms within the philosophy of education discipline have surely contributed, amongst other things, to greater clarification, but what is still

M.A. Peters, A. Britton and H. Blee (Eds.), Global Citizenship Education: Philosophy, Theory and Pedagogy, 169–185.

missing is the attempt to discuss the terms together and comprehensively in their definitional ground rather than separately and with regard to some of their nodal points. True, the importance of debating whether we must teach patriotism with or without obligations (White, 2001) and whether liberal patriotism is sensitive to cosmopolitan concerns (Callan, 1999) and the discussion of the tension between cosmopolitan universal rights and cosmopolitan respect for particularity (Todd, 2007) cannot be overestimated. However, debating our understanding of cosmopolitanism and patriotism ought logically to take place prior to exploring their relationship. In simpler terms, before quantifying the amount of patriotism and cosmopolitanism 'permitted' in teaching, we must ask: what is patriotism? What is cosmopolitanism?

Because this Chapter argues primarily for the need to redefine and reconceptualise these terms, the argument will focus on (a) the relationship of patriotism and cosmopolitanism as it has evolved and currently stands, and on (b) educational/philosophical positions regarding that relationship. For the aim is to substantiate the need to revisit the terms involved in citizenship education and to reconsider their relationship by showing how this is dependent on conceptions of the relevant terms.

THE RELATION OF PATRIOTISM AND COSMOPOLITANISM

To show why it is necessary to turn to definitions, the Chapter will first discuss how the relationship of the terms depends on our understanding of them and why, therefore, it cannot precede our effort to reconstruct their content. For instance, if one takes patriotism to be a form of chauvinism or takes cosmopolitanism to entail hostility to all particular attachments, the relationship of the two becomes one of incompatibility (Kleingeld, 2000, p. 317). The more the particular communal element is emphasised in patriotism and the generalisable in cosmopolitanism, the more the binary opposition 'cosmopolitanism versus patriotism' becomes consolidated. Many theorists take it for granted that the local and the global are irreconcilable and perhaps incommensurable dimensions of being, so that the development of strong patriotic feelings entails the lack of care for remote cultures. Likewise, the commitment to ideals of global solidarity and reconciliation appears to some as a cold and unattractive expression of lack of interest for one's specific community.[2]

The binary of 'nationalism versus unreflective universalism' has also accompanied polemics all along, manifesting the flip side, the border that not only separates each ideal from its own fall but also brings it in a dangerous proximity to it. For some adherents to cosmopolitanism, patriotism 'encourages unbridled and virulent chauvinism' and is held 'responsible for many of the most ghastly disasters in human history'. In the less appalling cases, 'patriotism usually appeals to the tradition and heritage of one or some dominant cultural groups, marginalizing and excluding minority groups belonging to the same nation' (Yonah, 1999, p. 379). For proponents of patriotism, cosmopolitanism reflects the imperialist, idealist and rationalist prejudices of an elitist group of intellectuals (Lu,

2000). In turn, some invert the charge of elitism so as to apply to communitarian detractors of cosmopolitanism (Lacroix, 2002, p. 949).

There is no compelling argument for accepting such a bipolar reasoning. Since the latter is often imposed by the narrowness of what counts as cosmopolitan or patriotic, it is imperative that philosophy covers much ground on the definitional and conceptual plane, prior to debating the theories that are constructed around current 'functional' conceptions. Already in the 18th and 19th centuries, when the polarisation was being solidified (Dewey, 1916/1993, p. 116), several philosophers, for example Condorcet, Rousseau, Kant, even Herder, understood cosmopolitanism and patriotism as compatible and complementary ideals. Of course, this fact speaks only for the theoretical possibility of constructing mediating and reconciling accounts and proves that there have been unexploited undercurrents going counter to the mainstream modern tendency; it does not establish that those accounts were convincing as such.

But what is important here is that the 'either/or' logic was not thought of as binding even then. And it shows how selective contemporary thinkers are when they treat Kant as the modern initiator of cosmopolitanism, while overlooking the many arguments he offers for theorising patriotic duty (Kleingeld, 2000). They are equally selective when they consider Rousseau exclusively a precursor of modern nation-state patriotism and overlook his cosmopolitan ideal of a common human nature. Dewey had set the record straight on this by identifying Rousseau as an emblematic figure of the 18th century individualist cosmopolitanism in education while acknowledging the strain in Rousseau that tended towards patriotism (Dewey, 1916/1993, pp. 114–116).

Let us now turn to the current tendency in most trends to impose this 'either/or' logic. It can be traced back to the separation of the social from the political in the modern imagination. As Gerard Delanty explains, one of the implications of such separation was the equation of cosmopolitanism with the political in opposition to the social. 'Cosmopolitanism thus reflected the revolt of the individual against the social world, for to be a "citizen of the world" was to reject the immediately given and closed world of particularistic attachments. Not surprisingly it became associated with the revolt of the elites against the low culture of the masses' (2006, p. 26). It is worth noting that cosmopolitanism in antiquity emerged from completely different considerations.[3]

Be that as it may, the public sphere usually took a different course from that of its mobile elites, and education serves as an example here. In becoming democratised, open to the masses, and increasingly dependent on state funding, education let the ideal of the citizen of the state surpass the ideal of the citizen of the world. In Dewey's words, 'education became a civic function and the civic function was identified with the realization of the ideal of the national state. The "state" was substituted for humanity; cosmopolitanism gave way to nationalism. To form the citizen, not the "man", became the aim of education' (1916/1993, p. 116). Yet the feeling that 'the social world as territorially given, closed and bounded by the nation-state and the class structure of the individual societies did not sit comfortably with the openness of the cosmopolitan idea, with its universalistic orientation' (Delanty, 2006, p. 26) was equally strong in the societies of the times. The current unresolved tension of theories of cosmopolitanism and patriotism (or the tension between the particular and the universal that some theorists locate within cosmopolitanism) may be regarded as a spectral presence of such 18th and 19th century false dichotomies.

Polemics contributed a great deal to entrenching the idea that cosmopolitanism as routes and patriotism as roots are opposing and conflicting. As is well-known,[4] many conservative thinkers saw in rootlessness an expedient detachment from patriotic duty and an opportunity for parasitic exploitation of various local resources without giving anything in return. To them, cosmopolitanism became a synonym of that rootlessness and had to be rejected wholesale for the sake of a wholehearted immersion in one's own culture and subservience to one's own country. Their progressive opponents often detected anti-Semitic motives in such a defence of patriotism, while emphasising the irenic significance of rootlessness against the role that patriotic passion played in exploiting the masses for nationalist purposes. Both parties, however, were so absorbed in the debate that they lost all sight of possibilities that cosmopolitanism and patriotism thus defined might even be tacit accomplices in global power relations. As a result, there were few serious attempts to redefine both terms and even the richness of older conceptualisations such as the Stoic or the Kantian was largely bypassed.

But the tendency to impose this 'either/or' logic can also be explained as a product of a particular socio-historical, faulty understanding of mobility as by definition other-oriented and other-sensitive. The centrifugal element of a decision to migrate, trade, travel and encounter foreign lifestyles and cultures was exaggerated in the 20th century to the point of expressing, ostensibly, a moral or emotive commitment to remote alternatives. It was thus identified with progressivism and contrasted with the supposedly inescapable parochialism of a rooted existence.

However, the hasty identification of cosmopolitanism and rootlessness (in their currently held conceptions) with progressivism may be easily subverted when we realise that mobility may assist the promotion of ethnocentric and imperialist concerns thus making common cause with an unacknowledged and ill-defined patriotism. When cosmopolitanism signifies merely constant exposure to various cultures and, by way of it, enrichment of existential choice, there is no guarantee that the cosmopolitan agent is less nationalist, exploitative or manipulative of otherness than any other agent who is immersed in her own communitarian ethos. In simpler terms, one may eat foreign food, listen to foreign music, abide by the law and travel or live abroad, without being truly cosmopolitan in the way s/he treats others or views cultural difference.[5] But even when cosmopolitanism is understood in governmental, institutional and legal terms, or relies on a narrow liberal sense of morality and duty, it still does not make enough room for perceiving and combating the myriad subtle oppressions of otherness that cannot be canalised in such moral and legal discourse (Papastephanou, 2002).

Ironically, cosmopolitanism can be shown to suffer precisely from the problems that it attributes to patriotism, that is, from expansionism and totalitarianism. It has appeared historically that the 'tourist', voyeuristic conception of cosmopolitanism has been an easy operation for the powerful, those who had opportunities for movement (and the positive self-image it created) and the theoretical freedom to combine it with all their other economic and political objectives. Some of those objectives were clearly imperialist and predatory (Harris, 2004)[6] and thereby at odds with a more complex and demanding conception of cosmopolitanism. Often, instead of having commitments to all people, the nomad cosmopolitan seemed commitments and obligations to no-one. In that case, Cicero's *ubi bene ibi patria* was taken to mean: where my profit lies, that land I will make my homeland, I will seize, exploit and shape it (e.g. by moulding the self-image (Fanon, 1967) of those I render subaltern) at will so as to make it a true, hospitable *patria* for me. Equally, whether his own country of origin would have been better (politically and ethically, through more egalitarian treatment of the other within and out), had he had a less outward and expansionist stance, this was of no importance to him. We must not forget that some of the most mobile people in the past were the slave traders: can one describe them as cosmopolitans on the grounds of their rootlessness without feeling that the term is dismally violated?

Rousseau overturned Cicero's dictum for other purposes,[7] but this reversal is very appropriate here for showing how easily cosmopolitanism and patriotism can make common cause in exploitation. Even in postcolonial times, Rousseau's (Yonah, 1999; Korsgaard, 2006) *ubi patria ibi bene* ['wherever (my) homeland, there is (my) well-being'] has been taken by the occidental footloose elites seriously enough to turn the whole world into a *patria* for them. No land is foreign to their economic activities, their employment potentials and their residence rights. No country is inhospitable to their ways of entertaining themselves in leisure time, that is, too different for their tastes. However, this does not always entail appreciation or even awareness of such privileges that derive from, and perpetuate, asymmetrical relations between economies and cultures (Bauman, 1998). Worse, managerial and other 'rootless' classes often appear so interest-driven and power-oriented that only the words 'sheer exploitation' and 'callousness regarding the effects of their actions on the environment and cultures' can describe their conduct. Thus, their 'patriotism' may not exactly signify a conscious commitment to their original community and its symbolic *forms* (e.g. their flag) but reflects their wholehearted immersion in the symbolic *content* (e.g. 'values' related to profit) of their own community as well as their substantive contribution to its *global material* reproduction.

Patriotism and cosmopolitanism may collaborate in a subterranean way to maintain and expand the stronghold of Western countries over the world. Their *prima facie* opposition and incompatibility collapse in cases where an arrogant and superior self-understanding of Occidental forces finds in the prospect of global mobility and action coordination a major outlet for its interests. If these ideals can display compatibility with regard to homogenising tendencies, it is crucial to examine whether they could also display compatibility with regard to more other-oriented and other-sensitive goals. Fanon's texts, not accidentally neglected by most contemporary liberalist cosmopolitan discourse, are monumental in paving the path to a modernist positive coupling of patriotism and cosmopolitanism. Resistance to colonial power and national insurrection should not turn the colonised into people of the past. Nationalist struggle is simultaneously a struggle for a future of cosmopolitan true justice. It is the author's view that to activate this possibility what is needed is a redefinition of both terms and a coupling of them with a comprehensive[8] theory of justice.

The 'either/or' tendency has been so strong that even some of the most elaborate efforts somehow to redefine cosmopolitanism and patriotism, for example, Martha Nussbaum's and Charles Taylor's respectively, focus on either one of the terms and give it priority over the other (Cohen & Nussbaum, 1996). In this way, the ideal they select appears purified of any negative implications or perhaps secret complicities. Hence the binary opposition is preserved while the option of reformulating both poles *in one theoretical framework* goes totally unnoticed. Worse, much confusion arises and affects not only philosophy but also political science and party politics and, by implication, philosophy of education. At least some of the inconsistencies and oscillations of the Left and the Right in their positive or negative reactions to globalisation and their ideological prior attachment to cosmopolitanism or patriotism attest to this lack[9] of sufficient theorisation and clarification of the concepts in question.

However, there have been efforts recently to mediate between the two camps producing very interesting syntheses such as various Kantian defences of the compatibility of cosmopolitanism and patriotism,[10] rooted cosmopolitanism (Ackerman, 1994; Appiah, 1996), embedded cosmopolitanism (Erskine, 2002) and Bellamy and Castiglione's (2004) cosmopolitan communitarianism.[11] Beyond the liberalist framework and within postcolonial theory, there have already been excellent endeavours, such as Neil Lazarus's (2002) and Benita Parry's (2003), to couple a revisited patriotism (termed nationalitarianism) with forms of cosmopolitanism or internationalism. Yet, even those attempts, especially the liberalist, require more thorough redefinitions and reconstructions. For it is not that any fresh redefinition would do, just by breaking the automatism of established meanings in an Arendtian (1989) sense of natality. Reconceptualisations need not only be new in the sense of being disruptive and unexpected but also well-researched, well-judged and well-argued.[12]

EDUCATIONAL PHILOSOPHICAL PREFERENCES

To substantiate why it is useful to turn to definitions and conceptions, three educational philosophical positions on the relationship between cosmopolitan and patriotic concerns are discussed here. It is the author's view that even some very sensitive and thoughtful (although diverging) accounts of that relationship could still benefit from 'first step' reconsiderations, as they might be termed, of established and well-worn meanings that, in some ways, lead their approaches astray. John White regards cosmopolitanism and patriotism as compatible, Eamonn Callan defends the view that liberal patriotism can cover the normative ground of cosmopolitanism without the latter's supposedly utopian ideological baggage, and

Sharon Todd focuses on the ostensibly internal contradictions of a cosmopolitanism that shifts away from patriotism.

White claims in this specific text[13] that patriotism and cosmopolitanism are compatible, but he does not define them or describe their relation in any detail. 'The proper virtue of patriotism can help to bind a liberal democracy together in pursuit of its ideals. It is not an alternative to cosmopolitanism' (White, 2001, p. 146). Are all possible ideals of a liberal democracy conducive to cosmopolitanism, or, at least, not alternative to it? And to what cosmopolitanism? One that simply promotes a cultural–pragmatic relativisation of one's roots? A cosmopolitanism of legality and global order? If yes, is it the cosmopolitanism of an inconsistent 'paper tiger', like the United Nations (Habermas, 2003, p. 39), or that of superpowers praying to God before unleashing a war in the name of political liberalism? Even if the vice of chauvinism is staved off by following the 'middle path' (White, 2001, p. 146) of compatible attachments to human beings down to ever narrowing circles (homeland, friends, family), are all anti-cosmopolitan tendencies attributable to chauvinism, so that its liberal containment would suffice in combating those tendencies? One may have no superior national feelings regarding others at all; perhaps no strong attachment (faulty or not) to a *patria* either. S/he may simply, however, view several others as sources of profit. Would s/he act in a cosmopolitan way in that case? Empirical synchronic and diachronic reality falsifies this hope.

Now, is it possible to provide a definition and, further, a conception of cosmopolitanism and patriotism that would be minimal enough so as to be a definition or a conception, but also comprehensive and specific enough to keep some distance from the undesirable duplicities (chauvinism as well as deeper and more materially motivated vices) of the terms? If it is not possible, it has to be explained why and in various ways, that is, either as a purely futile task, or a superfluous and unnecessary demand, or a Derridean aporetic, a necessary yet impossible effort. If it is possible and worth pursuing, as the author believes, then it should at least be hinted at. White's defence of patriotism would benefit from a discussion about the descriptive ground on which standard definitions of cosmopolitanism and patriotism are based and the limits such ground sets on the normative reach of these ideals.

White's implicit definition of patriotism is more comprehensive than alternative approaches. But this merit can stand out only through conceptual focus. For instance, White's patriotism can be shown to be more apposite than that of Charles Taylor. In his discussion of Nussbaum, Taylor (1996) describes patriotism as citizens' commitment to the common weal, as opposed to private interest, and renders patriotism the cement of society in structural–functionalist terms. His is an inward-looking patriotism, oblivious to the kind of patriotism that synchronically and diachronically has signified commitment to defending the freedom of a land, a people or a community against external aggression and expansionism. The most one gets from Taylor's theory in the latter direction is the cultural ecology of communitarianism that aims to prolong the viability of a culture and to protect its communal ethos against losses due to the competitive liberal marketplace of ideas. Unlike Taylor, White treats more thoroughly the concept of patriotism by stating

175

clearly (although not in such terms) its 'internal and external' content. As he writes, 'sometimes, as when Britain was under attack in 1940, [patriotism] is a matter of doing what one can to protect one's national group from attack'. We could take this as an example of outward-looking, or 'external', patriotism and add anti-colonial struggles of various peoples or the Iraqi resistance to the Western invasion as further examples of such patriotism. But he acknowledges the significance of another aspect of patriotism, the one termed above 'inward-looking' and traced in Taylor's text too. 'Sometimes patriotism can also take the form of shame or disgust that such discrepancies of wealth and life-chances can co-exist in the same national community; and of political action to rectify these' (White, 2001, p. 144). This is not necessarily a sign of unease on White's part regarding the elasticity of the term. The author believes that White would include both aspects equally in his conception of patriotism and he would have no objection to adding another variety, the one that combines the two aspects in feeling shame and regret when your homeland fails to treat ethically not only the other within but also the distant other, outside its borders, or the other as the totality of non-human biota. But this is precisely the point: that what is included in patriotism, what patriotism is and what it is not, and why, has to be spelled out and theorised along with an examination of how aspects of patriotism might relate.

White's account would also benefit from the definitional and reconstructive work that is necessary for sharpening the defence of patriotism that he rightly promotes and the coupling of it with the right kind of cosmopolitanism. White remarks that globalisation is not necessarily at odds with nationality and in doing this he offers an insight that very many contemporary theorists overlook, caught as they are in a self-deceptive enthusiasm and fascination with dispersal and diaspora. 'Economic forces may press in that direction; but culturally national attachments show no sign of weakening. Indeed, the more *cosmopolitan* we become, the more we tend to become aware at the same time of other national cultures and of the distinctive features of our own' (p. 146, emphasis added). It is an insight that helps us see, if we think it through to its implications, how it is possible to become less hospitable to otherness the more we encounter it, if we are unprepared intellectually, ethically and emotionally (that is, educationally) for such an encounter. Yet the implicit equation here of globalisation and our becoming cosmopolitan displays White's reliance on the current, standard conception of cosmopolitanism as transnational mobility or common legality. Such a conception conflates an empirical phenomenon with an ideal and makes cosmopolitanism seem like an accomplished reality (Papastephanou, 2005) by missing the normative gap that separates the two. A reformulation of the fashionable meaning of the cosmopolitan and the globalised self would preclude the employment of the adjective 'cosmopolitan' here, where 'globalised' would be more appropriate. The previous section of this chapter has shown that this is not just a terminological issue. You do not become more cosmopolitan just by becoming more mobile and adventurous. Proximity does not determine the way others are treated and cosmopolitanism in a redefined more cautious version, more aware of political subtleties, should be more about the treatment of others rather than about our contact and our agreement with them, as it tends to be now in pragmatic or legal–procedural accounts of cosmopolitanism.

Callan prefers liberal patriotism to world citizenship for reasons of the latter's utopianism. His worry is 'that the aspiration to world citizenship is utopian in an invidious sense, and educational practices inspired by the aspiration might often sacrifice the real if imperfect possibilities of patriotic attachment for an ideal that exists only in the fancy of its adherents' (1999, p. 199). Concerning utopianism, one may object that what counts as unreal or unrealisable depends on what one perceives as realistic impediments that render the ideal unrealisable, and, on this, liberalism needs much explanatory and justificatory work.

But what is more relevant here and emanates from his whole paper is that Callan prefers liberal patriotism because, in the way he defines it (p. 198), he considers it capable of accommodating obligations to distant others anyway. Thus, it seems that his well-argued objections to the received view of world citizenship do not point to a necessity to redefine cosmopolitanism, perhaps against the existing accounts of it that he finds undesirable. However, if we examine his account of what patriotism is capable of doing, we realise that much is still left to be done that requires either a further redefinition of his patriotism or a redefinition of cosmopolitanism and a placing of it alongside patriotism as two compatible and complementary ideals.

Like White's paper, Callan's too is a response and it would be unfair to it to examine it as supposedly exhaustive of his views on the issue. But it is very useful for what it *implies* regarding our concerns here. Callan and White single out chauvinism as the main reason for patriotism turning into a vice and their educational solution is to guide students away from chauvinism. 'The patriotic sentiment runs deep in many contemporary societies, and in its liberal form it can militate against the civic alienation and ethnic chauvinism that are among the most serious threats to the viability of mass democracy' (Callan, 1999, p. 199). Callan accepts or, at least, he does not question the 'cosmopolitan' view that 'the most egregious injustices in our world are commonly fuelled by hatred or indifference toward those who live and suffer beyond the borders of one's own country' (Callan, 1999, p. 197). He only tackles the charge that liberal patriotism with its emphasis on the just state rather than the just world is ostensibly insensitive to this fact. We notice again the psychologism that dematerialises conflict (and most conveniently the Western expansionist oppression of the rest of the world), as if material motives for expansion based on faulty conceptions of human needs and desires were irrelevant to injustices or as if they would vanish through merely learning that peoples are equal. Is it out of chauvinism that the *cosmos* as an environment and non-human biota is being destroyed? Liberalism thinks that it can have maximum ethical effects with only minimal theoretical concessions, without any radical shifts from its own priorities, its own perception of humanity as profit-seeking and the self as rational egoist.

This does affect Callan's conception of patriotism because a patriotism that considers itself hospitable to cosmopolitan concerns only due to its universalist principles of justice is blind to the fact that these principles do not secure on their own their cosmopolitan interpretation. They are too formal and minimal to meet a

177

more fleshy account of justice and too exculpating of their proponents. More clearly, Callan's liberal patriotism is not assisted by the universalist principles enough to perceive the simple fact that the western burgher who pursues his/her interest in remote places at the expense of the locals does not necessarily hate them. S/he may even not be indifferent to them, in the sense that s/he may have justified his/her conduct through all kinds of rationalisations that would interpret universalist principles in ways suitable, convenient to, and exonerating of, that conduct.

Patriotism is compatible and complementary to cosmopolitanism but it cannot replace it or dispense with it. For cosmopolitanism, as the author perceives it, is not about the false dilemma (obsolete since Kant (1992)) of the creation of a world state or not, or about world citizenship as participation in the global sphere in equal measure to participation in the local. Cosmopolitanism can be shown to be about the way distant others and the whole world of biota have been treated and still suffer from it as well as how some still profit from that treatment of *cosmos*. Cosmopolitanism supplies the voice of the other, it makes the complaint, the expectation, of the other be heard, so that the patriot will not judge the way his/her collectivity has treated others self-referentially, light-heartedly and introspectively. The betrayal of universalistic principles or their adaptation to the standard Occidental interpretive framework cannot be unveiled *foro interno*, without harkening to remote or interstitial others. On this inability, Callan's own omission of mentioning global redistribution of wealth and pending historical moral debts as an issue of patriotism and cosmopolitanism, as well as his possible relegation of it to the sphere of utopianism, is very telling.

Finally, to elaborate more on the need to revisit the terms, let us turn to the kinds of patriotism that are implicit in Callan's and White's texts. Civic patriotism 'is the love of ... shared political freedom and the institutions that sustain it. ... This kind of patriotism is of an inherently *political* nature and is not dependent on national or ethnic identity' (Kleingeld, 2000, p. 317). At first sight, being beyond the nation seems to secure a safe distance from chauvinism when the latter signifies illusions of national grandeur or claims to national superiority or outstanding quality. Being based on politics, civic patriotism appears reconciled with cosmopolitanism, if it can be argued that the principles determining it are truly universalisable. However, if that is not indeed the case, then we end up with illusions of political superiority this time and the pernicious, subtle assumption that our *patria* is closer to unquestioned principles and thus better than the *patria* of others.

Nationalist patriotism 'does not focus on the political commonwealth in which one is a citizen, but on the national group to which one belongs' (Kleingeld, 2000, p. 319). Because this focus is on the nation as one's own, 'instead of as the instantiation of a general ideal or as the bearer of particular qualities, there is no implication that one's own nation is *better* than others' (ibid, p. 320). Yet this does not rule out the possibility that this sense of belonging might obscure the responsibilities to outsiders, and no accommodation of justice is secured in the way that nationalist patriotism has so far theoretically been defined.

Unlike White's paper, which seems to promote a nationalist patriotism, Callan's paper adheres to a civic patriotism. Both are defensible within liberalism (Kleingeld, 2000). But neither theorist seems to justify this choice in a way that would make the preferred version of liberal patriotism stand out adequately. Each version of patriotism appears axiomatically stated; it does not emerge differentially from a contrast to other possible meanings. Even if that was not feasible in the particular texts, it was not mentioned as a considerable issue of either past or present or future research and this, in the author's opinion, proves a broader tendency in contemporary educational thought to select and draw from current and received views on such topics rather than realising the need for redefinitions and reconceptualisations of crucial notions.

A possible objection to my suggestion (and, indirectly, an explanation why a definitional–conceptual approach to these notions is being neglected) comes from 'the difficulty of defining' (Todd, 2007, p. 26) the terms. Todd states (p. 36, fn 1) that specifying cosmopolitanism positively and definitively is an 'uncosmopolitan' thing to do, because cosmopolitanism 'invokes an openness to the indefinite and gestures to an unknown "beyond" of the nation-state'. If this claim is weak and means that cosmopolitan responsibilities extend beyond any specific collective-ness, be it the nation-state, the region, social class, gender, and all other particular communities, it is indeed a valid and minimal requirement for making cosmopolitanism intelligible. Then, the question is, why is only the nation-state singled out in this statement? It seems that the claim is a strong one, presupposing that the *cosmos* is in a relation of opposition to the nation-state or any similar particularity rather than in a relation of set and subset. The former relation is one of mutual exclusion; the latter can be one of inclusion or complementarity.

Because of this strong claim, Todd describes as inherent contradiction (pp. 26, 27) something that can be seen merely as a tension, namely, the demand to embrace human rights in relation to the demand to respect particularity. The weaker position places the tension in a particular *conception* of cosmopolitanism (one that could be revisited or abandoned); the stronger locates the tension in the *concept* of cosmopolitanism. The author prefers the former and would argue that this tension is produced by failures in most Western discourse to theorise the dual demand for universality and particularity adequately; thus, taking issue with Todd's view that this 'double demand *inevitably creates a contradictory logic*' (p. 26, emphasis added). For particularity is not the opposite of universality, as it is usually theorised, but rather a subset of it.[14] Rather than being in endemic tension, particularity and universality are interconnected and equally present in cosmopolitan ethics. Once again, the problem is how we define cosmopolitanism and we realise that, ironically, the very Derridean efforts to stress the indefinitiveness and openness of conceptualisations are, in the end, those which consolidate conceptual essentialism by elevating *conceptions* to the onto-epistemological level of the *concept* and by regarding contingent tensions as onto-*logical* constants.

The author does not object to the openness and inconclusiveness of cosmopolitanism or of any other concept for that matter, and Todd's remark is valuable to that effect. What should be stressed instead is the gap between the essentialist character of the notion of a 'concept' and the fluid pluralism inherent in the notion of a 'conception', a well-known issue in general philosophy that underpins the tendency to speak about formulating *conceptions* even when our ultimate aspiration might be to approach something like the *concept* of a term. When redefinitions are suggested, it is not claimed that the latter will constitute 'the last word' on the subject. They will be revisable reflections of how the terms could be more comprehensively and plausibly grasped so as to clarify many issues at stake.

Despite the emphasis on openness, a specific definition of cosmopolitanism is clearly presupposed and conceptually essentialised through Todd's assumption of inevitability that was italicised above. It is a definition that connects cosmopolitanism negatively with the nation-state in a relation of opposition and transcendence (note the 'unknown beyond' in the first quotation above) and is, precisely because of this, a very specific and definitive position. Cosmopolitanism does not, by definition, gesture beyond the nation-state, firstly because as an ideal it predates political constructions of the 19th century (and it has not been a response to them), second because there is no compelling argument that cosmopolitanism be conceived as opposite to a commitment to a nation-state and third because there is no guarantee that what lies beyond the nation-state is automatically cosmopolitan (Papastephanou, 2005). Empires lie beyond the nation-state but thinkers do not usually treat them as exemplary of cosmopolitanism, with the exception of a small number who have, anyway, attracted much criticism for doing so.[15]

While acknowledging the difficulty of defining cosmopolitanism, Todd does rely on a very clearly demarcated and widely-held definition of it that excludes other, possible conceptions of cosmopolitanism. To her, cosmopolitanism comprises 'a political and ethical mission to embrace a sense of worldliness outside the confines of national belonging, where our neighbours are no longer those who are "just like us", but who exist in a global, as opposed to a national, neighbourhood. It is a *shift away from patriotism*' (p. 26, emphasis added). The very opposition of the global to the national without any qualifications is a first restriction of this, otherwise minimal, definition to a truly limited and specific account of cosmopolitanism, one that is unsuspecting of the gap that might separate the global from the cosmopolitan. Already 'the shift away from patriotism' determines the conceptual content of cosmopolitanism as incompatible or non-complementary to the ethical commitment to locality. Even if the intention is only to contrast cosmopolitanism to a very narrow form of nationalist commitment, the aphoristic disjunction effected by the distance involved in the phrase 'shifting away' suffices to impose a sense of wholesale indictment of patriotism and an unwillingness to examine the possibility of some compatibility of cosmopolitanism and patriotism. And it is no accident that, as Todd writes, these are, arguably, the 'historical and current invocations' of cosmopolitanism. In other words, they are not invocations coming from theoretical reformulations that might transcend or breathe new life into the historical and current contents of the term. The idea justifying the unwillingness to engage in definitional dialogue is usually that if we cannot grasp the concept of a term then we can sidestep the whole problem and move on to a head-on discussion of the term. Yet, there is no way of sidestepping definitions and their philosophical implications. What really comes about, instead, is a tacit reliance on workable, socially current definitions that in this way remain unshakeable and, worse, are thus elevated to the onto-epistemological status of concepts.

It is likewise no accident that when cosmopolitanism acquires more substance in Todd's text, its positive and definitive specification as exclusion of other possible contents becomes more apparent. 'Cosmopolitanism reveals a commitment to notions of "world", "transnational" or "global" citizenship, and also frames its pursuit of global justice largely along two lines: universal rights, on the one hand, and a respect for diversity, on the other' (p. 26). These two lines are exactly what makes Alain Badiou (2001, pp. 1–29) criticise both liberalism and Levinas' face-to-face ethics as secret accomplices in the promulgation of the western, tourist or voyeuristic treatment of world affairs. They could also be criticised from Andrew Dobson's 'thick cosmopolitanism' point of view (2006) for their presupposing too narrow a notion of moral obligation. People who have long been exploited cannot be said to be treated in a cosmopolitan way just when their universal rights are acknowledged and their cultural differences respected. And ongoing environmental damage affecting the poor and the rich differently (Dobson, 2006, pp. 173–4), while setting the liabilities of the latter in a different perspective, points to a new kind of obligations. Although not at odds with demands for rights and diversity, such obligations definitely go beyond them. What is more important, here, is that universal rights and respect for diversity are put centre stage (in Todd's text as much as in Callan's and White's) in a way that leaves the issue of justice as redistribution of wealth, not as supererogatory act of charity but as a moral duty emanating from diachronic and synchronic moral debts, out of the scope of cosmopolitanism. All in all, we notice that, even if we agree with other points of Todd's otherwise interesting and sensitive approach to the issue, we cannot accept that the difficulty of defining cosmopolitanism commits us to accept the historical and current invocations of the term and to leave minimalist cosmopolitanism (comprising only respect for human rights and diversity) unchallenged.

Another objection, the last one that can be dealt with in the present chapter, concerns the justification of the very need for patriotism prior to redefining it. This objection might be raised by White's and Callan's critics to whom their papers respond but also by proponents of the idea, as we encountered it in Todd, that cosmopolitanism is a shifting away from patriotism. If cosmopolitanism is love for the whole world that is always instantiated and tried out in particular situations, does it not cover the ground of patriotism anyway, rendering it expendable? To answer this, one may return to Kant. Kant ruled out the possibility of a world state because he saw in it a soulless despotism (1992, pp. 46–7, 90). This means that cosmopolitanism as world government is normatively undesirable and even dangerous, leaving us only the option of smaller configurations such as states coordinated by international law. In whatever form, national or multiethnic, such states require commitment and active participation on the part of their citizens.

Public affairs of any specific configuration are of such a complex nature that only the citizens belonging to that configuration are capable of a meaningful and consistent *vita activa* (Arendt, 1989) within its confines. Due to the limited human life span, as Kant observed (1992, p. 227), no matter how 'extrovert' we are, we cannot know or intervene in, say, the taxation system of a remote country, especially if that system has no dramatic effect to display and belongs only to the sphere of quotidian consideration. Thus, so long as a world state is both non-feasible and politically undesirable, what we may call 'internal patriotism', civic or national, is indispensable.

Regarding external patriotism, the argument is somewhat different but touches upon the confinements of human life span too. If a country exerts a subtle power (but no less intrusive for that matter) over another country; if the interests of the elites of the former translate into risks for the masses of the latter, it is very possible that we may never hear of it.[16] Those who suffer an injustice are alone in making it more globally known and in mobilising international attention, and hopefully, international law. Their patriotism as defence of their rights against external threat or against the indifference of the uninformed is, regrettably but pragmatically, their own battle. Even the decision of an impartial sympathiser to give them voice, to speak in their name – a rare thing anyway – does not alleviate this solitude. The only way by which external patriotism would become expendable, and, therefore, cosmopolitanism could shift away from it, would be by creating a just world in the sense that no political configuration or supranational groups and forces would be predatory, narrow-interest-driven or perhaps simply blundering. One might argue that, when and if that occurs, the need for patriotism, internal and external, could be reconsidered or made obsolete. Still, even the most extravagant utopia of a just state or a just world turning into reality would not be a static photographic arresting of time but a constant effort to preserve such justice, so that, if patriotism is in dialectical relation with justice, then, like all virtues, it can never be rendered obsolete.

CONCLUSION

The retreat from redefinitions and reconstructions affects education for citizenship negatively because of the unnecessary vagueness and mystification it introduces to it. Patriotism as love for one's community can be easily reconciled with a complex conception of cosmopolitanism as love for all biota, international legality and worldwide ethical responsibility, sensitive to diachronic and synchronic moral debt. Their reconciliation can be achieved through a comprehensive theory of justice capable of warding off any possible dangerous political implications and slippages to unreflective nationalism and chauvinism on the one hand and to an arrogant and facile globalistic internationalism on the other. Authorised by justice, they can be vigilant about causes of political evil that are more profound and subtle than chauvinism, thus diluting the double standards that usually confound students in classrooms regarding the scope of human responsibility.

If patriotism and cosmopolitanism mean, at their best, the ethical-political, intellectual and emotional worthiness of immediate proximity and annihilated distance, then it is evident that the empirical accomplished reality of spatiotemporally unhindered possibilities does not secure anything on its own. If globalisation is defined simply as the empirical evidence of such possibilities (Papastephanou, 2005), it cannot serve, on its own, a 'healthy' sense of cosmopolitanism and it is not on its own immune to the extended and camouflaged 'patriotism' of the powerful. Without the necessary ethical-political, intellectual and emotional interpretation of human entanglement (Papastephanou, 2002) [and, there, education has a huge task to address] the global may at best represent a 'tourist' enrichment of individual life-history. At worst, it may represent a more advanced form of *New Roman Times* through the anonymous, sweeping and uncontrollable sway of cyberspace, in other words, of *Times New Roman*.

NOTES

[1] On ideals having two sides that correspond to a desirable personhood and a desirable situation see, for instance, Doret De Ruyter (2003, pp. 469–70).

[2] See, for instance, some contributions in Cohen & Nussbaum, 1996. Along these lines, similar binary oppositions have emerged in recent theory in most traditions and persuasions – oppositions such as 'rootedness versus rootlessness', 'immobility versus fluidity' and 'identity versus hybridity or diaspora' (Isin & Wood, 1999).

[3] On the emergence of cosmopolitanism in antiquity see Nussbaum (1997, p. 34) and the course it took in medieval and renaissance times see Toulmin (1992, p. 68).

[4] See, for instance, Lu, 2000, p. 250, fn. 36; Waldron, 2000, p. 227.

[5] Jeremy Waldron (2000, p. 228) seems to totally miss this danger when he equates precisely such activities with being cosmopolitan.

[6] Such unethical 'cosmopolitan' mobility was the colonialism that was deriving justification from the argument of empty land (terra nullius). Foreign land was empty before the arrival of Europeans because its inhabitants did not use it properly (i.e. for maximum profit). In such context, European mobility meant justified exploitation on grounds of superior power over earthly productivity (Harris, 2004, pp. 170–171). For more on the violence of European colonial mobility, see Fanon (1967).

[7] On those purposes, see Korsgaard, 2006.

[8] I say 'comprehensive' to contrast it with more narrow notions of it such as the distributive (so as to add restorative justice for instance) and also to allude to its difference from Rawls' claim that contemporary political theory can do away with comprehensiveness and endorse political liberalism.

[9] It is a lack that often leads theory to conflating globalisation and cosmopolitanism. To overcome this predicament, political philosophy should draw and keep distinctions between globalisation as an empirical phenomenon, globalism as its discursive thematisation and cosmopolitanism as an ideal of global well-being (Papastephanou, 2005).

[10] For a summary of them, see Kleingeld, 2000, p. 315.

[11] For an exposition and critique of the latter, see Lacroix (2002, 951ff) to which Bellamy and Castiglione respond with their 2004 text.

[12] Kleingeld writes that 'rather than ahistorically trying to claim a single meaning for the term patriotism, one should acknowledge that some terms change their meaning over time or acquire additional meanings. In such cases, the point is not to determine which usage is wrong and which is right, but to distinguish the different meanings carefully' (2000, p. 318). Yet, in some cases, I believe, certain usages are too flat, unproductive and unhelpful regarding hidden semantic possibilities and thus less preferable than other usages.

13 This is not a criticism of the actual content of White's paper itself, for, being a response to critics, the paper is meant to address a different matter than the one I am discussing here. It is rather a criticism of the text's noticeable omission of acknowledging the need for redefinitions up to the reconstruction of different corresponding theories. The same holds for Callan's text too.

14 Although this requires a much broader and more detailed discussion, suffice it here to rely even on an intuitive understanding of cosmopolitanism: would that understanding allow us to name as 'cosmopolitan' one who is contemptuous of or insulting to those who do not share her religious or non-religious beliefs? Likewise, would we call 'cosmopolitan' a person who supports the expansionist foreign policy of his country on grounds of national interest at the expense of universal human rights?

15 See, for instance, criticisms of Hardt and Negri's *Empire* in Parry (2003) and Badiou (2003).

16 Even in more blatant cases such as wars, the complications and the stakes that escalated into crisis and matter immensely in judging fairly leave most observers (international referees notwithstanding) indifferent.

REFERENCES

Ackerman, B. (1994). Rooted cosmopolitanism. *Ethics, 104*(3), 516–535.

Appiah, K. A. (1996). Cosmopolitan patriots. In J. Cohen & M. Nussbaum (Eds.), *For love of country: Debating the limits of patriotism*. Boston: Beacon.

Arendt, H. (1989). *The human condition*. Chicago: The University of Chicago Press.

Badiou, A. (2001). *Ethics: An essay on the understanding of evil*. London: Verso.

Badiou, A. (2003). Beyond formalisation: An interview. *Angelaki, 8*(2), 111–136.

Bauman, Z. (1998). On glocalization: Or globalization for some, localization for some others. *Thesis Eleven, 54*, 37–51.

Bellamy, R. and Castiglione, D. (2004). Lacroix's European constitutional patriotism: A response. *Political Studies, 52*, 187–193.

Callan, E. (1999). A note on patriotism and utopianism: Response to Schrag. *Studies in Philosophy and Education, 18*, 197–201.

Cohen, J. & Nussbaum, M. (1996). *For love of country*. Boston, Beacon Press.

Delanty, G. (2006). The cosmopolitan imagination: Critical cosmopolitanism and social theory. *The British Journal of Sociology, 57*(1), 25–47.

De Ruyter, D. (2003). The importance of ideals in education. *Journal of Philosophy of Education, 37*(3), 467–482.

Dewey, J. (1993). The democratic conception of education. In D. Morris & I. Shapiro (Eds.), *John Dewey: The Political Writings*. Indianapolis: Hackett (Original work published 1916).

Dobson, A. (2006). Thick cosmopolitanism. *Political Studies, 54*, 165–184.

Erskine, T. (2002). 'Citizen of nowhere' or 'the point where circles intersect'? Impartialist and embedded cosmopolitanisms. *Review of International Studies, 28*, 457–478.

Fanon, F. (1967). *The wretched of the earth*. Harmondsworth: Penguin.

Habermas, J. (2003). Fundamentalism and terror: A dialogue with J. Habermas (interviewer: G. Borradori). In G. Borradori, *Philosophy in a time of terror*. Chicago: The University of Chicago Press.

Harris, C. (2004). How did colonialism dispossess? Comments from an edge of empire. *Annals of the Association of American Geographers, 94*(1), 165–182.

Isin, E.F. & Wood, P.K. (1999). *Citizenship and identity*. London: Sage.

Kant, I. (1992). *Political writings* (H. Reiss, Ed.). Cambridge: Cambridge University Press.

Kleingeld, P. (2000). Kantian patriotism. *Philosophy and Public Affairs, 29*(4), 313–341.

Korsgaard, O. (2006). Giving the spirit a national form: From Rousseau's advice to Poland to Habermas' advice to the European Union. *Educational Philosophy and Theory, 38*(2), 231–246.

Lacroix J. (2002). For a European constitutional patriotism. *Political Studies, 50*, 944–958.

Lazarus, N. (2002). The politics of postcolonial modernism. *The European Legacy, 7*(6), 771–782.

Lu, C. (2000). The one and many faces of cosmopolitanism. *Journal of Political Philosophy, 8*(2), 244–267.

Nussbaum, M. (1997). Kant and cosmopolitanism. In J. Bohman & M. Lutz-Bachmann (Eds.), *Perpetual peace: Essays on Kant's cosmopolitan ideal.* Cambridge, Mass.: MIT Press.

Papastephanou, M. (2002). Arrows not yet fired: Cultivating cosmopolitanism through education. *Journal of Philosophy of Education, 36*(1), 69–86.

Papastephanou, M. (2005). Globalization, globalism and cosmopolitanism as an educational ideal. *Educational Philosophy and Theory, 37*(4), 533–551.

Parry, B. (2003). Internationalism revisited or in praise of internationalism. *Interventions, 5*(2), 299–314.

Taylor, C. (1996). Why democracy needs patriotism. In J. Cohen & M. Nussbaum (Eds.), *For love of country: Debating the limits of patriotism.* Boston: Beacon.

Todd, S. (2007). Teachers judging without scripts, or thinking cosmopolitan. *Ethics and Education, 2*(1), 25–38.

Toulmin, S. (1992). *Cosmopolis.* Chicago: the University of Chicago Press.

Waldron, J. (2000). What is cosmopolitan? *The Journal of Political Philosophy, 8*(2), 227–243.

White, J. (2001). Patriotism without obligation. *Journal of Philosophy of Education, 35*(1), 141–151.

Yonah, Y. (1999). '*Ubi Patria – Ibi Bene*': The scope and limits of Rousseau's patriotic education. *Studies in Philosophy and Education, 18*, 365–388.

Marianna Papastephanou
University of Cyprus

JAMES C. CONROY AND ROBERT A. DAVIS

CITIZENSHIP, EDUCATION AND THE CLAIMS OF RELIGIOUS LITERACY

ABSTRACT

The current and conflicted interest in Global Citizenship Education has deep roots in the practices of values education, religious education and character education that flourished in the school and university systems of the Western democracies for much of the post-war period. These practices are not unproblematic and have themselves been sites of contestation between traditionalist conceptions of civic responsibility, liberal theories of autonomy and self-actualisation, and visions of social, cultural and economic empowerment to be achieved through radical educational critique of the structures of the social order. The language of Global Citizenship Education has retained much of the idealism and critical energy of the most progressive versions of values education, but it has, as a corollary, disavowed important elements of its ancestry in the philosophies of moral development and religious understanding. In reconceptualising these affinities, this chapter proposes an enrichment of the practices of Citizenship Education and its engagement with the forces of global change, arguing for the centrality of a renovated intercultural ethic to the authenticity of Citizenship Education.

INTRODUCTION

This essay explores two central concerns in and for Religious Education. The first is a marked decline in religious literacy – which is not to be confused with religious practice, or the active participation in religious observance that appears, at least in the former Christian strongholds of Western Europe, to be heading towards a terminal collapse (Scottish Executive, 2005). Rather, religious literacy denotes an acquaintance with, and an understanding of, the nature of religious experience, religious concepts and practices, together with some basic grasp of the complexities, contradictions and challenges of at least one religious tradition. Perhaps more than any of these, the promotion of religious literacy also entails serious and sustained engagement with religious language and its import, insisting that this be recognised as a necessary condition of successful education for citizenship in the modern polity – an undertaking quite distinct from the bestowal of assent or credence on any particular religious or theological claim.

M.A.Peters, A. Britton and H. Blee (Eds.), Global Citizenship Education: Philosophy, Theory and Pedagogy, 187–202.

The second concern of the present essay is the growing phenomenon of religious illiteracy and the effects of such illiteracy in reinforcing the hermetically sealed epistemologies of religious believers and religious sceptics alike. An integral concern of the argument is therefore with the consequences of such religious illiteracy for the conversations that take place in schools – and in the polity more generally – around the meaning of religion in a globalised society. The spread of religious illiteracy furthers, it can plausibly be argued, the declassification of those features of religion that appear, intellectually, emotionally and morally, to stand outside the normative liberal discourse of contemporary mass education – a discourse in which education is commonly prized as both the heir and the custodian of liberal principles. In exploring the shifting ratios of religious literacy and illiteracy, we intend to draw attention to the need for a long overdue reappraisal of the now pedagogically stipulative claim that the practices of Religious Education should be conducted within the frame of a morphological or typological method rooted in the principles of the phenomenological movement of the 1970s. This method supposedly freed Religious Education from its confessional shackles and enabled it to assume a credible position in the modern curriculum as an instrument for the promotion of core liberal values such as tolerance, pluralism and multicultural citizenship. In the process, this essay suggests, it may also have unintentionally deprived Religious Education of the resources to combat the mounting global threats to each of these values.

In the first part of the analysis we argue that the roots of religious illiteracy run deep, woven into the conflicted history of Western liberal thought and its interpretation of religion. In the second part we suggest that, in Britain at least, religious illiteracy is inextricably entangled in the pedagogical and regulatory assumptions governing Religious Education as a curricular area, particularly as these are expressed in the siren discourses of multiculturalism and its successor disciplines, such as Citizenship Education and Philosophy in Schools, now laying increasingly vocal claim to the traditional territories of Religious Education. It is a central contention of this essay that otherwise vibrant and necessary educational developments such as Citizenship Education are robbed of an essential validity in the era of globalised identities if their response to the question of religion remains constrained by the particular version of liberal critique that has come in the present time to dominate the encounter of religion, education and rationality in both our schools and the wider polity.

CONTEMPORARY CULTURE AND THE POLITICS OF RELIGIOUS LITERACY

Religious illiteracy currently takes many forms, and these seem to proliferate as the penetration of public life by the supposedly resurgent forces of religious atavism (and activism) extends into even the previously unassailable liberal educational jurisdictions of the Western democracies. The most egregious example of the failure of Western progressive elites to comprehend and respond to the contemporary rebirth of religious belief at the heart of seemingly secular polities can be seen most clearly in the bewildered response of the American Left to the re-election of President George Bush in 2004. All but incredulous before the appeal of Bush's conservatism to a huge and impossibly variegated religious constituency, progressive opinion in the United States found itself bereft of a cultural and religious lexicon for understanding the meaning of its own defeat and for interrogating the sources of its opponent's remarkable strength-in-depth (Giroux, 2004, pp. 415–425). Mesmerised by the resuscitation of a regressive religious language it had long believed politically extinct or inconsequential, Democratic thought strove vainly to reconfigure the expressly religious registers of the victorious Bush campaign as either redneck anachronism or as the latest convenient disguise of the neoconservative apologists for US corporate capital. The windy rhetoric of Michael Moore's *Fahrenheit 9/11* and the sneering and unfunny puerility of the popular 'Jesusland' cartoon represent only one dimension of a religiously illiterate politics of the Left that, even in electoral reverse, appeared unwilling and unable to acknowledge the culture of religious belief and practice as a mobilising and autonomous ethical and symbolic force within democratic society. Ironically, it is only as the Bush administration's flawed policy for the reconstruction of defeated post-Baathist Iraq has run aground on the rocks of Islamist resistance and ancient sectarian strife unpredicted by neoconservative strategy, that progressive opinion in the United States has finally rebounded from electoral despond, proving grimly that religious illiteracy was not, after all, the preserve of the liberal Left (Wimmer, 2003, pp. 111–134; Hogget, 2005, pp. 418–428).

The reasons for this widespread intellectual confusion lie in the peculiar history of modern Western responses to the question of religion and, in particular, to the historicist account of the rise and fall of religion that has been such a powerful motor in Enlightenment educational thought since the end of the eighteenth century. Within the parameters of this narrative, the dramatic global resurgence of religious, often reportedly 'fundamentalist', movements over the last three decades has caught many educators by surprise, since, according to the theory of modernisation of which Western education is such a powerful expression, religion was supposed to be doomed by the irresistible two-hundred-year advance of reason, secularisation and privatisation. The theory of modernisation presented educational thought with several alternative futures for the destiny of religion in the modern world, but neither a return of religion as a popular world-transforming force, nor its continuing – even renewed – capacity to shape human behaviour in accordance with non-material teleologies were expected to be among them. While few thinkers expected religion to disappear quickly or completely in the era of economic and social modernisation, many echoed the assessment given classic expression in the work of the sociologist Thomas Luckmann, in which religion was assigned to a transitional space in the private sphere where it would wither as the conditions of its existence (put simply, scarcity, subsistence and superstition) were steadily ameliorated (Luckmann, 1967, pp. 11–41). Religious institutions, it was assumed, would undergo a parallel process of internal secularisation, rapidly adapting to the requirements of modern social structures while maintaining a merely residual religious symbolism that would steadily mutate into alternative and wholly material forms of cultural meaning such as art and recreation (Wallis & Bruce, 1992, pp. 8–31). Some analysts, such as Robert Bellah, imagined that national ideologies or 'civil religions' would functionally replace religious traditions, or expected socially constructive religious values (such as charity or solidarity) to be absorbed into modern societies elsewhere in headlong retreat from traditional forms of religious observance (Bellah, 1970, pp. 20–53). Shed of its supernatural trappings, religion would become, in effect, a form of citizenship (as it now at least superficially appears to be in, for example, the Scandinavian countries). Few were prepared for the planetary resurgence of religions as transnational movements, or as the powerful, frequently illiberal shapers of religiously-constituted subjects they now once more aspire to be in many parts of the globalised world (Berger, 1999, pp. 1–19).

Efforts of social and educational theorists to respond to the return of religion have revealed widespread cognitive disarray within liberal opinion, which impacts damagingly on policy towards both Religious Education and Education for Citizenship. Some influential commentators have simply adjusted their interpretation of modernisation and secularisation, refined their understanding of the defensive character of cultural resistance, whilst insisting that the overall secularisation hypothesis remains fundamentally intact (Bruce, 2002, pp. 75–90). Examining the return of religion outside the modern West has allowed them to contextualise local religious revivals as still intrinsically a part of a modernizing process. Indeed, in a lingering if troubled indebtedness to Weber's 'Protestant Ethic' as a general theory of modernisation, several have claimed to discern a 'Puritan spirit' or an 'inner-worldly asceticism' in movements such as the Islam of commerce-rich Turkish Anatolia (Erdemir, 2005, pp. 937–951) or the state-supported enculturated Christianity of the burgeoning Chinese megacities (Overmeyer, 2003, pp. 307–316). Others have favoured precisely the converse of this analysis, denying entirely the existence of any global trend towards secularisation over the past two hundred years – not only in the pre-modern cultures of the developing world but also in the West itself. Rational choice theorists, such as Lawrence Young, have defended this seemingly startling proposition by explaining secularisation as an effect of religious monopolies (Young, 1997, pp. xi–xxii). Anchoring their understanding of religion in a transhistorical game-theory calculus with an ancestry in social darwinism, they have also concluded that people in the European Middle Ages – seen typically as the pinnacle of the age of faith – were not actually properly religious at all, because they did not function as the subjects of an authentic religious market or a genuinely competitive economy of alternative spiritual ideas. Dissatisfied with the dangerously circular and unfalsifiable nature of these claims, the sociologist Steven Warner has advanced a subtly different but related explanation (Warner, 1993, pp. 1044–1093). Warner's argument is highly historicized, and succeeds in emphasizing the differentiating features of American exceptionalism in direct contrast to what he sees as the undeniable European trend towards secularisation from the early modern period onwards. Warner maintains that there is a 'new paradigm' in the making for the study of religion in America in particular, which rejects an older hermeneutic based on the European experience of secularisation. Secularisation, he suggests, has not taken place in the United States, owing to the nature of American pluralism. Wherever religious pluralism and competition have predominated, secularisation has not happened since it is simply an effect of the monopolistic tendencies of European-style religious elites. Despite its Weberian antecedents, the 'new paradigm' – a term now widely adopted in Religious Studies – seriously underplays Weber's original account of the intrinsically *areligious* nature of modern institutions, especially capitalism and bureaucracy. The rationalisation processes initially set in motion by a religiously centred society contributed to the 'disenchantment' of the world, Weber's argument runs, by rejecting all 'irrational' means of attaining salvation and promoting the emergence of rationally organized institutional orders and systems of ethics. According to Weber, this process of disenchantment and secularisation removed the religious impulse from the central economic, political, cultural and educational institutions of society and freed them from religious regulation. In Western modernity it is therefore possible for a much-diminished version of religion to survive in the central institutions only if it adapts to their procedural logic of efficiency, performance and utility and contributes implicitly to their ongoing legitimation (Villa, 1999, pp. 540–552).

The consequence of this process for Religious Education as an element of the post-religious and Enlightened curriculum is to place it at the centre of a striking epistemological paradox: Religious Education participates in a disciplinary economy predicated precisely upon the delegitimation of organised religion as a zone of human flourishing, leaving it, uniquely, an oxymoronic subject – possibly the only subject in the curriculum the core concepts of which are regularly and relentlessly trashed beyond the boundaries of the school, and often inside them as well. It is this unresolved contradiction that disables the work of religious literacy and leaves the politics of citizenship frequently mute and uncomprehending before the discursive practices of a religiously-motivated legal and political programme such as that of the Bush Whitehouse, with its openly-declared war on secularism and its covert erosion of the Establishment Clause of the First Amendment. The deleterious effects on the separationist principle of a succession of test cases in US educational policy-making, surreptitiously championed by the Bush advisorate, remain poorly understood on the European side of the Atlantic. Similarly, intelligent and properly sensitised educational responses to the question of Islam are repeatedly impeded by the dominance of an educational paradigm that evacuates meaning from religious language and which is therefore compelled to translate faith into ethnicity, religious obedience into cultural submission. For dialogue with a religion largely untouched by the categorical distinctions issuing from the Enlightenment rationality and its hard-won discriminations, this is a potentially disastrous move, reinforcing all of the most alienating aspects of instrumental codification and separation, including those reproductive of racism and imperialism. In the face of the 'global citizenship' implied by the Muslim concept of the *Umma*, or the enfolding of political life into the daily exercise of religious obligation and theological judgement, Religious Education is rendered speechless, its foundational assumptions implicated in a worldview seen by many Muslims as constitutively hostile to the expression of faith (Halstead, 2004, pp. 517–529).

The re-emergence, or, better, re-affirmation, of religion as a political force of considerable magnitude across the world may itself be regarded as issuing from a religious illiteracy borne of the classically false Weberian dichotomy between public and private. Here a proper engagement with religion in the public school has been deemed *ultra vires*, with the consequence that it has been relegated to the back street of the mind, a place where the individual self is not required to subject to any kind of serious scrutiny his or her own relationship to the religious objects of consciousness. Curiously, and somewhat paradoxically, a similar kind outcome has issued from the particular approach to the teaching of Religious Education in Britain. Whereas in the United States the absence of Religious Education in the public school has fostered unthinkingness and the consequent growth of fundamentalism, in Britain a Religious Education that has failed to pay attention to the relationship between the self and 'religious objects' has also produced an unthinkingness manifest not as fundamentalism but as profound disassociation, lack of interest and scepticism deeply injurious to the project of a proper Education for Citizenship. This development, which makes it difficult, if not impossible, for the educational system to respond creatively to the 'return of religion' has its roots in a particular philosophy of Religious Education that arose in the 1960s and 70s in the British Isles, the lasting effects of which have yet to be fully appraised but which the emergence of Citizenship Education throws into fresh relief (Jackson, 2004, pp. 1–34).

THE PHENOMENOLOGICAL TURN AND
THE LOSS OF SELF IN RELIGIOUS EDUCATION

More often than not, judgements predicated on the wisdom of hindsight can appear facile. Nevertheless it is, on occasion, important to revisit and re-evaluate the effects of earlier theoretical developments that have had the consequence of shaping particular social and educational practices. In the case of Religious Education in Britain – and elsewhere – the work of Ninian Smart has been enormously influential in this respect. His theoretical – indeed, in his early work, theological – deliberations have been instrumental in shaping the attitudes, dispositions and methodologies of more than one generation of teachers. Generally, these developments have been judged in a very positive light, even if, more recently, some scholars have pursued a reappraisal of Smart's phenomenological approach. Aspects of this reappraisal amount to little more than an adjustment of tone and emphasis (O'Grady, 2005, pp. 227–237), reflective of a desire to infuse the original morphological method with the personal–spiritual approaches valued in certain 'therapeutic' models of educational growth. More searching examinations have taken criticism of Smart somewhat further (Wright, 1993; Wright, 2001, pp. 201–219; Barnes, 2000, pp. 315–352; Barnes, 2007, pp. 157–169), suggesting that the original phenomenological turn in Religious Education –

seen as a response to the inexorable advance of pluralism and pluralist philosophies – has been misguided and has shorn religion of its power to manifest a response to enduring and perfectly proper educational questions arising from the mystery of being (Thompson, 2004, pp. 61–73). In one important respect, the retreat from a phenomenological perspective in Religious Education is curious since, on any reasonable account of Phenomenology, a central purpose of its philosophical method has been not only to strip away the comforting familiarity of language and common perceptions that serve to mask our understandings of the world, but also – perhaps more importantly – its construal as 'a supremely personal affair ... We thus begin, everyone for himself and in himself, with the decision to disregard all our present knowledge' (Husserl, 1970, p. 4ff).

It is with these words that Edmund Husserl begins his discussion of the nature of the phenomenological enterprise as an endeavour to disclose the *'isness'* of things, including that of the intractable Self. Of course, there are some profound differences between the positions of Husserl and Smart, most particularly given Smart's interest in descriptive morphology as contrasted with the Husserlian enthusiasm for the apodictic. It would nonetheless be a mistake to imagine a chasm between philosophical phenomenology of a Husserlian kind and the descriptive task of, in Smart's terms, the *science* of religion. It can appear as if the one offers a nuanced and sophisticated account of philosophical method – which represents an unending effort to unearth the heraclitean relationship between the *cogito* and the objects of the world as the unmediated contents of consciousness – and the other a pre-philosophical and naively natural or realist account of things and objects. To do so is to regard the subtle timbre of Smart's position as crudely descriptive and consequently to underestimate it. In *The Religious Experience of Mankind*, Smart (Smart, 1971) does point out that in the study of religion, while the intention is to describe and not pass judgement on particular traditions, it is important to attend to the 'facts and feelings of religion ... it would be foolish to think that being "objective" means we only look at temples, churches, and outer behaviour. We must penetrate beyond what is publicly observable...How could we give a proper account of Paul's apostolate without referring to his shattering experience on the Damascus road?' (p.12). This echoes observations made in an earlier, much less well-known, volume in the Smart corpus, *The Teacher and Christian Belief* (Smart, 1966). Here Smart cautions against mixing up historical analysis and religious apologetic, arguing that it is

> foolish, uncandid and self-defeating. It is foolish because it fails to bring out the proper flavour of other faiths – of why they appeal to their adherents. It is uncandid because it smuggles argument into what should be a sympathetic description. It is self-defeating, because prejudice is easily detected and is usually interpreted as a sign of weakness. Thus it needs strongly to be stressed that the teaching of religion should attempt to move from inside other traditions: it should not seek to foist a Christian (or what have you) interpretation upon other faiths. (p. 47)

Given that plurality is undeniably a sealed assumption of modern political and social life, and a governing principle of Education for Citizenship, it is difficult not to be sympathetic to Smart's claims: indeed his thought can justly be regarded as in many senses constitutive of contemporary constructions of Religious Education. Working Paper 36 (Schools Council, 1971), which itself became the ground for Agreed Syllabuses in England and Wales – and a flotilla of subsequent policy documents in Religious Education throughout Britain – was deeply indebted to Smart's form of phenomenological engagement. All this is not enough, however, to redeem an important theoretical weakness in Smart's position, which, in turn, has arguably become amplified in the somewhat less dexterous hands of a great many classroom teachers. The key weakness in Smart's thought is the way in which intentionality is construed. For Smart, intentionality describes the relationship between the believer and the object of belief. Thus when we invite students to study religion we ask them to look not only at the particular cultural and material refractions of religious belief but also at what meaning these objects hold for the religious believer. To understand the material contents of religion – buildings, symbols, symbolic acts, liturgical practices and so on – we must necessarily understand how these things are regarded by the believer or adherent. Prima facie this seems like a reasonable requirement. As Wittgenstein first suggested, however, it is a far from straightforward enterprise (Barnes & Wright, 2006, pp. 65–77). Most precisely, it excludes from the engagement precisely that intentional relationship central to classical Husserlian phenomenology: the relationship between the cogito and the cogitata.

In the 'natural attitude', I am apt to imagine that I am a disinterested and divorced observer of the world of objects and relations about which I make certain kinds of judgements. These may of course include judgements about the intentionality of the Other with respect to the objects of her beliefs. If I am to grasp the nature of religious belief, however, then I have to be able to 'bracket out' my own perceiving. In other words, there is a need for the student qua observer to place herself, through the execution of the phenomenological epoché, in the frame of perception as part of that which is to be apprehended. The commonsense self, with all its inbuilt prejudices, needs itself to be part of that which is to be apprehended and consequently grasped. If I wish to examine a particular religious practice or belief, it is not that I stand outside, examining the liturgical practice of, for example, Holy Communion and how the believer sees and relates to the practice; rather, I place my own perceiving into the frame for apprehension. The 'I' is not anterior to the process. The reason for this is that 'the ego cogito precedes apodictically the fact that the world exists …The phenomenological attitude, with its epoché, consists in that I reach the ultimate experiential and cognitive perspective thinkable. In it I become the disinterested spectator of my natural and worldly ego and its life' (Husserl, 1970, p. 15; emphasis in text). Because Smart omits this part of the process of seeing things as they are, Religious Education crafted under his influence tends always to consist of effectively ignoring the determining presence of the self and all of the self's deepest affiliations. We wish to suggest that the absence of the self has a critical impact on the efficacy of such education and impairs its capacity to comprehend the role of beliefs such as religious ones in the formation of many, if not all, citizens. Since religion presents – in the terms made familiar by Hannah Arendt – a response to the complex interplay between hope as the condition of natality (Arendt, 1958) and anxiety as the condition of death (Heidegger, 1962), we cannot exclude the self which, like all selves, must live in the reflexive ambiguity that arises between these two poles. To do so is to create an imaginary condition where the engagement of the self is absent; it is thus not surprising that the erasure of such a crucial element leaves classroom students frequently devoid of key insights into the nature of religion, exacerbating religious illiteracy. If religious illiteracy is a problem in and for Religious Education then it may well be so because the pedagogical practices that emerged in the wake of Smart's thought disconnected the self as subject from the thing to be studied. While Smart may have been a much more sophisticated thinker than his acolytes, their pedagogical inadequacies are genealogically – indeed we might say genetically – linked to this major philosophical lacuna, which evacuates from the study of religion the perceiving, registering self.

Of course, there has been a drive to bridge this ontological gap with, in the British context, the express claim that Religious Education should be conducive to children learning from religion (SCAA, 1994) rather than through religion. Indeed, in a wide variety of syllabuses and Guidelines produced in the United Kingdom learning from religion appears as a sine qua non of Religious Education (Scottish Education Department, 1992). According to Nesbitt, among many others, a creative approach to Religious Education should include 'a reinforcement and affirmation of each child's experience of religion' (Nesbitt, 2001, p. 139). Such commitments might at first appear, prima facie, to suggest that the proposition summarised above – that the self has been evacuated out of Religious Education – is overstated and that the self remains integral to contemporary pedagogies in RE. There are, however, two observations that support the original claim. First, there is the difficulty that the 'Personal Search' strand currently favoured in Religious Education curricula substitutes for the activity of subjecting the self to the processes of the phenomenological reduction. In pedagogical practice, Personal Search has displaced the possibility of the phenomenological turn, since it offers only an attenuated notion of the self at the centre of the search. It is a form of self-reflection stripped of the costs, and the fruits, of choice and commitment. To understand and engage with the commitments of the Other is simultaneously to subject the self to an analogous form of scrutiny. In an interesting echo of Kierkegaard's concern in the Philosophical Fragments, the particular brand of Personal Search on offer in today's schools has little or no ethical import but is rather a kind of aesthetics. By this we mean that Personal Search is concerned largely to explore choices in the style of educational engagement rather than the existential substance of choice itself, from the import of which it bridles in something approaching embarrassment. Again, Personal Search takes the form of an essentially depoliticised engagement with issues of the moment in the public sphere. It is as if what people believed had nothing to do with how they acted in their relations with others. This is, once again, potentially fatal for the work of

Citizenship Education. Attempts by thinkers such as Audi to distinguish the public from the private in this manner tend to try to restrict the imprint of the private to the legislative arena (Audi, 1989, pp. 259–296). Even so accomplished a philosopher cannot forestall, however, the encroachments of the private. As we have argued in the first part of this essay, it is by no means clear that the public–private distinction works in quite the manner that liberals imagine and certainly not for religious communities striving to relate their beliefs to the making of citizenship. The point here is to suggest that it is a mistake to conceive of Personal Search as private search, and the self as somehow a neutral node in the study of the relations between the other and the objects of her consciousness. Again, we know enough of hermeneutics not to be beguiled by the illusory standpoint of the putatively neutral.

One further, pedagogical example may serve to shed light on the issue at stake here. Imagine a child reading a Harry Potter novel and declaring it a wonderful book. As an adult, parent, teacher, etc., we ask the child what was it that she found so wonderful. She replies that the relationship between Dumbledore and Harry was so rich and affectionate, or that Harry's reflections on his parents or his step parents were interesting or that the suspense was thrilling, or that she loved the idea of quidditch, and so on. Might one, at this stage not wish to observe that the reading child is likely to have been 'drawn into the book' through a range of imaginings about herself, the reader? She is not external to the action – her imaginings are those of one who is, at least partially, 'inside' the novel. Or, better yet, imagine the converse; that is, imagine asking a child not to get involved in the plot, to see herself as outside, to avoid imagining or empathising or sympathising. If we were to discover a child who knew all the words of a story or, a poem or play, but who expressed no engagement with it, we would be likely to say that the pedagogical endeavour had not been entirely satisfactory or successful. Where such a situation arises, we may admit that the child is indeed functionally literate, in that she knows to what objects words refer, but we are not likely to think her literate in the broadest sense of one who has learned and grown from the encounter with the story. The problem with religious literacy in the UK is that the very notion of such literacy has been increasingly articulated, adapted and contested in parallel with the advance of a National Literacy Strategy (or its cognates in Wales and Scotland) for the acquisition of competence in Reading and Writing and, in particular, with the specifically cultural ambitions of that strategy as a programme for the mediation of a shared and diverse cultural patrimony through the syllabus of English Literature and its associated disciplines in the Expressive Arts. This approach to literacy becomes, wittingly or otherwise, host to at least two problems. On the one hand it can be seen to reduce literacy to a form of functionality and, on the other, it can easily delimit the kinds of engagements deemed conducive to the well-being of the polity. In the case of the latter this may well include marginalising texts no longer regarded as appropriate to the reductionist aims of Citizenship Education in a consensual democracy. What then appears, rhetorically, as a claim to promote literacy, swiftly becomes rather more like its opposite – a reductio ad absurdum, reducing literacy to a mere cipher of basic cultural competence. The attempt by post-Smart morphologists to see Religious Education as an exercise in the observation of the Other and her relationship to the cogitationes of her cogito has, we wish to suggest, bred a parallel form of minimalist religious literacy focused upon everything except the central objects of religious consciousness.

RELIGIOUS LITERACY AND THE CRISIS OF LIBERAL CITIZENSHIP

This term 'religious literacy' is, in a technical sense, not new to the study of Religious Education in the United Kingdom. It has figured prominently and intriguingly in the work of thinkers such as Andrew Wright and Roger Homan (Homan, 2004, pp. 21–32) as a term for the ability (in Wright's words) 'to reflect, communicate and act in an informed, intelligent and sensitive manner toward the phenomenon of religion' (Wright, 2000, p. 11). Despite broad agreement with both Wright and Homan, we wish to suggest, as we have argued above, that it is necessary to subject oneself as the apperceiving subject to a special kind of scrutiny unavailable to conventional constructions of such literacy. The search for a way out of the impasse that traps authentic religious literacy between two mutually antagonistic ideologies, joined together by their shared attachment to unthinkingness, requires a revitalised Religious Education confidently equipped to interrogate the liberal settlement through which Religious Education's place in the contemporary curriculum is now determined and constrained. Religious Education may be both the catalyst and the beneficiary in this process, just as the grammar of a renovated religious literacy may paradoxically be drawn from the late Enlightenment genealogical methods that, historically, derived much of their energy from their concentrated assault on the truth claims of religion.

Bringing postmodernist, antifoundational perspectives to bear upon the academic and educational debates polarizing Free Exercise and Establishment Clause values in the United States, Stanley Fish has recently argued very persuasively for the impossibility of liberalism achieving the kind of 'neutrality' relative to religion envisioned by the Enlightenment legal-liberalism that has traditionally been invoked to support interpretations of the religion clauses in the US Constitution and its educational offshoots (Fish, 1997, pp. 2255–2333). Fish begins with the reiteration of the Nietzschean critique of liberalism's self-promotion, but also engages with writers who, having recognized the force of the antifoundational critique, have proposed what he terms a kind of 'superliberalism' that might be able to accommodate both religion and rationalism in a common neutral space. The real and unavoidable meaning of antifoundationalism, Fish insists, subverts this strategy of containment by showing that liberalism does not exist in anything like the form it purports to possess. While classical liberalism represents itself as a place of neutrality outside the partisan struggles that mark the contest of religious convictions, it is in fact a participant in these struggles, aggressively advancing its own values, which it masks as universal – values such as autonomy, individual freedom, and reasonableness – and circumscribing the concept of religion as private and personal in order better to police it through the unacknowledged violence of the liberal state. Liberalism – while affecting neutrality and tolerance – must be seen not as the impartial arbiter but as the temporary victor in an ongoing battle for the maintenance of what William Cavanaugh, following Nietzsche, has defined as its three 'religious' myths: the myth of the violent state as the rescue from violence, the myth of collusive civil society as free space, and the myth of dehumanizing economic globalisation as authentic, achieved catholicity (Cavanaugh, 2002).

While exposing the invocation of Enlightenment values by which even superliberalism would seek to justify itself, Fish and Cavanaugh emphasise that this move does not trap education in the condition of nihilism or relativism feared by some contemporary liberals. Indeed, the consequences are anti-relativistic. Fish has explained elsewhere that 'For me it is relativism when you slide away from the norms, histories, and practices of different cultures and groups and emphasize instead formal universal principles like equality and colour-blindness' (Fish, 1996, pp. 719–735). Fish is advocating abandonment of the pretence that any impartial universalism or neutrality is ultimately sustainable, urging that the illusion be dispelled by an open recognition that human beings in fact commonly perform evaluations from the partial perspectives of local, contingent commitments based upon a wide range of moral and spiritual investments. In strongly articulating the implications of antifoundationalism in the context of the relations of religion and the state, Fish is also implying that there is, and can be, no such thing as an irreducible separation of exterior citizenship and interior religious orientation. His antifoundationalist argument is correspondingly persuasive in its claim that reason – and citizenship understood as an instantiation of civic reason – is incapable of justifying liberalism exclusively from within its own resources. The values of liberalism will have to be understood as permanently engaged in struggle within a political and cultural domain no longer effortlessly protected by the axiomatic invocation of 'neutral' universal principles. While Fish and Cavanaugh have entered on to the disputed territory opened up by the deconstruction of liberalism, they remind educators in the arena of global civil society that there remains no normative basis – other than active religious literacy itself, we might say – for the complacent secular assurance that the resurgent 'conservative religions' of the post-modern age, eager to impose religious truths as universal law, will not eventually prevail. Indeed, the possibilities disclosed by antifoundationalism would seem to leave no certain philosophical defence against the displacement of liberalism by theocracy where the application of liberal principles – and liberal accounts of progress – appears to be obsolete, and hence of nugatory advantage in the resistance to encroachments of popular religion on the institutions of the secular State (Owen, 1999, pp. 911–924). On the eve of the Bush re-election in November 2004, Fish lamented before a UK radio audience the absence of a religious literacy that might have enabled progressive opinion to lay before the religious Right a series of convincing challenges to its brittle coalition of interests and the skilful concealment of difference on which it depended. 'The most fascinating political question of the age is how a series of conflicting confessions and belief systems that twenty years ago were in naked competition with one another have been forged in the United States into a moral and political alliance of breathtaking proportions' (BBC, 2004). This was allowed to happen, Fish implies, by the widespread delegitimation of religion, trivialising and reconfiguring the forms of religious life into readily-policable private transactions with little or no traction on the operations of civil society. At the same time, critiques of the liberalism's ineffectual response to the tightening grip of globalisation have pointed repeatedly to exactly those forces by which the contemporary return of religion is stimulated: the quest in popular consciousness for consolatory responses to the impersonal global threats that appear daily to menace humanity, and which further incentivise withdrawal behind the fences of faith in the face of the philosophical and ethical uncertainties of post-modernity. The 'return of religion' has arisen, Gianni Vattimo suggests, out of a popular mentality that is looking for a kind of 'God-as-foundation' (Vattimo, 1998, pp. 80–83). Religious fundamentalism gains credence as the popular will rejects those aspects of modernisation that it feels are destructive of the 'authentic roots of existence.' The late twentieth century disintegration of metanarratives occasioned by the spread of hypercapitalism, and tacitly applauded by critical theory, thus generated two contradictory outcomes. First, through its onslaught on Enlightenment rationality, critical theory accomplished a 'breakdown of the philosophical prohibition of religion'. Secondly, 'philosophy and critical thought in general, having abandoned the very idea of foundation, are not (or are no longer) able to give existence that meaning which it therefore seeks in religion'. Education for Citizenship that fails to acknowledge the gravity of this intellectual and spiritual crisis, and the perilous but compelling appeal of religious commitment as a transformative solution to it, signals its doubtful, even ignominious provenance in panic-stricken state-sponsored reactions to the loss of trust in democratic values and practices. Its activities then appear restricted always to the surfaces of educational experience, in contrast with religious movements that strive evermore stridently and persuasively to intervene in those depths of being and acting the very existence of which Education for Citizenship is prone either to ignore or declare educationally inaccessible.

FUTURES OF CITIZENSHIP

If Education for Citizenship is, in an important sense, an attempt to restore a participatory and resilient rationale of core humanist values to the tasks of modern education – albeit on more fully negotiated terms than in previous eras – it seems clear that procedural liberal-legalism is too attenuated a basis for the realisation of its chief objectives. Defenders of the strength and richness of liberalism, and the forms of non-instrumental rationality on which it draws, steadfastly resist what they see as an abridged account of its relationship to secularism, denying any necessary bias against religion in the conduct of defining liberal activities such as mass education. They oppose with equal vigour any choreographed dichotomy between liberalism and communitarian or 'narrativised' forms of identity-formation and moral development (of the kind associated with Macintyre), especially where such contrasts are contrived to liberalism's disadvantage by the repudiation of all normative statements of value (Carr, 2006, pp. 443–456). The artificial division between reductive procedural liberalism and enhanced communal initiation into 'traditions of virtue' is certainly of little utility in the work of building democratic civil society through the institutions of education. Nevertheless, it is interesting to observe that the defenders of liberal-democratic constructions of Citizenship Education, where they are prepared to recognize religion at all as a source of meaning and corporate civic identity, tend habitually to assimilate faith to culture and spiritual formation to character development. The claims of a radical religious literacy, which goes 'all the way down', may entail, in their recognition of the capacity of religion to make strange the encounter with both Self and Other, serious dissatisfaction with this manoeuvre. Religion may not be, after all, simply another cultural resource on which the processes of educated rationality work to clarify normative or universal values. Indeed, if the arguments pursued in this essay are correct, religion may serve to destabilise or unmask culture-exposing contradictions, complicities, fears, cruelties, taboos, hidden hopes and yearnings ideologically sublimated or neutralised by the operations of culture. Understood in these senses, religious literacy pushes Education for Citizenship into indisputably dangerous ground, largely uncharted by conventional forms of Enlightened educational inquiry. This process takes learning and teaching to a site where the deepest investments of the Self are both validated and interrogated; where the languages of faith have restored to them the energies of metaphysical commitment, and where the unappeasable longing for transcendence is recognised all too frequently to be in tension with the limitations of culture, society and all of the material and symbolic regimes imposed on selves and communities by an unjust world. The politics of citizenship can nonetheless be renewed by this synthesis, just as the concepts of 'religion', 'education' and 'citizenship' can emerge from a vibrant Religious Education classroom, each radically transformed by the interchange between them. The challenge to Citizenship Education is to validate this synthesis as a factor vital to the attainment of its goals and to confront the religious volatility of the globalised epoch in a spirit of confident, generous humanism free from the outmoded rationalisations of the past.

REFERENCES

Arendt, H. (1958). *The human condition.* Chicago: Chicago University Press.
Audi, R. (1989). The separation of church and state and the obligations of citizenship. *Philosophy and Public Affairs, 18*(3) (Summer), 259–296.
Barnes, L. P. (2000). Ninian Smart and the phenomenological approach to religious education. *Religion, 30,* 315–32.
Barnes, L. P. (2007). The disputed legacy of Ninian Smart and phenomenological religious education: a critical response to Kevin O'Grady. *British Journal of Religious Education, 29*(2), 157–169.
Barnes, L. P. and Wright, A. (2006). Romanticism, representations of religion and critical religious education. *British Journal of Religious Education, 28*(1), 65–77.
BBC (2004). *Night waves.* BBC Radio 4, 1 November 2004.
Bellah, R. (1970). *Beyond belief: Essays on religion in a post-traditional world.* New York: Harper and Row.

Berger, P. L. (1999). The desecularisation of the world: a global overview. In P. Berger *et al* (Eds.), *The desecularisation of the world: Resurgent religion and world politics*. Grand Rapids, MI: Eerdmans.

Bruce, S. (2002). *God is dead: Secularisation in the West*. Oxford: OUP.

Carr, D. (2006). The Moral roots of citizenship: reconciling principle and character in citizenship education. *Journal of Moral Education, 35*(4), 443–456.

Cavanaugh, W. T. (2002). *Theopolitical imagination: Discovering the liturgy as a political act in an age of global consumerism*. London: T. & T. Clark.

Erdemir, A. (2005). Tradition and modernity: Alevis' ambiguous terms and Turkey's ambivalent subjects. *Middle Eastern Studies, 41*(6), 937–951.

Fish, S. (1996). At the federalist society. *Howard Law Journal, 39* (3), 719-35.

Fish, S. (1997). Mission impossible: Settling the just bounds between church and state. *Columbia Law Review, 97*(8), 2255–2333.

Giroux, H. A. (2004). Beyond belief: Religious fundamentalism and cultural politics in the age of George W. Bush. *Cultural Studies Critical Methodologies, 4*(4), 415–425.

Halstead, M. J. (2004). An Islamic concept of education. *Comparative Education, 40*(4), 517–529.

Heidegger, M. (1962). *Being and time* (J. Macquarrie & E. Robinson, Trans.). London: SCM Press.

Hogget, P. (2005). Iraq: Blair's mission impossible. *British Journal of Politics and International Relations, 7*(3), 418–28.

Homan, R. (2004). Religion and literacy: observations on religious education and the literacy strategy for secondary education in Britain. *British Journal of Religious Education, 26*(1), 21–32.

Husserl, E. (1970). *The Paris lectures* (P. Koestenbaum, Trans. and Introductory Lecture). The Hague: Martinus Nijhoff.

Jackson, P. J. (2004). *The interface between religious education and citizenship education*. Birmingham: Farmington.

Luckmann, T. (1967). *The invisible religion: The problem of religion in modern society*. London: Macmillan.

Nesbitt, E. (2001). Religious nurture and young people. In C. Ericker & J. Ericker (Eds.), *Spiritual Education, Cultural Religious and Social Differences; New Perspectives for the 21st Century* (130-142).

O'Grady, K. (2005). Professor Ninian Smart, phenomenology and religious education. *British Journal of Religious Education, 27*(3), 227–237.

Overmeyer, D.L. (2003). Religion in China today: Introduction. *The China Quarterly, 174*, 307–316.

Owen, J.J. (1999). Church and state in Stanley Fish's antiliberalism. *The American Political Science Review, 93*(4), 911–924.

SCAA (1994). *Model syllabuses for religious education: Faith communities working group reports*. London: Schools Curriculum and Assessment Authority.

Schools Council (1971). *Working paper 36: Religious education in secondary schools*. London: Evans/Methuen.

Scottish Education Department (1992). *Curriculum guidelines 5–14: Religious and moral education*, Edinburgh: HMSO.

Scottish Executive (2005). *Analysis of religion in the 2001 census: Summary report*. Edinburgh: Scottish Executive.

Smart, N. (1966). The *teacher and Christian belief*. London: James Clarke.

Smart, N. (1971). *The religious experience of mankind*. London: Collins.

Thompson, P. (2004). Whose confession? Which tradition? *British Journal of Religious Education, 26*(1), 61–73.

Vattimo, G. (1998). The trace of the trace. In J. Derrida & G. Vattimo (Eds.), *Religion* (D. Webb *et al*, Trans.) (pp. 80–83). Stanford: Stanford University Press.

Villa, D. (1999). Max Weber: Integrity, disenchantment, and the illusions of politics. *Constellations, 6*(4), pp. 540–560.

Wallis, R. and Bruce, S. (1992). Secularisation: The orthodox model. In S. Bruce (Ed.), *Religion and modernisation: Sociologists and historians debate the secularisation thesis.* Oxford: Clarendon Press, pp. 8–31.

Warner, S. (1993). Work in progress toward a new paradigm for the sociological study of religion in the United States. *American Journal of Sociology,* 98, 1044–93.

Wimmer, A. (2003). Democracy and ethno-religious conflict in Iraq. *Survival, 45*(4), 111–134.

Wright, A. (1993). *Religious education in the secondary school: Prospects for a religious literacy.* London: David Fulton.

Wright, A. (2000). *Religious education, religious literacy and the literacy strategy.* Birmingham: Farmington.

Wright, A. (2001). Religious literacy and democratic citizenship. In L. Francis, J. Astley & M. Robbins (Eds.), *The fourth r for the third millennium: Education in religion and vales for the global future.* Dublin: Lindisfarne.

Young, L. A. (Ed.) (1997). *Rational choice theory and religion.* London: Routledge.

James C. Conroy and Robert A. Davis
University of Glasgow

LEONARD J. WAKS

COSMOPOLITANISM AND CITIZENSHIP EDUCATION

INTRODUCTION

Cosmopolitanism, a leading idea of classical era Stoics and enlightenment philosophies, is once again at the intellectual forefront. Geographer David Harvey declares that 'cosmopolitanism is back' (2000, p. 529). Historian David Hollinger points to a 'new wave' of cosmopolitan manifestos, declarations, and analyses, and sees this new cosmopolitanism as moving beyond the sterile disputes between liberal universalism and communitarianism (2003). Philosopher Kwame Appiah advances cosmopolitanism as a replacement for globalisation and multiculturalism as the central organising principle of our time (2006, p. xiii).[1] Rebecca Walkowitz (2006) posits a 'cosmopolitan style' that is transforming literature and all humanities disciplines (2006). After providing an account of this emerging cosmopolitanism (Section II), and locating its opportunities and constraints in contemporary metropolitan society, (Section III), the author then constructs a cosmopolitan framework for metropolitan citizenship education (Section IV). First a few words about cosmopolitanism itself.

The Cosmopolitan Idea

The root idea of cosmopolitanism is that of a community, a *polis*, as large as the world, the cosmos. A cosmopolitan is a member of this community, and a participant in its moral, political and cultural life. Cosmopolitans, in contrast with those with restricted loyalties to particular ethnic or national groups, extend themselves to other, or even all, peoples.

We may distinguish *moral–political* and *aesthetic–cultural* versions of cosmopolitanism. In the moral–political sense a cosmopolitan person is one who regards all people as though they were friends, neighbours and co-citizens. To be cosmopolitan in this sense is to accept moral responsibility, as both an individual and a citizen, for those beyond one's group. Rather than restricting one's moral responsibility to an in-group of friends, relatives and co-nationals to whom one owes special obligations, cosmopolitans in the moral–political sense both act charitably towards outsiders in an individual capacity, and promote governmental and trans-national policies to provide for their welfare.

M.A. Peters, A. Britton and H. Blee (Eds.), Global Citizenship Education: Philosophy, Theory and Pedagogy, 203–219.

In the second, aesthetic–cultural sense, a cosmopolitan person is one who exhibits a kind of multi-national sophistication. To be cosmopolitan in this sense is to be open to those from other places, take an interest in their cultural practices, learn about these practices through reading, travel, and personal contact, and even to shape a personal identity as *a* cosmopolitan through such experiences.

Cosmopolitanism and the Challenges of Our Era

Why is cosmopolitanism is coming to the fore today? One reason is that it offers an interpretive and normative frame for issues arising in the aftermath of globalisation; one, furthermore, that promises to be more illuminating and coherent than either nationalist or multi-culturalist alternatives.

Economic globalisation has extended capitalist exchange relations from North America, Western Europe and Japan to Asia, Eastern Europe and South America, bringing all of these regions within the information web of modern telecommunications and overnight courier services. Foods and consumer products from around the world are on our store shelves. Intermediate goods shipped overnight from distant factories and warehouses make up the parts of our domestic products. This compression of time and space makes everyone at least a virtual neighbour.

On social and cultural levels, both the economic prosperity of global centres and the erosion of traditional third-world economies have unleashed a wave of migration from the countryside to the cities and from poor nations in Asia and Africa to Western Europe and North America. Meanwhile the activities of trans-national corporations in producing and marketing goods for diverse world markets have forged working alliances between designers, engineers, marketers, financiers and insurers, and other knowledge professionals across the globe. Now many non-nationals are our *real* neighbours and working partners.

Just as the picture of the earth from outer-space created a concrete image of world as a geographic unity, the proximity of peoples from around the world at all economic levels – rich and poor, educated and uneducated – has given a more concrete sense in the popular mind to the idea of humanity as an inter-connected human community. This everyday cosmopolitanism is reinforced by the spread of world music, art, literature, religions, cuisines and architectural styles, and international celebrity culture, and the resulting post-modern cultural mélanges and fusions. Everyone with an Apple iPod and 99 cents can now aspire to and even attain a certain measure of international sophistication.

On a political level, many of the most pressing problems of our era, such as climate change and other environmental threats, the regulation of trans-national trade and migration, international terrorism, and nuclear proliferation transcend national borders and call for a coordinated global response. These problems generate global publics and social movements, and give rise to global non-governmental organisations operating within a world-wide civil society to address these problems through the United Nations and other agencies in the emerging world polity. After globalisation we can at least begin to experience ourselves not merely as members of an ideal world-wide community, but as members of a real, though still nascent, global political society.

A WORKING DEFINITION OF COSMOPOLITANISM

To explore the implications of these developments for civic education we will need more than a simple dictionary definition of 'cosmopolitanism'. Arriving at an up-to-date working conception will require that we review the historical and contemporary meanings of and debates about cosmopolitanism.

Cosmopolitanism as a Philosophy

The commitment to a *polis* as large as the *cosmos* pits cosmopolitanism as a moral notion against all forms of ethno-centrism and nationalism. Beyond this root notion, however, there are multiple competing philosophical conceptions of cosmopolitanism with different emphases, and it has been argued that no one conception is adequate (Vertovic & Cohen, 2003, 'Intro'). We thus have to discover or invent a conception upon which we can found a citizen education project. We begin by placing the idea in the history of philosophy.

Philosophy even in its pre-Socratic origins had a cosmopolitan strain. Pythagoras, Thales, and Democritus are all depicted by ancient biographers as having travelled widely to acquaint themselves with Babylonian and Egyptian science and mathematics and non-Greek religious literatures and practices. The Sophists critiqued by Plato were also depicted as cosmopolitan intellectuals teaching eclectic skills of argument and persuasion gathered from many cities. The Sophist Hippias is depicted by Plato (Protagoras, 337c7-d3) as telling a mixed group of Athenians and foreigners that 'I regard you all as kinsmen, familiars and fellow-citizens – by nature and not by convention, which is a tyrant over human beings and forces many things contrary to nature'.

Philosophical discussion of cosmopolitanism, classical and contemporary, has concentrated on this moral–political dimension. The 4th century BC cynic Diogenes of Sinope was the first philosopher explicitly to call himself a cosmopolitan, a 'citizen of the world' – a shocking statement in a world where one's city was such a fundamental feature of personal identity. Diogenes claimed that people could become reasonable and wise only if they liberated themselves from the limitations and narrow conventions of their cities. Diogenes' cosmopolitanism appears to be merely negative, however, in that he did not have a robust conception of a cosmopolitan community, and did not prescribe broad cosmopolitan obligations.

The Stoic philosophers took up the idea that a common human reason made all men brothers, and imagined an ideal brotherhood as wide as humanity. The Stoics actually conceived people as belonging to *two* communities, their historical group with its parochial ideas and conventions, and an idealised moral community governed by universal natural laws of reason. This notion of dual citizenship was taken up by early Christians as the view that individuals belong to both temporal (political and geographic) communities and to an ideal, universal, moral community of both Jews and Gentiles, the Kingdom of God. As Jesus advised, 'do unto Caesar that which is Caesar's, and unto God that which is God's'.

Kant, much influenced by the Stoics, conceived the universal laws of reason that free moral agents give to themselves as 'categorical imperatives' and the ideal moral community of humanity as the 'kingdom of ends'. Kant expanded this moral notion to the political realm, conceiving a federation of liberal republics as protector of universal human rights, especially the moral right of individuals as 'ends in themselves,' to develop freely and express their distinctly human capabilities. Human rights entailed a cosmopolitan duty: to resist the coercive guidance of any church or state. Kant's ideal of a world federation of liberal states was a direct inspiration for the League of Nations and the United Nations.

Current Debates about Cosmopolitanism

While it is reasonably straightforward to say what the word 'cosmopolitanism' has meant historically, it is more difficult to say precisely what it prescribes and forbids. Does it, for example, reject all special obligations deriving from one's national and ethnic communities, or only some of them? Is it for world government and the actualisation of a robust and fully integrated global society, or merely for qualifying national and local loyalties with more inclusive cosmopolitan ones? Does it prescribe cultural–aesthetic cosmopolitanism, or consider that kind of international sophistication hostile to moral–political cosmopolitanism? Conflicting answers have been given to all of these questions.

Special Obligations

A useful entry point to the current discussion of special obligations is Martha Nussbaum's (1994) uncompromising statement of strong moral–political cosmopolitanism coupled with an equally uncompromising cosmopolitan citizen education program. Calling all particular attachments and alleged special obligations to members of our own moral communities and nations 'arbitrary,' Nussbaum turned back to the Stoics and Kant and called for educating all young people to be 'citizens of the world' with obligations that extend globally. Several other prominent philosophers have advanced similar ethical ideas, challenging the special moral status we generally assign to our family members, friends, neighbours, and co-nationals. Why, they ask, do we unquestionably jump into a swimming pool to save a neighbour's child while knowingly doing nothing while so many children in Africa are dying from preventable diseases?[2] Are we not in so doing merely assigning those near and dear to us an unjustifiably privileged moral status?

Many authors flying the banner of cosmopolitanism, however, have distanced themselves from Nussbaum and these other so-called 'strong cosmopolitans'. They have rejected the moral demands of strong cosmopolitanism as 'incredible', arguing that if we accepted them we should all have to drop whatever we are doing, abandon those projects that make our individual lives worth living, and rush to 'save the children'. Certainly there must be more to life than that! Further, as few people would find such demands compelling, strong cosmopolitanism is from a practical point of view a weak basis upon which to build cosmopolitan political or educational projects.

In response, some strong cosmopolitans have argued that at least some special obligations are compatible with, or are even implied by, a universalist cosmopolitan ethic. Other cosmopolitans, however, have *weakened* the moral thesis by allowing that cosmopolitan moral claims must compete with other values and sources of moral obligation. David Held (2005), for example, claims that a cosmopolitan ethic is a framework only for the most basic rights, while Richard Miller (2005) argues that cosmopolitanism only requires moral *respect* for all people, not the moral *concern* that necessarily creates obligations for ameliorative action.

Individuals and the Nation State

Meanwhile, some cosmopolitans have questioned whether individual citizens are even the appropriate bearers of cosmopolitan moral obligations. Although individuals can do much on their own to end hunger or support peace or protect the environment, these ends might more properly be conceived as primarily those of collective rather than individual action. 'Ought' implies 'can'. While individual citizens can pressure their governments, governments possess the relevant levers of power. As a result, some cosmopolitans have concentrated not on individual morality but government policy. Noting that the actions of the European and North American powers have been largely responsible for third-world poverty, for example, Thomas Pogge (2005) has proposed a 'global resource dividend' to be provided by governments of rich nations for poor nations, not as a form of positive moral good but as reparation for moral harm.

A further question is the stance cosmopolitans should take to the institution of the nation state. John Dewey, among other cosmopolitan philosophers, pressed for a world government with its own courts, legislature, and executive with coercive powers. Liberal philosophers from Kant to Rawls, on the other hand, have feared that a consolidated power without effective checks could lead to global tyranny. Most contemporary cosmopolitans agree; they advocate strengthening the federation of nations with treaties and alliances, but not creating a world state; they caution against abandoning the nation state system, and even see it as potentially a useful instrument of cosmopolitan political action.

The Moral Contribution of Aesthetic–Cultural Cosmopolitanism

Some recent cosmopolitan ethicists, particularly strong cosmopolitans, have vigorously distanced themselves from aesthetic–cultural cosmopolitanism, portraying it as amoral and elitist. Roger Scruton, for example, puts it this way: 'in this sense the cosmopolitan is often seen as a kind of parasite, who depends on the quotidian lives of others to create the various local flavours and identities in which

207

he dabbles' (Scruton, 1982, p. 100). Not surprisingly, strong cosmopolitans have attempted to free the term entirely from such elitist associations. The idea has been to focus on *popular*, even everyday, forms of cultural exchange e.g., immigrant community gardeners sharing seeds for vegetables from their different countries. Against this distinction between elite (sophisticated) and popular cultural cosmopolitanism, however, in the information network era just about everyone can gain access to world music, world art, world food, and even international travel, so that aesthetic and cultural worldliness has itself *become* popular.

The opposition between aesthetic cultural and moral–political versions of cosmopolitanism is overdrawn. Christine Sypnowich (2005) has recently argued that cultural and aesthetic worldliness may be necessary for receptivity to and interest in others, as well as to effective moral engagement with moral problems affecting the diverse populations in cities and around the globe. Kwame Appiah (2006) makes a parallel argument that *because* (by definition) cultural cosmopolitans *are* interested in people around the world, they are likely also to take an interest in their problems and the conditions for their effective resolution. Rebecca Walkowitz (2006), moreover, has offered a sustained argument that even the self-fashioning gestures and affectations of Scruton's 'dabblers' are far from amoral and apolitical. Their various gestures, which Walkowitz brings together under the term 'cosmopolitan style', are public challenges to local conventions, nationalist projects, and uncritically embraced forms of so-called 'progress'.

Cosmopolitanism as a Synthesis of Liberalism and Communitarianism

One way of moving beyond such intra-cosmopolitan debates and locating the *core* of contemporary cosmopolitanism is to focus on its effort to move beyond the sterile debate between liberal universalism (e.g., Kant and Rawls) and communitarianism (e.g., Walzer and Sandel) that has dominated moral–political philosophy for decades; to see cosmopolitanism as a synthesis of those opposing theses.

Liberal Universalism

The liberal tradition in ethics and politics has been concerned primarily with the liberty of individuals, their freedom *from* both state institutions and social conventions *to* shape their own lives. A guiding idea for liberals is *autonomy*; the idea that individuals' lives and actions are in some sense their own to shape. Only lives in which individuals freely choose how to develop their unique capacities and satisfy their unique aspirations as part of overall plans of life can be *good* lives.

The fundamental moral right for liberals is the right of the individual to pursue his or her good. Thus a liberal political philosophy entails that society is best governed by neutral principles, those presupposing no particular conception of the good conflicting with or inhibiting the free, rational, autonomous development of citizens. Institutionally, this dictates state institutions emphasising fair procedures for resolving conflicts and distributing benefits, rather than promoting specific values. In education, for example, liberals have promoted free and equal provision of a 'standard issue' programme of basic cognitive skills and knowledge of academic disciplines, conceived as supplying necessary cognitive prerequisites for the free rational development of any life, and as neutral with respect to all of them.

Communitarianism

In the late 1970s and 1980s a number of philosophers including Michael Walzer and Michael Sandel argued that liberal universalism rests on an incoherent view of individuals as moral agents. Individuals, they argued, cannot step back and reflectively detach themselves *from* their communities of moral value to choose or shape a life. Rather, they are defined or constituted *by* their social attachments, as sons or fathers, daughters or mothers, neighbours, friends, co-religionists, compatriots. Their very identities, even their languages of moral reason, are bound up in their specific communities with defined roles and special obligations. They cannot coherently be conceived as *choosing* a plan of life; rather, they find themselves already 'thrown' into communities of moral value, shaped by habits and routines they have never chosen. Guidelines for good lives are already found *within* these communities, and reasons advanced against particular expectations and obligations can only be framed up within the internal languages of those communities. The only good lives are those shaped by, and closely attached within, an individual's communities of moral value.

Communitarians believe that the contemporary liberal moral landscape has undermined existing communities of moral value. By encouraging individuals to detach themselves from their communities in search of individual paths, it has merely blinded them to opportunities for living well within, and led them to reject any obligations for sustaining, these communities. As a result the traditional communities are eroding while individuals are set adrift, without firm moral guidelines or personal anchors.

In response, communitarians urge governments to promote and sustain national, religious and cultural groups as social bases upon which good lives can be built, to enter into partnerships with them to provide multi-dimensional assistance appropriate to their unique situations. Thus neighbourhood public schools, and even religious schools and schools serving distinct ethnic and racial groups, should be sensitive to the specific needs and cultural resources of their students and the surrounding communities. Communitarians thus reject 'standard issue' value-neutral programs in favour of charter schools and voucher programs that support existing communities of moral value.

The New Cosmopolitan Synthesis

The new cosmopolitanism is a synthesis of liberal universalism and communitarianism that accepts some communitarian insights while subjecting others to liberal critique.

Cosmopolitan Accommodations of Communitarian Insights. Cosmopolitans agree with the communitarian critique of liberalism's non-situated individualism. They agree that individuals do not and cannot simply 'choose' life plans in a vacuum, without regard for their social situations. Individuals' identities are formed as narratives, as ways individuals come to talk about themselves and their lives with others. Distinct repertoires of narrative forms are available in given ethnic or national societies, from which individuals construct and reconstruct more personal narratives with specific choices, values and ends. These personal narratives are framed within existing communal narratives about 'our people'. Thus, inevitably individuals find themselves already linked to others, bound in solidarity with them, and morally responsible to them. Ethnic and national identities are thus central components of individual life plans. They are not differences that don't make a moral difference; special obligations are not morally 'arbitrary'. Cosmopolitans respect special obligations to family, friends, neighbours and co-nationals as ineluctable elements of moral life.

The new cosmopolitans further agree that abstract liberal values, e.g., diffuse identification with 'humanity,' cannot fulfil the basic human need to belong. They further deny that particularistic identifications are necessarily atavistic or oppositional, although they are sensitive to these ever-present dangers. With good will, such identities can even be used as instruments of inter-group solidarity and the advancement of global human rights, as expressed in the lyric 'Black and White together, we shall overcome'. The new cosmopolitans thus see the real moral challenge not as assessing the moral status of ethnic identity per se, but rather of assessing specific forms of ethnic or national identification in terms of their differential potentials for cooperation or conflict.

Like communitarians, the new cosmopolitans value ethnic diversity as a source of interest and social renewal, and are sensitive to the conditions that sustain or threaten it. While they encourage individuals from all groups to enter into many associations – cultural, occupational and fraternal – beyond their narrow ethnic groups to form hybrid identities, they are sensitive that some forms of association can undermine individuals' identities and leave them adrift. Countering Salman Rushdie's praise for hybridity and impurity, Appiah notes that there can be as spurious a utopia of hybridity as of cultural purity.

Cosmopolitan Critiques of Communitarianism. For all that, the new cosmopolitans still share many basic principles with liberalism. They are *for* evermore inclusive identifications and solidarities, extending to identifications with the human community as a whole. These are, however, to be 'rooted' in identifications with family and friends, neighbours and co-nationals. While they are *for* cultural diversity, they are *against* any cultural pluralism that conceives distinct cultures as ineluctably different and incommensurate. The incommensurability thesis they take to be incompatible with any serious effort to advance trans-national human rights projects. While different communities of value may employ distinct moral vocabularies, cosmopolitans say, they can make practical accommodation if they wish to and are willing to make the effort. People share enough to start a conversation and navigate their way through it.

The new cosmopolitans, indeed, are sceptical about the very idea of distinct ethnic and national cultures to be protected and preserved. Cultures are dynamic instruments to further life, not museum pieces to be placed on pedestals and worshipped. Most ethnic 'cultures' (e.g., French Canadian culture, Afro-American culture) put up as objects to be preserved are in any case not really 'traditional'; they are inventions of sub-groups advancing new political projects or cultural visions. And even better chosen candidates for the status of 'traditional' cultures have continually received infusions from outsiders; no matter how far back we go there simply are no 'pure' cultures to preserve.

The new cosmopolitans *do not* join the communitarians in *rejecting* moral universals; they consider them potentially useful instruments for advancing global projects. They *reject* the idea that moral universals such as basic human rights are just 'ethnocentric' ideas of 'Western' culture, or are the enemy of differences worth preserving. They reject, for example, the idea of a special 'Asian form of human rights', put forward by apologists of suppressive Asian societies such as Singapore and Malaysia, to constrain individual speech and political action in the name of group cohesion.

The New Cosmopolitanism. Cosmopolitans are specialists at constructing the new without destroying the old. They are focused on the practical. Instead of theorising about constraints to inter-group communication and cooperation they look for actual opportunities and effective strategies *for* cooperative action. They assess efforts to advance human rights in terms not merely of morality but of practicability. They examine specific situations in which human rights are at stake, and carefully pick their fights. They reject 'incredible' moral claims about what everyone is morally obligated to do; they do not think that everybody's life projects should be put on hold while we devote ourselves to 'saving the children'.

They are, however, moral progressives, in that they look forward to new and better situations that can realistically be brought into being, rather than backward to any putative golden age of cultural purity. They seek to broaden solidarities among all groups around important common interests such as peace, environmental protection and the reduction of hunger and disease, recognising that different strategies will appeal to different groups – that there is no standard issue solution to fit every situation. In this sense they are pluralists, keen to accommodate cultural differences to achieve cooperative practical results. With this in mind it is now time to situate the cosmopolitan citizen education project.

COSMOPOLITAN EXPERIENCE AND THE CONTEMPORARY METROPOLIS

Education is preparation for life. Citizenship education is preparation for life as a citizen, that is, as a full member of civilized society. In this broad sense all education is citizenship education. Cosmopolitan citizenship education is preparation for life as a citizen with cosmopolitan attitudes and interests, capable of participating in cosmopolitan practices, those drawing upon contributions and resources of those from multiple ethnic and national groups on friendly and equitable terms.

Cosmopolitanism and the City

Such practices are rooted in cosmopolitan settings of cities and extended metropolitan areas. Cities, like philosophy, have been cosmopolitan from the beginning. Forming as centres of administration and exchange, at harbour seaports and cross-roads on trade routes, they have been magnets for people from the countryside and beyond the borders: producers and manufacturers, merchants, traders, craftsmen, seamen, travellers and adventurers, itinerant teachers, entertainers, charlatans, sex-workers. The existence of cosmopolitan zones for exchange, learning and apprenticeship, conversation and pleasure is among the most important characteristics of cities. We might say of municipalities lacking them that they are not *real* cities. Any cosmopolitan citizen education project must have metropolitan experience at its centre.

Cities, Exchange, and Cosmopolitan Friendship

Cities are centres of exchange, which is based on the principle of mutual advantage. One person has too many gallons of olive oil for immediate use, while another has too many bushels of wheat. At the margin, the gallon of oil given is worth less to its possessor than the bushels of wheat received, and vice versa, so the trade is a 'good deal' for both. This kind of exchange typically brings those from different places together: Attica had poor soil, good only for olives and grapes, while Egypt had rich soil producing wheat for bread. A bustling zone of exchange developed around Piraeus that eventually became one of the leading economic centres of the ancient world. The Greek verb 'to exchange', *kattallatten*, also meant 'to bring a stranger into friendship or into the community'. In his funeral oration, Pericles could boast that 'the magnitude of our city draws the produce of the world into our harbour, so that to the Athenian the fruits of other countries are as familiar a luxury as those of his own'.[3]

The profits from economic exchange can be re-invested in further trade, or in manufacturing, shipping, warehousing and other activities generating economic growth. Traders, financiers, sea captains, engineers, producers need meeting places to discuss new ideas and ventures, and thus have market areas, taverns and pubs, tea and coffee houses, and other cosmopolitan public meeting places developed.. Economic growth in turn becomes a magnet for still more outsiders – more craftsmen, labourers, seamen, teachers, entertainers, etc. Whole areas of cities and their suburbs become populated by migrants, some retaining their old ways, others forging hybrid identities and merging into the cosmopolitan life of the city.

Profits can also be spent on consumption, and cities also become magnets to high-end migrant artists and craftsmen providing objects of pleasure and status for wealthy citizens. Among many examples, the composers and musicians, artists and writers in 18th and 19th century Vienna came from throughout the Hapsburg Empire, from Bohemia, Hungary, Germany, Silesia, Poland and Northern Italy. Paris was another great international city peculiarly open to influences from outside, to trends circulating in other parts of the world. The great Impressionist and Post-Impressionist painters of late 19th century and early 20th century Paris included many outsiders, including the Dutchman Van Gogh, Spaniards Picasso and Gris, the Italian Amadeo Modigliani, the American Mary Cassatt. The new painting was influenced by Turner in England, Japanese prints appearing after 1855, African sculptures after 1880, and the pre-Roman Iberian sculptures so appealing to Picasso (Hall, 1998, p. 218). This process of cultural re-appropriation is the rule.

Non-Cosmopolitan Zones

Cities possess many areas of cosmopolitan exchange, and the encounters in these spaces can radiate out and impact the character of the entire city and its residents. But not every urban zone is cosmopolitan. Far from it! Cities are magnets to foreigners, and natives often withdraw to fortified settlements and shun new arrivals, who then group together in, or find themselves restricted to, ethnic 'ghettos'. This 'us vs. them' division often hardens native and immigrant identities as oppositional and blocks friendly and equitable, cosmopolitan inter-group exchanges.[4]

COSMOPOLITAN CITIZENSHIP EDUCATION

A cosmopolitan citizenship education project aims to soften oppositional identities and provide access to settings for cosmopolitan exchange. People form and strengthen cosmopolitan attitudes, interests and loyalties by engaging in such exchanges. Existing cosmopolitan settings, where people from different groups habitually and positively cooperate, whether in formal academic or 'real world' settings, thus play a singularly important role in this process. The project as a result aims primarily to (a) enlarge the cosmopolitan potential of academic settings and (b) establish access routes between them and the city.

Access and Barriers to Cosmopolitan Experience

Schools and colleges, like marketplaces and galleries and coffeehouses, can be favourable to cosmopolitan experience, but only if (a) an appropriate assemblage of ethnic and national groups is represented; (b) oppositional ethnic and national identities do not thwart their interactions; and (c) the faculties, school culture and curriculum actively promote cosmopolitan exchange.

'Real world' cosmopolitan groupings are generally structured as informal networks of practitioners, co-workers and assistants, students and apprentices, journalists and publicists and critics, financiers and dealers and clients, amateur camp followers, friends and lovers. Any of these can serve as sponsors, introducing newcomers and creating opportunities for them to display their talents and show they have something to contribute. Formal credentials may count for something, but in the non-bureaucratic network structure, capabilities and informal attributes count for more. Who you know and what you can do count for more than passage through a curriculum. Indeed, one aspect of 'cosmopolitan style', Rebecca Walkowitz (2006) notes, is a distrust of formal institutions of learning and cultural transmission.

What restricts access to cosmopolitan experiences in schools and 'real world' settings? Starting with schools, we may consider managed difference, and the diploma-credential systems, as major barriers to cosmopolitan experience.

The metropolitan geographic and political system of *managed difference* maintains distinct populations in their own designated spaces: city centre, ethnic neighbourhoods, underclass ghettos, working class and affluent suburbs, satellite cities (Abu-Lughod, 2000).[5] The school children in these different residential areas go to distinct and unequal schools in distinct, autonomous school districts. In the United States in particular, with its finely-structured system of local school districts, segregation by income and ethnicity, and inequality of educational provision, can be pronounced. As a result, students from a wide range of different national and ethnic groups are simply not brought into proximity, making cosmopolitan exchange impossible. Students from disadvantaged ethnic groups, confined to under-funded and segregated schools, also come to resent those more fortunate and are likely to form atavistic and oppositional ethnic identities, rendering themselves vulnerable to demagogic leaders who prey on their vulnerabilities and deepen their anti-cosmopolitan attitudes and interests. They are also likely to suffer from low self-esteem and to be vulnerable to self-destructive behaviours. These students are unlikely to develop proper work ethics or high levels of either basic cognitive skills or knowledge of academic disciplines. Thus they may have little to contribute, personally or intellectually, in inter-group exchange.

The *credential system* excludes potential teachers, whether domestic or foreign, possessing high-level skills in various real world practices and access to cosmopolitan networks, but lacking in formal teaching credentials. As a result school students are unable to acquire either the educational requisites or personal sponsors needed for access to cosmopolitan networks and experiences in the real world. Schools are thus neither cosmopolitan settings nor pathways to them.

Eliminating Barriers to Cosmopolitan Experience

Metropolitan regions have the resources for broadening cosmopolitan experience. Schools have to be made more inclusive and connections between schools and the 'real world' must be strengthened.

The Nationalist Barrier. With regard to the nationalistic and statist biases in the projects of state school systems, multiculturalists and postmodernists have for several decades challenged these, proposed non-biased alternatives and also taken note of countervailing multi-cultural and post-modern trends. Bill Readings, to take an extreme case, has asserted that the academy in the global era has been stripped of its nationalist ends and lies in 'ruins'. The author has recently argued (Waks, 2006) that the power bases of contemporary nation-states, as transformed by processes of globalisation, no longer require difference-denying national identities.

214

Forms of ethnic pluralism compatible with inter-group solidarity will be attractive to state leaders and national elites. Cosmopolitan educational projects may gain a surprisingly positive reception.

School District Barriers. One major barrier to inclusiveness is ethnic and class segregation by school districts, which have become merely tools of managed difference. While almost all of the major metropolitan regions of the United States are predominantly white, all of the city centre school districts are predominantly composed of disadvantaged minorities and immigrants. The neighbourhood district schools further isolate various ethnic and national groups. It is worth noting, however, that the district school is already under considerable strain. In the United States many state governments have suspended the authority of the local central city districts because of gross underperformance, and placed these districts under the control of state-appointed boards. In the wake of the national 'No Child Left Behind' legislation, underperforming schools have all been threatened with closure, and districts are now required to provide alternatives, including charter schools under private management, to their students. Meanwhile, many parents of both liberal and anti-liberal persuasion, sensing that their children are treated as mere numbers in the test-dominated, standard issue district schools, are pulling their school-aged children from these schools and placing them in privately operated charter schools or schooling them at home. As charter school and home-schooling opportunities grow, the district system is morphing into something new but still inchoate. It is now ripe for major overhaul.

Critics of both nationalist and cosmopolitan persuasions have worried about the exclusive, ethnic particularism of charter schools (Fuller, 2002), the social narrowness of home-based learning, and the increasing segregation of district schools as charter-school and home-school students leave the mainstream system (Wells, 2002). Kathleen Knight Abowitz (2001) has argued, however, that charter schools can be conceived not as spaces of ethnic isolation, but rather as spaces where distinct ethnic groups can both work toward curricular and extra-curricular arrangements suited to their needs and also prepare themselves for participation in the general public discussion. This is a paradigm new-cosmopolitan idea, serving to preserve the old (positive cultural identity) while building the new (inter-group exchange on more equitable terms). Terri Wilson (2006), however, has questioned whether the distinct ethnic groups placed in charge of their own charter schools can truly be motivated to engage with other groups in a broad public discussion, and whether the charter system can be set up to encourage it.

The way beyond the *school district* barrier is to re-conceive the multiple districts in the metropolitan area as elements in a metropolitan educational 'super-district'. Such an organisation would take on some responsibilities with respect to students in local district schools, charter schools, private and parochial schools and home-schools. These can include settings where children throughout the larger community can come together from time to time for cosmopolitan exchange. More will be said about this below.

The Diploma-Credential Barrier. In the United States, schools recruit teaching staff from restricted pools – people with credentials from teacher education programmes. These individuals usually have conventional ideas about teaching and curriculum. Through their school and work experiences they are linked to the school culture but not, with few exceptions, to the cosmopolitan networks of the city. They lack personal resources for cosmopolitan education and connections to others who possess them.

The way beyond this barrier is to recruit teachers from a larger pool and experiment with a variety of 'post-curriculum' learning approaches (Green, 1990). Schools would be more interesting places if their faculties could also include e.g., teachers from foreign countries with foreign qualification and talented, appealing, out-of-the-ordinary people without teacher credentials – writers and artists, intellectuals and travellers serving in part-time and limited term capacities. Such individuals can be selected carefully on the basis of their high-level practitioner knowledge and their established links to informal cosmopolitan networks. They can and should be drawn from a wide spectrum of ethnic and national backgrounds to serve as role models and guides. Of course bureaucratic rules and labour union restrictions would constrain this, but these are not carved in stone, and at the metro mega-district level no restrictions are entrenched.

Toward Metropolitan Regional Organization and Cosmopolitan Exchange

Metropolitan regional educational arrangements already exist. In the United States most of the several states already have regional or intermediate school districts to provide in-service teacher training, curriculum development, consultation and research for local school districts as their clients. Some of these districts even maintain regional schools. In one creative effort, the intermediate district in the Harrisburg region, in conjunction with a consortium of local districts, and in partnership with a non-governmental educational organisation, recently created the Capitol Area High School for the Arts. This school has a fixed student body like any district school, selected on the basis of portfolios and an interview. It makes available to suburban and rural students in the region Harrisburg's arts facilities and infra-structure, while also bringing middle class white students and poor minority students together under a single roof.[6] This is an example of a *metropolitan regional school.*

Regional Networks

The author has recently proposed a quite different *network* model for education in which a regional agency such as an intermediate district, in cooperation with local districts, charter schools, and private schools, and non-governmental organisations would establish *regional learning centres* (Waks, 2004). Unlike *regional schools*, which can only serve a handful of the region's students, the regional learning centres of the *network* could serve *all* the learners of the region on an intermittent basis, as meeting areas for inter-group learning and exchange. Local schools and districts would be preserved (the preservation of the old). But inter-group barriers would be moderated. Diversity would be established and maintained through the combination of face-to-face inter-group learning at the regional centres and coordinated, on-line inter-group learning activities at local school sites. The latter would involve on-line distance learning provided at the regional level, along with e-mail, listservs, web pages, blogs, social networks, and other means of day to day connection between learning centre sessions (the creation of the new).

Metropolitan regional educational networks consist of both (a) existing local or 'front line' educational facilities and providers, in mainstream or charter or private schools or homes, and (b) 'back-line' regional facilities and providers. In the back-line nodes, networked educators (c) draw upon personnel and facilities throughout the network to support both (i) *in-person* inter-group learning at the learning centres as well as (ii) local *networked* learning supporting and augmenting it. For example, in a regional poster or mural project, students from many ethnic and national groups, attending (a) neighbourhood district or charter schools, can attend periodic inter-group training workshops at (b) existing regional art colleges or other designated learning centres, while (c) under the coordinated supervision of back-line personnel from the centres and front-line local teachers, they could undertake project work at (i) the learning centres or (ii) their neighbourhood schools.

By retaining local educational agencies, including charter schools, the network draws on their specific strengths (e.g. as centres of community activity and focal points of neighbourhood identity and pride) even while undermining their role as instruments of ethnic isolation. The regional network participants, despite their local school attachments and ethnic identities, also form a larger metropolitan identity, just as major league sports fans now do. Thus the network bridges ethnic and national divides in concrete ways.

NOTES

[1] Appiah asks under what rubric shall we come to understand how peoples formerly living in distinct groups can be equipped to live together. In defence of 'cosmopolitanism', he proclaims: 'Not "globalization" – a term that once referred to a marketing strategy, and then came to designate a macroeconomic thesis, and now can seem to encompass everything and nothing. Not "multiculturalism," another shape shifter which so often designates the disease it purports to cure'.

[2] The philosophers Peter Singer and Peter Ungar are frequently cited as examples of this position.

[3] This point about the cooperation, mutual understanding and appreciation, and eventual friendship forged by strangers through exchange relations has been emphasised by Austrian economists such as von Mises and Hayek, and recently amplified in Paul Seabright's (2005) *The Company of Strangers*.

[4] Other situations involve inter-ethnic exchanges but are not inherently cosmopolitan: the ethnic resources of the participants have no play and contribute nothing to the exchanges that significantly affect the participants.

[5] Janet Abu-Lughod discusses systems of managed difference and provides detailed accounts of the process in New York, Chicago and Los Angeles throughout their histories.

[6] The Capitol Area School for the Arts was founded in 2001 by the Capitol Area Intermediate School District in partnership with Open Stage, a non-profit organisation for arts education. It provides intensive study of theatre, music, the visual arts, dance and film for students from 24 participating school districts.

REFERENCES

Abowitz, K.K. (2001). Charter schools and social justice. *Educational Theory*, *51*(2), 151–170.

Abu-Lughod, J. (2000). *New York, Chicago, Los Angeles: America's global cities*. Minneapolis: University of Minnesota Press.

Appiah, A.K (2004). *The ethics of identity*. Princeton: Princeton University Press.

Appiah, A.K (2006). *Cosmopolitanism: Ethics in a world of strangers*. New York: Norton.

Brock, G. & Brighouse, H. (Eds.) (2005). *The political philosophy of cosmopolitanism*. Cambridge: Cambridge University Press.

Calvino, I. (1978). *Invisible cities*, New York: Harvest.

Fuller, B. (2002). *Inside charter schools: The paradox of radical decentralization*. Cambridge, MA: Harvard University Press.

Green, A. (1990). *Education in state formation: The rise of education systems in England, France and the USA*. Basingstoke: Macmillan.

Hall, P. (1998). *Cities in civilization*. New York: Pantheon.

Harvey, D. (2000). Cosmopolitanism and the banality of geographical evils. *Public Culture, 12*(2), 529–564.

Held, D. (2005). Principles of cosmopolitan order. In G. Brock & H. Brighouse (Eds.), *The political philosophy of cosmopolitanism* (Ch. 2). Cambridge: Cambridge University Press.

Hollinger, D. (2003). Not universalists, not pluralists: The new cosmopolitans find their way. In S. Vertovic & R. Cohen (Eds.), *Conceiving cosmopolitanism* (pp. 227–239). Oxford: Oxford University Press.

Miller, R. (2005). Cosmopolitan respect and patriotic concern. In G. Brock & H. Brighouse (Eds.), *The political philosophy of cosmopolitanism (*Ch. 9). Cambridge: Cambridge University Press.

Nussbaum, M. (1994). Patriotism and cosmopolitanism [Special Issue]. *Boston Review, 19*(5).

Pogge, T. (2005). A cosmopolitan perspective on the global economic order. In G. Brock & H. Brighouse (Eds.), *The political philosophy of cosmopolitanism* (Ch. 7). Cambridge: Cambridge University Press.

Rawls, J. (1971). *A Theory of Justice*. Cambridge, MA: Harvard University Press.

Sandel, M. (1982*)*. *Liberalism and the limits of justice*. Cambridge: Cambridge University Press.

Scruton, R. (1982). *Dictionary of political thought*. London: MacMillan.

Seabright, P. (2005). *The company of strangers: A natural history of economic life*. Princeton: Princeton University Press.

Singer, P. (1972). Famine, affluence and morality. Reprinted in P. Singer (2000), *Writings on an ethical life* (pp. 105–117). New York: Ecco Press.

Stevens, M.L. (2001). *Kingdom of children: Culture and controversy in the homeschooling movement*. Princeton: Princeton University Press.

Synpnowich, C. (2005). Cosmopolitanism, cosmopolitans, and human flourishing. In G. Brock & H. Brighouse (Eds.), *The political philosophy of cosmopolitanism* (Ch. 5). Cambridge: Cambridge University Press.

Unger P. (1996). *Living high and letting die: Our illusion of innocence*. New York: Oxford University Press.

Vertovic, S. & Cohen, R. (2003). *Conceiving cosmopolitanism: Theory, context and practice*. New York: Oxford University Press.

Waks, L. (2004). The concept of the networked common school. *E-learning, 1*(2), 317–328. (Reprinted in M. Peters & J. Freeman-Moir, (Eds.) (2006), *Edutopias: New utopian thinking in education* (pp. 225–234). Rotterdam, The Netherlands: Sense Publishing.)

Waks, L. (2006). Globalization, state transformation, and educational re-structuring: Why postmodern diversity will prevail over standardization. *Studies in Philosophy and Education, 25*(5), 403–424.

Walkowitz, R. (2006). *Cosmopolitan style: Modernism beyond the nation*. New York: Columbia University Press.

Walzer, M. (1983). *Spheres of justice*. New York: Basic Books.

Walzer, M. (1984). Liberalism and the art of separation. *Political Theory*, *12*(3), 315–330.

Wells, A.S. (Ed.) (2002). *Where charter school policy fails: Issues of accountability and equity*. New York: Teachers College Press.

Wilson, T. (2006). *Civic fragmentation or voluntary association: Habermas, Fraser and charter school segregation*. Paper presented at the Annual meeting of the American Educational Research Association, San Francisco, 7–11 April.

Leonard J. Waks
Temple University, Philadelphia

TIMOTHY MURPHY

DIALOGUES ACROSS THE POND

Freire and Greene on the Citizenship Challenge in the Republic of Ireland

DEMOCRATIC PROCESSES AND CIVIC ENGAGEMENT IN THE RoI

Before moving on to consider the cornerstones of the democratic project in society, as elaborated by both Freire and Greene, it might be helpful to comment briefly on the general topography of the RoI in relation to democratic processes and civic engagement. Dunne, for example, alerts us to the fact that in the early decades of the state, the question of citizenship was perhaps assumed to be largely answered by a combination of nationalism and Catholicism (Dunne, 2002, p. 69). Such a perspective is certainly in tandem with Fitzgerald's contention that the pervasiveness of the Catholic moral code at that time probably restricted the extent to which alternative codes could also have been woven into the fabric of Irish society (Fitzgerald, 2005, p. 238). It is also consonant with O'Sullivan's erudite analysis of the cultural politics of Irish education, in his recently published work *Cultural Politics and Irish Education Since the 1950s* (O'Sullivan, 2005).

In this work, he distinguishes between 'theocentric' and 'mercantile' paradigms. The former, in his view, presents a view of education which is determined largely by unchanging principles 'based on a Christian view of human nature and destiny' (p. 112). There is ample evidence to suggest that following independence the Churches, both Catholic and Protestant, moved quickly to consolidate their dominant positions in their respective educational provenances. Peillon, for example, even contends that 'they succeeded in transforming schools which might have been, if not lay, at least neutral in religious matters into institutions which were directly controlled by the clergy, divided along religious lines and more and more committed to catechising' (Peillon, 1982, p. 148). The privileged position accorded to the Catholic Church in the provision of education in the RoI allowed for the exercise of a type of cultural hegemony which allowed it to build itself into the very 'vitals of the nation' (see Fuller, 2002, p. 10).

'THEOCENTRIC' WORLDVIEW

In the 'theocentric' worldview of the time knowledge was perceived as fixed and unchanging and the pursuit of it was ring-fenced for the principal purpose of illuminating the eternal truths. This is evident for example in the depiction of the

M.A. Peters, A. Brittes and H. Blee (Eds.), Global Citizenship Education: Philosophy, Theory and Pedagogy, 221–230.

aims and purpose of education as outlined in the 1971 *Primary School Curriculum: Teachers Handbook, Part 1*. It states that 'the scale of values in a society inevitably determines its educational aims and priorities. We in Ireland have our own scale of values. Each human being is created in God's image. He has a life to lead and a soul to be saved. Education is therefore concerned, not only with life but with the purpose of life (Department of Education, 1971, p. 12). As aforementioned, however, the symbiosis between Church and State was not confined to the sphere of education alone. Her influence extended into all of the vital socialising agencies of the State.

The net effect of the pervasiveness of the 'theocentric' paradigm, especially during the first half of the twentieth century, provided a favourable context for the emergence of a consensual conception of the social order throughout Irish society (Drudy & Lynch, 1993, p. 50). Such a view allows for the representation of society as an undifferentiated whole and educationally, then, according to Drudy and Lynch, this assumes 'that there is agreement within all sectors of that whole on what is the "public interest" or "collective interest" in education' (p. 50). Such a representation has also in their view forestalled the development of a critical structural analysis of the education system and of society more generally (p. 55). It would also lend credence to O'Sullivan's contention that conditions pertaining to the general democratic politics of the public sphere have been somewhat lacking in the RoI (O'Sullivan, 2005, p. 552). In particular, he points to the absence of any real 'generative dialogue' between the state and society that could cultivate 'a realization of the complexity, production, situatedness and functioning of interpretive frameworks in our lives' (p. 555).

There is a recognition here of schooling systems as sites of inquiry that provide spaces for the emergence of a learner's interpretive capacities. Such an acknowledgement would support the view that *Educating the 'Right' Way* (Apple, 2001) must involve developing a learner's capacity to ask the critical questions about 'the nature of "teachers" and "texts" and their relations to larger ideological, political, and economic dynamics' (Apple, 1986, p. 180). It would also be cognisant of Lynch's insistence that opportunities and spaces must be provided for the traditionally-silenced voices to be heard, those with 'the day-to-day experiential knowledge of injustice that is a necessary condition for informed decision-making' (Baker *et al*, 2004, p. 163). In the prevailing climate of the time, however, with the Catholic Church in such an ascendant position on the educational front, it was difficult to prise open a conception of the educational project that would accord such a high priority to the development of a learner's critical faculties.

'MERCANTILE' WORLDVIEW

The system of schooling that was existent at the establishment of the new Free State was to function without change for almost forty years (Peillon, 1982, p. 150). In the course of the 1960s, however, reform of the education system became a 'burning issue' and such reform was largely inspired by a push toward industrial development. Clancy would contend, for example, that in the wake of the adoption of a programme for economic development, with its commitment to economic growth and exported oriented industrialisation, 'the educational system would henceforth be assessed by its capacity to facilitate the achievement of these new economic objectives' (Clancy, 1986, p. 125).

This new phase in the development of Irish education was also marked by the publication of *Investment in Education* (1966). This report, which was prepared in collaboration with the Organisation for Economic Cooperation and Development (OECD), highlighted the gross under-investment in education in Ireland at that time. It also suggested that this situation represented a distinct disadvantage for Ireland in terms of the country's potential economic development. *Investment in Education*, then, was a wake-up call for the government and thereafter it was decided to substantially increase investment in education and that the State would take a more central role in the actual running of the system. Accordingly, *Educating the 'Right' Way* became synonymous with 'education as a business, students and their parents as customers, and teachers as mere functionaries who must satisfy the demand of their manager and clients' (Dunne, 2002, p. 86). Such a conception of the educational project is certainly congruent with O'Sullivan's depiction of the aforementioned 'mercantile paradigm' which contends that 'what education is for is a matter for consumers of the system, such as pupils, parents, civic leaders and business interests, to decide (O'Sullivan, 2005, p. 112). Dunne points out that in this new climate of mercantilism the civic remit of education becomes correlated to the contribution that it makes to national economic prosperity (Dunne, 2002, p. 70).

After considering the general topography of the RoI in relation to democratic processes and civic engagement, then, the author would be inclined to support Fitzgerald's position on the absence of an elaborate civic morality code there. It is in evidence that the development of such a code has been significantly restricted by the pervasiveness of the 'theocentric' and 'mercantile' paradigms at various phases in the development of Irish society.

CONVERGENCE IN DIVERGENCE: THE CITIZENSHIP CONSTRUCTS OF PAULO FREIRE AND MAXINE GREENE

In order to elicit the necessary conditions for the advancement of democratic citizenship in modern society, I have elected to focus on the educational work of Paulo Freire and Maxine Greene. It would be relatively easy for one to assume that there could be little in common between these educationalists, as they come from differing social backgrounds. Notwithstanding these differences, however, there is a remarkable congruence between them on the issue of democratic citizenship and particularly with respect to the pivotal role that education plays. But first, let us look a little more closely at the respective social contexts of each of these educationalists.

Freire was born in Recife, a part of Brazil that is familiar with extremes of poverty. In such a context, then, it is not at all unsurprising that, in his capacity as a professional educator, he committed himself toward the elaboration of a pedagogical approach that would equip the impoverished educands of Brazil to overcome their 'limit-situations'. In his view, such situations inhibit persons from realizing their full humanity, an instance of which would be recurrent poverty. The 'liberatory praxis' that he developed, then, attempts to provide spaces for learners to come together to re-create their own lived worlds so that 'through transforming action they can create a new situation, one which makes possible the pursuit of a fuller humanity' (Freire, 1970, p. 29). In this way, the future is perceived 'not as inexorable but as something that is constructed by people engaged together in life, in history' (Freire, 1998, p. 72). By contrast, Greene, had a privileged upbringing in Brooklyn, New York. As with Freire, she also decided to commit her life to education. As an educator, she became increasingly concerned about the manner in which persons, especially in the context of post-industrial, high-tech societies, like the United States, are inhibited from realising their full humanity (see Murphy, 2005). In a manner similar to Freire, she concerned herself with exploring a pedagogical approach that could enable the learner 'to let his consciousness take over, to enable him – in the face of mechanization and controls – to create himself as a human being, as a teacher capable of freeing other human beings to choose themselves' (Greene, 1973, p. 21).

FREIRE AND GREENE ON THE CORNERSTONES OF DEMOCRATIC CITIZENSHIP

Both of these educationalists, then, despite their differing social contexts, have convergent ideas on the significance of the educational project to effect human transformation, at both a personal and community level. Freire refers to this aspect of the educational endeavour as 'conscientization', which he refers to as 'the deepening of the attitude of awareness characteristic of all emergence' (Freire, 1970, p. 90). This deepening of awareness is also evident in Greene's concept of 'wide awakeness', which she describes as a heightened sense of agency in those we teach, empowering them 'to pursue their freedom and perhaps, transform to some degree their lived worlds' (Greene, 1995, p. 48). Notwithstanding the evident convergence of thinking here, it might also be helpful to consider what both of these authors consider to be the cornerstones of the democratic project, especially from an educational perspective. As already mentioned, such a consideration will allow for a more informed critique of the schooling system in the RoI.

It is evident from their writings, for example, that they both consider equality, freedom and social justice to be core, foundational prerequisites of the democratic project in education. There is also a sense in which each of these elements are inter-related, in the sense that when one is absent all are affected. Both would accentuate the public good of the educational endeavour as that space where students can identify and choose themselves, especially in relation to the aforementioned characteristics. Greene, for example, states that one of the primary aims of education is to motivate the young so that they 'can become principled enough, committed enough to reach beyond their self-interest and take responsibility for what happens in the space between themselves and others, what has been called the public space' (Ayers et al, 1998, p. xxxiv). The pivotal importance of the social justice dimension of the democratic project is clearly evident in Freire's contention that 'I cannot be a teacher if I do not perceive with greater clarity that my practice demand of me a definition about where I stand. A break with what is not ethically right' (Freire, 1998, p. 93). The import of this statement is also echoed in Greene's clarion call for educators to respond 'to those once called at risk, once carelessly marginalized, as living beings capable of choosing for themselves' (Greene, 1995, p. 42). Both Freire and Greene would also contend that the experience of freedom is an essential attribute of the democratic fabric of society. It is in Freire's words 'the indispensable condition for the quest for human completion' (Freire, 1970, p. 29).

THE CIVIC REMIT OF EDUCATION IN THE RoI – 'LIMIT-SITUATIONS'

At this juncture, it might be helpful to critically consider the extent to which the schooling system in the RoI is underpinned by such a democratic scaffolding, as that outlined by Freire and Greene above. There is certainly evidence of significant buckling on the equality and social justice fronts. It is even suggested that some schools in the RoI refrain from operating inclusive and progressive enrolment policies because they are concerned about losing their hard-won reputations (*Irish Times*, 2004). It has not been unknown for them to request pupils who were experiencing difficulties with their school work to move on to other schools in an attempt to secure the best possible profile for their schools in the competitive league table rankings (*Irish Independent*, 2004). The net result, however, from an equality and justice perspective is all the more contentious when one considers that it is often the poorest and most vulnerable sections of our communities who arc most impacted from such practices. It is evident then that for some students a form of pre-destination exists.

In the previous section, I also alluded to the fact that both of the aforementioned educationalists consider the experience of freedom to be an essential attribute of the democratic fabric of society. It might be helpful, then, to briefly consider the extent to which such an experience is characteristic of Irish school-going students. There is evidence to suggest that the full-development of these students is being inhibited by the extent to which success or failure in the educational system is being determined almost solely by the amount of points that one accumulates. This concern with respect to the one-dimensional conception of excellence in the current schooling system of the RoI is clearly articulated by Shelia Drudy in an article entitled 'Crude league tables are no measure of results' (Drudy, 2003). In addition, there is also evidence of a strong economic undertow to that same prevailing conception of excellence. An Irish second-level teacher, for example, recently commented that the social and personal development capacity of the Irish schooling system is being undermined by the extent to which it is currently being orchestrated by economic motives (*Irish Times*, 2005). A similar concern was echoed in the 1994 *Report on the National Education Convention* when it stated that an over-emphasis 'on economic and instrumentalist considerations in educational policy-making could have distorting effects, with deleterious consequences' (NECS, 1994, p. 9).

There is evidence to suggest, then, that the current schooling system in the RoI is being inhibited from realising its full democratic potential, especially in light of the aforementioned prerequisites, as elaborated by both Freire and Greene. The question still remains, however, as to how it might be possible to ameliorate the distorting effects of those same 'limit-situations', so that an understanding of education that 'incarnates the permanent search of people together for their becoming more fully human in the world in which they exist' (Freire, 1973, p. 96) can begin to take hold of the educational project.

THE CIVIC REMIT OF EDUCATION IN THE RoI – 'LIMIT-ACTS'

Freire and Greene exhibit an important convergence of thinking concerning the factors that could potentially lead to an eclipsing of the democratic capacity in education. What is significant about their work, however, is that neither of them stop at the mere naming of these factors. Instead, they invite learners to reach beyond their 'limit-situations' toward the untapped possibility of what can be. Such an understanding of the educational project is characteristic of the existentialist tradition in education, one which obviously had a very significant influence on the pedagogical orientations of both of these educationalists. Each of them would certainly resonate with Sartre's contention that it is 'on the day that we can conceive of a different state of affairs that a new light falls on our troubles and our suffering and that we decide that these are unbearable' (Sartre, 1956, p. 435). Such a conception of the educational project prompted me to explore teaching and learning opportunities for pre-service teacher educators that could allow for greater clarity and depth of understanding regarding the nature and meaning of the educational project in society, especially with respect to its democratic remit.

John Coolahan's article 'Teacher education and the teaching career in an era of lifelong learning' (Coolahan, 2002) clearly highlights the need for teacher-educators to have such informed understandings. Such understandings are accorded an even greater urgency in the context of a recent policy document from the OECD Directorate for Education on attracting, developing and retaining effective teachers (Directorate for Education, 2005). The *report* acknowledges that there is widespread recognition 'that countries need to have clear and concise statements of what teachers are expected to know and be able to do, and these teacher profiles need to be embedded throughout the school and teacher education systems' (p. 12). Do we want such statements to be framed solely according to a one-dimensional conception of excellence, as outlined by Drudy? Or, do we want our teachers to provide our students with learning opportunities that will equip them 'to step into their future as well-rounded and well-adjusted people' (Valarsan-Toomey, 1998, p. 52). Our current students ought to be provided with learning experiences that will encourage them to become the next generation's architects of the democratic project for society, paying particular attention to the aspects of equality, justice and freedom.

PRE-SERVICE TEACHER EDUCATION AT NUIG AND SERVICE-LEARNING

In the academic year 2004–2005, I invited pre-service teacher-education students to engage in service-learning activities, in partial fulfilment of their requirements for the 'Education and Society' foundations module. It was anticipated that such engagement would afford these students learning opportunities to expand and deepen their understandings on the nature and purpose of the educational project in society, especially with respect to its democratic remit. Each of the participating students submitted a reflective essay and, for that purpose, I alerted them to the fact that service-learning is a teaching/learning method that connects meaningful community service with academic learning, personal growth, and civic responsibility, so as to gain further understanding of course content, a broader appreciation of the discipline, and an enhanced sense of civic responsibility (AACTE, 2002). The following examples will clearly illustrate how engagement with service-learning activities can help to nurture the core democratic capacities of individuals.

One of the pre-service teachers, who elected to complete the service-learning option, decided to reflect on her involvement with the Outreach Society programme while completing her studies at the University of Limerick. As part of this programme, students from the university travel out to a community school in South Hill, a disadvantaged area of Limerick city with considerable socio-economic problems, and engage students for one-to-one tuition in English. The aforementioned student benefited greatly from her participation in this initiative, especially given that she is from a rural middle class background which did not bring her into significant contact with persons from lower socio-economic backgrounds. She acknowledged that she initially possessed an element of the 'cock-eyed' optimist when she became involved with the various outreach projects. The experience that she gained as an educator, however, through her involvement with service-learning allowed her to arrive at a richer understanding of what is involved in the educational project. In her own words, she came to realise that

> the principal aim of these projects was not to radically improve the students academically but to change their attitudes to education and the usefulness of it to them in their futures, something I didn't appreciate at the time and perhaps to enable them, as Maxine Greene suggests 'to see beyond the actual to a better order of things'. On reflection the experience for me was a formative one and had a significant impact on my decision to enter the teaching profession. According to Greene, teachers should 'challenge that which is taken for granted, the given, the bound and the restricted'. Teachers should also be taught, 'to educate our children to take responsibility for our collective well being' – aims I very much believe in and aspire to. To me teaching is about more than educating the child for our economy, which is of course important, but it has become the central focus of our education system.

Another pre-service teacher opted to complete her reflective essay on the experience that she had as a voluntary tutor with the Galway Adult Literacy Organisation. As with the previous service-learning participant, she also indicated that her involvement with the aforementioned organisation forced her to re-assess her comfortable middle class views on the efficacy of our current education system and that it also made her think more seriously about the processes involved in learning to read and write, something which most of us take for granted. As she commented:

> In order to become a successful tutor I had to put myself in the shoes of the student, and each student was unique. Did they prefer to process information visually or aurally or spatially? Was it possible to use their experience as a foundation for learning? I think this is why William Ayers musings on teaching struck such a deep chord – 'to reflect on the process of learning and teaching by consciously being in the role of one who doesn't know'. What service learning did for me was to remove the scales from my eyes and see that education should be about individuals and ensuring that each individual maximises their potential as a human being.

It is clearly evident then that this student benefited greatly from her involvement with service-learning. It helped her to clarify her own role as an educator. The transformative potential inherent in the project of educating, for example, is clearly evident when she describes what service-learning did for her, which she likened to removing the scales from her eyes. This vivid imagery, in my estimation, goes to the heart of the educational project. I am reminded of Greene's concept of 'wide awakeness'. Such a conception of the educational endeavour is extremely important, especially in the context of an educational system that is increasingly expected to process the young (seen as 'human resources') to perform acceptably on some level of an increasingly systematized world' (Greene, 1988, p. 12).

CONCLUSION

This chapter has attempted to outline the cornerstones of the democratic project in society, especially from an educational perspective. The democratic potential of the schooling system in the RoI was assessed, especially in light of the prerequisites as outlined by Freire and Greene. Such an analysis helped to identify the 'limit-situations' in the current schooling system, which effectively inhibit the full-flourishing of the democratic potential. The chapter concludes with a consideration of a specific instance of a 'limit-act' which, in the author's view, has the potential to ameliorate some of the more negative consequences of the aforementioned 'limit-situations'. In that regard, the reflective essays of two participating pre-service teachers are cited, so as to illustrate the potential of service-learning as a 'limit-act' to break-open our conceptions about the nature and purpose of the educational project in society, especially with regard to its democratic remit. If such learning is mainstreamed into our schooling system, it is possible that we might begin to arrive at a conception of the educational project that releases the creative imaginations of learners 'in the imaging of their own preferred futures and the kind of social order that might make such futures possible' (Reardon, 1994, p. 39).

REFERENCES

American Association of Colleges for Teacher Education (AACTE) (2002). Service-learning issue brief. Retrieved 18 September, 2007, from http://www.usm.maine.edu/servicelearning/pdf/sl know.pdf.

Apple, M. (1986). *Teachers and texts: A political economy of class & gender relations in education.* New York: Routledge & Kegan Paul.

Apple, M. (2001). *Educating the 'right' way: Markets, standards, God, and inequality.* New York: RoutledgeFalmer.

Ayers, W., Hunt, J. and Quinn, T. (1998). *Teaching for social justice.* New York: Teachers College Press.

Baker, J., Lynch, K., Cantillon, S. & Walsh, J. (2004). *Equality: From theory to action.* New York: Palgrave MacMillan.

Clancy, P. (1986). Socialisation, selection and reproduction in education. In P. Clancy, S. Drudy, K. Lynch & L. O'Dowd (Eds.) *Ireland: A sociological profile.* Dublin: Institute of Public Administration.

Coolahan, J. (2002). *The teaching career in an era of lifelong learning.* OECD Working Paper No. 2. Paris: OECD.

Department of Education (1971). *Primary school curriculum: Teacher's handbook, part 1.* Dublin: Stationery Office.

Directorate for Education (2005). Teachers matter: Attracting, developing and retaining effective teachers. Paris: OECD.

Drudy, S. (2003). Crude league tables are no measure of results. *Irish Times,* 9 September.

Drudy, S. & Lynch, K. (1993). *Schools and society in Ireland.* Dublin: Gill & Macmillan.

Dunne, J. (2002). Citizenship and education: A crisis of the Republic. In P. Kirby, L. Gibbons & M. Cronin (Eds.) *Reinventing Ireland: Culture, society and the global economy.* London: Pluto Press.

Fitzgerald, G. (2005). *Ireland in the world: Further reflections.* Dublin: Liberties Press.

Freire, P. (1970). *Pedagogy of the oppressed.* New York: Continuum.

Freire, P. (1973). *Education for critical consciousness.* New York: Continuum.

Freire, P. (1998). *Pedagogy of freedom: Ethics, democracy and civic courage.* New York: Rowman & Littlefield Publishers.

Fuller, L. (2002). *Irish Catholicism since the 1950s: The undoing of a culture.* Dublin: Gill and Macmillan.

Greene, M. (1973). *Teacher as stranger: Educational philosophy for the modern age.* Wadsworth.

Greene, M. (1988). *The dialectic of freedom.* New York: Teachers College Press.

Greene, M. (1995). *Releasing the imagination.* San Francisco: Jossey-Bass.

Investment in Education (1966). Report of the Survey Team appointed by the Minister for Education. Dublin: Stationery Office.

Irish Independent (2004, 27 March). When school league tables failed to pass the test.

Irish Times (2004, 12 May). Editorial.

Irish Times (2005, 27 September). In danger of drowning under a sea of paperwork. Teaching Matters.

Murphy, T. (2005). Maxine Greene and the democratic project in education: Signposts for the Irish educational system. *Journal of the Educational Studies Association of Ireland,* 24 (1), 55–64.

National Education Convention Secretariat (NECS) (1994). *Report on the National Education Convention.* Dublin: NESF.

O'Sullivan, D. (2005). *Cultural politics and Irish education since the 1950s.* Dublin: IPA.

Peillon, M. (1982). *Contemporary Irish society: An introduction.* Dublin: Gill and Macmillan.

Reardon, B. (1994) Learning our way to a human future. In: B. Reardon & E. Nordland (Eds.) *Learning peace: The promise of ecological and cooperative education*. State University of New York Press.
Sartre, J. P. (1956). *Being and nothingness*. New York: Gramercy Books.
Valarsan-Toomey, M. (1998). *The Celtic tiger: From the outside looking in*. Dublin: Blackhall Publishing.

Timothy Murphy
National University of Ireland, Galway

BRUCE CARRINGTON AND IAN MENTER

A 'COMMUNITY OF COMMUNITIES'?

Racism, Ethnicity and Education in Post-Devolution Scotland

INTRODUCTION

During the year 2007, a number of events were held to mark the 300th anniversary of the Act of Union that had led to the cessation of a Scottish Parliament. 2007 was also an historic year because it saw the installation of a new First Minister in the Scottish Parliament that had been (re-)established in 1999. Alex Salmond is the fourth person to hold this office, but unlike his three predecessors who were all Labour Party Members of the Scottish Parliament (MSPs), Salmond is the leader of the Scottish Nationalist Party. Although he is leading a minority government, the success of the Nationalist Party appears to signify a further major step in the process of decoupling of Scotland from the United Kingdom and in the re-assertion of a separate Scottish identity.

In this paper, that shifting political and cultural context is the backdrop to our consideration of the meanings of citizenship in Scotland and the ways in which those meanings relate to education policy and practice. The particular lens through which we examine these matters is ethnicity. The relationships between citizenship, national identity and ethnicity are complex within every society. The case of Scotland is one that may be especially interesting because of the particular histories and traditions of its peoples and because of the current political context outlined above.

At least until recent times, much more had been written about Scottish identity than about English identity (see, for example, Caunce *et al*, 2004). If for nearly three hundred years there had been only very limited political independence, then cultural features and especially 'traditions' were at the centre of questions of Scottishness. It has often been suggested that the three great institutional signifiers of Scottish cultural identity resided in the Church (the Kirk), the legal system and education. To some extent even this is one of the great myths of Scottish distinctiveness. Although the Church of England is the established church of the UK, the Church of Scotland and its organisations are very closely aligned to the Protestant Anglican tradition. Furthermore, one of the major features of Scottish culture is the longstanding tension, more pronounced in some localities than in others, between Roman Catholics and Protestants. These divisions are frequently referred to as sectarianism and have been a pronounced feature since nineteenth century immigration to Scotland from Ireland. The legal system has many

M.A. Peters, A. Britton and H. Blee (Eds.), Global Citizenship Education: Philosophy, Theory and Pedagogy, 231–243.

differences from those of England and Wales, making it difficult for a lawyer trained in one country to work in the other. The education system has indeed been distinctive, although throughout its history prior to 1999, it had been managed by a department of a UK ministry, the Scottish Office. During much of the twentieth century however, Scottish education was effectively managed from within Scotland, by a coterie of civil servants and senior educationists, who shared a common background and set of values, as described by McPherson and Raab (1988) and by Humes (1986). These arrangements were put under a considerable strain in the late 1980s when the Thatcher administration began to take a more avowedly interventionist stance towards education policy. It was remarkable that many of the most radical reforms in England during this time were effectively subverted or resisted in Scotland (see Paterson, 2003 for an account of this phase). We will return to some aspects of these tensions when we move in due course to consider some of the current curriculum provision in Scotland.

THE PEOPLING OF SCOTLAND

With just over five million inhabitants (2001 Census), Scotland's population is around one tenth of the overall population of the UK. More ethnically homogeneous than England (with a recorded 'visible' minority population in excess of nine per cent), minority ethnic groups comprise just two per cent of the total population of Scotland. (N.B. The corresponding figures for Wales and Northern Ireland are two per cent and one per cent respectively.) Pakistanis form the largest single minority ethnic group in Scotland, followed by Chinese and Indians. At the time of the 2001 Census, almost thirteen per cent of the country's 'visible' minority ethnic population described their ethnic group as 'mixed' (Scottish Executive, 2004).

When examined historically, it becomes very obvious that the Scottish population has many sources (see Ascherson, 2003). Early settlers of what is now Scotland came from Ireland and from Scandinavia. This in part is what has led to the significant linguistic diversity in Scotland, with Gaelic being an important language in the islands and parts of the Highlands, and Doric still being spoken in parts of the northeast. Perhaps the most unrecognised language form (both within and outwith Scotland) is Scots. It is perhaps most unrecognised because of its greater similarity to English than the other languages mentioned, although in the post-devolution context there is a growing awareness of Scots as a national language.

Throughout the modern period inward migration from Ireland has continued and there has been a constant and steady flow of people from England. Furthermore, the 'Scottish diaspora' has led to a large number of Scottish communities in many other parts of the world, including most Commonwealth countries and these communities have often been the origins of new arrivals (see Herman, 2003). The major places of settlement of migrants to the UK from the 'New Commonwealth' from the late 1940s onwards were undoubtedly in England. However, some significant communities, especially from the Indian sub-continent, did settle in

Scotland, most notably in and around Glasgow. Although 'visible' minority ethnic group members thus form a much smaller proportion of the total population in England, they do nevertheless share the experience of being severely under represented in public positions in most areas of cultural and economic life. Based on an analysis of the 2001 Census, de Lima (2005) finds:

> Despite the variations in size and ethnic composition, the minority ethnic population across the UK shared some similarities with regard for example, to age distribution, patterns of ethnicity, settlement trends, economic activity rates, vulnerability to poverty and inequalities (for example in relation to access to services and employment). (p. 138)

When the process towards formal devolution was underway during the late 1990s, Scotland, in contrast to England, was actually experiencing a declining population. The birth rate had fallen as in other parts of the UK and outward migration (including significant continuing movement southwards to England) was exceeding inward migration. The early devolved administrations identified this as a threat to Scotland's future prosperity and sought to reverse the trend. In particular there was a fear of a skills shortage in the labour market and hence the emphasis given to the promotion of a positive identity for Scotland abroad. These efforts however were (and continue to be) hampered by the fact that the Scottish government has no powers whatsoever in determining who should be allowed to settle in the country. The devolution settlement that was put in place at the end of the century set out clearly those powers that were to be devolved to the Scottish Parliament and those that were to be 'reserved' to Westminster in London. Nationality and immigration (incorporating all legislation relating to migration and asylum) were reserved. In essence this limitation means that the Scottish government has no part in determining who may call themselves Scots. Indeed all Scots legally remain subjects of the UK and hold UK passports. Perhaps this is at the core of why it is that questions of national identity continue to be so topical and often controversial. As de Lima (2005) puts it:

> Despite devolution, Scotland continues to operate within a neo-liberalist framework and can make limited changes given its limited powers to redress the fundamentally racist nature of immigration and nationalist legislation that has continued to shape race relations in the UK. (p. 152)

Policy relating to refugees and asylum seekers is one such area of controversy. While policy in this area has been the subject of considerable media attention throughout the UK, with the tabloid press helping to turn the term asylum seeker into an abusive epithet, the response in Scotland has been different. That is not to say that asylum seekers and refugees have not been subject to similarly racist experiences (see below). However, where Scotland has been seeking to increase the numbers of settlers, especially those with skills, asylum seekers and refugees have been seen as one partial solution to the problems of depopulation. There have been cases where complete families have been detained in special centres and then deported by the UK Home Office, to the consternation of those in their local communities and of politicians of all main parties.

The final most recent development in the demography of Scotland is one that has been shared with other parts of the UK: that is, the arrival of significant numbers of people from the so-called accession states in Europe, mostly those that were formerly part of the Soviet Union block. For example, the small, Polish communities that already existed in many Scottish towns and cities have now been supplemented by mainly young Poles who now play a key part in several sectors of the economy, most noticeably in service industries.

RACISM IN SCOTLAND

There are two questions that may be asked about the proposition that Scotland has been able to develop a reputation for 'tolerance' by comparison to England. Firstly, is that reputation actually based on reality and secondly, if it is, is that simply because the numbers of members of 'visible' minority ethnic groups are much smaller than they are in our southern neighbour? There is no satisfactory way to quantify racism in any society. There may be indicators such as racist attacks and other racist crimes, there may be employment figures or educational attainment figures that may relate to patterns of institutional discrimination, but with all such indicators, the meaning of the data may be limited by problems in reporting and/or by difficulties in isolating 'race' factors from other aspects of social differentiation. Nevertheless, what evidence we do have, actually indicates that many of the features of the experience of minority ethnic group members in England are also prevalent in Scotland. Furthermore the perception or claim that 'there is no problem here' may actually be seen as making the situation more serious than where 'the problem' is clearly acknowledged. Complacency in these matters can be very dangerous.

The problematisation of 'whiteness', that has been an important element in critical race studies (see, for example, Gillborn, 2006; Bonnett, 2000), has not emerged in any significant way in the Scottish context. Notwithstanding this, however, over the years Scots nationalists (along with their Welsh and Irish counterparts) have actively sought to eschew Anglo-centric constructions of British identity. On occasions, such attempts at 'nation-building' have led to acts of physical (as well as symbolic) violence directed against the English. Thus, in the 1980s, radical Welsh nationalists mounted a number of arson attacks on holiday homes owned by people from England. And although there was no parallel arson campaign in Scotland, there have been examples of what has been dubbed as 'anti-English racism', including some that were apparently deliberately provoked by xenophobic press reports during the 2006 World Cup football finals (Commission for Racial Equality, 2006). It should also be noted that there may be close links between sectarianism and 'Anglophobia'.

ETHNICITY, CITIZENSHIP AND NATIONAL IDENTITY

The Parekh Report, *The Future of Multi-ethnic Britain* (Runnymede Trust, 2000), provides various invaluable insights into changing conceptions of collective identity at a critical juncture in British history. Published in the wake of Scottish and Welsh devolution, the report opens with the following observation:

> England, Scotland and Wales are at a turning point in their history. They could become narrow and inward looking, with rifts between themselves and among their regions and communities, or they could develop as a 'community of citizens and communities'. (p. xiii)

Parekh and his colleagues are under no illusions that their liberal, pluralist and inclusive vision of national identity and citizenship is universally accepted and go to some lengths to show that class, gender, ethnic, religious, regional and local differences continue to provide a basis for conflict and disunity. They acknowledge that manifestations of racism, nationalism, xenophobia and ethnocentrism (including Anglo-centrism, sectarianism and Islamophobia) still present significant challenges to social cohesion and unity. However, despite their seemingly bleak assessment of the contemporary state of social, ethnic and community relations, they nevertheless argue that Britain must now embark on the process of 're-imagining' itself. According to Parekh *et al*, the starting point in any such debates about British national identity should be 'the recognition that England, Scotland and Wales are multi-ethnic, multi-faith, multicultural and multi-community societies' (p. 2). Commenting on the exclusive and invariably Anglo-centric nature of prevailing notions of national identity (especially prior to the run up to devolution), they also note that people across Britain increasingly view their own identities in complex and 'hybridised' terms (see, for example, Mac an Ghaill, 1999):

> Many customary images of Britain are England-centred – indeed southern England-centred – and leave many millions of people out of the picture. More and more people have multiple identities – they are Welsh-Europeans, Pakistani-Yorkshire women, Glaswegian-Muslims, English-Jews.

As well as devolution, this apparent challenge to narrow and exclusive constructions of Britishness is attributed to a range of factors, including: globalisation and 'glocalisation' (i.e., the growing emphasis on the importance of local and regional affiliation in a global context); the end of empire and the concomitant decline of Britain as a world power; post-war migration; Britain in Europe; and the development of social pluralism which has accompanied, among other things, a breakdown of class divisions, changing moral and sexual mores and a decline in organised religion.

Although there is a substantial body of published work on children's racial and ethnic identities (e.g., Connolly, 2001, 1998; Troyna & Hatcher, 1992; Carrington & Short, 1989; Aboud, 1988), there has been relatively little research into their constructions of national identity. Prior to devolution in the UK, Carrington and

Short (1995, 1996 and 1998) sought to plug this gap in the literature when they embarked on a series of case studies of 8- to 13-year-olds' notions of Britishness. Prompted by concerns about the possible influence of the assimilationist and exclusive constructions of national identity – such as those once proffered by the 'cultural restorationist' wing of the New Right (Ball, 1993) – this qualitative investigation drew upon one-to-one interviews with a socially and ethnically diverse sample of 320 children. The interviews were conducted initially with cohorts of 8- to 11-year-olds in three urban primary schools (two in North East England and one in the South East) and a suburban primary school in Edinburgh and, subsequently, with a cohort of 12- to 13-year-olds in an English urban middle school. The investigation was later extended to include a cohort of American 8- to 11-year-olds drawn from a suburban elementary school in Massachusetts (Short & Carrington, 1999; Carrington & Short, 2000). The comparative dimension allowed the researchers to examine claims made by Modood (1992) about the extent to which white English people may be less reflexive about their identities than other sections of the British population (both majority- and minority-ethnic), or that Americans are more likely than Britons to construe their national identity in a complex and 'hybridised' manner.

The interviews revealed a number of ethnic, regional and national differences in the ways in which the children described their national identity. For example, around a third of those from 'visible' minority ethnic backgrounds – whether British or American – saw it in 'hybridised' terms: e.g., 'Mum was born in England and she's British and my dad was born in Kenya. He's Kenyan [...] I'm both – a bit British and a bit Kenyan' (Prashant, 9 years); '... Puerto Rican, Dominican, Spanish or American' (Beatriz, 10 years); 'I'm mostly Chinese [but] I consider myself American' (Cindy, 11 years); 'British and Pakistani' (Wazir, 12 years). And while one in three of the white American children viewed themselves in a similar vein (e.g., 'I'd say Italian–American – I think I'm a little of both', Danny 10 years) their white English counterparts almost invariably saw themselves as simply 'British'. Although less likely than their American peers to view national identity in hyphenated terms, the older Scottish children were somewhat more inclined than their white English counterparts to eschew the simple epithet 'British' when describing their identity: e.g., 'Scottish and British', Claire, 11 years); 'I'm half British and half English' (Caroline, 10 years); 'I'm British and I'm Scottish' (James, 11 years). The Scottish children not only appeared to be less complacent about issues of citizenship and nationhood than their white English peers but, on occasions, were prepared to challenge Anglo-centric notions of Britishness: 'When people say you're British, they seem to think you're English – not Scottish. [...] A lot of people automatically assume that you're English and I don't really like that much, because we're not English!' (Ruth, 11 years).

Whether they construed their own identities in a unitary or 'hybridised' manner, very few of the children appeared to view national identity in exclusive or culturally homogeneous terms. Only a handful of children made comments that could be interpreted as racist, ethnocentric, xenophobic or nationalistic when responding to questions such as: 'What makes a person British/American?'; 'Is everyone who lives here in this country British/American?'; 'Is it possible to stop being British/American and become something else?'. Indeed the bulk of the children appeared to embrace a pluralist and inclusive constructions of nationhood and citizenship not dissimilar from that outlined by Parekh (Runnymede Trust, 2000). Other qualitative research, such as Howard and Gill's (2001) study of Australian children's construction of national identity, has drawn similarly optimistic conclusions about the impact of cultural pluralism on the young.

Notwithstanding this, however, more recent qualitative research into children's accounts of Welshness has suggested that the influence of racialised categories on children's thinking should not be entirely discounted (Scourfield & Davies, 2005). Working with 8 to 11-year-olds in six primary schools across Wales, Scourfield and Davies draw the following, somewhat less sanguine conclusions from their study:

> Although we have noted racialised discourses of Welsh identity, we can also report evidence of children resisting exclusive conceptions of national belonging and constructing broader more inclusive alternatives. (p. 102)

Some of the majority ethnic children in their study conflated Welshness with whiteness whilst others appeared to adopt an avowedly antiracist stance. The researchers go on to note that although the data on Black and minority ethnic children were 'limited' (i.e., restricted to just 11 individuals), it seemed to suggest 'a reluctance to claim Welshness and in particular a reluctance to use 'Welsh' as an umbrella identity within which other ethnic identities can be expressed' (pp. 104–105).

Research undertaken by Saeed *et al* (1999) with Pakistani-Muslim teenagers in Glasgow has revealed a similar ambivalence towards Britishness. Drawing on questionnaire data elicited from sixty-three pupils (aged between 14 and 17 years) from three state schools, the findings indicated that the young people attached greater importance to their Muslim identity (85%) and Pakistani heritage (30%) than other forms of identity. Notwithstanding this, however, when invited to complete the statement, 'In terms of ethnic group, I consider myself to', almost two thirds described their ethnicities in hyphenated terms, with 'Scottish–Pakistani' (22%) and 'Scottish-Muslim' (19%) being the most frequent choices. Others referred to themselves simply as 'Pakistani' (17%) or 'Muslim' (16%). Very few alluded to Britishness in their responses: indeed, just a handful used the epithets 'British–Pakistani' (5%) or 'British-Muslim' (3%) to describe their ethnicities. Conceivably, the timing of the research – that is, immediately prior to devolution – may have played a critical part in shaping the students' replies:

> It is perhaps within the new chemistries of identity created by the most radical shift in political power within the UK for three hundred years that the possibility of a new kind of Pakistani identity may require to be grasped. (Circumstantial and anecdotal evidence available seems to have pointed to widespread support for Scottish devolution among the Scottish–Pakistani

population, though in the in the absence of hard data we should not make too much of this supposition). (Saeed *et al*, 1999, p. 840)

The apparent commitment of the students in this study to a hyphenated Scottish identity is of interest for other reasons. In the UK, United States, Netherlands, Germany, Denmark, Belgium, France and other Western states there has been a steady growth of Islamophobia in recent years (e.g. Stone, 2004; van Driel, 2004). There can be little doubt that this hostility has been fuelled by the media-amplified, 'moral panics' which have ensued in the wake of the 'nine eleven' suicide attacks by Muslim extremists on New York and Washington in 2001, the subsequent terrorist bombings in London on 7th July 2005 and the war in Iraq. The increase in hostility towards Muslims in a number of countries has, in turn, led to mounting alienation within such communities, especially among the young.

The Report by the Commission on British Muslims and Islamophobia (Stone, 2004) reveals the pernicious effects of anti-Islamic prejudice and discrimination in a wide variety of contexts, including education. Although the Commission is not narrowly Anglo-centric in its concerns, the section of its report dealing specifically with *Identity and Education* draws entirely on examples from English schools to illustrate concerns about the adequacy of institutional responses to incidents of racism and religious hostility. Leaving aside this lacuna, other published work has pointed to the need for interventions to address racism and religious hostility in Scottish schools. It is to this research that we now turn.

As Arshad and Diniz (2003) have argued, prior to the establishment of the Scottish Parliament in 1999, antiracism and multiculturalism did not figure prominently in debates about educational policy and practice in Scotland. At a policy level, it was widely assumed that Scotland had 'good race relations' and that there was 'no problem here' (p. 910). Despite such claims, there is some recent evidence to show that colour racism may not be uncommon in Scottish schools. For example, Caulfield, Hill & Shelton's (2005) interviews with fifty-six 11- to 13-year-old minority ethnic pupils in the West of Scotland revealed that 'nearly all of the sample had experienced or witnessed racist behaviour in secondary school ... and some reported racist bullying and fights by ethnically based gangs' (p. 7). Although no allegations of racism were directed against school staff, the pupils expressed concerns about the effectiveness of institutional responses to such incidents, which were not dissimilar from those articulated by William Macpherson in *The Stephen Lawrence Inquiry* (Macpherson, 1999).

Anecdotal evidence about the extent of Islamophobia in non-denominational schools is provided by Finn (2003) in his observations about the factors which have led to lobbying for state-funded Islamic provision within Glasgow's Muslim communities.

> Moreover, contrary to the common and simplistic misconception about the value of social contact, Muslim parents do not report daily social contact in schools as lessening anti-Islamic prejudice. Instead, repeated questioning of their children's faith is judged to be hostile and leaves pupils with no option other than to become 'defenders of the faith' from a very early age. (p. 906)

In some ways this kind of reaction may be directly analogous to the development of sectarian views among young members of the Protestant and Catholic communities,

EDUCATIONAL RESPONSES TO CULTURAL AND ETHNIC DIVERSITY

How have educational policy makers and teachers in Scotland responded to ethnic, cultural and religious diversity and, in particular, to the challenges presented by racism, xenophobia and ethnocentrism (including sectarianism and Islamophobia)? What curricular and pedagogical strategies have been devised to promote an inclusive and pluralist conception of Scotland as a 'community of communities'?

It has been argued that educational responses to ethnic, cultural and religious diversity in pre-devolution Scotland were ill-defined and uncoordinated (Arshad & Diniz, 2003). Furthermore, despite the criticisms levelled against policies in the late 90s to promote ethnic equality and inclusion in English schools (Gillborn, 2001; Macpherson, 1999; Figueroa, 1999), the evidence suggests that progress had been slower in Scotland. Following devolution, however, there appeared to be a new impetus, stimulated not only by the political process but also by the publicity which had surrounded the publication of the Macpherson Inquiry in 1999. A Race Equality Forum was established which made recommendations about education policy as well as about many other areas of policy. However, a Scottish Executive-commissioned audit of these matters published in 2001 found that remarkably little had actually changed since devolution (Netto et al, 2001).

The publication of the discussion and consultation paper *Education for Citizenship in Scotland* (Learning and Teaching Scotland (LTS),[1] 2002) appeared to be the harbinger of a change in policy direction from a piecemeal and minimalist response to issues of identity and inclusion to something more systematic and comprehensive. The discussion paper offered schools the following unambiguous advice about the handling of issues such as racism and sectarianism:

> Education for citizenship must recognise the existence of such conflicts, and must help young people develop strategies for dealing effectively with controversy. These strategies include negotiation, compromise, awareness of the impact of conflict on the overall wellbeing of the community and the environment, and development of well-informed respect for differences between people. At the same time young people need to learn that although individuals should always be treated with respect, some of the views some people may hold, including those associated with racism and sectarianism, are a grave threat to the wellbeing of individuals and communities and must be opposed. (2002, p. 9)

However, four years after the publication of the discussion paper, HM Inspectorate of Education (HMIE) in Scotland reported that the response of schools to citizenship education had been patchy. They state:

Schools ... have increased their emphasis on citizenship. Many are giving some more attention to involving young people in decision making. Some have used curriculum inserts to explore issues such as citizenship and the law or anti-racism. However, practice is uneven within and across schools (HM Inspectorate of Education, 2006, p. 5).

Despite this apparently variability in practice, education for citizenship is a key element (i.e., 'cross-curricular theme') within the most recent curriculum initiative in Scotland, *A Curriculum for Excellence*. Furthermore, the LTS website is replete with exemplars showing how schools might engage with racism and religious prejudice and discrimination (including Islamophobia) and also counter enmity towards refugees and asylum seekers. The website also dispenses useful practical advice about measures that might be employed to promote an inclusive and pluralist conception of Scottish society. However, there are notable silences, especially in relation to white identities, a similar shortcoming to those identified in the English contexts described above (see also Gaine, 2007).

AN ALTERNATIVE APPROACH?

It is not clear that these recent approaches are likely to be any more successful than their predecessors in terms of ensuring inclusion and recognition of the hybrid identities that exist among young people in Scotland as in other parts of the UK (see above). In attempting to define a Scottish curriculum that is associated with a new national identity, there is the possibility of implicit support for Anglophobia, at the same time as there is a reasonable rejection of British Anglo-centrism.

A new approach would need to avoid the pitfalls of many earlier anti-racist approaches to education where, for example, white children find it difficult to identify their own ethnicity, and anti-racist education is somehow designed to be 'for' Black children and has the effect of excluding their White peers. This was found to have been the effect of the strong anti-racist approach taken at Burnage High School in Manchester, when an investigation was carried out following the playground murder of an Asian student (Macdonald, Bhavnani, Khan & John, 1989). More recently, a study carried out in England found that:

Teachers often referred to diversity and ethnicity in a way that focussed almost exclusively on minority ethnic groups and their cultures. White ethnicity, and the extent of diversities (including White British) within this, was not considered. (Maylor & Read, 2007)

But a new approach must also avoid the shortcomings of English citizenship education, which it has been argued, tends to focus only on knowledge about citizenship and democracy while ignoring the realities of social injustice that prevail and often ignoring the need for educational processes to be consistent with the values that the curriculum espouses (Menter & Walker, 2000).

An appropriate educational response to the complexity of contemporary society in post-devolution Scotland, is likely to be based on a recognition of the significance of spatial and social context. To be spatially context-sensitive is to suggest recognition of the significance of political boundaries and nations. To be socially context-sensitive is to suggest the significance of the demography of a school and its community. Young people are unlikely to develop a confidence in and understanding of their own identity unless they learn about their own history and geography and can relate these to the histories and geographies of others, whether those others are in the same school as them, in the same country or indeed wherever they are in the world.

A national identity within a democracy in a globalising world is no simple phenomenon, as is perhaps implied by recent pronouncements in England about British national identity and 'a core set of values'. As Modood has argued:

> The idea that there is to be a schedule of 'non-negotiable' value statements to which every citizen is expected to sign up is not in the spirit of open, plural citizenship. National identity should be woven in debate and discussion, not reduced to a list. For central to it is a citizenship and the right of all, especially previously marginalized or newly admitted groups to make a claim on the national identity. (Modood, 2007)

Writing soon after the establishment of the Scottish Parliament, the late Nigel Grant suggested, in somewhat colourful and emotive language:

> There is a chance – just a chance – that a multicultural education system can help Scotland rediscover herself, and escape from the twin dangers of inferiority complex and truculent jingoism, the oscillation between bombast and cringing that is our national curse, the outcome of centuries of preoccupation with the culture (or at least the power and prestige) of one neighbour rather than looking more clearly at herself and the world beyond the Channel, the Atlantic and the North Sea. (Grant, 2000, p. 66)

If the preoccupation with the one neighbour to the south has diminished considerably over the past years, it does not (yet) seem to have been replaced by a broader multicultural pluralism of the kind suggested by Grant. The opportunity is still here to fashion an educational approach that is suited to the economically, socially and culturally complex world in which we live. It remains to be seen whether *A Curriculum for Excellence* can be a vehicle for such developments.

NOTES

[1] Learning and Teaching Scotland (LTS) is an agency funded by the Scottish Executive with a remit for curriculum and professional development in education.

REFERENCES

Aboud, F. (1988). *Children and prejudice.* Oxford: Basil Blackwell.
Acherson, N. (2003). *Stone voices: The search for Scotland* (Rev. ed.). London: Granta.

Arshad, R. & Diniz, F.A. (2003). Race equality in Scottish education. In T.G.K. Bryce & W.M. Humes (Eds.), *Scottish education: Post devolution* (2nd ed.). Edinburgh: Edinburgh University Press.

Ball, S. (1993). Education, Majorism and the 'curriculum of the dead'. *Curriculum Studies, 1*(2), 195–213.

Bonnett, A. (2000). *Antiracism*. London: Routledge.

Carrington, B. & Short, G. (1989). *'Race' and the primary school: Theory into practice*. Windsor: NFER-Nelson.

Carrington, B. & Short, G. (1995). What makes a person British? Children's conceptions of their national culture and identity. *Educational Studies, 21*(2), 217–238.

Carrington, B. & Short, G. (1996). Who counts; who cares? Scottish children's notions of national identity. *Educational Studies, 22*(1), 203–224.

Carrington, B. & Short, G. (1998). Adolescent discourse on national identity: Voices of care and justice? *Educational Studies, 24*(2), 133–152.

Carrington, B. & Short, G. (2000). Citizenship and nationhood: The constructions of British and American children. In M. Leicester, C. Modgil & F. Modgil (Eds.), *Education, culture and values. Volume VI: Politics, education and citizenship*. London: Falmer.

Caunce, S., Mazierska, W., Sydney-Smith, S. & Watson, J.K. (Eds.) (2004). *Re-locating Britishness*. Manchester: Manchester University Press.

Caulfield, C., Hill, M. & Shelton, A. (2005). *The experiences of black and minority ethnic young people following the transition to secondary school*. Spotlight 93. Glasgow: The SCRE Centre, University of Glasgow. Retrieved 26 September, 2007, from <http://www.scre.ac.uk/spotlight/spotlight93 .html>.

Commission for Racial Equality (2006). World Cup is no excuse for anti-English racism. *News and Media*, 2nd June. Retrieved 26 September, 2007, from http://www.cre.gov.uk/default.aspx.locid-0hgnew0h1.Lang-EN.htm.

Connolly, P. (1998). *Racism, gender identities and young children*. London: Routledge.

Connolly, P. (2001). Qualitative methods in the study of children's racial attitudes and identities. *Infant and Child Development, 10*, 219–233.

De Lima, P. (2005). An inclusive Scotland? The Scottish executive and racial inequality. In G. Mooney & G. Scott (Eds.), *Exploring social policy in the 'New' Scotland*. Bristol: Policy Press.

Figueroa, P. (1999). Multiculturalism and anti racism in a new ERA: A critical review. *Race, Ethnicity and Education, 2*(2), 281–301.

Finn, G. (2003). 'Sectarianism': A challenge for Scottish education. In T.G.K. Bryce & W.M. Humes (Eds.), *Scottish education post devolution* (2nd ed.). Edinburgh: Edinburgh University Press.

Gaine, C. (2007). *We're all White thanks: The persisting myth about 'White' schools*. Stoke-on-Trent: Trentham Books.

Gillborn, D. (2001). Racism, policy and the (mis)education of Black children. In R. Majors (Ed.), *Educating our Black children*. London: Routledge/Falmer.

Gillborn, D. (2006). Critical race theory and education: Racism and anti-racism in educational theory and praxis. *Discourse: Studies in the Cultural Politics of Education, 27*(1), 11–32.

Grant, N. (2000). *Multicultural education in Scotland*. Edinburgh: Dunedin Academic Press.

Herman, A. (2003). *The Scottish enlightenment: The Scots' invention of the modern world*. London: Fourth Estate.

HM Inspectorate of Education (2006). *Education for citizenship: A portrait of current practice in Scottish schools and pre-school centres*. Edinburgh: HMIE.

Howard, S. & Gill, J. (2001). 'It's like we're a normal way and everyone else is different': Australian children's constructions of citizenship and national identity. *Educational Studies, 27*(1), 87–103.

Humes, W. (1986). *The leadership class in education*. Edinburgh: John Donald.

Mac an Ghaill, M. (1999). *Contemporary racisms and ethnicities: Social and cultural transformations*. Buckingham: Open University Press.

Macdonald, I., Bhavnani, R., Khan, L. & John, G. (1989). *Murder in the playground: The report of the Macdonald inquiry into racism and racial violence in Manchester schools.* London: Longsight Press.

Learning and Teaching Scotland (2002). *Education for citizenship in Scotland.* Glasgow: LTS.

Macpherson, W. (1999). *The Stephen Lawrence inquiry.* CM 4261-1. London: Stationery Office.

McPherson, A. & Raab, C. (1988). *Governing education: A sociology of policy since 1945.* Edinburgh: Edinburgh University Press.

Maylor, U. & Read, B. (2007). *Diversity and citizenship in the curriculum: Research review.* Research Brief RB819. London: Department for Education and Skills.

Menter, I. & Walker, M. (2000). How would a well educated young citizen react to the Stephen Lawrence inquiry? An examination of the parameters of current models of citizenship education. *The Curriculum Journal, 11*(1), 101–116.

Modood, T. (1992). On not being white in Britain: discrimination, diversity and commonality. In Leicester, M. & Taylor, M. (Eds.) *Ethics, ethnicity and education.* London: Kogan Page.

Modood, T. (2007, 23 May). Multiculturalism and nation building go hand in hand. *The Guardian,* p. 32.

Netto, G., Arshad, R., deLima, P., Almeida Diniz, F., Patel, V. & Syed, R. (2001). *Audit of research on minority ethnic groups from a 'race' perspective.* Edinburgh: Scottish Executive Central Research Unit.

Paterson, L. (2003). *Scottish education in the twentieth century.* Edinburgh: Edinburgh University Press.

Runnymede Trust (2000). *The future of multi-ethnic Britain: The Parekh report.* London: Profile Books.

Saeed, A., Blain, N., & Forbes, D. (1999). New ethnic and national questions in Scotland: Post-British identities among Glasgow Pakistani teenagers. *Ethnic and Racial Studies, 22*(5), 821–844.

Scottish Executive (2004). Analyis of ethnicity in the 2001 Census: A summary report. Retrieved 26 September, 2007, from http://www.scotland.gov.uk/Publications/2004/02/18876/32939.

Scourfield, J. & Davies, A. (2005). Children's accounts of Wales as racialized and inclusive. *Ethnicities, 5*(1), 83–107.

Short, G. & Carrington, B. (1999). Children's constructions of their national identity: implications for critical multiculturalism. In S. May (Ed.), *Critical multiculturalism: Re-thinking multicultural and antiracist education.* London: Falmer Press.

Stone, R (2004). *Islamophobia: Issues, challenges and action. A report by the Commission on British Muslims and Islamphobia.* Stoke on Trent: Trentham Books.

Troyna, B. & Hatcher, R. (1992). *Racism in children's lives: A study of mainly white schools.* London: Routledge.

Van Driel, B. (Ed.) (2004). *Confronting Islamophobia in educational practice.* Stoke-on-Trent: Trentham Books.

Bruce Carrington and Ian Menter
University of Glasgow

243

KLAS ROTH

MACINTYRE'S THEORY OF VIRTUE

An Ethics-for-Citizenship Education?[1]

A THEORY OF VIRTUE

MacIntyre begins his book *After Virtue* with a suggestive picture of what can happen when natural scientists suffer a catastrophe. He argues that moral language 'is in the same state of grave disorder as the language of natural science in the imaginary world' (1984, p. 2). He also argues that we nowadays only have fragments of moral conceptual schemes and that we have 'lost our comprehension, both theoretical and practical, of morality' (p. 2).

MacIntyre invites us to imagine that natural science has been blamed for causing a series of serious disasters in our environment. Because of this, people lynch, imprison and execute scientists, and destroy both their instruments and their books. Science teaching is also abolished. But later on some people start to revive science as a valuable contribution to life by collecting the remaining fragments. The grave problem is that there are only pieces of theories, parts of books and articles left, without their proper practices and context, and what is left is now being taught in schools. Teachers and students are therefore left with learning procedures that mostly mean memorising terms and fragmentised procedures without comprehending either the purpose or consequences or any proper understanding indeed of science at all.

MacIntyre concedes that people do not always behave like this. He argues that people have the capacity to handle epistemological crises in a more virtuous way than he portrays. In *Whose Justice? Which Rationality?* MacIntyre signifies a three-stage development in an epistemological crisis (1988, p. 362). First, there are too many problems which the current theories cannot solve. Secondly, there is a need to solve and explain the problems facing people. Thirdly, any new theory needs to solve and explain the new problems and explain the old ones.

He shows in both works that there are different conceptions of moral concepts such as virtue and justice; and that there is a 'diversity of traditions of enquiry, with histories, there are, so it will turn out, rationalities rather than rationality ...' (1988, p. 9). MacIntyre also shows that Western tradition embraces diverse conceptions, and not unitary conceptions of the concepts of virtue, justice and rationality. He argues too that there can be no solitary, single, unitary, substantive conception of these concepts, and he puts forward a theory of virtue which concedes that there is no unitary substantive conception of, for example, virtue.

M.A. Peters, A. Britton and H. Blee (Eds.), Global Citizenship Education: Philosophy, Theory and Pedagogy, 245–260.

MacIntyre argues that this concept requires three universal conditions that have to develop in a logical order, namely practice, narrative and tradition. Without these conditions, common to all actual conceptions of virtue such as Homer's, Aristotle's, the New Testament's and Aquinas', there could be no comprehensive understanding of the concept as such. These conditions are universal and substantive, according to him. He argues that every morally coherent conception of virtue has to involve a substantive account of these concepts in order to be comprehensible at all.

By virtue MacIntyre means:

> ... an acquired human quality the possession and exercise of which tends to enable us to achieve those goods which are internal to practices and the lack of which effectively prevents us from achieving any such goods. (1984, p. 191)

A virtue can be a disposition such as courage, honesty, justice or sincerity and can only be understood in human conjoint action in terms of practices.

To find out what, for example, honesty in communal life is, we have to observe what kind of practice is exercised and why that practice is counted a virtue. Any quality within a practice which is essential for achieving or sustaining practices of different kinds is a virtue, according to MacIntyre. Virtues function as a kind of glue binding people together in every practice by being, or functioning as, an overall good. Through exercising them, people find themselves involved in teleological action, that is, action inheriting an internal good achievable only through exercising them.

Practice

As mentioned earlier, virtues require practices, but virtues are in no way completely comprehensible in terms of practices (1984, p. 187). An account of them requires at least two more conditions, namely, narrative order and tradition. I will begin with practice, by which MacIntyre means:

> ... any coherent and complex form of socially established cooperative human activity through which goods internal to that form of activity are realized in the course of trying to achieve those standards of excellence which are appropriate to, and partially definitive of, that form of activity, with the result that human powers to achieve excellence, and human conceptions of the ends and goods involved, are systematically extended. (1984, p. 187)

He gives a few examples of what is considered to be a practice, such as football, architecture, farming, chess; but not throwing a ball or bricklaying. A practice is defined as involving at least two people regularly doing activities in agreement with rules and in which there is some kind of action involving, for example, training and an accord between people's judgements and definitions of these judgements. People have to agree on the procedures needed for achieving the goods internal to the activity and also on what is, or at least ought to be, the outcome of the practice itself.

Take football. It involves several people coordinating and cooperating in agreement with objectively defined rules accepted by those involved in the practice. Judgements and definitions thereof are regularly applied in agreement with the observable behaviour regulated and constituted by the rules applied in the practice. If the behaviour is not in agreement with the rules for the game, then football is not being practised.

The internal good is playing the game in order to win. Defined in relation to, for example, football, the good is also playing football well, that is, playing fair and fast, and coordinating the action so that cooperation between team members is regular and stable, quick and smooth. These goods are defined in relation to the game of football and they are the virtues exercised by good football players. They are also recognisable by those who have played, or are at least familiar enough with, football.

According to MacIntyre goods may be internal to a practice – such as football – or external, such as having status, gaining prestige, or achieving money and power. The practice can be exercised without the external goods, and understood without them. They can be, and in many cases are, important for the practice itself, but they are instrumentally achieved; that is, they can only be achieved by exercising the practice. However, if the external goods become more important for the participators and perhaps also for the spectators, and the practice becomes only a means to one or more ends achievable only for their own sake, then the internal goods become meaningless or lose importance. If this happens, the practice itself loses its meaning for participants and spectators alike. This suggests that any goods internal to an activity are more important for the practice itself than goods external to it.

Democracy or citizenship education considered as practices cannot then be exercised only as a means to an end, nor can they be achieved without the internal goods, such as freedom, justice, equality, and understanding and deliberation being practised by their practitioners, or so I will argue. A practitioner has to experience himself or herself as being free, equal and treated fairly in, for example, the education of deliberative, democratic citizens. A practitioner also has to act towards others in such a way that they too can be free, equal and treated fairly when deliberating knowledge, values and norms of action.

Democracy or citizenship education cannot survive as meaningful unless its internal goods are more achievable than its external goods. This means that any end achievable through a democratic process, such as the education of deliberative democratic citizens within a specific nation-state, cannot be settled once and for all at just one time and place. This education has to be settled from time to time, from place to place, in order to find out whether the internal goods are achievable and achieved, and to know how far people can be or are being educated in the sense required. In this respect, there is no ultimately final end concerning the internal goods, only temporary ends. Those lacking the experience of participation in sustaining and exercising the virtues internal to democracy and the education of deliberative democratic citizens, such as understanding and deliberation, cannot satisfactory evaluate or judge the goods internal to it. If democracy or citizenship education are viewed as ways of life in specific nation-states, then they cannot be sustained without being practised by its members and its virtues being acknowledged, reflected upon and criticised by them. And this can be achieved only if the members of a fully-fledged democracy are trained in exercising its virtues and by gaining knowledge of its principles, standards and rules; of its history, institution and practitioners.

To enter into a practice such as democracy or citizenship education in a specific nation-state is, according to MacIntyre 'to accept the authority of those standards and the inadequacy of my own performance as judged by them. It is to subject my own attitudes, choices, preferences and tastes to the standards which currently and partially define the practice' (1984, p. 190). This is an interesting observation. It is a situation that requires an individual entering or participating in a practice to have some understanding of the practice.

But entering and participating in a practice can mean initially accepting contemporary authorities and standards of conduct such as loyalty and patriotism, and recognising earlier ones as manifested in specific institutions and communities. But these are manifested only as the goods external to practices. Like other external goods they admit only competitiveness and the achievement and retention of properties in relation to individuals, unless the internal goods of the present practices are given adequate scope. The exercising of virtues internal to a practice means, in comparison to the exercising of external goods, the achievement of what is good 'for the whole community who participate in the practice' (1984, pp. 190–191), and not only for one or a few individuals.

In this respect MacIntyre criticises liberal individualism for its view that 'a community is simply an arena in which individuals each pursue their own self-chosen conception of the good life, and political institutions exist to provide that degree of order which makes such self-determined activity possible'(1984, p. 195). He argues that individuals never follow freely any 'conception of the good life'; they follow practices with ready-made standards of conduct, functioning as evaluative horizons against which individuals as citizens understand themselves and their ways of life. He also argues that liberalism in general, and Rawls' liberalism especially, expresses exactly the above propositional content, and that the key question is not 'What should I do?' but 'Who am I?' MacIntyre argues that liberals do not acknowledge the latter question as more basic than the former. He continues by claiming that the self as someone who freely makes choices and decisions cannot accomplish or even understand itself without understanding the stories in which the person is involved and by which the person is constituted. The key or prior question according to MacIntyre is not 'What am I to do?' but 'Who am I?':

> I can only answer the question 'What am I to do?' if I can answer the prior question 'Of what story or stories do I find myself a part?' We enter human society, that is, with one or more imputed characters – roles into which we

have been drafted – and we have to learn what they are in order to be able to understand how others respond to us and how our responses to them are apt to be construed. (1984, p. 216)

MacIntyre criticises liberalism for incorporating the false and illusory atomistic view that individuals can freely choose and make their own life. He claims that individuals cannot understand themselves or be understood in any proper sense without acknowledging that their identities, ends and beliefs are socially constituted. He claims that any individual, to understand what to do, has to recognise the story or stories within which he or she is structured narratively. The important questions for individuals, then, do not concern the individuals' choices, but self-understanding.

We see that MacIntyre argues against the liberal understanding of free choice and individuals as the makers of their own ways of life: he asserts that: 'we are never more (and sometimes less) than the co-authors of our own narratives' (1984, p. 213). He continues that it is 'only in fantasy [that we] live what story we please' (p.213). However, the idea that we are never more than co-authors of our lives does not necessarily contradict the liberal idea of being an individual with a possibility to make a choice, to reflect upon or reject a project or a way of life.[2]

Will Kymlicka and Stephen Mulhall challenge MacIntyre's interpretation of Rawls' liberalism and the liberal conception of free choice. First, Kymlicka points out that the role and function of freedom in liberalism, especially that of Rawls, is not that individuals strive for it for its own sake or value. Such an ideal of freedom would be empty (Taylor, 1979). Kymlicka argues in *Contemporary Political Philosophy* that freedom is not valuable in itself or the most valuable thing in life in liberalism (Kymlicka, 1990); more valuable are our projects and tasks. It is because they are so important to us that we ought to be free to reflect upon, change and possibly reject them. Kymlicka also argues that freedom is valuable as a necessary condition for fulfilling those projects and tasks we find important. This, for Kymlicka, is why liberals and especially Rawls argue that individuals ought to have the right to freely choose, revise and reject damaging regulated and constituted attachments, beliefs and ends.

Secondly, Stephen Mulhall, too, argues that MacIntyre misinterprets Rawls' liberalism. MacIntyre argues that for Rawls 'a society is composed of individuals, each with his or her own interest, who then have to come together and formulate common rules of life … [and that] individuals are … primary and society secondary, and the identification of individual interests is prior to, and independent of, the construction of any moral or social bonds between them' (MacIntyre, 1984, p. 250). But Rawls represents his view as a 'device of representation', and not as an ontological or epistemological view of the self as prior to or independent of society. Stephen Mulhall says that:

If we allowed our knowledge that we possessed a certain social status or talent to affect our choice, we would be permitting an inequality that is arbitrary from a moral point of view to distort our thinking about justice; we would not be treating people as equal. And if we allowed our knowledge that we were committed to a given conception of the good to influence our deliberations, we would be condemning those who had freely chosen or developed different commitments to unfair treatment by the state; we would not be treating people as free. (Mulhall, 1994, p. 208)

Mulhall argues that Rawls' theory does not imply or inherit the view of individuals as detached from attachments in a society, and that it does not view their interests as prior to or comprehended independently of constitutive attachments in society. The 'device of representation' is not, according to Rawls, an ontological claim about who individuals really are. It is not a statement about total neutrality, but only a device (and, according to Rawls, the best) for individuals to attempt to find a fair distribution of justice which views individuals as equals and free to pursue their own freely-chosen projects and tasks.

Narratives

The second condition – the narrative condition – for describing virtues is, says MacIntyre, necessary. No behaviour is intelligible without it: behaviour cannot be comprehended without characterising the intentions of the agent. Consider an individual bent over a book. What is he doing? Reading? Looking? Finding an answer to a specific question? Solving world mysteries? Hiding from the police? Identifying with the professor? We understand a person's specific behaviour only in terms of intentions and a specific narrative, according to MacIntyre. So if the narrative is that he is a professor bending over a book the person's behaviour is understood in those terms. And if his or her behaviour is reported in another narrative it will be understood in those other terms.

But this is not all. MacIntyre also argues that the narrative understanding of behaviour cannot be comprehended without also understanding the narrative's social setting and the historical character: '[a] social setting may be an institution, it may be what I have called a practice, or it may be a milieu of some other human kind' (1984, p. 206). An understanding of the individual bending over the book is, then, comprehended by understanding his or her intention, and by understanding, for example, the context within which the behaviour is settled. Bending over a book in a library, outside in a park, at a café, at home, by a grave, in front of a couple about to get married, all have different meanings, especially in causal relations with an intention spelled out. It is also central 'to the notion of a setting ... that a setting has a history, a history within which the histories of individual agents not only are, but have to be, situated, just because without the setting and its changes through time the history of the individual agent and his changes through time will be unintelligible' (pp. 206–207).

A person, then, is not a pre-historical, pre-cultural and pre-social character, according to MacIntyre, but someone whose beliefs, ends and goals are constituted and regulated by the social settings or narratives of which the individual is a part. His or her choices are not made in a vacuum, but always, for MacIntyre, within different narratives. An individual making choices is not making them *per se*, but always in some location with its history and as a citizen with his or her history. Intelligible behaviour cannot then be detached from beliefs, intention and social setting; and the understanding of individuals cannot, then, be detached in any strong sense from beliefs, intentions, social settings and narratives. And because of this, MacIntyre claims that Rawls' idea of 'an original position' is an illusion. Let us discuss this argument against Rawls' original position.

MacIntyre argues that some academic philosophers claim that rationality requires 'that we first divest ourselves of allegiance to any one of the contending theories and also abstract ourselves from all those particularities of social relationship in terms of which we have been accustomed to understand our responsibilities and our interests. Only by so doing, it has been suggested, shall we arrive at a genuinely neutral, impartial, and, in this way, universal point of view, freed from the partisanship and the partiality and one-sidedness that otherwise affect us. And only by so doing shall we be able to evaluate the contending accounts of justice rationally' (MacIntyre, 1984, p. 3). Rawls' method, the device of representation, is claimed to be universal in kind and abstracting from actual practices (which constitute our ends and goods in life, according to MacIntyre, Sandel (1995; 1992) and Taylor (1985a; 1985b; 1985c)).

Rawls on the other hand says that '[j]ustice as fairness is a political conception in part because it starts from within a certain political tradition' (1992, p. 189). It is not supposed to be universal in the sense that it can be used cross-culturally without taking into account actual practices in existing societies. It is true that Rawls enjoins us to abstract from our own interests, social position and particular endowments and to suggest ways to agree concerning matters of justice. It is therefore understandable that his method has been interpreted as an abstract, universal and trans-historical method and as an Archimedean point of departure from which justice is construed. But I am not sure that the method itself is to be understood as an abstract and universal device for rational, unencumbered, persons freed from the community's constituted practices. To me it seems that what he nowadays calls his 'device of representation' is more likely to be understood as a device for individuals to be free and able to question apprehensions of what is valuable in life within specific political traditions.

People should not, according to Rawls, be forced to accept any conception of what a good life in any society is. He says, 'the self is prior to the ends which are affirmed by it' (1973, p. 560). I interpret this in the following terms: individuals ought to be free to say no to or to choose any conception or apprehension of what a good life is or a lifestyle that they find valuable or non-valuable. The point is not that individuals should be interpreted as metaphysical subjects behind and absolutely free from authoritative conceptions and practices of what is valuable in life. Rather individuals ought to be free and able to question, analyse, criticise and revise any project, end, good or value in life through deliberation; justice as fairness, as a device of representation, can be used in this respect.

Rawls argues that his position is – I repeat – not ontological or epistemological, but is to be understood only as a 'device of representation'. He does not claim that individuals are what they choose to be, but that they can and do in fact have the capacity to make choices, and that his idea of 'the original position' can be used as a device for individuals to make a fair distribution of justice within the traditions of which they are a part.

It is therefore not clear whether there is any real difference between Rawls and MacIntyre concerning people's potential to reject their moral attachments and commitments. MacIntyre argues that 'the fact that the self has to find its moral identity in and through its membership in communities such as those of the family, the neighbourhood, the city and the tribe does not entail that the self has to accept the moral *limitations* of the particularity of those forms of community' (1984, p. 221). This suggests that MacIntyre and Rawls really do not differ concerning the individual's right to change his or her way of life. They do differ concerning the notion of the status of individual embeddedness, but not, as has been argued, concerning their rights to reject the goods internal to practices.

Traditions

The third stage in the account of the development of the logical order of virtues concerns traditions. MacIntyre is not precise in the same way when defining the concept of tradition as when defining the concept of practice, but it is still possible to review and assess the concept. First of all, traditions are constituted by a set of practices, which are both transmitted and reshaped through traditions. And a tradition which is in good order does have some goods which motivate and give direction to actions, and which constitute the understanding of the self involved in and participating in the practices of that tradition. Such goods are historically extended and embody the socially constituted selves. Every individual embedded in a tradition generally seeks and lives in accordance with the goods constituting the tradition. The narrative of the self is, therefore, to be understood against the background of practices and a wider social context that tradition is.

The practices in the tradition define the virtues, that is, the goods internal and external to the practices. And those in turn are sustained by tradition. Tradition also inherits specific views about rationality, which gives the intellectual understanding and legitimisation of how and why one set of practices and not another is to be pursued. A tradition which is living is in good order, and as such is not static, but dynamic. It is possible (or at least it should be) in a living tradition for individuals involved and participating in it to reflect upon, criticise, reconstruct and possibly reject practices within the tradition itself; but I am not sure that this concerns the traditions themselves. This is a problematic point to which I will return.

A tradition which is not in good order is one which lacks justice, truthfulness, courage and intellectual virtues (such as reflection, critique, reconstruction and rejection), and a tradition which lacks or risks lacking internal virtues also risks being corrupt and static (1984, p. 223). What, then, is a tradition? A tradition can be, as far as I understand, in political philosophy: liberalism, communitarianism, discourse ethics; in economics: a specific profession, craftsmanship; in science: Newtonian or Einsteinian physics; in philosophy: existentialism, hermeneutics, pragmatism; in religion: Judaism, Catholicism, Buddhism; and in philosophy of education: critical pedagogy, multiculturalism, etc. Any of these traditions can be static or dynamic. A debate may be going on in the institutions which are the bearers of a tradition concerning, for example, whether those practices constituting the tradition and the virtues internal to them are good as they are or whether and how they can and should be different.

A second characteristic of a tradition is that there can be what I briefly touched upon earlier, an epistemological crisis, here a crisis concerning internal standards for developing and assessing virtues, practices, problems and goods. The only way to overcome its crisis is, according to MacIntyre, to develop new ways of accounting the anomalies which have become too many, too problematic or both. This can be done by developing new concepts or synthesising rival conceptions of concepts such as democracy and democratic deliberation. The crisis can concern the text used in legitimising specific problems as serious and worth investigating, and in explaining problems and phenomena. The crisis can also concern the authorities that embody the practices and goods specific to a tradition and the institutions which are the bearers of practices.

MacIntyre points out, as we have seen, that there is no God's-eye-view for evaluating or assessing traditions or developing new ways of understanding and explaining phenomena (1988, p. 350). He also argues that one tradition cannot claim to be superior to any other (p.348). These ideas are similar to the ones articulated in a liberal tradition, that there cannot be any conception of goods, ends or beliefs that is or can be superior to any other. In this respect there is no difference between MacIntyre's and Rawls' conceptions of the status of an overriding good.

A third characteristic is that different traditions can meet and that the opponents can discuss their different ways of understanding and explaining phenomena of different kinds. This can be done in a two-stage development:

> The first is that in which each characterizes the contentions of its rival in its own terms, making explicit the grounds for rejecting what is incompatible with its own central theses although sometimes allowing that from its own point of view and in the light of its own standards of judgement its rival has something to teach it on marginal and subordinate questions. A second stage is reached if and when the protagonists of each tradition, having considered in what ways their own tradition has by its own standards of achievement in enquiry found it difficult to develop its enquiries beyond a certain point, or has produced in some area insoluble antinomies, ask whether the alternative and rival tradition may not be able to provide resources to characterize and to explain the failings and defects of their own tradition more adequately than they, using the resources of that tradition, have been able to do. (1988, pp. 166–167)

But passing from stage one to stage two requires empathy towards, and an intellectual insight into, both your own and the rival tradition:

In controversy between rival traditions the difficulty in passing from the first stage to the second is that it requires a rare gift of empathy as well as of intellectual insight for the protagonists of such a tradition to be able to understand the theses, arguments, and concepts of their rival in such a way that they are able to view themselves from such an alien standpoint and recharacterize their own beliefs in an appropriate manner from the alien perspective of the rival tradition. (1988, p. 167)

So far, I have tried to show that there seems to be no substantive difference between Rawls and MacIntyre. If I am correct then we can ask ourselves whether the basic goal of citizenship education only should be to initiate children and young people into specific narratives transmitted through education in specific nation-states, or whether such education also has to give them the possibility and perhaps even the right to understand each other and to deliberate the meaning and legitimacy of utterances whenever needed. I return to this issue in the next section.

GOALS OF CITIZENSHIP EDUCATION

As an analytical concept MacIntyre's definition of virtue is both interesting and valuable. It can help us to penetrate different virtues in different practices and traditions in order to find out what these virtues are and what practices sustain them. It may also indicate what virtues are not sustained and what practices are not being exercised. However, the definition seems problematic as a descriptive and normative concept. The former use is problematic because it does not make a clear distinction between 'good' and 'evil' practices, as pointed out by Elisabeth Frazer and Nicola Lacey in the article 'MacIntyre, Feminism and the Concept of Practice' (Frazer & Lacey, 1994). They observe that torture and rape can be defined as practices in agreement with MacIntyre's definition of practice. They also point out that he does not exclude or make an account of them in an attempt to evaluate which practices are worth exercising in a satisfactory way and which are not.

Frazer and Lacey point out two possible substantive and procedural ways in which the concept of practice could be interpreted so as to handle this problem (Frazer & Lacey, 1994). The first: there can be some basic goods which exclude 'evil' goods reachable, for example, through reason alone or through perception. But as these authors point out MacIntyre defines the concept of virtue in terms of practices and tradition, and he therefore excludes any objectivistic notion of virtue such as the Platonic conception of virtues reachable through reason alone. And as I have pointed out earlier, MacIntyre denies the possibility of any superior goods achieved through thinking or perceiving. Secondly, Frazer and Lacey also find the interpretation procedurally problematic since intellectually comprehended procedures can be respected in regimes which 'score high on substantive evil' (p. 275).

Another problematic issue is that MacIntyre defines the understanding of the goods internal to practices in terms of 'being experienced' without clearly explaining what he means by this concept. If 'being experienced' means intellectually experienced (that is, having a cognitive conceptual understanding of theses and arguments in rival traditions as well as the logical order between them, without using them in practices defined and exercised in the specific tradition), then apparently we can only understand them conceptually, not morally. If, on the other hand, 'being experienced' means to have lived or to live for a long time in a specific (rival) culture and/or tradition and that only by having done or by doing this can there be any deeper understanding of that tradition, then we face problems of understanding the different meanings embodied in the practices, and of adequately characterising conceptually and morally the protagonist's socially- and culturally-embodied meanings. We also face the problem of how to give a substantive critique and not only an intellectual critique of different cultures, traditions, practices and their internal goods in relation to their internal standards of achievement and assessments of ends, beliefs and goods.

The normative notion of the concept of virtue is problematic too, as pointed out by Seyla Benhabib (Benhabib, 1992). She argues that the integrative strand in MacIntyre's notion of practices and traditions leads to a notion of re-establishing value-based communities in which there are and should be consistent systems of values which the members of that community inherit and embody. This suggests that every member of such a community should be integrated within its specific values, practices and traditions. Will Kymlicka (1991, p. 56) shows that MacIntyre's 'embedded-self' view means that what is good for me is what is good for others in our community, and that we do not choose our lives but discover them. An individual who wants to know what to do has to become aware of the different narratives and histories through which his identities are constituted and regulated in, for example, education. These are not chosen, but discovered, according to MacIntyre. This, the normative notion of practices and traditions, deprives us of the possibility to reject them if they repress or neglect our possibilities to fulfil our projects and tasks.

MacIntyre's stress on practices, traditions and narratives tends to orient itself towards ethical life forms as constitutive for solidarity between citizens and their self-realisation and self-understanding. Citizens have positive rights to fulfil their life plans within those ethical communities in which social life is guaranteed and based on an objective ethical content, not on individual subjective rights. This tendency to narrow political discourse in terms of ethical life forms is questioned by Habermas (1984, p. 4). He argues that there cannot only be a hermeneutical approach in making social integration possible as a basis for self-understanding and self-realisation within ethical communities. Despite the importance of knowing where and who we are, political matters or questions cannot be reduced to questions concerning only such matters. Habermas argues that the formation of citizens gains support and power not from ethical convictions given in specific communities, as in MacIntyre's case, but from presuppositions for communicative action which are addressed and inquired among those concerned in discourse. The possibility to acknowledge and test these presuppositions in discourse (that is, how far they are understood and legitimised by all concerned) allows individuals intersubjectively to legitimise ethical matters motivated by the force of the better argument (Habermas, 1992).[3]

It seems too that questions concerning discourses in which self-understanding takes place are less pertinent than those concerning moral and pragmatic matters and queries. The questions of justice and of principles or presuppositions for communicative action are moral questions and as such are the most fundamental questions in a democratic society, according to Habermas. It can be put in this way: people can be regarded as equal in expressing their interests or in partaking in discourse, and they can be viewed as free from compulsion of any kind. Clearly, however, it is not enough for people to be equal or free from compulsion: this is not the only reasonable or even comprehensible way of viewing the concept of freedom since, viewed only thus, it becomes empty. Freedom from compulsion does not mean much unless individuals are viewed as free in a positive sense; that is, free to fulfil their wishes, tasks and projects. In this respect justice becomes important since the resources for whatever end are not endless, but have to be distributed in a fair way. Questions or principles of justice, then, according to both Rawls and Habermas, cannot be viewed only from the viewpoint of the specific life forms and ethical communities in which they operate. For these authors, the guiding idea is what is best for all, and not for specific individuals or specific groups of people; and I am inclined to agree.

It seems then that the difference between Rawls on the one hand, and MacIntyre on the other, in relation to Habermas[4] concerning the forming of citizens in a democratic society can be formulated as follows: Rawls emphasises the acceptance of practising political power in forming the democratic will of people, and MacIntyre emphasises the constitution of an ethical community as a presupposition for members in their achievements to form their ethical self-understanding. Habermas departs from both views. He accepts the importance of aggregating and balancing between interests, and he presupposes the embeddedness of individuals, but makes the procedures and presuppositions for political and democratic will-formation the centre. These are not universal in a substantive sense and do not remain totally constituted by, or within, specific ethical communities.

UNDERSTANDING AND SUCCESSFUL COMMUNICATION

MacIntyre claims, as seen from above, that virtues basically are understood in terms of practices, narratives and traditions, and he asserts that these conditions are necessary for understanding virtues. People communicating with each other linguistically can and do understand each other, and they can communicate successfully, understand each other. A question then is whether understanding or communicating successfully is a good internal to the practice of speaking a language in MacIntyre's terminology. At first glance it seems that speaking a language fits into the definition of a practice, that is, can be seen as a 'coherent and complex form of socially established cooperative human activity through which goods internal to that form of activity are realized in the course of trying to achieve those standards of excellence which are appropriate to, and partially definitive of,

256

that form of activity' (1984, p. 187); and that understanding is an internal good to such a practice. Speaking a language seems to be a human quality that enables us to come to understand each other. If seen as internal to speaking a language, this means that communication among those concerned has been or is successful, while if understanding is lacking then this prevents us from successfully communicating with each other. MacIntyre too, seems to say that an internal good such as understanding or communicating successfully cannot be understood without narratives and awareness of the intentions of the agent(s). Moreover, MacIntyre seems to assert that a child cannot learn to speak a language unless he or she is initiated into specific narratives expressed in a specific language; nor that teachers can teach students how to speak correctly unless they (teachers) 'have been educated into whatever discipline it is that they are to transmit' (MacIntyre, 2002, p. 5). If this is so, then it seems that children and young people can develop their capacity to understand and communicate successfully by being initiated into specific narratives and learning to use utterances as others do, as shown by teachers in educational settings as well as others outside these settings. However, I do not think that these conditions explain our *ability* to understand or communicate successfully with each other; nor that our ability to understand each other's utterances is necessarily understood as an internal good dependent upon narratives and traditions in MacIntyre's terminology. If this is correct then our capacity to understand or communicate successfully is not necessarily dependent upon our narratives or conventions, and human capacity to understand the meaning of utterances – interpreting each other successfully – is not necessarily dependent upon having been introduced into specific narratives; nor that successful communication requires such narratives or conventions in the form of socially or culturally established ways of using utterances relevantly similar in relevantly similar situations. Being able to speak and understand meaningful utterances does not then seem to be acquired through being taught, and learning, to use specific utterances as others do in relevantly similar situations.

Children and young people use or learn to use the same or similar concepts and utterances as others do: this is an act of learning and teaching. However, the fact that language users learn to use the same or similar concepts and utterances in the same or similar ways as others do does not explain the *meaning* of either those utterances or the capacity to understand or learn to understand meaningful utterances.

Meaning is not necessarily identical with use: two people can use the same or similar utterances in the same or similar ways in relevantly similar situations but mean something different. Two people can say 'I love you', to each other but not ascribe the same meaning to the utterance. One may be rehearsing a play and just want to use the utterance as such, while the other wants to communicate to the other that she really loves him. This shows that two people do not necessarily ascribe the same meaning to the same utterances used in communication. And MacIntyre seems to agree when he says that to 'identify an occurrence as an action is in the paradigmatic instances to identify it under a type of description which enables us to see that occurrence as flowing intelligibly from a human agent's intentions, motives, passions and purposes' (MacIntyre, 1984, p. 209). On the other hand he strongly emphasises the value and impact of narratives on peoples' intentions, beliefs and motives, as seen from the above.

Now it could be argued, as MacIntyre seems to do, that children and young people have to learn a language in order to communicate with other language users. And should they not learn a language they will not communicate successfully with others, that is, understand the meaning of specific utterances. Hence, it seems that they have to be initiated into specific uses of utterances within specific languages; otherwise they will be unable to understand the meaning of such utterances; or to develop their capacity to communicate successfully. If meaning were equated with use then it could possibly be suggested that someone – a child – will come to understand the meaning of specific utterances by using or learning to use the same or similar concepts as others do in relevantly similar situations. But this is not necessarily correct as seen from the above. According to Davidson (2001), our capacity to communicate successfully does not require conventions or narratives. He says that 'we should give up the attempt to illuminate how we can communicate by appeal to conventions' (Davidson, 1996, p. 475). Conventions or narratives do play an important role when people speak with each other, though. We often refer to specific uses of utterances in specific languages when we direct our attention to how people use them as others do in relevantly similar situations. But as MacIntyre says we cannot understand human behaviour without taking human intentions and beliefs into account, and this includes understanding the meaning speakers ascribe to linguistic utterances. Hence we cannot equate meaning with use; we also have to take the intentions and beliefs of the speakers into account when understanding or coming to understand the utterances in use.

What matters for successful communication is that 'the hearer assigns the meaning that the speaker intended' (Glüer, 2001, p. 55). And the ability to do this cannot be explained in terms of conventions or narratives, but in terms of speakers' ability to compose meaningful utterances from a finite numbers of words and in terms of being charitable when interpreting the meaning of the other's utterances. The best explanation of our capacity to speak meaningfully and understand the meaning of specific utterances seems then not to involve conventions or narratives or initiation into specific narratives or having used specific utterances as others do in relevantly similar situations. A better explanation seems to involve compositionality, that is, that the meaning of a complex expression is a function of the meaning of its parts and its mode of composition. It is also important that the listener ascribe the meaning the speaker intended to specific utterances and deliberate the meaning and legitimacy of utterances. That people do this in communication is probably correct in general, but not necessarily in every single case. Sometimes language users are uncertain of the other's intention or of whether the intention the other expressed was in fact his or her real intention. And the speaker, even, may be uncertain of what intention he or she had or has. It happen that language users express intentions other than those they really have!

These principles taken together seem to better explain our ability to communicate successfully and understand specific utterances (especially ones we have never heard before) than does the idea that we during our upbringing have been introduced into and imitated specific uses of utterances or so I have argued. Now if this is so, then a main goal of education and especially citizenship education cannot only be to initiate children and young people into specific narratives, but also to give them the opportunity or perhaps even the right to understand each other as charitably as possible and deliberate the meaning of utterances whenever they do not understand them or disagree, or are in conflict with each other. This presupposes that they are willing and able to handle and/or solve the disagreement and/or conflict peacefully and constructively.

SUMMARY

In this paper I have argued that MacIntyre's promising theory of virtue does not necessarily contradict liberal ideas or discourse-ethical ones, and that the theory seems to focus too heavily on the normative dimension of practices, narratives and traditions. I have also argued that a goal of citizenship education cannot only be to introduce children and young people to specific narratives or have them use utterances as others do or would do in relevantly similar situations.

Citizenship education in contemporary nation-states also has to enable those concerned to actualise charitable interpretations in order to develop their capacity to understand the other and to deliberate so as to develop their reflective and critical faculties and their capacity to make decisions which in principle can be legitimised by all concerned as participants in communication. To communicate successfully we not only have to understand each other as charitably as possible; we must also be able to deliberate the meaning and legitimacy of utterances whose meaning is not understood by those concerned, or when people disagree or are in conflict with each other. Now, if the above is correct then MacIntyre's theory of virtue does not, I have argued, seem to be an ethics-for-citizenship education unless it also takes into account the ideas discussed above.

NOTES

[1] An earlier version of this paper was published in my thesis: Roth, 2000, pp. 48–64.

[2] See also Roth, 2000, pp. 16–27 for a discussion on this issue.

[3] See Habermas (1992), pp. 43–115 for a discussion on a programme for philosophical justification.

[4] Habermas (1995) although empathic and admiring the intentions of Rawls's theory and its essential results, criticises Rawls (1995) for not clearly separating issues concerning the intersubjective justification of norms and the acceptance of principles of justice. The former is Habermas's concern and the latter Rawls's. Rawls claims to be dealing with issues of justification, but it turns out that he views justification, and not only acceptability, differently than Habermas does.

REFERENCES

Benhabib S. (1992). *Situating the self, gender, community and postmodernism in contemporary ethics.* New York: Routledge.

Davidson, D. (1996). A nice derangement of epitaphs. In A. P. Martinich (Ed.), *The philosophy of language* (3rd edition, pp. 465–475). Oxford University Press.

Davidson, D. (2001). Communication and convention. In *Inquires into truth and interpretation* (pp. 265–280). Oxford: Clarendon Press.

Frazer E. & Lacey N. (1994). MacIntyre, feminism and the concept of practice. In J. Horton & S. Mendus (Eds.), *After MacIntyre* (pp. 265–282). Oxford: Polity Press.

Glüer, K. (2001). Dreams and Nightmares. In P. Kotatko, P. Pagin and G. Segal (Eds.), *Interpreting Davidson* (pp. 53–74). Stanford: CSLI Publications.

Habermas J. (1984). *The theory of communicative action. Reason and the Rationalization of Society* (T. McCarthy, Trans.). Volume 1. Boston: Beacon Press.

Habermas J. (1992). Discourse ethics: Notes on a program of philosophical justification. In C. Lenhardt & S. Weber Nicholsen (Trans.), *Moral consciousness and communicative action* (pp. 43–115). Cambridge: Polity Press.

Habermas J. (1995). Reconciliation through the public use of reason: Remarks on John Rawls's Political Liberalism. *Journal of Philosophy, XCII* (3), 109–131.

Kymlicka W. (1990). *Contemporary political philosophy*. Oxford: Clarendon Press.

Kymlicka W. (1991). *Liberalism, community and culture*. Oxford: Clarendon Press.

MacIntyre A. (1984). *After virtue*. Notre Dame, Ind.: University of Notre Dame Press.

MacIntyre A. (1988). *Whose justice? Which rationality?* London: Duckworth.

MacIntyre, A. (2002). Alasdair MacIntyre on education: In dialogue with Joseph Dunne. *Journal of Philosophy of Education, 36*(1), 1–19.

Mulhall S. (1994). Liberalism, morality and rationality: MacIntyre, Rawls and Cavell. In J. Horton & S. Mendus (Eds.), *After MacIntyre* (pp. 205–224). Oxford: Polity Press.

Rawls J. (1973). *A theory of justice*. Oxford: Oxford University Press.

Rawls J. (1992). Justice as fairness: Political not metaphysical. In S. Avineri & A. De-Shalit (Eds.), *Communitarianism and individualism* (pp. 186–204). Oxford: Oxford University Press.

Rawls J. (1995). Reply to Habermas. *Journal of Philosophy, XCII* (3), 132–180.

Roth, K. (2000). *Democracy, education and citizenship. Towards a theory on the education of deliberative democratic citizens*. Stockholm: Stockholm Institute of Education Press.

Sandel M. (1992). The procedural republic and the unencumbered self. In S. Avineri & A. De-Shalit (Eds.), *Communitarianism and individualism* (pp. 12–28). Oxford: Oxford University Press.

Sandel M. (1995). *Liberalism and the limits of justice*. Cambridge: Cambridge University Press.

Taylor C. (1979). *Hegel and modern society*. Cambridge: Cambridge University Press.

Taylor C. (1985a). Atomism. In *Philosophy and the human sciences: Philosophical papers* (pp. 187–210). Volume 2. Cambridge: Cambridge University Press.

Taylor C. (1985b). What's wrong with negative liberty? In *Philosophy and the human sciences: Philosophical papers* (pp. 211–229). Volume 2. Cambridge: Cambridge University Press.

Taylor C. (1985c). Self-interpreting animals. In *Human agency and languages: Philosophical papers* (pp. 45–76). Volume 1. Cambridge: Cambridge University Press.

Klas Roth
Stockholm Institute of Education, Sweden

MARK OLSSEN

GLOBALISATION, THE THIRD WAY AND EDUCATION POST-9/11

Building Democratic Citizenship

INTRODUCTION

The possibility of acts of terror, whether committed by rogue states, or transnational groups, forces a new consideration of the themes of democracy, community and individual rights. And there must also, I believe, be a new understanding of what citizenship entails, and what the role of education is in relation to creating citizens. The new realisation that the world is full of dangers is leading to a reappraisal of the relations between the state and the individual and between collective interests and individual rights. What confronts us now, more than at any time since the 17th century, is the prospect of a new political settlement that involves a radical revision and restriction of traditional rights and liberties given to individuals. At the same time as states are encouraged to adhere to the 'steer-but-not-row' philosophy of neo-liberalism in economic affairs, in the political sphere the state's need to know, involving increased surveillance and data gathering for the purposes of fighting crime, fraud and preventing acts of terror, has now become an *explicit agenda of states*. What is being ushered in, indeed, is a new post-liberal political settlement. Within this scenario there are possibilities, openings and dangers. In this paper I will seek to reassess the significance of globalisation, neoliberalism, human rights, community, democracy and the role of education, taking the events of 9/11 into account.

NEOLIBERALISM, GLOBALISATION AND THE MOVE TO THE 'THIRD WAY'

Neoliberalism is that form of economic reason encapsulated in the notion of *homo economicus* which represents individuals as rational self-interested choosers, which was based on a revitalisation of neoclassical economic liberalism and which, as Peters (2001, p. 9) says 'has been remarkably successful in advancing a foundationalist and universalist reason as a basis for a radical global reconstruction of all aspects of society and economy'. During the last several years neoliberalism has been adapted, rescued one might say, under the mantle of the 'third way' which aims to retain the neoliberal concern with efficiency in the economic sphere while avoiding traditional policies of redistribution, still defining freedom in terms of

M.A. Peters, A. Britton and H. Blee (Eds.), Global Citizenship Education: Philosophy, Theory and Pedagogy, 261–281.

autonomy of action, but now mixed in with a concern for the values of social justice and democracy and increased involvement and participation in the local community.

Critics suggest that the 'third way' is an amorphous linking of disparate elements, lacking any distinctive economic policy, based upon an attempt to find a middle way. Giddens (2000, p. 163) suggests that the 'third way' is not an attempt to occupy the middle ground but rather is 'concerned with restructuring social democratic doctrines to respond to the twin revolutions of globalization and the knowledge economy'. What the 'third way' tries to do, in my view unsuccessfully, is theorise the need for a more active state intra-nationally in order to deal with the crucial national issues concerning social democracy, while retaining economic commitment to neo-liberalism as its central orientation to both domestic and global relations. In this sense, the 'third way' politics of New Labour in Britain maintains that it constitutes a melding of traditional concerns of social democracy while retaining the central neo-liberal insights over economic policy, the role of the state, and the need for accountability. This is the political discourse that presently dominates New Labour's policies towards education, health, crime, and the role of social services. Dubbed the 'new localism', it is based on the state philosophy of 'steer-but-not-row', and signals the end of the centrally planned welfare state as established in Britain in 1945. It entails the death of what British Prime Minister Tony Blair called a 'one size fits all' model of public service provision, whereby spending and direction was effected from the centre, moving towards a model whereby spending and direction is effected at the local level via the people directly affected and involved. As such, the 'third way' affects fundamentally a shift in the role of the state. As Tony Blair stated at the recently held Labour Party Conference at Bournemouth:

> Just as mass production has departed from industry, so the monolithic provision of services has to depart from the public sector. Out goes the big state. In comes the enabling state (Wintour, 2002)

This idea of an enabling state is central to 'third way' politics of New Labour, and to new policy initiatives on education and health. In education, it has involved the expansion and development of specialist schools as part of the 'post-comprehensive era'. This has resulted in new legislation to encourage successful specialist schools to operate autonomously, to expand, and to encourage school takeovers. Choice policies which enable parents to secure the school of their preference are being encouraged, and privatisation initiatives are also being encouraged in order to extend private sector involvement in public services through a proliferation of public-private partnerships (PPPs), and private finance initiatives (PFIs) and public interest companies (PICs). As such, the enabling state constitutes a model of semi-autonomous public services supposedly free of Whitehall control. Both schools and hospitals are being granted autonomy where they can establish new directions of travel. Controls on local councils are being released and voluntary organisations are being allowed to run public services. New Labour theorists, such as the New Economics Foundation, the New Local Government

Network, and the Institute of Public Policy Research represent this agenda as moving beyond old distinctions between the state and the market. The idea is that services funded by the state need not be run by the state. Such a model thus entails an increased role for the private sector and increased choice.

Whether this 'third way' model really does manage to reconcile neoliberal and social democratic agendas is a much-contested issue. Whether state control is any less, or any different, than it was in the pre-Thatcher years is indeed a meaningful question. Supposedly, according to Rhodes (2000), the new governance narrative which is espoused by New Labour is based on networking, partnerships, autonomy of providers, interdependence between organisations, and trust. The state's role is to facilitate and coordinate without treading on the autonomy of foundation hospitals, schools, or higher education institutions. In reality the state under-emphasises its control, for although it may not actively be delivering services, it can still be seen to be effecting control, and at least some studies claim that this control, rather than decreasing, is simply taking a different form (Rhodes 1997a, 1997b, 2000; Cloke et al, 2000, p. 130). In addition, in that the power of the state is being reorganised rather than reduced, in its relationship to local groups, the organisation of governance in networks and partnerships is producing new obstacles as far as traditional democratic forms of accountability are concerned. A governance model which delegates power to local agencies is producing problems relating to representation, accountability, openness to criticism, as well as to the rights of consumers or users. The ability of local agencies to work together, or coordinate service provision is offset by the differences in power and influence between them; by the adherence to traditional norms of exclusivity and non-cooperation; by the inequalities between the different partners or actors providing services in the state, voluntary and private spheres; and by the fragmentation of services across different sectors.

Thus, whether new models of governance based on networks and partnerships can constitute a solution to traditional forms of state bureaucracy or markets, or overcome the limitations inherent in forms of state bureaucracy or markets, is unlikely. Research by Rhodes (2000), Cochrane (2000), Cloke et al. (2000), Glendinning et al. (2002) and others cast doubt on whether patterns of state control have significantly altered, and whether ad hoc adjustments and interference are not constantly required to overcome inequities, unfairness, inequalities that arise when localistic solutions and policy operates. As Karl Polanyi (1944) observed with reference to the rise of the welfare state, the growth of central state involvement in economic and social policy arose not because of any pre-determined political plan or conspiracy, but because of the shear complexity of government. This complexity is likely to increase apace given the inherently individualist and self-serving nature of neo-liberal reason. In the end, the resources and manpower invested in 'steering' becomes as great if not greater than in 'rowing' until it is not clear what the differences between them are.

Indeed, we might be tempted to say that the bride is too beautiful, for any marriage of private investment with state 'steering' will likely result in a greater and greater role for the state as it attempts to level-out the bumps and potholes in the playing field, provide reasonable mechanisms of representation and accountability, and ensure some measure of rights and fair treatment for the unsuspecting and often unenlightened public whose education and welfare is at stake. This seems to be what is indeed happening in 'third way' policy delivery. In Britain, *Railtrack* which was privatised under Thatcher, has recently returned to public ownership due to the shear operational chaos that private ownership produced. More recently, *British Energy* has had to be bailed out by the State. The government had to underwrite its risks due to the sensitive place it occupies in the economy, which of course was one of the reasons for nationalising it in the first place. Under private ownership it has become obvious that neither managerial efficiency nor public safety are guaranteed. The history of the past year in Britain is littered with examples of the failings of privately run prisons, schools and hospitals. It is a situation, as Roy Hattersley (2002, p. 18) has quipped, of 'taxpayers servicing the debt, and shareholders receiving the dividends'.

If the 'third way' attempt to marry social democracy and neoliberalism in terms of governance is problematic, the rise of the 'third way' does suggest a more positive message in that it speaks to a more active state than was entailed under traditional laissez-faire models. Indeed, even if the state under the 'third way' seeks to change the form of its operation, from traditional bureaucracy to governance through networks, the model still speaks to the idea of a strong state. The idea of an enabling state is indeed quite compatible with a conception of the state that sets up the rules of the game, that passes legislation to enforce minimum conditions of acceptable treatment for all of the various groups in society (children, the aged, women, ethnic minorities, etc.,) and that seeks to ensure adequate protection and rights for all through the framing and introduction legislation. The notion of 'enabling', like that of 'steering' does not of itself speak to the size of the state, and conceivably, a state that 'steers' might be just as big as a state that 'rows'. At the same time, so long as the state can assure the important platforms of universal entitlement, equality of opportunity, and equality before the law, then the attempt to actively co-opt the citizenry in running their own lives can only be seen as positive and a major back-down from the discourse of a reduced state which became the catch-cry of neoliberal reason during the Thatcher years.

WHAT IS GLOBALISATION?

What is thus most positive about the third way's conception of the enabling state is the very recognition of a *role for the state* in an age of globalisation. The central thesis of the doctrine seems to suggest that the state can act as a powerful force to regulate and supervise and to initiate and direct policy within national contexts. This recognition of the power of the state would seem to contradict the thesis of a 'powerless state', as writers like Manuel Castells (1997) (who used this phrase as the title to a chapter), or Naomi Klein (2000), or Kenichi Ohmae (1990, 1995) have depicted, and which has been generally the dissertation of so many globalisation theorists of recent years.

264

In my view, globalisation does not spell the end, or even, necessarily, the demise, of the nation-state as an autonomous force. Writers who suggest that it does are failing to differentiate the different theses entailed in the notion of globalisation. In order to make this thesis clear it is important to distinguish the senses of globalisation. For a start we can note how this concept has functioned to displace other related concepts and theories to do with cultural, economic and political 'colonialism', 'neo-colonialism' or 'imperialism'. It is as if suddenly these more specific theories, which were more politically charged, and made explicit the relations of power and knowledge entailed in state actions in international affairs, were replaced by a more general concept where the relations of power are not so obvious, or were seen to be manifested in a different way. Yet, the concept is clearly important, and it has become more so post-9/11 in that it gives recognition to the undeniable fact that our lives are becoming more intertwined. This, it may be argued, has always been the case, and there is a certain sense in which that is true, as David Held (1995) has argued, but a number of twentieth century developments in technology, science, communication and travel, and economy have arguably increased or at least changed the sense in which it is so. From developments in communications technology, the mass media, the internet, the increasing availability and possibility of travel, the growth in multinational trade and international marketability of goods and services, the general growth in the circulation of money and goods, through to developments in science, and to the spread of knowledge and its democratisation, which make weapons of mass destruction and acts of terror as possible acts within the sphere of capability of private citizens, transnational groups and rogue nations, all serve to reinforce the 'intertwined' nature of our existence. 9/11 and Bali 02 have brought home dramatically the sense in which what happens in one part of the world effects what happens everywhere. Cultures mix through migration, education, GATS, news and information, ideas and fashions, brands and marketing. Terrorism increases, at the political level, the degree of inter-dependence in terms of political governance and regulatory arrangements between nation states and amongst transnational political and economic agencies and organisations such as the EU, WB, IMF, OECD, NAFTA, APEC and WTO.

The fact that globalisation is promoting greater integration between countries and regions is not of itself of concern. One must take each issue and each effect separately in order to assess its positive or negative consequences, and one must do this one issue at a time. That one can discern many issues of exploitation and oppression is clearly evident. At the cultural level, for instance, it can be observed that the spread of information technology and the communications revolution tends to operate as forms of imperialism, in that the ideas, images, and even language of communication is provided by the more powerful western states, led by the USA and Britain. If globalisation increases the speed and intensity of the circulation of ideas across the globe, then the effect on small relatively powerless states will be the same as has always been the case: the cultural and intellectual sovereignty of their customs, beliefs, and ways of life, will be undermined. At the same time, one must be open to the fact that there are some possible positive effects of globalisation. Recent moves to internationalise in higher education have resulted in the large-scale international movement of students and staff across national borders. PhD students at Surrey, to give one very local example, are now selected from many countries. Similarly, as with most universities, and many other institutions, higher education staff are recruited internationally. Growing internationalisation leads to increasingly innovative attempts to standardise procedures such as criteria of admission and recruitment, resulting in new forms of global communication and regulation. These trends, which are merely small examples of how global cooperation and exchange can have positive effects, are not without elements of injustice and oppression, of course, and this is especially so in that they are structured within neo-liberal economic frameworks. They are also not really new, but as with international travel and migration, the scale and scope have both increased. We can, in this sense, I believe, agree, at least in part, with Held (1995) in the relevance of a new concept of *cosmopolitanism*. This is so in a number of senses. Firstly, with changes to the material basis of culture in the West since the scientific revolution, but especially in the 20th century, it has become increasingly true that there are a great number of events and developments (Chernobyl, acid rain, oil slicks) which have impacts across national borders. Secondly, relatedly, in relation to international trade and 20th century economic developments, there have been huge increases in the global circulation of goods, ideas and information, and money, all of which are more global in terms of both the speed and scale of distribution than at any previous time in history. If these speak to a new sense of cosmopolitanism, which I see as an extension of the idea of republicanism, it is only partly in the sense elaborated by Held, however. For while both these developments clearly entail a growth in the importance of international agencies and regulatory bodies, as Hirst and Thompson (1996) argue, any mandate for the democratic functioning of these agencies still resides within individual nation states. It is at the national level, ultimately, that accountability resides.[1]

A NEW POLITICAL SETTLEMENT?

At the political level, globalisation can also be represented as a dynamic process. In that the scale and scope of communication and travel have increased, so we can say that since 9/11 the potential risks and dangers have also increased. It is at this level that 9/11 serves to denote a major epistemological-political break with previous discursive systems. Since 9/11 we can say indeed that there has been a keener interest by western states in the uniform global imposition of standard systems of security and surveillance which is altering the traditional nature of the relations between individuals and the state. What private individuals do in Bhagdad, Afghanistan, Cairo, Naples, London, or Auckland, or what they carry through airports, is now of vital concern to policy makers and ruling elites and some might argue, ordinary citizens, in America and Britain, and many other countries. In a way it has taken the prospect of terror to make us painfully aware of our inter-relatedness. The effects of this show the signs of crystallizing a new political settlement that has been perhaps embryonic as an emergent discourse for some time, but after 9/11 has been given a new impetus. Whether it represents a 'permanent settlement', or just a 'temporary tendency' is as yet uncertain, and while I will refer to the former, I leave open the possibility, and the hope, that it is only the latter. At least some early signs are appearing as emergent forms within the existing political milieu.

The emergent new tendency/settlement has two elements:

At an economic level, it is based on neoliberal freedom, which is now more obviously confined to the 'freedom of commerce', or to 'free trade'. In this sense, neoliberalism must clearly be seen as a particular element of globalisation in that it constitutes the form through which domestic and global economic relations are structured. Yet, neoliberalism is only one form of globalisation, and only pertains to economic globalisation. It is not something that has evolved naturally as a consequence of changes in technology or science. And it must not be confused with globalisation as such. Rather it must be seen as a specific economic discourse or philosophy which has become dominant and effective in world economic relations as a consequence of super-power sponsorship. Neoliberalism is a politically imposed discourse, which is to say that it constitutes the hegemonic discourse of western nation states. As such it is quite independent of the forms of globalisation that we have spoken of above, based as they are on changes in technology and science, nor can it be seen as part of their effects, although this is not to say that there is no relationship at all. Its major characteristics emerged in the USA in the 1970s as a forced response to stagflation and the collapse of the Bretton Woods system of international trade and exchange, leading to the abolition of capital controls in 1974 in the USA and 1979 in Britain (Mishra, 1999; Stiglitz, 2002). This made it extremely difficult to sustain Keynesian demand management. Financial globalisation made giant strides. Exchange rates were floated and capital controls abolished, giving money and capital the freedom to move across national boundaries. The changes in technology did certainly facilitate these changes, for developments in microelectronics and computers made it possible to shift financial reserves within seconds. To the extent that neoliberalism was effective it certainly compromised the autonomy of national governments in the sphere of managing their economies. This depended upon political alliances to support such policies however. By this I mean that there was nothing necessary about this decentring of the nation state. The very emergence of the 'third way', and of New Leftist traditional Labour adaptations within the 'third way', some of which are now claiming 'limits to privatisation',[2] make the latent power of the state in an age of globalisation eminently visible. The equation is not globalisation *or* the nation state but globalisation *and* the nation state.

At a political level the signs of what could be seen as a new post-liberal settlement is premised on greater control, increased surveillance, and an eclipse of liberal rights that have prevailed since the 17th and 18th centuries. Terrorism, as Charles Townsend (2002, p. 137) has noted, constitutes 'a calculated assault on the culture of reasonableness', which is central to democratic civic culture. Such a culture is epitomised by norms such as 'toleration', 'moderation', 'the principle of proportionality', and 'non-violence', which form the conditions for the exercise of civil liberties. Townsend (2002, p. 134) reports the conclusions of the Dutch political scientist Alex Schmid (1993) who has concluded that democracies experience weaknesses when faced with terrorism related to (a) freedom of movement, (b) freedom of association, (c) an abundance of targets, and (d) the constraints of the legal system.

While the liberal rights of free association and free speech make democracies slow to respond, some significant changes have come in a number of respects. Firstly, as concerns rights within the law, in respect to being imprisoned without being charged, and to being detained for an indefinite period. A relaxation of traditional judicial cautiousness has been introduced as the condition upon which the safety of each person can be assured. In Britain, the legislative basis was introduced in December 2001 in *the Anti Terrorism Crime and Security Act*, which introduced internment without trial or the necessity of levelling charges. October 2002 saw this Act being used to effect the imprisonment of the radical Muslim cleric Abu Qatada in London, who was suspected to be an Al Qaeda agent. This legislation and other legislation also enables state surveillance and control over banking and information resources.

A second sense in which traditional political settlement has altered relates to the doctrine of 'pre-emptive strike' (and the associated notion of 'regime-change') which supercedes the doctrine of deterrence or containment, which has been the bedrock of stability, and the traditional Westphalia model of international relations which established the principle of state sovereignty by a treaty signed in 1648. Under deterrence, a country could retaliate if its national borders were violated. Under the doctrine of pre-emptive strike, a country may anticipate aggression, and 'retaliate in advance'. This enables states to attack who they like, based solely on the perception of a threat. This represents a move beyond what Henry Kissinger called 'realpolitik' and castes aside traditional tenets of international law as well as UN and Nato charters. The new doctrine makes no qualification as to its use, so pre-emption becomes a new universal principle available to every nation. In addition, the new doctrine is not required to conform to international law, but can be justified as self-defence for individual countries to take action unilaterally. Except in these new circumstances, self-defence is redefined from meaning 'actual attack by another country' to 'perceived imminent attack'.[3]

In addition to these changes post-9/11 there has been a sharp increase in surveillance and data sharing which have effected changes in the conception of citizenship. As part of this there has been an increase in the demands for information in the name of the public interest which is affecting the boundaries between the private and public spheres. A recent *Guardian* feature on privacy (*Guardian*, 2002) documented a whole range of forms of surveillance across both the private and public spheres, including data trawling, data sharing, visual surveillance (CCTV), DNA testing, fingerprinting, communication interception, and identity cards. In Britain, where liberal protections of the individual privacy and autonomy have a strong tradition, a recent report has been published on privacy and data sharing which aims to balance the dual concerns of protecting the rights of the individual and the state's interest in collecting and sharing data more efficiently across various public and private agencies for the purposes of creating 'joined-up' government. Although critics are representing the report as a 'snooper's charter' enabling the state to know everything about you, and are doubtful, to use Charles Raab's (2002, p. 16) words, that 'the circle of privacy and data sharing can be squared', certain measures have been taken to protect the individual as well as minority groups within this legislation. These measures range from the establishment of a public services 'trust charter' and other devices which oblige all public services to state how data can be shared, how individual privacy can be protected, and how individuals can assert their rights, and the appointment of chief knowledge officers in state bodies with responsibility for managing data and overseeing an organisations privacy commitments. In addition, in Britain, there have been several pieces of legislation which help to protect the rights and interests of individuals. These range from the Human Rights Act, which aims to balance the needs of the state and the rights of the citizen, and is arguably one of the Blair governments most significant achievements to date; the Data Protection Act of 1998, which gives to all citizens the right to know who holds information about them (subject access), as well as rights to object and remedy errors; the Freedom of Information Act 1999, and the Regulation of Investigatory Powers Act 2000, both of which seek to ensure that the use of communication data are properly controlled with independent oversight and proper complaints procedures, and which introduce new and supposedly improved regulatory machinery which didn't previously exist. In addition, the Anti-Terrorism, Crime and Security Act of 2001, although it requires communications companies to retain basic details of internet activity longer than was the case previously, and to report suspicious and irregular activity, also forbids data 'fishing' and 'trawling' expeditions, confining access to information strictly in relation to specific inquiries about crime or terrorism.

A key question here relates to the issue that in tackling a minority or criminals or terrorists in our midst, are we not trampling on the rights of the vast majority of citizens? The answer to this is of course complex, but we must not see the issue in terms of privacy as a natural right of individuals pitted against the common good. The classical liberal conception of privacy is linked integrally to the conception of the self as the private, self-interested chooser who exists prior to society and is endowed with natural rights. What such a conception ignores is that such a conception is, as Foucault and others have identified, a fiction. Such rights are indeed internal, not antecedent to, community, and as such are not absolute. Moreover, as the framers of the recent Human Rights Act, as well as the European Convention of Human Rights, which was its inspiration, knew only too well, different rights and interests need to be kept in balance. Privacy, like autonomy and freedom, is rooted in human dignity and speaks to the demands for safety and respect. It is not, however, an absolute right, but must be balanced by the right to safety and security by all, including children, women, and employees.[4] In this balance of forces, the state must be seen as both a negative as well as a positive force. It is a negative force in that it protects the safety of all, and it is a positive force in that it empowers and enables people to shape their lives, constituting, as it were, a collective vehicle to achieve progressive change. This notion of positive freedom, which starts with the Greek polis, and can be seen evident in writers like John Dewey, sees the full development of human beings as only possible through active participation in the affairs of the community.

TOTALITARIANISM

This form of positive government was seen by liberals like Isaiah Berlin, Frederich Hayek and Karl Popper as likely to lead towards totalitarianism.[5] The classic liberal theory of totalitarianism sees it as a form of government that develops out of the structures of the positive state. For liberals a positive conception of liberty leads the state to promote a single substantive ideal of the good – a description of man as a spiritual being whose ultimate rationality and reality are grounded in a unified spirit. This leads to a nation state which imposes a substantive conception of the good life, eradicating individuality by a concern with 'normcentricity'.[6]

Positive freedom worries liberals. The positive view of freedom as active self-determination implies, says Berlin (1969), a distinction between two selves – a higher self that determines, and a lower self that is subject to determination. Berlin argues that in the history of political thought, it is all too easy for the higher self to become identified with the state or society, or with a particular political groups conception of what is 'rational'. Freedom then tends to become defined as obedience to what is rational, or obedience to the will of the state, or conformity to a predetermined pattern of thought or life. As a consequence, claims Berlin, positive freedom is transposed into the opposite of freedom: totalitarianism or tyranny.

In its extreme form, argues Nel Noddings (1996), it is claimed that the positive conception of liberty often leads to the promulgation of a single ideal – a description of 'man' as a spiritual being whose ultimate rationality and reality are grounded in a unified spirit. In this model, the state is seen as the expression of collective will (positive freedom), rather than the (mere) protector of individual liberties (negative freedom).

The total community equals fascism which equals the nation-state. If the state is right, then there is no room for dissent, and liberty is equated with full immersion in the community. Liberals claim that individuality is wiped out by 'normcentricity'. In this way, Eric Hoffer maintained that communities foster 'unity' and 'self-sacrifice' along with conformity to established norms. In Hoffer's words:

> Unity and self-sacrifice, of themselves, even when fostered by the most noble means, produce a facility for hating. Even when men league themselves mightily together to promote tolerance and peace on earth, they are likely to be violently intolerant towards those not of like mind. (Hoffer, 1951, p. 92)

While writers like Berlin, Popper and Hayek believe that any state, over and above a concern with negative liberties, constitutes a threat to the freedom of the individual, as if inherently unable to respect a diversity of lifestyles, their argument falters on a number of grounds which I have summarised more fully elsewhere,[7] and can only outline briefly in this context:

Firstly, their arguments technically rule out even a welfare state, for welfare rights are 'positive' rights, and for Hayek, the welfare state is the start of the 'slippery slope', leading down 'the road to serfdom'.

Secondly, it is neither logically or empirically entailed that a state that acts positively in terms of a specific substantive conception of the good, must ignore a respect for diversity and difference, or fail to respect the plurality of groups and sub-groups in the wider society. As postmodernists and others have suggested, the good can accommodate difference. To suggest, therefore, that any state that does not confine itself to the minimum protection of individual liberties, but acts in terms of a general substantive vision, even if conceived in sophisticated terms, will unleash a pressure towards 'unity' or 'normcentricity', is a flawed argument, for it assumes that a theory of the good cannot exist at an abstract enough level to accommodate diversity or pluralism. Further, it attributes a failure of democracy to the particular way the state acts, *as a general orientation*, rather than to a specific analysis of *particular* societies in *particular* historical circumstances.

Thirdly, the liberal theory of totalitarianism depends on presumptions that liberalism constitutes a neutral agenda where freedom is defined as the natural property of individuals outside of society. Based on this argument, writers like Berlin (1969) maintain that liberalism advocates no substantive conception of the good. The identification of a good is impossible, in Berlin's view, as individuals manifest such diversity of opinion over the nature of the good. Because of this irreducible pluralism over values and preferences, and consequent incompatibility over versions of the good, individual freedom is all that remains. It is only as a consequence of this axiom that the state can be represented as *the enemy*, rather than the *precondition*, of freedom.

Notwithstanding Berlin's view, it can be claimed that liberalism itself implies a substantive conception of the good. The argument by liberals that within its policy prescriptions liberalism does not invoke a particular preferred shape to society, or that it does not advocate the establishment of a social good over and above what individuals desire, cannot rule out substantive commitments about what society should be like. As Luke Martell (1992, p. 156) states:

> It all sounds very nice until you realise that what it does, in effect, is to let in just another particular substantive vision of society as consisting of the sum total of individuals' preferences over which individuals have no overall control. In this sense, liberalism is in fact a highly substantive doctrine – one which posits a competitive individualist society immune to overall democratic direction.[8]

Fourthly, as Steven Heyman (1992, pp. 81–82) claims with respect to Berlin's (1969) analysis of liberty, what is striking about it is the way it is distorted by the political circumstances in which the essay was written:

Berlin was writing in the late 1950s, at the height of the cold war. He casts the debate between negative and positive liberty as a crucial battle in 'the open war that is being fought between two systems of ideas' ... and between the political systems allegedly based on them – western liberal democracy and totalitarian regimes of the left and right. ... With the passing of the Cold War, it may be easier to understand the relationship between positive and negative liberty in our political tradition.

Although we must applaud classical and neoliberals for being against totalitarianism, their specific theoretical analysis as to *what causes* totalitarianism became mixed in with both 'left–right' politics and analysis of the role of the state in general, and 'Cold War' politics in particular. Although Heyman discusses this contention with specific regards to Berlin, I would claim the thesis is generally applicable to many others, *to varying extents*, including Hayek, Popper, and Plamenatz, to name but a few.[9]

With the passing of the Cold War, it can be more easily seen that liberal explanations as to the origins of totalitarianism are woefully inadequate. To the extent that there are dangers inherent in human societies, such dangers inhere in all sorts of society, and it is difficult to identify such dangers as belonging specifically to a particular form and organisation of the state, in promoting the conditions for positive or negative freedom. Although it is not possible to do justice to such a complex topic in the short space available here, any adequate explanation for the origins of totalitarianism must take adequate account of the *historical, political, cultural and economic specificity of particular states at particular locations in history*. What produces totalitarianism is not a particular gearing of state power (such as 'positive' or 'negative', or even 'holist', or 'piecemeal' engineering, to use Popper's terms), but quite simply, the *absence of democracy*, or of the *conditions* which enable democracy to flourish. On this criteria, the Marxist-Leninist regimes of Eastern Europe failed in that they lacked a strong or deep conception of democracy, as well as the range of specific *mechanisms* by which democracy operates. As democracy is a structural arrangement, with specific techniques and mechanisms and processes that can be analysed, the best way to safeguard against totalitarianism is by ensuring that the state is a *democratic* state, and by seeking to *deepen* the specific senses in terms of which democracy operates.

To the extent that the state is solely concerned with the negative goals supporting the protection of individual liberties, and does not focus on the expression of a public will, it will be poorly equipped to deal with terrorist attacks. To the extent that terrorism forces the liberal state to reveal its 'dormant will', liberals, who always thought that no such thing existed, will, of course, be perturbed.

Many, including myself, who support a 'positive' role for the state, while acknowledging that there are dangers in relation to this, as there are in relation to any form of social and political organisation, believe that the answer is best sought in the strengthening or deepening of democracy.[10]

RIGHTS TALK

The changes to traditional liberal safeguards and forms of governmentality, indicative of a new political tendency or settlement, outlined above, signal the sense in which certain liberal discursive patternings of power have constituted the taken-for-granted basis of western political and educational arguments over the last century. There was a time, not too far back, when the left saw 'rights-talk' as having little relevance to their discourses of emancipation or to educational programmes, seeing issues to do with 'rights' as either part of the regulatory politics of the bourgeois state, focussing too specifically on individual as opposed to collective concerns, or as part and parcel of Cold War politics. The events of 9/11 may hopefully reintroduce a concern for rights, and maybe other themes within liberal constitutionalism, in both educational and political research, as fundamental to emancipatory and progressive concerns. Indeed, it can be said that within what I am calling (following Held, 1995) *the new cosmopolitanism*, human rights and democratic justice must be called upon to fill the void of traditional concerns with socialist politics. In this sense, for educators, 9/11 has introduced much more pressing concerns, for one of the more important functions of education is in citizenship for democratic participation. This unfortunately is something that universal education in the western world has almost single-mindedly avoided during the 20th century. While it has been recognised that the concerns with literacy and numeracy and social studies have positive externalities for democratic citizenship, the emphasis has been on 'teaching' citizenship in the curriculum, rather than through involvement of students in the active decision-making processes of the school where it could be argued that democracy is learnt. As Walter Parker (2001, p. 9) has observed, citizenship education has largely been concerned with *learning about democracy* rather than *involvement in democracy*. What must be implemented is a form of citizenship education which is *extra-curricular*, focussing not only on what is taught in the classroom, but on *indirect* learning through participation in the governance of the school (the processes through which both school and classroom policies are made), in school-community forums, and in inter-school forums for broader educational-community relations.

A NEW MULTICULTURAL COSMOPOLITANISM

In this sense, the new cosmopolitanism must embody an educational conception of democracy which is truly *multicultural*. As well as aiming to promote the skills of sharing and deliberation through active participation in democratic processes of the school, what is brought home with the events of 9/11 is the need to involve students in democracy in a genuinely multicultural sense. For what is crucial in the world post-9/11 is that it is a global world which urges us to recognise those people and cultures who inhabit the world in addition to us, as those others who are inhabiting the cities, libraries, and schools that we think of as ours, a world which is increasingly cosmopolitan, if not in the sense that we all travel more, or at all, then certainly in the sense that what happens in one part of the globe now affects us all. Multicultural citizenship is now a matter of vital concern.

As democracy must respect multiculturalism, so multiculturalism must respect democracy. Democratic norms must necessarily cross-cut multicultural groups to protect three conditions: (1) the basic rights of all citizens individually and as groups (freedom of speech, thought, assembly, expression, lifestyle choice, etc); (2) that no person or group is manipulated into accepting values represented by public institutions; and (3) that public officials and institutions are democratically accountable in principle and practice.

Democracy in this sense must constitute a new universal. In this sense, it is a more basic set of procedural norms and rules than are the rights of any minority to do what they like. We must move away from any conception of multiculturalism whereby cultural minorities can be completely unresponsive to outside cultures, or where prohibitions against group members leaving the culture can be enforced. No minority and no culture, can guarantee their own survival forever, as openness to the world outside is a necessary principle of democracy. This openness is indeed a core principle of cosmopolitanism, which must infuse citizenship education post-9/11. The point here is that a democratic rights culture must underpin any conception of multiculturalism, so defined.

By making a 'rights culture' fundamental, in this sense, limits are placed upon the 'discourse of diversity' that multiculturalism entails. This does not mean that the recognition of distinct identities and differences, as argued for by multiculturalists, are not important. Liberalism has clearly failed to sufficiently acknowledge such insights from 'the politics of recognition', tending to represent justice as the *imposition of a single standard or rule* to all of the diverse groups within the social structure. Yet, while we can accept that multiculturalists have contributed something important in arguing for the recognition of distinct cultural identities, based on ethnicity, race, religion, gender or class, as Kymlicka (1999) has argued, such arguments cannot be used to legitimate 'internal restrictions' (e.g., prohibiting group exit) which violate or contradict democratic principles, or interfere with the rights of others individuals or groups. By the same token, multicultural advocacy may result in 'external protections' to counter group disadvantage or marginalisation. Such claims may themselves vary from one historical period to another, and should thus be deliberated and enacted through the democratic process itself.

Although multiculturalism advances a 'discourse of diversity', it is different from, and largely unrelated to, the 'discourse of diversity and devolution' advanced by neoliberalism. In that the multicultural stress on diversity has been influenced by postmodernist theorising, neoliberal diversity is sponsored by the market mechanism, which results in compounding and cumulative inequalities. With multiculturalism, diversity may also be dysfunctional to the extent that it undermines the degree of societal cohesion necessary for different groups to work and live together. The extent to which multicultural diversity reinforces norms of intolerance and conflict also takes on a new and altered significance post-9/11. Clearly the balance of contending forces between the common interests of society and the sub-groupings within it, and the overall extent to which diversity is *recognised* and permitted, is itself a question of democratic deliberation and adjudication, which may alter in different places and times.[11]

DEMOCRACY

The principle of democracy that I am talking about is *non-foundational* but *universal*. By this I mean that it is not based upon any fixed conception of human nature, or of a premise, as with Habermas, of universal rationality whereby conflicts can be redeemed dialogically through communicative action in the ideal speech community. Rather, the principle of democracy which we favour insists on the protection of human rights, recognises the distinctiveness of sub-cultures, ensures the principles of inclusion and openness, and ensures the universal application of the rule of law, and of open dialogue, not based upon any faith in rationality, but based purely on a principle of a *mutual interest in universal survival*. Thus, while such a conception of democracy is 'deliberative', it is pragmatically rather than epistemologically based.[12] This is to say that the safety of all is guaranteed *in the final analysis* on the basis of an interest in survival, and it is the same grounds which justify the culture of reasonableness, as well as liberal values such as freedom of association, expression, and the like. *In an age of terrorism, democracy is the condition upon which survival can best be assured.* Such a conception is universal to the extent that it is *willed*. The inspiration is Nietzschean rather than Kantian. It is also very Foucauldian in the sense that it constitutes *a universalism of democracy as a contingent discourse of open protection and facilitation in a world of dangers.*[13]

Although survival may justify democracy, as an end or goal it is too thin to be fully adequate, of course, for mere survival cannot possibly satisfy a complete account of life's ends and aims. And it may not be universally agreed to, if we mean by universal 'agreed to by all', for there are no doubt some, including 'suicide bombers', for whom it holds no sway at all. Ultimately, that is the choice of course, and certainly it focuses the concentration. For if democracy is the *precondition* of survival, then it requires a democratic mandate to be effective, even so.

Beyond this, it is possible to build a much richer conception of democracy on this basis. If survival is a final justification, and focuses our attention as to why democracy is important, survival with dignity resonates of a more traditional concern with *ends*. This, of course, is the classic conception of democracy as a doctrine based on the ultimate worth and dignity of the human being, as espoused in the republican tradition. Thus, it is not the narrow 'realist' theory of democracy that has been articulated and advocated by post-war American political science, commonly associated with the writings of Joseph Schumpeter's (1976) *Capitalism, Socialism and Democracy*, which refers to a narrow system of representative government and a means of changing governments through a system of elections (Hindess, 2000). Rather, if safety, dignity, and survival are to be possible, it must be deepened, once again, to refer to a substantive end which is something more than mere utility, but encompasses the well-being and safety 'of each and all' (Shapiro, 1999). Such a conception must once again entail a certain idea of participation and equality as well. While, some philosophers and political theorists will sense a resonance here with Rousseau's general will, this would be mistaken, for the model suggested here is not a totalising one, which presupposes unity between individual and collective, but a *detotalising* one that is based on the notion of general wellbeing, while recognising the diversity and differences between cultures and people. This is what I have referred to elsewhere as 'thin communitarianism'. The formulation owes its general inspiration to Foucault, whose conception of the 'equalisation of power relations' and 'non-domination', can be used to support, I argue, a general conception of democratic justice (see Olssen, 2002). In terms of social ontology such a conception can be thought of as similar to Martha Nussbaum's (1995, p. 456) 'thick vague conception of the good'. Nussbaum advances 'a soft version of Aristotelian essentialism' (p. 450) which incorporates a 'determinate account of the human being, human functioning and human flourishing' (p. 450). While in formal terms it recognises that all individuals and cultures have certain developmental and lifestyle needs, this 'internal essentialism' (p. 451) is 'an historically grounded empirical essentialism' (p. 451). As such, it is purely formal, for within this broad end, and subject to the limits necessary for its realisation and continuance, it permits and recognises a multitude of identities and projects and ways of life.

Attempts to reconcile diversity with social unity are not new. John Rawls seeks to account for a 'reasonable pluralism' within the context of the 'overlapping consensus', as the basis of 'justice as fairness' (Rawls, 1996: Lecture IV).[14] Arguments from postmodernists have also sought to throw new light on how difference and unity can be reconciled. For Foucault (1981, p. 69), the social whole is never a 'sealed' unity, or resistant to change, but is characterised rather by incompleteness, indeterminacy, complexity and chance (*aléa*). Such theorising by Foucault, and others, utilising models of non-linear complex causality,[15] has led to fresh interest in how freedom, creativity and difference can exist and be safeguarded in a community. Similar initiatives, relating to Foucault and other postmodernist thinkers, are summarised by William Corlett (1989) in his book *Community without Unity: A Politics of Derrridean Extravagance.*

DEEPENING DEMOCRACY THROUGH EDUCATION

If post-9/11 makes democracy of more pressing concern; our conception has moved a long way from a narrow theory of universal enfranchisement. To the extent that counter-terrorist action now constitutes an important item, it must itself be subject to the democratic norms of public visibility and critical scrutiny, together with open processes of deliberation and debate, as well as traditional rights of contestation in terms of the rule of law. If our substantive conception posits certain general ends, which allow for a degree of diversity and pluralism, our procedural view of democracy is as a multifaceted array of mechanisms and processes instituted to ensure the *inclusion, security* or *safety* (including sexual safety) as well as *development* and *opportunities* of all individuals and groups. In this respect research needs to focus on the means of *deepening* democracy to satisfy these goals. As a way of concluding this chapter, one might consider the development of research on all or any of the following themes:

- The concern with equality: The development of any conception of democratic justice must seek to deal with rather than avoid issues to do with distribution of resources and life chances. Given a rejection of the classical liberal fiction regarding entitlement to property based on a model of pre-social, possessive individuals who 'owe nothing to society', it is important to theorise the implications of a social ontological framework of community for considerations of democratic justice as it pertains to distributional ethics. Community in this sense is definable as an all-encompassing arena without fixed borders or unity, which comprises an assortment of values, norms and institutions that enable life to be lived. Such a conception of community recognises social ties and shared values, as well as practices of voluntary action and public institutions like education which constitute the conditions for stability and reproduction of society. Although neoliberal philosophers like Nozick have shifted political philosophy away from a concern with issues of distributive justice in recent years, my own view is similar to the nineteenth century social democrat L.T. Hobhouse who held that ones entitlement to rewards and gain must be balanced by one's obligation to society. What liberal conceptions of democracy obscured, in Hobhouse's view, was the inter-dependence between individuals and the social structure, or for the social and moral obligation of the society (acting through the vehicle of the state) to assist in arranging the social futures of each rising generation. As he argued in his book, *Liberalism* (1911, pp. 189–190), in his justification for redistributive policies of progressive taxation, the state has an obligation to enforce reasonable conditions of equality on the basis that while a society should provide the conditions for enterprise, all individuals are correspondingly indebted to society for the conditions and structures provided, and on this basis, individuals should contribute in direct proportion to the luck or good fortune they experience.
- The role of the state: The role of the state should be concerned with guaranteeing both negative freedom and positive freedom. Negative freedom involves the state's responsibility for ensuring the universal entitlements to safety and reasonable autonomy for all. The trade off in respect to privacy will be necessitated to the extent that these obligations are threatened. To the extent that greater surveillance is deemed necessary, the proposals must be themselves subject to democratic processes that ensure visibility, openness, deliberation and debate.

The state's obligations as regards positive freedom involve it in developing opportunities based on people's rights to inclusion and the development of their capacities. This obligation gives the state a role in the provision of social services, health care, and education. In brief, the role for the positively geared state lies in relation to socially directed investment decisions, to provide for the general conditions for all species needs and development, including education and training, and to create and maintain quality infrastructure such as schools, hospitals, parks and public spaces.

- The development of civil society: A vibrant civil society can constitute a check on the powers of government. Civil society refers to that sector of private associations relatively autonomous from the state and economy, which spring from the everyday lives and activities of communities of interest. Clearly, one principle of democracy is the idea of multiple centres of power, and of their separation, as suggested by writers like Montesquieu and de Tocqueville. Another principle of democracy is the right to contest, challenge or oppose. Institutions of civil society, as writers like Paul Hirst have maintained, can be seen to constitute an important powerful network of quasi-independent associations, which can strengthen democratic rule through checking the power of the state. If democracy is rule by the people, the ability, and opportunity to 'speak the truth to power', as Michel Foucault (2001) has put it, is itself one of democracy's crucial rights, indeed its very condition. According to Cohen and Arato (1992) civil society strengthens democracy in both a defensive and offensive sense. The defensive aspect refers to the way that associations and social movements develop forms of communicative interaction that support the development of people's identities, expand participatory possibilities and create networks of solidarity. The offensive aspect refers to how associational networks and institutions come to exert influence on, and constitute checks to, the state, and to each other.
- The role of education: the role of education is crucial for democracy, as educational institutions, whether compulsory or post-compulsory, intersect with, and therefore mediate between, institutions like the family and those of the state and the economy. Although formal institutions of education have been in the main public institutions, there is an important sense in which they are semi-autonomous from the state. This is not the neo-liberal sense where management and administration are devolved to the local school, but the sense in which the school's are located in, and represent local community groups. In this sense, schools are important as democratic organisations, through the particular way that they are connected to communities, through their ability to empower families, and involve minority groups in participatory projects. Education is also crucial as the central agency responsible for the production of democratic norms such as trust and political decision-making. This is to say, as Mill recognised in *Representative Government*, educational institutions are important as sites where democracy and self-government are learnt. Deliberative democracy is especially complex, for it involves not just norms and procedures of debate but norms and procedures of contestation, inclusiveness, tolerance, compromise, solidarity with others, generosity, care, the operations of forums, and of checks and balances, the use of sanctions and screens, and the separation of powers. In the republican tradition, schools are instrumental in the development of civic virtue and habits of good citizenship. This is what signals the real importance of

the 'knowledge economy'. For education is essentially important in its role of constructing democratic civic norms, and this must become one of the central aims of Government policy in this regard. It is not a case of 'brainwashing' or 'socialisation' but of teaching skills and establishing models of civic conduct based on tolerance, deliberation, conflict resolution, give and take, and trust. While educational processes depend upon fairness of political processes, and in the distribution of economic resources, education is necessary to construct the network of norms that permit both the market and democracy to function. As Philip Pettit (1999, p. 255) puts it, education represents a 'stark choice between the invisible hand and the iron hand: between a strategy of marketing and a strategy of management'. It is for this reason of course that education should ideally be *public, universal compulsory and free*. For if education is vital in constructing norms that nurture the market, it cannot be itself subject to the market's disorganising effects.

NOTES

[1] For a more nuanced discussion of cosmopolitanism, see Olssen, Codd & O'Neill (2003), Chapter 11.

[2] Guardian, Monday November 4th, 2002. A headline on page one read 'Brown camp seeks sell-off limit', revealing a faction in the government with a more cautious view towards privatisation. This reinforces a widely held view amongst journalists that within New Labour there are different factions on privatisation.

[3] Yet a third sign of a change in the political settlement is the ignoring of the Geneva Convention by the US in its imprisonment of suspected Al Qaeda terrorists at Guantanamo Bay, Cuba. Other possible signs include proposals in Britain in 2002 to do away with the 'double jeopardy' rule, which has traditionally prevented people from being tried twice, as well as proposals to restrict trial by jury, and to reveal a persons previous convictions.

[4] In legal terms, this idea of balance is covered by the 'principle of proportionality'.

[5] See Berlin (1969), Hayek (1935, 1944) and Popper (1945, 1961).

[6] See also Arendt (1958) and Talmon (1955).

[7] See Olssen (1996, 1998).

[8] This objection, which has been formulated many times by many writers, concerns the difficulty of distinguishing 'procedural' from 'substantive' goals (see Dahl, 1999, pp. 25–26; Honohan, 2002, p. 9; Sandel, 1982; Walzer, 1985; MacIntyre, 1984).. Given that even 'autonomy', or 'democratic citizenship' can be construed as 'substantive goals', on this basis, all states can be seen as having *some* substantive concerns.

[9] See Hayek (1944), Popper (1945, 1961), Plamenatz (1954, 1963). For a brief argument to this effect see Olssen (1996, 1998). A more substantial critique of the liberal theory of totalitarianism has yet to be made.

[10] Social democrats traditionally have supported a positive view of freedom. For a recent expression, see David Blunkett (2002), the current British Home Secretary, who writes 'I prefer a positive view of freedom, drawing on another tradition of political thinking that goes back to the ancient Greek polis. According to this tradition, we only become fully free when we share, as active citizens, in the government of the affairs of the community. Our identity as members of a collective political community is a positive thing. Democracy is not just an association of individuals determined to protect the private sphere, but a realm of active freedom in which citizens come together to shape the world around them. We contribute and we become entitled.'

[11] Sharon Gewirtz (2002) suggests that official government support towards state funding of 'faith-based' schools in England has altered post-9/11, suggesting that forms of religious separatism over education are being seen as socially dysfunctional for the production of democratic values, such as tolerance.

[12] It thus has the character of a 'settlement', rather than a 'consensus', or a 'reflexive equilibrium', although the latter concept (which is Rawls') may, in this view, form part of a broader conception of citizenship which the state seeks to democratically promote.

[13] My view is that 'survival' is a better basis to justify democracy than 'social contract'. However, it is not possible to explore the differences in this paper.

[14] While we can accept much of Rawls' argument in practice, it is Rawls' commitments to liberal contract theory that we find problematic and which prevents him from, amongst other things, developing a viable notion of community. (See Rawls, 1996)

[15] For Foucault's model of holism/particularism, or system/originality, see my brief summaries (Olssen, 1998, pp. 79–80; 2002, pp. 490–491). For a general account of theories of complex determination that are being used to explain how infinite possibilities, and unpredictable occurrences are derivable from a set of determined rules or structure, see Cilliers, 1998.

REFERENCES

Arendt, H. (1958). *The origins of totalitarianism*. London: Allen & Unwin.

Berlin, I. (1969). *Four essays on liberty*. Oxford: Oxford University Press.

Blunkett, D. (2002, 14 September). 'Civic rights'. In Big Brother: The secret state and the assault on privacy, Part two (pp. 22–23). *The Guardian*.

Castells, M. (1997). A powerless state. In *The information age: Economy, society and culture. Volume II: The power of identity*. Oxford: Blackwell.

Cilliers, P. (1998). *Complexity and postmodernism: Understanding complex systems*. London: Routledge.

Cloke, P., Milbourne, P., & Widdowfield, R. (2000). Partnership and policy networks in rural local governance: Homelessness in Taunton. *Public Administration, 78*(1), 111–113.

Cochrane, A. (2000). New Labour, new urban policy. *Social Policy Review, 12*, 184–204.

Cohen, J.L. & Arato, A. (1992). *Civil society and political theory*. Cambridge, MA: MIT Press.

Corlett, W. (1989). *Community without unity: A politics of Derridean extravagance*. London: Duke University Press.

Dahl, R. (1999). Can international organisations be democratic? A skeptic's view. In I. Shapiro & C. Hacker-Cordón (Eds.), *Democracy's edges* (pp. 19–36). Cambridge: Cambridge University Press.

Falk, R. (1995). *On humane governance*. Cambridge: Polity Press.

Foucault, M. (1981). The order of discourse (I. McLeod, Trans.). In R. Young (Ed.), *Untying the text*. London: Routledge.

Foucault, M. (2001). *Fearless speech* (J. Pearson, Ed.). Los Angeles: Semiotext(e).

Glendinning, C., Powell, M., and Rummery, K. (2002). *Partnerships, New Labour and the governance of welfare*. Bristol: Policy Press.

Giddens, A. (2000). *The third way and its critics*. Cambridge: Polity Press.

Gewirtz, S. (2002). Faith-based schooling and the invisible effects of September 11th: The view from England. Unpublished paper.

Guardian, The (2002) *Report on Privacy: Big Brother: The Secret State and the Assault or Privacy, Part Two*, 14th September. 24 pages, www.guardian.co.uk/bigbrother/privacy

Hattersley, R. (2002, 30 August). The silly season. *Guardian*, p.18.

Hayek, F. (1935). *Collectivist economic planning*. London: Routledge & Kegan Paul.

Hayek, F. (1944). *The road to serfdom*. London: Routledge & Kegan Paul.

Held, D. (1995). *Democracy and the global order*. Cambridge: Polity Press.

Hindess, B. (2000). Representative government and participatory democracy. In A. Vandenberg (Ed.), *Citizenship and democracy in the global era*. London: Macmillan Press.

Hirst, P. & Thompson, K (1996). *Globalization in question*. Cambridge: Polity Press.

Honohan, I. (2002). *Civic republicanism*. London: Routledge.

Hoffer, E. (1951). *The true believer*. New York: Harper & Row.

Kymlicka, W. (1999). Liberal complacancies. In S. Moller Okin (Ed.), *Is multiculturalism bad for women?* Princeton, N.J.: Princeton University Press.

Klein, N. (2000). *No logo*. London: Flamingo.

MacIntyre, A. (1984). *After virtue* (2nd edn.). Notre Dame: University of Notre Dame Press.

Martell, L. (1992). New Ideas of Socialism. *Economy and Society*, 21(2), 151–172.

Mishra, R. (1999). *Globalization and the welfare state*. Cheltenham: Edward Elgar.

Noddings, N. (1996). On community. *Educational Theory*, 46(3), 245–267.

Nussbaum, M (1995). Human functioning and social justice in defence of Aristotelian essentialism. In D. Tallack (Ed.), *Critical theory: A reader*. New York: Harvestor/Wheatsheaf.

Ohmae, K. (1990). *The borderless world*. New York: Harper Business.

Ohmae, K. (1995). *The end of the nation state: The rise of regional economics*. New York: The Free Press.

Olssen, M. (1996). In defence of the welfare state and publicly provided education: A New Zealand Perspective. *Journal of Education Policy*, 11(3), 337–362.

Olssen, M. (1998). Education policy, the Cold War and the 'liberal-communitarian' debate. *Journal of Education Policy*, 13(1), 63–89.

Olssen, M. (2002). Michel Foucault as thin communitarian: Difference, community, democracy. *Cultural Studies – Critical Methodologies*, 2(4), 483–513.

Olssen, M., Codd, J., and O'Neill, A-M. (2003). *Education policy: Globalisation, citizenship, democracy*. Sage: London.

Peters, M. (2001). *Education and culture in postmodernity: The challenges for Aoteroa/New Zealand*. The Macmillan Brown Lectures (Unpublished paper).

Pettit, P. (1999). *Republicanism: A theory of freedom and government*. Oxford: Oxford University Press.

Plamenatz, J. (1954). *Marxism and Russian communism*. London: Longmans.

Plamenatz, J. (1963). *Man and society: A critical examination of some important social and political theories from Machiavelli to Marx*. Volume 2. London: Longman Green.

Polanyi, K. (1944). *The great transformation*. Boston: Beacon Press.

Popper, K (1945). *The open society and its enemies*. London: Routledge.

Popper, K. (1961). *The poverty of historicism*. London: Routledge

Raab, C. (2002, 21 September). 'Data sharing: Privacy in the public interest'. In Big Brother, Part III. *The Guardian*.

Rawls, J. (1996). *Political liberalism*. New York: Columbia University Press.

Rhodes, R.W. (1997a). *Understanding governance: Policy networks, governance, reflexivity and accountability*. Buckingham: Open University Press.

Rhodes, R.W. (1997b). From marketization to diplomacy: It's the mix that matters. *Public Policy and Administration*, 12(2), 31–50.

Rhodes, R.W. (2000). Governance and public administration. In J. Pierre (Ed.), *Debating Governance*. Oxford: Oxford University Press.

Sandel, M. (1982). *Liberalism and the limits of justice*. Cambridge: Cambridge University Press.

Shapiro, I. (1999). *Democratic justice*. London: Yale University Press.

Schumpeter, J. (1976), *Capitalism, socialism and democracy* (5th Edition). London: Allen & Unwin.

Schmid, A. (1993). Terrorism and Democracy. In A. Schmid & R. Crelinsten (Eds.), *Western responses to terrorism*. London: Frank Cass.

Stiglitz, J. (2002). *Globalization and its discontents*. Allen Lane: Penguin.

Talmon, J. (1955). *The origins of totalitarian democracy*. London: Secker & Warburg.

Townshend, C. (2002). *Terrorism: A very short introduction*. Oxford: Oxford University Press.
Walzer, M. (1985). *Spheres of justice*. Oxford: Basil Blackwell.
Wintour, P. (2002, 12 October). Parties Consign welfare state to history. *Guardian*, p. 13.

Mark Olssen
University of Surrey

BARBARA CRUIKSHANK

REVOLUTIONS WITHIN

Self-government and Self-esteem

INTRODUCTION

This chapter is about the relationship between power and subjectivity in a democracy; and about the lines between subjectivity and subjection; and democracy and despotism. The ability of the democratic citizen to generate a politically able self depends upon technologies of subjectivity which link personal goals and desires to social order and stability; which link power and subjectivity. I begin with the contemporary self-esteem movement spearheaded by feminist Gloria Steinem and California legislator John Vasconcellos to show that programmes which attempt to enhance the subjectivity of women and the poor – strategies of empowerment, self-help, and democratic participation - are also practical techniques for the subjection of individuals. I go on to outline a history of the present 'state of esteem' beginning with the work of Alexis de Tocqueville. I locate the emergence of democratic self-governance in the advent of the social as a sphere of governability and expertise.

> What breach of order is it possible to commit in solitude? (Gustave de Beaumont and & Alexis de Tocqueville 1964, p. 72)

Some feminists have criticized Gloria Steinem's best-seller *Revolution from Within: A Book of Self-Esteem* (1992) for calling for a feminist retreat to personal life from the collective political front. Deidre English's (1992, p. 13) reservations about Steinem's book are typical: 'What is disturbing is to see the empowering therapy supplant the cause. The strategic vision of social revolution here has all but been replaced with a model of personal recovery'. Echoing Tocqueville, critics ask how is it possible to challenge the existing order from a solitary position? Is it possible to wage a real 'revolution from within'? Critics are afraid that feminism is going the way of Steinem's self-esteem movement and trading in collective action and confrontation for the solitude of self-reflection, the political for the personal.

I argue here that there is nothing personal about self-esteem.[1] In fact, what is remarkable and of political importance about Steinem's book is not where she directs her revolutionary subjectivity – to the personal or political fronts – but that she turns self-esteem into a social relationship and a political obligation. Self-esteem is not merely a misbegotten strategy for women's liberation as Steinem's

M.A. Peters, A. Britton and H. Blee (Eds.), Global Citizenship Education: Philosophy, Theory and Pedagogy, 283–298.

critics charge. The self-esteem movement is more than that; it is a movement that does not leave politics and power as they were, but seeks to constitute a 'state of esteem', a new politics and a new set of social relations.

Steinem's book is only a small part of the self-esteem movement made up of a whole range of experts, policy and social service professionals, and grass roots activists. The self-esteem movement, spearheaded by the California Task Force on Self-Esteem and Personal and Social Responsibility in 1983, promises to deliver a technology of subjectivity that will solve social problems, from crime and poverty to gender inequality, by waging a social revolution, not against capitalism, racism and inequality, but against the order of the self and the way we govern our selves. California Assembly Bill 3659, which established the Task Force on Self-Esteem and Social and Personal Responsibility, states that the social problems we face today have become ungovernable and that they seriously threaten democratic stability (California Task Force, 1990b) 'Government and experts cannot fix these problems for us. It is only when each of us recognizes our individual personal and social responsibility to be part of the solution that we also realize higher self-esteem' (ibid 1990a, pp. vii–viii). This is a social movement premised upon the limits of politics and the welfare state, the failures of American democracy, and upon the inability of government to control conflict; it is a 'revolutionary' movement seeking to forge a new terrain of politics and a new mode of governing the self, not a new government. In short, the question of governance becomes a question of self-governance in the discourse of self-esteem.

LIBERATION THERAPY

Personal fulfilment becomes a social obligation in the discourse of self-esteem according to an innovation which transforms the relationship of self-to-self into a relationship that is governable (California Task Force, 1990a, p. 22). Self-fulfilment is no longer a personal or private goal. According to advocates, taking up the goal of self-esteem is something we owe to society, something that will defray the costs of social problems, something that will create a 'true' democracy. Hence, the solution to the current 'crisis of governability' is discovered in the capacity of citizens to take action themselves, guided by the expertise of the social sciences and social service professionals.

A key finding reported by the California Task Force (1990a, p. 4) is as follows:

Self-esteem is the likeliest candidate for a social vaccine, something that empowers us to live responsibly and that inoculates us against the lures of crime, violence, substance abuse, teen pregnancy, child abuse, chronic welfare dependency, and educational failure. The lack of self-esteem is central to most personal and social ills plaguing our state and nation as we approach the end of the twentieth century.

Hardly a simple shot in the arm, self-esteem is a kind of 'liberation therapy' that requires a complete reorientation towards social problem-solving, as well as the mobilisation of an effort compared by advocates to landing on the moon or the discovery of the atom, and it calls for the mobilisation of 'every Californian' (1990a, p. vii). Such scientific innovations carried the burden of social stability, but the new science of the self places the hope of liberation in the psychological state of the people, especially poor urban people of colour to whom most of the 'social problems' listed above are attributed.

Self-esteem is a practical and productive technology available for the production of certain kinds of selves, for 'making up people', as Ian Hacking (1986a) might put it.[2] Self-esteem is a technology in the sense that it is a specialised knowledge of how to esteem our selves, to estimate, calculate, measure, evaluate, discipline, and to judge our selves. It is especially, though not exclusively, a literary technology.[3] A 'self' emerges out of confrontation with texts, primarily, or with the telling and writing of personal narratives, a practice Steinem refers to as 'bibliotherapy'. We can learn and perform 'bibliotherapy' upon ourselves or join any of the numerous agencies, associations and programmes set up to 'enhance' self-esteem. These are catalogued along with books and scholarly articles included in the bibliographic materials compiled by the California Task Force and in Steinem's book; compiling research is tantamount to delivering therapy.

One of the goals of the self-esteem movement is to elicit the participation of as many people as possible and that means hearing their personal stories and struggles with their lack of self-esteem. California legislator John Vasconcellos claims that his efforts to establish the California Task Force to Promote Self-Esteem and Personal and Social Responsibility grew first out of his own 'personal struggle despite repeated successes and achievements in my life – to develop my own self-esteem'. Second, his commitment to building self-esteem came from his experience with the State's budget that spent 'too little, too late [on] efforts to confine and/or repair our fellow Californians, whose lives are in distress and disrepair' (California Task Force, 1990a, p. ix). Similarly, Steinem links her personal lack of self-esteem to her role in the feminist movement, and her commitment to self-esteem is connected to the limits of politics.

Self-esteem programme goals include getting clients to write and tell their personal narratives with an eye to the social good. Narratives bring people to see that the details of their personal lives and their chances for improving their lives are inextricably linked to what is good for all of society. Steinem (1992, p. 29) insists that requiring teenage girls, for example, to write down their personal narratives, their feelings about teenage pregnancy and so on, can result in the prevention of teenage pregnancy. The girls construct a self to act upon and to govern in the process of writing.

Self-esteem is a way to subject citizens in the sense of making them 'prone to' or 'subject to' take up the goals of self-esteem for themselves and their vision of the good society. Thus we make our selves governable by taking up the social goal of self-esteem. As Foucault (1988, p. 146) explained, 'through some political technology of individuals, we have been led to recognize ourselves as a society, as a part of a social entity, as part of a nation or of a state'. A link is established between the individual's goal of achieving self-esteem and the social goal of eliminating child abuse, crime and welfare dependence. Those who undergo 'revolution from within' are citizens doing the right thing; they join programmes, volunteer, but most importantly, work on and improve their self-image. At all times, self-esteem calls upon individuals to act and to participate. 'The continuation and future success of our democratic system of government and society are dependent upon the exercise of responsible citizenship by each and every Californian' (California Task Force, 1990b, p. 102).

Self-esteem is a technology of citizenship and self-government for evaluating and acting upon our selves so that the police, the guards and the doctors do not have to. This relationship to our selves is directly related to citizenship because, by definition, 'Being a responsible citizen depends on developing personal and social responsibility' (California Task Force, 1990a, p. 22). Individuals must accept the responsibility to subject their selves; to voluntarily consent to establishing a relationship between one's self and a tutelary power such as a therapist, a social worker, a social programme, a parenting class, what have you. Consent in this case does not mean that there is no exercise of power; by isolating a self to act upon, to appreciate and to esteem, we avail ourselves of a terrain of action, we exercise power upon ourselves.

Those who have failed to link their personal fulfilment to social reform are lumped together as 'social problems', are diagnosed as 'lacking self-esteem' and are charged with 'antisocial behaviour'. Society needs protection from those who lack self-esteem, according to advocates. Obviously social science is the foremost expert on the needs of society, along with social workers and other professionals: philanthropists, policy experts, public health professionals, and politicians, to name a few.

I do not mean to underestimate the blatantly coercive and punitive measures taken by legislators, social workers and other professionals under the guise of liberation therapy. Very often, for example, women, say battered women, are coerced by the courts into participating in therapeutic programmes that aim at 'empowerment'. Mothers caught up in the juvenile court system are often forced to 'graduate' from parenting courses, group therapies, and the like before the custody of their children is secure. Foster care is an institution that is easily made into a coercive apparatus for preparing mothers to become the kind of mothers deemed appropriate by society, through legislation by philanthropists. The threat of taking children away is a primary tool of coercion.

But just as often, women are convinced to participate in their own 'empowerment' without threats. Governance in this case is something we do to our selves, not something done to us by those in power (Rose, 1990, p. 213). Democratic government, even self-government, depends upon the ability of the citizen to recognise, isolate and act upon their own subjectivity, to be governors of their selves. The ability of the citizen to generate a politically-able self depends upon technologies of subjectivity and citizenship which link personal goals and desires to social order and stability; which thus link power to subjectivity (Foucault, 1983).

The line between subjectivity and subjection is crossed when personal goals are aligned with those set out by reformers – both expert and activist – according to some notion of the social good. The norm of self-esteem links subjectivity to power; it 'binds subjects to a subjection that is the more profound because it appears to emanate from our autonomous quest for ourselves, it appears as a matter of our freedom' (Rose, 1990, p. 256).

The call for self-government and democracy is extended away from political institutions and economic relations by the self-esteem movement; the political goals of participation, empowerment and collective action are extended to the terrain of the self. Steinem turns around the feminist slogan, 'the personal is political', claiming that 'the political is personal'. Nikolas Rose (1990, p. 253) has shown how contemporary technologies of subjectivity (like self-esteem) promise a certain kind of freedom:

> not liberation from social constraints but rendering psychological constraints on autonomy conscious, and hence amenable to rational transformation. Achieving freedom becomes a matter not of slogans nor of political revolution, but of slow, painstaking, and detailed work on our own subjective and personal realities, guided by an expert knowledge of the psyche.

The liberation promised by self-esteem originates within the relation of self-to-self but is not limited to the self. Indeed, self-esteem is advocated as a strategy for the democratic development of the individual and society; it outlines a whole new set of social relationships and strategies for their development under the expert tutelage of 'liberation therapists'.

CONSTITUTING A STATE OF ESTEEM

The California Task Force to Promote Self-Esteem and Personal and Social Responsibility was charged by the state legislature with compiling existing research on the relationship between 'self-esteem' and six social problems: 'chronic welfare dependence', alcoholism and drug abuse, crime and violence, academic failure, teenage pregnancy and child abuse. Neil Smelser, a sociologist and member of the Task Force, admits the failure of social scientists to identify the lack of self-esteem as the cause of social problems.

> The news most consistently reported, however, is that the associations between self-esteem and its expected consequences are mixed, insignificant, or absent'. (Mecca et al, 1989, p. 15)

Despite the fact that a 'disappointing' correlation was found between the lack of self-esteem and the social problems listed, the Task Force forged ahead, calling for increased funding for further research (Mecca et al, 1989). Task Force members and the social scientists involved did not diagnose, empirically discover or even describe an already existing malaise and its cure. Instead, the social scientists devised methods to measure what was not there: the focus of research was on the lack of self-esteem and its (non)relation to social problems.

The Task Force included in its Final Report the following quotation from Professor Covington (California Task Force, 1990a, p. 44) who claims that self-esteem challenges us to be more fully human. In addition to being an object of scientific investigation and also an explanation for behaviour, self-esteem is above all a metaphor, a symbol filled with excess meaning that can ignite visions of what we as a people might become.

From the 'discovery' of an absence of the thing, social scientists have created a tangible vision of a 'state of esteem'. Here the social sciences can be seen as productive sciences; the knowledges, measurements and data they produce are constitutive of relations of governance as well as of the subjectivity of citizens. In devising the methods for measuring, evaluating and esteeming the self, social science actually devises the self and links it up to a vision of the social good and a programme of reform. In short, social scientists have helped to produce a set of social relationships and causal relations where before there were none.

Social science has been instrumental in generating a self capable of self-governance, but it is a decidedly unscientific enterprise. In the end, social scientists themselves eschew the importance of evidence:

> Our purpose is to build a prima facie case for the importance of self-esteem in the causation of violent crimes. Public policy does not wait for final proof in other realms. ... We see no need to be defensive about advocating the importance of self-esteem. (Scheff, 1989, p. 179)

The obvious question is why social science is a necessary member of a coalition for building a prima facie case for self-esteem. If the case is to be built prima facie, why call for more funding to gather evidence in the form of social science research? The answer lies, I think, in the productive capacities of social scientific research. It is social scientific research that produces the subject, as one who lacks self-esteem, and it is social science research that sets the terms for telling the truth of that subject. Finally, it falls to social science research to establish policy measures to regulate the subject according to that truth. In a turn of phrase taken from Pierre Bourdieu, from professing a faith in self-esteem for its liberatory properties, experts have turned self-esteem into a profession (cited in Rose, 1990, p. 256).

Social service providers and researchers earn high salaries from the self-esteem movement and new programmes are proliferating. 'Empowerment' and 'self-esteem' are almost mandatory in mission statements and grant applications for non-profit agencies. But it is a mistake to focus solely on the immediate economic and professional interests of service providers.[4] Programme directors and researchers may profit from the advances of the self-esteem movement, but that does not fully explain why or how people come to understand themselves as lacking self-esteem. It is equally partial to characterise self-esteem programmes as obscuring or neglecting the 'real' underlying causes (e.g., poverty, sexism, racism) of the lack of self-esteem. Self-esteem is not conceived on the level of ideology; it is not a ruse, a panacea, a cynical plot; it is a form of governance.

Again, despite the failures of social scientists to discern any scientific relationship between violence and self-esteem, a correlative (if not causal) relationship worked its way into law. I quote here from Assembly Bill No. 3659 which established the California Task Force (1990b, p. 104):

> The findings of the Commission on Crime Control and Violence Prevention included scientific evidence of the correlation between violent antisocial behaviour and a lack of self-esteem, to wit: 'A lack of self-esteem, negative or criminal self-image and feelings of distrust and personal powerlessness are prevalent among violent offenders and highly recidivistic criminals'.

The Task Force adapted the model of the Commission on Crime Control for their own 'citizens' effort' to secure funding for further research and took from the field of criminology its methods of applying and organising knowledge.

It is significant, of course, that the new technology of self-esteem is produced in part out of methods devised for the prevention of crime and the punishment and supervision of criminals. It is also important to remember that the language of empowerment and self-esteem emerged out of social movements. Liberation is clearly tied to discipline in the discourses of self-esteem in more ways than can be chronicled here, where just two will be mentioned. First, so-called 'welfare dependency', alcoholism, and teen pregnancy are pathologised and criminalised alongside violence, child abuse and illegal drug use. This move is accomplished by relating the 'low self-esteem' of the welfare recipient, for example, to the failure of the welfare recipient to act politically, to participate in their own empowerment, to engage their self in fulfilling the social obligation of 'responsible citizenship'. According to the report, welfare recipients are not fulfilling their responsibilities to society because of their lack of self-esteem, a deficiency demonstrated by their being on welfare in the first place.

Second, the knowledge originally applied to the government – control and reform of criminals and 'antisocial behaviour' – is now applied throughout the social body: the overt use of technologies of surveillance and control in the field of criminality are displaced by the technology of self-government applied to welfare recipients and alcoholics. From analysing the causes of the bloody Attica prison riot (a decline in the self-esteem of guards who were not consulted before their powers were reduced) reviewers leap immediately to the policy implications of that analysis for relationships between clients and staff, doctors and patients, teachers and students, parents and children (Scheff, 1989, pp. 192–193). The whole of society and all its designated 'social problems' become the location for the deployment of this new technology of subjectivity. A whole society of esteemed, quantified and measured individuals can replace a citizenry defined by their lack of self-esteem.

According to the California Task Force (1990a, p. 12), the 'social vaccine' must be applied at all levels of society: family, work, government; all areas of society must be integrated by the principles of self-esteem, personal and social responsibility:

> In the twenty-first century every government level in the state and each of its programmes are designed to empower people to become self-realizing and

self-reliant .... Every citizen (and non citizen as well) recognizes his or her personal responsibility for fully engaging in the political process, and he or she recognizes the possibility for positively affecting every other person in every situation and relationship.

The mixture of future and present tense notwithstanding, the discourse of self-esteem is aimed at constituting a just and democratic society. To get there, rather than revealing our opinions and persuading others to act with us in concert, 'self-esteem has to do with our reputation with our "selves" '. Constituting a state of esteem has nothing to do with traditionally conceived public life and speech. Today, a state of esteem can be founded upon the inner dialogue between self and self.

From the prison cell to the whole of society, individuals in isolation can act to bring about a social and democratic revolution. As Steinem (1992, pp. 9–10) puts it:

self-esteem plays as much a part in the destiny of nations as it does in the lives of individuals; that self-hatred leads to the need either to dominate or to be dominated; that citizens who refuse to obey anything but their own conscience can transform their countries; in short, that self-esteem is the basis of any real democracy.

Given the possibility of thus aligning political power and personal empowerment in the self, we can return to Tocqueville's question about the possibility of isolated resistance to the established order.

A NEW SCIENCE OF POLITICS

From Foucault and from feminism we have learned how individuals come to understand themselves as the subjects of sexuality and gender, respectively. Similarly, I am arguing that individuals learn to recognise themselves as subjects of democratic citizenship and so become self-governing. As with technologies and discourses of sexuality and gender, it is possible to give a history of the fabrication of citizen-subjects and of their relation to the social order. But what Foucault and feminism have not elaborated, Alexis de Tocqueville took as a guiding question, namely, why do these forms of power, citizenship and subjectivity emerge only with democracy? How does governance become a question of self-governance in a democracy?

The capacities of citizens to govern their selves as well as the conditions of self-government underwent dramatic changes in the transition from republican to democratic government in the Jacksonian America that Tocqueville visited. The 1830s marked the birth of mass democracy, the social as a sphere of government, the development of social science, and the demise of the republican public sphere.[5] Moreover, the difficulties that Tocqueville encountered in distinguishing despotism and democracy reveal that self-government not only entails the exercise of subjectivity, but also the subjection of the self.

290

Ostensibly, democracy liberated political subjects, thus transforming them overnight into political citizens. A society in which a citizen is subject to the rule of another is, ipso facto, not a democracy. Tocqueville (1961a, p. 62) permanently enlivened the argument for local and decentralised government when he distinguished citizens from subjects: 'Yet, without power and independence, a town may contain good subjects, but it can have no active citizens'. The democratic citizen who participates directly in government, in self-rule, thereby avoids subjection. However, the line between the subjectivity of the citizen and their subjection was not clear, as Tocqueville himself discovered. By the time he finished the second volume of *Democracy in America* (1961b), he seemed unable to distinguish either democracy from its tendencies toward despotism, or the subjectivity of the masses from their subjection.

Both despotism and democracy relied upon isolated and powerless citizens, according to Tocqueville. Under despotism, subjects were simply unfree and isolated. In a democracy under conditions of equality, citizens are isolated and made powerless by the freedom granted to each singly; while they are free, they are relatively powerless as isolated individuals. Hence, the power of numbers becomes the *sine qua non* of democratic power and stability. In order to exercise self-government, citizens must act in concert and combine forces to wield any power and to guard against the tendency of democracies toward despotism.

However, the same democratic conditions – individual equality and individual freedom – made combining numbers very difficult.

As in ages of equality no man is compelled to lend his assistance to his fellow-men … every one is at once independent and powerless. These two conditions, which must never be either separately considered or confounded together, inspire the citizen of a democratic country with very contrary propensities. (Tocqueville, 1961b, p. 352)

Getting independent citizens to participate and take an interest in the life and well-being of society was no small task. In a chapter titled 'That the Americans Combat the Effects of Individualism by Free Institutions', Tocqueville insists that local and associational freedoms – political freedoms – are the only guards against despotism because they ensure the capacity of citizens to govern themselves actively by providing the training and the taste for freedom.

Yet the features of despotism and democracy led citizens to neglect their political freedoms which, from disuse, were rendered powerless against despotism.

Equality places men side by side, unconnected by any common tie; despotism raises barriers to keep them asunder: the former predisposes them not to consider their fellow – creatures, the latter makes general indifference a sort of public virtue. (Tocqueville, 1961b, p. 123)

Tocqueville recognised that while the police and the state can prevent action with outright domination and force, they cannot produce the active cooperation and participation of citizens. Democratic governance relied upon a productive rather than a repressive form of governance (see 1961b, p. 91). To govern a democracy,

Tocqueville called for a 'new science of politics' (1961a, p. lxxiii). Democratic participation was not clear-cut or naturally occurring, it was something that had to be solicited, encouraged, guided, and directed. Hence, the new science of politics must develop technologies of citizenship and participation.

Isolated in their freedom from one another, individuals required an artificially created solidarity, namely, a science of association. 'In democratic countries the science of association is the mother of science; the progress of all the rest depends upon the progress it has made' (1961b, p. 133). Even the legal recognition of associations, previously considered a dangerous source of disorder, was not enough to ensure democratic order if citizens could not be led to exercise their political freedoms; the capacity of citizens to exercise self-government itself had to become a matter of government.

In short, the threat of despotism and disorder did not come from the unruly, but from the indifferent citizens, the apathetic (1961b, p. 124).

> Citizens who are individually powerless, do not very clearly anticipate the strength which they may acquire by uniting together; it must be shown to them in order to be understood (1961a, p. 140).

Citizens had to be made to act; they must first know how to get together, to amass themselves to act in concert, and second, they must desire to do so. The former could be accomplished through the science of association; the latter was a matter of what Tocqueville (1961b, p. 162) called 'enlightened self-interest', or 'interest rightly understood':

> When men are no longer united among themselves by firm and lasting ties, it is impossible to obtain the cooperation of any great number of them unless you can persuade every man that his private interest obliges him voluntarily to unite his exertions and the exertions of all the others.

Persuading citizens voluntarily to tie their self-interest and their fate to society was the key to stability without the use of force.

The republican preoccupation with civic virtue – overcoming one's self-interest to take up the common interest – was replaced, according to Tocqueville, by the discipline that led to actions inspired by 'enlightened self-interest'. Democratic political action is further distinguished by a 'general rule' that links citizens to society:

> The principle of interest rightly understood produces no great acts of self-sacrifice, but it suggests daily small acts of self-denial. By itself it cannot suffice to make a man virtuous, but it disciplines a number of citizens in habits of regularity, temperance, moderation, foresight, self-command; and, if it does not lead men straight to virtue by the will, it gradually draws them in that direction by their habits. (1961b, p. 147)

Tocqueville learned about discipline and enlightened self-interest from his study of prisons. As others have pointed out, Tocqueville learned that prison discipline could 'make up' good citizens even if it could not produce virtuous men (Dumm,

1987; Boesche, 1987, p. 201). However, we must not make too much of the prison as a model for democratic government (Miller, 1987, p. 201). The prison may serve as a perfect model for despotism, but not for democracy. The task Tocqueville set himself was to discover those aspects of democracy that could be mobilised against despotism, despite the similarities between the two forms of governance.

Both democracy and despotism were completely new forms of governance in that neither were distinguished by any particular set of institutions. Tocqueville claimed that neither despotism nor democracy was a form of government so much as a kind of society. The condition of democratic equality and individual isolation led to a contradictory propensity of democratic citizens, on the one hand, to become ungovernable in their independence, and on the other hand, wholly to submit in powerlessness to any authority powerful enough to command them.

> I am persuaded, however, that anarchy is not the principal evil which democratic ages have to fear, but the least. For the principle of equality begets two tendencies: the one leads men straight to independence, and may suddenly drive them into anarchy; the other conducts them by a longer, more secret, and more certain road, to servitude. (Tocqueville, 1961b, p. 345)

Tocqueville's new science of politics, then, is not concerned with political institutions, but with preserving democratic freedom and the power of citizens within the realm of the social.

The ties that citizens must cultivate are not political, but social (associational); their fabrication marks the dislocation of the political, the state, and the emergence of 'the social' in the nineteenth century alongside the birth of the social sciences. Associations – organised to build bridges, to develop the arts and sciences, to do business – were useful for cementing the individual citizens' desires and goals to a vision of what is good for society. With no apparent coercion or centralised state action, voluntary associations ensured a united citizenry and a stable society.

Democracy entailed the transformation of politics from an activity dependent upon a conception of public (as opposed to private) life, to a matter of social life and the life of society. For democracy to meet the requirement of getting individuals to act together in concert as citizens, Tocqueville (1961b, p. 124) initially sounded a common republican theme:

> As soon as a man begins to treat of public affairs in public, he begins to perceive that he is not as independent of his fellow-men as he had at first imagined, and, that, in order to obtain their support, he must often lend them his co-operation.

However, in a mass democracy, as opposed to a republic, a single public sphere could not extend far enough to impress upon all the citizens their need of each other to maintain stability. Republican self-government was understood to be a part-time activity taking place within the restricted public sphere and over matters of public (shared) importance; freedom and politics were located in the restricted public sphere. In a democracy, on the other hand, democratic freedom and hence

293

the activities of self-government underwent a dislocation and were to be found instead in associations and in the capacities and actions of individuals. The capacity of citizens to be self-governing in a republic depended upon institutions that disappeared under the conditions of democracy. Tocqueville claimed that the legislators of American democracy knew that a single public sphere could not extend the awareness of mutual dependence upon an isolated citizenry. Hence, the whole of society had to be 'governmentalised' and venues constructed for citizens to take care of organising and governing themselves.

> The legislators of America ... thought that it would be well to infuse political life into each portion of the territory, in order to multiply to an infinite extent opportunities of acting in concert, for all the members of the community, and to make them constantly feel their mutual dependence on each other. (Tocqueville, 1961b, p. 125)

Multiple public spheres for the exercise of citizenship were developed beyond the states, counties, cities and other geographically-based spheres. These new spheres were civil, racial, professional, economic, and social. By politicising or 'governmentalising' as many areas of social life as possible, by multiplying as far as possible the number of public spheres, citizens were held responsible for the promotion of social stability.

Still, what was it that distinguished democracy from despotism? The answer does not lie in politics or institutions, but in the relationship of the individual to society. Again, Tocqueville (1961a, p. 66) was struck by the absence of visible official governmental powers and actions in America. Moreover, he was dumbstruck and terrified by the invisible governance to which citizens were subject:

> the species of oppression by which democratic nations are menaced is unlike anything which ever before existed in the world .... I seek in vain for an expression which will accurately convey the whole idea I have formed of it. (1961b, p. 380)

What Tocqueville called 'despotism', for lack of a better expression, he describes as a condition of holding society − its interests, privileges, wisdom and power − above the individual.

> The idea of intermediary powers is weakened and obliterated; the idea of rights inherent in certain individuals is rapidly disappearing from the minds of men; the idea of the omnipotence and the sole authority of society at large rises to fill its place. (1961b, p. 349)

Powers of government then, are transferred from the government and from the individual onto society at large; society is granted 'the duty, as well as the right ... to guide as well as to govern each private citizen' (1961b, p. 348).

We have traditionally understood Tocqueville to be holding out the threat of the tyranny of the majority or society writ large as a threat to the subjectivity, actions and independence of individuals. However, for Tocqueville, democratic government is not a question of pitting the individual citizen against collective society. Society has no agency or power of its own to wield. The dangerous tendency in a democracy is not toward tyranny, or visible forms of domination, or forced conformity, but toward an invisible and gentle subjection. The tutelary power of associations, which could lead citizens to exercise their subjectivity and to act upon their enlightened self-interest, could also lead citizens into complete subjection. 'Every man allows himself to be put in leading-strings, because he sees that it is not a person or a class of persons, but the people at large that holds the end of his chain' (Tocqueville, 1961b, p. 383). Citizens obey the call of society at large and are self-guided, without chains, without force; they quietly place themselves in the hands of society and mobilise themselves in society's interest.

Tutelary power is easily combined with outward forms of political freedom because it is society at large, not a class or a tyrant, that places citizens in chains. That which stands above is society. The individual citizen was not pitted against the majority but was artificially linked to the majority by discipline and association. The distinction between despotism and democracy rests on the degree to which tutelary powers act for individuals rather than guiding them to act for themselves. 'The proper object therefore of our most strenuous resistance, is far less either anarchy or despotism, than that apathy which may almost indifferently beget either the one or the other' (Tocqueville 1961b, p. 432). It is upon the small and daily routines of social life that self-government depends.

Subjection in minor affairs breaks out every day, and is felt by the whole community indiscriminately. It does not drive men to resistance, but it crosses them at every turn, till they are led to surrender the exercise of their will. (1961b, p. 383)

CONCLUSION

Tocqueville overestimated the tendency of democracies toward despotism because he underestimated the successes of the social sciences, social reformers, and their development of the social. Beaumont and Tocqueville (1964, p. 80) found prison reformers in the US somewhat overzealous: 'Philanthropy has become for them a kind of profession, and they have caught the monomanie of the penitentiary system, which to them seems the remedy for all the evils of society'. Today, self-esteem is our reformers' monomanie. It is an innovation in the means of governing a democratic society.

Self-esteem is but one in a long line of technologies of citizenship. Democracy is entirely dependent upon technologies of citizenship which are developed, to list only a few examples, in social movements, in public policy research, sciences of human development, and as is well-documented, discourses of republican motherhood (Mink, 1990). The constitution of the citizen-subject requires technologies of subjectivity, technologies aimed at producing happy, active and participatory democratic citizens. These technologies rarely emerge from the Congress; more often, they emerge from the social sciences, pressure groups, social work discourses, therapeutic social service programmes, and so on. Their common goal, nevertheless, is to get the citizen to act as his or her own master.

They begin with the acknowledgement that democratic government is limited in its capacity to govern. Democratic government is one that relies upon citizens to voluntarily subject themselves to power. Here is the State of California (California Task Force, 1990a, p. 37) saying go ahead and democratise the family, the work place, the schools:

> Sometimes we feel that if we create democracy in the home, work place or school, we will undercut someone's authority and encourage irresponsibility. In fact, democracy works well only when we all exercise self-discipline and personal and social responsibility.

The goal is to deepen the reach of tutelary powers intended to enhance the subjectivity of citizens.

Of course, not everyone can be vaccinated and those who lack self-esteem will abuse, haunt, rob, reproduce and otherwise bring ill health back upon the social body. Self-esteem means about as much as 'positive thinking' meant in the 1970s and 'empowerment' meant in the 1980s, and 'enterprise' meant in the 1990s. We are not entering the age of an all-powerful therapeutic state, or a state of complete subjection for we are still citizens. Yet thousands of people now define their lack of power and control in the world as attributable to their lack of self-esteem. Needless to say, Gloria Steinem is spokeswoman for one of the largest feminist associations, NOW, and today she attributes the failures of her political career and the feminist movement to her lack of self-esteem.

More importantly, a state government document like the one considered here does not create citizen-subjects by itself. Discourse is not literally constitutive. Nor do the therapists, mothers, and politicians who vaccinate citizens with self-esteem bear the responsibility for creating citizen-subjects. Self-rule remains essential to democratic stability, and so the relationship of self-to-self is a political relationship, although one that is more dependent upon voluntarily applied technologies of selfhood than upon coercion, force, or social control engineered from above.

Self-esteem advocates, including Steinem, do not recognise the extent to which personal life is the product of power relations. Steinem fails to realise the extent to which personal life is governed and is itself a terrain of government. The 'inner voice' to which she teaches us to listen is the voice of pure and unremediated self-knowledge. She assumes that women have a natural subjectivity that is hindered or repressed by power, rather than shaped and constituted by power. Steinem fails to grasp the difficulty of distinguishing subjectivity from subjection.

Self-esteem is a social movement that links subjectivity and power in a way that confounds any neat separation of the 'empowered' from the powerful. Most importantly, the self-esteem movement advocates a new form of governance that cannot be critically assessed by mobilising the separation of public from private, political from personal. Too much is left out by critics of the self-esteem movement who continue to think of power and resistance in paired opposition: individual and collective, public and private, political and personal. What these criticisms omit, in the author's view, is the extent to which the self is (like inequality, poverty and racism) not personal, but the product of power relations, the outcome of strategies and technologies developed to create everything from autonomy to participatory democratic citizenship. External powers act upon the terrain of the self, but we also act upon ourselves, particularly according to models of self-help, like the self-esteem movement. To use the words of Hacking (1986b, p. 236), '[Critics] leave out the inner monologue, what I say to myself. They leave out self-discipline, what I do to myself. Thus they omit the permanent heartland of subjectivity'. We might add that they leave out self-government, how we rule ourselves.

Tocqueville attributed to the general 'equality of conditions' shared by American citizens the greater role in generating stability. What has become evident since is that even in a society deeply divided by inequalities of race, class, and gender, political stability is relatively secure and overt resistance is rare. While the absence of open conflict is notable, social science that proposes a lack of something – a lack of resistance, a social movement, a consciousness of race, class or gender, a lack of self-esteem – is productive science.

This chapter has outlined a history of the present 'state of esteem'. That history shows how self-governance is an invention of, and crucial to, modern democracy. These claims about modern democratic forms of power help us to understand how, for example, poor single mothers on welfare who are enrolled in self-esteem programmes become subjects, even as they are subjected to forms of power and government. The failure of a women's movement united across race, class, gender and sexuality is due as much to the means by which we are 'empowered' as to any 'lack of self-esteem'.

NOTES

[1] Nikolas Rose (1987) offers a compelling account of the limitations of feminist critique based on the public/private division which has influenced my arguments here.

[2] Consider, for example, the following publication titles included in California Task Force (1990b): Stewart Emery, *Actualizations: You Don't Have to Rehearse to Be Yourself* (New York: Irving Publications, 1980); Morris Rosenberg, *Conceiving the Self* (Melbourne, FL.: Robert E. Krieger Publishing, 1979); Virginia Satir, *People Making* (Palo Alto, CA.: Science & Behavior Books, 1988).

[3] For a discussion of the political and constitutive nature of narrative strategies, see Nancy Armstrong (1987); Carolyn Kay Steedman (1986); and for a study of narrative across social scientific, journalistic and fictional discourses, see Anita Levy (1991).

[4] For a compelling and insightful account of the economic interests of the middle-class in service provisions to the poor, see Theresa Funiciello (1990). Although Funiciello fails to see that the social services are a form of governing the poor, she does clearly articulate the relationship between the social science professions and income redistribution. From p. 38: 'What became the professionalization of being human took off, bloating under government contracts. For every poverty problem, a self-perpetuating profession proposed to ameliorate the situation without altering the poverty'.

[5] Denise Riley (1988) points to the tangled history of women's citizenship and the emergence of the social as a sphere of governance and science, especially pp. 44–66.

REFERENCES

Armstrong, N. (1987). *Desire and domestic fiction: A political history of the novel*, Oxford: Oxford University Press.

Beaumont, G. de & Tocqueville, A. de (1964). *On the penitentiary system in the United States and its application in France*. Southern Illinois: University Press.

Boesche, R. (1987). *The strange liberalism of Alexis de Tocqueville*. Cornell University Press.

California Task Force to Promote Self-Esteem and Personal and Social Responsibility (1990a). *Toward a State of esteem: The Final Report*. Sacramento, CA.: California Department of Education.

California Task Force to Promote Self-Esteem and Personal and Social Responsibility (1990b). *Appendices to 'Toward a state of esteem'*. Sacramento, CA.: California Department of Education.

Dumm, T. (1987). *Democracy and punishment: The disciplinary origins of the United States.* University of Wisconsin Press.

English, D. (1992, 2 February). Review in *New York Times Book Review, p. 13.*

Foucault, M. (1983). The subject and power. In H.L. Dreyfus & P. Rabinow (Eds.), *Michel Foucault: Bond structuralism and hermeneutics* (2nd ed.). Chicago: University of Chicago Press.

Foucault, M. (1988). The political technology of individuals. In L.H. Martin, H. Gutman & P.H. Hutton (Eds.), *Technologies of the self.* University of Massachusetts Press.

Funiciello, T. (1990, November/December). The poverty industry: Do governments and charities create the poor? *Ms. Magazine*, p. 38.

Hacking, I. (1986a). Making up people. In T. Heller, M. Sosna, & D. Wellberg (Eds.), *Reconstructing individualism: Autonomy, individuality, and the self in Western thought.* Stanford University Press.

Hacking, I. (1986b). Self-improvement. In D.C. Hoy (Ed.), *Foucault: A critical reader.* Oxford: Basil Blackwell.

Levy, A. (1991). *The other woman: The writing of class, race and gender, 1832–1898.* Princeton: Princeton University Press.

Mecca, A., Smelser, N. & Vasconcellos, J. (Eds.) (1989). *The social importance of self-esteem.* University of California Press.

Miller, P. (1987). *Domination and power.* London: Routledge & Chapman Hall.

Mink, G. (1990). The lady and the tramp: Gender, race and the origins of the American welfare state. In L. Gordon (Ed.), *Women, the state, and welfare.* Wisconsin University Press.

Riley, D. (1988). *Am I that name? Feminism and the category of 'women' in history.* University of Minnesota Press.

Rose, N. (1987). Beyond the public/private division: Law power, and the family. *Journal of Law and Society,* 14(1).

Rose, Nikolas (1990). *Governing the soul: The shaping of the private self.* London: Routledge & Chapman Hall.

Scheff, T., Retzinger, S.M. & Ryan, M.T. (1989). Crime, violence, and self-esteem. In A. Mecca, N. Smelser & J. Vasconcellos (Eds.), *The social importance of self-esteem.* University of California Press.

Steedman, C.K. (1986). *Landscape for a good woman: A story of two lives.* New Brunswick, NJ: Rutgers University Press.

Steinem, G. (1992). *Revolution from within: A book of self-esteem.* London: Little, Brown and Company.

Tocqueville, Alexis de (1961a). *Democracy in America* (H. Reeve, Trans.). Volume 1. Schocken Books. (1989).

Tocqueville, Alexis de (1961b). *Democracy in America* (H. Reeve, Trans.). Volume 2. Schocken Books.

Barbara Cruikshank
University of Massachusetts

EMERY J. HYSLOP-MARGISON AND ALAN M. SEARS

CHALLENGING THE DOMINANT NEO-LIBERAL DISCOURSE

From Human Capital Learning to Education for Civic Engagement

INTRODUCTION

Neo-liberalism has dramatically shifted the context of contemporary society by dismantling the public mechanisms that previously protected individuals from the ravages of 'capitalism with the gloves off' (McLaren & Farahmandpur, 2000, p. 26). Within the sphere of education, public schools and universities have not escaped the influence of neo-liberal policies, as these institutions are focused more and more on human capital development and far less on critical inquiry into the economic, social and political conditions that lie at the heart of democratic citizenship. Universities, once a bastion of social critique and intellectual freedom, face increasing pressure to conform to the dictates of neo-liberal regimes and a corporate hegemony that places profit over people (Chomsky, 2002). In this chapter and in response to this trend, the authors argue that educators must mount a more concerted resistance to the myriad of contemporary challenges to authentic citizenship education. We propose that meaningful democratic dialogue requires revealing neo-liberal ideologies to students and reclaiming such educational concepts as lifelong learning, critical thinking and literacy as primary democratic learning practices (Hyslop-Margison & Sears, 2006).

THE NEO-LIBERAL CONTEXT: PRIVATE PROFIT AS A PUBLIC GOOD

The 1970s witnessed a dramatically shifting political and economic paradigm among virtually all industrialised countries. These nations, including the US, Canada, Great Britain and other members of the then G7, were about to suffer a series of crippling recessions that continued throughout the decade. In *Das Kapital* Marx accurately predicted that capitalism, by its very nature, experiences inexorable and recurring crises of over-accumulation that inevitably result in unavoidable cycles of economic decline (Marx, 1933). In periods of over-accumulation like the 1970s, capital becomes so plentiful that industry cannot dispose of its product profitably and production is therefore correspondingly reduced. The tightening of consumer spending through increased interest rates results in widespread job losses among the working class members of society. The

M.A. Peters, A. Britton and H. Blee (Eds.), Global Citizenship Education: Philosophy, Theory and Pedagogy, 299–315.

economy eventually recovers from each over-accumulation crisis but with each recovery the entire cycle begins all over again with every subsequent collapse, according to Marx, more serious than its predecessor.

The economic fallout from the over-accumulation crisis of the 1970s and early 1980s impacted negatively on many citizens of the world's industrialised democracies. As industry limited production and lending institutions tightened the reins on available capital, mass layoffs of workers throughout the manufacturing and transportation sectors occurred to protect corporate profits. Interest rates witnessed a significant jump that in turn prompted a dramatic increase in the number of personal and small business bankruptcies (Hyslop-Margison & Welsh, 2003). One noted economist describes the fiscal decline of the 1970s as 'a disaster that would rival the great crash of 1929' (Mahar, 2003, p. 39). Many members of the working class lost their jobs, homes and savings as they struggled to carve out a new niche for themselves in the emerging leaner, and decidedly meaner, neo-liberal order.

Neo-liberalism has not only redefined the role of the democratic citizen but also our understanding of what constitutes the national or state interest. As the Cold War faded with a triumphant capitalist victory, most notably symbolised by the demolition of the Berlin Wall and the collapse of the Warsaw Pact, the challenges facing Western democracies became increasingly viewed in economic terms rather than in political or moral ones. Success no longer depended on winning hearts and minds from communism to capitalism but in maintaining the economic stature and advantage of the corporate class. The complete collapse of Eastern European and Soviet communism removed the only substantial obstacle to unfettered capitalism. With the spectre of socialism all but vanished from the political horizon, capital was free to reach into the far corners of the globe for new exploitative opportunities. In the *Communist Manifesto* Marx and Engels (1998) anticipated this global assault by observing that,

> The bourgeoisie, by the rapid improvement of all instruments of production, by the immensely facilitated means of communication, draws all, even the most barbarian, nations into civilization. The cheap prices of its commodities are the heavy artillery with which it batters down all Chinese walls, with which it forces the barbarians' hatred of foreigners to capitulate. It compels all nations, on pain of extinction, to adopt the bourgeois mode of production; it compels them to introduce what it calls civilization into their midst, i.e., to become bourgeois themselves. In one word, it creates a world after its own image. (p. 40)

In the two decades preceding the 1970s, governments from industrialised countries adopted a range of policies and programmes that enhanced quality of life for many of their most vulnerable citizens. In Canada, unemployment insurance programmes, national healthcare and enhanced social assistance programmes protected the most susceptible members of the population from slipping below subsistence levels of income. In the US, where the welfare state was far less instantiated in a national consciousness founded on romanticised notions of rugged

300

individualism, 'from 1950 to 1970, in a period of unparalleled economic growth, Welfare Liberalism scored its success and created something close to a national consensus' (Bellah *et al*, 1986, p. 262). In his classic analysis of the evolution of democratic citizenship British theorist T.H. Marshall was so sanguinely confident of the progress made on social equality issues by the 1950s that he predicted social rights would soon hold the same status in Western democracies as civil and political rights: 'The modern drive to social equality,' he wrote, 'is the latest phase of an evolution of citizenship which has been in continuous progress for some 250 years' (Marshall, 1992, p. 7).

Many of the considerable social gains accrued through welfare state policies were lost or substantially rolled back during the next two decades of trickle down economics. By 1990 the industrialised world was a radically different sort of place where vulnerable citizens were often left without meaningful public mechanisms to protect them from the rather ruthless application of market economy principles (Giroux, 2003). The attack on the welfare state reflected not only a reduction in available social programs but also a much more fundamental shift in prevailing ideology and citizen beliefs. Since 1970, neo-liberalism in the US has gained virtually complete control over the political consciousness of Americans and has enjoyed considerable success in convincing even those citizens most victimised by its principles of its supposed merit (Bellah *et al*, 1986).

The welfare state polices of the 1960s and 1970s proved counterproductive to corporate interests because they interfered with the raw supply and demand market principles that form the foundation of unregulated capitalism. When workers are provided with the opportunity to choose between drawing sustainable unemployment benefits and working for an unsustainable minimum wage many understandably select the former. This has the net impact of shrinking the available labour pool and therefore driving wages upward. The upward pressure on wages caused consistently high inflation and, as a result, corporate profits stagnated throughout many sectors of the economy. It was an enviable situation for workers who made considerable inroads in overcoming the exploitative mechanisms of surplus labour. Given their political lobbying power and considerable control over the economic fortunes of industrialised countries, however, it was a situation that corporations were simply unwilling to tolerate.

With the tide of public sentiment now effectively turned against the more liberal welfare state governments of the period, as well as against labour unions, widespread corporate political support for candidates such as Margaret Thatcher in Britain and Ronald Reagan in the US contributed to their election and ultimate re-election. Reagan and Thatcher were both enthusiastic advocates of neo-liberal economic policies and embraced the logic of vulgar capitalism with the same reverence and sense of inevitability as the law of gravity. *Reaganomics,* with its trickle down dregs to the economically disadvantaged, increased job growth significantly in the form of low paying service sector positions. The drop in unemployment corresponded with a rapid drop in actual worker earnings (Hyslop-Margison & Welsh, 2003). In the US, perhaps the ideal prototype of Milton Friedman's economic policies with their trickle down presuppositions, almost a

301

quarter of the population, or approximately 60 million people – many of them working full and part time retail and service industry jobs – now live as members of the so-called underclass (Sadovnik *et al*, 2001).

In their book *The Right Nation: Conservative Power in America,* Micklethwait and Wooldridge (2004) argue that over the past 40 years the political right in the US has built an intellectual infrastructure that almost completely dominates contemporary public policy debates. Various groups forming this infrastructure, well funded and well coordinated in their ideological mandates, maintained that the demands of labour, rather than the excesses of the corporate class, were responsible for driving industrialised nations to their economic knees. Conservative ideologues in the US, from intellectual William F. Buckley to radio talk show host Rush Limbaugh, effectively used this claim to manipulate public opinion in favour of their corporate allies. The corporate lobby convinced the general public that countries could not expect to be internationally competitive unless unions and workers accepted significant labour market reorganisation. In many places where labour has not complied with this agenda, jobs have been simply shipped 'offshore' to various developing countries with a readily available supply of cheap labour.

With the widespread retrenchment of the welfare state, governments from industrialised nations were forced to redefine themselves to justify their new role in the emerging neo-liberal global order. They achieved this objective by cooperating more fully with the demands of free enterprise and reducing all public policy decisions to questions of market economy efficiency (Young, 1990). The role of government within neo-liberalism became that of creating optimum conditions for the practice of global economics in a social order totally committed to the logic of the marketplace. This commitment not only affected the quality of employment workers might expect to find in the shifting and unstable conditions of the new labour market, but also influenced environmental spending, social programs such as Medicare and, of course, the focus of public and higher education

The dominant political and educational discourse suggests that the logic of the neo-liberal market is irrefutable and, therefore, it has been naturalised for citizens within neo-liberal nations. This logic is expressed ideologically and validated as 'common sense' by powerful institutions such as the International Monetary Fund (IMF), the World Bank and the Organization for Economic Cooperation and Development (OECD). Mike Harris, the former neo-liberal premier of Ontario, Canada, gained power in 1995 by asking citizens to join him in a 'Common Sense Revolution' premised on significant cuts in four areas: taxes; government spending; barriers to job creation (including workmen's compensation premiums and progressive labour legislation); and the size of government (Harris, 1994). Perhaps the foremost expert in the field of ideology and how it influences social thinking, Terry Eagleton (1991), argues that making problematic and contestable assumptions part of *common sense* thinking is a familiar ideological strategy to manipulate public opinion.

Ironically, the impetus to spread democracy itself is one area where neo-liberal ideology is perhaps most powerfully expressed. Speaking to a conference concerned with issues facing emerging democracies in Eastern Europe and the former Soviet Bloc, US political scientist Benjamin Barber (1995) warned about four myths that often accompany movements to spread democracies: democracy is easily exportable from one context to another; appropriate constitutional and legal structures are all that is needed for democracy to flourish; democracy depends on heroic leadership; and, the myth he describes as the most insidious, democracy is synonymous with free markets. Barber points out that capitalism cannot produce many of the public goods necessary for democracy such as public health and social safety nets and warned his audience not to be seduced by the mythic logic of an inextricable link between unfettered markets and democracy.

Almost ten years later Barber sees the same myth being perpetrated in the present US desire to spread democracy to the nations of the Middle East. His book *Fear's Empire: War, Terrorism, and Democracy* contains a chapter titled, 'You Can't Export McWorld and Call it Democracy' in which Barber argues that in the administrations of both Bill Clinton and George W. Bush the term '*market democracy* [emphasis in original] was used to suggest that democracy is synonymous with the free market' (Barber, 2003, p. 155). For Barber, unquestioned capitalism is not the same as democracy and often undermines the latter by creating a dangerous privatisation that 'effectively gives public power away, yielding it to private elites beyond scrutiny and control. In the name of liberty it destroys democracy by annihilating the good of the public (the *res publica*) in whose name democratic republics are constituted in the first place' (Barber, 2003, p. 162).

The naturalisation of neo-liberal ideology is widely evident in a range of contemporary curricula that typically describe present circumstances to students in terms that suggest either their inevitability or social desirability. Neo-liberal ideology removes the economic sphere from moral or social discussion by portraying these latter realms of discourse as entirely dependent on the former. In other words, appropriate social and moral action is determined by what works for the market, and what works for the market, according to the prevailing logic, is neo-liberalism. All other spheres of life are correspondingly designed to address the needs of the marketplace and any interference with market logic becomes unthinkable let alone possible. Habermas observes that we are witnessing the total invasion of what he describes as the *life world* by the creation of false needs and the decline of pubic spaces (Habermas, 1996). The life world for Habermas consists of those fundamental human experiences and interactions that generate a sense of peace or individual wellbeing, and provides the necessary community and intellectual space for critical democratic discussion.

THE NEO-LIBERAL ASSAULT ON EDUCATION

With the revised role of government in neo-liberalism reduced to that of creating optimum market conditions, public policy development faced concerted attack in the final two decades of the twentieth-century. Nationally owned resources and services were routinely sold to the private sector predicated on the view that such sell offs would necessarily increase productive efficiency. Public education did not escape the shift toward privatisation as evidenced by the growth of the school choice movement, especially in the US. Consistent with the unquestioned faith in competition and micro level accountability as the means to correct all possible social and economic ills, neo-liberalism demanded that schools and teachers be held directly accountable for student academic fortunes through the development of standardised testing. As an ideological mechanism, these tests effectively mask the structural causes of academic underachievement and unemployment by viewing educational problems as individual rather than social failures. With complete disregard for resource inequity, economic disparity and other structural impediments to education, the belief developed, encouraged by private enterprise, that schools could be improved by creating a parallel charter school system to compete with the public variety.

In spite of their traditional role as the gatekeepers of intellectual freedom, universities have not escaped the drift toward human capital preparation and other instrumental demands of the marketplace. Faced with huge public expenditure reductions, universities are increasingly becoming institutions focused on technical training rather than on creating informed and engaged democratic citizens (Giroux, 2003). At one of the authors' institutions, Concordia University, courses are marketed under the slogan 'real knowledge for the real world,' an idea that effectively reduces learning to social efficiency precepts by implying there is a real social world beyond that shaped by human agency and decision-making. In the US, a significant number of research chairs are entirely corporate sponsored with the attending obligation to direct research agendas towards issues that pay corporate dividends.

Increasingly, universities see their relationship with students within a business model framework with students often described as clients or customers of the university rather than as members of a scholarly community with rights and responsibilities in shaping community life. A recent article appearing in a University of Toronto publication extolled that university's new focus on students as customers who deserved good service as a smart move not for delivering quality education but for nurturing long term alumni loyalty – and presumably financial contributions (Lighthall, 2006). This commodification of education shows up not only in marketing and customer service campaigns directed at students, parents and alumni but in an increasing focus on universities as providers of commodities (in the guise of credentials) rather than education. Almost forty years ago social critic Ivan Illich (1971) argued that Western educational institutions had already substituted credentialing for educating, an observation even truer today.

Current reductions in public funding for universities precipitate intense competition within and between faculties for available private and public grants. The ability to attract funding into the university is now typically viewed as a fundamental tenure requirement. The research funded by these grants often poses little challenge to the neo-liberal structure because it either neglects society as a primary unit of analysis or manifestly embraces prevailing human capital objectives. The focus of this research is often grounded far more in the idea of social and economic utility than in fostering democratic critique. The idea that a university experience is about intellectual growth, social debate and democratic dialogue has been largely usurped by the neo-liberal objectives of customer service, credentialising, technical training and instrumental learning. In the current university milieu, faculty are often reduced from their democratic role of social critic or public intellectual to that of entrepreneurial researcher or clerical proletariat labour (Aronowitz, 2001).

The ability and right to criticise public figures and government policy is obviously central to democratic societies. In the post-September 11, 2001, US it has become dangerously unpopular for educators at all levels to criticise the Bush administration's direction and decision-making on domestic and foreign policy. Those public figures and academics who do so, such as recently illustrated by the case featuring University of Colorado professor Ward Churchill, run the risk of either personal attack or, in this particular case, the almost complete ruination of one's professional reputation. Giroux (2003) refers to the present political context as *emergency time*, or a period during which the general public is easily manipulated through fear and anxiety to accept government action and policy that it would otherwise reject. Emergency time creates a period when criticism of government policy is rejected as being counter to a conception of a greater public 'good', and civil liberties are undermined without public criticism as state power increases exponentially.

It is critically important that universities respect and protect the democratic right of individual dissent so long as that dissent does not explicitly threaten the well being of other citizens. The public space for social critique must be protected even when dissent runs counter to mainstream or popular thinking. Obviously, no one is obligated to accept Ward Churchill's controversial contention that the financial bureaucrats situated in the World Trade Center who succumbed to the unfortunate terrorist attacks were akin to 'little Eichmanns', but he deserves the opportunity to state that opinion and support it on the basis of some attending argument. To reject the position simply on the grounds that it is 'offensive' or counter to generally-held public opinion undermines the basic principles of democratic and intellectual discourse. The attack on Professor Churchill symbolically reflects a growing and profoundly disturbing trend within the US that routinely persecutes or ridicules anyone who challenges neo-liberal ideology or questions US foreign policy. Within such a milieu, democracy is endangered because the scope of circulating ideas and public debate is narrowed to predetermined assumptions and objectives that comply with a single point of view. Even those holding alternative perspectives tend to withhold their views under such conditions due to fear of subsequent persecution. Thankfully, with the recent shift in US political power, new spaces are seemingly appearing that allow for more trenchant critiques of the Bush administration's domestic and foreign policy decisions although voiced mainstream alternatives remain somewhat ambiguous.

An education system designed to respond to the needs of the marketplace predictably appears radically different from one focused on preparing students for the responsibilities of democratic citizenship. The No Child Left Behind (NCLB) legislation in the US, for example, does not contain a single reference to either democracy or democratic citizenship. Neo-liberal culture is naturalised to students in public and higher education as an unchangeable social reality rather than critiqued as an ideological movement imposed by special corporate interests on citizens of industrialised democratic societies. Outside the strictures of the global market, education in the neo-liberal order conveys to students that there are simply no longer any meaningful choices to be made. Throughout contemporary career education curricula in particular, and in a variety of ideologically manipulative ways, students are expected to prepare for an uncertain occupational future and are discursively convinced that such conditions are beyond the scope of their own political agency. Pedagogical tools of social critique such as critical thinking, lifelong learning and literacy are all influenced by the neo-liberal shift toward instrumental instruction. As a result, schools fail to prepare students as democratic citizens who possess the necessary understanding and dispositions to decide politically between various social possibilities. Instead, students are portrayed as mere objects in history and inculcated with a consumer-driven worldview devoid of imagination, hope or alternative social visions.

One of the most interesting curricular vehicles for truncating students' ability to participate as agents in shaping their world is the return of civics to the school curriculum. Both Ontario and British Columbia recently reintroduced civics courses to the high school curriculum under neo-liberal governments; Mike Harris's government in Ontario and Gordon Campbell's in British Columbia (Ontario Ministry of Education, 2005; British Columbia Ministry of Education, 2005). While both of these curricula take a generally activist approach to citizenship and focus on encouraging citizen engagement, an idea the authors applaud, the move to centralise citizenship education in civics courses rather than infusing it more widely in the curriculum implies that civic action ought to be limited to the overtly political sphere and does not include action to shape economic systems, society more generally, or vocational experience.

EXPOSING NEO-LIBERAL IDEOLOGY TO STUDENTS

A pedagogical feature too often lacking in educational preparation for democratic citizenship is instruction that provides students with a basic understanding of how ideology shapes individual and cultural consciousness. If our students are expected to make autonomous and democratic political choices about society, then providing them with understanding about the mechanisms of ideology and *false consciousness* becomes a pivotal educational objective. To remedy the present lack of attention schools pay to this problem, the term *ideology* should be introduced to students relatively early to empower them with a concept that effectively names and exposes the manipulative forces in their culture. Ideology, especially in the current era of modern media and technological invasion, has a potentially profound and lasting impact on student consciousness that may impede their ability for autonomous preference formation. Without providing students with some opportunity to examine the impact of ideology on consciousness shaping, the hope of achieving a meaningful, or what Apple describes as a *thick democracy,* is seriously undermined (Apple & Aasen, 2003).

One effective pedagogical approach to open up student consideration of the ideologies that underlie contemporary Western society is to present historical or contemporary alternatives. Feminist scholars have provided insightful critiques of liberal and formal democratic conceptions of citizenship and democracy (Arnot & Dillabough, 2000). In addition, there is a considerable body of academic scholarship on citizenship emerging from Asia that challenges the privileging of individuals over communities and proposes alternative social and economic frameworks other than neo-liberalism for political and social organisation in democratic societies (Lee *et al,* 2004). Either or both of these frameworks could provide valuable education strategies for opening up the taken-for-granted nature of existing social, economic, labour market and working conditions.

Giroux (2003) underscores the potential contribution of Marxism in contemporary education by suggesting it affords an effective vehicle to highlight the ravages of neo-liberal capitalism. Unfortunately, these potentially valuable contributions are presently part of the *null curriculum* because of an economic and ideological context that depicts all components of Marxism in typically sinister terms, read as the archenemy of the capitalist discourse embracing freedom and democracy. The null curriculum is a powerful indoctrinating force that denies students access to available intellectual culture and manipulates them instead to value only that content contained in the *formal curriculum*, in this case, neo-liberal assumptions, policies and consequences.

Marx's base/superstructure model, arguably the foundation for *critical theory*, offers an excellent pedagogical device to illustrate to students how economic forces direct or control ideas within capitalist culture. The model reflects Marx's view that those individuals who control the economic base of society also control the dissemination of prevailing ideas and values. The economic base contains such elements as the means of production and distribution, the means of communication and the financial institutions that control capital. According to Marx, the individuals who control these various economic forces also control a culture's major ideas, and they shape these ideas to protect their own hegemonic and class based economic interests. Introducing the base/superstructure model to students relatively early in their education can help them better understand how culture is saturated with ideas and values emanating from powerful individuals, organisations and groups. It reveals in a very concrete visual way the relationship between economic power and ideological influence, and alerts students to how their own ideas, sometimes self-damaging ones, are often the result of these intersecting forces.

RE-APPROPRIATING DEMOCRATIC EDUCATIONAL CONCEPTS

Consistent with the neo-liberal assumptions propelling reform in education, many organisations influencing contemporary policy development within education advance a human capital construct of lifelong learning designed to address unstable labour market conditions (Hyslop-Margison & Naseem, in press). Contemporary conditions generally include recurrent occupational displacement and instability that combine to undermine the job security of workers. The human capital construct of lifelong learning is designed to ensure that students, as future workers, passively accept the occupational uncertainty they will inevitably confront in the new global economic order. For example, the World Bank Group endorses the following conception of lifelong learning:

> In the 21st century, workers need to be lifelong learners, adapting continuously to changed opportunities and to the labor market demands of the knowledge economy. Lifelong learning is more than education and training beyond formal schooling. A comprehensive programme of lifelong-learning education for dynamic economies, within the context of the overall development framework of each country, encompasses all levels. (The World Bank, 2004, p. v)

From this perspective, lifelong learning involves the constant upgrading of skills to ensure workers remain responsive to contemporary labour market demands. By blurring the distinction between the constructed nature of society and natural reality, thus ignoring Searle's crucial distinction between brute facts and social facts, this discourse conveys to students that their role is simply preparing for an inevitable and unstable future rather than engaging with or democratically transforming their political, economic and social landscapes (Searle, 1995).

The authors believe that the stakes in the battle for lifelong learning are enormously high. The human capital discourse portraying lifelong learning as a labour market adjustment strategy undermines the ability of students to act as democratic agents of social change. Democratic forms of pedagogy view humans and society as unfinished, subject to continual evaluation and transformation. As dynamic subjects in history, students, respected as lifelong learners, have a right to influence economic conditions and, in the process, create a more just, stable and caring social experience. From a democratic perspective, then, we should not ask our students to accept an ahistorical view of the world that represents social reality and labour market conditions as fixed and unchangeable, and that reduces their role to mere social adaptation (Hyslop-Margison & Naseem, in press).

The area of literacy education represents another example where the instrumental assumptions of neo-liberal ideology dominate the curriculum. The 1998 Ontario Secondary Schools Detailed Discussion Document issued by the Ministry of Education explored several possible purposes for education that eventually precipitated large-scale curricular reform in the Canadian province. These purposes range from preparing students for the workforce to preparing students as reflective individuals and engaged democratic citizens. The Ontario Ministry of Education concluded that meeting both of these objectives required enhancing the literacy 'skills' of students. In a ministry brochure titled *Literacy in Ontario: The Rewards are for Life*, the functionalist assumptions supporting the ministry's vision of literacy are revealed: 'Literacy skills are needed every day – at work, at home, at school, in the community. These skills help people to take part in further education and training, as well as to find and keep jobs'. The emphasis on simply encoding textual messages for instrumental application in the workplace without considering the broader social context from which that information emerges undermines the democratic participation of learners by ignoring their role as rational agents in social construction (Hyslop-Margison & Pinto, in press).

The political perspective represented in many of the current literacy practices in the province of Ontario and elsewhere reveals a monolithic neo-liberal agenda that denies students access to alternative worldviews. This agenda interferes with the fundamental democratic right of students to act as political agents of social reconstruction by transforming the social, economic and labour market circumstances they confront. Students are depicted by literacy imperatives as objects of, rather than subjects in, the construction of social reality. Freire (1970) explains how critical forms of literacy learning counteract this type of politically paralysing and decidedly undemocratic education: 'In problem-posing education, [students] develop their power to perceive critically the way they exist in the world with which and in which they find themselves; they come to see the world not as static reality, but as a reality in process, in transformation' (p. 78). In critical literacy, students learn to give democratic voice to the vocational and social challenges they presently confront and develop a deep understanding that social change is a real possibility. This understanding is central to the democratic learning advocated by Freire who 'taught us that, for social transformation to take place, it is important for students to understand and give voice to their personal struggles' (Darder, 2002, p. 155).

Through Ontario's current educational initiatives, students learn to view and name the world through a corporate dominated discourse that conveys particular values, assumptions and expectations. By way of an alternative, the primary objective of critical literacy in democratic education is heightening student awareness on how discourse influences our view of social reality. Apple (2000) describes this alternate conception as 'critical literacy, powerful literacy, political literacy which enables the growth of genuine understandings and control of all the spheres of social life in which we participate' (p. 42).

Even in the area of critical thinking, current curriculum constructs tend toward an instrumental reasoning approach that ignores the social and economic context as a primary unit of analysis. Critical thinking is widely portrayed as a problem solving strategy to generate technical solutions within a naturalised market economy system. Five Steps to Better Critical Thinking, Problem Solving, and Decision Making, for example, a business resource created for teachers, emphasises the daily practical challenges that workers might expect to confront: 'Some problems are big and unmistakable, such as the failure of an air freight delivery service to get packages to customers on time. Other problems may be continuing annoyances, such as regularly running out of toner for an office copy machine' (Guffey, 1996, p. 10).

British Columbia's Business Education reflects a technical rationality focus more directly by suggesting that, 'Critical thinking is an important aspect of all courses. Instruction should include opportunities for students to justify positions on issues and to apply economic and business principles to particular circumstances' (British Columbia Ministry of Education, 1998, n.p.). The Iowa City Community School District Career/Business Education high school curriculum describes problem solving as 'an employability skill required by employers' (Iowa City Community School District, 2003, n.p.). The Missouri Department of Elementary and Secondary Education's Division of Vocational and Adult Education maintain that critical thinking skills help students 'solve everyday, practical problems' (Missouri Department of Elementary and Secondary Education, 2003).

These constructs of critical thinking promote technical rationality and instrumental reasoning by encouraging students to address problems from a limited perspective that ignores wider workplace, labour market, and socio-economic issues. When students are tacitly or openly discouraged from engaging the social and economic forces shaping contemporary experience, their democratic right to participate in directing these forces is correspondingly undermined. Indeed, the moral imperatives of education within a democratic society require students to be provided with the necessary knowledge and dispositions to make informed choices about current political and social conditions, and entertain possible alternatives to improve these conditions (Hyslop-Margison & Armstrong, 2004).

The authors contend that education adopting a critical thinking approach based on democratic learning pursues the following principles of inquiry:
- Critical thinking that respects democratic learning considers the social and economic context a legitimate unit of analysis;
- Critical thinking that respects democratic learning encourages the political engagement of students in shaping the conditions that determine their social and political lives;
- Critical thinking that respects democratic learning places neo-liberalism, or *any other* ideology, in a historical context that promotes student understanding of society as a dynamic and evolving process;
- Critical thinking that respects democratic learning provides students with alternative viewpoints on possible social and economic structures;
- Critical thinking that respects democratic learning fosters critical dispositions among students by providing continuous opportunities for social, economic and political critique. (Hyslop-Margison & Armstrong, 2004)

Although the idea of epistemic virtue has been largely neglected in education, we believe it provides teachers with another effective strategy to pursue democratic learning objectives. Perhaps the primary strength of epistemic virtue involves its avoidance of the conceptual confusions present in current critical thinking constructs. Whereas non-virtue theories of knowledge consider epistemic justification in terms of evidence requirements or evaluation procedures, virtue epistemology understands justified belief in terms of epistemic, or intellectual, virtues. Again, the intellectual virtues consist of personal qualities, character traits, and dispositions rather than problem-solving strategies, heuristics or meta-cognitive critical thinking skills. Since the intellectual virtues are dispositions and character qualities students can be habituated to their development throughout the curriculum.

Any pedagogical approach that successfully enhances the intellectual development of students must include both an epistemological and a dispositional component. Unlike the neo-liberal discourse on critical thinking that neglects these requirements, virtue epistemology reflects a coherent recognition of their combined importance. Montmarquet (1993) suggests, for example, that the epistemologically virtuous individual aspires toward three interrelated general objectives: to discover new truths; to increase one's explanatory understanding; and to hold true rather than false beliefs. By encouraging students to discover new truths and increase their explanatory understanding, the intellectual virtues initially compel students to expand their subject knowledge relevant to a particular problem.

An example of how this initial virtue might be applied involves student discussion of neo-liberalism. Rather than a teacher simply lecturing about, condemning or advocating the prevailing social and economic order, students would be encouraged to learn as much information as possible about neo-liberalism for themselves. What are the major arguments in favour of and against neo-liberalism, and what does the available evidence suggest on its efficacy? If students are habituated to accumulate such information in advance of rendering any decision or judgment on a topic, they can avoid the rash opinions and *ad hominem* attacks that often dominate contemporary debates on key social and political issues. Instead, they understand that background knowledge provides the initial and foundational component to any meaningful reflective judgment and withhold such judgment in the absence of adequate knowledge and understanding. This type of student reflection is critical in protecting learners from ideological manipulation.

The intellectual virtues we advocate for application in citizenship education cannot be understood exclusively in terms of a general desire to acquire additional knowledge and enhance explanatory understanding. Other personal qualities are obviously required for epistemic success since they impact directly on how evidence is interpreted. In addition to the general epistemic virtues, Montmarquet (1993) identifies a list of regulatory virtues, or second order virtues, and classifies them in three additional distinct categories: Virtues of impartiality include personality traits such as openness to the ideas of others, willingness to exchange ideas, and a lively sense of one's own fallibility; virtues of intellectual sobriety oppose the excitement and rashness of overly enthusiastic commitment to truth claims; and finally, virtues of intellectual courage include a willingness to entertain and examine potential alternatives to popular ideas, perseverance in the face of opposition from others, and the determination to see an inquiry through to the end.

We reiterate our point that these virtues not only afford a solid basis for critical thinking but are consistent with the underlying values – or virtues – of democratic practice. Barber (2003), for example, argues that the central democratic value is humility. 'After all,' he writes, 'the recognition that I might be wrong and my opponent right is the very heart of the democratic faith' (p. 138). In writing about some of the fledgling democracies in Eastern Europe, Schöpflin (2001) makes a point similar to ours that both substantive knowledge and dispositions are essential to democratic practice. Having the form of democracy without an underlying commitment to democratic values leaves democracy largely unrealised. He observes that 'post-communist systems were consensual, a consent that was expressed regularly in elections and through other institutions, but were not democratic in as much as democratic values were only sporadically to be observed' (p. 110). He proceeds to argue that societies have what he calls first and second order rules. 'First order rules include the formal regulation by which every system operates, like the constitution, laws governing elections, procedures for the settlement of conflict and the like' – the substance of democracy. Second order rules are the informal tacit rules of the game that are internalised as part of the virtues of democracy. In a democracy these second order rules include 'key democratic values of self-limitation, feedback, moderation, commitment, responsibility, [and] the recognition of the value of competing multiple rationalities' (p. 120).

These more specific second order virtues are designed to regulate the general objective of epistemic conscientiousness because, as Montmarquet (1993) observes, 'Bare conscientiousness by no means guarantees a proper orientation toward one's own or others' beliefs, and this is why the qualities we have been enumerating seem so necessary to intellectual inquiry and integral to our notion of a virtuous inquirer' (p. 25). Although the personal qualities identified as epistemic virtues may be construed as habits, teachers and students must remember that they are not mindless habits, and this is where subject knowledge and understanding once again play a pivotal role. As Montmarquet (1993) explains, 'one is trying to arrive at the truth [and most importantly] be guided by the evidence' (p. 41).

The problem, then, with the accumulation of knowledge and information in the absence of these other regulatory virtues is that dogmatic commitment to certain beliefs remains possible. If teachers or students, ideologically committed to neo-liberal principles, are wrongfully dismissive of evidence pointing to the tragic consequences of neo-liberal policies, then the impartial judgment consistent with intellectual virtue is unattainable. As difficult as it may be, even those of us who oppose neo-liberalism within a democracy must be open to the possibility that our beliefs are in error and remain perpetually cognisant of our epistemic fallibility. However, in situations where we are convinced that the preponderance of available evidence points in the direction we support, we must also possess the intellectual courage not to yield to political or professional pressure.

Unlike critical thinking, epistemic virtue represents an ideal to be strived toward rather than a measurable standard to achieve. The intellectual character consistent with democratic citizenship developed through virtue epistemology will not appear after a single lesson or even after an entire course, but reflects instead the educational journey of a lifetime. Although we have provided a general framework for this approach, the epistemic virtues cannot be neatly compartmentalised for fragmented instruction, nor can they be clearly marked for easy assessment. Many teachers and students may find the amorphous and often inconstant nature of the epistemic virtues profoundly disturbing during an era marked by curriculum standardisation and high stakes assessment. To those individuals, we might simply suggest that in spite of educational rhetoric to the contrary, there are no quick and facile recipes to enhance the knowledge, understanding, and citizenship development of students.

Critical thinking, framed within an intellectual virtues approach, has the capacity to promote a more complete and democratic understanding among students of the various forces shaping contemporary social experience. When students develop such an understanding, and the necessary dispositions to transform that knowledge into practice, they are empowered as democratic citizens to influence the quality of their own lives. Unfortunately, as we have illustrated, current models of critical thinking in education are often conceptually problematic, epistemologically incomplete, virtually ignore dispositions, and merely promote technical rationality aimed at improving human capital efficiency within difficult labour market and working conditions. The challenge for democratically minded teachers, then, is expanding the unit of analysis to explore the social, economic, and political boundaries of contemporary social experience.

Truly democratic educators are committed to pedagogical approaches that politically empower students in their personal lives. A critical, liberating and democratic education considers political participation and social justice, including the right to satisfying and financially rewarding employment, as fundamental democratic objectives. For critical thinking to achieve its full pedagogical potential, it must encourage students to assume a far greater measure of decision-making power over the policies influencing their lives. This means challenging the human capital assumptions and corporate dominated educational reform movements that reduce critical thinking to technical rationality and a transferable employability skill, and correspondingly preclude serious critique of morally questionable social, economic, and labour market practices. The authors would suggest that critical thinking respecting foundational rationality and pursuing an intellectual virtues approach can meet the pressing challenge of creating politically informed subjects in the democratic construction of social experience rather than mere objects of labour market efficiency.

CONCLUSION

The authors sincerely hope that this chapter provides teachers at various levels with the knowledge, understanding, strategies and, perhaps most importantly, the incentive to counter the neo-liberal polices that threaten to turn our remaining public spaces in education into realms of instrumental human capital preparation. As educators we must fully appreciate our inter-generational obligation to students and to future citizens, and work to protect the rapidly fading ideals that lie at the heart of our cherished democratic life. The choice before us is a relatively simple but critically important one for the future of our democratic societies: Do we create students as future citizens who view themselves as mere objects in history, or do we create learners who view themselves as dynamic political agents of personal and social improvement? From an educational perspective that respects the principles of democratic learning and intellectual freedom, the answer is abundantly clear and our responsibility as educators exceptionally compelling.

313

REFERENCES

Apple, M., & Aasen, P. (2003). *The state and the politics of knowledge.* New York: Routledge Falmer.

Arnot, M., & Dillabough, J. (Eds.) (2000). *Challenging democracy: International perspectives on gender, education and citizenship.* London: Routledge.

Apple, M. (2000). *Official knowledge: Democratic education in a conservative age.* 2nd Edition. New York: Routledge.

Aronowitz, S. (2001). *The last good job in America.* Lanham: Rowan and Littlefield.

Barber, B.R. (1995). *The future of civil society.* Paper presented at the Strengthening Citizenship and Civic Society Conference, Prague, June 2–6.

Barber, B. (2003). *Fear empire: War, terrorism and democracy.* New York: W. W. Norton & Company.

Bellah, R., Masden, R., Sullivan, W.M., Swidler, A. & Tipton, S.M. (1986). *Habits of the heart: Individualism and commitment in American life.* New York: Harper and Row.

British Columbia Ministry of Education. (1998). Business Education. Victoria, BC: Author.

British Columbia Ministry of Education. (2005). Civic studies 11. Victoria, BC: Author.

Chomsky, N. (2002). *Media control: The spectacular achievements of propaganda.* 2nd edition. New York: Seven Stories Press.

Darder, A. (2002). *Reinventing Paulo Freire: A pedagogy of love.* Boulder, CO: Westview Press.

Eagleton, T. (1991). *Ideology: An introduction.* London: Verso.

Freire, P. (1970). *Pedagogy of the oppressed.* New York: Herder & Herder.

Giroux, H. (2003). *The abandoned generation: Democracy beyond the culture of fear.* New York: Palgrave Macmillan.

Guffey, M. (1996). *Business communication: Process and product.* Cincinnati, OH: South Western College.

Habermas, J. (1996). *Between facts and norms: Contributions to a discourse theory of law and democracy: Studies in contemporary German thought.* Cambridge, MA: MIT Press.

Harris, M. (1994). *The common sense revolution.* Retrieved March 09, 2005, from http://www.ontariopc.com/feature/csr/csr_text.htm.

Hyslop-Margison, E. J., & Armstrong, J. (2004). Critical thinking in Career Education: The importance of foundational rationality. *Journal of Career and Technical Education, 21*(1), 39–49.

Hyslop-Margison, E.J., & Naseem, A. (in press). Career education as humanization: A Freirean approach to lifelong learning. *Alberta Journal of Educational Research.*

Hyslop-Margison, E. J., & Pinto, L. (in press). Critical literacy for democratic learning in career education. *Canadian Journal of Education.*

Hyslop-Margison, E.J. & Sears, A. (2006). *Neo-liberalism, globalization and human capital learning: Reclaiming education for democratic citizenship.* Dordrecht, the Netherlands: Springer.

Hyslop-Margison, E. J., & Welsh, B. (2003). The skills gap myth. *Journal of Educational Thought, 37*(1), 5–21.

Illich, I. (1971). *Deschooling society.* New York: Harper & Row.

Iowa City Community School District. (2003). Career/business education. Retrieved October 22, 2003, from http://www.dese.state.mo.us/divvoced/facs_curriculum.htm.

Lee, W.O., Grossman, D.L., Kennedy, K.J. & Fairborther, G. P. (2004). *Citizenship education in Asia and the Pacific: Concepts and issues.* Norwell, MA: Kluwer Academic Publishers.

Lighthall, W.D. (2006). *Viewing students as customers: Delivering quality student services becoming top priority to nurture loyal alumni in the long run.* Retrieved February 14, 2007, from http://www.news.utoronto.ca/bin6/060724–2477.asp.

Mahar, M. (2003). *Bull: A history of the boom, 1982–1999: What to know about financial cycles.* New York: HarperBusiness.

Marshall, T.H. (1992). Citizenship and social class. In T. Bottomore (Ed.), *Citizenship and social class.* London: Pluto Press.

Marx, K. (1933). *Das Kapital.* London: J.M. Dent.

Marx, K., & Engels, F. (1998). *The communist manifesto.* London: Verso.

McLaren, P., & Farahmandpur, R. (2000). Reconsidering Marx in post-Marxist times: A requiem for postmodernism? *Educational Researcher, 29*(3), 25–33.

Micklethwait, J., & Wooldridge, A. (2004). *The right nation: Conservative power in America.* New York: Penguin Press.

Missouri Department of Elementary and Secondary Education (2003). *Family and Consumer Sciences (FACS) curriculum and resources.* Retrieved from http://www.dese.mo.gov/divcareered/facs_curriculum.htm.

Montmarquet, J. (1993). *Epistemic virtue and doxastic responsibility.* Lanham, MD: Rowan & Littlefield.

Ontario Ministry of Education (2005). *The Ontario curriculum grades 9 and 10: Canadian and world studies.* Toronto: Author.

Sadovnik, A., Cookson, P. & Semel, S. (2001). *Exploring education: An introduction to the foundations of education.* Boston: Allyn and Bacon.

Schöpflin, G. (2001). Liberal pluralism and post communism. In W. Kymlicka & M. Olpalski (Eds.), *Can liberalism be exported? Western political theory and ethnic relations in Eastern Europe* (pp. 109–125). Oxford: Oxford University Press,.

Searle, J. (1995). *The construction of social reality.* New York: The Free Press.

The World Bank (2004). *Lifelong learning and the knowledge economy. Summary of the Global Conference on Lifelong Learning, Stuttgart, Germany, October 9–10, 2002.* Retrieved 25 September, 2007, from http://siteresources.worldbank.org/EDUCATION/Resources/278200-099079877269/547664-1099079984605/lifelong_KE.pdf.

Young, R. E. (1990). *A critical theory of education: Habermas and our children's future.* New York: Teachers College Press.

Emery J. Hyslop-Margison and Alan M. Sears
University of New Brunswick

315

JAMES A. BANKS

CITIZENSHIP EDUCATION AND DIVERSITY

Implications for Teacher Education

Adapted from: Journal of Teacher Education, January/February, 2001, 52(1), 5–16

INTRODUCTION

Because of the increasing racial, ethnic, cultural, and language diversity in the United States, effective teachers in the new century must help students become reflective citizens in pluralistic democratic nation-states. In this article, I argue that citizenship education needs to be reconceptualised because of the increased salience of diversity issues throughout the world. A new kind of citizenship education, called multicultural citizenship, will enable students to acquire a delicate balance of cultural, national, and global identifications and to understand the ways in which knowledge is constructed; to become knowledge producers; and to participate in civic action to create a more humane nation and world (J.A. Banks, 1997a). Teachers must develop reflective cultural, national, and global identifications themselves if they are to help students become thoughtful, caring, and reflective citizens in a multicultural world society.

This chapter consists of two major parts. In the first, I describe the theoretical and conceptual goals for citizenship education in a pluralistic democratic society. In the second, I describe how I implement these goals in one of my teacher education courses. The tone and style of the second part of the article are more personalised than those of the first part because I describe how the theory that I have developed is implemented in my own classroom.

Balancing Diversity and Unity

Most nation-states and societies throughout the world are characterised by cultural, ethnic, language, and religious diversity. One of the challenges to pluralistic democratic nation-states is to provide opportunities for cultural and ethnic groups to maintain components of their community cultures while at the same time constructing a nation-state in which diverse groups are structurally included and to

M.A. Peters, A. Britton and H. Blee (Eds.), Global Citizenship Education: Philosophy, Theory and Pedagogy, 317–331.

which they feel an allegiance. A delicate balance of unity and diversity should be an essential goal of democratic nation-states.

The challenge of balancing diversity and unity is intensifying as democratic nation-states such as the United States, Canada, Australia, and the United Kingdom become more diversified and as racial and ethnic groups within these nations become involved in cultural and ethnic revitalisation movements. The democratic ideologies institutionalised within the major democratic Western nations and the wide gap between these ideals and realities were major factors that resulted in the rise of ethnic revitalisation movements in nation-states such as the United States, Canada, and the United Kingdom during the 1960s and 1970s.

These nations share a democratic ideal, a major tenet of which is that the state should protect human rights and promote equality and the structural inclusion of diverse groups into the fabric of society. These societies are also characterised by widespread inequality and by racial, ethnic, and class stratification. The discrepancy between democratic ideals and societal realities and the rising expectations of structurally excluded racial, ethnic, and social-class groups created protest and revival movements within the Western democratic nations.

THE NEED FOR A NEW CONCEPTION OF CITIZENSHIP EDUCATION

Because of growing ethnic, cultural, racial, and religious diversity throughout the world, citizenship education needs to be changed in substantial ways to prepare students to function effectively in the 21st century. Citizens in the new century need the knowledge, attitudes, and skills required to function in their ethnic and cultural communities and beyond their cultural borders, and to participate in the construction of a national civic culture that is a moral and just community that embodies democratic ideals and values, such as those embodied in the Universal Declaration of Human Rights. Students also need to acquire the knowledge and skills needed to become effective citizens in the global community.

Citizenship education in the past, in the United States as well as in many other nations, embraced an assimilationist ideology. In the United States, its aim was to educate students so they would fit into a mythical Anglo-Saxon Protestant conception of the 'good citizen'. Anglo-conformity was the goal of citizenship education. One of its aims was to eradicate the community cultures and languages of students from diverse ethnic, cultural, racial, and language groups. One consequence of this assimilationist conception of citizenship education was that many students lost their first cultures, languages, and ethnic identities. Some students also became alienated from family and community. Another consequence was that many students became socially and politically alienated within the national civic culture.

Ethnic minorities of colour often became marginalised in both their community cultures and in the national civic culture because they could function effectively in neither. When they acquired the language and culture of the Anglo mainstream, they were denied structural inclusion and full participation into the civic culture because of their racial characteristics.

318

Citizenship education must be transformed in this new century because of the large influx of immigrants who are now settling in nations throughout the world, because of the continuing existence of institutional racism and discrimination throughout the world, and because of the widening gap between the rich and the poor.

The US Census (US Bureau of the Census, 1998) projects that 50% of the US population will consist of ethnic minorities of colour by 2050. The percentage of ethnic minorities in nation-states throughout the world has increased significantly within the past 30 years. In many Western nations, the ethnic minority population is growing at significantly greater rates than is the majority population. Institutionalised discrimination and racism are manifest by the significant gaps in the incomes, education, and health of minority and majority groups in many nation-states. Ethnic, racial, and religious minorities are also the victims of violence in many nation-states.

In the United States, the share of the nation's wealth held by the wealthiest households (0.5%) rose sharply in the 1980s after declining for 40 years. In 1976 this segment of the population held 14% of the nation's wealth. In 1983 it held 26.9% (Phillips, 1990). In 1997, 12.7% of Americans, which included a higher percentage of African Americans and Hispanics (8.6% of non-Hispanic Whites, 26.0% of African Americans, 27.1% of Hispanics) were living in poverty (US Bureau of the Census, 1998).

Cultural Communities and Multicultural Citizenship

Citizens should be able to maintain attachments to their cultural communities as well as participate effectively in the shared national culture. Cultural and ethnic communities need to be respected and given legitimacy, not only because they provide safe spaces for ethnic, cultural, and language groups on the margins of society, but also because they serve as a conscience for the nation-state. These communities take action to force the nation to live up to its democratic ideals when they are most seriously violated. It was the abolitionists and not the founding fathers in the United States who argued that freedom and equality should be extended to all Americans. African Americans led the civil rights movement of the 1960s and 1970s that forced the United States to eradicate its system of racial apartheid.

Okihiro (1994) points out that people and groups in the margins have been the conscience of the United States throughout its history. They have kept the United States committed to its democratic ideals as stated in its founding documents: the Declaration of Independence, the Constitution, and the Bill of Rights. He argues that the margins have been the main sites for keeping democracy and freedom alive in the United States. It was the groups in the margins that reminded and forced America to live up to its democratic ideals when they were most severely tested. Examples include (a) slavery and the middle passage, (b) Indian removal in the 1830s, (c) the internment of Japanese Americans during World War II, and (d) segregation and apartheid in the South that crumbled during the 1960s and 1970s in response to the African American-led civil rights movement. In *The Story of American Freedom*, Foner (1998) makes an argument similar to Okihiro's:

The authors of the notion of freedom as a universal birthright, a truly human ideal, were not so much the founding fathers who created a nation dedicated to liberty but resting in large measure on slavery, but abolitionists ... and women. (p. xx)

A new kind of citizenship is needed for the 21st century, which Kymlicka (1995) calls 'multicultural citizenship'. It recognises and legitimises the right and need of citizens to maintain commitments both to their ethnic and cultural communities and to the national civic culture. Only when the national civic culture is transformed in ways that reflect and give voice to the diverse ethnic, racial, language, and religious communities that constitute it will it be viewed as legitimate by all of its citizens. Only then can they develop clarified commitments to the commonwealth and its ideals.

The Assimilationist Fallacy and Citizenship Education

An assimilationist conception of citizenship will not be effective in the 21st century because it is based on a serious fallacy. The assimilationist assumes that the most effective way to reduce strong ethnic boundaries, attachments, and affiliations within a nation-state is to provide marginalised and excluded ethnic and racial groups opportunities to experience equality in the nation's social, economic, and political institutions. As they begin to participate more fully in the mainstream society and institutions, argues the assimilationist, marginalised cultural and ethnic groups will focus less on their specific concerns and more on national issues and priorities (Patterson, 1977).

When ethnic groups experience equality argues the assimilationist, ethnic attachments die of their own weight. The assimilationist views the ideal society as one in which there are no traces of ethnic or racial attachments. All groups will share one dominant national and overarching culture; people will forsake their ethnic cultures when they are structurally included in the national civic culture and community.

Apter (1977) calls the assimilationist position the 'assimilationist fallacy'. This position holds that as modernisation occurs, ethnic groups experience social, political, and economic equality, and commitments to ethnic and community attachments weaken and disappear. Ethnicity, argues the assimilationist, promotes division, exhumes ethnic conflicts, and leads to divisions within society. It also promotes group rights over the rights of the individual.

As Apter (1977) keenly observes, the assimilationist conception is not so much wrong as it is an incomplete and inadequate explanation of ethnic realities in modernised, pluralistic, and democratic nation-states. Ethnicity and assimilationism coexist in modernised democratic nation-states. As Apter suggests,

The two tendencies, toward and against [ethnicity] can go on at the same time. Indeed, the more development and growth that takes place, the more some [ethnic] groupings have to gain by their parochialism. (p. 65)

Ethnicity and modernity coexist in part because of what assimilationists call the 'pathological condition'; that is, ethnic groups such as Mexicans in the United States and Afro-Caribbeans in the United Kingdom maintain attachments to their ethnic groups and cultures in part because they have been excluded from full participation in the social, economic, and political institutions of their nation-states. However, members of marginalised ethnic groups, as well as more privileged ethnic and cultural groups such as Greeks and Jews in the United States, maintain ethnic affiliations and ethnic attachments for more fundamental psychological and sociological reasons. Ethnicity helps them to fulfil some basic psychological and sociological needs that the 'thin' culture of modernisation leaves starving. Apter (1977) comments insightfully on this point:

[Ethnic revival] is a response to the thinning out of enlightenment culture, the deterioration of which is a part of the process of democratization and pluralization. ... Assimilation itself then vitiates the enlightenment culture. As it does, it leaves what might be called a *primordial space* [italics added], a space people try to fill when they believe they have lost something fundamental and try to recreate it. (p. 75)

Multicultural citizenship education allows students to maintain attachments to their cultural and ethnic communities while at the same time helping them to attain the knowledge and skills needed to participate in the wider civic culture and community.

Helping Students to Develop Cultural, National, and Global Identifications

Citizenship education should help students to develop thoughtful and clarified identifications with their cultural communities and their nation-states. It should also help students to develop clarified global identifications and deep understandings of their roles in the world community (Diaz *et al*, 1999). Students need to understand how life in their cultural communities and nations influences other nations and the cogent influence that international events have on their daily lives. Global education should have as major goals helping students to develop understandings of the interdependence among nations in the world today, clarified attitudes toward other nations, and reflective identifications with the world community.

Developing a Delicate Balance of Identifications

Non-reflective and unexamined cultural attachments may prevent the development of a cohesive nation with clearly defined national goals and policies. Although we need to help students to develop reflective and clarified cultural identifications,

321

they must also be helped to clarify and strengthen their identifications with their nation-states. However, blind nationalism will prevent students from developing reflective and positive global identifications. Nationalism and national attachments in most nations of the world are strong and tenacious. An important aim of citizenship education should be to help students develop global identifications and a deep understanding of the need to take action as citizens of the global community to help solve the world's difficult global problems.

Cultural, national, and global experiences and identifications are interactive and interrelated in a dynamic way. Writes Arnove (1999),

> There is a dialect at work by which ... global processes interact with national and local actors and contexts to be modified, and in some cases transformed. There is a process of give-and-take, an exchange by which international trends are reshaped to local ends. (pp. 2–3)

Students should develop a delicate balance of cultural, national, and global identifications. However, educators often try to help students develop strong national identifications by eradicating their ethnic and community cultures and making students ashamed of their families, community beliefs, languages, and behaviours.

Cultural, national, and global experiences and identifications are developmental in nature, that individuals can attain healthy and reflective national identifications only when they have acquired healthy and reflective cultural identifications, and that individuals can develop reflective and positive global identifications only after they have realistic, reflective, and positive national identifications (J.A. Banks, 2001). These identifications are dynamic and interactive; they are not discrete.

Individuals can develop a clarified commitment to and identification with a nation-state and the national culture only when they believe that they are a meaningful part of the nation-state and that it acknowledges, reflects, and values their culture and them as individuals. A nation-state that alienates and does not structurally include all cultural groups into the national culture runs the risk of creating alienation and causing groups to focus on specific concerns and issues rather than on the overarching goals and policies of the nation-state.

Multicultural Citizenship Education, Knowledge, and Action

To help students acquire reflective and clarified cultural, national, and global identifications, citizenship education must teach them to know, to care, and to act. As Paulo Freire (1985) points out, students must be taught to read the word and the world. In other words, they must acquire higher levels of knowledge, understand the relationship between knowledge and action, develop a commitment to act to improve the world, and acquire the skills needed to participate in civic action. Multicultural citizens take actions within their communities, and nations to make the world more humane. Multicultural citizenship education helps students learn how to act to change the world.

322

To become thoughtful and effective citizen actors, students must understand the ways in which knowledge is constructed and how knowledge production is related to the location of knowledge producers in the social, political, and economic contexts of society. Multicultural citizenship education must also help students to become knowledge producers themselves and to use the knowledge they have acquired and constructed to take democratic social and civic action.

I have conceptualised five types of knowledge that can help educators to conceptualise and teach about knowledge construction (J.A. Banks, 1996): (a) personal/cultural knowledge, (b) popular knowledge, (c) mainstream academic knowledge, (d) transformative academic knowledge, and (e) school knowledge. Although the categories of this ideal-type typology can be conceptually distinguished, in reality they overlap and are interrelated in a dynamic way. *Mainstream academic knowledge* and *transformative academic knowledge* are briefly defined below because these concepts are used in the discussion in the second part of this article.

Mainstream academic knowledge consists of the concepts, paradigms, theories, and explanations that constitute traditional and established knowledge in the behavioural and social sciences. An important assumption within mainstream knowledge is that objective truths can be verified through rigorous and objective research procedures that are uninfluenced by human interests, values, and perspectives (Homans, 1967).

Transformative academic knowledge consists of the concepts, paradigms, themes, and explanations that challenge mainstream academic knowledge and that expand the historical and literary canon (J.A. Banks, 1996, 1998; Limerick, 1987). Transformative scholars assume that knowledge is influenced by personal values, the social context, and factors such as race, class, and gender. Whereas the primary goal of mainstream academic knowledge is to build theory and explanations, an important goal of transformative knowledge is to use knowledge to change society to make it more just and humane.

The Knowledge Construction Process and Student Identifications

The knowledge construction process describes the ways in which teachers help students to understand, investigate, and determine how the implicit cultural assumptions, frames of reference, perspectives, and biases within a discipline influence the ways in which knowledge is constructed. When the knowledge construction process is implemented in the classroom, teachers help students to understand how knowledge is created and how it is influenced by the racial, ethnic, social-class, and gender positions of individuals and groups.

When students participate in knowledge construction, they challenge the mainstream academic metanarrative and construct liberatory and transformative ways of conceptualising the US and the world experience. Understanding the knowledge construction process and participating in it themselves helps students to construct clarified cultural, national, and global identifications and to become knowledgeable, caring, and active citizens in democratic societies.

IMPLICATIONS FOR TEACHER EDUCATION

Helping Teachers to Develop Clarified Cultural and National Identifications

Teachers need to develop reflective cultural and national identifications if they are to function effectively in diverse classrooms and help students from different cultures and groups to construct clarified identifications. Several characteristics of US teachers and teacher education students make it difficult and problematic for them to develop reflective cultural and national identifications.

Most of the nation's teacher education students are middle-class White females who have little experience of other racial, ethnic, or social-class groups. Even when they come from working-class backgrounds, teacher education students tend to distance themselves from their class origins and to view themselves as middle class in their values, perspectives, and behaviours. This occurs in part because White students who come from lower- and working-class communities and cultures – like students of colour – must distance themselves from their primordial cultures to experience academic and social success in educational institutions. This is true not only in the United States but in other nations, as is epitomised in this statement by a Canadian Ukrainian who recalls his school experiences (Diakiw, 1994):

> This [school] was not an environment in which I was able to talk proudly about my heritage. I retreated and assimilated as fast as I could. I was ashamed of my background. I was particularly embarrassed about my parents. Compared to my friends' parents, mine seemed ignorant and crude. … I visited in their homes but not until the end of grade thirteen did I invite any friends to mine. Only then did I realize that despite the differences in culture and wealth, my parents were among the best. (p. 54)

When teacher education students from working-class backgrounds distance themselves from their class origins, they become less able to connect their childhood experiences with those of low-income and working-class students of colour. Consequently, they are less likely to develop an empathetic understanding of students whose behaviours and values conflict with those of the school's mainstream culture (Erickson, 2001).

One of the consequences of the monocultural experiences and the privileged racial and class status of many White college students in teacher education programs is their tendency to view themselves as noncultural and nonethnic beings who are colour-blind and raceless. Consequently, they often view race and culture as something possessed by outsiders and others and view themselves as 'just Americans'. These kinds of perceptions and perspectives often lead majority group students to ask these kinds of question during class discussions: 'Why do we have to focus on race and other kinds of differences? Why can't we all be just Americans?'

The culturally isolated experiences of most of my teacher education students, reinforced by their assimilationist high school education and the popular culture, result in their accepting without question the metanarrative of US history that has

324

dominated the nation's curriculum since the late 1800s. The metanarrative that is institutionalised within the nation's schools, colleges, and universities is called 'American exceptionalism' by historians such as Appleby (1992) and Kammen (1997).

The institutionalised metanarrative conceptualises the development of US history as a linear movement of Europeans from the east to the west coast of the United States, a movement that was ordained by God to bring civilisation to the West, which was a wilderness and a frontier. These words connote that the lands on which the Native Americans lived were uninhabited until the Europeans arrived in the West.

Frederick Jackson Turner (1894/1989), in a paper presented at the 1893 meeting of the American Historical Association that was destined to become a classic, characterised the frontier as 'the meeting point between savagery and civilization' (p. 3). Turner's characterisation of the West epitomises the metanarrative that is institutionalised in the nation's schools, colleges, and universities. However, the established metanarrative, which I call 'mainstream academic knowledge' (J.A. Banks, 1996) and which Apple (1993) describes as 'official knowledge,' has been strongly challenged by transformative scholars within the past 30 years (C.A.M. Banks, 1996; Limerick, 1987). The use of concepts such as *wilderness, frontier,* and *westward movement* are legacies of Turner's frontier thesis and the times in which he lived and worked. Cherry McGee Banks (1996) describes the serious limitations of the mainstream metanarrative:

> By telling part of the story and leaving other parts of the story out, meta-narratives suggest not only that some parts of the story don't count, but that some parts don't even exist. The exclusive nature of meta-narratives, their canonized place in formal school curricula, and the extent to which they are woven into the societal curriculum result in meta-narratives producing a feeling of well-being and comfort within society and their validity rarely being questioned. (p. 49)

The strong and persistent challenge that transformative scholars of colour and women have directed toward mainstream academic knowledge since the mid-1960s has resulted in significant curriculum changes in the nation's schools, colleges, and universities and in textbooks. However, despite these substantial changes, many of the concepts, perspectives, and periodisations of the mainstream meta-narrative are still deeply embedded in the curriculum, in textbooks, and in the popular culture.

Helping Teacher Education Students Rethink Race, Culture, and Ethnicity

To develop clarified cultural and national identifications, teacher education students must be helped to critically analyse and rethink their notions of race, culture, and ethnicity and to view themselves as cultural and racial beings. They also need to reconstruct race, culture, and ethnicity in ways that are inclusive and that reveal the ways in which these concepts are related to the social, economic, and political structures in US society (Nieto, 1999; Omi & Winant, 1994).

Teacher education students need to understand, for example, the ways in which the statement, 'I am not ethnic; I am just American,' reveals the privileged position of an individual who is proclaiming his or her own unique culture as American and other cultures as non-American. A statement such as 'I don't see colour' reveals a privileged position that refuses to legitimise racial identifications that are very important to people of colour and that are often used to justify inaction and perpetuation of the status quo. If educators do not 'see' colour and the ways in which institutionalised racism privileges some groups and disadvantages others, they will be unable to take action to eliminate racial inequality in schools.

In an important ethnographic study of a school, Schofield (2001) found that teachers who said they were colour-blind suspended African American males at highly disproportionate rates and failed to integrate content about African Americans into the curriculum. Colour blindness was used to justify inaction and the perpetuation of institutionalised discrimination within the school. Colour-blindness is part of the 'racial text' of teacher education which, as Cochran-Smith (2000) points out, teachers and teacher educators must 'unlearn'.

In the first course I teach for teacher education students, I incorporate readings, activities, lectures, and discussions designed to help students construct new concepts of race, culture, and ethnicity. Most students in the course are White women. These activities are designed, in part, to help the students 'unlearn racism' and to read the 'racial text' of US society and popular culture (Cochran-Smith, 2000). Assignments include a personal reflection paper on the book *We Can't Teach What We Don't Know: White Teachers, Multicultural Schools* (Howard, 1999) as well as a family history project.

In his book, Howard (1999) describes his personal journey as a White person to come to grips with racial issues and to become an effective educator. He speaks in a personal and engaging way to White teachers. In their reflection papers, my students describe their powerful reactions to Howard's book and how it helps them to rethink their personal journey related to race and their ideas about race. Howard makes racism explicit for most of my students for the first time in their lives.

In their family history project, the students are asked not only to provide a brief account of their family's historical journey but also to give explicit attention to the ways in which race, class, and gender have influenced their family and personal histories. Although the family history project is a popular assignment, most of the students have to struggle to describe ways in which race has influenced their family and personal histories because race is largely invisible to them (McIntosh, 1997). Gender is much more visible to my women students. More of the female than male students are able to relate gender to their family and personal stories in meaningful ways.

Challenging the Metanarrative

A series of activities in the course is designed to help students examine the US metanarrative, to construct new conceptions and narratives that describe the development of US history and culture (which I call transformative knowledge), and to think of creative and effective ways to teach new conceptions of the American experience to students. These activities include historical readings, discussions, and role-playing events about US ethnic and racial groups (J.A. Banks, 1997b), with the emphasis on the history of ethnic groups of colour. The perspectives in these historical accounts are primarily those of the groups being studied rather than those of outsiders.

The perspectives of both insiders and outsiders are needed to give students a comprehensive understanding of US history and culture. However, I emphasise the perspectives of insiders in this course because my students have been exposed to outsider perspectives for most of their education prior to my course. I also focus on insider perspectives because one of the most important goals of the course is to help students learn how to challenge and critically analyse the mainstream metanarrative they have learned during their high school and college years.

The historical readings in my course are supplemented by videotapes that powerfully depict the perspectives of ethnic groups of colour on historical and contemporary events. These videotapes include *The Shadow of Hate: A History of Intolerance in America* (Guggenheim, 1995), which chronicles how various groups within the United States, including the Irish, Jews, and African Americans, have been victimised by discrimination. One of the most trenchant examples of discrimination in the videotape is the description of the way Leo Frank, a Jewish northerner living in Atlanta, became a victim of anti-Semitism and racial hostility when he was accused of murdering a White girl who worked in a pencil factory he co-owned.

The Leo Frank case provides the students an opportunity to understand the ways in which race is a social construction, is contextual, and how the meaning of race has changed historically and continues to change today (Jacobson, 1998). Leo Frank was considered Jewish and not White in 1915 Atlanta. In a lecture, I provide the students an overview of Karen Brodkin's (1998) book that describes the process by which Jews became White in America and what the experiences of Jews and other White ethnics, such as the Irish and Italians, reveal about the characteristics of race in the United States.

Brodkin (1998) argues that Jews had to assimilate mainstream American behaviours, ideologies, attitudes, and perspectives to become White. Among the important attitudes they had to acquire, she argues, were the institutionalised attitudes and perceptions that mainstream Whites held toward groups of colour. Brodkin argues, as does Toni Morrison (1992), that Whites defined themselves in opposition to African Americans, and that this oppositional definition was one important way in which disparate groups of White ethnics were able to form a collectivity in the United States and to construct themselves as one cultural and identity group.

Ignatiev (1995) describes the ways in which the Irish, like other White ethnic groups, became White by acquiring mainstream White values and behaviours directed against ethnic groups of colour. My students are always surprised to learn how the meaning of race has changed through time and that the idea that Whites are one racial group is a rather recent historical development.

327

I use a videotape that deals with a contemporary Native American issue to relate historical events to current issues and to help the students understand the ways in which our nation's past and present are connected. *In Whose Honor?* (Rosenstein, 1997) chronicles the struggle of Charlene Teters, a Native American graduate student, to end the use of a Native American chief as a football team mascot at the University of Illinois in Champaign-Urbana. The team is called The Fighting Illini, after Chief Illiniwek. During halftime, a student dresses up as Chief Illiniwek and dances. Teters considers the chief and the dance sacrilegious and demeaning to Native Americans. The videotape describes the social action taken by Teters to end the tradition, as well as the strong opposition by the board of trustees and alumni who want to maintain a tradition that is deeply beloved by vocal and influential alumni and board members. The people who defend the 70-year-old tradition cannot understand how anyone can find it offensive.

In Whose Honor? helps the students understand how the construction of Indian in US society is controlled by mainstream institutions, including the mainstream media. Through questioning and discussion, I help the students relate Columbus's construction of the Native people of the Caribbean as Indians, Cortés's construction of the Aztecs as savages, Turner's construction of the West as a wilderness, and the selection of Chief Illiniwek as a mascot. We discuss the following questions to uncover ways in which these events are connected (J. A. Banks, 2000):

1. Which groups have the power to define and institutionalise their conceptions within the schools, colleges, and universities?
2. What is the relationship between knowledge and power? Who exercises the most power in this case study?
3. Who benefits from the ways in which Native Americans have been and are often defined in US society? Who loses?
4. How can views of Native Americans be reconstructed in ways that will help empower Native American groups and create more justice in society?

An Unfinished Journey

My project to help teacher education students develop reflective cultural and national identifications is a work in progress that has rewards, challenges, unrealised possibilities, conflicts, and – at times – frustrations for my students and me. My work on global identifications and issues is incomplete and episodic. Each time I teach the course, I feel that I do not have enough time to deal with cultural and national issues. Global issues remain mostly an unrealised and hoped-for goal. Making links when discussing cultural and national issues is the extent to which I deal with global issues in the course.

The class is an unfinished journey for the students and me in several important ways. It is a beginning of what I hope will be a lifelong journey for my students. I realise that one course with a transformative goal can have only a limited influence on the knowledge, beliefs, and values of students who have been exposed to mainstream knowledge and perspectives for most of their prior education. Students are required to take a second multicultural education course in our teacher education program. Also, other members of the teacher education faculty are trying to integrate ethnic, cultural, and racial content into the foundations and methods courses.

My course is also an unfinished journey because I am still trying to figure out how to achieve the delicate balance of showing respect for my students while at the same time encouraging them to challenge seriously their deeply held beliefs, attitudes, values, and knowledge claims. I am also trying to conceptualise effective ways to determine the short-term and long-term effectiveness of the course. The opinions of most of my students when the course ends are encouraging. However, I do not know the relationship between these opinions and the behaviour of the students when they become teachers.

When I taught the class in fall 1999, 21 of 25 students wrote positive and detailed responses to the following question on the University of Washington's standardised course evaluation form: 'Was this class intellectually stimulating? Did it stretch your thinking? Yes, No, Why, or Why not?'

However, I worry about the 4 students in this class of 25 who merely checked Yes in answer to the question and made no further comments. The responses of these 4 students evoke these questions: What are the meanings of their terse responses? In what ways might these 4 students differ from the other students who wrote detailed comments? Do they need a different kind of course and a different set of experiences? How will these 4 students, as well as the other 21 students, view the experience in my course a year after they have been teaching? Will the course make a difference in the ways in which they teach and deal with multicultural content? I was heartened to read in a study reported by Ladson-Billings (1999) that some of the students in a teacher education program who had been 'the most resistant to the program's emphasis on equity and diversity issues feel that it has been most beneficial to them in their teaching' (p. 116).

My observations of my students during this 10-week course, reading of their reflection papers and other papers, listening to their class discussions, having conversations with them, and studying their end-of-class course evaluations indicate that most of my students attain some of the important course objectives. They develop an understanding of how knowledge is constructed, how it relates to power, and how the mainstream metanarrative privileges some groups and marginalises others. They also develop a better understanding of race, culture, and ethnicity and begin the process of questioning some of their assumptions about these concepts. Perhaps most important, most of my students begin to view their own cultural and racial journeys from different and more critical perspectives. I believe that these critical perspectives will help them to develop more reflective cultural, national, and global identifications.

Teachers with the knowledge and skills I teach in my course are better able to interrogate the assumptions of official school knowledge, less likely to be victimised by knowledge that protects hegemony and inequality, and better able to help students acquire the knowledge and skills needed to take citizen action that will make the world more just and humane.

ACKNOWLEDGMENT

Different versions of this article were presented at several conferences as keynote addresses in 2000, including the 44th Annual Meeting of the Comparative and International Education Society San Antonio, Texas, March 8 to 11; the 20th Anniversary Conference of the Intercultural Education Society, Sophia University Tokyo, Japan, May 26 to 28; and the Fifth International Conference of the National Council for the Social Studies, University of Calgary, Canada, June 28 to July 1. I wish to acknowledge the helpful and thoughtful feedback I received from the participants at these conferences. I am grateful to Cherry A. McGee Banks, Geneva Gay, Walter C. Parker (colleagues at the University of Washington), and Marilyn Cochran-Smith for their thoughtful comments on an earlier draft of this article.

REFERENCES

Apple, M.W. (1993). *Official knowledge: Democratic education in a conservative age.* New York: Routledge.

Appleby, J. (1992). Recovering America's historic diversity: Beyond exceptionalism. *Journal of American History, 79*(2), 419–431.

Apter, D.E. (1977). Political life and cultural pluralism. In M.M. Tumin & W. Plotch (Eds.), *Pluralism in a democratic society* (pp. 58–91). New York: Praeger.

Arnove, R.F. (1999). Reframing comparative education: The dialectic of the global and the local. In R.F. Arnove & C.A. Torres (Eds.), *Comparative education: The dialectic of the global and the local* (pp. 1–23). New York: Rowman & Littlefield.

Banks, C.A.M. (1996). Intellectual leadership and African American challenges to metanarratives. In J. A. Banks (Ed.), *Multicultural education, transformative knowledge, and action: Historical and contemporary perspectives* (pp. 46–63). New York: Teachers College Press.

Banks, J.A. (1996). The canon debate, knowledge construction, and multicultural education. In J.A. Banks (Ed.), *Multicultural education, transformative knowledge, and action* (pp. 3–29). New York: Teachers College Press.

Banks, J.A. (1997a). *Educating citizens in a multicultural society.* New York: Teachers College Press.

Banks, J.A. (1997b). *Teaching strategies for ethnic studies* (6th ed.). Boston: Allyn & Bacon.

Banks, J.A. (1998). The lives and values of researchers: Implications for Educating citizens in a multicultural society. *Educational researcher, 27*(7), 4–17.

Banks, J. A. (2000). The social construction of difference and the quest for educational equality. In R. S. Brandt (Ed.), *Education in a new era* (pp. 21–45). Alexandria, VA: Association for Supervision and Curriculum Development.

Banks, J. A. (2001). *Cultural diversity and education: Foundations, curriculum and teaching* (4th ed.). Boston: Allyn & Bacon.

Brodkin, K. (1998). *How Jews became Whitefolks and what that says about race in America.* New Brunswick, NJ: Rutgers University Press.

Cochran-Smith, M. (2000). Blind vision: Unlearning racism in teacher education. *Harvard Educational Review, 72*(2), 157–190.

Diakiw, J. (1994). Growing up Ukrainian in Toronto. In C. E. James & A. Shadd (Eds.), *Talking about difference: Encounters in culture, language and identity* (pp. 49–55). Toronto, Canada: Between the Lines.

Diaz, C. F., Massialas, B. C., & Xanthopoulos, J. A. (1999). *Global perspectives for educators.* Boston: Allyn & Bacon.

Erickson, F. (2001). Culture in society and in educational practices. In J.A. Banks & C.A.M. Banks (Eds.), *Multicultural education: Issues and perspectives* (4th ed., pp. 31–58). New York: John Wiley.

Foner, E. (1998). *The story of American freedom*, New York: Norton.

Freire, P. (1985). *The politics of education: Culture, power, and liberation*. New York: Bergin & Garvey.

Guggenheim, C. (1995). *The shadow of hate: A history of intolerance in America* [Videotape] (Available from: Teaching Tolerance, 400 Washington Avenue, Montgomery AL 36104)

Homans, G.C. (1967). *The nature of social science*. New York: Harcourt Brace.

Howard, G. (1999). *We can't teach what we don't know: White teachers, multiracial schools*. New York: Teachers College Press.

Ignatiev, I. (1995). *How the Irish became White*. New York: Routledge.

Jacobson, M.F. (1998). *Whiteness of a different color: European immigrants and the alchemy of race*. Cambridge, MA: Harvard University Press.

Kammen, M. (1997). *In the past lane: Historical perspectives on American culture*. New York: Oxford University Press.

Kymlicka, W. (1995). *Multicultural citizenship: A liberal theory of minority rights*, New York: Oxford University Press.

Ladson-Billings, G. (1999). Preparing teachers for diversity: Historical perspectives, current trends, and future directions. In L. Darling-Hammond & G. Sykes (Eds.), *Teaching as the learning profession* (pp. 86–123). San Francisco: Jossey-Bass.

Limerick, P. N. (1987). *The legacy of conquest: The unbroken past of the American West*. New York: Norton.

McIntosh, P. (1997). White privilege: Unpacking the invisible knapsack. In V. Cyrus (Ed.), *Experiencing race, class, and gender* (2nd ed., pp. 194–198). Mountain View, CA: Mayfield.

Morrison, T. (1992). *Playing in the dark: Whiteness and the literary imagination*. Cambridge: Harvard University Press.

Nieto, S. (1999). *The light in their eyes: Creating multicultural learning communities*. New York: Teachers College Press.

Okihiro, G. (1994). *Margins and mainstreams: Asians in American history and culture*, Seattle: University of Washington Press.

Omi, M., & Winant, H. (1994). *Racial formation in the United States* (2nd ed). New York: Routledge.

Patterson, O. (1977). *Ethnic chauvinism: The reactionary impulse*. New York: Stein & Day.

Phillips, K. (1990). *The politics of rich and poor*. New York: Random House.

Rosenstein, J. (Writer, Producer, Ed.). (1997). *In whose honor? American Indian mascots in sports* [Videotape] (Available from New Day Films, 22D Hollywood Avenue, Ho-ho-kus, NJ 07423; 888-367-9154)

Schofield, J.W. (2001). The colorblind perspective in school: Causes and consequences. In J.A. Banks & C.A.M. Banks (Eds.), *Multicultural education: Issues and perspectives* (4th ed., pp.327–352). New York: John Wiley.

Turner, F. J. (1894/1989). The significance of the frontier in American history. In C.A. Mimer II (Ed.), *Major problems in the history of the American West* (pp. 2–21). Lexington, MA: Heath.

US Bureau of the Census (1998). *Statistical abstract of the United States*, 118th ed., Washington, DC: Government Printing Office.

James A. Banks
University of Washington, Seattle

STEPHEN J. MCKINNEY

IMMIGRANTS AND RELIGIOUS CONFLICT

Insider Accounts of Italian, Lithuanian and Polish Catholics in Scotland

INTRODUCTION

In the last twenty years there has been an enormous surge of academic interest, research and writing in the history of the post-Reformation Irish Catholic community in Scotland. This history has been examined in a variety of articles and specialist books and has become an important feature of some recent histories of Scotland. The vast majority of writers in this area come from some form of Scottish/Irish Catholic background and represent not only the growth in scholarship in this area, but an upsurge of Catholic scholars and wider acknowledgement in the academy that this is a legitimate area of research. One of the key aspects of this history is the religious sectarianism and hostility encountered by the Catholics of Irish origin. While acknowledging this valuable contribution to research, this chapter focuses on less well-known and less well-researched groups in the history of post-Reformation Catholicism – the Italian, Lithuanian and Polish Catholics – and the comparable experience of sectarianism and hostility encountered by these groups. The examination of these groups leads to a connected discussion of their relationship with the much larger group of Catholics of Irish origin. The chapter will examine the history of these three groups mainly from the writings of authors who belong, in some way, to these groups. The limited number of sources and perspectives, and the nature of these sources, clearly restricts the claims that can be made concerning the histories of these groups, but this chapter strives to raise greater awareness of these histories and sources and encourage further research.

This chapter will begin by examining the nature of the sources of the history of the Irish, Italian, Lithuanian and Polish Catholics and the insider status of the writers and their views. The next section will briefly sketch the history of the sectarianism experienced in post-Reformation Catholicism (initially within the Irish Catholic community). The chapter will then examine each of the groups (the Italians, Lithuanians and Poles), their experience of sectarianism and hostility, and their relation to the wider Catholic community in Scotland. The conclusion briefly compares and contrasts the experiences of these three groups.

M.A. Peters, A. Britton and H. Blee (Eds.), Global Citizenship Education: Philosophy, Theory and Pedagogy, 333–349.

INSIDER STORIES

Contemporary scholarship in Scotland has examined and discussed the arrival of a number of diverse immigrant groups to Scotland between the eighteenth and twentieth centuries: Jews, Asian, Italians, Lithuanians, Poles and Irish. The Irish Catholics constitute the largest single group and the vast majority of Catholics in contemporary Scotland are descended from large-scale Irish Catholic immigration in the nineteenth century. The history and impact of this particular group have been explored in some depth: the arrival of the Irish Catholics and the hostile response of the (sometimes violent) local populace and the Scottish establishment; employment opportunities and the socio-economic progress of the Irish Catholics; bigotry and sectarianism; Catholic schooling; the contemporary relation of the Catholic community and the wider Scottish community; the possible futures for this Catholic community (Bradley, 1995, 1998, 2000; Conroy, 2001, 2002; Devine, 1991, 2006; Boyle and Lynch, 1998; Finn, 1999, 2000, 2003; Gallagher, 1987, 1991; McKinney, 2007).

Many of the writers focussing on these topics belong to, or have some links with, the Scottish Catholic community and represent a variety of approaches to claiming the stake of the Irish Catholics in the socio-economic, cultural, religious and educational history of Scotland in the nineteenth and twentieth centuries. A number of writers, for example, have sought greater public recognition for the importance of the position, if not the pivotal role, of the Irish Catholics in the rapid growth and success of the Industrial Revolution in Scotland (Damer, 1990, p. 52; Devine, 2006, pp. 487–488). Most of these writers present some form of 'insider account', coming from an 'insider source' – someone who writes about a particular group but also identifies, partially or completely, with the aims, objectives and views of that group. Often they are the only people who have the interest and impetus to write about the particular group in any depth – the group may have been treated in a superficial, perfunctory or distorted way in 'official' histories (De Vos, 1995, p. 17).

This impetus is not unique to Scotland:

> We are also witnessing a revolution in the recording of social and cultural history. Today's ethnic minorities are not content to remain mute; they too, seek to be heard. The defeated and the oppressed, now literate, are themselves contributing their interpretations to the writing or rewriting of history, adding their own and, where facts fail, creating or deepening their own sustaining mythologies. (De Vos, 1995, p. 16)

There are dangers, however, that the insider account can lack a critical edge: by failing to have a broader perspective; by being defensive; by exaggerating or even minimizing difficulties encountered by the group; by championing the group or championing factions or certain perspectives within the group. Insider accounts, for example, are more likely to discuss challenges faced by the group, rather than challenges caused by the group. There is a tendency to be less critical when evaluating commonly held assumptions within the group and the views of fellow insiders.

The growth of these 'insider accounts' in Scotland is not confined to the Catholics of Irish descent. The histories of the Jews (Collins, 1987, 1990; Daiches, 1987; Glasser, 1986) and Asians (Maan, 1992) in Scotland are also being recounted. The other Catholic immigrants – Italians, Lithuanians and Poles – have often been referred to in histories of Scotland, or even in discussions of post-Reformation Catholicism, in footnotes or in a cursory way, but their stories are also now being told as Italian (Colpi, 1991, 1993; Pieri, 1997, 2005; Rossi, 1991; Ugolini, 2000), Polish (Ziarski-Kernberg, 2000) and Lithuanian (Miller, 1998; O'Donnell, 1998, 2000) authors provide a fuller account of the origins and development of their immigrant groups, usually based on a more thorough examination of original documentary sources, secondary sources and, increasingly, an analysis of collections of oral histories (the insider status provides ease of access for obtaining oral histories). The history of the Italians, Lithuanians and Poles in Scotland will be examined mainly from insider accounts. These were relatively small groups, but most of their members shared the Catholicism of the Irish Catholic immigrants and all were to experience hostility and vehement sectarianism in Scotland, some of which has only recently been disclosed. A brief overview of sectarianism in Scotland will be given in the next section to provide the context for the discussion of these other Catholic groups.

SECTARIANISM

Jack McConnell, Scotland's First Minister, has borrowed the description of sectarianism as Scotland's 'secret shame' from James MacMillan and has repeatedly used this phrase in the highly publicised efforts of the Scottish Executive to tackle Sectarianism (e.g. *Guardian Unlimited*, 2002; BBC News, 2005). The words 'sectarianism' and 'sectarian', when applied to religion, refer to intra-faith divisions within a variety of faith groups, and recent documentation in Scotland has recognised the scope of contemporary sectarianism in Scotland that includes, for example, the Islamic groups in Scotland (Learning and Teaching Scotland, 2006). Within the scope of this chapter, however, sectarianism will refer exclusively to divisions within Christianity in Scotland, and the term will be used to refer to tension between groups labelled as 'Catholics' and 'Protestants' – an inter-denominational tension that is rooted in complex historical issues of religion, immigration and cultural identity (Finn, 1999, 2003). Agreed definitions, or descriptions, of sectarianism and identification of expressions of sectarian attitudes and activities in Scotland and elsewhere, have often proved to be highly problematic and elusive, e.g. the record of the Scottish Summit on Sectarianism held in 2005 avoids this problem by containing neither a definition nor a description of sectarianism (Scottish Executive, 2005). One of the challenges, then, is to establish an adequate generalisation, or generalised definition, that can be effectively applied to specific instances of sectarianism. Some definitions of sectarianism appear to be too general, focussing on the attitudes prevalent in sectarian activity, but less focussed on the expressions, or manifestations, of sectarianism (Groome, 1998; Bruce *et al*, 2004). A recent definition from Learning and Teaching Scotland appears to be more useful:

> A narrow-minded following of a particular belief by members of a denomination that leads to prejudice, bigotry, discrimination, malice and ill-will towards members, or presumed members, of another denomination. Sectarianism can occur in different ways, either at an individual, group, cultural or institutional level. (Learning and Teaching Scotland, 2006)

This definition identifies the roots of sectarianism, some of the expressions and sociological levels. It does, however, still seem to be too general as it does not provide more concrete examples of how these expressions (prejudice, bigotry, discrimination) are actualised. Perhaps, given the difficulties encountered, it is better to adopt a definition as a 'working' definition – such as the developed and nuanced 'working' definition constructed by Liechty and Clegg for their research into sectarianism in Northern Ireland (2001, pp. 102–103):

> Sectarianism ... a system of attitudes, actions, beliefs and structures, at personal, communal and institutional levels, which always involves religion, and typically involves a negative mixing of religion and politics. (Sectarianism) arises as a distorted expression of positive human needs, especially for belonging, identity and the free expression of difference... and is expressed in destructive patterns of relating: hardening the boundaries between groups; overlooking others; belittling, dehumanising, or demonising others; justifying or collaborating in the domination of others; physically or verbally intimidating or attacking others.

This provides complex psychological and religious root causes of sectarianism. Furthermore, Liechty and Clegg discuss sociological 'levels' of sectarianism (personal, communal and institutional) *and* they provide some examples of these expressions of sectarianism. While acknowledging that this working definition has limitations, not least in the application of a contemporary heuristic tool to historical situations, and, like all working definitions, could be revised, it is proposed that this working definition will be adopted in this chapter.

The origins of sectarianism in Scotland are perceived to be rooted in the arrival of a large number of Irish Catholics in the mid to late nineteenth century. They came to Scotland desperate to escape the devastating effects of the famines and subsequent deprivation and destitution (Collins, 1991, pp. 1–11). They gathered in the industrial cities and towns seeking employment and, at times, competing with the local population for jobs (Devine, 2006, pp. 487–488). They arrived in large numbers and often settled in areas that were already dangerously over-populated, and they arrived in Scotland resenting the British authorities because they did not provide properly organised relief schemes in colonial Ireland (O'Tuathaigh, 1985, p. 21). The Irish Catholic immigrants harboured deep-rooted suspicions that this was the result of a lack of willingness as much as a lack of resources (Foster, 1988, pp. 318–344).

The Irish Catholic immigrants appeared to present a threat to the Presbyterian tradition of Scotland. The Church of Scotland arose as a direct result of the Protestant Reformation in Scotland in the mid sixteenth century, adopting a Calvinist Protestant theology which was more radical than Lutheran theology and more extreme in its rejection of Catholicism (Brown, 2000, pp. 258–259). After the Union of Parliaments of 1707, the Church of Scotland, in the absence of a unique Scottish parliament, had become a strong focus for Scottish identity and was perceived by the Scots and by outsiders as the 'embodiment of Scottishness' (Robbins, 2000, p. 252). The Irish Catholic immigrants, then, appear to have presented an unwelcome and serious challenge to the Church of Scotland, as the established form of reformed Christianity and as the 'embodiment of Scottishness' and symbol of identity (Gallagher, 1991, p. 34).

The incorporation of Catholic schools into the state education system in 1918 – a move not welcomed by all sectors of Scottish society – provided a public and visible focus for sectarianism (Bruce, 1985, pp. 43–44). Another public and visible focus for sectarianism was the large numbers of Irish Catholic (or immediate descendants) employed, almost exclusively, in heavy industry and manufacturing. The depression between the two World Wars was to prove a catalyst for concerted sectarianism as 'foreign' Irish Catholic workers were used as scapegoats for the economic ills besetting society. The racist and sectarian ferment brewed by figures like John White and John Cormack was to be a heady draught – attractive, albeit briefly, to many in Scotland (Brown, 1991; Devine, 2006; Kelly, 2003). Later, in the early 1950's, a Church of Scotland report articulated concerns about the 'menace' of the Catholics of 'alien' origin (Brown, 2000, pp. 272–273). The rise of the ecumenical movement in Scotland in the 1960's, however, brought an end to any explicit sectarian or anti-Catholic discourse in the institutional Church of Scotland (Brown, 2000, pp. 275–281). Some academics now question the extent of sectarianism in contemporary Scotland and suggest that the problem has been exaggerated (Bruce et al, 2004). Nevertheless, sectarianism, or at least sectarian attitude, appears to continue to exist as a feature of contemporary Scottish life within some forms of post-religious/cultural tribalism in Scotland (McKinney, 2007). The above account of the history of sectarianism in Scotland has been frequently recounted and discussed, in different ways, but what is less frequently recounted and discussed is that the Irish Catholics were not the only Catholic group to suffer sectarianism between the eighteenth and twentieth centuries in the history of Scotland. The chapter will now look at brief histories of the Italian, Lithuanian and Polish Catholics in Scotland.

ITALIAN CATHOLICS

The Italians, fleeing poverty caused by increased population and outdated agricultural practices, initially arrived in Scotland in some number between 1870 and 1913 (Colpi, 1993, p. 155). They created employment for themselves in the catering industry: ice cream cafés and fish and chip shops and tended to disperse throughout Scotland. The number grew to around 6,092 in 1927 (Colpi, 1991, pp.

32–33, 74–75). Devine (2006, pp. 515–517) and Maan (1992, pp. 26–28) state that the Italians encountered little hostility between the two world wars as they appeared to present little threat to employment, unlike the Irish, Lithuanian and early Polish Catholics. Crucially, the Italians were not concentrated in any specific areas (Farrell, 1983, p. 15). The insider stories from the Italian community, however, present a more complex picture of the challenges faced by the Italian community in Scotland. Ugolini (2000), a researcher of oral history, states that:

> It has become commonplace to assert that the Italians were well received in Scotland with favourable comparisons made with the other large immigrant groups of the nineteenth and early twentieth century, the Irish and the Lithuanians. Indeed there is a tendency to romanticize the presence of Italians in Scotland and to avoid addressing the more painful reality of how the Italians were treated. (p. 34)

She states that the history of the Italian community in Scotland requires deeper research. She points out, for example, that hostility towards the Italians was not confined to the outbreak of World War II, as suggested by Devine and Maan – hostility and sectarianism arose previously and was intensified in Scotland at the time of the unpopular Italian invasion of Abyssinia in 1935 (Ugolini, 2000, p. 35). Pieri recalls the reaction from some of his customers at the family fish and chip shop in Glasgow:

> The 1930s had been a period of political turmoil in Europe. Italy's invasion of Abyssinia and Mussolini's intervention in the Spanish Civil war had created a wave of ill feeling against Italy in the general population. The childhood taunts of 'dirty wee Tally' had given way to more frequent, forceful and insulting remarks about my nationality from some of the more drunken and belligerent types who made up a good percentage of our night-time clientele. 'Dirty wee Tally' had given way to 'Tally Bastard'. (Pieri, 1997, p. 8)

Pieri also recalls being excluded, like many Italians in Scotland, from golf clubs because he was both Italian and a Catholic (Pieri, 1997, p. 9; 2005, pp. 147–149). This verbal intimidation represents a destructive pattern of relating and the exclusion from the golf clubs, within the description of Liechty and Clegg of sectarianism, represents a form of institutional sectarianism that hardened the boundaries of exclusion for this immigrant group.

Colpi (1991, pp. 85–89, 92–93, 101) points out that during the time between the wars, many Scottish Italians responded positively to Mussolini's attempts to encourage exiles to celebrate their Italian culture. Glasgow became the most important focus for fascism outside London (Colpi, 1993, p. 163). Not all of the Italians in Glasgow or Scotland, however, were in sympathy with the political ideals of fascism and refused to engage in this resurgence of Italian culture prompted by fascism, but the public perception of a widespread association between the Scottish Italians and fascism was to have 'devastating effects' (Colpi, 1991, pp. 102–105; Rossi, 1991, pp. 10–12; Pieri, 2005, pp. 66–68). When Italy declared war on Britain on June 10, 1940, there were riots and demonstrations against Italians throughout Scotland, including the looting of the cafés and shops (Colpi, 1991, pp. 105–108; Pieri, 2005, p. 93). Another consequence of the wartime suspicion of the Italian community was the internment of Italian men aged between 17 and 60. The memoirs of Pieri (1997) and Rossi (1991) provide personal accounts of life in the internment camps and the absurdity of the internment of many harmless Italian civilians from Scotland. Many of the Italian men were transported overseas and, tragically, some Scottish Italians were drowned when the Arandora Star, carrying Italian internees, was torpedoed en route to Canada.

The complexity of the wartime hostility towards the Scottish Italians requires further examination. Pieri (2005, p. 94) and Colpi (1991) suggest that the viciousness of the 1940 riots in Scotland was partly fuelled by anti-Catholicism:

> These anti-Italian riots were particularly widespread and vicious in Scotland due, perhaps, to the religious bigotry prevalent in that society. A long-standing hatred and fear of Catholics could well have been partly responsible for the violence vented on this night. (Colpi, 1991, p. 105)

Although there were mixed motives for this violence, this physical intimidation and attack of others is one of the expressions of sectarianism identified by Liechty and Clegg. This combination of xenophobia and sectarianism (the Italians being recognized as belonging to the wider Catholic group) is, in one sense, ironical because according to Colpi, the Italians often felt estranged from the legalistic and colourless 'Irish' Catholicism which had developed in Scotland – an Irish Catholicism which had culturally formed, led and dominated Post-Reformation Catholicism in Scotland (1991, pp. 240–241). Some Italian priests from England had ministered to the Italians in Scotland in the late 19th and early 20th centuries and a permanent Italian priest was established in Glasgow in 1918. Later in the 1950s to 1970s, monthly Italian Masses were celebrated in Glasgow. There was some discussion about establishing an Italian parish in Glasgow in the late 19th century but a combination of factors prevented the Italians from sustaining any kind of pressure for this initiative: working practices of the Italian community (irregular hours); geographic dispersal; and a rift between the two main Italian groups in Glasgow (dependent upon village of origin). The Irish-dominated Catholic Church in Scotland was reluctant to progress the initiative beyond discussion because it preferred a policy of internal integration (Colpi, 1993, pp. 160–165).

Ugolini (2000, p. 35) states that the treatment of the Italians during World War II appears to have had a profound effect on older Italians. This concurs with the findings of Colpi (1991, pp. 99–101, 195) who states that the deeply wounding effect of the Arandora Star and internment in the Italian community were combined with ambivalence concerning the pre-war support for fascism and distress because Italy lost the war. This has created difficulties for researchers like Ugolini and Colpi, because older Italian people are reluctant to speak about the past, especially the war, not just to oral historians but also to the younger generations of Italians (Ugolini, 2000, p. 34). The hostile and possible sectarian treatment of the Italians and the deep silence in the older generation, both currently being researched, has not, ultimately, prevented the growth and prosperity of the Italian community in Scotland. The Italians re-established themselves in Scotland in the post-war years, although this was partly due to the later influx of Italian immigrants. They continued to work in the catering industry, though some have entered the professions and the public sector. Those who have remained in business, catering or other forms, appear to have retained some form of Italian identity – more so than those who have entered the public sector (Colpi, 1991, pp. 43, 191–199). Some of the Italians, then, continue to exist as an identifiable group and various organizations, such as the Dante Alighieri Society, celebrate the Italian language and culture (Pieri, 2005, pp. 147–149). The appointment of two Catholic bishops of Italian descent in Scotland and the celebration of an annual Mass in Italian in Glasgow's Catholic cathedral (and reception) suggest a greater acknowledgement of the cultural complexity of the Scottish Catholic community. Colpi (1993, pp. 166–167), however, argues that the establishment of an Italian church would have provided an invaluable focus for the Italian Catholics and helped retain a greater sense of identity and community. The Lithuanians, by contrast, were to experience enormous difficulties in trying to preserve any kind of cultural and national identity.

LITHUANIAN CATHOLICS

A small group of Lithuanians (probably numbering about 7,000 in 1914) emigrated from poverty and cultural and religious suppression by the Russians between 1880 and 1914. They settled in Scotland and worked in the mining areas, especially Ayrshire and Lanarkshire, but were, curiously and erroneously, always referred to as 'Poles'. They formed a vibrant and colourful community (Miller, 1998, pp. 4–7, 16–21, 53, 57, 149). Maan (1992, pp. 30–32) acknowledges that the Lithuanians experienced hostility on their arrival, and as they settled in:

> Being of the same faith and the same colour of skin, there were no strong barriers between the Scottish and Lithuanian peoples. (p. 31)

Maan's statement, however, is based on an inadequate understanding of the nature of Christian denominational sectarianism in Scotland and perception of difference in colour as the fundamental basis of racism. In stark contrast, Miller, a member of the Lithuanian community, states that their Catholic faith and foreign origin meant that Lithuanians were often discriminated against:

> Probably the main thing they brought with them was their religion. To the Calvinistic Presbyterian country of Scotland they brought and diligently pursued the Roman Catholic faith. The traditional religious bigotry, particularly in the west of Scotland, meant that there were two reasons why the Lithuanians suffered ostracism and prejudice: a) they were foreigners, and b) they were Catholic. Having suffered almost a century of Russian

persecution this treatment was nothing new to them and they persevered in practicing their faith .... (Miller, 1998, p. 70)

James Keir Hardie, the Socialist leader, often spoke publicly and vehemently against the Lithuanians, perceiving them as a threat to local employment (Reid, 1978, p. 122; Miller, 1998, pp. 23–24). Hardie's antipathy towards the Lithuanians can be contrasted with his 'sympathy' for the aspirations of the Irish Catholics – he even appeared on the platform of an Irish Home Rule Rally in Glasgow on St Patrick's day in 1888 (Handley, 1947, p. 277). The large number of Irish Catholics constituted a large and useful voting constituency unlike the smaller and more vulnerable group of Lithuanian Catholics, though Hardie also viewed the Irish with some suspicion because they too were immigrants (Morgan, 1975, pp. 26–27; Reid, 1978, p. 79). Later, in the economic crisis of the 1930s, when Scottish society sought to blame the continued presence of immigrant workers, however long established, for widespread economic depression, many Lithuanian men changed their names and concealed their ethnic identity to gain employment. This demonising of a small immigrant group (Liechty and Clegg) was partly due to their status as immigrants and partly due to their Catholic religion.

The Lithuanian struggle to gain acceptance in the workplace was mirrored in their struggle to retain their own cultural expression of Catholicism within a predominantly Irish Catholic church (O'Donnell, 1998, 2000; Grace, 2002, pp. 8, 77). O'Donnell, a member of the Lithuanian community, states that the Lithuanians in Scotland received visits from Lithuanian priests based in England in the late 19th century but were anxious to secure their own chaplain. In 1898 it was agreed that a Lithuanian priest, Fr Vincent Warnagaris (the first of a series of Lithuanian priests), would reside in a parish in the Archdiocese of Glasgow under the jurisdiction of the local parish priest and would minister to the widespread Lithuanian settlements (O'Donnell, 1998, pp. 171–175).

The position of Lithuanian priest was funded by the Lithuanians themselves which meant that they paid church dues twice, to maintain the local church and also the Lithuanian chaplain. The priests, however, helped in the retention of a sense of Lithuanian identity – the presence of the priest, fluent in Lithuanian, combined with language classes helped to promote the language. The priests were to the fore in the internal strife with the pro-Marxist Lithuanian groups in Scotland (O'Donnell, 2000, pp. 167–178). The Lithuanians also petitioned for a Lithuanian Church in Bellshill, a request which was refused on a number of grounds: the Lithuanians were small in number and were not perceived as a permanent community; the Archdiocese of Glasgow may have regarded the Lithuanians as a threat to unity (1998, pp. 176–183). O'Donnell suggests that a Lithuanian church would have helped preserve language culture and identity:

... it seems fairly obvious that the institutional Catholic Church in the West of Scotland had little sympathy for the ethnic aspirations and outlook of the Lithuanians.

... The diocesan authorities were willing to allow and assist in organizing a supply of chaplains for the community. However, for reasons that had largely to do with the position of the Catholic Church in Scotland, they were not willing to accept that the community had any need, or right, to have its own church or parish. To the extent that a national Church was perhaps essential to such a small community if its culture was to thrive, it can be argued that the policy of the Glasgow Archdiocese was of key importance in the process of Lithuanian assimilation. (p. 183)

This assimilation was hastened in the inter-war years with the break-up of the traditional mining communities, including Lithuanian communities, and the dispersal to new housing – the relatively small numbers of Lithuanian families found themselves isolated from each other and marriage outside the community became common (Miller, 1998, p. 138). The Lithuanian language, preserved mainly as a 'spoken' language, became obsolete (Boyd, 1983, pp. 32–34). O'Donnell comments:

As Scotland enters the twenty first century, the Lithuanian community, first established here around a century ago, has been largely assimilated into the general Scottish community. (O'Donnell, 2000, p. 185)

Miller, an elderly member of the Lithuanian community, predicted in 1998, that with the passing of his generation, the Lithuanian community and culture in Scotland will disappear (p. 150). As Miller's generation does disappear, this will also be the end of Scottish Lithuanian insider accounts and possibly social historians sufficiently motivated to further examine the history of the Lithuanians in depth. The Poles, especially in Glasgow, have a much higher profile than the remnants of the Lithuanian community, although they face some interesting developments in their continued existence as an identifiable group in Scotland.

POLISH CATHOLICS

Prior to the outbreak of World War II, very few Poles had settled in Scotland, but some Polish Jews had settled in the late nineteenth century and a small number of Polish Catholics worked in the mines in Lanarkshire, alongside the Lithuanians, before World War I (Ziarski-Kernberg, 2000, pp. 17–19, McKinney, 2004, p. 31). Ziarski-Kernberg, a member of the Polish community, points out that these Polish Catholics experienced the same hostility and sectarianism as the Lithuanians:

The opposition to the 'Poles' was not influenced by the national origins of the immigrants. Religion was the issue because most of the 'Poles' were Catholics. Before 1914 anti-Catholicism in Scotland was very strong in the industrialized West, the Lothians, Fife and the Central Belt.

In Lanarkshire...some Protestant Scots regarded the 'Poles' as being very similar to the Irish. As in the case of the Irish, the 'Poles' were resented for being Catholic, for an alleged fondness for drunkenness and violence, and for apparently being willing to serve the mine-owners as cheap, unskilled labour and strike-breakers. (Ziarski-Kernberg, 2000, p. 19)

The Poles were subjected to belittling and demonizing stereotyping of their alleged 'national' and 'religious' characteristics but, despite this and their small number, they gained respect from their fellow workers because of their willingness to join and fully participate in trade unions and union strike activity (pp. 19–22). Another, much larger, influx of Poles into Scotland was to occur at the beginning of World War II and these Poles, at the end of the war, were also to experience sectarianism and hostility.

At the onset of World War II exiled members of the Polish Army were based in Scotland, mainly in Lanarkshire and the Borders (pp. 31–49). By 1945, there were 24,287 Polish servicemen in Scotland (p. 68). After the War the proposed repatriation of the Poles was not as successful as the British Government had hoped. Many Poles did not want to return to life under a communist regime. For some Scots, the continued presence of a large number of Polish troops which was welcome in wartime, became a nuisance, or even a threat, in peace time – there were fears that demobbed and settled Poles would compete for jobs and housing (Ziarski-Kernberg, 2000, pp. 74–75, 111; Sword *et al*, 1989, p. 296).

Some opposed the continued presence of the Poles because they were Catholic. Ziarski-Kernberg cites as an example an anti-Polish demonstration in Edinburgh on 3 June 1946 which was attended by 2,500 people:

The chief organizer of the demonstration was John Cormack, an Edinburgh councillor who was better known as a leader of the Protestant Action Society. His dislike of the Poles was motivated by the fact that the majority of Poles were Catholics. He was also influenced by Communist newspapers, such as 'The Daily Worker' and 'Pravda', which he quoted during the meeting. According to Cormack, the Poles were to blame for the queues and the food shortages, for the economic depression of Scotland, and for the shortage of housing. He accused the majority of Poles of being murderers and rapists. (Ziarski-Kernberg, 2000, p. 120)

This representation of the Polish Catholic immigrant group as a social burden and as an inherently morally depraved people can be interpreted as an attempt to dehumanise the Poles. Cormack had a long history of organizing anti-Catholic demonstrations and disrupting public Catholic meetings. He was particularly successful at gaining public support in the inter-war years (the influence of extremists such as Cormack diminished considerably in the post-war years). In this incident he provides an example of the consistency of his anti-Catholic stance: he was normally opposed to the socialist Labour Party in Scotland, because the majority of Catholics supported it, but was willing to quote communist propaganda to attack the Polish Catholics (Bruce, 1985, pp. 88–106).

In spite of such sectarian and xenophobic outbursts, it became clear by 1947 that the majority of the Poles would remain in Scotland and that they were, in fact, needed for the rebuilding of the industrial base of the Scottish economy (Ziarski-

Kernberg, 2000, p. 123; Sword *et al*, 1989, pp. 256–257). The Poles were employed in a wide variety of trades and professions and were spread throughout Scotland: organised Polish community life flourished in Glasgow and Edinburgh, but also in Falkirk, Dundee, Fife, Kirkcaldy, Dunfermline, Aberdeen and Perth (Ziarski-Kernberg, 2000, pp. 171–181). The Polish Catholic community appears to have developed a good relationship with the Catholic Church in Scotland. Perhaps the trauma of the war years, the post-war rebuilding and the renewed Catholic vision of Vatican II have all contributed to a greater appreciation of pluriformity of religious culture and cultural expression. Currently, the Polish community has a number of Polish Catholic chaplains (Glasgow, Edinburgh and Falkirk) (Sword *et al*, 1989, p. 401).

The Polish community does face some interesting contemporary challenges. Many Poles married Scottish women and this caused difficulties in the continuation of Polish identity and culture (Ziarski-Kernberg, 2000, p. 66; Sword *et al*, 1989, p. 401). Up until recently, the number of 'Polish born' had dramatically decreased and the future of the Polish community and the Polish organizations depended upon the interest and commitment of the second generation of Poles (Ziarski-Kernberg, 2000, pp. 214–216).

INCLUSION IN CONTEMPORARY SCOTLAND

The writers of Irish Catholic descent have staked a claim in Scottish history for their group and have sought to redress some of the recorded historical inaccuracies and imbalance. The writers of Lithuanian, Italian and Polish descent, while much smaller in number, have also staked a claim in Scottish history for their groups and have sought to establish the historical contribution of these groups to Scotland.

The history of the Irish Catholic community in Scotland is scarred by incidences of sectarianism, and, it has been argued, the social progress of the Catholics hindered by anti-Catholic employment practices and often aided by coincidental advantages (Devine, 2006, pp. 498, 652–653; Gallagher, 1987, pp. 252–254; Maver, 1996, p. 281). The three immigrant groups above, as has been seen, also faced sectarianism and hostility at some point in the history of their presence in Scotland and often at times of economic crisis. The development of insider accounts has provided a voice for these immigrant groups and alternative perspectives on Scottish social history from the 19th and 20th centuries. A fuller account of the history of Scotland's 'secret shame' is being exposed.

It has further emerged that the Italians and the Lithuanians did not always have a comfortable relationship with the larger wider Catholic community of Irish descent – an intra-denominational tension that paralleled the inter-denominational tension. The growth of the post-Reformation Catholic community in Scotland in the 19th and early 20th centuries has been dominated by a particular national-cultural form of Catholicism. It is claimed that the 'Irishness' and 'Catholicity' of this larger immigrant group alienated the Scottish population and these identifying features were to be the source of tension and conflict. Arguably, this tension and conflict partly helped to provide the impetus for the self-preservation and maintenance of

Irish Catholics, but possibly precluded the inclusion of other national-cultural forms of Catholicism – a drive for unity and combined critical mass, possibly inevitably, rather than pluriformity of cultural expression, resulting in what could be described as a form of 'cultural imperialism' (expression used by Grace, 2002, p. 7) within post-Reformation Catholicism. O'Donnell and Colpi suggest that this 'cultural imperialism' was probably experienced, at various times, by the Lithuanians and the Italians. The Poles appear to have fared better in more recent times.

The experience of the Poles in the mid to late 20th century may partly be the result of changes of attitude within the Catholic Church in the last fifty years. Catholicism has always described itself as 'universal' (*Catechism of the Catholic Church*, 1999, pp. 831–832), though Groome (1996) suggests that 'inclusive' may be a better, more contemporary, term than 'universal':

> To claim to be the great Catholic tradition of Christianity is rather pretentious. Some Christian communities settle for naming themselves by a central doctrine (Baptists) or after their first mentor (Lutherans), or by their form of government (Presbyterians) and so on. Our claim to be 'Catholic' should confront us with our sins of exclusion and sectarianism and even challenge us to become an inclusive community with hospitality and openness to all. (Groome, 1996, p. 123)

Groome's comments can be applied to inclusion *within* the Scottish Catholic community, which, according to some authors, has not always demonstrated 'universality' or 'inclusion' towards other national-cultural expressions of Catholicism and, in at least one instance, according to members of the Lithuanian community, appears to have contributed to the demise of a national-cultural expression of Catholicism in Scotland. In more recent times this inclusion appears to have been practised.

Further research is required to uncover the extent of the sectarianism and hostility experienced by the Italian, Lithuanian and Polish Catholics in Scotland. The relation of each of these immigrant groups to the Catholic community in Scotland also requires deeper research. As Lithuanian voices emerge, it becomes clear that they will be short-lived and it is probably too late to salvage their cultural heritage in Scotland. The Italian community continues to have a strong presence in Scotland, but the passing of the older generation in the Italian community silences the voices that provided oral stories of the more tragic aspects of Scottish Italian history, preventing the deepening of these revealed stories. The Polish presence in Scotland, still young, and boasting a more positive experience in Scotland, has been increased by the incorporation of Poland in the EU and ease of access to Scotland for employment. The issue will be how incoming Poles configure themselves in relation to the local community, the Polish community and Catholic Church. All of this will be crucial for the continued existence of a distinctive Polish Catholic community in Scotland.

CONCLUDING DISCUSSION

What are the implications of the findings of this research for 21st century Scotland and contemporary concepts of global citizenship? Accounts of these historical experiences of hostility and sectarianism, it has been argued, are only beginning to emerge, and as the Scottish Executive publicly denounces and acts against contemporary racism and sectarianism, there is a pressing need to review, and learn from, the history of these two social evils in Scotland. Although this chapter has focussed on Christian sectarianism, the misunderstanding of Maan must be strongly countered – racism is not necessarily an issue of colour. This is recognised in the *One Scotland* campaign (Scottish Executive, 2007) which states that racism is 'conduct, words or practices which disadvantage or advantage people because of their colour, culture or ethnic origin'. This broader definition of racism is applicable to the findings of this research and this broader definition and understanding will become increasingly important as the number of Polish workers continues to increase in Scotland.

Discrimination against an immigrant group has complex historical, cultural and socio-economic causes and is often related to the national-cultural heritage of the immigrant group, but, as has been seen, can also be explicitly related to the religious affiliation or denomination of the immigrant group. Religion and religious identity are often integral to an immigrant's self-identity and to the self-understanding of an immigrant group – the preservation of a national-cultural heritage often includes a religious dimension. Discrimination towards an immigrant group because of their religious affiliation or denomination, as demonstrated in the working definition of Liechty and Clegg (2001), can be expressed in destructive patterns of relating that impede the possible integration (or assimilation) of the immigrant group. This form of discrimination and destructive patterns of relating would appear to be antithetical to any authentic conception of the aims and outlook of a 21st century global citizen. The conception of a global citizen, as outlined by Oxfam (1997), for example, is the idea of someone who:

- is aware of the wider world and has a sense of their own role as a world citizen
- respects and values diversity
- has an understanding of how the world works economically, politically, socially, culturally, technologically and environmentally
- is outraged by social injustice
- participates in and contributes to the community at a range of levels from local to global
- is willing to act in order to make the world a more equitable and sustainable place
- takes responsibility for their actions.

Although there is no explicit mention of religion or religious identity (nor in Oxfam's *Education for Global Citizenship: A Guide for schools*, 2006) in this frequently-used conception of a global citizen, Oxfam state that this conception is not 'set in stone'. Drawing from the history of sectarianism in Scotland, the aims for the global citizen in contemporary Scotland could be configured thus:

- is aware of the wider world, including the *religious* dimension, and has a sense of their own role as a world citizen
- respects and values diversity, including *religious* diversity
- has an understanding of how the world works economically, politically, socially, culturally, technologically, environmentally, and *religiously*
- is outraged by social injustice, including *sectarianism*
- participates in and contributes to the community at a range of levels from local to global, recognising local and global affiliation to *religion*
- is willing to act in order to make the world a more equitable and sustainable place, including *religious* equality
- takes responsibility for their actions, and does not engage in activity related to social evils such as *sectarianism*.

While this emphasis on awareness and respect for religious diversity may not cohere with some secular political and media agendas, and this re-configuration of the conception of the global citizen could be contested, it is coherent with both the deeper implications of the Scottish Executive's action against racism and sectarianism and with the findings of this research. Importantly, this re-configured conception of the global citizen does not just apply to Christianity and Christian sectarianism, but can, arguably, also be applied to other forms of emerging religious discrimination and sectarianism in contemporary Scotland that relate to the newer immigrants who have arrived in Scotland.

REFERENCES

BBC News (2005). Team bid to tackle Sectarianism. *BBC News website*, January 6, 2005. Retrieved February 14, 2007, from http://news.bbc.co.uk/1/hi/scotland/4150833.stm.

Boyd, J.A. (1983). Lithuanian. In J.D. McClure (Ed.), *Minority languages in central Scotland* (pp. 15–21). Occasional Papers 5. Aberdeen: Association for Scottish Literary Studies.

Boyle, R. and Lynch, P. (Eds.) (1998). *Out of the ghetto?* Edinburgh: John Donald Publishers.

Bradley, J. (1995). *Ethnic and religious identity in modern Scotland*. Aldershot: Avebury.

Bradley, J. (1998). Sport and the contestation of cultural and ethnic identities in Scottish society. *Immigrants and Minorities*, *17*(1), 127–150.

Bradley, J. (2000). Catholic distinctiveness: a need to be different? In T.M. Devine (Ed.), *Scotland's shame* (pp. 159–174). Edinburgh: Mainstream Publishing.

Brown, S.J. (1991). Outside the covenant: The Scottish Presbyterian churches and Irish immigration, 1922–1938. *The Innes Review*, XLII (1), 19–45.

Brown, S.J. (2000). Presbyterians and Catholics in twentieth-century Scotland. In S.J. Brown & G. Newlands (Eds.), *Scottish Christianity in the modern world* (pp. 255–281). Edinburgh: T&T Clark.

Bruce, S. (1985). *No Pope of Rome: Anti-Catholicism in modern Scotland*. Edinburgh: Mainstream.

Bruce, S., Glendinning, T., Paterson, I. & Rosie, M. (2004). *Sectarianism in Scotland*. Edinburgh, Edinburgh University Press.

Catechism of the Catholic Church (1999). London: Geoffrey Chapman.

Collins, B. (1991). The Origins of Irish immigration to Scotland in the nineteenth and twentieth centuries. In T.M. Devine (Ed.), *Irish immigrants and Scottish society in the nineteenth and twentieth Centuries* (pp. 1–18). Edinburgh: John Donald Publishers.

Collins, K.E. (Ed.) (1987). *Aspects of Scottish Jewry*. Glasgow: Glasgow Jewish Representative Council.

Collins, K.E. (1990). *Second city Jewry*. Glasgow: Scottish Jewish Archives.

347

Colpi, T. (1991). *The Italian factor: The Italian community in Great Britain*. Edinburgh: Mainstream.

Colpi, T. (1993). The Scottish Italian community: Senza un campanile? *The Innes Review, XLIV*(2), 153–167.

Conroy, J. (2001). A very Scottish affair: Catholic education and the state. *Oxford Review of Education, 27*(4), 543–558.

Conroy, J. (2002). Catholic education in Scotland. In M.A. Hayes & L. Gearon (Eds.), *Contemporary Catholic education*. Leominster: Gracewing.

Daiches, D. (1987). *Two worlds*. Edinburgh: Canongate Publishing (First published, 1957).

Damer, S. (1990). *Glasgow: Going for a song*. London: Lawrence & Wishart.

Devine, T.M. (Ed.) (1991). *Irish immigrants and Scottish society in the nineteenth and twentieth centuries*. Edinburgh: John Donald Publishers.

Devine, T. M. (2006). *The Scottish nation 1700–2007*. London: Penguin Books.

De Vos, G. (1995). Ethnic pluralism: Conflict and accommodation. In L. Romaucci-Ross & G. De Vos (Eds.), *Ethnic identity: Creation, conflict and accommodation* (pp. 15–47). Walnut Creek: Altamira Press.

Farrell, J. (1983). Italian. In J.D. McClure (Ed.), *Minority languages in central Scotland* (pp. 15–21). Occasional Papers. No 5 Aberdeen: Association for Scottish Literary Studies.

Finn, G.P.T. (1999). Sectarianism. In T.G.K. Bryce & W.M. Humes (Eds.), *Scottish education* (pp. 869–907). Edinburgh: Edinburgh University Press.

Finn, G.P.T. (2000). A culture of prejudice: Promoting pluralism in education. In T.M. Devine (Ed.), *Scotland's shame* (pp. 53–88). Edinburgh: Mainstream Publishing.

Finn, G.P.T. (2003). Sectarianism. In T.G.K. Bryce & W.M. Humes (Eds.), *Scottish education* (pp. 897–907). Edinburgh: Edinburgh University Press.

Foster, R. F. (1988). *Modern Ireland 1600-1972*. London: Allen Lane.

Gallagher, T. (1987). *Glasgow: The uneasy peace*. Manchester: Manchester University Press.

Gallagher, T. (1991). The Catholic Irish in Scotland: In search of identity. In T.M. Devine (Ed.), *Irish immigrants and Scottish society in the nineteenth and twentieth centuries* (pp. 19–43). Edinburgh: John Donald Publishers.

Glasser, R. (1986). *Growing up in the Gorbals*. London: Chatto & Windus.

Grace, G. (2002). *Catholic schools: Mission, markets and morality*. London: Routledge.

Groome, T. (1996). What makes a school Catholic? In T. McLaughlin, J. O'Keefe & B. O'Keeffe (Eds.), *The contemporary Catholic school* (pp. 107–125). Falmer Press: London.

Groome, T. (1998). *Educating for life*. Allen, Texas: Thomas More.

Guardian Unlimited (2002). Scotland clamps down on Sectarianism. *Guardian Unlimited* website, December 5, 2002. Retrieved February 14, 2007, from http://www.guardian.co.uk/print/0,4561695-103602,00.html.

Handley, J.E. (1947). *The Irish in modern Scotland*. Cork: Cork University Press.

Kelly, E. (2003). Challenging sectarianism in Scotland: The prism of racism. *Scottish Affairs, 42*, 32–56.

Learning and Teaching Scotland (2006). *Sectarianism*. Retrieved February 14, 2007, from http://www.ltscotland.org.uk/antisectarian/whatIsSectarianism/aboutsectarianism/index.asp

Liechty, J. and Clegg, C. (2001). *Moving beyond sectarianism*. Dublin: The Columba Press.

Maan, B. (1992). *The new Scots*. Edinburgh: John Donald.

Maver, I. (1996). The Catholic community. In T.M. Devine and R.J. Finlay (Eds.), *Scotland in the twentieth century* (pp. 269–284). Edinburgh: Edinburgh University Press.

McKinney, S.J. (2004). Jewish education and formation in Glasgow: A case study. *Journal of Beliefs and Values, 25*(1), 31–42.

McKinney, S.J. (2007). Symbol or stigma? The place of Catholic schools in Scotland. *The Catalyst* [Commission for Racial Equality]. Retrieved February 14, 2007, from http://www.catalystmagazine.org/Default.aspx.LocID-0hgnew0ox.RefLocID-0hg01b00100k.Lang-EN.html.

Miller, J. (1998). *The Lithuanians in Scotland*. Isle of Colonsay: House of Lochar.

Morgan, K. O. (1975). *Keir Hardie*. London: Weidenfeld and Nicolson.

O'Donnell, E. (1998). 'To keep our fathers' faith ...' Lithuanian immigrant religious aspiration and the policy of west of Scotland Catholic clergy, 1889-1914. *The Innes Review, 49*(2), 168–183.

O'Donnell, E. (2000). Clergy ministering to Lithuanian immigrants in Scotland, 1889-1989. *The Innes Review, 51*(2), 166–187.

O'Tuathaigh, M.A.G. (1985). The Irish in nineteenth century Britain: Problems of integration. In R. Swift and S. Gilley (Eds.), *The Irish in the Victorian city* (pp. 13–36). London: Croom Helm.

Oxfam (1997). *What is global citizenship?* Retrieved February 14, 2007, from http://www.oxfam.org.uk/coolplanet/teachers/globciti/whatis.html.

Oxfam (2006). *Education for global citizenship a guide for schools*. Retrieved February 14, 2007, from http://www.oxfam.org.uk/coolplanet/teachers/globciti/downloads/gcguide06.pdf.

Pieri, J. (1997). *Isle of the displaced*. Glasgow: Neil Wilson.

Pieri, J. (2005). *The Scots-Italians*. Edinburgh: Mercat Press.

Reid, F. (1978). *Keir Hardie*. London: Croom Helm.

Robbins, K. (2000). Establishing disestablishment: Some reflections on Wales and Scotland. In S.J. Brown & G. Newlands (Eds.), *Scottish Christianity in the modern world* (pp. 231–254). Edinburgh: T&T Clark.

Rossi, G. V. Rev. Mgr. (1991). *Memories of 1940*. Glasgow: Glasgow University Department of Italian.

Scottish Executive (2005). *Record of the summit on sectarianism*. Edinburgh: One Scotland, Scottish Executive. Retrieved February 14, 2007, from http://www.scotland.gov.uk/Publications/2005/04/2193329/33313.

Scottish Executive (2007). *One Scotland*. Retrieved February 14, 2007, from http://www.onescotland.com.

Sword, K., Davies, N. and Ciechanowski, J. (1989). *The formation of the Polish community in Great Britain 1939-1950*. London: School of Slavonic and East European Studies.

Ugolini, W. (2000). The Italian Community in Scotland: Insights from Oral History Research. In M. Rose & E. Rossini (Eds.), *Italian Scottish identities and connections* (pp. 31–39). Edinburgh: Italian Cultural Institute.

Ziarski-Kernberg, T. (2000). *The Polish Community in Scotland*. Hove: Caldra House.

Stephen J. McKinney
University of Glasgow

DORET DE RUYTER AND BEN SPIECKER

THE WORLD CITIZEN TRAVELS WITH A DIFFERENT VIEW[1]

INTRODUCTION

'I am urging that we should learn about people in other places, take an interest in their civilizations, their arguments, their errors, their achievements, not because that will bring us agreement, but because it will help us to get used to each other' (Appiah, 2006, p. 78).

The Netherlands is a country in which citizens are able to lead a flourishing life. Most inhabitants are happy, can live the life they prefer and earn a decent income. And although the welfare system of our country is being revised, every citizen receives medical care, the disability allowance is not broken down and children receive appropriate education. Additionally, most people tend to be good citizens. They respect the laws of the liberal democracy: they respect the freedom rights of other citizens and tolerate their conceptions of the good. It is, however, true to say that there is a lot of debate about the decline in the adherence to public norms and values, which particularly focuses on the inappropriate social behaviour of youngsters: a recent report of the scientific counsel for government policy (*WRR*) (2006) showed that there is a growing number of citizens who do not feel attached to the Dutch society and have become somewhat outsiders. These worries are given a lot of media attention which tends to give the impression that the liberal democracy is under threat, but this seems to be an overstatement due to the one-sidedness of the coverage; most inhabitants are decent citizens.

The fact that the Dutch tend to be good citizens of their nation state, does not mean, however, that they are good global citizens too. It is even fair to question if they are good European citizens. One of the main reasons that this question arises is that the majority voted against the constitution of the European Union in 2005. Although it would be simplistic to conclude that the people who voted 'no' do not consider themselves as European citizens (for there were various reasons for people to oppose to the constitution) many did believe that it would not be beneficial to them to be subjected to a European constitution instead of a Dutch one. In other words, they preferred to remain Dutch citizens instead of becoming European subjects. This evaluation is, however, based on a strict conceptualisation of 'citizen', namely as being a person who is a subject of a government and an inhabitant of a particular nation or conglomerate of nations. Whether or not this conceptualisation is to be preferred, is one of the topics of our contribution.

M.A. Peters, A. Britton and H. Blee (Eds.), Global Citizenship Education: Philosophy, Theory and Pedagogy, 351–363.

We begin with an exploration of the conceptual differences between the notions of citizen and world citizen. The former, in our view, primarily refers to the social-political domain, whereas the latter primarily has a social-cultural content and is often used in a metaphorical sense. A person can be a proper Dutch citizen but not qualify as a European or world citizen when she fully misses the knowledge and understanding of the many different cultures and traditions. Although citizen and world citizen can be conceived as two different concepts, it is also possible to perceive these two concepts as two stages in the development of citizens, namely minimal and maximal citizenship, which together form a one-layered concept. This will be further explored in the third section. The fourth section focuses on one of the characteristics of a world citizen, namely being culturally competent. In the fifth section we describe education towards national citizenship in a genre-rich culture and education for world citizenship, to conclude that there need not be as many differences between being a citizen of a nation state and being a citizen of the world as authors like Nussbaum seem to have suggested, which means that educating children to become good citizens of a genre-rich liberal democracy could be sufficient for their education towards world citizenship.

CONCEPTUAL CLARIFICATION

We do not have to give an extensive account of the meaning of 'citizen' as used in our daily language. The *Oxford English Dictionary* gives two entries that concisely describe its meaning as "An inhabitant of a city or (often) of a town; esp. one possessing civic rights and privileges, a burgess or freeman of a city" and "A member of a state, an enfranchised inhabitant of a country, as opposed to an alien". Both descriptions demonstrate that the notion of citizenship refers to the social-political domain, where persons are being perceived in terms of their relation to a state or nation. Moreover, they are being identified as belonging to a particular state or nation, which allows them to think of others as strangers or aliens. Interestingly, this seems to rule out the idea of world citizen, unless one assumes the existence of extraterrestrial aliens. Of course, one might argue that the conception of citizenship that draws upon the distinction between the insider and outsider or the familiar and the alien is archaic as well as politically dubious and that this does not diminish the possibility of using the concept of world citizen (see for instance Nussbaum, 1997). In our view, however, the concept of world citizen cannot be fully grasped within the social-political domain, but needs to be conceived primarily in social-cultural terms. While being a citizen of a nation or a federation of states draws upon a political language game, this does not seem to be the most appropriate one for world citizenship. There is a different type of identification required for a world citizen than of soil, a state, the law, and fellow inhabitants.

World citizens are persons who are able to identify with cultural expressions and fellow human beings (note the change in terms: from inhabitant to human being). In order to be called a world citizen, it is necessary that one adheres to public rules in a minimally moral sense (not to kill or steal) and in a political sense: one has to respect the rights of other people to live according to their own world view or culture, unless their way of life inhibits the rights of others to do the same, but it is also necessary for one to have an interest in and understanding of cultures as well. On the other hand, a world citizen is not merely a world traveler or an enthusiastic reader who cherishes the acquaintance with other cultures for her own interests, entertainment or development only, because she does not necessarily have the political capacities required of world citizens. Our conceptualisation corresponds with the two strands that Appiah believes to intertwine in the notion of cosmopolitanism. 'One is the idea that we have obligations to others, obligations that stretch beyond those to whom we are related by the ties of kith and kind, or even the more formal ties of a shared citizenship. The other is that we take seriously the value not just of human life but of particular human lives, which means taking an interest in the *practices and beliefs* that lend them significance' (2006, p. xv; italics by authors).

Although 'citizen' and 'world citizen' can be conceived as two different concepts, it is also possible to perceive them as two stages in the development of world citizens, namely minimal and maximal citizenship.

A MINIMAL AND MAXIMAL SENSE OF CITIZENSHIP

Being a citizen in the minimal sense means that a person is able to speak and read the dominant language, has the disposition to abide by the law and has moral, political and social knowledge. Although this level is sufficient for being a citizen and maybe characteristic for most inhabitants of a nation state, it is not a level that persons – or educators – should aspire towards. After all, a citizen in the minimal sense is equipped to participate in a nation's labour market or the nation's economy, but does not necessarily have an interest in or contribution to the cultural dimension of the nation state. And this, in our view, is precisely the distinction between the minimal and maximal sense of citizenship. Being a citizen in the maximal sense does not only differ from minimal citizenship in the level of the aspects mentioned, but also in a qualitative respect: a citizen in the maximal sense is someone who is culturally competent too. Our main focus will be on this last criterion, for only if a person is a citizen in the maximal sense, can she be a world citizen. In our view many liberal conceptions of citizenship are too confined. These conceptions of citizenship are not necessarily minimal or easily achieved, but they tend to overlook the necessary condition of cultural competence. Therefore, we may question if the educational aims of civic education are too limited. Reference to the French tradition of the distinction between *citoyen* and bourgeois may be somewhat helpful here. The citizen as bourgeois conceives herself as a client of the state, that is, a person who makes use of the provisions of the state for the benefit of herself only. The citizen as *citoyen* on the other hand is a person who actively engages in discussions about the arrangements for a well-ordered society; the latter activities presuppose that this person is well-versed in the social and cultural traditions of her country.

In Western liberal democracies and in some political philosophical views, the freedom of the individual tends to be presented as being not only the central but also the most important principle of liberalism. Being a citizen of a liberal democracy in this sense means being free from tyrannical powers of the state and other institutions (state-related or not). Popular interpretations may even lead to the legitimization of the freedom to satisfy all kinds of needs and ultimately to a self-serving or egocentric attitude. It is not surprising that this leads to a common criticism of the liberal conception of the citizen: this person does not sufficiently take into account the interests of others and develops a superficial attitude of consumerism. This is, however, a one-sided interpretation or caricature of the views of one of the main founding-fathers of liberalism, J.S. Mill. According to Skorupski (2006), Mill stresses also, or primarily, the development of artistic, intellectual and idealistic motives and aims of the citizen. His view of education is that of a balanced development of all faculties. In this respect Mill might have been influenced by 'Germano-Coleridgean' ideas (Skorupski, 2006, p. 27). According to this conception of citizenship, a citizen is also a culturally and intellectually well-developed person who contributes to the cultural enlightenment of a nation, to phrase it in rather grandiose terms. Equally, a culturally rich nation makes possible the development of the cultural abilities of a citizen, which in a totalitarian society is clearly much more difficult because of the ban on other cultural or religious expressions. Afghanistan under the Islamic fundamentalist Taliban or Mao's communist cultural revolution are but two examples that illustrate this point. This conception is obviously diametrically opposed to the current view that liberalism would lead to value neutralism. It also has consequences for conceptions of civic education in which there is one-sided attention for the fostering of civic virtues. We will return to this issue in the next section. One issue needs to be mentioned before we come to that.

In Western Europe, liberal politics have developed out of the wish to leave behind the bloody wars on religion. The focus on differences in religions has contributed to the fact that there is a narrowing of vision towards other domains of life, most particularly cultural diversity and the diversity of genres within the cultural domain. This narrowing of vision to the religious domain still dominates contemporary Dutch discussions on diversity. For instance, there is an ongoing debate about Article 23 of the Dutch constitution that protects freedom of schooling. Parents have the constitutional right to send their children to a school that has the same religious identity as they wish to pass on to the children themselves. And the discussion focuses on the question of whether or not religiously based schools are a threat to the cohesion of society. This is at least an impoverishment and one-sided vision on the cultural richness of our society. For, understanding and tolerance of the religion of others can flourish only within a wider cultural framework. The government of The Netherlands seems to confine itself to ensuring the freedom of religion, whilst the duty to enlighten citizens in a wider societal and cultural sense is neglected on the basis of her acclaimed neutrality. The embarrassment felt by some cultural minorities about their marginal position, which is visible in relatively low levels of participation in societal and cultural life, finds an outlet by stressing original religious roots, which can lead to the radicalisation of apparently integrated minorities. This does not enhance the understanding of the differences between ethno-cultural communities and leads to a one-sided focus on religious difference. Thus, we concur with Sen's claim that it is a mistake and ethically wrong to equate people with only one part or aspect of their identity. In *Identity and Violence*, Sen (2006) argues that one of the major mistakes in the current political debate is that people are thought to have a singular identity, which is tied up with their religion or their culture. In his view, people's identity consists of a variety of aspects, for instance their gender, social roles, personal characteristics and their membership of diverse communities. This means that it is impossible to assume that people of a religious community are similar. Although they share a religion that is very important to them, their identities tend to be highly diverse, because they identify with other aspects, including the cultures of the communities they belong to, too.

CULTURAL COMPETENCY

We already stated that a citizen in the maximal sense is also a person who contributes to the civilisation of the society in which she lives. She is not only active in the political domain, in other words she does not only foster civility, she often also actively plays a modest part in the cultural flourishing of the society. For instance, parents will introduce their children to diverse cultural expressions and try to enthuse their children to learn as much about them as possible. In other words, parents assist their children to become culturally competent.

A culturally competent person has cultural knowledge about cultural artefacts and cultural practice as well as the disposition to value them on their own merits. Cultures generate different forms of cultural artefacts and practices, like music, literature, scientific and technological findings, and visual art, as well as different kinds of social practices, like the ways in which children are being raised, ways in which adults interact and what is deemed appropriate in dressing, eating, etc. These cultural and social practices can be distinguished further into genres. This idea has been eloquently developed by the philosopher Joseph Raz.

Joseph Raz defends a social dependence thesis, which consists of two theses: 'The special social dependence thesis claims that some values exist only if there are (or were) social practices sustaining them. The (general) social dependence thesis claims that, with some exceptions, all values depend on social practices either by being subject to the special thesis or through their dependence on values that are subject to the special thesis' (2003, p. 19). According to Raz, values exist where there is a practice that sustains those values, even though people may not be aware that their acting is based on the values that underlie the practice. The way in which Raz perceives of the relation between value and practice is, on the one hand, in terms of a necessary relation, i.e. a value will only come into existence within a social practice, but on the other hand, seemingly contingent, as he claims that values are not dependent on the original practice to remain of value; practices are necessary for the origin of values, but not for their continuity. Practices can change without the values necessarily disappearing. This means that Raz's theory is not a form of social relativism, because the values are only dependent on social practices for coming into existence, not for their recognition afterwards or by others. Neither is his theory conventional, he claims, because a practice is not the reason for the value of the value: it is the reason for its existence. Although there may be disagreement about the ways in which standards or concepts are interpreted, such disagreements affirm the objectivity of values, according to Raz, for 'the disagreements are contained within a framework of shared views' (2003, p. 51).

The special dependence thesis seems to apply primarily to cultural values, 'because sustaining practices are a necessary condition for it to be possible for these values to be instantiated, and the possibility of instantiation is a condition for the existence of values' (Raz, 2003, p. 33). There are four classes of values whose instantiation do not depend on a sustaining practice, namely (a) pure sensual and perceptual pleasure; (b) aesthetic values of natural phenomena; (c) many enabling and facilitating values like freedom or justice, and (d) the value of people, and of other valuers who are valuable in themselves. The last two categories, however, can be related to the special dependence thesis via the general dependence thesis: they only have a point or are of value if they enable people to value the socially dependent values. The value of these values is therefore, at least partly, dependent on the social dependence thesis.

The social dependence thesis leads to value pluralism, i.e. that there are many distinct values and there are incompatible values, but not to relativism. The ground for saying that an action or object is good is relative to a particular genre, but this verdict is unrestricted, i.e. it is absolute. This resonates with Mill's liberal elitism that 'recognises the objectivity and hierarchy of values, the vital distance between great, good and bad, ...' (Skorupski, 2006, p. 55). A piece of art, but also social arrangements, can be judged with criteria that belong to their genre. For instance, we can argue that a restaurant with three Michelin stars is a good restaurant, because of the distinguished cuisine, but we can also say that a fast food restaurant that serves a good meal quickly is good. Both are good, but on the basis of the criteria that belong to different genres. This allows us to say without contradiction that works of art or social arrangements that are completely different are both good.

It is possible to think of genres at different levels of generality: a genre could be paintings, sculptures, buildings (or churches, palaces, utility buildings, etc.), music or literature, but one could also think of genres at a more specific level. Paintings could, for instance, be divided into the genres of medieval, baroque, manierism, impressionism, expressionism, minimal art, etc. For each genre there are different criteria. Whilst Michelangelo is considered to be one of the best examples of the manieristic style or genre, the paintings of Van Gogh are deemed to be of excellent quality within impressionism. The level at which the term 'genre' is applied, should in our view be based on pragmatic grounds. It depends on the variety of coherent groups of practices that are sufficiently distinct from others within a relatively general genre, as to whether or not it is sensible to think of genres at a more specific level. In the rest of this chapter, different levels of generality will therefore be used next to each other.

Although it is not possible to compare the value of genres to each other and for instance claim that the best in opera is better than the best in pop music, it is possible to make absolute claims about quality within genres on the basis of the criteria that define the genre. Thus, one is not a cultural relativist, if within the genres one believes one's judgement to be non-relative. In our view, a world citizen is able to recognise a great variety and differing levels of genres and make a judgement about an artefact or practice in relation to the genre, and is able to discuss her judgement with other world citizens. For instance, knowing the work of Shakespeare, which does not necessarily require having read all his plays and sonnets, means that one is also able to appreciate the way in which his work has been used in other cultural artefacts in other cultures, like operas of Verdi (e.g. Macbeth, Otello or Falstaff or movies of Kurusawa (e.g. Ran and Throne of Blood). As Appiah claims: 'Because you respond, with the instinct of a cosmopolitan, to the value of elegance of verbal expression, you take pleasure in Akan proverbs, Oscar Wilde's plays, Basho's haiku verses, Nietzsche's philosophy. Your respect for wit doesn't just lead you to these works: it shapes how you respond to them' (Appiah, 2006, p. 26). Another, more contentious example, is that a world citizen is able to compare the way in which women are being displayed, willingly, for the erotic pleasure of others in Playboy, to the way in which Geisha's work for the sensuous pleasures of men. Both are not involved in a sexual act with the observer who watches them with the intention of being sensuously aroused. But obviously, in the case of a Geisha this is taken at a completely different level: the purpose of her company does not consist of a sexual dimension only. Her task is to satisfy diverse appetites of men, among which their aesthetic desires and sense of self-esteem. This also explains why a centrefold or playmate of the month does not need to have any specific (cultural) knowledge or capacities and therefore does not require any training, whereas the education of a Geisha is a long-term process covering a vast amount of knowledge and competencies, ranging from performing a tea ceremony to being able to play instruments and converse about a variety of subjects. This also explains why a Geisha is a good example of a cultural practice in which women work to please men and featuring in Playboy is not, although some, including feminists and orthodox believers, would argue that such a practice is ethically wrong per se.

It is important to note that cultural and social practices are not static. We agree with Appiah (2006) that it would be, in our terms, naively romantic to presume that there are pure or traditional cultures uninfluenced by other traditions or to put it in normative terms that it is a bad thing that cultures influence each other. However, we do believe it is possible to suggest that world citizens will appreciate the good examples within the genres and will contribute to the continued existence of those practices. This may be a potential power against the consumer market forces that flood the world with their products. Although we would not go so far as to suggest that the opening of a McDonald's near the Chinese wall is a blemish on Chinese culture[2], we do think that the attitude of those Western Europeans and Americans to go out of their way to find a hamburger in a Chinese city is not characteristic for a world citizen. That such an attitude may be found amongst philosophers of education too, may be illustrated by our experience in Nanjing where some delegates at a conference on global citizenship moved heaven and earth to have a full English breakfast or ventured out in the early morning into the city to visit McDonald's or KFC instead of eating the well prepared rice, noodles and soup.

Another misunderstanding that may have arisen from our account is that a world citizen uncritically accepts and values all cultural and social practices per se. Of course, our proposal of genres and the possibility of evaluating practices within the genres does already suggest otherwise, but we want to expand on this a bit further. A world citizen is firstly able to determine to which genre a practice belongs, in other words he is able to apply the standards that characterise the genres. For instance, he would know the difference between an arranged and freely encountered marriage. Secondly, he is able to compare the practice he encounters to the standards of quality of the genre. For instance, if the son believes that his mother knows best with whom he can marry, the practice of an arranged marriage can be called good. If he would feel trapped or forced into a particular arrangement he believes to be wrong, the practice cannot be interpreted as a good example of the genre. To be able to do that it is paramount that he understands the practice well. This means that he will apply diverse criteria, because practices serve different aims. For example, an Indonesian Wajang play can be valued because of its aesthetic worth, for instance that the show was well performed and was a treat to the eye, but also has to be evaluated in terms of its authentic expression of the religious and ethical values that underlie the play. A play performed in a Western hotel, purely for the aesthetic pleasure of the tourists would be a worse example than one that was performed for the sake of itself. Thirdly, a world citizen will also evaluate the practice she encounters from an ethical perspective. World citizens are able to appreciate cultural artefacts for their aesthetic value or rites of passage for their social value, but can at the same time disvalue the accompanying cultural practices or can appreciate the aesthetic values of artefacts but be highly critical of current political and moral circumstances. For instance, one can be in awe of the beauty and grandeur of Maya temples while at the same time being abhorred by the practice of offering people to the gods that occurred within the temples. Equally, while there may be good reasons for valuing the practice of hunting by tribes who live on the animals they have caught, it would be much more difficult to value this practice by otherwise noble men and women who hunt after purpose-bred animals for the sake of pleasure. The ethical evaluation of a world citizen is related to the other characteristic we mentioned earlier: her civility. World citizens are both able to evaluate a practice in terms of its genre and to criticise it on the basis of her ethical or moral intuitions.

The ethical evaluation of an artefact or practice the world citizen encounters can take a twofold character. Firstly, she can evaluate the ethical quality of them, if they belong to a genre that has ethical standards as well. Secondly, the (historical) artefacts and practices are set within an existing societal configuration as well. It would, in our view, be a one-sided depiction if world citizens were characterised primarily in terms of their ability to adapt themselves to living around the globe (for instance Nussbaum, 1997). Although it is a necessary condition for world citizenship to be able to live outside her own country, she is not a cultural or moral relativist. Therefore, we would dare to claim that world citizens would not be able to live in countries – unless as an activist – in which human lives are being threatened. Proponents of economic globalisation tend to overlook precisely this point.

CITIZENSHIP AND (CIVIC) EDUCATION IN A GENRE-RICH LIBERAL DEMOCRATIC NATION

In the former sections we have described a world citizen as a person who not only has political capacities and dispositions, but also aims to understand cultural practices in all their dimensions and who is able to evaluate these on the basis of the standards of the genre as well as her moral intuitions, which again are related to her political qualities. We suggested perceiving of world citizenship as a maximal level of citizenship to which adults themselves as well as educators should aspire. In this section we will address only three of the questions that might be asked, but we believe them to be the central ones. The first question is whether or not children need to encounter the cultures, have to know, have read or have seen the good and diverse practices of the genres in order to become world citizens. Secondly, we are interested in the curricular implications, and thirdly we want to take a closer look at the demands on the teachers.

With regard to the first question, we believe it is not necessary that one experience all the genres before one is able to apply the standards to a new practice one encounters. Of course, in order to be able to make a balanced evaluation, one has to have an understanding of the background to the practice; one cannot simply apply the standards, although it is fair to say that the more culturally literate one becomes, the easier it is to do so. It is, however, necessary to encounter a diversity of genres, for being raised within a singular cultural practice, would mean that one would have grave difficulty in understanding the concept of genre. Thus, in order to become a world citizen one needs to live in a genre-rich society. Living in a genre-rich society, however, is not sufficient; one has to be an active participant. For this, one needs to be introduced into the practices. Parents and teachers need to lead children into diverse cultural genres. For instance, although China is a genre-rich culture, most Chinese are not well-educated and therefore it is virtually impossible for them to become world citizens. This argument also regards fundamentalist parents, who wish to ensure that their children become unquestioningly abiding adherents of the religion of the parents (see for instance De Ruyter, 2001; Spiecker, De Ruyter & Steutel, 2006). Although the children grow up in a genre-rich environment, parents aim to prevent their children from encountering other cultures. Spinner-Halev (2000) may be right in claiming that the influence of mainstream culture is unavoidable and that children will necessarily be affected, but this is actively undermined by the parents: children are not invited to explore the cultural artefacts and practices in order to discover their worth, but they are taught that these artefacts and practices are untrue or unworthy. All practices are laid on the Procrustean bed of the holy book of the respective religions and evaluated by that single standard. Fundamentalist education is therefore incompatible with education for world citizenship.

Of course, the media, most particularly the internet has drastically changed the accessibility of cultures and thereby the possibility of becoming a world citizen. Although one has to have an understanding of the concept of cultural genres, what has substantially changed is that one does not have to travel to learn about other cultures in the world. Thus, we might say that it has become easier to develop into a world citizen, since accessing the world is possible from your home. Has this also increased the necessity or importance of becoming a world citizen? We think it has, because one needs to be able to truly appreciate what one sees or hears. The internet may have a facilitative role in developing world citizens, but like the hedonistic world traveller it is not sufficient. Also, for the internet to have true value to a person and present more than interesting but ill-understood artefacts, etc., one needs to have an understanding of the genres.

Education into a genre-rich culture is not sufficient for world citizenship, because it is crucial for being a world citizen that one respects the rights of others and evaluate the political, social and moral qualities of societies. Citizens in liberal democracies are, or more precisely should be, taught to do so. Civic education in liberal democracies comprises learning the liberal democratic virtues regarding other citizens, which are obviously not confined to citizens within a particular nation state, as well as the capacities and disposition to be critical about the government, political parties and organisations of the civil society, which are clearly generalisable to other nations as well.

With regard to the second question, our suggestion is that there are two consequences for the curriculum: civilization and civility should be part of the curriculum. Although in most western liberal democracies, the study of history and culture has been part of the curriculum of primary and secondary schools, these have been trimmed down quite substantially. It might even be correct to talk about the cultural deficit of education.

It is important to note that we do not argue that it is a duty of citizens to become world citizens or citizens in the maximal sense. Some citizens do not have any desire to become world citizens and do not need to, because their scope is relatively limited. There will also be citizens who are unable to become citizens in the maximal sense, for it requires both intellectual and aesthetic capacities and dispositions that not everyone will be able to develop to the level required. We do suggest that all citizens have a right to develop into a world citizen and that therefore the government has the duty to provide an education that enables children and youngsters to do so.

The discussion about the curricular implications of civic education seems to focus primarily on the capacities and dispositions citizens need in order to maintain or contribute to the flourishing of the system of a liberal democracy. It is argued that children need to learn what it means to be a member of a democracy, for instance that they have to be able to vote on the basis of a critical evaluation of programmes of political parties, and what the implications are of living in a liberal state – for instance that they have to respect the rights of their fellow citizens and tolerate their views and opinions. This side of civic education is necessary, but not sufficient for world citizenship as we have argued in the preceeding sections. These characteristics are sufficient for the minimal level of citizenship, but not for the maximal level of a world citizen and we might even question if these characteristics are sufficient for being a citizen in a genre-rich liberal democracy. Since most liberal democracies are pluralistic or multicultural, we suggest that the flourishing of the cultures within society requires an active interest of citizens in each other's culture.

There is a discussion about the content of culture in the curriculum too. In The Netherlands this focuses on what should belong to the Canon, i.e. what every child should know about the history of the civilization of our country. Interestingly, however, although teaching children about the Canon is perceived as being part of civic education, the content consists primarily of the perceived important aspects of the history of Dutch culture. Therefore, the Canon assists children to become knowledgeable Dutch citizens, but not ones of the pluralistic society which the Netherlands nowadays is. Part of the one-sidedness may be explained by the perceived threat of losing what is deemed to be the Dutch identity. With the influx of immigrants and in reaction to the celebration of multiculturalism as well as the enlargement of the European Union, many citizens – not only the right-wing 'Blut und Boden' adherents – were anxious to restore in Dutch children an attachment to their own history and culture. Various objections can be made: for instance the one we already mentioned that there are no cultures that have not been influenced by other cultures and that therefore to understand one culture, one has to have knowledge of the others as well. Our main objection, however, is that the induction of children into a Dutch Canon is not conducive to their development into world citizens and that therefore the Dutch government does not meet her duty to assist children in this respect. Our objection is not that this education addresses a singular culture, because the Dutch culture consists of diverse genres, but that it lacks attention to cultures that seemingly have not had an influence on Dutch religion, literature, rituals, etc. And these cultures are also present in our current society, most notably the Islamic cultures. While educating children into the genre-rich society the Netherlands nowadays is – which would be sufficient for their education towards world citizenship – a confinement to the important Dutch achievements diminishes this possibility. Our suggestion would therefore be to widen the Canon to the world. Of course, it is impossible to learn everything in school or even in one's entire life, so our suggestion should be interpreted realistically: children need to learn to understand different genres when they meet them; they do not have to know them all.

Thus, culture should be part of the curriculum and this should be in terms of a wide variety of genres. We suggest that it should not only be interpreted in terms of introducing literature from various genres, like poems, novels, scientific literature and from different cultures, but also in terms of exploring artefacts, religious practices, scientific inventions, rites and rituals.

The final question we want to address concerns the qualities of the teacher. Do teachers have to be world citizens themselves? This may seem to be too demanding, but we suggest that this is not the case. Teachers need to be civil, i.e. have the disposition and capacity to be citizens of a liberal democracy, and they need to be civilised: they need to have an interest in cultural practices and artefacts and need to be able to understand and evaluate these. This is also something teachers learn throughout their careers. Because they have to teach the genres they will become better interpreters of the genres. It also implies that Teacher Education should address the cultivation of cultural literacy; the tendency both in The Netherlands and in the UK to structure Teacher Education around competencies, which unfortunately do not seem to encompass the extensive cultural competencies we suggest they should have, gives rise to doubt that student teachers are currently sufficiently equipped to be called world citizens themselves.

CONCLUSION

We conclude that educating children to become citizens of a liberal democratic nation that is culturally genre-rich is sufficient for assisting them to become citizens of the world, although educators may wish to widen the scope of the cultural baggage they offer children. We believe that if children are inducted into diverse genres they will want to become world citizens, because they will want to know as much as they can about cultural artefacts and practices.

Raising the standards of education for world citizenship is important for all children because it is a way of showing respect for people and their cultural artefacts and practices, but it may be particularly significant for children of cultural minorities, who in the Netherlands are immigrant families. Firstly, these children may feel that their culture is taken more seriously. Secondly, children whose parents are culturally illiterate are not given sufficient opportunity to develop the capacities and dispositions of world citizenship. These are not stimulated by the parents, because they lack these capacities themselves and because they tend to orient themselves towards their country of origin, for instance by watching the Arabic TV channels via a satellite dish. These channels are in some cases subsidized by radical Islamic movements or groups, which means that children are prone to learn one interpretation of genres only, namely the one based on the religious world view. This may have the effect that youngsters retreat into their own culture and only take seriously the ideas of their own leaders.

This view on the importance of education for world citizenship also shows that it is not only valuable for Western citizens who, confronted with globalisation, need to be able to interact and trade with people from around the world, but also for immigrants into Western liberal democracies. Children of immigrants will feel that their culture is taken seriously and they will profit from world citizenship education in becoming culturally literate. This sheds another light on the importance of education for world citizenship.

NOTES

[1] This paraphrases Richard Peters' view that 'to be educated is not to have arrived at a destination; it is to travel with a different view' (1965, p. 110).

[2] That the consumer market may have destructive consequences for people living in other cultures is not the subject of this paper, although the following quote from Larson does stick: 'Youth lose their rich cultural heritage and the systems of meanings, support, and social control that were part of traditional society, typically getting little in return, except poverty and unrealizable hopes of material achievement' (Larson, 2002, p. 13). However, he immediately reassures us by adding that in his own experience adopting a material lifestyle does not necessarily imply that youngsters change their core values and beliefs.

REFERENCES

Appiah, K.A. (2006). *Cosmopolitanism: Ethics in a world of strangers.* London: W.W. Norton.

De Ruyter, D.J. (2001). Fundamentalist education: A critical analysis. *Religious Education, 96*(2), 193–210.

Larson, R.W. (2002). Globalization, societal change, and new technologies: What they mean for the future of adolescence. *Journal of Research on Adolescence, 12*(1), 1–30.

Nussbaum, M. (1997). *Cultivating humanity: A classical defense of reform in liberal education.* Cambridge, MA.: Harvard University Press.

Peters, R.S., (1965). Education as initiation. In Archambault (Ed.), *Philosophical analysis and education.* London: Routledge & Kegan Paul.

Raz, J. (2003). *The practice of value.* Oxford: Oxford University Press.

Sen, A. (2006). *Identity and violence. The illusion of destiny.* London: W.W. Norton.

Spiecker, B., de Ruyter, D.J. & Steutel, J.W. (2006). Taking the right to exit seriously. *Theory and Research in Education,* 4(3), 313–327.

Skorupski, J. (2006). *Why read Mill today?* London: Routledge.

Spinner-Halev, J. (2000). *Surviving diversity: Religion and democratic citizenship.* Baltimore: The John Hopkins University Press.

Van der Donk, W.B.H.J., Jonkers, A.P., Konjee, G.J. & Plum, R.J.J.M. (Eds.) *Geloven in het publieke Domein. Verkenningen van een dubbele transformatie.* Amsterdam: Amsterdam University Press.

Doret de Ruyter and Ben Spiecker
Vrije Universiteit Amsterdam

FRANCIS J. O'HAGAN

ROBERT OWEN AND THE DEVELOPMENT OF GOOD CITIZENSHIP IN 19TH CENTURY NEW LANARK

Enlightened Reform of Social Control?

INTRODUCTION

This chapter examines the ideological significance of the early 19th century experiment in education introduced by Robert Owen at New Lanark and its implications for contemporary students and educators. Furthermore it aims to address the question of the efficacy and feasibility of organised field studies to New Lanark as part of the curriculum and as a source for the education of young people designed to enhance their appreciation of issues related to citizenship. Should Robert Owen's experiment at New Lanark therefore be hailed as an ideal that Scotland should cherish? Might students, teachers and pupils (not only from Scotland, but from the world beyond) benefit from analysing and interpreting afresh this 19th century utopia in the 21st century? Is it a useful case study for education for global citizenship in a contemporary world?

THE CONCEPT OF CITIZENSHIP IN CONTEXT

The concept of citizenship has emerged prominently in Scotland, Britain and the wider world over recent years. The adoption in the UK of 'Citizenship Tests' for immigrants, the proposals for identity cards for all UK citizens and the inclusion of 'Citizenship' as one of the five main educational priorities of the Scottish Government are only some indications that citizenship is a concept 'whose time has come'. Faulks (2000, p. 1) has described citizenship as a 'momentum concept' and explains that the reason for its universal appeal is that the idea of citizenship contains both individualistic and collectivist elements: it recognises the dignity of the individual, as a citizen with certain rights, but at the same time reaffirms the social context in which the individual acts – a social context that introduces the ideas of community, mutual respect and civic responsibility. Humes (2002) cites other examples of why the concept of citizenship has been important recently both in the UK and internationally – riots in towns such as Burnley, Oldham and Bradford, and the position of asylum seekers in a number of European countries. *A Curriculum for Excellence*, when identifying the purposes of the schools curriculum in Scotland, states that the fundamental purpose of the curriculum is to

M.A. Peters, A. Britton and H. Blee (Eds.), Global Citizenship Education: Philosophy, Theory and Pedagogy, 365–379.

enable young people to develop their capacities as successful learners, responsible citizens, confident individuals and effective contributors (SEED, 2004).

The Scottish consultation document on *Education for Citizenship* (LTS, 2000) defines its overall goal as 'the development of capability for thoughtful and responsible participation in political, economic, social and cultural life'.

The citizenship agenda can be used by different groups for different purposes and Faulks (2000, p. 1) provides a useful insight into the current interest in citizenship when he observes that radicals and conservatives alike feel able to utilise the language of citizenship in support of their policy prescriptions.

In a similar manner, Robert Owen has been adopted and praised by commentators from both ends of the political spectrum. Paradoxically, he has been described as both the 'Father of Socialism' and as the 'Father of Scientific Management' as a result of his social experiment at New Lanark. For this reason, among others, his 19th century utopia provides a useful case study for education for global citizenship in the contemporary world.

HISTORY OF THE NEW LANARK SITE

In 2001 the historic village of New Lanark was designated as a UNESCO World Heritage Site and this makes the case for the study of New Lanark even more compelling. The first year of the new millennium was a key moment in what had been a long history marked by highs and lows. After having passed into the possession of a rope work company in the 1950s and subsequently falling into a dilapidated state in the 1960s, New Lanark received a new lease of life in the 1970s. New Lanark Conservation Trust – its stated aim being to preserve New Lanark as a sustainable community with a resident population and new opportunities for employment – was formed in 1974 as a charity dedicated to the restoration and development of the historic village. The Trustees serve in a voluntary capacity. New Lanark Trading Ltd. and New Lanark Hotels Ltd. are wholly owned subsidiaries of the Trust and surpluses generated by these companies are returned to the Trust for reinvestment in the project.[1] What of the origins of this remarkable site?

Although Robert Owen (1771–1858) is now the name most closely associated with New Lanark, the unique cotton spinning community was in fact established in 1785 by the prominent Scottish entrepreneur David Dale (1739–1806) who ran it from its inception in 1785 until New Year's Eve, 1799. A typical development of the water power stage of industrialisation, it was, however, quite exceptional in scale, having four massive mills employing more than 2000 workers, including many women and children (Donnachie, 1993, pp. 17–58). Dale had a reputation as a philanthropic employer and his regime was soon noted and celebrated for its humanity (Donnachie, 2004, p. 145). He was a deeply religious man, who from the age of thirty had been a lay preacher in an Independent church in Glasgow, learning Greek and Hebrew so that he could study the Bible more effectively. At New Lanark he paid better wages and provided better working conditions than any employer of his time. He built good houses with effective sanitation for his workers and gave them opportunities for education. While from our contemporary perspective some aspects of working life appear extremely harsh, they were, relative to this time in history, 'good conditions'. For example, the 500 orphans, whom he collected from Edinburgh and Glasgow poorhouses, worked 11½ hours a day (with sometimes 2 additional hours of schooling) and received no holidays except Sundays which Dale permitted because of his religious objections to Sunday work (MacPhail, 1956, p. 73–74).

It was, however, Robert Owen, David Dale's more famous son-in-law, who made New Lanark one of the showpieces of European industry in the 19th century. Owen took over management of New Lanark on 1 January 1800 and ran it until December 1824.

Donnachie's research has been invaluable in focusing on how Owen's agenda at New Lanark emphasised improved factory conditions (in particular for children), popular education, citizenship, planning, environment and, ultimately, cooperation. Owen also had progressive views on gender relations, marriage and birth control, to which he often alluded, though he rarely articulated these directly (Donnachie, 2004, p. 146).

In particular, from 1 January 1814, when he acquired what he considered to be more enlightened partners, Owen accelerated and broadened the scope of his 'social experiment' in relation to childcare, education, healthcare and cooperative shopping; these are still held up as examples of enlightened reform for the amelioration of social conditions.

Anderson (1995) cites Owen's influences and the central place education had in them:

> The desire to change society by changing individuals was a feature of utilitarian doctrines, which had affiliations with the Scottish Enlightenment, but reached Scotland in an updated form through the influence of Jeremy Bentham. Utilitarians believed in universal education as the instrument of human progress, and their 'environmentalist' psychology sought to achieve social harmony by moulding the individual character and personality from earliest childhood. (p. 33)

These ideas, in a radical form, inspired Owen's experiments at New Lanark. Owen wrote extensively on the subject of education and in order to determine whether his experiment in education represented enlightened reform or simply mechanisms of social control it is necessary to examine the situation at that time and assess the motives that lay behind his experiment.

ROBERT OWEN: BACKGROUND

Robert Owen was born in Wales in 1771 and, after an apprenticeship in the textile retail trade, moved to Manchester where he progressed quickly through the various levels of the cotton industry and became manager of one of the largest businesses in Manchester in a period of substantial expansion in the industry. He travelled widely for his firm and during a visit to Glasgow met Dale's daughter, Anne

Caroline Dale. Dale sold New Lanark to Owen and his partners for £60,000 in 1799 and in the same year, Owen married Anne Caroline Dale. After a short period in Manchester, Owen and his new wife returned to New Lanark where he became managing partner from January 1, 1800. Over the next 25 years, as managing partner to three groups of collaborators, Owen made huge profits and at the same time gained an international reputation as a humanitarian, educationist and creator of a model industrial community (Pollard & Salt, 1971).

Owen's first impression of New Lanark was that it had great potential for profit but that the workforce was in need of serious attention and improvement:

> The population lived in idleness, in poverty, in almost every kind of crime, consequently in debt, out of health and in misery .... (Owen, 1813, p. 14)

He describes the workpeople who he found to be dirty in their habits and houses, intemperate and demoralised, and writes of the community:

> It may with truth be said, that at this period they possessed almost all of the vices and very few of the virtues of a social community. Theft and the receipt of stolen goods was their trade, idleness and drunkenness their habit, falsehood and deception their garb, dissensions, civil and religious, their daily practice; they united only in a zealous systematic opposition to their employers. (p. 16)

He immediately set about improving the economic performance of the mills. First he replaced the managers whom he thought were inefficient with his own management which included fellow Welshman, Robert Humphreys. He made clear his intention to reassert control over the labour force and to establish tighter discipline, to the extent that, amongst his contemporaries, he acquired very rapidly the reputation of being a very strict man (Butt, 1971, p. 523).

ROBERT OWEN IN HISTORICAL CONTEXT

It is fundamentally important to emphasise that the unplanned growth and development of towns was one of the major social problems at this time in the 19th century. This expansion was inseparable from the main political issues of the day such as parliamentary reform and the perceived threat of revolution. There were minor outbreaks of machine breaking, riots and strikes during the time that Owen was at New Lanark and he thought that he could solve the problems of what he interpreted as a bitter class struggle. Paradoxically, one of the features of his management is that he was regarded as an ideal employer by his workforce at the time. The most obvious manifestation of this occurred after 1807–8 when there was a minor cotton famine arising from American policy and the increased price of cotton, so much that, in Owen's view, it was uneconomic to keep the mills open. He closed the mills down but kept the labour force on at their normal wages. After this gesture he seems to have had no problems of faith, trust or loyalty from his labour force.[2]

Two main questions arise that must be addressed. First, why was New Lanark and Owen's experiment there of such significance during this period? Second, were Owen's experiments in education and community living 'enlightened reform' or 'mechanisms of social control' or both?

There are three main reasons why Owen's experiment at New Lanark was of particular significance at this time in history: urban population increase; a growing interest in the purposes of education; and the issue of social control. The population of Britain more than trebled between 1800 and 1900, despite significant emigration. The political problem of the 19th century – an epoch unprecedented in that it was preserved from warfare on the Western European mainland for much of its duration – was how to provide for the needs of the new urban populations. A rapidly changing mass urban society had taken the place of a stable agricultural community. In practice, the government tried to meet the needs of the urban poor with welfare legislation and came to realise that a national system of education would have to be put into place. Education would be used as an instrument of enlightened reform and/or a mechanism of social control. How the masses were to be educated, and whether the education they received would have a moralising influence on them, were two questions that needed to be addressed urgently.

In addition to this, during the 19th century, there was growing interest in education outside the sphere of Royal Commissions and state intervention. Among the chief exponents of a reforming educational philosophy then were figures of the intellectual stature of John Stuart Mill (1806–1873), Matthew Arnold (1822–1888), John Ruskin (1819–1900), Frederick Denison Maurice (1805–1872) and Charles Kingsley (1819–1875). It was precisely at the time when these formidable minds were deliberating about the purposes of education that Owen attempted his ambitious practical experiment in education at New Lanark.

Owen believed strongly that the violence of character in the working classes was fostered by their environment. Deeply influenced by Claude Adrien Helvétius (1715–1771) and his belief in the total influence of external circumstances, rational government and educational provision, Owen's experiment, as he saw it, was successful in proving the truth of the principle that the character is formed for, and not by, the individual. Politically the most considerable of the *philosophes*, Helvétius combined an abstractly rationalistic account of human nature – generalising Locke's doctrine that the human mind is at birth a blank slate, a *tabula rasa* in Locke's terminology, acquiring its entire character from environmental influences by which it is completely malleable – with a rejection of Locke's rationalistic ethics in favour of a clear and explicit utilitarianism (Kenny, 1994, p. 329). Helvétius held that morality is not innate; it must proceed from education, 'education makes us what we are'.[3] Like Condillac (Etienne Bonnot, Abbé de Condillac, 1714–1780), Helvétius took a radical empiricist position, that man was born a *tabula rasa* and formed his knowledge from the senses and association of ideas. A radical hedonist, Helvétius also argued that actions and judgments are generated by the natural desire to maximise pleasure and minimise pain. Consequently, human behaviour is completely determined by education and social environment.

369

In April 1812, at a dinner in Glasgow in honour of the educationist Joseph Lancaster, Owen made his first public statement that '...we can materially command those circumstances which influence character...',[4] and it is clear from the context that he was thinking of the effects of education on a community. Similarly the famous passage in the first essay of *A New View of Society* referred to the influence of the environment on a community:

> Any general character, from the best to the worst, from the most ignorant to the most enlightened, may be given to any community, even to the world at large, by the application of proper means; which means are to a great extent at the command and under the control of those who have influence in the affairs of men. (p. 1)

During the 19th century in Britain, it became increasingly recognised by employers, churchmen, educationists and politicians that the Industrial Revolution created, as Owen called it, a 'ferocity of character' among the labouring classes, and Owen was particularly determined to moderate this. To Owen, enlightened reform and mechanisms of control need not be mutually exclusive. They could in fact be complementary. One way to handle the 'ferocity of character' was to change the forms of schooling so that the younger generation would be brought up in new ways. In Owen's view, the problems of mass production and mass schooling were essentially the same. They were about balancing productive efficiency with social regulation. At the heart of Owen's educational programme was the determination to create a disciplined, docile but contented population for his factory. Initially Owen saw the problem simply as one of establishing habits suitable for factory life, but increasingly he believed as well that it was necessary to establish a certain mental outlook, on the part of the children in particular and the workers in general, and his experiments or innovations in education are a response to that. He believed that if children could understand their place in the world through, for example, History lessons or Geography lessons, they would be better prepared to appreciate and understand their place in the world as, in Owen's words, 'workpersons' or 'domestics'.[5]

This is evident in sentiments such as:

> ... the children are, without exception, passive and wonderfully contrived compounds; which, by an accurate and previous subsequent attention, founded on a correct knowledge of the subject, may be formed collectively to have any human character. And although these compounds, like all the other works of nature, possess endless varieties, yet they partake of that plastic quality, which by perseverance and judicious management, may be ultimately moulded into the very image of rational wishes and desires. (Owen, 1813, p. 11)

Owen was a paternalistic employer and the ideals of the society at New Lanark were imposed from above. Miles removed from the large industrial towns, Owen carefully established his microcosmic kingdom where his absolute rule determined what was good for people. His use of devices such as the 'silent monitor' and the establishment of the 'Institution for the Formation of Character' strongly suggest an extended regime of social control. Further evidence of this is the fact that he fined people for drunkenness, for immorality and for stealing. He even fined them if their homes were untidy. But at the same time he eased the cost of living by providing cheap food in the village store, free entertainments, free lunches and schooling for the young, and this undoubtedly constituted enlightened reform at that time. The romantic ideal he strove towards was that of the simple community of his childhood in Wales, with a benevolent gentry and contented workforce. Owen's experiment at New Lanark was utopian and was, literally and figuratively, a considerable distance from Glasgow.

The idea that human beings were '... passive and wonderfully contrived compounds which may be formed to have any character and be ultimately moulded into the very image of rational wishes and desires' did not *only* apply to the children in New Lanark, nor was it only relevant to the school day. At night too, in the Institute for the Formation of Character, the adult workers were encouraged to come to evening classes, to concerts or to use the library. It was a centre for adult education where the courses included health and hygiene, domestic economy and thrift. By the standards of the early 19th century in Scotland these were certainly enlightened reforms, although the contemporary poet, Robert Southey, was scathing about some of Owen's practices (Southey, 1929, published posthumously). Referring to Owen's description of the inhabitants of New Lanark as 'human machines', he said:

> But I never regarded man as a machine: I never believed him to be merely a material thing; I never for a moment ... suppose, as Owen does, that men may be cast in a mould (like other parts of his mill) and take the impression with perfect certainty.

Southey added:

> He keeps out of sight from others, and perhaps from himself, that his system instead of aiming at perfect freedom, can only be kept in play by perfect power.

Despite his criticisms of Owen, Southey described him as 'one of the three men who have in this generation given an impulse to the modern world' and continued:

> Clarkson and Dr Bell are the other two. They have seen the first fruits of their harvest. So I think would Owen ere this, if he had not alarmed the better part of the nation by proclaiming, upon the most momentous of all subjects, opinions which are alike fatal to individual happiness and to the general good .... A craniologist, I dare say, would pronounce that the organ of theopathy is wanting in Owen's head, that of benevolence being so large as to have left no room for it.

On New Year's Day, 1816, when he was opening the Institute for the Formation of Character, Owen addressed the inhabitants of New Lanark as follows:

What ideas individuals may attach to the term 'Millennium' I know not; but I know that society may be formed so as to exist without crime, without poverty, with health greatly improved, with little, if any misery, and with intelligence and happiness increased a hundredfold; and no obstacle whatsoever intervenes at this moment except ignorance to prevent such a state of society from becoming universal.

In the same year, 1816, he also published the full version of his *A New View of Society*, which proclaimed (among much else) that 'the best state will be that which shall possess the best national system of education' (Owen, 1927, p. 73). The Institute for the Formation of Character was, in effect, a community education centre and in his speech at its opening Owen outlined his visionary plans for an astonishingly progressive and enlightened system of education which he believed was the key to a happier society and universal harmony.

Under Owen's management, the cotton mills and village of New Lanark became a model community, in which the drive towards progress and prosperity through the new technology of the industrial revolution was tempered by a caring and humane regime. New Lanark had the first Infant School in the world, a crèche for working mothers, free medical care, comprehensive education and evening classes. Leisure and recreation were not forgotten; there were concerts, dancing, music-making and pleasant landscaped areas for the benefit of the community. The village attracted international attention in the early19[th] century (Donnachie, 2004). While at New Lanark, Owen demonstrated management policies that are now widely recognised as the precursors of modern theories relating to human resource management, as well as skilful and ethical business practice. His work inspired infant education, humane working practices, co-operation, trade unionism, and garden cities.

Owen looked forward to the new Millennium with optimism and with confidence (Donnachie, 2004) and wrote in 1841:

It is therefore, the interest of all, that every one, from birth, should be well educated, physically and mentally, that society may be improved in its character, – that everyone should be beneficially employed, physically and mentally, everyone should be placed in the midst of those external circumstances that will produce the greatest number of pleasurable sensations, through the longest life, that man may be made truly intelligent, moral and happy, and be thus prepared to enter upon the coming Millennium.

As a consequence of Owen's contributions and philosophy, he was first taken up by the Fabian Society in the early years of the 20th century as they searched for an authentic voice of British socialism in contrast to the communism of Karl Marx. Owen had moved into the socialist pantheon for three main reasons. First, he had spoken up for the Tolpuddle Martyrs (Hopkins, 2000, p. 5; Gregg, 1971, p. 179; Powell, 2002, p. 47). Second, his mills at New Lanark represented an alternative model to the actual 'dark satanic mills' elsewhere that disfigured lives and landscape. Third, he stood for co-operatives rather than existing capitalist hierarchies.

In recent years some historians, notably Butt, Finlayson and Hamilton have questioned Owen's standing as an unambiguous figure in socialist hearts and minds. Some argue that Owen's rightful place in history is as a Victorian industrialist, a man who believed in enlightened reform but knew that enlightened reform was often the most effective way of making huge profits.[7] As Butt (1971) comments: "... business efficiency and good morals went hand in hand!"

Should Owen therefore be regarded as 'the father of British socialism', 'the founding figure of all co-operation', 'the instigator of all things co-operative'? If, like the co-operative society, we see Owen in this light, he was a great social reformer; he founded a mill which could only be described as the most progressive of its time. On the other hand, should Owen be regarded as 'the prince of cotton spinners', 'the founding father of scientific management'? – in which case the reality of his career at New Lanark is that he was a self-made businessman and capitalist who used sophisticated mechanisms of social control to achieve his utopian ideas alongside profit.

When Owen came to New Lanark in 1800 he was placed in charge of the largest cotton mills in Scotland with a labour force of around 2,000. This business had been created over a sixteen year period and was considered to be '...one of the most humanely conducted factories in the Empire' (Cole, 1953, p. 44). Owen's debt to David Dale therefore perhaps was greater than he would lead readers to believe in his later writings and particularly in *The Life of Robert Owen, Written by Himself* (Owen, 1857, pp. 57–59). However favourably the conditions for child workers at New Lanark compared with those elsewhere, they were still firmly situated within a capitalist logic of production. Owen had seen appalling examples of cruelty and exploitation in Manchester, Leeds and elsewhere and considered the practice of using child labour both abhorrent and inefficient and set out to do away with it. His first improvement at New Lanark was to get rid of unreliable child labour recruited from the charity houses and to employ local village women instead. The practice of employing children of less than ten years of age was discontinued and their parents were advised to allow them to acquire health and education until they were ten. This was enlightened reform, but in a statement of his intention to extend the children's time at school until the age of twelve, there is a hint of the capitalist with a thorough knowledge of cost-efficiency:

> ... far better it would be for the children, their parents and society that the first should not commence employment until they attain the age of twelve, when their bodies would be more competent to undergo the fatigue and exertions required of them. (Owen, 1813, p. 18)

Neither were the motives behind the education of the children completely enlightened, unselfish or altruistic, as is evident from Owen's words:

> By the arrangements formed for the education of children, they will be trained regularly for their employment, and all their habits, bodily and

mental, formed to carry them to a high state of perfection; and this alone, in its consequences, will be of incalculable advantage for the concern; for to these people are entrusted the care and use of nice and valuable machinery, with a great variety of materials requisite for the business. (Owen, 1812)

On the other hand Owen saw that the employment of children at too young an age had been the real weakness in Dale's educational scheme and by refusing to employ any child under the age of ten and by improving the conditions for adult workers Owen had created the opportunity to put into practice educational projects which, by any standards, would have to be considered as more enlightened than any that had been envisaged at the time. He soon became involved in cost accountancy and he costed every production process within the mills in an attempt to improve production flows and raise productivity and profitability. He installed new machinery and streamlined production. He also applied what he regarded as the latest management practices, some of which were of his own devising, notably, the use of the 'silent monitor' which was hung on the front of each machine and was used to assess the workers' performance on a daily basis, thus encouraging peer competition among the workers.

Owen's methods were certainly productive but his success at New Lanark coincided with a period of great unrest in the large industrial cities he had left behind. Industrial expansion had brought with it the exploitation of factory labour, chronic overcrowding in slums and profound poverty. Owen observed this potentially dangerous situation from the rural security and safety of New Lanark.

Owen had grand schemes and his appeal to spread his ideas was addressed to the elite in society, people like William Wilberforce, the Prince Regent, Lord Liverpool and political leaders of the day. He believed that society should reform itself from the top and not from the bottom – for Owen that was the key lesson of the French Revolution. Owen associated with royal dukes and government ministers and carried the message of New Lanark to Europe (1818) and Ireland (1822–1823).

His activities generated worldwide interest among reformers, because he seemed to offer solutions to critical social and economic problems that had arisen after the Napoleonic Wars. Unlike the radicals of the time, he appeared to eschew political action which might upset the existing order. So apart from the community he had made famous, the charismatic Owen became a celebrity, attracting large audiences, including many women. As an agent for social and cultural change, the benevolent Mr. Owen thus became a major attraction in his own right (Donnachie, 2000, pp. 133–155). Donnachie's research reveals the types of visitors that came to New Lanark at the time. The entries in the visitors' book for 1795 and 1825 highlight a preponderance of lawyers, merchants, clergy, naval and army officers. Doctors and teachers, including those from colleges and universities, are also evident. Most of the visitors had a professional interest in the place: cotton merchants; doctors concerned about public health; clergy or ministers of the Kirk involved in the administration of poor relief; or teachers interested in the school and its curriculum. Although perhaps not professionally involved, the remaining 90% of male visitors probably had enough interest in social reform to see Owen's community for themselves as they made their way to the nearby waterfalls on the River Clyde. Foreigners had similar backgrounds, as social reformers, educators, merchants and industrialists. There were also many diplomats, government officials and civil servants interested in industry or education (Donnachie, 2004).

In numerous other countries, therefore, Owen's ideas were acknowledged and his memory honoured. When 20th century socialists rediscovered Owen after his death, they ignored the side of him that did not fit their historical vision. It is important to realise that, in a sense, Owen was a figure of myth as well as a figure of reality. It would be just as appropriate to describe him as one of the founding fathers of scientific management – Robert Owen, this prophet of modern management, who kept his workforce employed even during times of slump, has been largely ignored until relatively recently. Tarlow (2004) points out that Owen's self-proclaimed utopian community at New Lanark was a cotton mill and, irrespective of the amelioration of conditions for his Scottish labourers, continued to process cotton grown on American plantations under institutionalised slavery. Paradoxically, Owen dedicated one of his books to William Wilberforce, the abolitionist, and was himself a forthright campaigner against slavery (Harrison, 1969, p. 22).

Visitors from all over the world are still interested in the social experiment that Owen carried out at New Lanark. Is there a case, therefore, for promoting New Lanark as a venue for field studies for school pupils, students, teachers and educators in general and those with an interest in citizenship and education? The interpretive framework is certainly in place. Donnachie (2000) examined early visitor data, typologies, origins, occupational profiles, motivations, and visitor experiences. A high proportion of visitors, he concludes, were interested in social and educational reform, as well as seeing romantic scenery. It also suggests that, in line with Owen's agenda, the interpretation of the site for modern visitors is strongly influenced by similar social, educational, cooperative and environmental concerns (Donnachie, 2004).

McKinlay (2006) follows the lead of Michel Foucault and his central text for historians *Discipline and Punish* (1977) by focusing on the influence of Jeremy Bentham upon managerial theory and practice and the case of Robert Owen at New Lanark. Arguing that business history has become an increasingly inter-disciplinary space and has been rejuvenated as a result, McKinlay uses the cases of Bentham, Owen and New Lanark as the basis for a discussion of Foucault and the implications of Foucault's work for business history.

Tarlow (2004) emphasises that utopia is a 'hot topic' in academia, and adds: 'Moreover, Utopia is a place where a number of disciplines have converged, including architecture, history, geography, art history, film criticism, and social and political philosophy' (p. 304).

She cites New Lanark as an example of a place where the ideas developed in a communitarian setting were significant in wider society:

> ... the educational methods pioneered in Owenite communities were widely influential and provided models for the establishment of national educational programmes in Europe and North America, even after the collapse or transformation of Owen's own communities at New Lanark, New Harmony, and Queenswood. (Tarlow, 2004:306; see also Kumar, 1991, p. 77)

Harrison (1989), in his assessment of the legacy of Robert Owen, draws out of Owenite thinking a fundamental belief in the capacity of humans to bring about their own destiny. Tarlow (2004) argues that this belief is equally evident in most other utopian thought and that personal power rather than the power of a benevolent state or the fulfilment of an obscure economic force, can bring about the ideal state.

In November 2004, the Scottish Executive published *A Curriculum for Excellence: The Curriculum Review Group* alongside *A Curriculum for Excellence: Ministerial Response*. These documents are expected to be extremely influential in shaping the Scottish Curriculum over the next decade at least. The authors of *A Curriculum for Excellence* have the stated objective of 'decluttering the curriculum' (SEED, 2004); in other words, reducing the compulsory elements of the curriculum in Scottish schools. Undoubtedly New Lanark has a strong claim to be included in a pared down curriculum in schools, colleges and universities, and as an essential field study destination for people of all ages.

Now that the major restoration programme on site has been completed, the marketing, promotion and reception of visitors have become a major element in the workload of the staff at New Lanark. Educational visits have constituted a major proportion of group visits to New Lanark. The site is seen as being of national significance for the study of the industrial revolution and environmental studies. Schools are prepared to travel considerable distances to get to it even from abroad and, among the schools visiting, there has been a general balance between primary and secondary schools.

Many museums and heritage sites attract predominantly primary school groups but in New Lanark there has been a deliberate policy of tying the visit closely to the needs of the curriculum. There are few areas of the curriculum which cannot be taught more effectively by involving the pupils in fieldwork, which can play an important role in enriching and expanding the different areas of the curriculum. Indeed, a major advantage of fieldwork is that it emphasises the unity and coherence of the curriculum and demands the use of skills, knowledge and evidence drawn from a wide spectrum of disciplines. Many of the outcomes and strands described in curriculum guidelines in schools and universities contain targets which can be partially met through systematic attention to fieldwork since it offers opportunities to develop a range of skills associated with, for example, planning, collecting and analysing evidence, hypothesising, discussing and debating, recording and presenting, applying skills and presenting solutions, interpreting and evaluating, and writing reports, dissertations and articles.

There can be little doubt that fieldwork, in general, has a motivating effect on pupils and students, especially when they see the direct relevance of studies they are undertaking to their own lives. Fieldwork at New Lanark can contribute greatly to the development of aesthetic values since it is a location of particular cultural and scenic significance. It has the potential, therefore, to form an important bridge between school work and the world outside school. The connection between the lives of others in the past, the child's, pupil's or student's life today, and the contributions both have made and can make to the world of which they were or are a part, can be more clearly illustrated. The development of informed attitudes to the environment is yet another important issue where the fieldwork experience, involving contact with the environment through immediate local or national environmental issues, offers considerable scope for fostering such attitudes and raising pupil and student awareness as it poses important questions for education for citizenship in a contemporary world.

New Lanark is unique in that the industrial history, the social history, the superb restoration and the beautiful natural environment have been brought together to produce a truly living and thriving village with a wide range of attractions for visitors. What Hewison described as 'the true continuity between the past and the present' (Hewison, 1987, p. 143) is also very evident in the interpretation of New Lanark for modern visitors in the 21st century.

CONCLUSION

Having made his fortune at New Lanark, Owen embarked latterly on a career as social critic and great inspirer of social movements of his time. He had by that time, however, earned his place in the histories of economic thought, enlightened reform and educational thought. As a result of his pioneering work in social reform, New Lanark became internationally famous.

Owen is seen by some as an internationally recognised pioneer of enlightened management. At the beginning of the 19th century New Lanark attracted attention as a model village and one of the great sites of Scotland. At the beginning of the 21st century it has enjoyed something of a renaissance as one of the greatest sites of Scotland with its unique buildings, sense of history, industrial archaeology and natural setting.

The educational value of visiting New Lanark is not merely about reaching conclusions but about the educational experience itself. The fact that this chapter itself does not reach a conclusion about whether Owen's work at New Lanark constitutes enlightened reform or social control or, indeed, something of both, is not crucially important. Visitors, including school children, are left to ponder the paradoxes of Owen's approach and legacy for themselves. One of the things that *A Curriculum for Excellence* is trying to address is life beyond industrial society – a post-industrial ethic for a post-industrial economy. New Lanark illustrates the capacity that human beings have to take charge of seemingly impersonal processes. It demonstrates that human beings can re-invent their civilisation. It will be up to the next generation to adjudicate New Lanark for themselves. Furthermore, in a context where there are growing concerns about the working conditions of young people in some developing economies, the site may also provide pause for reflection, as well as an impetus for an active response by children, in relation to contemporary issues as well as historical events.

For these reasons Robert Owen's experiment at New Lanark should be hailed as an ideal that should be cherished. There can be little doubt that great benefits would accrue from analysing and interpreting this attempt at utopia. It is, therefore, a most useful case study which contributes towards the enhancement of education for global citizenship in the contemporary world.

NOTES

[1] See website at http://www.newlanark.org (last accessed on 31st January 2007).

[2] BBC Television Timewatch broadcast on BBC 2 on 1/05/1984. This programme examined three Victorian buildings: the Empire Building, the Victorian Asylum and the New Lanark Mills. The programme was presented by John Tusa, reporter David Drew produced by Andrea Conway, executive producer, Timothy Gardam, edited by Bruce Norman and featured contributions from: Geoffrey Booth, President of the North West Pioneers Cooperative Society, John Whyte, former works manager, Professor John Butt of the University of Strathclyde and Dr. Geoffrey Finlayson and Dr. David Hamilton of the University of Glasgow.

[3] Helvétius, C.A. 'Discourse XXX', Ch. 30, in *The Oxford Dictionary of Quotations New Edition* (1981), Oxford: Oxford University Press, p. 244.

[4] The Glasgow Herald, 20 April, 1812, as recorded in Owen, 1857.

[5] BBC Television *Timewatch* documentary, broadcast on BBC2 on 1/05/1984.

[6] Extract from Robert Owen's 'Address to the Inhabitants of New Lanark', New Year's Day, 1816.

[7] BBC Television *Timewatch* documentary, broadcast on BBC 2 on 1/05/1984.

REFERENCES

Anderson, R.D. (1995). *Education and the Scottish people*. Oxford: Clarendon Press.

Butt, J. (Ed.) (1971). *Robert Owen: Prince of cotton spinners*. Newton Abbot: David & Charles.

Claeys, G. (1991). *A new view of society and other writings by Robert Owen*. Harmondsworth: Penguin Classics.

Claeys, G. (1993). (Ed.) *Selected works of Robert Owen*. 4 Vols. London: Pickering.

Cole, G.D.H. (1930). *Life of Robert Owen*. London: Macmillan.

Cole, M.I. (1953). *Robert Owen of New Lanark*. London: MacMillan.

Davidson, L. and Hardy, D. (1992). *Thinking of heritage: The case for New Lanark*. Geography and planning paper No 27. Enfield, England: Middlesex Polytechnic.

Donnachie, I. and Hewitt, G. (1993). *Historic New Lanark: The Dale and Owen industrial community since 1785* (2nd ed.). Edinburgh: Edinburgh University Press.

Donnachie ,I. (2000). *Robert Owen: Owen of New Lanark and new harmony*. East Linton: Tuckwell Press.

Donnachie, I. (2003). Education in Robert Owen's new society: The New Lanark Institute and school. *The encyclopaedia of informal education*. Retrieved 18 September, 2007, from http://www.infed.org/thinkers/et-owen.htm.

Donnachie, I. (2004). Historic tourism to New Lanark and the Falls of Clyde 1795–1830: The evidence of contemporary visiting books and related sources. *Journal of Tourism and Cultural Change, 2*(3), 145–163.

Faulks, K. (2000). *Citizenship*. London and New York: Routledge.

Foucault, M. (1977). *Discipline and punish: The birth of the prison*. Harmondsworth: Penguin.

Gregg, P. (1971). *A social and economic history of Britain, 1760–1970*. London: Larousse Harrap.

Harrison, J.F.C. (1969). *Robert Owen and the Owenites in Britain and America*. London: Routledge and Kegan Paul.

Harrison, J.F.C. (1989). The legacy of Robert Owen. In D. Hardy & L. Davidson (Eds.), *Utopian thought and communal experience* (pp. 11–16). Geography and planning paper 24. Enfield: Middlesex Polytechnic.

Hewison, R. (1987). *The heritage industry: Britain in a climate of decline*. London: Methuen.

Hopkins, E. (2000). *Industrialisation and society: A social history, 1830–1951*. London: Routledge.

Humes, W.M. (2002). Exploring citizenship and enterprise in a global context. *Citizenship, Social and Economics Education, 5*(1), 17–28

Kenny, A. (Ed.) (1994). *The Oxford illustrated history of western philosophy*. Oxford: Oxford University Press.

Kumar, K. (1991). *Utopianism*. Milton Keynes: Open University Press.

Learning and Teaching Scotland (LTS) (2000). *Education for citizenship: A paper for discussion and consultation*. Dundee: Learning and Teaching Scotland.

McKinlay, A. (2006). Managing Foucault: Genealogies of management. *Management and Organisational History, 1*(1), 87–100.

McLaren, D. (1999). *David Dale of New Lanark*. Glasgow: Caring Books.

MacPhail, I.M.M. (1956). *A history of Scotland*. Book 2. London: Edward Arnold.

New Lanark (n.d.) Retrieved 31 January, 2007, from http://www.newlanark.org.

Owen, R. (1812). A statement regarding the New Lanark Establishment. In G. Claeys (Ed.) (1993), *Selected works of Robert Owen*. London: Pickering & Chatto.

Owen, R. (1813). *A new view of society: Second essay on the principle of the formation of human character*. London: Cadell & Davies.

Owen, R. (1857). *The life of Robert Owen, written by himself: With selections from his writings and correspondence*. Vol. 1. London: E. Wilson. (New edition, 1967, London: Cassell.)

Owen, R. (1927). *A new view of society and other writings*. Everyman edition. London: Dent.

Podmore, F. (1906). *Robert Owen, a biography*. London: Allen & Unwin.

Pollard, S. and Salt, J (Eds.) (1971). *Robert Owen: Prophet of the poor*. London: Macmillan.

Powell, D. (2002). *Nationhood and identity: The British state since 1800*. London: I.B. Tauris.

Scottish Executive Education Department (SEED) (2004). *A curriculum for excellence: The curriculum review group*. Edinburgh: Scottish Executive.

Southey, R. (1929). *Journal of a tour in Scotland in 1819*. London: Murray.

Tarlow, S. (2004). Excavating utopia: Why archaeologists should study 'ideal' communities of the nineteenth century. *International Journal of Historical Archaeology, 6*(4), 299–323.

Francis J. O'Hagan
University of Glasgow

JULIA PREECE

A SOCIAL JUSTICE APPROACH TO EDUCATION FOR ACTIVE CITIZENSHIP

An International Perspective

INTRODUCTION

The concept of citizenship is now widely discussed – in terms of citizenship status, citizenship identity, civic responsibilities and agency (active citizenship). It can involve a set of values as well as a legal framework. Formal curricula for citizenship education have been introduced across the world; for example in South and East Asia, Africa, Europe, North America and the Pacific. Education about or for these citizenships can promote passivity or exclusion for some or critical consciousness for others (Mundel & Schugurensky, 2004; Bisch, 1995), though the tendency is towards 'civics' as volunteerism rather than critical engagement with the wider issues of human rights, minorities and sustainable development. It is argued here that in this era of globalisation, citizenship education needs to give equal consideration to these wider global issues. In many parts of the world, for instance, citizens by national status do not have equal rights in their own country (Hames, 2006, writing about black women in South Africa) and immigrants or minorities often struggle to acquire citizenship identities from their host country (Nordberg, 2006, on the Roma in Finland; Nyamjoh, 2007 on the distinction between black and white, male and female minorities and immigrants in South Africa and Botswana). The ways in which such individuals and social groups negotiate meaningful identities and effective participation is often dependent upon the kind of educational opportunities they receive to enable them to interrogate injustices, learn problem solving and ethical decision making skills and appreciate democratic values.

Since the literature on this topic is now extensive, this paper examines citizenship education and emerging issues in a small selection of countries mostly from the global South – as this is the locus where the concept of a universal citizenship education is most challenged. I then explore emerging concepts of social justice, finishing with Martha Nussbaum's (2006) 'capabilities' notion of social justice as a strategy for focusing on education for critical, active and ethical citizenship. Finally I briefly explain some common features of non-formal education provision and suggest that the non-formal system provides better opportunities for radical citizenship education of the kind that would take a social

M.A. Peters, A. Britton and H. Blee (Eds.), Global Citizenship Education: Philosophy, Theory and Pedagogy, 381–393.

justice perspective as its starting point because it provides more scope for flexible, context-driven learner needs.

COUNTRY PERSPECTIVES ON CITIZENSHIP EDUCATION

We will see from these short extracts that citizenship education is often bound by national histories that shape and inform attitudes to nation-building, unity and independence. We will also see that such influences change over time, depending on emerging political goals.

Bernadette Dean has conducted surveys of attitudes and schooling for citizenship education in Pakistan. Her recent study of citizenship education in Pakistani schools (2005) suggests that the curriculum does not sufficiently distinguish between Islamic and citizenship education, thus tending to encourage a passive citizenship which reproduces government ideology of the time. She tracks the evolution of current practice across the country's own history of colonialism and military rule. Citizenship education was initially guided by 'the principles of universal brotherhood ... social democracy and social justice ... democratic virtues of tolerance, self-help, self-sacrifice' (p. 36), with a focus on national unity, and with the aim of generating loyal citizens, but nevertheless using a two tier education system borrowed from the West. Later, after a military coup in 1977, the focus was on developing patriotism and universalisation of basic education and rights, thereafter focusing on the development of citizens as practising Muslims, and thereby excluding non-Muslim Pakistanis from being Pakistani citizens, as well as excluding women from equal citizenship. Subsequent policy focused on character building and creation of a productive and useful workforce. Her Canadian International Development Agency-funded project reviews the Pakistan social studies curriculum. Dean concludes that its approach tends to support gender inequalities, reproduces some factual distortions and was inclined to focus on government rather than citizen agency. Where parent teacher associations or student councils exist these are usually viewed as 'simply' a formality (2005, p. 45). Values explicitly focus on instilling knowledge and understanding for becoming good Muslims. These, whilst not always contradictory to democratic citizenship skills, fail to address concepts such as human rights or social action for a more just society. Opportunities for democratic participation are rarely practised. Dean's recommendations include the development of more interactive pedagogical styles, opportunities for extra curricular community programmes and collaborative learning.

In contrast, Park (2006) identifies a non-formal Centre for Civic Education in Pakistan which promotes active citizenship among out-of-school young people and youth groups, where the focus is on youth themselves, exploring public policy problems in communities, researching problems, evaluating and developing their own solutions in the form of a public policy and action plan, with a view to presenting policy plans to panels of civic-minded community members.

Park (2006) also highlights several community-based learning approaches for citizenship education across the globe – though the focus is usually on enhancing solidarity and community service – where people learn to engage in volunteer activities and thereby acquire social skills, civic skills and dispositions, helping to foster caring for others. Promotion of volunteerism even in civil society, therefore, is strong in many countries, rather than promotion of critical citizenship.

Taking a Southern African country which is often claimed to be a shining example of democracy on this continent, Adeymi *et al* (2003) examine the effectiveness of citizenship education in Botswana schools. Here citizenship education is taught through Social Studies classes. The focus is on 'good citizenship' based around the core national principles of democracy, development, self-reliance and unity. Appreciation of 'society, culture and sense of citizenship' is the core theme (p. 36), along with life skills such as problem solving and critical thinking. The study was conducted in order to examine teacher preparedness for this subject. Even within this thematic focus for good citizenship, half the teachers surveyed felt that they would benefit from further training to achieve their educational goals, implying that citizenship as a subject of study would benefit from closer conceptual analysis, as well as more critical appreciation of its aims. But, as with the literature on Pakistan, Scanlon (2002) has highlighted that in Botswana it is the NGO community that educates more on human rights issues, though this initiative to influence the more passive institutional approach has been criticised at school level as undermining school discipline. The focus in Botswana is on encouraging respect and harmony rather than challenging the status quo, in keeping with its national 'Vision 2016' document which advocates education for 'kagisano' (peace) (Presidential Task Group, 1997).

Similar stories of this uneven approach to citizenship education can be found across the globe. So Astiz and Mendez (2006) describe the challenges in Argentinian schooling systems for engaging with citizenship for nation building whilst at the same time recognising the nation's relationship to a wider world and its principles of political and social rights. Lack of recognition of specific issues within curriculum materials means that text books may reproduce discriminatory attitudes and, in their effort to encourage harmony, for example, 'do not contribute to exploration and critical analysis of the historical tension between Buenos Aires and the provinces' (p. 194). Civic education in this country, they point out, is more about political socialisation – to promote universal liberal values – than how to address cultural difference, minorities or social justice issues. The goal is usually to educate the ideal citizen.

Koshmanova (2006) describes the Ukraine's current emphasis on nationalism as a reaction to former Soviet control. 'Schools were entrusted with the duty of the "patriotic upbringing" of the nation's children' (p. 107). As a result, the pluralistic status of ethnic minorities is marginalised and teaching is premised on a belief that education should be monocultural (p. 114), and critical reflexivity on matters of democracy and citizenship are limited: 'students understand tolerance as passive acts of enduring others and of non-resistance to people who may have different viewpoints' (p. 115).

Not all countries have a negative story to tell. Arko-Cobbah (2005), in South Africa, shows how citizenship education has been framed within an understanding of the country's historical context of apartheid. He states that the South African national curriculum 2005 does attempt to inculcate a sense of unity, but also core values of social justice, equity, and democracy, to develop critical, active citizens. Programmes range from 'teaching young peoples about democracy, to voter education programmes, and neighbourhood problem-solving programmes that bring individuals in contact with local authorities for purposes of promoting collective action to benefit local communities' (p. 1). The formal curriculum aims to develop well-informed citizens and a value system that fosters 'unity within diversity'. Concepts of justice and equality are now part of the vocabulary of citizenship education in the context of national consciousness, political literacy and rights and duties of citizens, particularly in view of South Africa's historical context where citizen identity and legal status were unequal among different social groups. Civil society organisations are also very active and able to enforce accountability and critical dialogue, building on a history of civil disobedience during and after the apartheid regime – such as the Western Cape anti-eviction campaign in 2000 (Miraftab & Wills, 2005).

There are several critiques of the system and approaches to citizenship education. Arnot (2006), for instance, asks: Do we educate *for* citizenship or *about* citizenship, since our educational goals inevitably have implications for what kinds of skills or awareness we choose to focus on? Moreover many, like Cornwall and Molyneux (2006), raise questions about the legitimacy of western notions of citizenship and human rights education in contexts where liberal rights agendas and realities of people's lives are significantly different. Nyamnjoh (2007) argues, for instance, that:

> The mistake has been to focus analysis almost exclusively upon institutional and constitutional arrangements, thereby downplaying the hierarchies and relationships of inclusion and exclusion informed by race, ethnicity, class, gender and geography that determine accessibility to citizenship in real terms. (p. 79)

Miraftab and Wills (2005) argue too that it is not enough, particularly in the global South, to promulgate an unproblematic, liberal notion of citizenship rights and obligations. Even though there may be equal statutory rights and obligations for citizens, the reality for many poor people or people from formerly colonised nations is that there are 'disjunctures between the form and substance of citizenship' (p. 202). This means that for some citizens such as the anti-eviction campaigners in South Africa, it is necessary for people to conduct 'civil disobedience' and create their own spaces for citizenship activity beyond the 'invited spaces' provided through statutory provision. Critical citizenship activity, therefore, is sometimes messy.

Changing political regimes do, of course, open up opportunities for more critical approaches to citizenship. Harber (2002) makes a connection between the general advances in citizenship education to greater levels of democracy and civil society in nations. With a focus again on Africa he provides examples of country contexts where education has not played a part in furthering democracy (usually in authoritarian regimes) but also contexts where innovative initiatives are taking place to address these issues. He argues that education per se does not contribute to democratisation; we need to consciously design education in a way that fosters democratic values and behaviours.

There is no shortage of external programme offerings for citizenship education. One example comes from UNESCO (1998). Here UNESCO provides an online Citizenship and Human Rights course which looks at citizenship issues in the context of the school and wider community, with a section on understanding citizenship through the concept of democracy, and which invites exploration of civil and political rights as well as the notion of the good citizen as the responsible citizen, whilst also encouraging dialogue and interaction.

Oxfam, too, contributes. Its (2002) curriculum for Global Citizenship provides a handbook for primary teaching that addresses: values and attitudes, including commitment to social justice, concern for the environment, valuing and respecting diversity, concern for others, nurturing a sense of identity and self esteem; skills for critical thinking, the ability to argue effectively, to challenge injustice and inequalities, skills for cooperation and conflict resolution; knowledge and understanding of concepts such as social justice and equity, diversity, globalisation and interdependence, sustainable development, peace and conflict.

Whilst the above external citizenship programmes encourage attention to very similar vocabulary, it is less clear how one can encourage social justice values which are embedded in different contexts and value systems. We are now increasingly becoming more interdependent for our world's sustainability. It is important, therefore, to explore how it may be possible to develop international citizenship values whilst continuing to respect socio-political cultural differences and contexts, as well as understanding how notions of citizenship in formerly colonised countries are influenced by their histories and objectives for national development. A social justice agenda that encapsulates these complexities, it is argued, will create opportunities for more ethical and analytical approaches to citizenship education.

The next section of this paper, therefore, focuses on some of the tensions around the discourse of social justice itself before offering at least a partial solution to a universal concept of citizenship education.

SOCIAL JUSTICE

The writer who has had most influence on discussions about social justice is Rawls. His (1972) *Theory of Social Justice* is primarily concerned with a concept of justice as 'fairness' manifested through a political conception of the principles by which the good things in life (economic and social) are distributed according to need, desert, merit and equality. This formal commitment to distributive justice reflects the welfarist policies of the time which claimed to redistribute goods on the basis of meritocracy. One example of this is the secondary education system of the time in the UK, which had evolved into a two-tier system of academic and vocational education (Gewirtz, 2002) where children's academic or vocational future at the age of 11 was judged on a single examination result. This approach did not consider whether all children had experienced equitable nurturing and education up to the age of 11.

Rawls has been critiqued by Sen (1992) as inadequately addressing issues of difference and tolerance (including tolerance of different political positions). Sen sees Rawl's concept of distributional justice as focusing too much on ensuring that certain outcomes are achieved, rather than considering the freedoms required to achieve those outcomes. So, for instance, someone with a disability may have access to a higher level of wealth or possessions (primary goods) than a non-disabled counterpart (outcomes achieved), but they may have more difficulty in converting those primary goods into 'basic capabilities' (freedoms) that would enable them to take part in community life or move from one location to another: 'neither primary goods, nor resources more broadly defined, can represent the capability a person actually enjoys' (Sen, 1992, p. 82). In other words, even though good things in life may be distributed or available to all, some people are better able to make use of those goods than others, simply because their life circumstances are not hindered by environmental or other social barriers to participate in the goods. Sen also argues that the converse could apply. That is, two people with the same capabilities (freedoms) will not necessarily choose to achieve the same outcomes (functionings). According to Sen, Rawls has placed too much emphasis on assuming that everyone has the same common goals, thus only emphasising the need to ensure people have the appropriate distribution of primary goods as the means to freedom. Sen prefers to focus on what freedoms one actually has, rather than the means alone.

This critique of Rawls, whilst recognising that he provides an important starting point for analysing social justice, is continued by a number of feminist writers. Their central theme is a concern with the politics of recognition and the relationships that structure society (Young, 1996; Nussbaum, 2006; Fraser, 1997; Gewirtz, 2002). So Fraser (1997) in our postmodern world of instability and diversity asks that we shift our central focus of justice from one of redistribution to one of recognition. She points out that we not only have disparities in income and wealth, but also capabilities (the things we are able to say and do, such as accessing clean water, education, healthcare, paid work, nutrition, safety, freedom of speech). Fraser argues that the theory of distributional justice must be integrated with a theory of cultural justice. This means, for example, looking at whether women are given equal recognition in their cultural contexts when judgements are made about distribution of resources such as credit facilities. The importance of challenging cultural and socioeconomic injustices that are 'rooted in processes and practices that systematically disadvantage some groups of people' (Fraser, 1997, p. 12) are central to this argument. There are many instances where women in South Africa, for instance, have legal rights, but custom and tradition prohibit women's claims to property and land use (Hames, 2006). Fraser (1997) acknowledges that the redistribution–recognition dilemma is not easy to resolve, but an awareness of the tensions and multiplicities of injustices that intersect at race, gender, ethnicity and other levels will at least minimise some of the potential conflicts.

Gewirtz (2002) introduces a relational dimension to these tensions. The relational dimension 'refers to the nature of the relationships that structure society' (p. 140). This brings us to theorise issues of power and how we treat each other. *Relational* justice asks us to examine the 'informal and formal rules that govern how members of society treat each other'. Whilst distributional justice focuses on ensuring everyone receives their due, based on judgement of what they are worth, relational justice examines how that judgement is made – what are the inter-connections between individuals in society (family, cultural, ethnic or other) that impinge on people's ability to access opportunities, or even make their voice heard?

> We have opportunities if we are not constrained from doing things or if the conditions within which we have opportunities depends upon the enabling possibilities generated by the rules and practices of the society within which we operate, and by the ways in which people treat each other in that society. (Gewirtz, 2002, p. 142)

So, whilst international agencies may support micro-credit as an empowerment strategy for poor women in India, the fact that women are then denied opportunity to build on that credit or open bank accounts because their husband refuses to give permission, or custom denies them the opportunity to access markets that would enable them to make a profit from their small businesses, means that distributional justice fails to take account of relational issues. This results in citizenship capability as 'unfreedom' and limitation of achievement (in Sen's word, 'functionings').

Gewirtz's (2002) solution to this tension draws on Iris Young, suggesting that we need to pay more attention to the relationships that structure society – examining the effects on others of what we do and have as a result of attitudes and internalised practices. In terms of social justice, do policies and behaviours support or subvert exploitation, marginalisation, recognition or respect? One example of socially unjust policies can be seen in the World Bank and IMF structural adjustment conditions for low-income countries where international aid was made dependent upon reduced public spending. This impacted on distribution of free education, resulting in non-participation by the poorest and most vulnerable in those countries. What such examples demonstrate is that it is important to take account of context that includes social relations, culture and history when making social justice claims for citizenship based on need, desert and ability to benefit.

In spite of these caveats, Nussbaum (2006) attempts to develop a universalist position for social justice. She bases her argument on three unsolved problems of social justice identified as: lack of recognition for people with impairments; extending justice to all world citizens (as opposed to those determined by the national state); and including the treatment of non-human animals as a social justice issue.

Drawing on Sen's political economy concept of capabilities as 'freedoms' in terms of poverty eradication, and supporting his position that Rawls fails to examine outcomes for social justice, Nussbaum converts these freedoms, into ten central human entitlements, or capabilities, necessary for living a life of dignity. She argues that these capabilities are mutually supportive and should be respected and implemented by all governments. She further argues that they cannot be implemented from a purely political perspective. Capabilities are defined as 'what people are actually able to do and be' – but now they are also 'informed by an intuitive idea of a life that is worthy of the dignity of the human being' (p. 70). The introduction of 'intuition' adds a new, but also contestable dimension to the debate. By this means she allows for context-specific interpretation, but demands that we challenge people to look beyond the status quo and the tendency to be satisfied with 'adaptive preferences'. In other words she challenges hegemonic situations in society where women's or minorities' unequal treatment is inscribed in practices and attitudes in the name of tradition or culture. Citizenship education that is based on examining the extent to which these capabilities are in operation for every individual would take us beyond simply identifying the existence of human rights. It would challenge us to examine whether those human rights are freely accessible. The central human capabilities are briefly summarised as freedom to:

- Life – to live healthily and long
- Bodily health – including nourishment and reproductive health
- Senses, imagination and thought – informed and cultivated by adequate education
- Emotions – attachment to things and beings
- Practical reason – critical reflection
- Affiliation – living with others, consideration of others, respect, dignity
- Other species – concern for the world of nature
- Play – able to enjoy leisure
- Control over one's environment – including participation in political decision making, ownership of property, and equal rights to employment, or establishing meaningful relationships of personal choice (pp. 76–77).

Walker (2006) explores the degree to which Nussbaum's list adequately addresses a capability approach to education for social justice in a co-educational school environment in South Africa. She concludes that:

> The lens of capability directs our attention to any sources of unfreedom that might constrain genuine choices and how diverse individuals are affected. For example, violence and harassment of female pupils by their male peers and by teachers continues to be endemic in large numbers of black schools. (p. 180)

If the adoption of a capability lens facilitates our unearthing of injustices, perhaps this will in turn facilitate a social justice approach to citizenship education that will help to prevent future injustices.

A social justice perspective for citizenship education, therefore, might wish to explore the extent to which the girl child has freedom to go to school and learn about reproductive health, the extent to which she is able to make choices about who she wishes to marry, how many children she wants, the opportunity she has to live free from violent behaviour towards her body and property. Does she have freedom to take part in community and political decision-making bodies, freedom to learn and reflect critically on her and others' social or political circumstances? Does she have self respect? And so on. Similar comparisons can be made to people with disabilities whose freedom to employment, mobility or opportunity to make meaningful relationships are curtailed by environmental or social barriers. A central question to ask would be whether some people get more opportunities to convert their resources (distribution of good things in life) into capabilities (freedom to use and access those goods) than others. Some of these issues in different cultural contexts would need close scrutiny and challenge normative practices. But they may open up opportunity for debate about rationales for certain practices in terms of motivation or power relations for instance.

So how might a universal citizenship education programme function? This final section suggests some of the ingredients necessary for a capabilities approach to citizenship education.

CITIZENSHIP EDUCATION AND SOCIAL JUSTICE

I have discussed elsewhere (Preece, 2006) – as have others – that the education system itself may adopt socially just or unjust practices in terms of pedagogy, learner-centredness and criticality. I have also, in the same paper, offered a typology of educational processes and outcomes which can facilitate, to a greater or lesser degree, capability-based theories of social justice for education. The social justice-friendly educational typology privileges learner-centred pedagogical practices that encourage discussion, reflexivity, relevant curricula for learner context and needs, including using Young's (1996) proposals for other culturally relevant forms of communication such as proverbs or story telling. The educational outcomes would be less concerned with individual achievements or maintaining the status quo, but leaning more towards perspective transformation (changing mindsets) and generating more involvement in decisions that affect communities' or individuals' lives.

In order to see how a capabilities approach for citizenship education might operate, I take an example drawn from a non-formal educational programme for out-of-school girls in Malawi (Hogg 2005) as a starting framework for interrogating Nussbaum's list. Hogg describes one instance of adapting the girls' curriculum in order to be of practical value to their context:

> We learnt that ... it is the learners and their communities who determine more precisely what touches the reality of their lives. For example, in practice, teaching the girls that flying ants, mice, beans and groundnuts are a valuable source of protein was more useful than examples using meat and eggs. According to some girls, 'Eggs are sold, left to hatch, or given to the men. If there is meat locally, the men have that too'. (pp. 661–662)

Nussbaum's capability approach might encourage us to interrogate to what extent such an adapted curriculum is preventing life, compromising bodily health or bodily integrity. Discussions amongst the girls might ensue that claim these

389

alternative sources of protein do not compromise these capabilities. On the contrary, an attempt to secure eggs might risk vulnerability to bodily security in the form of beatings. Similarly senses, imagination and thought are being encouraged through potentially imaginative ways of preparing meals from these resources. However, to what extent is freedom of choice curtailed, or freedom of expression, in articulating the discriminatory denial of certain kinds of food on grounds of gender? To what extent would emotions of anger be undermined if attempts to complain were undertaken? A critical citizenship analysis would raise the girls consciousness of the apparently unjust distribution of certain forms of good. Nussbaum's inclusion of 'practical reason' as engagement in critical reflection might, however, also result in the girls articulating the wider economic value of selling eggs or letting them hatch, or that equipping men with the nutrients of limited meat supplies equips them with muscle strength to do any available manual work so that the girls are enabled to go to school. The same reasoning might also stimulate analysis of the extent to which such rationales are premised on power relations rather than consensus – for instance, women also do heavy manual work.

Further examination of Nussbaum's capabilities in relation to these girls' lives draws us beyond the above quotation. But the concept of affiliation – which Nussbaum elaborates as being able 'to live with and toward others ... to imagine the situation of another' (2006, p. 77) is relevant to understanding community living in situations of poverty. Whilst understanding that, it could also be used to explore whether girls have a say in how they want to live their lives, or whether it is poverty itself which constrains their opportunities and also denies them a voice in challenging gender or other forms of discrimination. Similarly, is it poverty or culture that denies them access to recreational activities? In terms of being able to live in harmony with nature, how much is the education system enabling these girls to utilise their local resources sustainably when such resources are poorly supplemented by communication networks or access to new technologies? Perhaps more poignantly, how much is increased education about human rights enabling the girls to have greater control over their political and material environment so they may participate equally with their male counterparts or those who are able to work for a living wage? It seems that an examination of the central human capabilities raises many questions, and challenges the learner to think creatively about the extent of their freedoms in relation to others. But in themselves, do they equip the learner with increased agency to act or use goods that are freely available?

It seems that the capability approach challenges us to ask what education enables us to do and be, rather than solely focusing on education for productivity and employment (though this could, of course, also be a capability). It also challenges us to ask how capabilities can develop agency and autonomy that translate into opportunity and life choices. But decision-making and use of agency to challenge injustices is dependent upon the individual's choice of *whether* to act. So we must also ask, Who, in different contexts, has opportunities for active citizenship? If we explore the tensions for justice that is based on need, desert and ability to benefit, we should then be able to identify which people get more opportunities to convert their resources into capabilities than others. From here a focus on consideration, caring and concern for others should lead us to reconsider injustices. We cannot assume, of course, that everyone is at the same emotional level when these questions are asked. It is not clear that a common outcome would be achieved in social justice terms. But an education that stimulates these debates is more likely to produce consideration of the consequences of outcomes that are rationalised under the name of social justice. It is a form of education that takes us beyond information-giving and requires the facilitation of a discursive critique of contextually-framed issues rather than facts.

The non-formal education that is practised through civil society movements, and out-of-school agencies is likely, as indicated in the early part of this paper, to be less constrained by government policy and standardised curricula. It is arguably better positioned to engage with issues that centre round Nussbaum's core freedoms for living a life with dignity. But it is not inconceivable that such programmes could also be undertaken through the formal school system, given appropriate training in the pedagogical approach. The Oxfam programme discussed earlier in this paper offered some indication that social justice is a core part of the skills, attitudes, knowledge and understanding required for citizenship activity. Nussbaum's list of capabilities might provide a framework for exploring how to interrogate social justice issues in different global contexts and assess whether these ten freedoms are indeed universal if adapted to context.

CONCLUSION

In this paper I have argued that current citizenship education is at best uneven and at worst inadequately focused. The concept of social justice should be a central tenet of citizenship education, thus encouraging a more critical analysis of our world and its complexities. However, social justice perspectives must take account of context, culture and the power relations that often frame actions and attitudes in the name of social justice. In Nussbaum's principles this must include a more intuitively-led analysis to try and remove us from normative discourses that simply make invisible and silence those already silenced and invisible, who are most at risk from injustices. The extent to which her capabilities approach is potentially universal must be tried and tested. A capabilities exploration of social justice in relation to the context of Malawi out-of-school learners in a non-formal education environment, suggests that a lesson on nutrition and health could encourage critical engagement with accepted norms and notions of fairness in relation to particular contexts, but a citizen's decision to act would depend on the extent of the individual's motivation and their existing freedoms to act. Whilst the formal system could adopt a capability curriculum, it is suggested that civil society or non-formal systems, unconstrained by government-driven curricula, are more likely to engage in this kind of learning. Although a social justice approach to citizenship education is not in itself going to emancipate the unemancipated, it provides people with the critical skills to question and raise awareness of their citizenship rights and responsibilities within an informed context.

REFERENCES

Adeyemi, M. B., Boikhutso, K and Moffat, P (2003). Teaching and learning of citizenship education at the junior secondary level in Botswana. *The Journal for Pastoral Care and Personal/Social Education, 21*(2), 35–40.

Arko-Cobbah, A. (2005). 'Quest for democratic citizenship in South Africa: Curriculum 2005 and citizenship education in perspective'. Paper presented at PESA 2005, Hong Kong. Retrieved from http://www.pesa.org.au/html/documents/2005-papers/Paper-01_Albert_Arko-Cobbah.doc.

Arnot, M. (2006). Freedom's children: A gender perspective on the education of the learner-citizen. *Review of Education, 52*, 67–87.

Astiz, M. and Mendez, G. (2006). Education for citizenship: The argentine case in comparison. *Education, Citizenship and Social Justice, 1*(2), 175–200.

Bisch, P.M. (Ed.) (1995). *A culture of democracy: A challenge for schools.* Paris: UNESCO.

Cornwall, A. and Molyneux, M. (2006). The politics of rights: Dilemmas for feminist praxis. An introduction. *Third World Quarterly, 27*(7), 1175–1191.

Dean, B.L. (2005). Citizenship education in Pakistani schools: Problems and possibilities. *International Journal of Citizenship and Teacher Education, 1*(2), 35–55.

Fraser, N. (1997). *Justice interruptus.* London: Routledge.

Gewirtz, S. (2002). *The managerial school: Post-welfarism and social justice in education.* London: Routledge.

Presidential Task Group (1997). *Vision 2016: Towards prosperity for all.* Gaborone: Presidential Task Group.

Harber, C. (2002). Education, democracy and poverty reduction in Africa. *Comparative Education, 38*(3), 267–276.

Hames, M. (2006). Rights and realities: Limits to women's rights and citizenship after 10 years of democracy in South Africa. *Third World Quarterly, 27*(7), 1313–1327.

Hogg, A. (2005). Finding a curriculum that works under trees: Literacy and health education for adolescent girls in rural Malawi. *Development in Practice, 15*(5), 655–667.

Koshmanova, T. (2006). National identity and cultural coherence in educational reform for democratic citizenship: The case of Ukraine. *Education, Citizenship and Social Justice, 1*(1), 105–118.

Miraftab, F. and Wills, S. (2005). Insurgency and space of active citizenship. *Journal of Planning Education and Research, 25*, 200–217.

Mundel, K. and Schugurensky D. (Eds.) (2004). *Lifelong citizenship learning, participatory democracy and social change.* Toronto: Transformative Learning Centre, OISE/University of Toronto.

Nordberg, C. (2006). Claiming citizenship: Marginalised voices on identity and belonging. *Citizenship Studies, 10*(5), 523–539.

Nussbaum, M. (2006). *Frontiers of justice.* London: The Belknap Press/Harvard University Press.

Nyamnjoh, F.B. (2007). From bounded to flexible citizenship: Lessons from Africa. *Citizenship Studies, 11*(1), 73–82.

Oxfam (2002). *Global citizenship: The handbook for primary teaching.* London: Oxfam.

Park, B. (2006). The community-based learning approach for citizenship education: An instrument for attaining a lifelong learning society. *Citizenship Teacher and Learning, 2*(2), 85–97.

Preece, J. (2006). 'Non-formal education for social justice and inclusion in developing countries'. Paper submitted to Compare and presented at BAICE Annual Conference, Belfast, September 8–10.

Rawls, J. (1972). *A theory of justice.* Oxford: Clarendon Press.

Scanlon, C. (2002). 'Educating for peace: Politics and human rights in Botswana'. Unpublished seminar presentation, 27 March.

Sen, A. (1992). *Inequality re-examined.* Oxford: Oxford University Press.

UNESCO (1995). *Declaration and integrated framework of action on education for peace, human rights and democracy.* Paris: UNESCO.

UNESCO (1998). *Citizenship education for the 21st century.* Retrieved 11 September, 2007, from http://www.unesco.org.

Walker, M. (2006). Towards a capability-based theory of social justice for education policy-making. *Journal of Education Policy, 21*(2), 163–185.

Young, I. (1996). Communication and the other: Beyond deliberative democracy. In S. Benhabib (Ed.), *Democracy and difference.* Princeton, New Jersey: Princeton University Press.

Julia Preece
Centre for Research and Development in Adult and Lifelong Learning (CRADALL)
University of Glasgow

ALI A. ABDI

CITIZENSHIP AND ITS DISCONTENTS

Educating for Political and Economic Development in Sub-Saharan Africa

INTRODUCTION

With the geographical and quasi-political decolonisation of Sub-Saharan Africa (hereafter, Africa) from the late 1950s into early 1960s, there was a widespread expectation with respect to the possible 're-citizenising' of previously subject populations in the sub-continent. After a while, though, it became clear that, via the economic and cultural hegemony of the West, Africa was actually slowly being recolonised through the twin tragedies of European and American global policies and the exclusionist, degenerative and corrupt behaviours of the sub-continent's postcolonial elite. And if things were not bad enough, the ushering in of organised globalisation, with its post-1980 rapid intensities and extensities (see Held & McGrew, 2002), added to the continuing marginalisation of Africa. With those in place, came the fall of the Eastern Bloc, followed by such triumphalist exhortations (from the neo-liberal camp) as Francis Fukuyama's *End of History and the Last Man* (1993), which hastily told us, among many other things, that the promise of liberal democracy will now be harnessed by all.

Before the fall of the Eastern bloc in the late 1980s, most African governments were successful in playing the bi-polar world induced superpower card, which was readily available to them as a result of the global rivalry between the Americans and the Russians. While military coups d'état and other violent changes of political regimes were more common than now, it was also the case that via the support of either superpower, a high number of army dictators, corrupt civilian elites and single family dynasties stayed in power for decades. It was from the early 1990s, therefore, that most African countries started to adhere, theoretically at least, to the exegesis of some democratic rule (as was demanded by Western powers). However one defines and/or practises democracy, though (e.g., government by all, or government by the few who supposedly represent the rest), hardly anything that corresponds to that has developed in the nearly two decades of African democracy. So much so that in Julius Ihonvbere's terms (1996), with so much institutional weakness inherent in the processes of democratisation that started in the decade of the 1990s, Africa may have found itself at the threshold of another false start, and may have mainly succumbed to elite driven forms of what Zakaria (2004) calls illiberal democracy, which did not ameliorate either the political and/or socio-economic rights of the masses. And in early 21st century, most of the people in the

M.A. Peters, A. Britton and H. Blee (Eds.), Global Citizenship Education: Philosophy, Theory and Pedagogy, 395–407.

continent (there are a few exceptions, including political South Africa, Botswana, to some extent Ghana, and economic Uganda) can hardly claim any viable citizenship rights that can be operationalised for better liveable contexts.

It is on the basis of these realities that I am advancing this call for citizenship development, which despite the disappointments with the current political structure, should still aim for a socially inclusive perspective that assures what may still be the most effective way to achieve these rights, i.e., strengthening the accountability plateau of the national political public space (Abdi *et al*, 2005; Gyimah-Boadi, 1998; Ihonvbere, 1996; Burnell, 1995). The rationale here should not be too complicated to see and analyse. If the effective and development-oriented management and distribution of national resources, especially in areas where the capacity of the private sector is either very weak or quasi-non-existent, should be dependent on a transparent and socially responsive political structure, then people's well-being and their citizenship rights would be best achieved by correcting and sustaining the inclusiveness of the political component.

As Tully (2005, p. 3) correctly notes, 'when the governed act as citizens and demand a say in the practices of governance to which they are subject, they bring this practice under shared authority: that is, under the shared authority of citizens and governors in negotiation [thus democratising] the practice of governance.' This is also related to what Ottonelli (2002, p. 236) calls the 'fundamental principle of political justice' which requires that

> whoever is permanently subject to the laws of a country should have a voice in their making, and whoever partakes in the economy of a country should also participate in the social benefits deriving from that economic cooperation.

With Africans not having much say in either the governance structures or the economic interactions that mostly determine their lives, it should go without saying that if Africa is to reverse the trends of global de-linking it is currently exposed to, all countries in the region must exercise proactive and practically viable programs of political participation. Political participation as a multidimensional construct and practice should go beyond the simple act of voting, and should involve citizens fully involved in defining and acting within and through their country's political processes, objectives and results.

As an introductory work on these topics, therefore, this chapter analyses select theoretical pointers that are discursively brought together to highlight the importance of citizenship development in all the actualities of the African continent. But political development is not an automatic historical event, and could only be achieved if and when it permeates public space and discourse. As should be understood, there is an assumption here that as things are today in our world and while democracy, however it is defined and practiced, is not a perfect system of governance, it at least seems to achieve more positive outcomes for more people than other things that have been tried in the recent history of our world. In the following, I will present some brief pointers on the actualities of African development, followed by a generalised historicisation of education and development in Africa, the role of citizenship education and an attached perspective on the need for economic democracy. In general, the unproblematised deployment of the terms 'democracy' and 'development' in the text of the chapter is intended to indicate their generalised usability, and no postmodernist or post-structuralist critiques of the cases will be undertaken at this point in time.

ACTUALITIES OF AFRICAN DEVELOPMENT

Development as a theoretical construct and its attendant practices, and with some disciplinary and measurable attachments, gained an ongoing importance since the end of the Second World War. As Maggie Black (2002) notes, inherent in the construction of the idea was a sense of responsibility, albeit a misguided one, by the industrialised countries to help the backward nations of the world. Here, one should immediately discern the modernist intentions that are encoded; we should, of course, know that the world was 'developing' in its different and diverse ways for some millennia before that, but this post-War period should at least pertain to development as a new attempt to homogenise all people's comparative relationship with prospectively standardised notions of material, physical and later, mental well-being. In the African case specifically, we can probably talk about the continent's development in the past 50 or so years. Before that, almost all of Africa was under colonial rule whose effects were counter-development and mainly focused on the maximum exploitations of the continent's human and natural resources (Abdi, 2002; Rodney, 1982; Nyerere, 1968).

At any rate, and regardless of the pragmatism of the overall intentions, advancement possibilities in those 50 years did not respond to the development expectations of the people. In many cases, the general continental situation was characterised by the realities of closura politica and maladministration, which all led to failed economic and governance programmes, environmental degradation and the resulting droughts and famines. These were later complemented by the post-Cold War fragmentation of a number of countries that either became stateless (Somalia), quasi-stateless (Zaire), in full civil war (Liberia and Sierra Leone), under the onslaught of genocide (Rwanda in the 1990s, and potentially Sudan and Chad now), and, at times, on the brink of self-destruction (Burundi). In addition, the almost fragile political structures in most other parts of the continent continue to be problematic, for what was supposed to be the enlightened and relatively educated second generation of leaders who did not live up to the expectations of the public.

It is the case, therefore, that what has been labelled in Bayart's 1993 book, *The State in Africa: the Politics of the Belly*, where public office and public funds were not being stipulated for social development, but for the personal enrichment of those who were entrusted with the management of these resources, may unfortunately be still true. Again, this is an Africa whose share in world trade in manufactured goods was falling from 0.4% in the early 1960s to 0.2% in the late 1980s (Kennedy, 1993), an Africa that was spending about US$13 billion on foreign debt servicing in 1995, twice what was spent on healthcare and education combined in that same year (*The Globe and Mail*, 1996, p. A10). It is also an Africa where, in most countries at least, living standards have been declining since the 1970s (Tsie, 1997). With Africa so peripheral in development terms to most of the world, therefore, it might not surprise us that in the early 1990s (and surely into the 21st century) new ethnocentric exhortations were coming from some quarters in the West, including this one from William Pfaff (1993, pp. 2, 6) who, in the influential publication *Foreign Affairs*, wrote this:

> Much of what Africa needs, to put it bluntly, is what one could call a disinterested neo-colonialism. Africans acknowledge the immensity of their crisis and the need to consider hitherto unacceptable remedies .... The democracy movement, which in the past years produced a series of national conferences to end dictatorships, is foundering. Fewer than a third of Sub-Saharan Africa's governments have anything resembling multiparty politics.

Here, Pfaff's points, while interesting from the perspective of a very distant observer who wilfully ignores the long historical and cultural realities that would determine people's capacity to oppose the continuities of colonial subjugations, could also actually dilute the meanings of any citizenship rights Africans could have achieved after military-based colonialism. That is, by displaying the continent's citizenship and general development problems as inherent in the nature of Africa, his potentially influential observations could have been very effective in adding to Africa's problems of underdevelopment and marginalisation. Instead of blaming the African people, which is apparently what he is doing, for what went wrong with the continent, Pfaff and his ilk should have known that despite the reality of African leaders mostly betraying the promise of independence, Africa's collective structural problems were, to the larger extent, the result of global market forces, complemented by the tenacity of the imperial order that has selectively recolonised Africa's politico-economic spaces for the ideological demands of American institutions such as the International Monetary Fund (IMF) and the World Bank (Leys, 1996). Indeed, these and their allied international financial institutions (IFIs) were instrumental in imposing the draconian governance and public resources management schemes known as Structural Adjustment Programs (SAPs), which due to the pressures they put on the average African family, have always been counter to the basic citizenship rights of survival and development (Schatz, 2002; Tsie, 1997; Eyoh, 1996; Cheru, 1995). Indeed, James Tully's admirable analytical position would give us a more reliable perspective in the case. Tully (2005, p. 6) writes:

> [When] the formal colonies were dismantled, local political power was transferred to, or taken back by, westernized capitalist or socialist elites during colonization. While the decolonized (but not de-imperialized) dreamed of diverse forms of citizenship, self-reliance, local democracy, alternative modernities or a dialogical perspective among diverse populations, the westernized elites, trapped and sometimes seeing their personal interests in economic, military, technological and debt dependencies

of the existing imperial relationships, were constrained to what colonialism began: the destruction, overriding or subordination of local communities, economies and legalities, and the rapid development of nationalizing subaltern regimes of uniform modern citizenship and civilization dominated by the economies of the former imperial powers, or face the overwhelming force of military and financial power as we have been seeing lately in many parts of the world.

Tully's observations actually go to the core of what went wrong with the citizenship rights of so many whose postcolonial expectations were thrown, to use just one deformalised expression, to the dogs. In fact, one could describe these historical trajectories as triply 'de-citizenising' tragedies where the problems of colonialism were continued by the postcolonial elite, always complemented by the global threat to maintain the selectively disjunctured citizenship realities that were imposed at will on populations that are seen as perennial subjects for the interests of the West and its economic and military power. But again, even when so many in Africa and elsewhere are 'de-citizenised', at least some of their agency, unless they are killed in direct military campaigns, is never taken away. Hence, the important point that although the citizenship situation in current Africa is not developmentally constructive, and while there will be a number of social and other intersections where someone has failed the people, the move forward in citizenship rights should not be compromised from now on, and I agree with Gyimah-Boadi (2004), Sandbrook (2000), and Van de Walle (1997) that in the thick of all the changes that are needed, aiming to fix the political platform with transparent and accountable governance and economic structures that are fully entrenched in the national public spaces, would be the most important outlet for tangible and African development. To achieve that, one needs to re-engage and analyse the education system in historical and current perspectives.

THE ROLE OF EDUCATION IN SOCIAL DEVELOPMENT

As Soltis (1988) correctly noted, all forms of education including (for me at least) traditional, pre-colonial learning in Africa, and all current forms of formal education and informal systems, involve an element of citizenship training. That is, as everything we learn shapes the way we understand and respond to our social and physical environments, it helps us ascertain the way we interact with others, thus heavily influencing how we comprehend and seek out our rights and responsibilities in any given temporal and spatial intersections of life. Especially as a social development platform where, for our purpose, the focus will be on introducing ameliorative possibilities in the political, economic, educational, cultural, technological and affective/emotional aspects of people's lives, the role of most learning programmes will either be catalysts for, or will act against, the goals of citizenship education. As such, it is important to note that all learning dispensations in pre-colonial traditional systems of education in Africa were formulated with a tangible, albeit sometimes implicit, element of citizenship education. These systems of learning analysed and explained, among other things, social responsibilities, the relationship between the ruler and the ruled, and the economic and environmental rights of groups and communities (Rodney, 1982). With the arrival of colonialism, though, as Nyerere (1968) and Rodney (1982) pointed out, local projects and programmes of educational and social development were portrayed by colonial powers as exclusively inferior to European ways of learning and knowing, thus relegating Africa's epistemic and epistemological projects to the fringes of the colonised landscape.

For me, and I am sure for many others, this could be seen as a widespread project of 'de-citizenising' people in the context of important life systems that they were born into, and with which they have established select ontological centres that defined both their existential and metaphysical worlds. Despite those colonialism-driven accusations and annulments, though, the fact remains that pre-colonial, African traditional systems of education were informed and characterised by advanced notions and practices of instruction that were established many years before the advent of European conquest, which could be officially dated from late 16th to mid-20th century (Van Sertima, 1991; Diop, 1990; Jackson, 1970). In addition, one must pragmatically adhere to the reality that if peoples who live in different parts of the world were allowed to design and implement their own systems of education, based on an extensive analysis of their needs and expectations and which would sustain their lives and intergenerational relationships, then expectedly Africans might have more effectively managed their complex life systems if they were able to develop those corresponding educational programmes. As such, Tanzania's former philosopher-statesman, Julius Nyerere (1968, p. 268) should be right when he writes:

> The educational systems in different kinds of societies in the world have been, are, very different in organization and content. They are different because the societies providing the education are different, and because education, whether it be formal or informal, has a purpose. That purpose is to transmit from one generation to the next the accumulated wisdom and knowledge of society, and to prepare the young people for their future membership of the society and their active participation in its maintenance and development.

Perhaps one step further, during colonialism, one would not have expected programmes of citizenship education to be part of colonial education. As was the case, colonialism did not have any intentions of educating and developing a cadre or more of critical African citizens, who by ascertaining and appreciating their citizenship rights, would become an apparent danger to the corporeal of the colonial project. And in the postcolonial situation, two important educational realities that were not conducive to citizenship development took place. The first one was by omission where almost all new African countries did not alter the basic foundations of colonial education, further entrenching the supremacy of school curricula that did not remedy the 'de-citizenising' schemes that have been inscribed on the bodies and minds of the people. This onslaught of existentially inferioritising life systems were also instrumental in relegating Africans to third or even fourth class status in the lands of their birth (Memmi, 1991). The second was by commission, and was related to how the new ruling class was loathe to develop any viable and globally- or locally-informed political education programmes that would affirm the citizenship dossier of the public. Instead, in the few cases where there were any notions of citizenship education, the limited civics instruction programmes were mainly formulated and implemented to create quasi-docile subjects whose loyalty to military rulers and civilian dictators was total and sustainable.

Later, with the move to democracy mentioned above, one should have expected more tangible projects of citizenship development through education, for as Dewey (1926) cogently noted, people cannot be expected to adhere to new systems of governance without critically understanding the character of those systems. If things went right on the citizenship front at least, since the processes of democratisation started in the early 1990s, we should have seen by now the beginning of the 'creation' of new citizens whose presence in the national public space accords them the capacity to achieve life systems that are both politically and economically endowed. To reaffirm again, though, with the reconstitutionalisation of the old order and labelling of it as a democracy, in most of these countries the quality of citizenship enjoyed by people in supposedly democratising Africa did not improve that much (Joseph, 1998; Hutchful, 1997; Mbembe, 1990). The transformative nature of the desired citizenship is important here, for in order to create citizens, one must identify with the whole political tradition and its derivatives so as 'to make a claim about one's moral identity; [and] to commit oneself to continuing a particular story because one thinks it is morally worthy of continuance' (Callan, 1997, p. 125). Those identities and the accompanying worthy stories of citizenship should, for me at least, enlarge the circumference of the genuine and institutionally traceable claims of a large and increasing number of stakeholders. And to return to the perspective of social development that is desired here, the entrenchment of citizenship rights, however they might be achieved, should always remain the sine qua non for the horizontal achievement of this and related platforms of life.

THE ROLE OF EDUCATION IN RE-IMAGINING CITIZENSHIP

To reiterate, educational programmes in both colonial and postcolonial Africa did not enhance the citizenship rights of people. On the contrary, these types of education actually increased and sustained multiple layers of subjugation for the population. In effect, it should also be noted that subsequent schemes of colonial education, mainly in their capacity to de-culture and 'de-linguicise' the colonised, were one of the most potent weapons of imperialism. In the context of those realities and into the current situation, therefore, one should not underestimate the role of education, whether formal or informal, to achieve the opposite of what it has achieved for colonialism and oppressive post-independence dictatorships in Africa. That is, the critical potential of education to decolonise the psychosomatic existentialities of people, including the recasting of deformed identities (Abdi, 1999), and restructuring false generalisations and misrecognitions that have done so much damage in the lives of people (Taylor, 1995).

In addition, the counter-hegemonic educational programmes that are needed to de-subject perennially subjected populations (see Mamdani, 1996), would also contain in their kernel multi-centric and therefore, global citizenship notations that should induce, to use a Freirean perspective (see Freire, 2000), an anti-oppressive liberating praxis that can pulverise, one has to hope, rigid, citizenship suppressing platforms that have become of longue durée. Indeed, while one has to consider the possible pragmatics of this project, we must also realise that the task will not be simple, for as they say, any destruction is always much simpler than the reconstructive capacities that should follow it. The good news though, is that unless it is rescinded by post-education practices (on daily, yearly or level basis) that are intentionally oppressive, all forms of learning could at least yield some elements of social thinking that endow the interactive faculties of individuals and communities. But sometimes we also need to go for a certain pedagogical design, especially in the current African situation, that goes beyond the general course of education. A new design that deliberately aims for the establishment of citizenship education projects that teach people about the historical characters of their marginalisation, complemented by intensive but clear disquisitions that effectively explain their rights vis-à-vis the powers that be.

It is the case that because humanity has been afflicted with constant doses of oppression, political education, in different forms and capacities, has been with us for a long time. It was Plato, for example, who in his *Republic*, spoke about how extensive and ongoing political education can bring about, even maintain, a just society. Plato's pupil Aristotle followed by writing in his *Politics*, that liberty and equality could be safeguarded when and if all persons would participate in the running of their government. Here, one must be tempted to take the classic philosophers to task, as their societies in early Greece were not very open to a horizontal political space, but the main point here should be that the theories espoused by these philosophers were aiming for an ideal that might have been present either, in their communities and in others since then. What is also true is that the practical implications of these pointers would be good for any society that wants to achieve positive citizenship results that inform the lives of people.

Beyond the need, the use and the desirability of citizenship education in Africa, one must also anticipate that with more people learning about their political rights and responsibilities and, in the process, expectedly becoming proactive citizens of their countries, the overall culture of the political space and, by extension, economic space, could be forever altered. In that setting, a return to the old, highly unequal order may be difficult, i.e., as the creation takes hold of a critical mass of citizens who are educationally endowed enough to counter-weigh any repressive practices that might be brought about by some 'politiciens malins' (cunning politicians) who would be longing for the privileges that were lost, we may see new beginnings in Africa and elsewhere. Again, Dewey (1926) should be right when he emphasised the relationship between the important value of effective mass education which can sustain the place of an educated citizenry that refuses to be oppressed. Specifically in Africa, an interesting project of political education with clear social aims (Education for Self-Reliance) was formulated by Tanzania's Nyerere (1968). This program, which was based on the philosophy of Ujamaa or villagisation, was intended to create a practical and ongoing relationship between education and rural communities. And while many see it as having had a limited success, the fact remains that with the onslaught of global capitalism so focused on defeating it (McHenry, 1994), it never had a chance to move forward and be judged on its own merits.

Therefore, to achieve the project of citizenship we are seeking via the critical deployment of inclusive citizenship education, some important things have to happen. One of these is the need for educators, educational researchers and policy makers to acquire a poly-perspective historico-cultural and politico-economic understanding of the regimes of oppression that this new political education should encounter. In a, perhaps, less nuanced version of the case, one should not lose sight of the weight of history in changing systems that need to be changed. So while taking into account the subsequent programmes of the 'de-citizenising' platforms and how to practically counter them, this new and rightly imagined citizenship education must also study and understand the current division of world power including the dominant, indeed, predatory place of the forces of globalisation such as the ubiquitously powerful multinational corporations that are not interested in the creation of citizens, but rather in the establishment of a world culture where all are consumers of the products the multinationals produce. In addition, our re-imagined citizenship education must also explain the reasons for the growing gap between the haves and have-nots in almost all parts of the world. Indeed, the most effective way to combat this gap, which cannot be sustained at its present rate and speed, is to situate and explain it as a stark denial of the rights of people whose resources, labour and consumerism (the latter, only when they can) are actually enriching the world of the wealthy and the powerful who are mostly in the so-called advanced democracies in the West.

Here, one should wonder how people in the West and the several non-Western developed regions of the world would justify their place vis-à-vis the 60 percent of the world's population who live on less than a dollar per day, especially when in the past 10 years or so, the rhetoric of global citizenship has been increasing in these same countries. If global citizenship, beyond the very ambitious Kantian notion of the 'kingdom of ends', would minimally aim for a global economic, educational and environmental justice (Noddings, 2005) and an ethical attachment that seeks those (Dower, 2002; Dower & Williams, 2002), then the privileged citizens of the First World, must realise that 'the wretched of the Earth', to deploy a Fanonian characterisation (Fanon, 1968) will not eat either the conceptual foundations or the rhetorical offshoots of citizenship or democracy. To repeat, therefore, the noble project to 're-citizenise' former citizens via the reconstructive prospects of political education will aim for the expansive establishment of a human rights project that decolonises the state-society and market-based interactions of life. These should be complemented by the even more urgent decolonisation of the mind (see Nandy, 1995; Wa Thiong'o, 1986) for especially Africans and others of the same current life trajectories. Here, I am also reminded of the Freirean notion that decolonising the oppressed is just half the liberation program, so perhaps decolonising the haves would also induce in them a desirable sobriety to see the effects of the price of their prosperity on their fellow global citizens.

Expanding Citizenship: The Need for Economic Democracy

Educating for political development in Africa will always be important, but even if that is achieved more effectively than has been the case, the achievement will still, be hollow unless it is accompanied by tangible programmes of livelihood improvement. While I have already mentioned the economic development issue above, because of the emphasis I am placing on the issue, I still would like to say more about it here. As the world is moving towards or already selectively achieving 'the knowledge economies of the 21st century' (and Africa has to be there), the main category determining factor here will be the availability of a well educated work force that can produce more than it consumes, i.e., can produce goods for export, and can compete, in its overall productivity and in the general quality of goods it creates, with all others in a continually globalising world. These will be the inescapable, main intersections of viable economic development for Africans and their states in the coming decades. Without inclusive and long-term economic development, which could only be possible via expansive and improving programmes of education that are timely and relevant, African democracies, regardless of their qualitative dispositions and even with the desired political improvements, will not keep their promise and may find it difficulty to meet the increasing expectations of the African public. Hence the prospectively horizontal point: economic democracy, which can only happen when all Africans who study and work hard can justly achieve discernible upward mobility, and which is a function of learning possibilities that target those that need them most, should be the direction where Africa's future should heading.

Beyond that, regimes of economic democracy need not be limited to decreases in unemployment rates, wage increases, or more viable purchasing power for the public. In fact, these will not be detached from political accountability and transparency in the sense that both speak about a level of institutional fairness and justice that indemnify the stakes of those who would otherwise be marginalised. As such, beyond viable educational programmes and the right to viable and liveable contexts, one should speak about ensuring the rights of workers and their dependents vis-à-vis the state, private local employers and foreign multinationals. In that vein, economic democracy also ushers in hitherto absent but interactively effective regimes of personal enhancement and social development schemes that once they are established, should self-perpetuate and in the process, could herald the beginning of the still elusive horizontal development possibilities that the masses are yearning for. Needless to say, the prospective to achieve these, will not be limited to activities that take in the local space, but would also include those that are practised outside Africa.

Indeed, deliberately established projects that include the appreciation of African commodities and other exports to their rightful values, complemented by the elimination of draconian loan practices that are draining Africa's finances will be important. These should be intermeshed with interventionist African government policies (in the Keynesian sense) that create national employment programmes that are supported by workers' rights, insurance programmes, viable pension possibilities and control of prices, which could all change the now chronic poverty and general crisis situations in the continent. After all, even if we were to stay with liberal democracy in its purest forms, a situation that may not bode well for an African space where community needs and interdependencies could supersede the rights of the individual, we should still be talking about effective state apparatuses that mediate social and economic interactions so individuals and groups get their rights and live up to their responsibilities. In addition, these should not be construed as advocating for the primacy of the neo-liberal agenda where market forces control everything. While open commerce and competitive market relationships could have a wider positive impact in the long run, these may not be immediately helpful in precarious economic situations, and the unleashing of the undiluted market forces might simply sustain the current status quo whereby, in most African countries, a few wealthy people and those attached to them in one way or another, are thriving at the expense of the perennially deprived majority. As such, in the emerging schemes of citizenship education, the possibility of de-subjecting citizens has to have an economic component that 'pragmatises' the imperative to live more viable, productive and secure lives.

CONCLUSION

In this chapter, I have attempted to problematise the locations of citizenship rights and the possibilities of citizenship education to ameliorate life systems in the African situation. To a limited but convenient extent, I have descriptively borrowed from the historical trajectories that should have shaped the current outcomes in a continent that would be the least endowed, educationally, economically and politically, in the world. One of the main catalysts that led to what we are seeing today was the experience of colonialism that subjugated people to the extent that, after independence, those who learned the most from colonial schools, the African government elites, more or less continued the imperial projects that denied people their basic citizenship rights. Finally, with the fall of the Eastern Bloc at the end of the 1980s, African governments had to obey the West's aid requirements and at least declare themselves as democratic states. But contrary to the expectations of the people and the world, most of these 'democracies' became democratic in name only, and for the African public the political forum did not improve that much, while the economic situation actually worsened. It is on the basis of these realities that I have suggested viable intentions and programmes of citizenship education that aim to strengthen the rights of citizens in the diverse contexts they come into contact with, and deal with the institutions of their states. Here, I have emphasised that even if citizenship mainly talks political development, we need to go one step further, and practically call for what I have called economic democracy in a context where due to intensifying livelihood pressures since the early 1990s, many are blaming this vaguely understood thing called 'democracy' as mainly responsible for their employment and income woes. While I am not claiming to have found any new remedies that would change the situation immediately, I strongly believe that strengthening people's citizenship rights including their economic liquidities, could herald more inclusive social development possibilities for the African public.

REFERENCES

Abdi, A. (1999). Identity formations and deformations in South Africa: A historical and contemporary overview. *Journal of Black Studies, 30*(2), 147–163.

Abdi, A. (2002). *Culture, education and development in Africa: Historical and contemporary perspectives.* Westport, CT: Bergin & Garvey.

Abdi, A., Ellis, L. & Shizha, E. (2005). Democratic development and the role of citizenship education in Sub-Saharan Africa with a case focus of Zambia. *International Education Journal, 6*(4), 454–466.

Bayart, J.-F. (1993). *The state in Africa: The politics of the belly.* London: Longman.

Black, M. (2002). *The no-nonsense guide to international development.* Oxford: Verso.

Burnell, P. (1995). The politics of poverty and the poverty of politics in Zambia's third republic. *Third World Quarterly, 16*(4), 675–690.

Callan, E. (1997). *Creating citizens: Political education and liberal democracy.* Oxford: Clarendon Press.

Cheru, F. (1995). The World Bank and structural adjustment programmes. *African Insight, 25*, 236–240.

Dewey, J. (1926). *Democracy and education.* New York: Macmillan.

Diop, C. A. (1990). *Civilization or barbarism: An authentic anthropology.* Brooklyn, NY: Lawrence Hill Books.

Dower, N. (2002). *Introduction to global citizenship.* Edinburgh: University of Edinburgh Press.

Dower, N. & Williams, J. (Eds.) (2002). *Global citizenship: A critical introduction.* New York: Routledge.

Eyoh, D. (1996). From Economic crisis to political liberalization: Pitfalls of the new political sociology in Africa. *African Studies Review, 39*, 43–80.

Fanon, F. (1968). *The wretched of the earth.* New York: Grove Press.

Freire, P. (2000). *Pedagogy of the oppressed.* New York:Cotinuum. (First published, 1970.)

Fukuyama, F. (1993). *The end of history and the last man.* Toronto: HarperCollins.

Gyimah-Boadi, E. (Ed.) (2004). *Democracy and development in Africa: The quality of the progress.*, Boulder, CO: Lynne Rienner.

Gyimah-Boadi, E. (1998). The rebirth of African liberalism. *Journal of Democracy, 9*, 18–31.

Held, D. & McGrew, A. (2002). *The global transformations reader: An introduction to the globalization debate.* Cambridge, UK: Polity Press.

Hutchful, E. (1997). Militarism and problems of democratic transition. In M. Ottaway (Ed.), *Democracy in Africa: The hard road ahead.* Boulder, CO: Lynne Rirnner.

Ihonvbere, J. (1996). On the threshold of another false start? A critical evaluation of pro-democracy movements in Africa. *Journal of Asian and African Studies, XXXI*, 125–142.

Jackson, J. (1970). *Introduction to African civilizations.* Secaucus, NJ: The Citadel Press.

Joseph, R. (1998). Africa, 1990–1997: From abertura to closure. *Journal of Democracy, 9*, 3–17.

Kennedy, P. (1993). *Preparing for the twenty-first century.* New York: Random House.

Leys, C. (1996). *The rise and fall of development theory.* Bloomington, IN: Indiana University Press.

Mamdani, M. (1996). *Citizen and subject: Contemporary Africa and the legacy of late colonialism*. Newhaven, NJ: Princeton University Press.

Mbembe, A. (1990). Democratization and social movements in Africa. *Africa Demos, 1*, 4.

McHenry, D.E. (1994). *Limited choices: The political struggle for socialism in Tanzania*. London: James Curry.

Memmi, A. (1991). *The colonizer and the colonized*. Boston: Beacon Press.

Nandy, A. (1997). The decolonization of the mind. In M. Rahnema & V. Bowtree (Eds.), *The post-development reader*. London: Zed Books.

Noddings, N. (Ed.) (2005). *Educating citizens for global awareness*. New York: Teachers College Press.

Nyerere, J. (1968). *Freedom and socialism: A selection from writings and speeches, 1965–67*. Oxford: Oxford University Press.

Ottonelli, V. (2002). Immigration: What does global justice require? In N. Dower & J. Williams (Eds.), *Global citizenship: A critical introduction*. New York: Routledge.

Pfaff, W. (1993). A New Colonialism? Europe must go back to Africa. *Foreign Affairs, 4*, 2, 6.

Rodney, W. (1982). *How Europe underdeveloped Africa*. Washington, DC: Howard University Press.

Sandbrook, R. (2000). *Closing the circle: Democratization and development in Africa*. Toronto: Between the Lines.

Schatz, S. (2002). Structural adjustment. In G. Bond & N. Gibson (Eds.), *Contested terrains and constructed categories: Contemporary Africa in focus*. Boulder, CO: Westview Press.

Soltis, J. (1988). Foreword. In R. Pratte, *The civic imperative: Examining the need for civic education*. New York: Teachers College Press.

Taylor, C. (1995). *Philosophical arguments*. Cambridge, MA: Harvard University Press.

The Globe and Mail (1996). January 11, p. A10.

Tsie, B. (1997). States and markets in southern African development community (SADC): Beyond the neo-liberal paradigm. *Journal of Southern African Studies, 22*, 75–98.

Tully, J. (2005). *Two meanings of global citizenship: Modern and diverse*. Paper presented at the Meanings of Global Citizenship Conference, University of British Columbia, Canada, September 2005.

Van de Walle, N. (1997). Economic reform and the consolidation of democracy in Africa. In M. Ottaway (Ed.), *Democracy in Africa: The hard road ahead*. Boulder, CO: Lynne Rienner.

Van Sertima, I. (1991). The lost sciences of Africa. In I. Van Sertima (Ed.), *Blacks in science: Ancient and modern*. New Brunswick, NJ: Transaction Books.

Wa Thiong'o, N. (1986). *Decolonising the mind: The politics of language in African literature*. London: Heinmann.

Zakaria, F. (2004). *The future of freedom: Illiberal democracy at home and abroad*. New York: WW Norton.

Ali A. Abdi
University of Alberta

YUSEF WAGHID

DEMOCRATIC CITIZENSHIP, PHILOSOPHY OF ISLAMIC EDUCATION AND MADRASSAH SCHOOLING IN SOUTH AFRICA

INTRODUCTION

Three fundamental Islamic educational institutions related to schooling include the *maktab* (elementary school or pre-primary school), *masjid* (mosque) and *madrassah* (public school, namely primary and secondary school) (Waghid, 1996, pp. 35–37). In this chapter I show that madrassah schooling in South Africa does not show much promise for achieving some of the public goods associated with a liberal conception of democratic citizenship education, namely achieving a collective identity, confrontational public deliberation and the recognition of, and responsibility for, the rights of others. Firstly, I explore a liberal conception of democratic citizenship education with reference to the seminal ideas of Seyla Benhabib and Eamonn Callan. Therefore, I discuss a philosophy of Islamic education with reference to just actions such as *ijtihād* (rational argumentation), *shūrā* (mutual or deliberative engagement) and *ikhtilaf* (diversity, pluralism, disagreement). I argue that these just actions can potentially cultivate constitutive goods of democratic citizenship education. Finally, with reference to a case study of forty *madāris'* (Muslim schools) I show how difficult it seems for these schools to achieve some of the public goods linked to a liberal conception of democratic citizenship education.

TWO LIBERAL CONCEPTIONS OF DEMOCRATIC CITIZENSHIP EDUCATION: THE VIEWS OF SEYLA BENHABIB AND EAMONN CALLAN

In this chapter I explore a liberal conception of democratic citizenship education as espoused by Seyla Benhabib (2002) and Eamonn Callan (1997). According to Benhabib (2002, p. 169), democracy and citizenship can co-exist because the former frames education as a process of active consent and participation, whereas the latter designates the sense of belonging people demonstrate when socialised into educative practices. Active participation and belonging are both conceptually connected to some form of engagement in relation to someone else – I participate with others in a conversation, so I engage with them; and I belong to a group where members are in conversation with one another, so I engage with them by being attached to the conversation. On the one hand, by active participation Benhabib

M.A. Peters, A. Britton and H. Blee (Eds.), Global Citizenship Education: Philosophy, Theory and Pedagogy, 409–420.

(2002, pp. 133–134) means that people are free and equal moral beings who attempt to influence each other's opinions by engaging in a public dialogue in which they examine and critique (in a civil and considerate manner) each other's positions, while explaining reasons for their own. On the other hand, by belonging is meant that people are committed to the task of education through being more accountable to the process and deepening their attachment to it. Moreover, for Benhabib democratic citizenship education (more specifically, educating people to become democratic citizens) would at least be constituted by three interrelated aspects: collective identity, privileges of membership, and social rights and benefits.

Firstly, educating people to be democratic citizens has to take into account people's linguistic, cultural, ethnic and religious commonalities (Benhabib, 2002, p. 162). The idea of finding a civil space for the sharing of different people's commonalities is based on the understanding that people need to learn to live with the otherness of others whose ways of being may be deeply threatening to their own (p. 130). And, by creating a civil space, referred to by Benhabib (p. 127) as 'intercultural dialogue', whereby people can enact what they have in common and at the same time make public their competing narratives and significations, people might have a real opportunity to co-exist. In this way they would not only establish a community of conversation and interdependence (that is, they share commonalities), but also one of disagreement (that is, they do not share commonalities) without disrespecting others' life-worlds (pp. 35, 41). Put differently, when people are engaged in a conversation underpinned by interdependence and disagreement, they engage in an educative process with a collective identity – they share commonalities. And educating people to become democratic citizens involves creating civil spaces whereby they can learn to share commonalities and to respect the differences of others.

Secondly, educating people to be democratic citizens involves making them aware of the right of political participation, the right to hold certain offices and perform certain tasks, and the right to deliberate and decide upon certain questions (Benhabib, 2002, p. 162). The point is that people need to be educated to accept that they cannot be excluded from holding certain positions or performing certain tasks on the basis of their cultural differences. They have the right to participate, to be heard and to offer an account of their reasons 'within a civil public space of multicultural understanding and confrontation' (p. 130). Of particular importance to this chapter is the notion of educating people about the right to deliberate and decide on certain questions. What this implies is that we should recognise the right of people capable of speech and action to be participants in the moral conversation whereby they should have the same rights to various speech acts, to initiate new topics and to ask for justification of the presuppositions of the conversation (p. 107). Only then do people become participants in an educative process underpinned by democratic citizenship.

Thirdly, democratic citizenship education also involves educating people about their civil, political and social rights. Such a process would educate people about the rights to protection of life, liberty and property, the right to freedom of conscience, and certain associational rights, such as those of contract and marriage – all civil rights. People would also be educated about the rights of self-determination, to hold and run for office, to enjoy freedom of speech and opinion, and to establish political and non-political associations, including a free press and free institutions of science and culture – that is, political rights. And they are educated about the right to form trade unions as well as other professional and trade associations, health care rights, unemployment compensation, old-age pensions, child care, housing and educational subsidies – that is, social rights (Benhabib, 2002, pp. 163–164).

In essence, following Benhabib, a democratic citizenship education aims to cultivate public pedagogical spaces (in associational and non-associational networks such as schools, universities, religious sites and clubs) whereby people can be educated about one another's shared commonalities and to respect cultural differences (where culture represents people's shared values, meanings, linguistic signs and symbols). A democratic citizenship education would also educate people to deliberate in such a way as to offer an account of one's reasons and in turn listen to the reasons of others, and to recognise and respect people's civil, political and social rights. An education which takes into account these issues is underpinned by democracy and citizenship. I shall now elucidate a framework of democratic citizenship education as articulated in the seminal ideas of Eamonn Callan.

Like Benhabib, Callan (1997, pp. 221–222, 73) also makes a cogent argument for democratic citizenship education as being constituted by at least the following aspects: cohesive political identity, public deliberation and responsibility for the rights of others. Firstly, democratic citizenship education, particularly in pluralistic free societies, makes urgent the task of creating democratic citizens who share a sufficiently cohesive political identity (Callan, 1997, p. 221). By this he means that such a conception of democratic citizenship education 'honours the sources of diversity that thrive within the boundaries of a strong common citizenship, and yet supports a judicious tolerance to ways of life that conflict with some of its demands'. The pursuit of a collective political identity without discounting the differences of others could do much to prevent ethnic hatred and religious intolerance (p. 221).

Secondly, Callan (1997, p. 215) favours a conception of public deliberation characterised by the distress and belligerence (that is, a rough process of struggle) of confrontation (as recognised by Benhabib) that will naturally give way to conciliation as moral truth is pieced together from the fragmentary insights of conflicting viewpoints. For him, the idea of public deliberation is not an attempt 'to achieve dialogical victory over our adversaries but rather the attempt to find and enact terms of political coexistence that we and they can reasonably endorse as morally acceptable' (p. 215). Through public deliberation, participants disturb doubts about the correctness of their moral beliefs or about the importance of the differences between what they and others believe (a matter of arousing distress) accompanied by a rough process of struggle and ethical confrontation – that is, belligerence (p. 211). If this happens, belligerence and distress give way eventually to moments of ethical conciliation, when the truth and error in rival positions have been made clear and a fitting synthesis of factional viewpoints is achieved (p. 212). This is an idea of public deliberation – with which I agree – where no one has the right to silence dissent and where participants can speak their minds. In the words of Callan (pp. 201–202) 'real moral dialogue (as constitutive of democratic citizenship education), as opposed to carefully policed conversations about the meaning of some moral orthodoxy, cannot occur without the risk of offence, an offence-free school would oblige us to eschew dialogue'.

Thirdly, Callan (1997, p. 73), unlike Benhabib, does not merely call for recognition and respect of other's rights (whether civil, political or social) within a democratic citizenship education agenda, but he also stresses the importance of taking responsibility for the rights of others. In his words, taking rights seriously means 'accepting appropriate responsibility for the rights of others, not just making a fuss about our own' (p. 73). For instance, people who champion the right to employment in South Africa also consider as important the cause of others to take responsibility to meet the needs of those who are jobless. Such an understanding of democratic citizenship education could potentially extend the mere recognition of, and respect for, others' rights to a position whereby we assume appropriate responsibility for the rights of others.

This brings me to a discussion of whether a philosophy of Islamic education can engender democratic citizenship.

A PHILOSOPHY OF ISLAMIC EDUCATION: IS THERE SPACE FOR A LIBERAL VIEW OF DEMOCRATIC CITIZENSHIP?

In this section I shall explore whether a philosophy of Islamic education has the potential to engender a liberal view of democratic citizenship, with specific reference to a collective or cohesive political identity, confrontational public deliberation and recognition of, and responsibility for, the rights of others.

There exists sufficient evidence to suggest that the philosophy of Islamic education embeds tenets of democratisation (Esposito & Voll, 1996, p. 7), negotiation and protest politics (Eickelman & Piscatori, 1996, p. 108), liberalism and totalitarianism (Hrair Dekmejian, 1995:220), and *ijtihad* – rational argumentation on the basis of the Islamic sources, that is, the Qur'an and Sunnah[1] (Goldberg, 1993, p. 248). Thus, it seems as if Islamic sources on the philosophy of Islamic education's potential to engender a liberal form of democratic citizenship are ambivalent on the view that quietism and totalitarianism are also identified as tenets in this philosophy. For the purposes of this chapter, I shall explore those aspects of the philosophy of Islamic education which desirably connect with the constitutive meanings of a liberal conception of democratic citizenship education – collective or cohesive political identity, confrontational public deliberation and recognition of, and responsibility for, the rights of others.

But first I have to look at how Islamic sources interpret the notion of democracy. Some Islamic scholars claim that democracy has strong tendencies towards nihilism and immorality and, furthermore, calls for the abolition of Islam (Abed, 1995, p. 125). Others strongly contest this claim on the basis that nihilism and immorality can only thrive under conditions of dictatorship, which undermine the self-respect of people on the basis that dictatorships (such as those in some Muslim countries) are established on the basis of fear and the inculcation of terror in the hearts and minds of people (El-Effendi, 1991, p. 88). I support the latter view, because democratic principles propound that people should be respected as persons who have a legitimate right to settle their affairs by *shūrā* or 'good counsel and constructive criticism to rulers and fellow citizens alike' (Abd al-Rahim, 1987, p. 13). Dictatorships which deny people the right to articulate their views against totalitarian rulers (as in some Middle Eastern countries) are more inclined to breed nihilism, in particular dissatisfaction with a state which restricts people's freedom. In this regard, Kamali (1993, p. 34) makes the claim that the Islamic political system has nothing in common with dictatorship or theocracy, and has some characteristics of democracy. However, Kamali also holds the view that the Islamic political system does oppose the sovereignty of people and restricts their freedom, because the will of the people can never be above the *shari'ah* (Islamic law) (Kamali, 1993, p. 35). But then, for the *shari'ah* to become the supreme law in Islamic states, governments would require a democratic political procedure which can elicit the support of the majority of people in favour of such a system of rule. Thus, the idea that an Islamic state cannot be a democracy and that Muslims cannot be democratic citizens seems misplaced (El-Effendi, 1991, p. 90). If Muslims can act as democratic citizens, what is there potentially in an Islamic education system which can contribute towards guiding people to act as democratic citizens?

This brings me to a discussion of what constitutes a philosophy of Islamic education? To be more specific, what makes Islamic education what it is? A philosophy of Islamic education, like any other type of education, is constituted of a formal element (that which makes a concept what it is) and material elements or the ways in which Islamic education is realised. The formal element of Islamic education is *adab* or the appropriate use of knowledge (*'ilm*), reason (*nutq*), intellect (*'aql*) and heart (*qalb*) – more specifically one's physical, intellectual and spiritual capacities – to perform acts (*'amal*) of justice (*'adl*). For this reason, the rationale (formal element) of Islamic education aims to produce a just person: 'The *just* man is he who effects such *adab* unto his self, resulting in his being a *good* man [sic]' (al-Attas, 1991, p. 24). Some of the material elements of Islamic education include: *fiqh* (that is, religious insight and discernment which brings about piety or *taqwa,* which became associated with jurisprudence); *tawhid* (that is, knowledge of spiritual reality and truth which became associated with the science of dialectics); and *tadhkir* (that is, admonition which became associated with story-telling and the reciting of poems) (pp. 36–37).

For the purposes of this chapter, my emphasis is on an exploration of 'acts of justice' connected with a philosophy of Islamic education. These acts of justice would be discussed in relation to the constitutive meanings of democratic citizenship education earlier elaborated on, namely collective or cohesive political identity, confrontational public deliberation and recognition of, and responsibility for, the rights of others.

The first act of justice related to the realisation of a philosophy (including formal and materials elements) of Islamic education prominently referred to in Islamic sources is *ijtihād* – literally meaning rationality. In a well-known *Hadith* the Prophet is reported to have said: 'When a judge making a decision exerts himself [sic] and makes a correct decision, he will have a double reward, and if he errs in his judgement, he will still merit a reward'.[2] Elsewhere I have shown that *ijtihād* is a form of rationality which seeks to achieve justice (Waghid, 1996, p. 30). This idea of *ijtihād* differs from the very narrow juristic notion that links *ijtihād* to reasoning as a last resort to be employed solely by Muslim jurists to determine the permissibility of some action according to the Shari'ah, when the Qur'an and Sunnah are silent and earlier medieval Islamic scholars had not judged on the matter (Khan, 2005, p. 44). This view of *ijtihād* is parochial in the sense that rationality can only be invoked once it has been discovered that the primary sources of Islam are silent on a matter and no medieval scholar has addressed the issue – a view which leads to intellectual stagnation on the part of those who are not Muslim jurists. A liberal conception of *ijtihād,* used by non-jurists and supported by me, is deeply influenced by a type of moderate Islam which is reflective, self-critical, democratic and pro-human rights. Whereas for moderate Muslims *ijtihād* is the preferred method of choice for socio-political change, for militant Muslims, military *jihād* is the first option and *ijtihād* is not an option at all (p. 41). In my view, liberal *ijtihād* ought to be constituted by a type of reasoning which not only demands that one offers a justifiable account of one's reasons, but also that one is required to engage carefully with other points of view so as to arrive at independent interpretive judgements – even though at the same time one enters into controversy with other rival standpoints or articulations (MacIntyre, 1990, pp. 231–232). On the one hand, engaging carefully with other points of view involves advancing reasoning from within a particular point of view, preserving and transforming the initial agreements with those who share the point of view. On the other hand, entering into controversy with other rival standpoints involves both revealing what is mistaken in a rival standpoint in the light of one's understanding, and conceiving and reconceiving one's own point of view against the strongest possible objections to that offered by one's opponents. By implication, a liberal account of *ijtihād* firstly demands that a text (Qur'an or Hādith) be read in a way whereby one sets out the range of possible interpretations of the text, and identifies and evaluates the presuppositions of this or that particular argument in the text; and secondly, a text should be read in a way whereby the reader is put to question by the text as much as the text by the reader, that is to say, the reading prompts one to engage in systematic controversy. And the importance of reading a text in this way is that the outcome of one's reading is not the final (conclusive) answer, but rather a rational (interpretive) judgement which itself must be subjected to critical scrutiny by others who engage in similar intellectual debate free from the imperatives of constrained or unconstrained agreement.

Only when a liberal form of *ijtihād* is applied will the possibility exist for Muslim learners to begin to question, debate, undermine – all those critical qualities necessary to articulate and practise a more moderate form of Islam, that is, one which not only aspires for change through the rational mind, but also cultivates respect for persons through deliberative engagement. Through the use of liberal *ijtihād* 'moderate Muslims aspire for a society – a city of virtue – that will treat all people with dignity and respect [Qur'an, 17: 70]. There will be no room for political and normative intimidation [Qur'an, 2: 256]' (Khan, 2005, p. 41) – no space for *jihād* in the form of unacceptable acts of aggression against humanity. The Qur'an clearly favours a form of *ijtihād* whereby Muslims engage deliberatively with others (mutual action or *shūrā*) and rationally justify their arguments on the basis of critical engagement with the interpretive judgements of others (*amruhum shūrā bainahum*) (Qur'an, 42: 38). Now if one considers that *ijtihād* (rational argumentation) aims to achieve *shūrā* (mutual or deliberative engagement), it can be claimed that *ijtihād* is capable of achieving public deliberation – a constitutive feature of democratic citizenship education. What follows from this is that a philosophy of Islamic education whose aim is to achieve justice through *ijtihād* cannot be considered as incommensurate with an important feature of democratic citizenship education, that is, public deliberation. However, the question remains whether *shūrā* (mutual deliberation) should be confrontational – that is, arousing distress and accompanying belligerence. An appropriate example of the embodiment of confrontational public deliberation in the history of political Islam is Caliph Ali's treatment of the *Khawarij*. According to Yūsuf al-Qaradāwi, Muhammad Mahdī Shams al-Dīn, Fahmī Huwaydī and Louyay Safī (cited in Alibasic, 1999, p. 259), only violent action is prohibited in public deliberation (*shūrā*), because Caliph Ali condoned 'verbal assault' on the *Khawarij* people, who excommunicated him and his companions. Another precedent from Caliph Ali induced one of the famous Muslim jurists, Abu Hanifa, to say that it is unlawful to imprison or punish those who oppose and disagree with legitimate and just caliphs (Mustafa, in Alibasic, 1999, p. 262). In other words, in Islamic discourse public deliberation can be ethically confrontational as witnessed in the relationship between Caliph Ali (who was left with feelings of moral discomfort as a result of being verbally undermined) and the *Khawarij* people.

Secondly, the practice of *ikhtilaf* (diversity, pluralism, disagreement), considered as an offshoot of *ijtihād,* is also a way through which justice can be achieved (Alibasic, 1999, p. 258). Some Muslims perceive *ikhtilaf* as a necessary evil and feel uneasy about it, while others consider it as a source of flexibility and resourcefulness in the *Shari'ah* (Islamic law) (Al-'Alwani, 1994, pp. 11–19). Now considering that both the Qur'an and Sunnah call for the unity of the Muslim community,[3] it can be claimed that interdependence and consensus are highly prized in Islamic practices – an idea which has some connection with reaching a shared compromise (Callan, 1997) and finding shared commonalities (Benhabib, 2002). In this way, a philosophy of Islamic education has the potential to cultivate a collective community – an idea constitutive of democratic citizenship education. But this collective community – what Muslims would refer to as *ummah* – can be attained by giving consideration to *ikhtilaf* (disagreement). In other words, in a collective community there also exists disagreement or the recognition that there are not always commonalities amongst people that can be shared, but that the different 'life worlds' of people be respected under the pretext of recognition of difference or pluralism. In this way, *ikhtilaf* as a just Islamic educational activity has the potential to engender democratic citizenship and, more specifically, a collective community of interdependence and disagreement.

Thirdly, the Qur'anic dictum *la ikraha fi–al-din* (non-coercion) implies that people have the right to oppose, as well as freedom of religion, conscience and expression as corroborated by Qur'anic injunctions: 'You are not one to compel them by force' (*Surah Qaf*, 50: 45); 'Will you then compel humankind against their will, to believe' (*Surah Yunus*, 10: 99); and 'Revile not you those whom they call upon besides Allah, unless they out of spite revile Allah in their ignorance' (*Surah al-An'am*, 6: 108). Not only do these verses point out the importance of recognising the rights of people to make their own choices, but also our responsibility to ensure that others enjoy their rights (whether social, political and civil) which might be different to ours. Of course, the only condition seems to be that people do not commit an injustice against others, for instance, disparaging others' Gods or perhaps their Prophets. In other words, our responsibility to ensure the rights of others, say, to freedom of speech, ends as soon as injustice to others begins. This means freedom of expression should not become what Gutmann (2003, p. 200) calls 'an unconstrained licence to discriminate' – only if one avoids that does one act responsibly, that is, 'within the limits of doing no injustice to others' (p. 200). Put differently, the right to free and unconstrained expression ends when injustice to others begins. One can no longer lay claim to being responsible and just, if one advocates a particular point of view that entails excluding certain individuals – that is, discriminating invidiously against others (particularly those individuals in society most vulnerable and who lack the same expressive freedom as those who are excluding them) on grounds such as gender, race, sexual orientation, ethnicity and religion (p. 200). So, if those who want to be offensive to others, whether it be the Taliban who castigate Buddhists, al-Qaeda who practise anti-Semitism, the Danish cartoonists who caricature Islam's prophet, radicals who attempt to take out reputable Islamic scholars (such as the Egyptian Noble Prize laureate for literature), or soldiers who humiliate and torture prisoners of war, then their actions cannot be left unconstrained and irreversible. The point I am making is that such unconstrained and irresponsible actions are in fact unjust and do not offer any possibility for cultivating democratic citizenship.

I shall now explore whether some *madaris* in the Western Cape province of South Africa cultivate a philosophy of Islamic education commensurate with some of the aims of democratic citizenship.

ON THE (UN)DESIRABILITY OF DEMOCRATIC CITIZENSHIP THROUGH
MADRASSAH SCHOOLING?

In this section of the chapter I analyse some of the practices in *madaris* in the Western Cape, focusing on a snapshot of forty schools in which semi-structured interviews were conducted with madrassah educators. These *madaris* are located in five areas: Strand–Macassar–Stellenbosch–Wellington, Athlone–Gatesville–Lansdowne, Bo–Kaap–Woodstock–Kensington, Mitchells's Plain, and Grassy Park–Lotus River–Ottery. The primary aim of this research was to investigate whether madrassah schooling in contemporary Muslim schools in one of the nine provinces in South Africa can potentially engender democratic citizenship education and whether these schools see their roles as contributing towards producing democratic citizens. Consequently the interviews were structured around three main questions: What constitutes madrassah schooling? Do madrassah schooling practices create opportunities for dialogical action? and Does teaching and learning in *madaris* relate to issues of democracy and citizenship?

Firstly, it seems as if madrassah schooling is primarily concerned with inculcating in learners the tenets of Islam such as cleanliness, prayer (*salah*), fasting and pilgrimage – that is, teaching learners to be good 'practical Muslims'. By far the majority of educators emphasised the importance of teaching the Qur'an, specifically its memorisation in rote fashion, and the learning of invocations / supplications (*duahs*) and *ahadith* in order for Muslims to acquire a heightened sense of piety or God-consciousness (*taqwah*). Although some educators indicated that madrassah schooling is in some ways linked to contemporary societal issues such as teaching learners to respect life, others' property and the rule of law, by far the majority of educators did not conceive madrassah schooling as having anything to do with what learners learn in public schools, for instance, biological, physical and technological, economic and management sciences.[4] In this way there seems to be a bifurcation between madrassah schooling (as education in the religious sciences) and public education (as education in the rational, non-revealed sciences) to the extent that some madrassah educators claim that only the former type of education would secure a Muslim's place in paradise in the afterlife – an untenable view which assumes that, for instance, learning 'respect for life' has nothing to do with learning about the biological natures of humans and animals. However, the fact that madrassah schooling aims to inculcate in learners respect for life, others' property and the rule of law, it can be argued that it has the potential to contribute towards engendering democratic citizenship education, because the latter is concerned with learning, for instance, to respect others and to abide by the rule of law. This is so despite the fact that most educators claimed that their teaching has no links with democracy and citizenship.[5] However, whether madrassah schooling in its current form actually cultivates in learners the capacity to assume responsibility for ensuring the rights of others seems unlikely at this stage, because during the interviews some educators claimed that education in their schools 'has been isolated from world affairs'. This suggests that learning to share commonalities and to respect the differences of others might not be so easy, because madrassah schooling seems to be quite an insulated activity.

Secondly, some educators claimed that occasionally they do engage learners through discussion, open debate and questioning, as two educators at different *madaris* remarked: 'We don't want the children just to sit and take in what we tell them' and 'We don't just dictate'. This suggests that madrassah schooling has some affinity towards dialogical action: 'In introducing new topics learners are allowed the opportunity to engage in conversation or dialogue'. Yet, by far the majority of educators acknowledge that little or no opportunity is established whereby learners can question particular viewpoints. As aptly put by one educator: 'We do not encourage learners to think critically or participate (actively) in the lesson due to time constraints and large classes' and 'No time is given for children to engage with a specific topic'.[6] Thus, in the main, dialogical action is not necessarily implemented in madrassah schooling. One gets the impression that the preponderance of rote learning somehow makes it difficult to use dialogue as a mode of educating learners. By implication madrassah learners are not necessarily taught to be critical, because the practice of mutual deliberation (*shūrā*) so highly regarded in normative Islamic education seems to be absent from madrassah schooling.

Thirdly, most of the educators seem to be oblivious to issues related to democratic citizenship education, because learning about the latter requires that one engages dialogically with co-educators and learners. As some educators remarked: 'Our curriculum is not linked to citizenship and democracy ... we focus on the child becoming a good person', and 'The purpose of my teaching is not grounded in politics' – as if learning to be a good person is unrelated to being a good citizen in a democratic post-apartheid South Africa. Educators in most of the schools consider their role to be teaching the *din* (religion) and not to concentrate on democracy and citizenship. Thus, it seems as if madrassah schooling focuses on teaching a form of Islam which can remain 'uncorrupted' by issues which involve 'secular education' – that is, democratic citizenship education is not considered as Islamic education.

CONCLUSION

Madrassah schooling in South Africa seems to be overwhelmingly biased towards cultivating Islamic moral beliefs (mostly the essentials of the Islamic faith such as belief in God, His angels, revealed books, prophets, eschatology, good and evil, prayers, fasting, charity, pilgrimage and selected historical moments in Islam – mostly involving the life of Prophet Muhammad) – and values (particularly respect for others, greeting, supplications, sayings of the prophet and reading and memorisation of the Qur'an) in learners – 'Our purpose is to produce good Muslim persons'. In some instances, although minimally, these beliefs and values are taught through debate, discussion and questioning. Otherwise, rote learning seems to be very dominant in madrassah schooling.[7] Therefore, it seems rather unlikely that madrassah schooling could engender deliberative engagement. Or, madrassah schooling seems unlikely to produce moments of public deliberation which could disturb doubts about the correctness of their moral beliefs or about the importance of differences between what Muslims and non-Muslims believe accompanied by ethical confrontation.

Finally, not a single madrassah educator mentioned the importance of teaching acts of justice such as *ijtihād* (rational interpretive judgements) and *ikhtilaf* (pluralism and disagreement). By implication, it does not seem likely that the idea of cultivating a collective identity with others who are not Muslim – whereby both parties can learn to share commonalities and to respect one another's differences – will soon materialise in South African madrassah schooling. This, of course, makes the achievement of democratic citizenship even more unlikely. However, as a glimmer of hope for South Africa's fledgling democracy, madrassah schooling does focus on teaching learners to be good Muslims, in particular what it means to respect human and non-human life. This is where the potential lies for madrassah schooling to begin to extend what it means to be a good Muslim to ideas which involve being a good citizen, in particular learning to recognise and take responsibility for people's civil, political and social rights.

NOTES

[1] The Qur'an is considered by Muslims as the divine message of God (Allah) and the Sunnah refers to the embodiment of the message in the life experiences of the Prophet Muhammad.

[2] Hasan, Sunana Abi Dawud, 3:1013, Hadith no. 3567.

[3] Qur'an: al-Anfal, 8: 46; al-An'am, 6: 16, 159; al-'Imran, 3: 103, 105; al-Shura, 42: 13; al-Rum, 30: 31; and al-Anbiya, 21: 92.

[4] The *madaris* mostly function as complementary to the public school education system and are held after the completion of a normal school day. These *madaris* are mostly home-based and mosque-based schools in which the majority of the educators do not have any formal qualification (although some are professionally trained as educators).

[5] For instance, one educator claimed: 'The purpose of my teaching is not grounded in politics ... I concentrate more on values and morals of Islam and how to shape or educate Muslims'.

[6] Usually madrassah schooling lasts for about 1–2 hours in the late afternoon, that is, after learners have been dismissed from public schools.

[7] The memorisation of the Qur'an (in its entirety or passages) is considered as the most important aspect of madrassah schooling. This does not necessarily occur with an understanding of the messages of the Qur'an.

REFERENCES

Abd al-Rahim, M. (1987). The roots of revolution in the Quran, *Dirasat Ifriqiyya,* (3), 10–11.

Abed, S.B. (1995). Islam and democracy. In D. Graham, & M. Tessler, (Eds.) *Democracy, war, and peace in the Middle East* (pp. 105–115). Bloomington: Indiana University Press.

Alibasic, A. (1999). The right of political opposition in Islamic history and legal theory: an exploration of an ambivalent heritage, *Al-Shajarah,* 4(2), 231–296.

Al-'Alwani, J. (1994). *The ethics of disagreement in Islam* (A.S. Al-Shaikh-Ali, Ed.; A.W. Hamid, Trans.). Herndon, VA: The International Institute of Islamic Thought.

Al-Attas, M.N. (1991). *The concept of education in Islam.* Kuala Lumpur: International Institute of Islamic Thought and Civilisation.

Benhabib, S. (2002). *The claims of culture: Equality and diversity in the global era.* Princeton: Princeton University Press.

Callan, E. (1997). *Creating citizens: Political education and liberal democracy.* Oxford: Oxford University Press.

El-Effendi, A. (1991). *Who needs an Islamic state?* London: Grey Seal.

Esposito, J. & Voll, J. (1996). *Islam and democracy.* Oxford: Oxford University Press.

Eickelman, D. & Piscatori, J. (1996). *Muslim politics.* Princeton: Princeton University Press.

Goldberg, E. (1993). Private goods, public wrongs and civil society in some medieval Arab theory and practice. In Goldberg, E. Kasaba, R. & Midal, J. (Eds.). *Rules and rights in the Middle East: Democracy, law and society.* Seattle: University of Washington Press.

Gutmann, A. (2003). *Identity in democracy.* Princeton: Princeton University Press.

Hrair Dekmejian, R. (1995). *Islam in revolution: Fundamentalism in the Arab World.* Syracuse, NY: Syracuse University Press.

Kamali, H. (1993). Characteristics of the Islamic state. *Islamic Studies, 32*(1), 34–35.

Khan, M (2005). Islamic democracy and moderate Muslims: The straight path runs through the middle. *American Journal of Islamic Social Sciences, 22*(3), 39–50.

MacIntyre, A. (1999). *Dependent rational animals: Why human beings need the virtues.* Chicago, IL: Open Court.

Waghid, Y. (1996). In search of a boundless ocean and new skies: Human creativity is a matter of *a'mal, jihad* and *ijtihad. American Journal of Islamic Social Sciences, 13*(3), 353–365.

Waghid, Y. (1997). Islamic educational institutions: Can the heritage be sustained? *American Journal of Islamic Social Sciences, 14*(4), 35–50.

Yusef Waghid
Stellenbosch University

YVONNE M. HÉBERT

THE EMERGENCE OF THE CHILD-AS-CITIZEN
IN CANADA

The conception of the child-as-citizen emerged in the 20th century as the most recent of many conceptions of childhood. The meaning of child-as-citizen depends largely upon the webs of political and economic beliefs of each era about young people, throughout Canada's history. With the revival of citizenship education today, in a neo-liberal globalising context, the conception of the child-as-citizen is central to current concerns regarding teaching and learning in the context of intense educational reform. How educators understand young people is critical to their ability to comprehend themselves as social actors and to their capacity for acting upon society to achieve their intellectual and career goals as well as state-established goals, in reciprocal transformations of self, school and society. If young people are to succeed as thinkers, as creators, as learners, and as humans who make valuable contributions to society, it is necessary to know who young people are as citizens and how this is fundamental to education for democracy.

The notion of conception refers to a specification of the attributes of children distinguishable from those of adults (Archard, 2004). Conceptions of children differ with respect to their boundaries, dimensions and divisions. Each conception makes claims about how long it lasts, thus establishing boundaries; about the qualities that distinguish it from another, thus making precise its dimensions; and how important these differences are, thus specifying its significant divisions. Conceptions then are social constructs as well as biological categorisations. An individual may hold a conception about childhood and youth; a conception may also be widely held, in which case it may be part of a prevailing ideology.

In this chapter, ideology refers to a complex of interrelated ideas and values that constitutes a universe for cultural practice, including educational practice that is infused with economic and political significance (Hoffman, 2003). Taken for granted as common sense, hegemonic ideologies provide a certain social stability and cohesiveness (Osborne, 1996). Since such positions are largely accepted as part of the natural order of things, dominant groups do not need to resort to force to maintain their power except in times of crisis. Quite importantly, hegemony contains elements of commonality that genuinely cut across society and must be negotiated and maintained. Its stability can never be assumed as it is challenged, resisted, diverted, and put to uses other than those intended. In the process, hegemony often changes its shape, as conceptions have gradually for childhood and youth.

M.A. Peters, A. Britton and H. Blee (Eds.), Global Citizenship Education: Philosophy, Theory and Pedagogy, 421–443.

The story is told from multiple perspectives, weaving in historical, sociological, philosophical and cultural considerations as required for explanatory purposes. For the purposes of this chapter, I present briefly the historical evolution of the child as social actor in Canada, and then focus upon the development of social policies and a body of rights including child rights in the most recent century up to the present day. In the telling, particular attention is given to agency, individuality, autonomy, power, emotional expression, voice, and social role, all of which are important to citizenship in (neo)-liberal democratic contexts in a country such as Canada. Of particular interest is the relevance of prevailing conceptions of childhood to the emergence of the child-as-citizen.

BEGINNINGS OF THE STORY

Childhood, as we know it today, was invented in the philosophical, social and economic context of rising modernity of the 17th and 18th century Europe, as separate and distinct from the adult (Archard, 2004; Canella, 1997; Cunningham, 2000; O'Neill, 2004). Childhood ended at the age of seven, with a change of attire marking the passage to adulthood. This was consistent with the separation of mind and matter, with reason as the means to knowledge. Children were recognised as a distinct group that needed protection from a corrupt society. Homes for foundlings were established in this period as part of changing social norms, moving towards new expressive forms of sentimentality and caring (Ariès, 1962; Cunningham, 1998; de Mause, 1974; Laneyrie-Dagen, 1995). When sufficient adult labourers became available, children who had previously been employed in factories had to be protected. Running in the streets was deemed socially unacceptable. Thus, the school became the perfect vehicle for the construction, protection and reformation of the child.

With the spread of literacy and the rise of nationalism, the conception of childhood encapsulated in the middle-class or bourgeois family model became increasingly dominant across all social strata in Western countries (Rooke & Schnell, 1983, 1982). This conception informed the influential work of Jean Piaget (1896-1980), the first to make scientific observations of children. He proposed that children individually construct their worlds from inside out, a process that is both self-directed and self-regulated. The modern commitment to scientific truth, objectivity, reason, and progress is well illustrated in his descriptions of the child as a developing scientist, systematically examining problems in the real world, hypothesising and learning how to solve problems through discovery. He privileged the mental over the active, thinking over doing, abstract over the concrete, adult over child, rationality over irrationality, and ultimately believed in the innocence of children, assuming that the child responded to his questioning independently of culture, context or the power relationship present in the interview situation (Piaget, 1957). The spread of the bourgeois conception of childhood reached its apogée after the Second World War. Child development studies, their application in early childhood education, and the development of moral reasoning by Kohlberg, were all based on Piagetian stages of progressive development. Thus, the conception of the bourgeois child came to be widely held in terms of autonomy and protection.

Precursors to Children's Rights in Early Canada

Children and youth are critical to the establishment of a new country through their labour and through their eventual leadership and responsibility for the future. Throughout the early years of the period of colonialisation, the well-being of young people was of utmost concern, as it was important in a harsh climate, that children be self-reliant, autonomous and strong individuals, capable of taking up the challenges of nation-building. Four examples are given of children as social actors: French-Canadian and Métis children in colonial times, children as sites of identity struggles in western expansion, collier boys' strikes in Nova Scotia, and the Chinese school strike in Victoria.

Children in Colonial Canada

Children and youth were constructed differently in the New World than on the European continent. The political economy of extraction from the new world to enrich the old, the minimal influence of the church and state, and the mixed origins of the European settlers tempered the entrenchment of customs and community bonds (Janovicek, 2003: 35). Consequently, the children of New France in the 18th and 19th century and Métis children in the Pacific Northwest in the 19th century changed the boundaries of childhood (Shipley, 1995) and their lives were characterised by their own individuality, agency and autonomy.

Termed '*les petits sauvages*' by French observers, the new world children were encouraged to be self-reliant, as families adapted old world practices to suit social and economic patterns of colonial life (Moogk, 2003). Young girls from privileged families played, read their choice of books, and attended convent school. Young boys of 12-14 rode their horses in the public square, cursed, spat, and swore, to the dismay of some leaders who wished to fine the parents. Working class children toiled as servants in the homes of the rich, as labourers on the piers and on farms.

Schooled as early as 1832, Métis children of fur traders in the Pacific Northwest developed a Métis consciousness which transcended the class structure of the Hudson's Bay Company as well as the cultural heritage of their parents, to create a sense of self that was neither white nor Indian (Larsell, 1932; Pollard, 2003). Métis children acquired a value system and lifestyle uniquely their own. They became social actors upon their world and upon themselves as autonomous individuals. In the face of widespread racial prejudice, the young Métis strengthened their identities as new world people, perpetuating a transcultural identity and consciousness throughout their lives (Pollard, 2003). What is important, in both examples, is that children themselves understood the outside world's view of them and challenged the image of themselves as inferior people wherever and whenever they could, becoming agentive and independent in the process.

CHILDHOOD DURING WESTERN EXPANSION

With Confederation in 1867 followed by western expansion from the 1870s to the 1930s, children and youth were conceptualised as cultural, economic and political commodities, in the context of economic and political ideologies and with powerful nationalising agendas as blueprints for progress. Schools were seen as the socialising agency for citizenship, nation-building, and training for the age of industrialisation (Davey, 2003), in which young people constructed themselves under the constraints of power relations.

During this period, children's cultural and civic identifications became the battleground for two nations warring within one state, tensions that continue to characterise the Canadian political and cultural scene. School rights had been entrenched in the British North America Act of 1867, the Manitoba Act of 1870, and the Territories Act of 1875 according to religion, Protestant and Catholic, which was, at the time, contiguous with language. Nonetheless the French school question raged in the Northwest from the 1870s through the early 1930s, challenging the very basis of Confederation. The British-Canadian residents of the Northwest were determined that the Prairie provinces should be English and Canadian (Friesen, 1984: 217; McLeod, 1979). The struggle pitted the Anglican bishops, the Orange Lodges and the Ku Klux Klan against the French Catholic bishops and community leaders (Baergen, 2000). Many petitions and requests for remedial legislation were made to Ottawa. In Manitoba, French as a language of instruction in schools was terminated by the provincial government in 1890, restored in 1897 as part of an English-dominant bilingual programme, and abolished again in 1916 (Friesen, 1984). In 1901 when both provinces became autonomous, one hour of optional instruction in the upper grades, after school hours, in languages other than English could be given, if trustees passed a resolution to that effect (McLeod, 1979). Yet by 1931, Saskatchewan removed all provisions for the teaching of French except the one-hour provisional course.

Thus the harsh assimilative process begun in the late 1880s had run its course, with anti-French forces also sweeping up schools established by immigrant groups in their own languages (Sutherland, 2000; Bruno-Jofré, 1996; Mahé, 1993). Intolerant of linguistic heterogeneity and cultural difference, Canada's newest region did not provide the bilingual promises of Canadian confederation. Not until the passage of the Canadian Charter of Rights and Freedoms some fifty years later, in 1982, was legal recognition granted to linguistic school rights of parents of official language minorities, thus reinstating the school as the agency for protecting children's civic and cultural identifications and for building a bilingual country.

The Collier Boys in Nova Scotia

In the coal mines of Nova Scotia from the late 1880s into the 1920s, the collier boys were responsible for hauling coal by horse, for dragging sledges on all fours, and for ventilating the mines by letting air in through trapdoors, demonstrating "resilience and self-reliance". At Victorian mines where "expansion and technical progress" were most pronounced, child labour was most extensive, "often requested by fathers who wished to have their contribution to support the family" (McIntosh, 2003: 80, 78). Boys as young as 12-14 years objected to travelling to dangerous sections of mines, to being disciplined, to being restricted to boys' work until the age of eighteen. In response to any of these harsh conditions and to discriminatory pay, the boys could strongly object and cause a strike in one, two or even three mines. Concerned middle-class women reformers lobbied for the protection and schooling of the young miners. By virtue of successive school acts which established a framework for a common school system, compulsory taxation for school upkeep, as well as compulsory attendance, the impact on the colliery boys was profound. By 1908, legislation prohibited from working in the mines, any boy between the age of twelve and sixteen who had not completed grade seven. Child labour came to an end in 1923 with the passage of the Mines Act, which prohibited collier work for anyone under the age of sixteen. Thus, a general concern for the child's welfare pushed the boy from the workforce while establishing rights to a minimum level of education.

The Chinese School Strike in Victoria

In September 1922, Chinese students organised a strike in Victoria to protest against segregation into schools for Chinese students only. At a signal from one of the most studious boys, rows of Chinese students vanished on the way to the segregated schools leaving the principal standing alone in the middle of the roadway (Stanley, 2003). The deadlock between the Chinese community and the Victoria School Board lasted for the entire school year. The resistance had been preceded by many instances of violent attacks by white boys bullying Chinese boys. In light of such racist incidents, many Chinese parents enrolled their younger children, especially girls, in a Chinese-language day school rather than a public elementary school where their children were endangered. The depth of resentment was enormous for the second generation, the sons and daughters of merchants and professionals, who had a great deal to lose, as this was perceived as an effort to segregate and to prevent them from learning English well. Challenging white hegemony, the Chinese community invented a common identity as Chinese with the community-based Chinese Free School, established in the interim, bringing together speakers of several dialects. Knowledge of written Chinese was essential to the organisation of the resistance, drawing upon a network of day and evening Chinese-language schools.

Illustrating the complex interplay between conceptions of childhood and issues of youth, sex, class and race, these examples also serve to establish a strong link between dominant conceptions of children and the treatment afforded those who were not members of the bourgeoisie. Marginalised and rendered voiceless and invisible, such children and youth were gradually constructed as inferiors: dependent and distinct from adult males, as irresponsible and necessitating protection within strong patriarchal forces in English Canada. Yet, as in the Colonial period, children and youth acted upon society. Thus, conceptions of children and youth as social actors gradually emerged, which contributed to middle-class movements for the rights of children.

TRANSFORMING EDUCATION AND CONCEPTIONS OF CHILDHOOD

In the context of a national transformation, the new social policies of the next era focused on the rearing of the child within family, maintaining and protecting health, transforming society by means of schooling, and preventing him/her from becoming a burden on society (Sutherland, 2000; Houston & Prentice, 1988). The 'new education' in 1915 in Ontario agreed upon the importance of the home in shaping the next generation; an aggressive policy of Canadianisation through education; and various reforms, such as agriculture as a school subject, manual training, domestic science, and consolidated schools. In the 1920s, unions raised objections that schools were discriminating against working class children and that history textbooks had a militaristic bias, an objection shared by feminists across the country. Pledged to cooperative principles, organised farmers on the Prairies were critical of citizenship education as subordination, saw the schools as vehicles for another kind of social transformation, and called for a social interpretation of citizenship (Osborne, 1996).

The post World War II period saw the re-introduction of human rights. Adding to civil and political rights, emerging social and economic rights included the universal rights of children to education and welfare as an avowed national aim and international idea for post war social policy (Marshall, 2003). To achieve freedom through social security and human welfare, while replacing Anglo-centric patriotism with a national ideology that celebrated social policies (Blake, 1995), Prime Minister Mackenzie King introduced family allowances, the first universal social programme in Canadian history. Closely tied to this initiative was the enactment of compulsory schooling in Québec, the most significant social policy of the Québécois government of the times. The introduction of family allowances as the cornerstone of the children's agenda successfully sold Canada's new post-war social programmes in the 1945 federal election (Marshall, 2003).

The next action on the children's agenda addressed Indigenous education. In 1946, a joint committee of the Senate and House of Commons recommended Indian integration into the dominant society. The revised Indian Act of 1951 permitted the federal government to enter into financial agreements with provincial and other school authorities for Indian children to attend public and private schooling for non-Indians.

The growing hegemony of the middle-class family pattern among Canadian working classes accompanied the development of the welfare state, fuelling moral and social reform movements aimed at inculcating the norms of the bourgeois family model among so-called deviant populations (Chunn, 2003). In Ontario and British Columbia, the enactment of legislation was directed at poor children and the adults responsible for them, to oblige compliance with middle-class standards of morality and family life. A concern for order and a more disciplined society motivated educational reformers who called for greater social efficiency. Social reconstruction was the new goal until the mid-century.

Based on new understandings of children and society, modern education had five purposes: to teach youngsters the means for social control; to disseminate knowledge; to meet the public demand for social improvement; to meet the demand for industrial efficiency via practical subjects; and to make each individual into a productive social unit (Sutherland, 2002). A belief in the scientific method replaced religious beliefs in the education system of the progressivism era. Self-motivated students with cooperative work habits fitted perfectly into the bureaucratic machinery of industry. Several educational initiatives of this era contributed to the emergence of human rights.

Children as Inquirers and Citizens

Reaching a number of Canadian provinces in the late twenties and early thirties, the principles of progressive education affected the notion of citizenship education, in the thinking of leaders if not in actual school practice (Bruno-Jofré, 1996). Although progressive education was borrowed from John Dewey and derived from an older New Education movement in Europe, Alberta's educational establishment was inspired by an educational philosophy that was revolutionary, transformative, and representative of the regeneration of humanity and society (Mazurek, 1999). Children and youth were re-conceptualised as scientific inquirers and discoverers, as self-motivated cooperative individuals, and as participants in democracy. The concern for individuality and for students' future role in a democratic society were made very clear in the approach to Social Studies as a school subject in Manitoba as well as in Alberta (Bruno-Jofré, 1996).

The discourse on citizenship and common polity was construed differently in the 1920s than in the 1930s. In the first half of the 1920s, emphasis was placed on appropriate behaviours, neatness and memorisation. By comparison, the discourse of the 1930s into the early forties, under Dewey's influence, began to advocate meeting individual needs of students and to produce citizens for what turned out to be a poorly articulated ideal democratic society. The discourse of citizenship in the Thirties did not explore critically and concretely understandings of democracy within socio-economic contexts (Bruno-Jofré, 1996). Textbooks and curriculum continued the marginalisation of women and various forms of racism while British-orientation, Anglo-conformity and patriarchal dominance continued unabated.

Children as Marginalized and Passive Recipients

A sustaining universalising ideology made those who did not fit into it, into second-class citizens, for example, Aboriginal and French-Canadian children and adolescents. The most telling failure of progressive education was the inability to deal with the bilingual and culturally plural nature of Canada. French Canada was portrayed in history books as a romantic relic from earlier times; the achievements of New France were celebrated, as was the British conquest, while passing over its scathing dismissal of French Canadian history, literature, culture and people. Québec's reservations about Confederation were similarly omitted in a rush to celebrate Canadian nationhood. In Alberta, French was taught, but as a foreign language. Proposals to require the study of both French and English at the secondary and university levels were given polite hearings but no action would be taken. Resistance and informal accommodation of conflicting interests often took place at the local level. In Manitoban communities, homogeneous groups such as Mennonites and French-Manitobans struggled to preserve their religion and language, e.g., in the township of Sainte Anne, well into the 1950s (Ross, 1997).

The education of Aboriginal children and youth continued to be assimilative, ignored in the curriculum or portrayed in old stereotypes (Osborne, 1996: 46). Modelled upon the industrial school, day-schools and residential schools continued to operate, in which part or most of the day was spent in work to prepare for entry into the labour market at the lowest rungs of the social ladder (Barman, 2003; Barman, Hébert & McCaskill, 1987, 1986). Combining economics with racism, this education for inequality was made possible by the serious under-funding of Aboriginal education, lodged in the hegemony of white supremacy and Anglo-conformity. Enclosed in residential and day schools under federal jurisdiction, the autonomy and voices of Aboriginal children were silenced for several decades. These were not to be heard until adulthood when safe places for expression were found (Perreault & Vance, 1990). Aboriginal peoples, French Canada, women and immigrant groups were all neglected and schooled for inequality.

Emergence of Human Rights: Children as Bearers of Rights

Canadians participated in the international development of children's rights, an exposure that had a profound impact on the evolution of domestic support. The Canadian Council of Child Welfare printed and circulated the Geneva Declaration of the Rights of the Child (1924) across the country. The notion of children's rights evolved and broadened over the next two decades to include rights for all children, spreading the discourse of universality. Children's social citizenship was an important principle for political action on the part of labour unions and educators alike. The economic and social commitments of the post-war social policy were translated into measures to protect the children of Canada from want, malnutrition and inadequate educational opportunity, as an integral measure of social security in the broadest sense. For Aboriginal parents, they came to receive payment of family allowances directly like all Canadians, without having to pass by the Indian agent of the federal bureaucracy. Finally, the notion of children's rights increased their individual sovereignty. The language of universal rights and images associated with universal programmes helped to homogenise the experiences of girls and boys, rural and urban children, at a time when the large majority of child labourers were poor daughters and farmers' sons (Marshall, 2003).

In 1948, the Universal Declaration of Human Rights, first drafted by John Humphrey, a Canadian law professor then head of the UN secretariat's Division of Human Rights, was adopted by 58 member states. However in the 1940s and

1950s, there was a contradictory tendency in Canada to promote children's universal rights yet to subordinate them to political expediency. Canada was embarrassed into endorsing the UN Declaration by its presence in a group of abstaining, repressive countries. Behind the work of John Humphrey and many others was a profound transformation of the political culture that led to and consolidated the formation of universal welfare programmes. Yet Canadian children were supplied only with minimum levels of welfare and education, a profound ambiguity intricately connected to the social and political history of Canadian families (Marshall, 2003).

Conceptualising children and youth as scientific inquirers and discoverers, as participants in democracy and as bearers of rights, reflected a radical change in hegemonic ideologies and socio-political and educational thinking about young people. Challenging the bourgeois conception of childhood as a time of preparation for the future, these new conceptions recognised the historical realities of children in Canadian contexts and the contemporary emphasis on living in the present. Thus, the working class girls, the colliers boys in Nova Scotia, Métis children in the Pacific Northwest, and the young people of New France, to name but a few, were precursors of lives to come decades later, in which young people were recognised as being entitled to human dignity during their childhood and youth. Young people became subjects in the here and now, social actors who are self-motivated, cooperative individuals, and who are capable social actors upon themselves, others and society. The youth as radical straddled more than one conception, as social actors and citizens, as well as troublemaker who insisted on certain ways of being treated by others. Nonetheless, competing conceptions placed children and youth in positions of dependency to enforce middle-class views of young people among those who are not. This perpetuated the negative view of the bourgeois child as a dependent, possibly as a ward of juvenile court; as a recipient, unequal, marginalised and passive.

CHILDHOODS WITHIN ACTIVISM AND NATIONAL IDENTIFICATION, 1960S-1980S

Profound social change continued, with the beginnings of the Quiet Revolution in Québec in the fifties and the Royal Commission on Bilingualism and Biculturalism through most of the Sixties. Parliamentary endorsement of the new policy, multiculturalism in a bilingual framework, in 1971, marked the growing assertiveness of Aboriginal peoples, rising provincial challenges to the increased role of the federal government, a concern for Canadian identity and independence from Americanising economic and cultural forces. Two official languages were established as well as an approach permitting groups to maintain their cultures. All of these forces challenged social cohesion, public education, and the meaning of citizenship.

Influences on the educational establishment combined to mount a comprehensive attack on progressive education in the 1950s. Teachers did not have adequate resources or preparation. Open-ended inquiry meant that absolutist answers to moral, social, cultural and political questions were suspect. Some groups complained that traditional social and ethical values were being undermined and insisted that this approach be discontinued (Mazurek, 1999). Universities criticised progressive education for having abandoned all standards of rigour, contributing to the decline of intellectual traditions (Neatby, 1953). Submissions to the national Massey Commission on the Arts in 1950 were consistently scathing in their criticisms of the lack of academic quality (Osborne, 1996).

Post-industrial influences created demands for reforms in line with economic and political requirements. Educational mandates and systems were obliged to keep up with the seemingly insatiable demands of industry and bureaucracy in the new technocratic society (Mazurek, 1999). Increased levels of technical and intellectual skills were required as the economy changed fundamentally. The next educational response was obvious: a return to a core of essential knowledge and disciplines, and a reaffirmation of traditional values. In Alberta, the Cameron Report (1959) redefined schooling by enshrining core subjects in highly specific curriculum; introducing standardised testing to measure achievement levels; instilling a work ethic and citizenship training. Powerful forces however were already beginning to reshape the country.

The rise of prosperity in the Sixties and, especially, the discovery and exploitation of oil generated a powerful momentum to economic and social change, leading once again to educational reform. The booming prosperity resulted in a chronic shortage of personnel especially in technical fields and the professions, including a serious teacher shortage; an explosion in the budgets and student populations in schools and post-secondary institutions; and an increase in schooling options (Mazurek, 1999).

The 1960s heralded an era of considerable social and cultural innovation and experimentation. Knowledge was recognised as deeply personal. Embodied knowing is inescapably participatory, organic rather than mechanistic, and constructed in social, communal, interactive and discursive contexts (Polanyi, 1958, 1969). A sense of empowerment gripped youth and the sense of the dawning of a new age was in the air. This feeling took shape in overt rebellion against tradition and authority, in the sexual revolution and drug use, in the redefinition of identity through humanistic psychology and cooperative living arrangements, and in a more direct democratic participation in the student rights movement and demonstrations. The Sixties generation would not be content to fit into the pre-existing mould of previous generations.

In 1967, Canada celebrated the centenary of Confederation. Several challenges were identified for the next hundred years: a concern for an inadequate knowledge of Canada and its history, Québec separatism, regionalism and Americanisation (Hodgett, 1968). The Canadian studies movement ensued, with a call for pan-Canadian understanding and a heightened sense of Canadian identity. Curriculum concerns focused on the lack of coherent vision of Canada as a distinct society and an absence of emphasis on local and regional priorities (Osborne, 1996).

An increased awareness and emphasis on world affairs permeated schools in the 1970s and 1980s as a result of changing immigration patterns (Osborne, 1996). With the introduction in 1967 of a non-racist merit system based on a system of points (Isajiw, 1999), 1.6 million people entered the country from 1968 to 1977, originating mostly from Asia and the Caribbean, and from 1968–1976, another 35,000 people from Czechoslovakia, Tibet, Uganda, Chile, Vietnam and Cambodia. Most immigrants settled in Toronto, Vancouver and Montréal, raising concerns about the overly rapid growth of cities, the shifting density and composition of the Canadian population, and labour force shortages, in light of a declining birth rate, signs of a looming recession and resurgence in racism.

Examples of new conceptions of childhood and youth emerging in this period include children's rights to a cultural education; the return of the French school question as collective rights and parental control of education; new approaches to citizenship education and Canadian identities; children as bearers of rights; and the emergence of youth studies with multiple images.

Children's Access and Rights to a Cultural Education and Identity

In the 1970s, schools responded quickly to the federal policy call for bilingualism within a multicultural context, thanks in part to the very effective lobbying efforts of the Canadian Parents for French who wanted better second language programmes for their children. French Immersion programmes were established, first in Saint Lambert, a suburb of Montréal, and spread rapidly across the country. Supplementary funding was provided under federal-provincial transfer agreements. Student exchange programmes were organised spanning English-French provincial boundaries.

The 1972 policy of the National Indian Brotherhood, *Indian Control of Indian Education*, marked a clear change of paradigm in Aboriginal education (Kirkness, 1972). Discussions between First Nations and the state shifted school governance and responsibility to First Nations parents and communities. As a result, residential schools were phased out, and federal day schools dropped considerably in number. Aboriginal controlled schools hired more Aboriginal teachers, infused cultural elements into curriculum, and introduced language classes (Royal Commission on Aboriginal Peoples, 1997; Castellano et al, 2000). For the most part, Aboriginal authorities have had no control over transfers of educational services for children who attend provincial schools off reserves, mostly in urban contexts. More recently, Aboriginal authorities have gained more involvement in negotiating agreements for educational services by outside authorities. At the end of the 20th century, philosophical and sociological work outlined the foundations and principles of Indigenous knowledge, pedagogies, as well as strategies and processes of enfranchisement (Battiste, 2002, 2000; Barman et al, 1987, 1986; Castellano et al, 2000; Schissel and Wotherspoon, 2002).

Collective Rights and Parental Control of Education

In 1982, the Canadian Charter of Rights and Freedoms redefined what it was to be Canadian, resulting in what became known as 'Charter identities', in relationship to clauses guaranteeing gender rights, linguistic school rights for official language minorities, Aboriginal and multiculturalism rights. This document went well beyond civil, political and socio-economic rights, to establish a fourth generation of rights, cultural rights which are collective in nature (Hébert & Wilkinson, 2002).

The impact of the Canadian Charter of Rights and Freedoms on education was far-reaching. Applying to official language education in minority contexts, Section 23 guarantees school rights to parents who were schooled primarily in French. Francophone communities across all sectors were mobilised, first in the Maritimes then elsewhere across the land, to raise the consciousness of parents, educational and political leaders, and to make good use of research to support claims and actions. Obtaining parental control of francophone education necessitated several court cases emanating from parental mobilisation and action in jurisdictions across the country reaching the Supreme Court (Hébert, 1993; Bastarache, 1986). The Alberta School Act was amended, thirteen years later in 1995, to be consistent with the Charter. Other court cases followed across the land; the arguments for equity in education becoming increasingly sophisticated with each case, dealing with identity, self-esteem, and finally the curriculum. As a result, francophone schools districts with parental control of education, all flowing from the Charter, were established across the country in the eighties and nineties (Martel, 1991).

New Approaches to Citizenship Education and Canadian Identities

Influenced by the Canadian Studies movement, a new citizenship education informed curriculum changes in the Social Studies programme of studies. New in the 1970s-1980s was the attention paid to the relationship between developed and developing countries, the role which countries such as Canada should play in fostering economic and social development, as well as an increasing interest in environmental issues (Osborne, 1996). This new approach to political education, with children and youth as active citizens, occurred in social studies classrooms, environmental studies, home economics, law, and other subjects, frequently enough to constitute a trend and form part of a new conception of citizenship education. A less politicised version of this approach saw the inclusion of community service as an element of school curricula, attention paid to the Canadian Charter of Rights and Freedoms (1982) and law-related education.

Children and Youth as Bearers of Rights

An increased awareness of international and human rights education returned to the public agenda. The legally binding UN Convention on the Rights of the Child (1989) includes protection rights such as the right to life, survival and development; as well as protection from abuse, neglect and exploitation

432

(Verhellen, 2000). Rights to access include information, social security, and the highest level of health and education. Participation rights include the right to express an opinion; freedom of thought, conscience and religion; freedom of association; and protection of privacy. These rights acknowledge children as meaning-makers and as citizens. Containing civil, political, social, economic, and cultural rights, the Convention demands a comprehensive and interactive interpretation, setting a standard for future human rights instruments and for the human rights project as a whole. To date, 191 states including Canada have ratified the CRC, with the exception of the USA and Somalia. This almost universal ratification is a unique milestone in the history of human rights.

The introduction and implementation of children's rights marks a shift of paradigm in conceptions of childhood and youth (Archard, 2004; Howe & Covell, 2005; Verhellen, 2000). The prevailing social construction of childhood, flowing from the Enlightenment and defined as a stage of preparation for adult life, has had and continues to have enormous consequences for children and for those who relate to them. Children had been defined as not yet knowing, not yet competent, and not yet being. By defining childhood as a stage of preparation and youth as transition, young people were in a sense, waiting to become future performers. New understandings of childhood led to widespread advocacy of children's right to enjoy their rights in the present rather than wait for the future. With the passage of the Convention on the Rights of the Child (1989), children are recognised as individuals entitled to human dignity, as bearers of rights like all human beings. The ratification of the UN Convention on the Rights of Children (CRC) provided a more general basis for conceptions of childhood and youth as social actors and active citizens. The Convention's meanings for educational policy, curriculum and pedagogy are yet to be fully understood in policy and practice.

Emergence of Youth Studies with Multiple Images

In the mid-sixties, young people were the source of considerable concern about their non-conformism, their apparent delinquent and deviant behaviour. Sociologists and psychologists alike tried to guide the young towards the prevailing model in society: the *American Way of Life,* born after WWII. In 1965, sociologists in Québec believed that the youth of the day would henceforth shape society (Rioux, 1969). At the time, 'youth' as an object of study or as an historical subject was elevated to the status of a deviant attempting to act on society. Young people have since been portrayed at various times as collective actors, as a passive mass, as individuals or subjects, or a cohort (Dumas et al., 1984; Molgat, 1998).

In more recent decades, three approaches stand out in the representations of youth in recent decades (Gauthier, 2001). In one approach, the young are confronted with a new situation, such as victimisation, recognition of a new stage of life, youth's new place in the structuring of society, relating youth to a broader vision of changes occurring in society and generating active subjects. Describing the same nature, the second approach is centred more on the new problems likely to emerge during the time in which autonomy is being acquired outside the family home but before the stable building of a couple and family, offering an image of youth in trouble and another one of youth as victims of the structural change. Informed by a decade long body of research, a third approach determines how society exercises on the social conditions of the young with regard to culture, education, the labour market and entry into adult life (Rocher, 1988, 1973). Social stratification studies exploded the widely held monolithic myth of youth, that young people's social characteristics cannot be lumped into a single notion or category (Bernier, 1980). From this perspective, student protests are explained in terms of class struggle, the main issue being that of social mobility (Mahcu and Bélanger, 1972). This is an image, from French-Canadian sociology, of youth as a group, at the heart of the moral and educational designs of society.

Thus, this period heralded major shifts in society with concomitant changing conceptions of childhood and youth, with the Canadian Charter and the UN Convention on the Rights of Children providing the legal transformative bases. The recognition that children need a cultural education flowed from the federal multiculturalism in a bilingual framework policy of 1971. Marginalised groups made great strides in obtaining equity rights to self-determination and to parental control of education. With the youth activism of the sixties and the subsequent creation of youth studies as a field of study, the basis for self-determination of action and policy-making expanded from a cultural basis to a generational one.

SHIFTS OF MEANING, CHILDHOODS AND IDENTITIES, 1990S – PRESENT

Changes rolled on, incessantly. Two recessions at the outset of each decade, the 1980s and 1990s, put enormous pressure on schools districts to do more with less funding. Conservative ideas that had germinated in the 1970s grew and came to fruition with the restructuring of elementary schools and post-secondary educational systems, one to two decades later. Part of a 'back to basics' movement, serious attacks on public education and especially on teachers, ensued as the first step in reducing and restructuring education in a globalising economy. Shifts of meaning redefined citizens as consumers; new forms of racism emerged; equity was taken up as an issue of parental choice, rather than as claims for inclusion and fair treatment of the disadvantaged and minorities.

Child and Citizen as Consumer

Shifts of meanings, which typify this period, can best be seen in citizenship education. The citizen is now primarily a consumer of goods and services, and the student as a client of educational services. The logic of globalisation, in its economic form, requires that claims of statehood be set aside. The 'rights of the marketplace' claimed by multinational corporations as unfettered sales are packaged as rights of the consumer. The claims of citizenship and capitalist economies are contradictory, as was pointed out in the fifties by T. H. Marshall, for historically, states have curbed the imperatives of the market place. Although the marketplace requires free movement of labour, it is on the basis of citizenship within countries that rights to organise unions, satisfactory minimum wages, unemployment insurance, and rewarding work can be justified (Osborne, 1996). The conception of the child as a consumer may be construed as incorporating the power of the consumer, but this view disregards the market's manipulation of the youthful individual who has been recreated for the good of the corporation rather than the common good (Isin and Wood, 1999; Klein, 2000).

Canadians are not immune to the messages of American movies and media. Images of children shifted from the centrality of character that demanded Victorian discipline, habit and frugality, restraint and inner development, to a culture of personality which promotes spontaneity, outward projection, and self-realisation through consumption (King, 2001). Such images of childhood offered a point of confluence for competing models of childhood. Children now appear in advertising and were soon thereafter addressed directly in targeted advertising. Childhood was redefined as part of the self-indulgence and leisure pursuits of a consumer society. The redefinition of the child-as-consumer has taken almost a century to consolidate fully and explicitly.

Parental Choice as a Shift of Meaning of Equity

Parental choice of schooling is part of a suite of democratic options, with the Charter schools still largely within the public education system in Canada, offering specialised schooling, such as a focus on science education or on traditional approaches to learning. While such options have yet to demonstrate superior results, the pressure to offer alternatives has resulted in school districts making available specialised forms of education for middle-class parental choice. This shifts the meaning of equity from collective rights for the disadvantaged. With the move into the 21st century, the notion of equity is refocused to refer to the non-codified individual rights of parents to choose among a range of educational options. This co-opts minority rights and generalises them so as to attenuate and erase notions of racism and discrimination while further favouring the privileged middle and upper classes (Kallen, 2003; Robert & Tondreau, 1997; Baker, 1981).

Delayed Adulthood and Extended Youth

Responding to longer periods of time spent on schooling and job entry, youth has been extended up to the age of thirty, by governmental agencies and researchers alike (Gauthier & Pacom, 2001). Certain rituals or indications that marked the transition from youth to adulthood, such as departure from home, marriage, child-rearing responsibilities, or entry into the job market, no longer suffice to delineate adulthood. Just as childhood and youth have been redefined over historical time, blurring the line between youth and adulthood, now maturity is being transformed within the context of the decline of authority and structure. Delayed maturity is highly relevant to educational policy-making and practice. If the child/adult distinctions no longer pertain to late modern or postmodern societies, then the relevance of adulthood, its duties and responsibilities are called into question, as is the relevance of childhood as a distinct life-stage and of the child-as-citizen.

The New Racism and Blaming the Victim

In order to maintain the status quo of inequality in the face of an anti-racist egalitarian national ideology under the Canadian Charter, majority authorities in education and other sectors of society shifted their ideological stance from a focus on inherent 'biological' racial inferiority, to a focus on 'natural' cultural difference. This shift does not, however, alter the fundamental premise of white supremacy: that of blaming the victim for social and economic problems perceived as a 'natural' consequence of group differences and framed in a language of innocence which disguises its insidious intent by referring to egalitarianism, social justice, and common sense (Kallen, 2003; Baker 1981).

Moral panics surrounding school shootings, inner-city gang activities, schoolyard bullying and child/youth killers are part of a larger ideology set in a cultural and economic context. Children and youth are a source of cheap, obedient, and disposable labour for multi-national food and clothing industries. Youth as fertile consumers spend their meagre earnings on products of the same industries, making their labour fundamental to the survival of global capital (Schissel, in press). Youth culture is portrayed as evil, creating fictions of youth as devils, as feminist she-devils and bigoted gangs. Canada has the highest youth incarceration rates of all industrialised countries and locks up more youth than adults although there is far more adult crime (Schissel, 1997; in press). Demonising youth is also applied broadly to Canadian immigrant and Aboriginal youth. Punishment is ideological, delineated largely on the basis of placement in the socio-political realm, thus violating the civil liberties of children and youth under the pretext of ensuring the safety of society. Thus, children and youth are denied their democratic place, while the corporate sector depends on their labour and their spending.

NEW IDENTITIES: SOCIAL NETWORKS, STRATEGIC AND EMOTIONAL COMPETENCES

For contemporary youth, social networks are lived in real places and times. These may also leap across geographical and virtual distance and be organised into constellations of networks (Massey, 1998; Pattison, 1994; Carrasco, Rose & Charbonneau, 1999). More specifically, immigrant youth negotiate and interpret social relations for their own social and political purposes, gradually changing their friends in an integrative process, taking into consideration the constraining, challenging and empowering possibilities of categories of race, identity, and culture, yielding a more dynamic and nuanced notion of self and other, as revealed in several case studies in Calgary, Toronto, Edmonton and Vancouver (Hébert et al, 2004; Hébert et al, 2002; Anisef & Kilbride, 2003; Hagan et al., 2003; Bannerji, 2000, 1993; Kelly, 1998a, b; Beynon et al, 1998).

Meeting the challenge of creating new identities, young people are familiar with their rights, believe in multiculturalism, have strong views about being a Canadian and tend to be comfortable with their cultural group belongings (Lee & Hébert, 2007; Hébert & Racicot, 2001). Most importantly, they are strategic, either paying attention to detail, abstracting and synthesising meaning, or dwelling on contextualised social relations (Lee et al, 2001). Finally, these young people respond to new challenges with the development of an emotional competence consisting of skills and strategies that are sensitive to the nature of the problem as controllable or not (Hébert, Berti et al, 2003). In all sectors - family, community, school and youth - there is variation across groups of youth of immigrant origins, with regard to the nexus between bonding, bridging and linking capital and its impact on the strategic process of integration and of educational outcomes, thus sharpening and blurring conceptions of children and youth.

CONCLUSIONS AND CONSEQUENCES

Conceptions of childhood and youth are social constructs, contingent upon a wide variety of factors and circumstances, cultural traditions and rituals, and historical variations. Many moral, socio-economic, political and legal influences have shaped these changes over time, including the appearance of a more liberal Christianity, the growth of industrial and agricultural productivity, the spread of literacy and the rise of a middle class, the greater emancipation of women, and enlarged notions of citizenship (Strong-Boag, 2002; Postman, 1982). Four particular processes have been instrumental in extending childhood and shaping youth in the Canadian context: the advent of schooling at all levels; the post-war development of teenage youth culture in advertising and through the media; the increasing regulation of family life; and the fundamental shift in the experience of childhood, from one where all children contributed to the family economy to one where they constitute a net cost to that economy (Cunningham, 1998; Hollands, 2001). In other words, the more emotionally valuable children become, the longer they are perceived as children rather than adults.

Social representations of childhood and youth are what Bourdieu would term intellectual and cultural capital (1972), whatever be their degree of organisation, coherence, validity, subjectivity and explication. Some representations tend to be descriptive or explanatory; others are scholarly, popular or based on experiential knowledge, or simple beliefs and opinions. Still others are more openly normative or prescriptive, expressing values, rules, ends, models or projects, that is, desired states of reality (Perrenoud, 1993). For Bourdieu, capital remains largely practical, escaping the conscious awareness of subjects, making up a generative lexicon of practices that often function in an illusory fashion as freedom and improvisation. These broad schemata sustain thoughts and actions, in minor accommodations of their important differentiation, coordination and transformation.

The democratic conception of children and young people is based on understandings, developed over at least three decades, of the child as social actor, as an active participant in his/her own life. Although this process culminated with the Convention on the Rights of the Child adopted by the UN in 1989, legally binding on all signatory parties, this too in Canada continues to interact with economic, cultural and political contexts, constituting power relations as well as spatial and temporal boundaries. As outcomes of negotiation, struggle and human agency, children and youth construct themselves as social agents able to decide their being and their future.

There is nonetheless, a social representation that is extremely vulnerable to market forces, that of the child-as-citizen in juxtaposition with child-as-worker/consumer. The latter conception runs through all of Canada's history: the notion of children and youth as producers, buyers and commodities. In the colonial period, children's labour was a survival strategy of the family, the colonisers and the fur trade. During Confederation and Western expansion into the 1920s, child labour was extensive and its excesses led to child labour laws, further supporting the middle class conception of the child as dependent upon adults and free to play, rather than to labour until adolescence and adulthood. The rise of prosperity in the 1950s and 1960s, followed by recessions at the outset of the 1980s and 1990s, made explicit the economic and political agendas underpinning educational reforms, turning citizens into consumers, shifting meanings, equity and identities.

Pluralism presents a very real challenge to the ever-expanding democratic conception of children and youth. The raging debates on the French school question were resolved in the Thirties so as to maintain only one possible hegemonic view of the self. During the era of progressivism, the child was conceptualised as a scientific inquirer and meaning maker, as liberated thinker and as social actor, a conception that was embodied in the middle-class view of childhood, moving towards a later conception of the independent learner as part of neo-liberal ideals of citizen autonomy. The following period saw the emergence of Charter identities, individual and collective rights including francophone school rights and Aboriginal cultural rights, as well as a conscious deliberate construction of a society respectful of self and others, in diverse and multifaceted lives.

Educational policy makers and researchers have a responsibility to understand the democratic conception of children and youth, by recognising the forces that shape them, the indeterminable character of the realities of young people, and their possibilities as deliberative inquirers, social actors and active citizens. Beyond the critique of deterministic frames of reference of neo-conservative institutions and forces, young people must be recognised with all their self-creating potential, as whole individuals and as valuable members of particular socio-political and cultural groupings, that is, as citizens (Pacom, 2001). As fully-fledged citizens replete with civic, political, social and cultural rights and privileges, young people in Canada are themselves able to see great richness of detail hidden behind images of others (Jover & Reyero, 2000). By virtue of their profession, educators are called upon to see and to support the strengths, legitimacy, diversity and vitality of the child-as-citizen.

The consequences of this analysis of the contextualised emergence of the democratic conception of childhood are relevant to wider considerations of the reform of future educational policies, services and practices. First, this chapter did not dwell upon the meanings of the clauses of the UN Convention on the Child, for this is available elsewhere in a combination of elegant insight and critical prose (Alderson, 2002; Archard, 2004; Casas, 1997; O'Neill, 2004; Howe & Covell, 2005; Verhellen, 2000). The tensions between autonomy and protection have been amply documented and are at the very heart of young people's social engagement as valid forms of democratic participation. Second, schooling has always been shaped in terms of broad political and economic realities, alternating and consolidating three basic goals of schooling which are intellectual, social and democratic. Third, conceptions tend to escape the awareness of subjects, with broad schemata of thought and feeling sustaining most operations and actions, at the price of minor accommodation to the processes of differentiation, coordination and transformation of ways of thinking and acting. This is the case of the democratic conception, which reaches out to engagement, commitment, diversity and respect for others, understood by Canadian children and young people to mean social participation, deliberation, and interaction in school and society. Fourth, conceptions of young people are closely tied to those of women, family models, and aspirations to a better life. Supporting families and women, as well as the civic, political, and cultural identity formation of children and youth, is likely to bring about not only improved student achievement, but also to create good, critical yet effective Canadian citizens. Fifth, the democratic conception is especially closely connected to the neo-economic ideology of a globalising society. Instead of surrendering to global forces that exploit young people, it becomes necessary, then, to focus our energies on democracy as the organising force in the daily lives of children and youth. As part of this focus, it also becomes necessary to address the inequalities and ignorance that challenge plural models of governance for creating long-lasting liberal democracies.

REFERENCES

Alderson, P. (2000). *Young children's rights.* London: Jessica Kingsley.

Anisef, P. & Kilbride, K. M. (Eds.) (2003). *Managing two worlds.* Toronto: Canadian Scholars Press.

Archard, D. (2004). *Children: Rights and childhood* (2nd ed.). London: Routledge.

Baergen, W. (2000). *The Ku Klux Klan in Central Alberta.* Red Deer: Central Alberta Historical Society.

Baker, M. (1981). *The new racism: Conservatives and the ideology of the tribe.* London: Junction Books.

Bannerji, H. (Ed.) (1993). *Returning the gaze: Essays on racism, feminism and politics.* Toronto: Sister Vision Press.

Bannerji, H. (2000). *The dark side of the nation: Essays on multiculturalism, nationalism and gender.* Toronto: Canadian Scholars' Press, Inc.

Barman, J. (2003). Schooled for inequality: The education of British Columbia Aboriginal children. In N. Janovicek & J. Parr (Eds.), *Histories of Canadian children and youth*, Toronto: Oxford University Press.

439

Barman, J., Y. Hébert, Y., & McCaskill, D. (Eds.) (1986). *Indian education in Canada, Vol. 1: The legacy*. Vancouver: UBC Press.

Barman, J., Y. Hébert, Y., & D. McCaskill (Eds.) (1987). *Indian education in Canada, Vol. 2: The challenge*. Vancouver: UBC Press.

Bastarache, M. (Dir.) (1986). *Les droits linguistiques au Canada*. Montréal: Les Éditions Yvon Blais Inc.

Battiste, M. (2002). *Indigenous knowledge and pedagogy in first nations education: A literature review with recommendations*. Ottawa: Indian and Northern Affairs Canada (INAC).

Battiste, M. (Ed.) (2000). *Reclaiming indigenous voice and vision*. Vancouver: UBC Press.

Bernier, L. (1980). *Génération, maturation et conjoncture: Une étude du changement d'attitudes dans le Québec des années 1970*. Montréal: Coll. Cahier d'ASOPE, 10, Université de Montréal.

Beynon, J. D., Toohey, K., & Kishor, N. (1998). Do visible minority students of Chinese and South Asian ancestry want teaching as a career? Perceptions of some secondary school students in Vancouver, B.C. *Canadian Ethnic Studies, 30*(2), 50–72.

Blake, R. (1995). Mackenzie King and the genesis of family allowances in Canada. In R. Blake & J. Keshen (Eds.) *Social and welfare policy in Canada: Historical readings*. Toronto: Copp Clark.

Bourdieu, P. (1972). *Esquisse d'une théorie de la pratique*. Genève: Droz.

Bruno-Jofré, R. (1996). Schooling and the struggles to develop a common polity, 1919–1971. In R. Bruno-Jofré & L. Grieger (Eds.) *Papers on contemporary issues in education policy and administration in Canada: A foundations perspective*. Winnipeg: University of Manitoba.

Carrasco, P., Rose, D. & Charbonneau, J. (1999). La constitution de liens faibles: une passerelle pour l'adaptation des immigrantes centro-américaines mères de jeunes enfants à Montréal. *Études ethniques au Canada/Canadian Ethnic Studies, 31*(1), 73–91.

Casas, F. (1997). Children's rights and children's quality of life: Conceptual and practical issues. *Social Indicators Research, 42*, 283–298.

Castellano, M. B., Davis, L., & Lahache, L. (Eds.) (2000). *Aboriginal education: Fulfilling the promise*. Vancouver: UBC Press.

Chunn, D. (2003). Boys will be men, girls will be mothers: The legal regulation of childhood in Toronto and Vancouver. In N. Janovicek & J. Parr (Eds.), *Histories of Canadian children and youth*. Toronto: Oxford University Press.

Cunningham, F. (2002). *Theories of democracy: A critical introduction*. London: Routledge.

Cunningham, H. (1998). Histories of childhood: Review essay. *The American Historical Review, 103*(4), 1195–1208.

Davey, I. (2003). The rhythm of work and the rhythm of school. In N. Janovicek & J. Parr (Eds.) *Histories of Canadian children and youth*. Toronto: Oxford University Press.

de Mause, L. (Ed.) (1974). *The history of childhood*. New York: The Psychohistory Press.

Dumas, S., G. Rochais, G. & Tremblay, H. (1982). *Une génération silencieusement lucide?* Québec: Gouvernement du Québec.

Friesen, G. (1984). *The Canadian prairies: A history*. Toronto: University of Toronto Press.

Gauthier, M. (2001). The social construction of youth in French Canadian sociology. In M. Gauthier & D. Pacom (Eds.) *Spotlight on Canadian youth research*. Sainte-Foy: Les Presses de l'Université Laval.

Gauthier, M. & Pacom, D. (Eds.) (2001). *Spotlight on Canadian youth research*. Sainte-Foy: Les Presses de l'Université Laval.

Hagan, J., Dinovitzer, R. & Parker, P. (2003). Choice and circumstance: Social capital and planful competence in the attainment of the 'one-and-a-half' generation. Web site: http://www.ceris.metropolis.net/VirtualLibrary/education/hagan1/hagan1.html retrieved on 21 January 2003.

Hébert, Y., Lee, W-S. J., Sun, X. S. & Berti, D. (2004a). Relational citizenship as social capital: Immigrant youth's mental maps of their friendships. *Encounters in Education, 4*, 83–106.

Hébert, Y., Sun, X. S. & Kowch, E. (2004b). Focusing on youth: Social capital, diversity and educational outcomes. *Journal of International Migration and Integration, 5*(2), 229–249.

Hébert, Y., Berti, C., Lee, W-S. & Afatsawo, C. K. (2003). Life stories of Canadian immigrant youth: Evidence of emotional competence. Paper presented at the 6th National Metropolis Conference, Edmonton.

Hébert, Y., Lee, W-S., Sun, X. S., & Berti, C. (2003). Canadian citizenship and national identity: Forms of local attachment among youth. Paper presented at the conference on *Lifelong Citizenship Learning, Participatory Democracy, and Social Change: Local and Global Perspectives*, Transformation Learning Centre, Ontario Institute for the Study of Education, University of Toronto.

Hébert, Y. & Wilkinson, L. (2002). The citizenship debates: Conceptual, policy, experiential and educational issues. In Y. Hébert (Ed.), *Citizenship in transformation in Canada*. Toronto: University of Toronto Press.

Hébert, Y. M. & Racicot, C. (2001). Relations identitaires et citoyennes à l'école dans l'Ouest canadien. In M. Pagé & F. Ouellet (Dirs.) *L'Éducation à la citoyenneté*. Sherbrooke : Association mondiale des sciences de l'éducation et Éditions du CRP.

Hébert, Y. (Dir.) (1993). L'évolution de l'école francophone en milieu minoritaire. Numéro thématique de la *Revue canadienne des langues vivantes/Canadian Modern Language Review, 49*(4).

Hoffman, D. (2003). Childhood ideology in the United States: A comparative cultural view. *International Review of Education, 49*(1-2), 191−211.

Hodgett, A. B. (1968). *What culture? What heritage?* Toronto: Ontario Institute for Studies in Education.

Hollands, R. (2001). (Re)presenting Canadian youth: Challenge or opportunity? In M. Gauthier & D. Pacom (Eds.) *Spotlight on Canadian youth research*. Sainte-Foy, QC: Les Presses de l'Université Laval.

Houston, S. E., & Prentice, A. (1988). *Schooling and scholars in nineteenth century Ontario*. Toronto: University of Toronto Press.

Howe, R. Brian & Covell, K. (2005). *Empowering children: Children's rights education as a pathway to citizenship*. Toronto: University of Toronto Press.

Isajiw, W. (1999). *Understanding diversity: Ethnicity and race in the Canadian context*. Toronto: Thompson Educational Publishing, Inc.

Isin, E. & Wood, P. (1999). *Citizenship and identity*. London: Sage Publications.

Janovicek, N. (2003). Colonial childhood, 1700−1880. In N. Janovicek and J. Parr (Eds.), *Histories of Canadian children and youth*. Toronto: Oxford University Press.

Jover, G. & Reyero, D. (2000). Images of the other in childhood: Researching the limits of cultural diversity in education from the standpoint of new anthropological methodologies. *Encounters on Education, 1*, 127−152.

Kallen, E. (2003). *Ethnicity and human rights in Canada: A human rights perspective on ethnicity, racism, and systemic inequality* (3rd ed.). Toronto: Oxford University Press.

Kelly, J. (1998a). Experiences with the white man: Black student narratives. *Canadian Ethnic Studies, 30*(2), 95−111.

Kelly, J. (1998b). *Under the gaze: Learning to be Black in White society*. Halifax: Fernwood.

King, R. (2001). The Kid from *The Kid:* Jackie Coogan and the consolidation of child consumerism. *The Velvet Light Trap, 48*, 1−17.

Kirkness, V. (1972). *Indian control of Indian education*. Ottawa: National Indian Brotherhood.

Klein, N. (2000). *No logo*. Toronto: Vintage Canada.

Laneyrie-Dagen, N. (1995). *Les grands événements de l'histoire des enfants*. Paris: Larousse.

Larsell, O. (1932). An outline for the history of medicine in the Pacific Northwest. *Northwest Medicine, 31*, 484.

Lee, W.-S. J. & Y. Hébert (2007). The meaning of being Canadian: A comparison between 1st generation and non-immigrant youth in Calgary. *Canadian Journal of Education, 27*(2), 497−520. Web site: http://www.csse.ca/CJE/Articles/CJE29-2.htm

Lee, W.-S. J., Hébert, Y., Parel, R. & Racicot, C. (2001). *Learning to read, spatiality, and strategic competence of immigrant youth in Western Canadian High Schools*. Paper presented at the annual conference of the Canadian Society for the Study of Education, Université Laval.

Mahé, Y. (1993). L'idéologie, le curriculum et les enseignants des écoles bilingues de l'Alberta, 1892–1992. *Revue canadienne de langues vivantes, 49*(4), 687–703.

Maheu, L. & Bélanger, P. (1972). Pratique politique étudiante au Québec. *Recherches sociographiques, 13*(3), 310–342.

Marshall, D. (2003). Reconstruction politics, the Canadian welfare state, and the ambiguity of children's rights. In N. Janovicek & J. Parr (Eds.) *Histories of Canadian children and youth.* Toronto: Oxford University Press.

Marshall, T. (1964). Citizenship and social class. In T. Marshall, *Class, citizenship, and social development.* New York: Doubleday.

Martel, A. (1991). *Les droits scolaires des minorités de langue officielle au Canada: De l'instruction à la gestion.* Ottawa: Commissariat aux Langues Officielles.

Massey, D. (1998). The spatial construction of youth cultures. In T. Skelton & G. Valentine (Eds.), *Cool places: Geographies of youth cultures.* London: Routledge.

Mazurek, K. (1999). Passing fancies: Educational change in Alberta. In T. Harrison & J. Kachur (Eds.), *Contested classrooms: Education, globalization and democracy in Alberta,* Edmonton: Parkland Institute and University of Alberta Press.

McIntosh, R. (2003). The boys in the Nova Scotia coal mines: 1873–1923. In N. Janovicek & J. Parr (Eds.), *Histories of Canadian children and youth.* Toronto: Oxford University Press.

McLeod, K. (1979). Politics, schools and the French language, 1881–1931. In D. Jones, N. Sheehan & R. Stamp (Eds.), *Shaping the schools of the Canadian West.* Calgary: Detselig.

Moogk, P. (2003). Les petits sauvages: The children of eighteenth-century new France. In N. Janovicek & J. Parr (Eds.), *Histories of Canadian children and youth.* Toronto: Oxford University Press.

Molgat, M. (1998). *L'insertion résidentielle des jeunes.* Thèse de doctorat, Université de Montréal.

Neatby, H. (1953). *So little for the mind.* Toronto: Clark Irwin.

Osborne, K. (1996). Education is the best national insurance: Citizenship education in Canadian schools, past and present. *Canadian and International Education/Éducation Canadienne et Internationale, 25*(2), 31–58.

Pacom, D. (2001). Beyond positivism: A theoretical evaluation of the sociology of youth. In M. Gauthier & D. Pacom (Eds.), *Spotlight on Canadian youth research.* Sainte-Foy: Les Presses de l'Université Laval.

Pattison, P. (1994). Social cognition in context: Some applications of social network analysis. In S. Wasserman & J. Galaskiewicz (Eds.), *Advances in social network analysis.* Thousand Oaks, CA: Sage Publications.

Penner, N. (1978). The making of a radical: Winnipeg in the 1930s. In I. Abella & D. Millar (Eds.) *The Canadian worker in the twentieth century.* Toronto: Oxford University Press.

Perreault, J. & Vance, S. (1990). *Writing the circle: Native women of Western Canada.* Edmonton: NuWest Publishers.

Perrenoud, P. (1993). La formation au métier d'enseignant: Complexité, professionnalisation et démarche clinique. In *Compétence et formation des enseignants.* Trois-Rivières, QC: La Coopérative universitaire de Trois-Rivières.

Piaget, J. (1957). The child and modern physics. *Scientific American, 197,* 46–51.

Polanyi, M. (1969). *Knowing and being.* London: Routledge & Kegan Paul.

Polanyi, M. (1958). *Personal knowledge: Towards a post-critical philosophy.* Chicago: University of Chicago Press.

Pollard, J. (2003). A most remarkable phenomenon: Growing up métis: Fur traders' children in the Pacific Northwest. In N. Janovicek & J. Parr (Eds.) *Histories of Canadian children and youth.* Toronto: Oxford University Press.

Postman, N. (1982). *The disappearance of childhood.* New York: Delacorte Press.

Report of the Royal Commission on Education in Alberta 1959 (1959). Edmonton: Queen's Printer.

Rioux, M. (1969). *Jeunesse et société contemporaine.* Montréal: Les Presses de l'Université de Montréal.

Robert, M. & Tondreau, J. (1997). *L'école québécoise: Débats, enjeux et pratiques sociales.* Anjou, QC : Les éditions CEC Inc.

Rocher, G. (1988). L'étudiant et la modernité. *Revue de l'Université de Moncton, 21,* 1.

Rocher, G. (1973) *Le Québec en mutation.* Montréal: Hurtubise HMH.

Rooke, P. & Schnell, R. (1983). Discarding the asylum. In P. Rooke & R. Schnell (Eds.) *From child rescue to the welfare state in English-Canada, 1800–1950.* Lanham, MD: University Press of America.

Rooke, P. & Schnell, R. L. (1982). Guttersnipes and charity children: Nineteenth century child rescue in the Atlantic Provinces. In R. L. Schnell & P. Rooke (Eds.) *Studies in childhood history, A Canadian perspective.* Calgary: Detsileg Enterprises Ltd.

Ross, C. (1997) *Franco-Manitobans and the struggle for the preservation of religion and language: Public schools and the township of Ste Anne, 1946–1955.* M. Ed Thesis, University of Manitoba.

Royal Commission on Aboriginal Peoples (1997). *For seven generations: An information legacy of the Royal Commission on Aboriginal Peoples.* Ottawa: Libraxus Inc..

Schissel, B. (1997). *Blaming children: Youth crime, moral panics and the politics of hate.* Halifax: Fernwood Publishing.

Schissel, B. & Wotherspoon, T. (2002). *The legacy of school for Aboriginal people: Education, oppression, and emancipation.* Toronto: Oxford University Press.

Schissel, B. (In Press). Justice undone: Public panic, and the condemnation of children and youth. In C. Krinsky (Ed.), *The sky is falling: international perspectives on moral panics.* Columbia: Columbia University Press.

Shipley, D. (1995). Families and domestic routines: Constructing the boundaries of childhood. In S. Pile & N. Thrift (Eds.), *Mapping the subject: Geographies of cultural transformation.* London: Routledge.

Stanley, T. (2003). White supremacy: Chinese schooling, and school segregation in Victoria: The case of the Chinese students' strike, 1922–23. In N. Janovicek & J. Parr (Eds.), *Histories of Canadian children and youth.* Toronto: Oxford University Press.

Strong-Boag, V. (2002). Getting to now: Children in distress in Canada's past. In B. Wharf (Ed.), *Community work in child welfare.* Toronto: Broadview Press.

Sutherland, N. (2002). *Growing up: Childhood in English Canada from the Great War to the age of transition.* Toronto: University of Toronto Press.

Sutherland, N. (2000). *Children in English-Canadian society: Framing the twentieth-century consensus.* Waterloo, ON: Wilfred Laurier University Press.

Verhellen, E. (2000). Children's Rights and Education. In Osler, Audrey (Ed.), *Citizenship and democracy in schools: Diversity, identity, equality.* Stoke on Trent, UK and Sterling, USA: Trentham Books.

Yvonne M. Hébert
Faculty of Education, University of Calgary

HANS HOOGHOFF

EDUCATION *IMPLIES* CITIZENSHIP

Developing a Global Dimension in Dutch Education

INTRODUCTION

Both Scottish and Dutch education systems have long reputations for high quality. The Scottish system is seen as one that has been characterised as liberal, egalitarian and democratic. While internationally there is a trend towards increasing homogeneity of curricula, there remains in the Scottish educational psyche, I would argue, the spirit of the democratic intellect. Long may that continue.

The promotion of active citizenship and social integration is high on the agenda in the Netherlands, in Europe and in the rest of the world. Social developments lead to new requirements for schools as part of their pedagogical task. Interdependence is increasing worldwide. Whereas in the past things that happened in China or Brazil hardly seemed to affect us at all, nowadays they can have great consequences closer to home. We become more and more aware that we must regard the earth as one coherent, interdependent system. The challenge this presents to schools is very considerable. That challenge is to ensure that the idea of interdependence becomes central to the learning and teaching process.

Contrary to what often seems to be the case, the quality of our society is not determined exclusively by economic factors. It is above all determined by underlying social mores which in the recent past have in educational policy terms heavily emphasised the importance of the world of work and economic development (Senge *et al*, 2000). But societal values change over time and there is an increasing recognition of the centrality of wider cultural dimensions of learning as determinants of educational provision.

I take the view that living together effectively in the early 21st century requires us to value and celebrate the creative tension created by diversity and connectedness. My premise is that living together effectively is something we can learn, and something we *have* to learn. That is the basis for education for citizenship.

In the Netherlands, the debate on citizenship was accelerated recently after the violent death of Theo van Gogh, a filmmaker and writer, who openly criticised the current influence of Islamic culture on Dutch society.[1]

On 1st February 2006 some legal provisions[2] concerning active citizenship and social integration were put into effect. Since then, primary and secondary schools have the task of preparing their pupils for participation in a multicultural society.

M.A. Peters, A. Britton and H. Blee (Eds.), Global Citizenship Education: Philosophy, Theory and Pedagogy, 445–458.

Pupils have to learn about their fellow pupils and contemporaries from other cultural backgrounds and how to deal with living in a culturally diverse society. Citizenship education is no abstract issue: it impacts directly on social behaviour in our streets, schools and communities.

Citizenship has been explicitly incorporated in the new Dutch core objectives (Ministry of Education, Culture and Science, 2006). It is for the individual school to choose approaches that are in tune with their particular religious or pedagogical viewpoints. It is, however, easy to write down objectives and desirable results, but that is a long way from the point at which they might be achieved. Unpredictable developments and social trends such as migration, technological revolution and religious revivalism make it more and more important that schools handle citizenship in a responsive and effective way. Schools have to deal with more than just academic issues. Schools must also participate in the development of reflective adults, who are able to approach social topics with an open and critical mind.

In this chapter I would like to ask, from a Dutch perspective, a number of questions about education for global citizenship. I'd like to ask if these resonate with the Scottish experience and to consider ways in which we as a community of shared interests might address some of the challenges of implementing global citizenship.

My chapter is built around the following questions:
- What is the essence of citizenship in school education?
- Is citizenship actually a school subject?
- Are schools already in fact practising education for citizenship?
- What do approaches to citizenship education in Scotland, England, and the Netherlands tell us about implementation strategies?
- What criteria might we use to determine the effectiveness of education for global citizenship?

WHAT IS THE ESSENCE OF CITIZENSHIP IN SCHOOL EDUCATION?

Globalisation: A Rationale

The speed of information exchange and travel, and the dominant influence of modern communication media lead to a decreasing distance between the different parts of the world. The economies of different countries are increasingly closely related to one another, allowing a vast world trade system to blossom.

However, whilst these factors have led to huge improvements that have changed the lives of millions of people, one in five of the world's population still lives in extreme poverty. They lack access to basic healthcare, education and clean water, with little opportunity to improve their condition. There is increasing acknowledgement of the far-reaching impact of levels of global poverty. For example, environmental damage, exacerbated by poverty, does not stop at national boundaries.

The worldwide distribution of western culture via the media has led to western producers overrunning and almost overruling the lifestyles of other cultures and their associated norms and values. As a reaction to this dominant influence a revival of especially regional, national, religious and cultural awareness is coming about; and Scotland is, of course, one example of this phenomenon.

But issues of poverty, human rights, peace and safety as well as the environment increasingly require a sound international approach. We are all too well aware that many problems can only be solved if we work together on an international basis. All these issues concern every citizen, including young people. Young people already have an interest in proper preparation for world citizenship and for their future in a continuously changing world. They also need to be helped to understand that they can play a small but important part in determining developments in cooperation and integration and that they can contribute to the solution of international issues. Encouraging critical reflection on current developments and problems perhaps best does this. The optimistic hope is that young people will be increasingly able to determine and assess their position both in their own community and in the wider world.

WHAT IS THE ESSENCE OF CITIZENSHIP IN SCHOOL EDUCATION?

Unity in Diversity: Unum in Pluribus

In the future internationalisation or sustainable globalisation will continue to change our economic, cultural, political and educational structures. It is not unthinkable that individual states will gradually lose autonomous functions as education systems grow towards one another.

There is also an increasing trend towards common visions of curriculum, the exchange of practical examples and participation in collaborative projects. We can see that education ministries of different states increasingly adapt their education policies according to the results of international comparative research such as TIMMS (Mullis *et al*, 2003).

At the same time, however, regions within countries promote and advance their *own cultural identity* and they request political recognition and economic protection. Private prevails over universal and the parties involved consider the preservation of their own language, values and habits to be more essential than a common national culture. One risk in such a trend is that it might lead to insularity and the creation of 'communities within communities'.

Nation states will increasingly have to anticipate decentralised forces and in the long run will not be able to put themselves forward as the keepers *of a unitary culture.* The multi-ethnic society, consisting of a large variety of cultural minorities, will develop further and further. At the same time, certain political and social groups will try to enforce a reactionary non-inclusive social order, at the expense of a just and humane society.

A prime task and responsibility for education systems is to create a pedagogically and ethically responsible climate in the institution of the school (Bron, 2005), as well as an environment that is physically and psychologically safe, enabling students to fully develop their talents. The challenge is complex.

447

WHAT IS THE ESSENCE OF CITIZENSHIP IN SCHOOL EDUCATION?

Implementation Issues

Since the beginning of the 1970s there has been a call for a greater social dimension in education in the Netherlands. Since then different interest groups have tried to capture the attention of education and have tried to secure a permanent position in the school curriculum (Hooghoff, 1997). These groups have promoted a broad variety of themes and issues, including conflict management, emancipation, developing countries, human rights, holocaust, homosexuality, technology, intercultural education, environmental issues, the European dimension, health and citizenship.

Common characteristics of these cross-curricular themes are that they:
- Concern a social or political item
- Can be incorporated into different school subjects
- Pay considerable attention to values development and values communication
- Emphasise an active and participating role for the student.

Initially the interest groups, often private organizations and NGOs, engaged themselves in the production of teaching resources in all shapes and sizes. Gradually they discovered that with this method only a small number of schools was reached and the use of the resources was limited.

In the Eighties, the Dutch government decided to establish legal regulations for core objectives for primary and secondary education (age group 4 to 15), just as Scotland had National Guidelines set out in the 5–14 programme. The aim was to have a structural position of compulsory subjects within core objectives.

In the Dutch education system the core objectives and the examinations constitute the directive framework for textbooks. Moreover, commercial textbooks are the most important teaching materials for Dutch teachers. This is why the interest groups, who were advocating particular educational themes, were very keen to have these themes anchored in learning standards. But to what extent can textbooks capture the central ideas and issues of values development, social engagement and active citizenship?

Besides the cross-curricular themes, a number of general skills were also agreed as compulsory as well as part of all the core objectives and subject areas. They include problem-solving skills, active and independent learning, mastering communicative competencies. This is, of course, similar to Scotland's core skills approach. They represent minimum competence levels and all schools are supposed to meet the core objectives.

While the introduction of such metaskills has been thought by many to be helpful in providing young people with capabilities necessary for effective engagement in the world of work, what do they do in helping promote social cohesion and interdependence?

IS CITIZENSHIP ACTUALLY A SCHOOL SUBJECT?

Reviving Active Citizenship Education in the Netherlands

The Dutch Ministry of Education, Culture and Science defines citizenship as:

> willingness and capability to be part of a community and to make a positive contribution to this community. (Ministry of Education, 2006)

Schools, while obliged to pay attention to active citizenship and social integration, have the freedom to determine *how* they are going to integrate citizenship in their current curriculum, thus avoiding adding a new school subject – something similar to the Scottish approach.

Citizenship is not just another of the long list of social *themes* that schools are encouraged to attend to, it is about 'functioning well' meaning active participation, taking responsibility for one's own actions, contributing to one's living environment and showing a willingness to engage in democratic behaviour. Education in this understanding *implies* citizenship. Or, in other words, to quote a school leader:

> The pupils' social development is not achieved in one lesson period a week, I tell my teachers we are working on it throughout the whole week.

But why should citizenship be part of school education? In the first place, because for the pupils school is the most direct form in which society manifests itself. In the classroom, in the schoolyard, in the canteen they are confronted with processes, manners of behaviour and events that also occur in 'real' society, such as differing opinions, rows, bullying, violence, but also the formation of groups, sympathy, cooperation and participation and involvement. At school, pupils are stimulated to express their opinions and to substantiate them with well-founded arguments. They learn to respect people with different opinions. They become aware of their social rights and duties.

However, school is not the only place where education takes place. For many pupils the situation at home, within their religious group, in the peer group, in the street, in clubs has a more powerful influence on their development into democratic citizens than education at school. (*Non scolae sed vitae dicimus*: the street is the school for life). Therefore, the expectation of the effects of citizenship education must be put into perspective. Schools cannot be made wholly responsible for how future citizens manifest themselves. Schools cannot compensate for the range of social and cultural factors that impact on young people's world views and behaviours.

At the same time schools must go on creating a pedagogical climate and educational practices such that an open and respectful learning environment based on democratic values is guaranteed. School is a training ground, and ought to be a forum for democratic citizenship.

The cross-curricular character of citizenship education demands a coherent approach, which clarifies the effects for school, pupils and society. Citizenship should become visible through the actions and behaviours of motivated and

449

professional teachers. But, we must recognise that as a professional group teachers are rather conservative, and many, particularly in the secondary sector, do not see education for citizenship as their responsibility. They take the view that their responsibility is for the teaching of specific subjects, not cross-curricular themes. In such a context how can we advance the importance of education for citizenship?

While there is no doubt that education for citizenship has been given high priority at a policy level, the extent to which schools have altered their practices in response to these policies is less clear (see Education Inspectorate, 2007).

Clear and widely supported educational viewpoints form the basis for the introduction of citizenship into the school curriculum, possibly combined in some instances with religious principles. It is thought important to lay the basis of citizenship at an early age and to build on that by introducing more complex aspects over time. Valuable citizenship experiences can be gained within and outside school. Some aspects of citizenship are already part of the curricula for different subjects or can be integrated fairly easily, but citizenship in education also demands different content, and above all different ways of learning with more action oriented activities within and outside school. The cross-curricular character of citizenship demands a coherent approach which clarifies the effects for the school as an organisation, the pupils and society. Citizenship in schools needs to become visible.

WHAT DO APPROACHES TO CITIZENSHIP EDUCATION IN SCOTLAND, ENGLAND, AND THE NETHERLANDS TELL US ABOUT IMPLEMENTATION STRATEGIES?

A Selective Comparison between English, Scottish and Dutch Approaches to Implementation

Undertaking a comparison of the approaches and evaluations, to date, of citizenship education in England, Scotland and Holland provides some interesting insights. In England, The National Foundation for Educational Research (NFER) is monitoring citizenship in education in a nine-year project. In 2005 a survey was conducted among 13,000 pupils, teachers and school managers (NFER, 2006). Some significant conclusions were that:
- Between 2003 and 2005 there was increasing attention given to citizenship's place in the curriculum.
- Teachers had a preference for teaching it as a separate subject.
- Really 'active citizenship' hardly had a place at all in education.
- Young people like to be part of a community.
- The introduction of citizenship in schools is not unproblematic.
- Educational policy and legislation are necessary if citizenship education is to be consolidated.

The main conclusion of this survey was that citizenship has made an entry into schools' planning processes, but there is still a long way to go.

The English school inspectorate (OFSTED) also reports on the development of citizenship education. In 2006 they came to the conclusion that, in spite of the government's initiative to make citizenship a spearhead in the fight against extremism, schools did not succeed in making pupils politically and socially competent. Only a minority of schools had embraced citizenship as a theme. Many schools do not establish the link with current local, national or international topics and the manner in which politicians handle them (OFSTED, 2006).

OFSTED concluded that it would be best to teach citizenship as a separate subject. Chief Inspector David Bell was in favour of striving after world citizenship and defined a world citizen as a person

who knows how the world is put together, who is angry about injustice and is willing and able to do something about it. (Bell, 2005)

Bell argued that it was not the textbook but the newspaper with current news items that was the best teaching resource for this aspect of education.

The approach recommended in Scotland and applied in many Scottish schools is not to teach citizenship as a separate subject, but to embed it in the curriculum and the whole school organisation. The basic objective is to prepare young people for political, social, economic and cultural participation in society.

One of the objectives of education for citizenship is to stimulate the development of personal values, and to make pupils aware of common social values.

Education in 'values' is a complex and challenging enterprise, where the contribution of the school is one of many influences. I think a basic principle in the Scottish approach is that the school can play an important role in the development of personal values – political, social and spiritual – through a sustainable and sustained emphasis on responsible behaviour and care for others.

But this is only one side of effective citizenship education programmes. They must also enable pupils to become critical and independent thinkers. This means that young people must be able to communicate and challenge ideas and viewpoints in debate and in dialogue.

In 2006 the Scottish school inspectorate (HMIE, 2006) stated that, among other things, the above-mentioned approach had led to:
– Schools involving pupils more in decision making.
– Where schools had a proactive approach to pupils' participation, pupils succeeded better in identifying with the activities of the school and the community.
– Schools were more aware of the importance of an effective personal and social development programme.

HMIE pointed out, however, that improvements were necessary with respect to the following points:
– More schools must assess their curriculum with respect to the embedding of citizenship.
– In citizenship education, schools must put more emphasis on the relation between values and citizenship.

- Citizenship programmes must incorporate more themes relating to world citizenship. In particular, the theme of 'sustainability'.
- The professional development of teachers in citizenship still lags behind policy expectations.

We can conclude that there are two striking points in the Scottish approach:

- The intention is to incorporate situations into educational practice, which give pupils the opportunity to *experience* democratic citizenship.
- As opposed to OFSTED's argument in England, Scotland is in favour of an integrated approach of education in citizenship instead of teaching it as a separate subject.

And while we may have views on the good sense of the Scottish approach, we know that implementation is proving to be a challenge.

In Holland a recent annual 'state of the art' report on education (Dutch title: *De staat van het onderwijs*) the Dutch school inspectorate stated that most schools already engage in some way or another in active citizenship and social integration (Education Inspectorate, 2007). What is often missing, however, is a wider vision of its purpose and a systematic approach. Perhaps this is also true in Scotland.

How, for instance, does the school react to undesirable opinions and attitudes of students? What does the school do to offer pupils and staff from an increasingly diverse set of cultural and ethnic backgrounds a safe physical and psychological environment in which to learn?

It is not easy to define specific objectives for citizenship in education, given that it is arguably as much about values formation and attitudinal development as the acquisition of a body of knowledge. In the long run, professional and political consensus on both the purposes of education and the nature of society, when taken with empirical knowledge and examples of good practice are more likely to lead to a more normative understanding of the desirable outcomes of education for citizenship as well as a more adequate basis on which to assess effectiveness. This is, of course, a shift in emphasis many would argue is needed across the curriculum as the shortcomings of an overemphasis on narrow measurable objectives are increasingly recognised.[3]

Problems and Opportunities

Society and politicians ask repeatedly to put a range of current social topics on the school agenda. The continuously changing social priorities cause a constantly changing demand on schools. For example, the increasing diversity of Dutch society led to the compulsory topic *Intercultural Education*. In order to promote the EU, Brussels launched the *European Dimension*; the indignation about the loss of social norms gave rise to rethinking the locus of *Moral Responsibility* in schools; and of course governmental concern with voter apathy and disinterest has led to *Education for Citizenship*. Furthermore, since the 1970s schools have been expected to pay regular attention to international issues, such as developing countries, human rights and environmental issues.

Not only is too much asked of schools, but they are expected to be able to contribute significantly to the reduction of negative social trends. The available teaching time is limited, and there is a strong view that complying with too many claims on the curriculum will fragment the teaching programme even though an underlying idea in all cross-curricular themes is the idea of 'connectedness'.

The question remains: what is the *'added value'* of cross curricular themes and issues if time is taken from the subject-teaching programme to address particular current social issues? Is the subject-based curriculum still the most adequate way of organising learning? Might it be helpful in securing a more holistic and coherent approach to curriculum planning if a criterion for the inclusion of any theme such as, for example, global citizenship, was the extent to which it contributes to the realisation of the school's fundamental educational purposes.

Research and experience with national education projects on social and political topics, such as environmental education and the global dimension, have shown that a directive curriculum framework, that is, one which states the intended learning objectives, the contents, the array of teaching methods, assessment of knowledge and skills, as well as the relationship to subject-specific curricula, seems to be an important condition for reaching the intended goals (Boersma & Hoogshoff, 1993; CIDREE, 1998).

But how can such a directive framework do justice to the very ideas at the heart of education for citizenship? How can it cope with ideas such as the importance of alternative viewpoints; the right to dissent; the opportunity to adopt alternative lifestyles; the validation of difference? All of which are central to participative citizenship. This presents education systems with something of a dilemma.

Does the problem lie with teachers' inability or unwillingness to see themselves as having teaching responsibilities beyond a subject curriculum; or does it lie with schools becoming too focused on test scores and a subject-based curriculum? Or is it a failure on the part of politicians to 'follow through' with the resource and training implications of innovative and additional curriculum components? Or is it a loss of confidence on the part of the system to jettison aspects of the existing curriculum that are no longer relevant?

WHAT CRITERIA MIGHT WE USE TO DETERMINE THE EFFECTIVENESS OF EDUCATION FOR GLOBAL CITIZENSHIP?

The Need for Evaluation

Significant priority has been given to exchange and cooperation initiatives as a means of enhancing learning about the international and global dimensions of education. But there is little research evidence on the effects of such programmes. The policy of the next few years has to change from stimulation and facilitation, to a more structured incorporation of global aspects into the mainstream activities of educational institutions.

Some key starting points will have to include:

- Consideration of the implications of programming international activities as a permanent part of the policy of education institutions.
- The assessment of additional educational resources on internationalisation, but in relation to the national innovation objectives for primary and secondary education.
- The formulation of quality indicators for the systematic evaluation of the programmes for exchange and cooperation.
- How participation can remain broadly accessible for pupils, students and teachers, but also move from the individual to consideration of mechanisms that enable participation in international collaboration at institutional level.

The questions I set out at the beginning of this chapter require continued consideration. Across Europe the reasons for the priority given to education for citizenship have been as much about the preoccupations of politicians as with the intrinsic educational value of learning about the nature of democratic citizenship. Nevertheless, whatever the motivation, this aspect of young people's educational entitlement forces us to reconsider the extent to which young people's *experience* of school education is consistent with active democratic participation in a pluralist society. The essence of effective citizenship is activity not passivity. How does such an assertion fit into the constraints of current curriculum planning and teaching?

In considering what is a trans-national issue it might seem reasonable that we should take active steps to learn from each others' experiences and research findings. Unfortunately, too often the lead time for curriculum evaluation lags too far behind the demands of politically-driven curriculum imperatives to allow formative input that might enhance effective implementation strategies. Perhaps the development of new, innovative approaches to curriculum research and evaluation would enable more rapid, and hence useful, comparisons to be made across themes of interest to a number of education systems (HMIE, 2006).

The SLO Project Core Affairs: An Agenda for Cooperation

The Netherlands Institute for Curriculum Development (SLO) is carrying out a comparative research project regarding design and implementation of common aims and contents in basic education across Europe (Core Affairs, 2007). The research activities are based on the results of a previous project, focused on curriculum development in a (de)centralised context in some European countries (Kuiper *et al*, 2005).

In almost all European and western-oriented countries, there is an on-going debate about what belongs to the *core of education* and what aims are desirable to strive for or to attain. In Scotland *A Curriculum for Excellence* is part of that debate. The debate is not only for the education community: it needs to take place across several layers of society, involving a variety of stakeholders such as social policy makers, administrators, religious and community groups, parents, business and industry.[4] The debate gives regard to the formative and qualifying values of education for individuals as well as for society. It relates to skill development, preserving and transferring cultural heritage, global citizenship and social responsibility, as well as respect for, and fulfilling of, common values and societal norms.

The debate also concerns the wish for stabilisation and reinforcement of the economic position through effective and useful investments in competence and knowledge development. In the debate there are contradictions in the weighing of the interests of distinguished stakeholders; for example, business and industry, politicians of different parties, parents, teacher groups, academics and philosophers. No less problematic are differing views as to the functions of education; for example, is it principally about economic development, or is it at source about cultural identity, or is the fundamental obligation personal formation? In this turbulent environment governments and other educational authorities have to make their decisions, which should be relevant, guaranteeing and supporting a sustainable quality of education for the 21st century.

Dutch education policy is facing some dilemmas. After a period with a strong focus on social relations and accents on equal opportunities, designed in a uniform structure with a common content, society changed in the direction of accepting and even valuing social diversity, with consequences for educational policy. What we see now is a tendency towards deregulation and increasing autonomy. This is also the case in Scotland.

The research project '*Core Affairs*' investigates the development, the determination and the maintenance of a common core in education, in a more or less (de)centralised policy context. More specifically, the researchers in the project are looking at what is being considered as the common core and aims in several European countries (Scotland, Finland, Sweden, Germany); for example:

– What resources are being used?
– What motives for choices are used?
– What might a common core look like?
– Which stakeholders are involved, their level of commitment and ownership?
– What are the intended and realised effects of common content and mutual aims?

CONTRIBUTION TO THE DISCUSSION FOR 'CHANCES FOR GLOBAL EDUCATION'

There is a large quantity and variety of sources available on conceptual frameworks, training programmes, educational support resources (multimedia), educational concepts and successful school programmes for global education. These have been developed over recent years, but with limited success. If this assumption is correct, does it mean the challenge concerns implementation rather than development? And if this is true, what are the reasons for the low levels of interest in global education and the marginal position it occupies in education?

Can obstacles be identified, and are there any mechanisms for tackling them in the near future? And what would this require in the way of knowledge, infrastructure and support?

Some possible barriers to implementation are:

- The changes are not in accordance with school practices and at much too high a level of ambition, resulting in teachers failing to have any real sense of ownership.
- There is no adequate support structure, professionally coordinated, for the long term.
- No implementation and evaluation policy at school level has been formulated, resulting in ad hoc procedures in different schools.
- The nature of the concept of global education has been insufficiently defined in terms of knowledge and skills for the student, resulting in constant reinterpretations which interfere with the implementation process.
- There is a lack of interest in the subject on the part of students and their parents, hence vital support is lacking.
- Not everybody is committed to globalism.

All these points can be confirmed on the basis of numerous international research studies (for example: Bolt et al, 2006; Fullan, 2001a; Fullan, 2001b; Senge, 1990; Senge et al, 2000). However, in my opinion it remains curious that so little has been learned from disappointments and failing reform operations all over the world.

Perhaps the time has come to conduct a thorough analysis of the highs and lows of global citizenship education and to ask ourselves whether, in this case, realism would not be better than idealism.

If we believe that democratic processes offer the best prospects of a just and humane future, schools play an important role. Although many things are often laid down in a school's 'mission statement', in practice these are often empty rhetoric. Policy makers, administrators and managers are often stuck on academic priorities and leave democratic citizenship aside.

Academic studies do not guarantee our humanity, nor do they support democracy. Let me quote Ghandi who, when asked what he found the saddest thing in life, said: *'the small heart of those who are the most developed'*.

If we truly cherish democracy we must strive after education systems that increase young people's capability to look critically and empathetically at the lives of others across the globe.

NOTES

[1] The clearest example of this is in the film 'Submission', where Ayaan Hirsi Ali (former member of Dutch parliament) calls the tune. The film concerns the alleged mistreatment of women in some Islamic families. The film shows the bodies of Muslim women battered by their family members, or because they were sentenced for (alleged) indecent behaviour. Some Muslim groups regard the film as blasphemous, which caused vehement reactions, and eventually led to the murder of the film producer Theo van Gogh.

[2] Act of 9 December 2005, saying that active citizenship and social integration should be incorporated in the Primary Education Act, the Act on the Centres of Expertise and the Secondary Education Act, to stress the obligation of schools to contribute to the integration of pupils into Dutch society. (For the original text in Dutch please consult Staatsblad 2005, 678). The Act was effectuated on 1st February 2006 (Staatsblad 2006, 36).

[3] There has been in recent years a tendency across Europe (cf. England, Wales, the Netherlands) to relax the number and specificity of learning objectives within national curriculum requirements. This has been in response to concerns that assessment requirements have been excessive and also in recognition that failure to secure important wider learning outcomes, together with an unhelpful fragmentation of learning, can be the result of a curriculum specification which is too detailed.

[4] A literature study on attainment targets in lower classes of Dutch secondary education (Studulski & Timmerhuis, 2007) states that many stakeholders, especially in a decentralised context, play an important role in defining these targets.

REFERENCES

Barker, C.M. (2000). *Education for international understanding and global competence*. Report of a meeting convened by the Carnegie Corporation of New York. Retrieved 20 September, 2007, from http://www.carnegie.org/pdf/global.pdf.

Bell, D. (2005, 2 November). *Education for democratic citizenship*. Guardian Unlimited web site. Retrieved 20 September, 2007, from http://education.guardian.co.uk/ofsted/story/0,,1606888,00 .html.

Boersma, K. & Hooghoff, J.H.W. (1993). *Leerplanontwikkeling en educaties in Nederland*. [Curriculum development and cross-curricular themes in the Netherlands]. Enschede: Netherlands Institute of Curriculum Development (SLO).

Bolt, L. van der, Studulski, F., Vegt, A. van der & Bontje, D. (2006). *De betrokkenheid van de leraar bij onderwijsinnovaties. Een verkenning op basis van literatuur* [The involvement of the teacher in educational reforms. An exploration on the basis of literature]. Utrecht: Sardes.

Bron, J. (2005). *Een basis voor burgerschap: Een inhoudelijke verkenning voor het funderend onderwijs* [A basis for citizenship: An exploration for elementary and the first stage of secondary education]. Enschede: SLO.

CIDREE (1998). *Across the great divides. Report of the CIDREE collaborative project on cross curricular themes*. Dundee: CIDREE.

Core Affairs (2007*). A comparative study about motives, functions, sources, design and implementation of common aims and contents in Europe in basic education*. Enschede: Netherlands Institute of Curriculum Development (SLO). (Forthcoming.)

Education Council (2003). *Onderwijs en burgerschap* [Education and citizenship]. The Hague: Education Council.

Education Inspectorate (2006). *Toezicht op burgerschap en integratie* [Monitoring citizenship and integration]. Utrecht: Education Inspectorate.

Education Inspectorate (2007). *De staat van het onderwijs: Onderwijsverslag 2005/2006* [Education, a state of the art report on education 2005/2006]. Utrecht: Education Inspectorate.

Fullan, M. (2001a). *The new meaning of educational change* (3rd edition). New York: Teachers College Press.

Fullan, M. (2001b). *Leading in a culture of change*. San Francisco: Josey-Bass.

Her Majesty's Inspectorate of Education (HMIE) (2006). *Education for citizenship: A portrait of current practice in Scottish schools and pre-school centres*. Edinburgh: HMIE.

Hooghoff, J.H.W. (1997). *Global and development education*. Nagoya University, School of Education., Nagoya, Japan.

Kennedy, J. (2005). 'Civic virtues' en democratie. In *In de Marge*, 14, pp. 11–30. Amsterdam: Blaise Pascal Instituut VU.

Kerr, D. & Nelson, J. (2006). *Active citizenship in INCA countries: Definitions, policies, practices and outcomes*. Final report. London: QCA & NFER.

Kuiper, W., Akker, J. van den, Hooghoff, H. & Letschert, J. (2005). Curriculum policy and school practice in a European comparative perspective. In *Curriculum development re-invented*. Proceedings of the invitational conference on the occasion of 30 years SLO 1975-2005, Leiden, the

Netherlands, 7–9 December 2005. Enschede: SLO. Retrieved from http://www.slo.nl/themas/00153/Currdevelopment_re-invented_on_line_versie.pdf.

Ministry of Education, Culture and Science (OCW) (2004). *Koers primair onderwijs: Ruimte voor de school* [Setting out the course for primary education: More scope for the school]. Den Haag: OCW.

Ministry of Education, Culture and Science (2006). *Kerndoelen primair onderwijs* [Core objectives for primary education]. Den Haag: DeltaHage.

Mullis, I.V.S., Martin, M.O. & Foy, P. (2003). *International mathematics report.* Boston: TIMMS International Study Center.

National Foundation for Educational Research (NFER) (2006). *Active citizenship and young people: The citizenship education longitudinal study 2006.* Slough: NFER.

Office for Standards in Education (OFSTED) (2006). *Towards concensus? Citizenship in secondary schools.* London: OFSTED.

Senge, P.M. (1990). *The fifth discipline: The art and practice of the learning organization.* New York: DoubleDay.

Senge, P., Cambron-McCabe, N., Lucas, T., Smith, B., Dutton, J. & Kleiner, A. (2000). *Schools that learn.* New York: Random House Inc.

Studulski, F. & Timmerhuis, A.H.B. (2007). *De kerndoelen voor de basisvorming. Een analyse op basis van literatuur.* Utrecht: Sardes.

Hans Hooghoff
Netherlands Institute for Curriculum Development (SLO)
The Netherlands

EVELYN ARIZPE AND JAMES MCGONIGAL

GLOBAL CITIZENS, LOCAL LINGUISTS

How Migrant Children Explore Cultural Identity through Vernacular Texts

INTRODUCTION

This chapter is about migrant children's cultural identity and their emergent intercultural understanding, which is to say it is centrally about children listening to language and making sense of new texts in new locations. In all sorts of ways, this is an uncertain experience for them and progress is often hidden or hesitant. When the chosen texts are carefully matched by their teachers to the children's new place of residence, however, a space can open up that is more than local, in which home and school literacies, classroom and playground languages, and personal and ethnic identities can be explored.

We are going to focus here on children's fiction in a range of genres written in varieties of Scots language. Lowland Scots is the main heritage language of Scotland, along with the more ancient Gaelic language of the Highlands and Islands, and is spoken or understood by well over a million Scots in a variety of regional forms, as opposed to the fifty thousand or so remaining who now speak Gaelic. Whereas the Scottish English that is spoken by most educated adults in Scotland in formal situations approximates to Standard English (with some noticeable differences in usage and accent) the 'broader' more ancient Lowland Scots is the language that marks out Scotland as significantly different from the rest of the United Kingdom, and carries significant signals of identity, culture and values.

What is offered through such local texts, then, is different from what Standard English holds out to immigrants as a passport to educational success and (perhaps) to social integration. Vernacular literature, which in the research project described here meant stories, poems and cartoons in Scottish English as well as in broader Lowland Scots, possesses something of the outcast status as a language that migrant or asylum-seeking children recognise: for it is in some senses a forbidden language in schools, fit for children to use in the playground but not for classroom or curriculum. For historical and political reasons, within a contemporary Scotland exploring the potential of a devolved parliament within a UK unionist framework, Scots language is a strong marker of identity, whether of nationality or of social class or of age. Scottish children sometimes use it almost as a badge of protest against the adults who would standardise them into English, although they do recognise the usefulness of English in relation to literacy, travel and trade.

M.A. Peters, A. Britton and H. Blee (Eds.), Global Citizenship Education: Philosophy, Theory and Pedagogy, 459–476.

Immigrant parents respond even more keenly to such global advantages of Standard English: but Scots language offers their children another sort of passport to social integration with their dialect-speaking peer group. It can also serve as a key to unlocking some of the mysteries of Scottish identity: it offers a way of exploring the prejudices, humour and values of the new society within which they are striving to develop their own shifting and multilingual identities.

In Scotland, consultation on a national Languages Strategy to address the increasingly multilingual nature of society is ongoing at the time of writing, and we will return to this issue below. Firstly we should briefly consider the broader issue of citizenship education in a period of significant political and cultural change, since our work with vernacular fiction lay at the intersection of literacy, linguistic and citizenship activities in Scottish schools.

CITIZENSHIP EDUCATION IN SCOTTISH SCHOOLS

In 2002, the Scottish Executive's national curriculum development agency, Learning & Teaching Scotland (LTS), published the discussion paper *Education for Citizenship in Scotland* which sets out to review the principles of citizenship and their implications for teaching and learning and to develop existing policies and practices. One of its core themes is that 'the development of capability for citizenship should be fostered in ways that motivate young people to be active and responsible members of their communities – local, national and global' (LTS, 2002, p. iii). The document recognises that the process of 'globalisation' involves 'a growing sense of interconnectedness of peoples and places' which is being promoted by information and communications technology. It stresses that

> young people's education in school and early education settings has a key role to play in fostering a modern, democratic society, whose members have a clear sense of identity and belonging, feel empowered to participate effectively in their communities and recognise their roles and responsibilities as global citizens. (LTS, 2002, p. 3)

While these aims are laudable and essential for understanding and solving conflicts in today's world, this idea of developing a 'clear sense of identity and belonging' is not easy in a nation which, as a whole, has a complex history relating to these two issues. In Scotland, the ambiguous status of native Scots language (the LTS document does not mention language even though it is one of the clearest markers of 'belonging') together with residual Protestant-Catholic sectarianism makes 'identity' a fraught issue. The document includes various examples of Scottish secondary schools that are approaching citizenship in creative ways, including one which focuses on equal opportunities and anti-racist education. None of these projects, however, includes looking at issues of Scottish identity and language.

Our project, in contrast, brings together issues of identity, culture and citizenship within an exploration of imaginary textual worlds that relate significantly to children's socio-linguistic reality. In the case of Scotland, that reality has become even more complex after Devolution: it has seemed more important than ever to define what it is that has kept this country 'Scottish' rather than 'English' or 'British'; and yet, at the same time, the place of Scotland within the political unity of the United Kingdom has had to be sustained. Increasing numbers of migrant workers and asylum seekers (the former encouraged by the Scottish Executive in order to re-balance an aging and declining workforce, and the latter dispersed from the South of England in order to 'manage' political and social concerns there) further complicate the situation.

General educational programmes on citizenship hardly touch upon such issues of national cultural identity and the place of migrant children's cultures within that. The LTS website offers a list of projects which involve education for citizenship. Although there are some which address integration, appreciation of diversity and promote understanding of different faiths and sectarianism, there is still no project which deals directly with Scottish identity issues. Many teaching and learning resources and methodologies are used within education for global citizenship, and yet children's literature, where imagination and reflection on children's emotional, social and ethical lives best combine, is often overlooked within these resources. While non-fiction books about children in other countries are often used, there has been no major focus on the discussion that can arise from fiction books set in other countries or in Scotland, or that have a particular focus on identity and citizenship.

USING SCOTTISH TEXTS IN MULTILINGUAL CLASSROOMS

Our project was born of the question: What do children from ethnic minority families make of Scotland and Scottish culture and identity, as reflected in the texts they encounter inside and outside school? A second question followed from that: How do they make sense of these texts and relate them (if they do) to their own experiences, to their countries of origin and to their home culture?

Groups of asylum-seeking children, economic migrants, refugees, second-generation immigrants and indigenous children were given experiences of reading and discussing stories, poems and comics set in a Scottish context, some of which contained strong elements of different dialects of Scots language and Scottish settings. The study also looked at the interaction of the home and school literacy practices of these children, and at the current context of educational policies in Scotland regarding bilingualism, multiculturalism and citizenship.

Children's literature can provide an enjoyable space for those new to a language and culture to explore unfamiliar elements through words and images (whether visual or textual). If there is a supportive classroom environment, it can become a 'third space' (Bhabha, 1994), an imagined context shaped by narrative within which emergent bi-culturate children can negotiate and construct identities without fear of 'getting it wrong'. The interaction of teachers and pupils around a text can lead to a better understanding, for everyone involved, about how texts work within a particular cultural situation and also about what it is that readers bring from their own cultural backgrounds to the meaning-making process. Although there is now a growing body of research on the subject of how minority ethnic readers make sense of children's literature in English (Bromley, 1996; Laycock, 1998; Colledge, 2005; Walsh, 2000, 2003; Coulthard in Arizpe & Styles, 2003; Arizpe, 2006), involving pupils from a wide variety of ethnic backgrounds and different genres of texts, there have been no comparable studies in the Scottish context.

In Scotland, as we have said, the authorities have had to tread a fine line between promoting fluency in English, re-valuing Scots and rescuing Gaelic while at the same time respecting the language diversity that immigrants bring with them. The challenges involved in sustaining and developing community languages so that a newly devolved Scotland might gain 'the benefits of defining itself as a multilingual nation, in which linguistic, cultural and ethnic pluralism is treated as the norm and not as a problem' (Landon, 2001, p. 34), have been usefully analysed within the broader context of national and European language and cultural planning by Joseph Lo Bianco in his *Language and Literacy Policy in Scotland* (2001). Here Scots language, by the criteria of its range of social and regional uses, and 'its elaboration, literature and comprehension between it and southern British English ... lays claim to recognition and warrants acceptance as a [separate] language' (Lo Bianco, 2001, p. 6). He therefore treats it within a policy framework of educational provision for modern European languages, Gaelic, minority and community languages and British Sign Language, all of which are taught in Scottish schools. A key difference between Scots and other minority languages, however, is recognised to be the historical neglect and misrepresentation of the language, and even hostility towards it in school contexts, where developing children's competence in Standard English has understandably been a key concern for teachers and parents. The resulting absence of statistical information about the use and teaching of Scots means that

> positive moves in policy are continually challenged, delayed and frustrated. Many educational measures that could be sustained from a better information base are made difficult because they cannot legitimately be based on secure information. (Lo Bianco 2001, p. 9)

Our Scottish books project, funded by the Scottish Executive, contributes to that need for an information base in respect of language and culture. It can provide answers to some of the questions that Lo Bianco raises about how Scots is represented in schooling, what pedagogy is to be used and what attitudes are exhibited towards it. The research activity in itself might contribute in a small way to the necessary language planning process of 'prestige-allocation' that is necessary for Scots (in a way that is very different from the language planning needs of the other heritage language, Gaelic).

Languages and their literatures from this perspective are strongly linked to preparing the ground for the kind of citizenship necessary within a national context that is not single or homogenous. Lo Bianco argues for dynamic notions of culture that prepare young people for substantive participation in the political community. As a combination of knowledge and skill, bilingualism and multiple-literacy must be counted as powerful additions to human capital. (Lo Bianco, 2001, p. 25)

There is awareness within this wider vision, too, of the ways in which technological changes in society have brought increasing need for a multi-modal approach to literacy in which 'previously separate channels of literacy, visual, audio, gestural, iconic combine with the textual format to produce a hybrid and very complex kind of literate practice' (Lo Bianco, 2001, p. 40). This becomes particularly apparent among the children in our study, as their understandings of a new culture emerge from a complex and sometimes contradictory series of messages and interpretations through home or community languages, sacred languages, playground and classroom languages, and electronic or media literacies. Our focus on visual aspects of illustrations in the chosen Scottish texts, and children's drawings in response to narratives, relates to this.

The influence of Lo Bianco's work can be seen in the Scottish Executive's draft Languages Strategy (for example, in its inclusion of British Sign Language), which is in various ways a positive response to the multilingual nature of contemporary Scotland. However, as with the mismatch noted above between citizenship education and Scottish curricular resources, the rationale for the Languages Strategy appears less comprehensive than the detailed rationale published in the Executive's *Citizens of a Multilingual World* (2002). Specifically, it lacks engagement with crucial issues surrounding the interconnections between language, identity and power. There remains an impression that languages other than English might be neglected or treated in a tokenistic manner: these are to be 'celebrated' in schools and society, a word that seems vague in practical terms. 'Confident engagement with cultural diversity' might be more meaningful in the present context.

The study of languages, particularly foreign languages, is presented and emphasised in this Strategy as a communicative tool which enables mobility within the European job market and as a means of accessing 'economic opportunity' (Scottish Executive 2007, pp. 3, 5, 6). The case for second and third language acquisition, whether it be local heritage or foreign, is of course greater than that, and includes access to, understanding of and respect for other cultures and communities as well as a range of cognitive benefits, all of which are acknowledged in *Citizens of a Multilingual World*. By emphasising the economic benefits for the resident population, including migrant communities within it, the wider vision of a greater comprehension of language, culture and communities within Scotland and elsewhere is overlooked. Yet this type of intercultural understanding is a vital contributory ingredient to the development of an international 'outward looking [Scottish] society' (Scottish Executive, 2007, p. 4). Children's understanding of an international view of the world and an appreciation of Scotland's place within it must be based on, and balanced with, a confident sense of identity derived from an informed view and knowledge of Scotland's own cultural and linguistic heritage, which has long been treated with disrespect within educational settings.

IMMIGRATION TO GLASGOW: CONTEXT, POLICIES AND RESEARCH

Our study took place in Glasgow, a city that has been a particular site of immigrant life in Scotland for at least 150 years. Different waves of migration have formed the city: Irish, Highland Gaelic, Jewish, Polish, Lithuanian, Italian, South and East Asian among others. New groups continue to arrive. Some of these early groups have become integrated into the 'white' population of the city but there are still strong community ties, mainly along religious and cultural lines, among some groups such as the Scots-Irish.

At the beginning of the 21st century, Glasgow had a residential population of over 600,000, making it the largest city in Scotland. Natural change and out-migration has meant that the city's population has been declining for several years. However, this decline is now slowing down and the ethnic minority population has been increasing. Data on immigration shows that 34% more foreign born people were living in Scotland in 2001 compared to 1991, making it one of the fastest growing rates in the UK. The city has a higher black and minority ethnic population than Scotland as a whole, although still predominantly 'white' (nearly 95%). Although there are no exact statistics for asylum-seekers and refugees, 5640 were receiving accommodation and subsistence in 2005 from the National Asylum Support Service under its dispersal scheme which began in 2000. They come from 54 countries, with Turkish, Pakistani, Iraqi, Iranian and Somali refugees being the largest national groups.

Lewis' (2006) report on public attitudes towards asylum seekers in Scotland suggests that a more positive attitude in this country (compared to England) may be due to the positive discourse of the Scottish Executive and of the Scottish media, who have promoted a more welcoming attitude and a more positive image of asylum seekers. Lewis also suggests that 'a strong sense of national identity and pride may also increase tolerance, as people do not fear their culture may be damaged' (Lewis 2006, p. 9). However, the study found people in Glasgow were generally hostile to asylum seekers and made little distinction between them and settled ethnic minority communities. Yet many parents felt it was beneficial for their children to mix with others and had come to know immigrant families through them. This suggests the importance of creating opportunities for meaningful contact between groups; and one of the key spaces where this might take place is the local school.

Research in Scotland on ethnic minority education has increased over recent years, exploring the contradictions that emerge as pupils go through the process of integration into their new schools. Powney et al (1998) carried out a review for the Scottish Executive on research into ethnic minority education in Scotland. In terms of language issues and bilingualism, their findings showed that more resources were invested in teaching English as a second language than in providing greater opportunities for developing community languages. The reviewers referred to

American research which has shown that in order for bilingualism to be positive, both languages must be developed. They recommended more research in the areas of school ethos, the curriculum, home and school links, and language awareness issues.

Since this review's publication, many of its key topics have been further investigated (Netto *et al*, 2001) and, because of legislative changes which have focussed on equal opportunities, some have led to new policy documents. Stead *et al* (1999) found that whatever their background, and even if they had little knowledge of the Scottish education system, immigrant parents placed great importance on education and getting their children into school was among their first concerns. However, parents were also aware of the consequences of entering education in a new country:

> They expressed pride that their children spoke English so well and understood life here apparently so easily in comparison with themselves. However, they felt deep regret when this brought loss of the home language and history. (Stead *et al*, 1999, p. 3)

Another contradiction found by the researchers was that, although pupils also placed high value on education and wanted to 'catch up', they did not want attention drawn to them as 'different' (Stead *et al*, 1999, p. 5). Our project with its shared whole-class experience of different, distanced or 'forbidden' language as a key element, was responsive to such feelings. Its literacy focus also carries forward the work of Arshad *et al* (2005), some of whose findings are significant for constructing a picture of the interaction between home and school literacies, such as the high value pupils placed on a school's efforts to recognise diversity (by understanding the importance of other languages, faiths and traditions).

In 2005, Learning and Teaching Scotland produced *Learning in 2 (+) Languages*, a document which identifies good practice in supporting children who are accessing the curriculum through English as an additional language. It provides a general introduction to bilingualism and its advantages in terms of a greater linguistic and critical awareness, and encourages schools to be more proactive in addressing needs and raising achievement of bilingual pupils through taking account of the cultural and linguistic background of pupils, being aware of the problems with assessment and helping them achieve their potential. Among other things, this is done by creating a more multicultural, multilingual classroom through books, language assistants, and collaborative work. Our project extended that multilingual emphasis by involving the excluded local Scots language of playground and street, and making it part of classroom discourse and discussion.

A CHANGING SCOTTISH CURRICULUM FOR LANGUAGE?

Issues of social inclusion are involved here, as with other aspects of the Scottish Executive's focus on developing social capital through the networks and norms that build the trust and reciprocity to create local communities and wider civil society. One of the key aims of the Executive's Cultural Strategy is 'Promoting

Scotland's languages as cultural expressions and as means of accessing Scotland's culture' (Scottish Executive, 2000, p. 23). If children of present-day immigrant communities are to become the Scots of the future, then the development of confident literacy and linguistic awareness of Scotland's full language variety, at regional and community levels, is vital for both individual and general socio-economic development.

Such concerns also inform the new *Curriculum for Excellence* that is being developed to help Scottish schools meet the needs of pupils in a changing world, recognising that Scotland's rich diversity of languages offers rich opportunities for learning and global interconnections. Website guidance for schools includes much that is relevant to our research, with regard to the development of successful learners, confident individuals, responsible citizens and effective contributors. Schools and teachers wishing to develop topics in Scottish literature in line with such guidance can now draw on a range of new publications and resources in Scots language publishing for children, some of it funded by a Scottish Executive that recognises its importance as part of the linguistic and cultural heritage of young people.

A specifically Scottish focus is particularly important, within the changing demographic patterns of language and culture in contemporary Scotland, increasingly open to economic migration and educational change within a global perspective. Globalisation has paradoxically been a spur to recovery of local and historical identities, through the realisation that tourism and other 'cultural industries' would benefit from a greater focus on the distinctiveness of Scottish culture, including its languages, literature and arts.

Curriculum guidance on Scottish culture included in *English Language 5–14 National Guidelines* suggests that Scottish writing and writing about Scotland should permeate the curriculum (SOED, 1991, p. 68). That this aim remains debatable or unfulfilled arises from the complex series of causes, both cultural and educational, described above. A key difference between Scots and other minority languages is recognised to be a historical neglect, misrepresentation or hostility towards it in school contexts, where developing children's competence in Standard English has understandably been a key concern for teachers and parents. There is a resulting absence of statistical and pedagogical information about the use and teaching of Scots, which this project begins to address.

OPENING DOORS ON SCOTTISH TEXTS

Our research took place in two Glasgow primary schools with a significant intake of immigrant and refugee children from different areas of the city, north and south of the River Clyde: Sir James Kelvin Primary (an impressively large Victorian building overshadowed by three decrepit-looking high-rise buildings and set to merge with two other schools from the area) and St Margaret's Roman Catholic Primary (dating from the 1920s and 1930s expansion of denominational education in Glasgow, in another working class area with a reputation for social problems, and also dominated by even taller high rise flats, in which dispersed asylum seekers from London and South East England were housed). Both schools having falling rolls, of 190 and 325 respectively, and indeed it is only the presence of half its intake from asylum seeking families that keeps Sir James Kelvin Primary School viable. Nineteen languages are spoken there and 85.1% of the pupils are on free school meals (this is the normal indicator of social deprivation in Scotland's schools; the average for Glasgow primaries is 41.4%). St Margaret's Primary School has approximately 18% of its pupils from refugee or asylum-seeking families. At least fifteen languages are spoken and 58.7% of pupils are on free school meals. Both schools offer language support and build upon the skills of bilingual pupils, and both are keen to develop links with the community.

In these schools we worked with two classes of P6 pupils, between 10 and 11 years old, and then with smaller groups of ethnic minority children and native Scots. The countries of origin of the 14 bilingual pupils and/or their parents were Pakistan, Latvia, Iran, Iraq, Turkey, Rwanda, Congo, Algeria and Somalia. Their heritage languages included Urdu, Panjabi, Farsi, Latvian, French, English, Dutch, Hungarian, Turkish, Rwandan, Kurdish, Congolese, Arabic and Somali, among others.

The texts we read with the children were either written by Scottish authors, set in Scotland, or used Scots language. They were selected for their potential appeal to 10 year olds. We used different genres such as picture books, short stories, poems and comics. Whole class sessions of about 45 minutes were held, in which poems and texts from two anthologies of Scottish writing for children, *My Mum's a Punk* (Breslin *et al*, 2002), and *Blethertoun Braes* (Fitt & Robertson, 2004) were read and discussed. After the discussions, the Scots children were given a brief writing task which also included drawing. Small group sessions were then held in a nearby room with ethnic minority pupils, reading and discussing a wider range of texts.

They were told that we were carrying out research about Scottish books for children, and looking for 'Scottish clues' that make these particular books Scottish, and we asked them to help us 'be detectives' in this search. For each small group session, the researchers read the text first. Difficult words or concepts were explained either during or after the reading. A series of pre-determined questions were then asked, although there was room for following children's line of thinking or bringing up other issues. Some of the questions were specific for each text, others were more generic, for example:

– Would you describe this as a Scottish book? What makes it Scottish?
– If this happened to someone in another country, would there be anything different about the story or the pictures?

We also asked questions about the children's own language and literacy and about the texts they encountered at home.

LANGUAGE AND CITIZENSHIP

Our findings, as documented in the Final Report to the Scottish Executive (Arizpe & McGonigal, 2007), give a full exploration of key issues of literacy, language and identity, considering the children's experience at home and school, their perceptions of Scotland and Scottish people, home literacy practices, and their responses to the chosen texts and often skilful strategies for making sense of them. Their discussions of Scots language and Scottish texts offered particularly interesting insights, as these revealed conflicting aspects of identity between countries of origin and current residence. The role of the school in supporting them through this transition also emerged, with points for further research or development.

We cannot discuss all these findings here, but we will focus on four main topics which provide insights into how language interacts with a developing notion of belonging and citizenship. First, the language that children speak at home and within their communities has a defining impact on their identities; indeed, language was one of the main markers of similarities and difference. For example, Gabriel, originally from Congo and a Christian, and Abdul, originally from Algeria and a Muslim, had established a particular link because of their French-speaking background. The local 'street' language was perceived by both sometimes as a threat, but also as a way into social integration. Second, the Scots language and accent was beginning to mark the immigrant children as 'Scottish', whether they were aware of it or not, and this contributes to the way in which the indigenous children perceive and welcome them. Third, the Scottish stories that children hear, both in the community, at school and in the media, 'clued' them into the values and experiences of the Scots and encouraged them to enter a dialogue where they could share their own personal and cultural stories. Finally, issues specific to identity emerged from the discussions which point to the need to open up these issues and so help the children see where they are placed as 'new' citizens.

Although there was an awareness of 'Scottishness' in the texts, there was little personal identification with being Scottish at this stage of the children's development within their new society. However, empathy with the books' characters and conflicts did allow these 'new Scots' to discuss their own experiences, differing interpretations and cultural values, their responses to local and standard language usage, and their impressions of the new or different society in which they might one day play a part. Such talk, mediated in part through the language of the texts (that is spoken by their Scottish fellow-pupils in the playground but rarely sanctioned in the more formal language lessons of the classroom) proved valuable in permitting these children to align unspoken or contradictory experiences through imaginative texts, within supportive group frameworks.

Language at Home and in the Community

Several of the pupils in the sample spoke more than one foreign language at home, although they were not always able to read and write in all of them. They often acted as interpreters for younger siblings or parents whose English was less confident than theirs. Heritage languages were encouraged and practised, in after-school lessons if these were available. They struggled to maintain facility in the home language, as English became their frequent daily mode of expression and study, but were helped by communication with family members overseas and the presence of home language books or comics. Most parents were anxious for their children to maintain their heritage language, and attempted to achieve this by making them speak it at home and, in some cases, teaching them themselves. However, learning English was equally a commitment of many immigrant parents, and bilingual support teachers commented that some were prepared to neglect their own language in favour of the children learning English, despite their advice that concepts learned in the mother tongue transfer more easily into learning in the English medium.

As for the language the children heard on the streets and the playground, the connotations were mainly negative because it was associated with violence and threatening behaviour, particularly from 'teenagers'. Teachers pointed out that some of the first words even very young immigrant children learned, sometimes without being aware of their meaning, were swear words. At the same time, they began to pick up Scots words and Scottish accents and frequently used words such as 'wee' (small) and 'disnae' (does not). Immigrant children need to learn to distinguish between 'Scots' language, popular 'slang' and 'bad words', something many Scottish children themselves find difficult to do. The children were aware of its lower status, but they were also curious and aware of the difference between Scots and English and between different Scottish accents. As one bilingual support teacher commented:

> … even in conversation they notice right away what is Scottish and what is not Scottish. Yes they are very clear on Scottish accents, the way people in Scotland speak and the words we use and how different it is from the rest of the country. (Jenny, SJK)

The pupils' keenness to explore Scots language was evident when we gave them notebooks to write down anything 'Scottish' they observed or heard or read in the time between our visits. Several, sometimes with the help of a Scottish classmate, made long lists of Scottish words (and some not so Scottish slang) and their English equivalent. Umay had a few on her list, phonetically written. She also included a translation in brackets: *'wid'* (would), *'ryt'* (ok), *'yiz'* (you plural) and *'jist'* (just). The children enjoyed discussing the way Scottish people spoke and offered many oral examples such as *'cannae dae it'* (cannot do it), *'no a wisnae'* (no, I was not) and *'wan'* (one). Rafiq was able to identify 'kelpie' (a word he had never come across before) as a Scottish word because *'it sounds like one'*, which suggests that immigrant children develop an ear for the sounds used in Scots.

Making Sense of the Language in Scottish Texts for Children

The perception of Scots as 'slang' is not surprising, given the complex cultural and political history of Scotland. Matthew Fitt, editor of the Itchy Coo series of Scottish texts for children, is currently exploring this perception in the context of raising the literacy performance and motivation of disaffected older primary school boys (in particular) in a current Scots language project at Letham Primary, Livingston (see http://www.literatureinlearning.org for an outline of this work). Lo Bianco (2001) and Corbett *et al* (2003) both emphasise status building as a key focus in the maintenance of minority languages such as Scots.

The texts using Scots language were a novelty in both schools. When we asked teachers what they thought the immigrant children made of the texts with Scots words, one of the teachers said that *'they would enjoy it, it would make sense to them to see the words written on the page and connect the words with what they hear'*. The class had responded positively to the materials the researchers had brought in and the teacher thought *'it would be good to use it more with them'*. However, both she and a bilingual support teacher were cautious about exposing the immigrant children to Scots at an early stage, before they had a 'good grasp' of English. They also thought the parents might wonder what point there was in learning Scots, a view confirmed by some migrant pupils who reflected their parents' negative attitude to Scots language.

'Wee Grantie' was one of the stories we read to the whole class. Briefly, this is a lively first-person narrative in Scots dialect in which a young boy narrates an out-of-school episode involving 'Wee Grantie', a rather annoying classmate who is always tagging along and talking 'rubbish'. The author cleverly reveals that the reason for Grantie's behaviour is that his parents' attention is concentrated on his young sister, who has spina bifida. The narrator is sympathetic up to a point, but still cannot resist joining in the teasing of Grantie, raising issues of both friendship and bullying.

The teacher at Sir James Kelvin PS thought that although the spelling was unfamiliar, most of the pupils, both Scots and ethnic minority, had enjoyed the story

> ... because of the language the boys used, especially the boys, in this area, I think they identified ... the phrases that were used, they picked up on them really quickly and identified them as something that they would use.

After reading this story we asked the class to either describe what would happen if 'Wee Grantie' came in through the door of their classroom or to draw a picture of him. In their texts and pictures the ethnic minority children incorporated Scottish words and spelling as well as showing an understanding of the plot and sympathy for the boy, for example:

> If wee Grantie was joining us in our school he will be a wee bit silly and annoying (sic) to other children. But I will not treat him like the children in the book. (Datse)

Scots words or phrases were also included in many of the other drawings that pupils in both schools made for us.

Another example of an activity which helped to clarify language usage in Scots and English was when the researchers asked the ethnic minority pupils to fill in one of the final (blanked out) speech bubbles in an episode from *Oor Wullie* (a traditional Scottish comic strip) where Wullie, having been given extra homework as a punishment for reading the *Beano* comic in school instead of his textbook, is caught by his pals reading his history book in the gang hut instead of the *Beano*. The pupils had to imagine, in Scots, what Wullie's pals were saying to him as they banned him from their hut. At first, Gabriel used English, *'Get out of here, you are banned forever'*, but after hearing the others, he changed his suggestion to *'Get oot o' here, you wee TP [teacher's pet]!'* Neylan's suggestion was expressed in a perfect Scottish accent: *'Och you get out of here, you've brought shame to the Fat Boab's shed. Get oot o' here, ye bring shame tae us!'*

It was clear that indigenous Scottish pupils were very much aware of the difference between their usual language and how they were expected to talk at school. As one girl said: *'It's different at school, you're not supposed to talk like this but we do in the interval'*. Therefore, reading a text in Scots was both enjoyable and a recognition of 'their language' in print – in other words, if it was in a book, it was not just 'slang'. However, they did mention that they sometimes found it difficult to understand the words because of the way they were 'spelled', because it made them look different from the way they sounded. This seemed to happen even if the dialect words used were not exactly the same ones they used themselves or heard from their families. The loss of many (mainly rural) dialect words is also increasing in urban contexts, under the impact of media and social diversification, yet many of the Scottish children, particularly boys, responded positively to the sounds and meanings of these culturally specific expressions.

During one session, the researcher tried to 'translate' a bit of a poem from the *Blethertoun Braes* anthology into English and asked what difference it would make if these poems were written in English. Most pupils thought it did make a difference; the reasons they gave for it being better in Scottish were that *'it's more entertaining'*, *'it's funny'*, *'it rhymes better'*, *'it sounds better'*, *'more special'*, *'more individual'*, *'it makes a challenge to read'* and, tellingly, *'it makes it more exciting cause it's in our language'*. Referring to the language in 'Wee Grantie', one boy said it made the story *'funnier'* and more *'believable'*. Echoing the teacher at Sir James Kelvin Primary School, the teacher at St Margaret's said she thought the boys in particular 'identified' with the language and context of the texts, and she was surprised that we had kept the attention of even the more disruptive Scottish boys during the whole class sessions with the texts. Again, this links with Matthew Fitt's research referred to at the start of this section.

Making Sense of Scottish Stories

Living in Scotland means coming into contact with Scots language, but also hearing, interpreting and assimilating both English and Scottish 'stories', from oral, written and media sources. Even pupils who had been here for less than a year were already making references to these stories, some of which were encountered in the school curriculum. At the same time, previous knowledge and experience of texts in other languages were clearly involved in the immigrant children's interpretations of Scottish stories, and intertextual connections were made.

Our data points to the significant consequences of reading and discussing Scottish children's literature with children in Scottish schools. It is not because these texts are better written than any other British children's literature or because they contain Scots language rather than English, but because they provide a very specific site for pupils to explore issues of identity and culture: an enjoyable path into the stories of the country in which they now live and a 'safe' space to talk about their own stories. For example, the Scottish texts we chose provoked discussion about how and when we use particular local language forms, about codes of behaviour and relationships, about the values inherent in arguments, or the consequences that follow from the decisions we make.

Although we have said that there is nothing essentially 'better' about the use of Scottish texts, of course there is a sense in which only Scottish texts will do. For this is the non-Standard English of the playground and the street – subversive, quick-witted, rough and ready – that immigrant children have to learn in order to 'belong', and that native-born Scottish children of whatever ethnic origin also speak or understand.

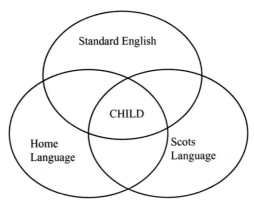

Figure 1

If we imagine a Venn diagram (Figure 1) with the child at the centre of interlocking circles of Standard English (the language of power and learning), Home language (the language of roots and ethnic identity), and Scots language (the language of new or potential identity and local culture), then it is plain that Scots texts and language can achieve effects that other texts cannot, since they touch the complex actualities and tensions of the refugee's present linguistic world, and, in the way of all creative texts, gather them into a temporary and pleasurable unity. It may be worth noting that both researchers were themselves working out of a migrant consciousness and sense of cultural difference, as well as an enjoyment and appreciation of Glasgow and its people. This was, we hoped, clear to all the children in the project.

Themes of the supernatural and of Scottish family life were the focus of interested discussion by both native Scottish and migrant pupils, who all agreed that reading stories about a culture in its own local language helped them to understand it better.

Through shared reading and discussion, it can also introduce the readers to all kinds of 'stories' from other cultures, as the mixed group works together to make sense of the new story in the light of past reading or life experience. As some comments revealed, texts which portray particular nationalities can lead to discussions about stereotypes and identities, key issues in developing citizenship among young people, both indigenous and immigrant.

Making Sense of Identity

We found that ethnic minority pupils' response to Scottish literature involves the story of their own identities and the interpretative practices they have acquired as well as their perceptions of their host culture. Among the stories we are told and that we tell ourselves is the story of our own identity. Experiences at home and school, in both the heritage country and new country, affected the way in which these ethnic minority pupils imagined their identity. The children seemed to understand that all of them were affected by issues of 'belonging' even though they did not often voice them directly. This was clear in the way they not only offered linguistic support when someone in the group was talking about their experiences and backgrounds, but also contributed with encouraging nods and sympathetic interventions as they perhaps recognised bits of their own stories in those of others.

Many interventions began with the phrase: 'in my country...' regardless of how long the ethnic minority children had been in Scotland. The fact that many of their families will actually be leaving Scotland as soon as they get their permission to stay in Britain was another factor which contributes to the complexity and instability of identity construction among these immigrant children, according to their teachers. Because most of the asylum-seeking families were sent to Scotland as part of the UK government's dispersal programme, many have neither family nor extended community networks here. As soon as they are allowed to stay, they go back to England, to London and other cities with large communities, such as Manchester or Birmingham. In the meantime their time in Scotland is clouded by the possibility of deportation, of being forcefully removed from their houses and sent back to countries where they feel their lives are in danger. If Scotland may be the country that sends them back, it is not surprising that they do not begin to feel 'Scottish', no matter how long they've been here. On the contrary, this may make them cling to their original identities and avoid integrating.

We asked the children whether they felt Scottish in any way and, if not, if they thought they ever would. The girls in particular said their mothers did not want them to become 'Scottish', citing the 'bad' behaviour of many Scottish young people – swearing, fighting, drinking, or taking drugs – as a reason. For some of the Pakistani boys who had been in Scotland longest or even been born here, it seemed to be the first time they had thought of their dual identity and they did not have a confident answer to the question 'Do you feel you are Scottish?'

CONCLUSION: NEW CITIZENS AND OLD CULTURES

The implication is that political aspiration towards new citizenship needs to attend to the emotional and intellectual patterns of an earlier cultural and linguistic life that continues within the host community. That life is partly sustained through new media and technology that allow easy interaction across continents. Although we need to treat with caution widely-held notions about the potential of multicultural children's literature to create understanding across cultures, local dialect writing for children, by problematising the standard forms of classroom communication through its vernacular energies, can open a door into an authentic sharing and validation of diverse cultural experience. By hearing characters speak in the language and accents of Scottish youngsters they know, ethnic minority children begin to attend more keenly to differences and similarities operating at the human level in their new community of school and locality.

As for immigrants to Scotland, our research made it clear that even second generation ethnic minority children were uncertain about their identities. For the children of asylum seekers and refugees, who might only be in Scotland for a few years, there was no sense of 'belonging' to their new country and it was hard to see how that sense could change if their futures were so uncertain. School heads and staff were clearly positive in their support of migrant pupils, stressing the key aim of providing a safe environment in which the qualities of intelligence and commitment that these children brought to the school community could flourish. And the children too were positive about the kindness of the teachers (although a few echoed what we took to be parental views about the lack of strict discipline to enforce a quicker pacing of schoolwork).

But as for their learning to 'participate effectively' in their local communities (as educational policy would strive for), their socio-economic circumstances along with anxieties about aggression from indigenous or other local residents imposed severe limitations. In the sense that most of our ethnic minority children regularly used ICT to interact with family and friends beyond Scotland, they were indeed 'global citizens'. However, they were also global citizens in a more negative sense of that term, as they now belonged nowhere in particular, and even though they spoke several languages most were not completely literate in any of them.

Local books, however, and particularly picture books (all our texts were selected partly on the basis of lively visual support of the narrative) can help integrate migrant children's visual and electronic literacy with the language and values of the social context where they now find themselves. If a curriculum for global citizenship implies 'asking questions and developing critical thinking skills ... acknowledging the complexity of global issues; revealing the global as part of everyday local life ... and understanding how we relate to the environment and to each other as human beings' (Oxfam, 2006, p. 3), then a crucial way of achieving such understanding is through reading books about children in different cultures, hearing their different voices, and making connections with one's own heritage and home experience. Books provide a safe space for these questions to be raised and explored: an imagined locus which still provides a habitation for the human within a dislocated world. The local library was one of our migrant children's favourite places, and classic children's stories often sat beside bilingual or trilingual dictionaries on their shelves. We reckoned that both were vital to survival in a strange land.

REFERENCES

Arizpe, E. & Styles, M. (2003). *Children reading pictures: Interpreting visual texts.* London: Routledge Falmer.

Arizpe, E. (2006). Young interpreters: Affective dimensions of bilingual children's response to pictures. In J. Enever& G. Schmid-Schönbein (Eds.), *Picturebooks and primary EFL learners.* Munich: Langenscheidt.

Arizpe, E. & McGonigal, J. (2007). *Learning to read a new culture: How immigrant and asylum-seeking children experience Scottish culture through classroom books.* Final report to funders: Scottish Executive.

Arshad, R., Diniz, F. A., Kelly, E., O'Hara, P., Sharp, S. and Syed, R. (2005). *Minority ethnic pupils' experiences of school in Scotland.* Edinburgh: Scottish Executive Education Department.

Bhabha, H. (1994). *The location of culture.* London: Routledge.

Breslin, T., McGonigal, J. and Whyte, H. (Eds.) (2002). *My mum's a punk.* Dalkeith: Scottish Children's Press.

Bromley, H.(1996). 'Madam! Read the scary book, Madam': The emergent bilingual reader. In V. Watson & M. Styles (Eds.), *Talking pictures.* London: Hodder & Stoughton.

Colledge, M. (2005). Baby Bear or Mrs Bear? Young English Bengali-speaking children's responses to narrative picture books at school. *Literacy*, 39, 24–30.

Corbett, J., McClure, D. and Stuart-Smith, J. (Eds.) (2003). *The Edinburgh companion to Scots.* Edinburgh: Edinburgh University Press.

Fitt, M. and Robertson, J. (Eds.) (2004). *Blethertoun Braes.* Edinburgh: Itchy Coo.

Landon, J. (2001). Culture and community. *Multicultural Teaching, 20*(1), 34–37.

Learning and Teaching Scotland (2002). *Education for citizenship in Scotland: A paper for discussion and development.* Learning and Teaching Scotland. Retrieved 20 September 2007 from http://www.LTScotland.com/citizenship.

Learning and Teaching Scotland (2005). *Learning in 2 (+) languages.* Learning and Teaching Scotland. Retrieved 20 September 2007 from http://www.ltscotland.org.uk/inclusiveeducation/Images/LearningInTwoPlusLanguages_tcm4-306089.pdf.

Laycock, L. (1998). A way into a new language and culture. In J. Evans (Ed.), *What's in the picture? Responding to illustrations in picture books.* London: Paul Chapman.

Lewis, M. (2006). *Warm welcome? Understanding public attitudes to asylum seekers in Scotland.* Institute for Public Policy Research. Retrieved 20 September 2007 from http://www.ippr.org/ecomm/files/warm_welcome.pdf.

Lo Bianco, J. (2001). *Language and literacy policy in Scotland.* Stirling: Scottish CILT.

Netto, G., Arshad, R., deLima, P., Almeida Diniz, F., Patel, V. and Syed, R. (2001). *Audit of research on minority ethnic issues in Scotland from a 'race' perspective.* Scottish Executive Central Research Unit.

Oxfam (2006). *A curriculum for global citizenship. A guide for schools.* Oxfam GB.

Powney, J., McPake, J., Hall, S. and Lyall, L. (1998). *Education of minority ethnic groups in Scotland.* SCRE Research Report 88. Edinburgh: Scottish Council for Research in Education.

Scottish Executive (2000). *Creating our future ... Minding our past: Scotland's national cultural strategy.* Edinburgh: Scottish Executive.

Scottish Executive (2002). *Citizens of a multilingual world.* Scottish Executive Publications. Available at http://www.scotland.gov.uk/library3/education/mwki-00.asp. Accessed 23 May 2007.

Singh Ghuman, P.A. (1994). *Coping with two cultures.* Clevedon: Multilingual Matters.

Scottish Executive (2007). *A strategy for Scotland's languages consultation document.* Scottish Executive Publications. Retrieved 20 September 2007 from http://www.scotland.gov.uk/Publications/2007/01/24130746/1.

Scottish Office Education Department (SOED) (1991). *National guidelines English Language 5–14.* Edinburgh.

Stead, J., Closs, A. and Arshad, R. (1999). *Refugee pupils in Scottish schools.* Spotlight 74. Edinburgh: Scottish Council for Research in Education.

Walsh, M. (2000). Text-related variables in narrative picture books: Children's responses to visual and verbal texts. *The Australian Journal of Language and Literacy, 23,* 139–156.

Walsh, M. (2003). 'Reading' pictures: What do they reveal? Young children's reading of visual texts. *Reading, 37,* 123–130.

Evelyn Arizpe and James McGonigal
University of Glasgow

GEORGE DEI

ANTI-RACISM EDUCATION FOR
GLOBAL CITIZENSHIP

INTRODUCTION

This chapter explores the connections between anti-racism and global citizenship
education. It utilizes a critical anti-colonial discursive framework to theorize the
nature and extent of colonial/colonising relations in schooling, drawing on the
implications for knowledge production, subject identity formation and the pursuit
of agency for resistance. It is shown that a critical anti-colonial prism to
understanding school practices offers possibilities for charting the course/path of
global citizenship education. In order to create a truly democratic society we must
see inclusion and inclusiveness as key. Inclusion means addressing questions of
equity and social difference as primarily power issues. Inclusion calls for education
to connect questions of race identity, difference and representation with power and
knowledge production in schooling. In such discursive, intellectual and political
undertakings what role can be assigned to the on-going calls for anti-racism
education? The saliency and centrality of race and differences means that we pay
attention not only to the cultural wars around knowledge production, but also to the
racial politics of schooling. Consequently, the paper will argue that an important
challenge for global citizenship education is to connect human rights and
citizenship concerns, with a critical and anti-racism practice that is anchored in a
politics of difference to address the myriad oppressions in society. In responding to
this challenge the paper will ask some pertinent questions about race, difference
and the asymmetrical power relations that refract upon everyday schooling
(including classroom) practice. In conclusion, the discussion will highlight some
important challenges for educators in pluralistic communities who are veering into
the road of educational equity and social justice for the minoritised and
disadvantaged.

ANTI-RACISM EDUCATION AND EDUCATING FOR GLOBAL CITIZENSHIP

Anti-racism encompasses an understanding of race and its intersections with other
forms of difference (gender, class, sexuality, (dis)ability, language, religion and
culture). But anti-racism education is more than a discourse or a theory of society
and human relations. It is an action-oriented educational strategy to deal with
racism, White power, and White privilege, including how these concepts intersect
with other forms of difference and oppression (i.e., classism, sexism, homophobia,
ableism, language and religious discrimination). These sites of violence and

*M.A. Peters, A. Britton and H. Blee (Eds.), Global Citizenship Education: Philosophy, Theory and
Pedagogy, 477–490.*

contention can arguably be among the many challenges that confront the making of a 'global citizenship'. For, when we connect anti-racism with global citizenship broader macro-social questions of colonialism, imperialism and human enslavement are implicated in how we come to understand notions of nationhood, citizenship and community belonging. These are questions of power and resource sharing to ensure equity, fairness and justice. These issues also necessitate a collective societal response to ensure that all citizens of the global community attain both self- and collective actualisation. One major site of self-identity and equitable empowerment could be within an educational environment. Pertinent questions about race, difference and the asymmetrical power relations that refract upon everyday schooling, including classroom practices are necessary when assessing global citizenship. However, the challenge for today's educators working in pluralistic communities is in finding ways to join the path for educational equity and social justice, particularly for the minoritised and disadvantaged bodies in our school system. I argue in this chapter that an important challenge for global citizenship education is to connect human rights and citizenship concerns, with a critical anti-racism practice. Indeed, the primary task of anti-racism education is to address the myriad of oppressions in society that lie anchored in the politics of difference.

One can draw similar lines between the directives of anti-racism education and those of educating for global citizenship. By utilising a critical anti-racist discursive framework we come to understand the nature and extent of colonial/colonising relations in schooling and education, drawing on the implications for knowledge production, subject identity formation and the pursuit of agency for resistance (see Dei, 1996, 2006). Anti-racism offers possibilities for charting the course of global citizenship education by helping to raise and address power issues that create social inequities and implicate our sense of belonging and connectedness to communities. To create a truly democratic society we must see inclusion and inclusiveness as key. Inclusion means addressing questions of equity and social difference as primarily power issues. Inclusion also calls for education to connect questions of race, class, gender, sexual identity, (dis)ability, and religion, ensuring representation with respect to power and knowledge production in schooling and education. In discursive, intellectual and political undertakings of global citizenship what role can be assigned to the on-going calls for anti-racism education? The saliency and centrality of race and difference (within issues of class, gender, sexual, disability, language and religion) means that we pay attention not only to the cultural wars around knowledge production, but also, to the racial politics of schooling and education.

It is also important to acknowledge the shift in gaze away from race and anti-racism as part of a backlash against speaking of race in the first place. It is fashionable today to speak of the limits of anti-racist theory and critical race scholarship. When such scrutiny is brought upon discussions of race and anti-racism I wonder if anyone is also speaking about the limits of post-structuralism, post-colonial theory, and/or post-modernism? We theorise in many forms and for critical, oppositional and indigenous scholarship it is crucial to acknowledge the different epistemologies that multiple learners bring to the academic table. Lived experiences, especially surrounding issues of race, are acceptable forms of knowing and knowledge that need to be heard and taken seriously within the academy. For race is part of every identity and discursive space. Just as Omi and Winant suggested over a decade ago: 'Race is present in every institution, every relationship, [and within] every individual' (Omi & Winant, 1994, p. 159). This is the case not only for the way society is organised – spatially, culturally, in terms of stratification, and so on – but also for our perceptions and understandings of personal experience. Thus as we watch the videotape of Rodney King being beaten, compare real estate prices in different neighbourhoods, size up a potential client, neighbour, or teacher, stand in line at the unemployment office, or carry out a thousand other normal tasks, we are compelled to think racially, to use racial categories and meaning systems in which we have been socialised. Despite exhortations both sincere and hypocritical, it is not possible or even desirable to be 'colour-blind'. This is a profound and astute reading of modern society, and only the intellectually naïve could dismiss this observation. We are indeed defined by our contemporary existence, as well as our location in history, and the ways we contest and imagine the future with its possibilities.

In undertaking a critical scholarly engagement concerning the possibilities of anti-racism for citizenship education, questions of politics and identity are central. Consequently, I want to affirm that 'race matters' conceptually, theoretically, geographically and politically. Anti-racist scholars and workers are engaged in transformative politics for social change. The task of anti-racism is not simply to complicate space, subjectivities, identities and scholarship. Our rhetorics of belonging must connect us to a politics of social transformation. The critique of White dominance, power and privilege is a by-product of the politics that allow us to get to such a transformation. There have been successes around the question of representation in our (educational) institutions that would not have been possible without a vigorous focus on questions of identity and the link to knowledge production. This does not mean the world is all about the politics of identity. But we cannot dismiss the power of such politics which has ensured that our institutions have remained White.

So how can race be evoked in discourse within the current curriculum and global citizenship education? Are there consequences and risks in speaking race for different bodies? For many of us (particularly as racial minority scholars) addressing race is not entirely an academic choice, an option or a luxury. Race matters to our lived experiences and a silencing of race simply masks a form of intellectual hypocrisy. We are repeatedly told that (as racial minority scholars) we cannot marginalise ourselves and neither can our academic pursuits create 'academic reservations' or 'ghettoes'. We need to critically interrogate what we mean by these 'ghettoes' and/or 'reservations'. I don't see my scholarship on race and anti-racism, or even my presence in the academy, in terms of a ghetto. The challenge of addressing ghettoisation is something for the academy or our institutions to address. In fact, the challenge is for dominant scholars and so-called academic scholarship to hear what subordinate voices are saying rather than putting pressure on critical/oppositional voices to tailor the message to suit dominant ears. To listen to subordinate voices can be a form of academic re-colonisation. The shift from a 'politics of negotiation' to a 'politics of transformation' (Dei *et al*, 2004) requires that the onerous call for change in the academy be placed on dominant bodies and scholarship. This does not mean that minority bodies will fold their arms and be silent. Critical/oppositional scholarship should highlight the voices that have long been subordinated rather than mimic dominant theories and scholarship. This is vital and imperative since within the Western academy today Eurocentric mimicry is a big problem for minorities.

A common argument thrown out against anti-racism and social equity work is their moralistic use and practice of highlighting race in society. Indeed, it is a form of intellectual arrogance to posit that anti-racists pursue their goals on the back of the disenfranchised and the marginalised. What is class, gender, sexual, queer politics about that is different from racial politics? Do we understand unified discussions between racial minority scholars and community colleagues on oppression and social exclusions as bourgeois intellectual pre-occupations? It is interesting how we sometimes hold up critical (and oppositional discourses) to a higher level of scrutiny than we do other intellectual practices that sustain the status quo. Unless our work engages local communities and partnerships, we as scholars and intellectuals are considered to be 'milking' (if you will) certain spaces and bodies, and unnecessarily trespassing across boundaries. The crucial and most important point in terms of our engagement is the ethics and ethicality of our scholarship. Critical anti-racism work and global citizenship education provide voices to the voiceless, and the avoidance of acknowledging that fact lends itself to a questionable ethical debate on those who suggest otherwise.

In order to understand the connections of race and anti-racism to global citizenship education we must bring a history and context to racism. The academic purpose is thus not to trace the inception of racism back to some original historical moment in time, as if racism were a thing of the past, but to discern continuities in the present; that is, within the contemporary political economy of globalisation. While acknowledging the complexities, specificities and paradoxes of racism across time and space, it is important not to confuse issues when theorizing about race and racism or interpret decisive actions as a means to paralyse debate. An examination of the literature on critical race theories and anti-racist education exposes internal contestation, but also makes it possible to tease out continuities and divergences that have shaped the field over time. An historical approach serves to articulate how old formulations pertain in the present; that is, to recognise old constructions of racial hierarchies when they re-emerge in new forms. Whereas pseudoscientific definitions of race have been discredited as problematic in fixing categories of human beings and assigning attributes to them, racism persists in deeply embedded pernicious assumptions that underpin policies and practices, with very real effects on people's lives, in terms of education, employment, housing, immigration, and the criminal justice system. A simple linear historical analysis belies the complexity and paradoxes of how racism is reconstituted in different places at different times. Rather than pursuing elusive, essentialist 'origins' back through linear-historical time, a genealogical approach seeks connections and broadens the field in order to identify the discursive practices or discourses that dominate in and across institutionalised structures.

A more practical working definition takes racism to be an ideology embedded in the policies and practices of society that discriminate against and/or present barriers to certain groups, based on assumptions ascribed to physical markers of difference, which promote differential power relations and inequity. Without dwelling on definitions of cultural, systemic, institutional and individual racism, suffice it to say that these various overlapping forms constitute multiple facets of racism that rely upon a critical mass of consent. Whereas the finer distinctions are useful in understanding the complexities of racism, they have been reviewed adequately elsewhere (for example, Scheurich & Young, 1997). The cultural reproduction theories of the 1970s (Bowles & Gintis, 1976; Bourdieu & Passeron, 1977; Bourdieu, 1985) have since been superceded by post-structural or post-modern theories in the academy. An integration of structural and post-structural theoretical orientations provides a corrective to the inherent problems of either primary orientation (Carlson & Apple, 1998; Carlson, 1997). This helps to alleviate a structural determinism, without lapsing into an apolitical cultural relativism, both of which tend to downplay human agency. Integrating theory with practice is central to anti-racist projects.

At this stage it is only fitting to raise a very pointed question: Why anti-racism? There are no definite answers for this simple question. However I would venture to list a few thoughts. These are not conclusive and I respect the knowledge of others to differ and/or to add: First, contrary to popular rhetoric we have not gone and cannot go beyond race, especially when we are in denial. Race and difference provide the context for power and domination in our society. Second, there is growing hostility toward affirming race and there is a need for anti-racism to challenge the complacency, silencing, and hostility towards race and racialised bodies. Indeed it is important that we distinguish 'the discomfort of speaking race' from 'the urgency and necessity of addressing the race/racial problem'. Third, racism is not situational, nor a situated event. Anti-racism calls for the engagement of history, social structures and relations (both past and present) as well as questions of institutional responsibility. Fourth, no doubt oppressions have many things in common (such as, all oppressions work within structures; oppressions are intended to establish advantage/disadvantage; oppressions also lead to a process of 'Othering' groups with material consequences). At the same time, it is maintained in anti-racism discourse that oppressions are not equal in their consequences. The sixth point is the fact that Whiteness, despite complications of gender, sexuality, class and ethnicity, is a system of dominance and we cannot do away with racism without addressing the oppressive aspects of Whiteness. The seventh point involves the seduction of (White) privilege. Within our institutions racially minoritised bodies at times assume some of the trappings of Whiteness in a bid to gain acceptability and credibility. For example, we see the constant distancing of self from a community that has been labelled, totalised and essentialised through such racist terms as 'criminal', 'deviant' and 'subversive'. Eight, we need to speak of the qualitative value of justice, which is to say that ethics and ethicality of our (anti-oppressive) politics require we become strategic and counteract the majorities' propensity to sweep race under the carpet, notwithstanding perceived and real glaring racial inequities. Ninth, that 'goodness' and 'racism' can co-exist within us. These are not contrary claims. We affirm this in anti-racist practice to uncover the limits of Whites engaging in defensiveness and a pedagogy of guilt when charged as 'racists'. Finally, we need anti-racism because it is good education for all. If one cannot appreciate 'anti-racism education' can we conveniently then conclude that one must like 'racist education'? My point is that when it comes to racial politics and discourse there is no such thing as a neutral stance. Dominant bodies often like to assume the position of racialised neutrality to avoid speaking about issues of complicity and responsibility.

Critical anti-racism education, therefore like citizenship education requires a dialogue about race, nation, power and community belonging. Citizenship education follows through with further discussions on rights and responsibilities. At a more discursive level it is guided by a need for collective spaces where people can air their positions about equity and social (in)justice and be able to critique White privilege without reproach and punishment. This need for a collective space is not, in the old conventional thinking, affirming the 'freedom of speech' argument where we would resist policing the discursive space. In fact, I am more interested in creating a collective responsibility to disrupt the burden that marginalised bodies carry, particularly when it is our experiences that are presented for dissection in such conversations, at the same time as the carriers of power are vested with some kind of responsibility to absolve their guilt and to de-racialise. Who and what is the nation, the subject and the citizen? How do questions of power, history and responsibility implicate these discussions?

Those of us who embark on critical and sometimes oppositional discourses are often told to bring more diverse and complicated or complicating framings into our work. In particular in anti-racism practice there are often calls to evoke the ties between micro-politics and macro-politics. Oftentimes what we present as the 'alternative' has itself become the normalised/normalising theoretical framing. Education cannot be anti-intellectual nor neutral. Specifically we need critical reflection in order to rupture the oft-repeated assertion that all educators want 'tools' to work with, rather than 'ideas or theories' that underpin such discussions. The divide is not only problematic but it ensures that educational practitioners and theorists remain in their own cocoons without engaging knowledge broadly to compel social change. When racial minority bodies enter our institutions, their mere presence is only part of the solution to the problem of representation. The presence of these bodies marks the possibilities of 'destabilising' the institutions. This may not always be welcome or what others have in mind. So the question of how these bodies are supported, how they are given resources to sustain their work, and how such work receives recognition and credibility are all critical questions to ask of our institutions. Global citizenship education is part of building a community of citizens and a responsible citizenry. If this is not citizenship education I am not sure what is.

The neo-liberal appropriation or co-option of such terms as accountability, quality, standards, and competence brings with it the risk of depoliticised readings of what these notions evoke and the implications in the struggle for social equity and justice. For example, accountability is now seen more in terms of fiscal responsibility and ensuring that the 'community' is served well for its dollars. But a different reading of accountability highlights institutional and state responsibility to diverse communities, and particularly to marginalised communities. 'Excellence' now means gearing schools towards the 'best' and brightest'. Excellence is defined in dominant, restrictive ways that heavily favours test scores and academics rather than a holistic interpretation that combines the 'social' and 'academic'. Education, knowledge and the school system are generally seen as apolitical, value-free, objective and fair. Within the school system the conventional understanding is that all young people have an equal chance to succeed. Those who struggle in school have themselves to blame. If they can only put themselves to the task, then excellence can be achieved. It is this mindset that justifies the one-size-fits-all approach to schooling, and vehemently opposes radical thinking to structure the relations and cultural politics of schooling. The mindset remains that 'structures must be left intact, as they have worked well for all who care to take advantage of opportunities'.

For global citizenship education to be truly transformative it must challenge the neo-liberal denial of difference and the necessity to maintain homogeneity of educational spaces. Global citizenship education must most assuredly fracture societal notions of 'excellence', 'responsibility', 'accountability', 'culture', 'race' and the macro-social politics of schooling and education.

Admittedly, we all have stakes in intellectual engagements. We also use different discursive lenses to offer social interpretations. Sometimes these observations are lost on some critics. Howard (2007), in speaking about what he calls 'Critical Race Africology', cautions about the intellectual paralysis engendered in progressive politics when we pit race against culture. While we need to be critical of culturalist interpretations of race and racism, we should be equally careful not to dismiss the usefulness of culture as a source of knowledge and resistance to Eurocentric dominance. We cannot get bogged down on culture and culturalist interpretations. Culture is living and it affects our day-to-day experiences. Anti-racism does not deny culture and the efficacy of cultural politics. Culture can be a site of knowledge and resistance, yet racism is more than just culture and politics. There is a tendency for an uncritical post-modernist stance to deny the saliency of race and also to begin to question anti-racist politics by privileging culture and cultural politics. As noted repeatedly, schooling is a culturally, politically and racially mediated experience for students. This reading requires that we employ both race and culture critically as analytical tools for examining young people's schooling experiences.

What are we to make of race and racial permutations today? I pose this question primarily because of the intellectual entanglements and clever discursive manipulations of avoiding the hard contemporary facts that trap our conversations.

We see race but are denied the voice to call it what it is. A claim of the 'illusion of race' is meaningless in the face of its social and political effects and consequences. The 'morality' of our shared collective existence is confronted with the 'immorality' of racial injustice when we are being told repeatedly to deny the intellectual tools that allow us to discursively articulate this disjuncture. Personally, I do not find this intellectual hypocrisy surprising given that the same people who deny a place for morals, ethics and morality in debates on existential questions of justice are the same people who deny our basic humanity in the face of glaring power inequities in society. So herein lies the ontological dilemma. On the one hand, we are confronted with what is a moral imperative to go beyond race and the categories of difference. On the other hand, we are confronted with harsh inequities that make false and benign claims of our shared humanness and basic frailties. This means we need to articulate carefully what we define as 'global citizenship'. Who belongs to this community and who feels a sense of entitlement or marginality within this community? We also need to critically understand how identities are reclaimed, affirmed, repositioned and/or denied through global citizenship.

In coming to terms with the social disconnect about belonging to a 'global citizenry' and the intellectual disjuncture of sharing in an epistemic community that understands injustice and power inequity, we are urged to spread the pain and injury of racial discourse. The blame and pain for racial injustice and bigotry that we see all around us is camouflaged in the blind faith that we are all human and connected without interrogating issues of power and resources. The 2005 Hollywood movie CRASH is a good example of what I mean here (see Howard & Dei, 2007). Oftentimes, what is lost in discourse about the banality of race/racism and the collective implications of all subjects is the moral and social distinction between the oppressor and oppressed as understood through the prism of White dominance (see also Karenga, 1999). This leaves us to reflect on the tremendous responsibility taken on by those working for social change who have historically held power and influence in all our institutions. Those with White privilege must understand their relative positions of power and influence. Of course White racial identity like all identities is complex. But, the White body must be read in their multiple locations of class, gender, and sexuality. The body must also be read in the extent that Whiteness is occupied as an assumed place of complacency, privilege and entitlement. Many times (and with some exceptions) this assumed position is notable for inaction and a desire to protect the status quo. A theorisation of the intersectionality of oppression equally risks falling into such traps when asymmetrical relations of power are not situated in our analysis of how we are differentially privileged and oppressed at the same time. It is a kind of uncritical take on power that is 'all there and not yet here'.

Karenga (2007b) notes that our world today is afflicted with hollow claims of freedom, justice and democracy. Our educational institutions promote these claims as not only real, but obtainable for all. It is self-delusionary to think that these are possibilities that currently exist for all citizens. Unfortunately, sometimes racialised learners even 'consciously or unconsciously participate in this acute denial and embrace the self delusion of [Western society] as a land founded on freedom and conceived in justice' (p. 9). By being complicit in denying the power of race, anti-racism, class, gender, and sexual politics we are paralysed by the inability to change our social realities. White racial domination is justified as the normal and moral way of reason and life. Karenga asserts further that what is seen as 'high ideals' carry within them 'both hidden and expressed values and a vision which are dreams for White folks, but a nightmare for Black people and other peoples of color' (p. 9).

Critical anti-racism does not lend any credence to the proposition that Black victimisation, for example, is the rallying cry for Black radical politics. The roots of Black radical politics are lodged in the effects of colonisation and its aftermath, and the necessity for a politics of decolonisation to claim our basic humanity as racially oppressed peoples. We have survived as a people through our collective 'agency, adaptive vitality and indomitable spirit' and 'much of our success is not from opportunities "given" but from opportunities made and seized at critical moments' (Karenga, 2007b, p. 9). The school system has an intellectual and emancipatory obligation to teach students such knowledge. Yet in schools all learners, and particularly the racially oppressed, are taught not to voice race and racism. There always appears to be a consequence for crying race and racism. But the evocation of race is not to voice oneself as the victim. Critiques of racialised bodies always placing themselves as 'victims' can be largely overblown (if not disingenuous) since this emancipatory distancing has its limits. At the end of the day all oppressions leave behind victims that are badly wounded, emotionally, spiritually and physically.

Local communities have been at the forefront of anti-racist politics and struggles for change. Criticisms of anti-racism that deny this fact can only be deemed as scholarly perilous acts. Fanon (1963) long ago spoke about helping the Black person free himself/herself of 'the arsenal of complexes that has been developed by the colonial environment' (p. 30). As a community, the racially oppressed need a more coherent analysis of the impact of colonialism on the human psyche, especially at a time when the dominant voice sets the agenda and terms of social engagement. There will always be resistance but this does not mute the fact that the dominant voice seeks to dictate and define. Part of the struggle for decolonisation is a positive reclamation of our myriad identities for resistance. Race and racial identities are part of who we are as a people, including all aspects of our class, gender, sexuality, language, religion, (dis)ability, etc. The experiences of racism can produce parallels in our thinking about the effects of oppression, as well as divergence in frames of reference in our analysis of race and its social impact. Race is still salient in our lived experiences.

Are there some lessons to point to as we rethink 'global citizenship? One of the greatest contributions of indigenous peoples to global knowledge is the understanding of humanism, i.e., the love and generosity for humanity, the inter-relations of rights and responsibilities, the connections of the individual to community (see also Du Bois, 1969). For example, Frantz Fanon speaks of the enduring sense of self criticism as an 'African institution' (see Fanon, 1963, pp. 47–48). African humanism (also shared by other indigenous peoples) espouses the ethical ideals of social justice and a concern for collective human good in the world. This humanism is also an ethical and spiritual tradition which calls on us to care for the vulnerable, support social change and continue the historical struggles for freedom and rights 'of all humans' (Karenga, 2007a). It is about understanding the African saying that 'I am because We are, and because We are, therefore I am'.

The current call for a return to a new humanism is not new especially if one critically interrogates the ideas and philosophies behind the reclaiming of this knowing. Perhaps what is new is the power of reinvigorating this humanism and the respectability that has been afforded it in a culture and climate so adverse to human justice, freedom, and social equity for it. As has been noted race does not create biological, ontological, epistemological, nor axiological divides. Rather race and racism are tied to powerful histories and exclusions that cannot be swept under the carpet with claims of our basic humanity and humanness. We speak of race and racism to ingrain the notion that we cannot hide from historic, contemporary and on-going injustices. Race and racism are part of our institutional fabric and culture. Silence on race does not negate the perniciousness of racism, nor can a 'post-race script' necessarily enshrine justice.

Furthermore, Karenga (2007b) speaks of African humanism as about African peoples 'spiritual and ethical traditions, and [focus] on mutual care and concern, common ground and shared work, responsibility and struggle for [the just world] we all want and deserve' (p. 9). There is little doubt that this humanism inspires all oppressed minds with a new faith and hope in helping to rediscover the potentials of all colonised peoples. The African and indigenous humanism of old was to offer the world what European rationalism failed to offer; that is, the love for humanity in general. This 'New Humanism' will be an emerging consciousness among all racialised, oppressed working peoples, emphasising the role of ideas and social forces in development, and speaks about hope not despair, for example, in the case of Africa speaking 'to the capacity of the continent to resuscitate itself from terminal collapse' (Ragwanja, 1997, p. 5).

The possibility of human relationality does not mean we negate aspects of our identities. There needs to be a shift in thinking away from the individual and self to the group and community and to recognise the connections between self and groups, intersections of different identities and experiences, as well as a balance in those relationships. To begin to talk about and describe a balance of social space depends on a preparedness to acknowledge our different histories and the asymmetrical power relations that govern how we each can claim a place of belonging. The consciousness of our existence as racialised and colonised bodies cannot be dismissed in a desire for a new humanism. Humanism is about shared histories and connected identities. We are all a people rooted in history, culture and knowledge. Indigenousness is about being rooted in a place. The post-colonial claims of hybridity may deny this rootedness but there are others who would reclaim this rootedness for a purpose. This history and politics of being rooted in a place (and culture) means we have had, and continue to experience, separate realities. It does not mean our realities are not intersected but that to some of us resistance will come naturally, socially and politically. And yet our histories are contingent. There is a search for congruence in multiple knowledges about our collective existence which must come to grips with the propensity for the dominant to universalise these experiences. So the key question is: Under whose terms do we engage in this search for congruence and possible synthesis of different knowledges and experiences?

There is power in the pursuit of broader politics against global and international capitalism, neo-colonialisation, Western militarism and the extension of the claws and tentacles of the Empire. But such politics cannot be pursued by downplaying the saliency of race and other identities in our lives today. Critical global citizenship is about a quest for liberty, fraternity, justice, equality and peace. To paraphrase Frantz Fanon, 'a nation which undertakes a liberation struggle to uphold these ideals of global citizenship rarely condones racism' (cited in Diawara, 1996, p. 3). The quest for such critical global citizenship may lie on a 'universal road beyond skin colour', shunning the thesis of 'irreducible difference' in our contemporary racial politics. Critical global citizenship is in many ways 'an international movement, with a promise of universal emancipation' (Diawara, 1996, p. 5).

Again, I reiterate the importance for the struggle for community and coalition building in not subsuming race and racial struggles under international capitalism. Race is still salient, as a powerful currency and category of what I would term 'anti-different racism', the exploitation and enslavement of oppressed peoples, as well as the force of White supremacy and the continuing economic domination of the West. These facts in themselves point to the necessity for the struggle against racism to be fought on a global, international level. To deny the power of anti-racist politics is to put our collective struggles in peril. As a racial minority anti-racist educator I work with an important knowing: We have enough Whites denying the identity of Whiteness as privilege such that as minoritised bodies we do not need to lend credence to such politics of denial. Diawara (1996) makes an important observation when he notes that in contemporary debates on universalism, it is easy to see that people 'who refute the existence of race ... are among the same groups that deny the large majority of [racialized peoples] access to the political, economic, and cultural means which will enable them to move beyond the simple determinism of colour' (p. 6).

Identities and the identifications we make in belonging to a society revolve around feelings of inclusion in which identities and subjectivities are recognised as significant for how we experience everyday life. In effect then, global citizenship is about community building. In the current post-modern context, the notion of 'community' brings forth claims about essentialism and the perceived dangers of such discursive claims. But there are important distinctions to be made when community is claimed. There is a particular politics of essentialism that speaks about the project of collective resistance informed by collective histories and struggles. Race victimisation and the enslavement of racialised, particularly Black/African, bodies is one such history. For example, it can be argued that European slave traders knew the Africans they were deciding to trade as human slaves. There were particular identity claims made. Similarly we look at contemporary politics in which Black, Asian and Aboriginal bodies are criminalised and encoded with notions of deviancy, subversion, terrorism and laziness. This is a form of essentialism pursued by the dominant voice to distance itself from these racialised bodies. So how do we respond to such politics? Anti-racism education is relevant here. Our response should not be simply denying our racial identities but rather bringing counter readings to such identities and what it means to belong to communities.

In the context of global citizenship asserting one's individuality is important. But so is defining bounds that tie individuals in communities. We are not simply a sea of individuals. While claims of individuality and individual rights are reinforced and rewarded in Euro-American society there is no absence of group claims. For example, it is perfectly clear that White bodies claim group/collective rights when it is to their advantage. Anti-racism teaches that the defence of White power, privilege and sense of entitlement that goes with having a White racial identity is not simply an individual act. So, perhaps for the importance of a racialised political solidarity, we also have to confront the debilitating intellectual practice of some racially minoritised bodies who tend to distance themselves from a 'community' in part because of the dominant tendency to inferiorise racialised bodies. In their politics these racialised bodies understandably may be vehemently and vigorously hanging on to their individualities. While these strategies can be read as resistance and claims of individual agency, it is often much more than that. Such claims are asserted to gain White acceptability and to show 'I am not like them', given the context in which citizenship is being defined. We are confronted with Eurocentric measurements of what is deemed acceptable, normal and respectable of the citizen. Dominant bodies feel a sense of comfort when these claims of individuality are made using White/dominant reference points. These claims further a project of the dominant to conscript the idea of a fractured community in order to deny responsibility and accountability.

So we are presented with a tension: how to claim and positively assert a collective belongingness while at the same time dealing with a historical fact of essentialising racial differences in ways that deny our basic humanity. Obviously, there is an urgency to address the concerns of communities of differences such that race, class, gender, sexuality, religion and language differences cut through community affinities and become acknowledged and respected. For example, a pan-ethnic vision of unity cannot be built without acknowledging the diverse and contingent politics of difference embedded in the notion of community. Anti-racism and global citizenry education is about creating spaces for self-definitions as well as resistance to imposed definitions. As racialised bodies we are continually being asked to tone down our intellectual politics (a critique informed by an arrogance of knowing what is best for 'us', etc.). We are continually being put on the defensive for the positions we take.

In a recent correspondence with a colleague (Provost, personal communication, 2007) she pointed out to me that sometimes as racial minority scholars, in highlighting the essence of 'cooperative individuality' and in reclaiming our identities and voices, we come across as having suffered from the virus of 'rugged individuality'. This is why it is important for 'the' small voice to be acknowledged as an equal and albeit different voice. Anti-racism has never called for a denial of individuality. However, there is a big difference between the assertion of a 'competitive individual' with no claims to community and that of a 'co-operative individual' who is nurtured by the community. The sense and respect for the individual as shared by most epistemes and ways of knowing is not in doubt. What is at stake is the reward for rugged individualism and the creation of a global citizenry in a capitalist social formation.

In the modern state, racially minoritised communities are under an assault which can be called a form of emotional, cultural, spiritual, economic and psychological violence. It leaves us to ponder over certain questions. How are we to understand the ways the oppressor uses his power, wealth, privilege and weapons to maintain and sustain such dominance? How does the oppressed resist the oppressor's dominance and subjugation of the former's basic humanity, soul and spirit? How do we make the transgression for revolution and resistance to denial of our humanity, freedom and injustice? Given the wars we are witnessing today, who are truly the peace lovers? Is modern peacemaking now becoming an act of violence and terrorism (e.g., bringing peace at the barrel of a gun)? Who is afraid of the oppressed using violence to retain their humanity and survival? How do we respond to the social, spiritual, material, and emotional death of the oppressed? There is spiritual carnage and a massacre of the soul, and how do we respond to that as oppressed peoples? Creating awareness of these questions through an anti-racist and anti-colonial perspective can only strengthen the virtues of global citizenship education.

However, educating and education cannot happen in isolation. The strength of global citizenship education lies in its inherent foundation to facilitate learning through collective and community action. Educators need to be using critical anti-racism strategies in an effort to mould a global citizenry built on respect for a diverse society. We as anti-racism practitioners need to address the continuing insidious routine in which our institutions marginalise discussions of difference, and bring voice to the knowledge and lived experiences of the oppressed. Global citizenship education will afford healing of the injured spirit and wounded psyches of our youth through bridging the gaps and forming alliances within community groups. On top of all of this, we must work to deal with the violence of racism if global citizenship if is to mean anything to the racially oppressed. Austin (2006) points out that Fanon saw violence as a 'cathartic act'. Consequently he (Fanon, 1963) did not prescribe violence: he merely diagnosed it and sought to explain violence. However, we cannot take this assertion as a licence to mute violence as a cunning way of denying on unpleasant past. How much of such violence continues today but is not spoken? Is this not a form of amputating the past and/or denial of the present? What is the concern over reading Fanon as prescribing violence? What are we afraid of? Colonialism was a violent encounter. Racism and forms of oppression today are violent acts and institutionalised practices.

ACKNOWLEDGEMENTS

I want to thank Terri-Lynn Brennan of the Department of Sociology and Equity Studies, Ontario Institute for Studies in Education of the University of Toronto (OISE/UT) for reading and commenting on an earlier draft of this chapter.

REFERENCES

Austin, D. (2006, 23 October). Frantz Fanon's diagnosis. *Toronto Star*.

Bourdieu, P. (1985). The genesis of the concepts of habitus and field. *Sociocriticism*, *2*(2), 11–24.

Bourdieu, P. & Passeron, J. (1977). *Reproduction in education, society and culture*. Thousand Oaks, CA: Sage Publishers.

Bowles, S. & Gintis, H. (1976). *Schooling in a capitalist America: Education reform and the contradictions of economic life*. New York: Basic Books.

Carlson, D. (1997). *Making progress: Education and culture in new times*. New York: Teachers College Press.

Carlson, D. & Apple, M. (Eds.) (1998). *Power/knowledge/pedagogy: The meaning of democratic education in unsettling times*. Boulder, CO: Westview Press.

Dei, G.J.S. (1996). *Anti-racism education in theory and practice*. Halifax: Fernwood Publishing.

Dei, G.J.S. (2006). Mapping the terrain: Anti-colonial thought and politics of resistance. In G.J.S. Dei & A. Kempf (Eds.), *Anti-colonialism and education: The politics of resistance*. Rotterdam: Sense Publishers/Peter Lang Publishers.

Dei, G.J.S., Karumanchery, L. & Karumanchery-Luik, N. (2004). *Playing the race card: Exposing White power and privilege*. New York: Peter Lang Publishers.

Diawara, M. (1996). *Pan-Africanism and pedagogy*. Retrieved 26 September, 2007, from http://www.blackculturalstudies.org/m_diawara/panafr.html.

Du Bois, W.E.B. (1969). *The souls of Black folk*. New York: Penguin. (Original work published 1903.)

Fanon, F. (1963). *The wretched of the Earth* (C. Farrington, Trans.). New York: Grove.

Howard, P. (2007). *CRASH: Colliding positions on what counts as racially progressive: A critical race Africology*. Manuscript submitted for publication.

Howard, P. & Dei, G.J.S (Eds.) (2007). *Crash politics and anti-racism: Interrogating the liberal discourse of race*. Manuscript submitted for publication.

Karenga, M. (1999). Whiteness studies: Deceptive or welcome discourse? *Black Issues in Higher Education, 16*(6), pp. 26–28.

Karenga, M. (2007a, 15 February). The racial reliability of Obama: An unworthy and contradictory conversation. *Los Angeles Sentinel*, p. A9.

Karenga, M. (2007b, 22 February). The flawed founding of America: Jamestown and Herrenvolk democracy. *Los Angeles Sentinel*, p. A9.

Omi, M. & Winant, H. (1994). *Racial formation in the United States: From the 1960s to the 1990s* (2nd Ed.). New York: Routledge.

Ragwanja, P. (1997). Post-industrialism and knowledge production: African intellectuals in the new international division of labour. *CODESRIA Bulletin, 3*, pp. 5–11.

Scheurich J. & Young, M. (1997). Coloring epistemologies: Are our research epistemologies racially biased? *Educational Researcher, 264*, 4–16.

George Dei
Sociology and Equity Studies
OISE, University of Toronto

PENNY ENSLIN

BETWEEN EUROPE AND AFRICA

Against Regionalism in Citizenship Education

INTRODUCTION

The enlargement of the European Union in 2004 and 2007 represents not only the growth of political structures beyond the nation state and a more peaceful and prosperous Europe. For a continent that colonised much of the world and gave it two world wars, this seems a welcome step towards world peace, wider respect for human rights, and the consolidation of liberal democracy in Eastern Europe. And the opportunities that these developments present for education for democratic citizenship are obvious. Indeed, the growth of the European Union has prompted various educational initiatives that aim to develop European citizenship (Smith & Print, 2003).

One view of the consolidation of European citizenship perceives it as evidence of how regional democracy promotes world peace. This position might be defended by reference to one contemporary interpretation of Kant's notion of perpetual peace through 'pacific federation' (Kant, 1970). This defence of regional institutions of governance holds that while world government is unfeasible and potentially tyrannical, regional democracy, as exemplified in the European Union, is both a sensible compromise and potentially a move towards closer global union at a future date.

A prominent defender of regionalisation within a cosmopolitan model of democracy is David Held, who identifies political regionalisation as a short-term objective of the cosmopolitan model of democracy:

> ... the cosmopolitan model would seek the creation of an effective transnational legislative and executive at regional and global levels, bound by and operating within the terms of the basic democratic law. This would involve the creation of regional parliaments (for example in Latin America and Africa) and the enhancement of the role of such bodies where they already exist (the European parliament) in order that their decisions become recognized, in principle, as legitimate independent sources of regional and international regulation. (Held, 1995, pp. 272–273)

Held speculates (1995, pp. 283–284) on the potential of regional governments to address old ills by eroding the geopolitical splits that characterised the world between 1945 and 1998. While there could be new dangers, at least the growth of

M.A. Peters, A. Britton and H. Blee (Eds.), Global Citizenship Education: Philosophy, Theory and Pedagogy, 491–501.

regional structures would reduce the sort of infighting that has characterised relations between nation-states until now. Regionalism could reduce partisan rivalries and pave the way for a new democratic order between nation-states.

I question Held's optimism, and will consider the international context of citizenship education, under conditions of accelerating globalisation, from the perspective of the developing world. Taking into account recent attention to the notion of cosmopolitan justice and cosmopolitan citizenship, I will suggest that regionalisation as exemplified in the 'new Europe' is in tension with cosmopolitan democracy and education for cosmopolitan citizenship.

In taking issue with regionalism and the idea of European citizenship, I concede that in its conception, if not yet in practice, European citizenship promises rights, freedoms and benefits, as well as active citizenship for millions of Europeans. Yet we should also take into account that severe regional conflicts continue in other parts of the world – some of them posing a threat to world peace, most notably those in the Middle East and the Gulf Region. Since 9/11 the greatest threat to peace in North America and Europe from organised violence has shifted from armed conflict between national governments to terrorism and the American state's response to it (supported by some European governments). By contrast, in the developing world the complex factors that continue to undermine peace and to subvert democratisation remain: ethnic and religious strife, political instability, dictatorship, military coups, civil wars, genocide, corruption, abuse of human rights, disease, and weak civil society – and most crucially ongoing and increasing poverty largely as a consequence of the economic and political domination of the rich states of the north.

If these concerns about current threats to world peace are well founded, they raise important questions about the aims and conceptualisation of education for European citizenship. A regionalism that strengthens Europe while leaving democratic citizenship underdeveloped in poor countries is problematic. For although Africa, for example, has recently revived the African Union and found a home for its parliament, the strengthening of Europe and its citizens' power, in a regional structure that pursues European interests as successfully as it already does, will favour European interests, rather than world peace and the global benefits of citizenship.

A just distribution of wealth is a necessary condition for global peace not only in that peace is undermined by poverty. Equality between the world's regions is also a matter of developing assertive, critical, active citizens in all states, so that global justice can be pursued among partner communities equally able to assert their claims.

Current conceptions of citizenship in the north, including European citizenship, stand in grotesque contrast to the increasing impoverishment of the south, where the very possibility of citizenship as the degree of engagement available to citizens of the north is remote. These claims prompt the conclusion that only cosmopolitan or global citizenship can provide a defensible conceptual underpinning for citizenship education.

DAVID HELD'S COSMOPOLITAN MODEL OF DEMOCRACY

Numerous political theorists have taken up the debate on the implications of globalisation for government, democracy and citizenship. (Some of these implications have special relevance for the problems of citizenship education, to which I will turn later.) One of the most prolific commentators on this set of issues is David Held (e.g. 1995, 1998, 1999, 2002, 2003), who defends a cosmopolitan conception of democracy's future, in which the European Union exemplifies a regional response to globalisation in the form of 'new mechanisms of collaboration, human rights enforcement, and new political institutions in order not only to hold member states to account across a broad range of issues, but to pool aspects of their sovereignty' (1998, p. 108).

As a prominent commentator on the meaning and impact of globalisation, Held is careful to stress that globalisation is not new, but a process that can be traced to the spread of world religions, through to Europe's 'Age of Discovery' and the conquests that carved out its empires (Held, 2003, p. 160). What distinguishes the recent phase of globalisation is its pace and reach. Interregional and intercontinental interaction is faster and more intense, as we witness in electronic communication, the global economy, international financial markets, and the size and power of multinational corporations. Apart from creating the more obvious transnational problems like environmental degradation, the spread of HIV/AIDS and drug trafficking, globalisation 'involves a stretching and deepening of social relations and institutions across space and time such that, on the one hand, day-to-day activities are increasingly influenced by events happening on the other side of the globe, and, on the other, the practices and decisions of local groups or communities can have significant global reverberations'. (Held, 1998, p. 13)

These reverberations are triggered and felt unequally. Emphasising the uneven effects of globalisation for different contexts and individuals, Held claims that globalisation gives 'differential, unequal and uneven access to the dominant organisations, institutions and processes of the new emerging global order' (1998, p. 14). In this new order there is 'differential access' to power to control and influence the conditions in which groups and individuals find themselves. Access to global resources, infrastructure and networks is hierarchical and uneven. I will return later to the implications of Held's acute observations about the inequalities fostered by globalisation and their implications for citizenship and democracy education across the globe's regions.

Held observes that the consolidation of democracy since about 1990 has been accompanied by growing challenges posed by transnational and cross-regional problems that transcend the traditional jurisdiction of nation states, and by international corporations and institutions that are unaccountable to the citizens of those states. Suggesting the need to ask whether the nation state can remain the central focus of democratic theory, given the extent to which global trade, financial flows, the actions of multinational corporations, communication and media, transnational environmental problems and transnational political, legal and security organisations operate across and above the reach of individual states, he has argued that nation states should not continue to be regarded as the only locus of legislative authority inside their borders (Held, 1995, p. 233).

In his defence of cosmopolitan democracy, Held proposes an expanding complex of institutions and procedures with global scope, 'given shape and form by reference to a basic democratic law, which takes on the character of government to the extent, and only to the extent, that it promulgates, implements, and enforces this law ... . [O]nly by buttressing democracy within and across nation states, can the accountability of power in the contemporary era be strengthened' (1999, p. 84). Democracy no longer has an obvious home, but would operate through 'cosmopolitan democratic law' in the first place, followed by such transnational bodies as regional assemblies and transnational referenda, accountable international organisations and a reformed United Nations that includes an elected assembly representative of the people of democratic states. Crucially, for Held, this is not a single world state with formal uniform citizenship for all the world's people. Political agents, whether individuals or groups, are members of various local and international communities that overlap with each other. They are citizens of the multiple political communities that affect them. Within a framework of cosmopolitan democratic law various self-governing associations constitute an overlapping system of authority which for Held portends 'the recovery of intensive and participatory democracy at local levels as a complement to the public assemblies of the wider global order; that is, a political order of democratic associations, cities and nations as well as of regions and global networks. The cosmopolitan model of democracy is the legal basis of a global and divided authority system – a system of diverse and overlapping power centres, shaped and limited by democratic law' (1995, pp. 234–235). It presupposes that a plurality of identities will persist.

Held thus proposes a conception of cosmopolitan citizenship that embraces local, national, regional and global memberships. In his recent work (2003), Held elaborates briefly on the ethical basis of cosmopolitanism, sketching features that include a capacity for mediation between cultures, fostering dialogue between traditions. 'Political agents who can "reason from the point of view of others" are better equipped to resolve, and resolve fairly, the challenging transboundary issues that create overlapping communities of fate' (2003, pp. 168–169). This requires that all acknowledge that ultimately individuals (rather than groups) are the units of moral concern, whose claims should be impartially treated.

Held's defence of cosmopolitan democracy and its ethical basis points us to some challenges for citizenship education, now shifted from its usual location in the context of a nation-state whose future citizens are taught about their rights and responsibilities as its members. The requirement that all citizens of a cosmopolitan order acknowledge that all others are equally units of moral concern reflects current debates about global justice, for there are elements in Held's broader account of globalisation that implicitly acknowledge obstacles to the principle of equal moral concern as well as to the very possibility that all could effectively stake their claim to equal concern under democratic conditions. Held points to what he aptly calls the 'moral gap' between the privileged and the disadvantaged in the global distribution of goods (2003, pp. 163–164). He also observes that even as governance becomes dispersed at multiple levels, identity and representation remain more locally sited (2003, p. 166) But his work's major focus is more on institutional and procedural responses to globalisation than on normative responses to it, and for its fuller educational implications we need to note developments in cosmopolitan theory viewed more broadly, especially in recent theories of cosmopolitan justice.

Globalisation has created a new order in which duties of justice have wider scope than to fellow citizens of a nation state; they now have global reach (Moellendorf, 2002; Pogge, 2002). Guarantees of human rights 'has been the principal change in the relationship of national and international law which has undermined the very idea of sovereignty being located on one level of governance' (Delanty, 2000, p. 79). The discourse of national sovereignty has been successfully undermined by that of human rights. Moellendorf argues further that the forms of association that now characterise relationships across state boundaries mean that global duties can no longer be overridden by duties to compatriots. How extensive are duties of global justice? For Pogge (1989) their scope is wide, including positive duties to assist those disadvantaged by global inequality, as well as negative duties in terms of which those who influence and benefit from a global order that adversely affects some are obliged to contribute towards compensating them and improving the international order. Significantly for my focus here, Pogge (1989, p. 180) regards equalizing of educational opportunities as an especially appropriate means of addressing global injustice. (See Enslin & Tjiattas, 2004, for detailed discussion of positive and negative duties of global justice in education.)

What are the chances of democratisation through regional democratic structures succeeding in a context in which citizens of poorer countries and their communities are systematically further disadvantaged by illiteracy, underfunding of education and consequent lower rates of completion of primary, secondary and tertiary education?

For in spite of the indications described by Held and others (e.g. Dryzek, 2000) of a growing international system, in which problems and conflicts are addressed, much of the capacity and location of the growing cosmopolitan public sphere lies in the wealthier countries. For institutions to be democratic, they need to secure citizen participation. This applies to regional and global institutions as much as to local and national ones, especially if we look to them to foster transnational democracy and cosmopolitan justice. For Moellendorf, 'only some sort of globalisation-from-below … represents a realistic strategy for a more egalitarian global order' (2002, p. 175). I take the notion of globalisation-from-below to comprise significant participation by citizens in making decisions that affect them and in bringing those institutions whose actions affect their lives to account. In a globalised world, this requirement places far-reaching demands on democratic processes, across national and regional boundaries. But although there is a growing cosmopolitan public sphere, exemplified in the European public sphere (Delanty, 2000, p. 120), whose informality makes it less susceptible to the self-interested influences of the international business elite, this informal public sphere is more likely to flourish in areas of the globe with sufficient resources and where established democratic traditions make it less vulnerable to state interference and repression.

Given the conditions of differential access to power and control over their material conditions, what kind of relationship can we envisage between citizens in rich and in developing countries, as part of a democratic cosmopolitan order? The contrast between Europe and Africa as sites of citizenship gives pause for thought.

REGIONALIZATION: THE EUROPEAN MODEL AND AFRICA'S PROSPECTS

It is hard to disagree with Held's claim that the European Union is a remarkable achievement, given Europe's circumstances at the end of the Second World War. (1998, p. 108) Its growth as a regional body that has successfully promoted forms of collaboration through new institutions is undeniably impressive. Not that these developments have gone without debate about what they mean. Europeans (and others) have argued about what 'Europe' means: is there such a thing as European culture? Is there a European identity? Is 'Europe' centrally a cultural, an economic, or a political entity?

Viewed from outside, debates on the meaning of Europe look less significant than those about its effects as a regional power on poorer countries. As Delanty comments (from inside): 'there are many "Europes" and ... the one that has become prevalent today is very much one of exclusion and not inclusion' (1995, p. 156). Warning against the danger of an 'unreflected idea of Europe', Delanty's view is that: 'the only adequate idea of Europe is one that is connected to anti-racism and stands unequivocally for post-national citizenship' (1995, p. 163). Much of the debate around these issues focuses on the exclusion of immigrant groups within European societies and on further immigration and the treatment of asylum seekers. But if we take the cosmopolitan position seriously they apply too to the relationships between Europeans and *all others*.

The European Union's democratic deficit has received much attention by political commentators and the media, who have lamented European citizens' lack of interest in European politics and, relatedly, their limited influence over the decisions made on their behalf by European political institutions, to which Pogge adds a third deficit: that European citizens have enjoyed a negligible role in the design of their European institutions (1997, p. 163).

Much effort has been devoted to educating Europeans about democratic citizenship in Europe (Smith & Print, 2003). In policy development, research, creation of networks and teaching resources and materials, attention has been paid to the task of developing a sense of European citizenship, a shared democratic culture and a common vision of active, participatory citizenship in which citizens engage democratically, even at the level of the European Parliament. But even bearing in mind that, for example, the Erasmus Programme for Curriculum Development includes global responsibility as well as social justice, and that the ideal has embraced a vision not only of citizens who are critical, responsible and inclined to participate but also of an emphasis on peace itself, these efforts still have a clear and unsurprising regional focus.

Whether European institutions are able or not to reduce the democratic deficit through educational interventions and institutional reform, what is important for my purposes is that, viewed from the developing world, Europe is primarily an economic entity, prospering with the help of rules of exchange designed to allow rich countries to call the shots. Resources available for fostering citizenship are greater, simply because of the availability of funding alone. Even if the notion of 'European' identity is not ultimately coherent, it may be productive in fostering a stronger continental democracy better able to respond to the declared needs and interests of its citizens. Other things being equal, a stronger shared identity probably does create greater political coherence and focus efforts towards the pursuit of economic self-interest.

By contrast with Europe, some African countries are among the poorest in the world. The continent has been subject to poverty, political instability and war since decolonisation. These factors both reflect the weakness of political authority and undermine efforts to democratise. With weak states, weak civil society and under-resourced educational systems, they are in Held's terms rarely initiators of events and influences that reverberate in other parts of the globe. Instead, they are usually on the receiving end of the worst consequences of globalisation, with fewer resources to counter their limited access to its benefits.

Recent regional developments in Africa aim to address these problems. The African Union (loosely modelled on the EU) has been revived and the African parliament whose role will initially be to advise the AU has begun to meet in Midrand, South Africa, where its permanent home is being established. The New Partnership for Africa's Development (NEPAD) is tasked with the role of halting the marginalisation of Africa by globalisation.

NEPAD'S strategic framework document adopted in 2001 declares poverty eradication, development and halting the marginalisation of Africa by globalisation (as well as the empowerment of women) as among its primary objectives. Democracy and good government, human development and education feature prominently in a vision that candidly acknowledges the continent's political weaknesses among its problems:

> Many African governments did not empower their peoples to embark on development initiatives to realize their creative potential. Today, the weak state remains a major constraint on sustainable development in a number of countries. Indeed, one of Africa's major challenges is to strengthen the capacity to govern and to develop long-term policies. At the same time, there is also the urgent need to implement far-reaching reforms and programmes in many African states. (NEPAD, 2001, p. 5)

The document acknowledges shortcomings in the policies pursued by many African countries after independence, as well as the effects of patronage and corruption, and failures of leadership. But it also emphasises the effects of structural adjustment programmes in undermining of social services. Contrasting

497

widespread poverty with its richness in resources, it criticizes European protectionism while urging Africans to take responsibility for Africa's recovery. It declares that African leaders, with new political will, are committed to an agenda for renewal of the continent, including promoting democracy and human rights, and pursuing accountability. Government will be transparent and accountable.

NEPAD and the AU are much younger than the EU. They are still to be tested, especially on their commitment to peer review of fellow African governments, but they deserve time to prove their worth. My interest is in the prospects for success of the AU compared with the achievements of the EU. Comparisons from an unequal base are inappropriate, but much is at stake. If democratisation and the development of citizenship require resources, globalisation-from-below is a daunting project in Africa. This is not so only because of the uneven effects of globalisation; the inter-relatedness of these two projects go further than that, as indicated by growing evidence of the complicity of rich countries in maintaining global inequality and its political consequences.

In his work on cosmopolitan justice and global inequality, Thomas Pogge contrasts growth in the global economy with an increase in global inequality, with large numbers of the world's population excluded from the prosperity brought to some by economic progress. Quoting data now widely available, Pogge observes that 'if the European Union had its proportional share of this misery, we should have over 51 million malnourished people and over 1.1 million poverty-related deaths each year' (2003, p. 118). Most importantly, Pogge argues against the widespread assumption that the causes of global poverty can be adequately explained by reference to causes within the poor countries alone.

Pogge shows how developed countries' economic exploitation is tied up with those countries' democratic deficit. He considers the social causes of persistent poverty, challenging the assumption that the causes of poverty in poor countries lie within those countries themselves, in flawed policies and institutions and in the actions of elites who are oppressive and corrupt. Not only ought we to take into account the role of rich states in fostering a vicious cycle in creating rules that allow them to help themselves to a disproportionate share of the world's wealth. Furthermore, the global order plays an influential part in maintaining corrupt government and oppression in developing countries. Bribes paid to obtain public contracts in developing countries, with the costs priced into the contracts, cause huge losses in the quality of the service provided, often for goods that are either unneeded or even harmful. This in contexts where the differences in power and wealth between the elite and the general population are so great that the latter can do little to make their governments accountable to them. International borrowing privilege exacerbates poverty and corruption by enabling unpopular governments to stay in power, imposing the heavy debts thus accumulated on even democratic successors, and providing incentives in the form of future borrowing privileges for coups (Pogge, 2003, pp. 120–130).

If these factors characterise relationships between developed and developing countries, what are their implications for global citizenship and for education for the cosmopolitan order envisaged by David Held?

MARTHA NUSSBAUM AND EDUCATION FOR COSMOPOLITAN CITIZENSHIP

Martha Nussbaum's defence of education for cosmopolitan citizenship takes us some way towards understanding the challenge of educating all for equal global citizenship. She defends 'the very old ideal of the cosmopolitan, the person whose allegiance is to the worldwide community of human beings' (1996, p. 4), arguing (against the nationalist's stance) that our primary moral allegiance is to all human beings.

Nussbaum notes how the Stoics followed Diogenes the Cynic's lead in claiming to be a 'citizen of the world', by arguing that we each live 'in two communities – the local community of our birth, and the community of human argument and aspiration. We should regard our deliberations as, first and foremost, deliberations about human problems of people in particular concrete situations, not problems growing out of a national identity that is altogether unlike that of others' (Nussbaum, 1996, p. 12).

Also like Held, Nussbaum does not presuppose either a world state or that the cosmopolitan citizen has no local loyalties, noting that for the Stoics citizens of the world are thought of as 'surrounded by a series of concentric circles' (Nussbaum, 1996, p. 9), moving outwards from the self, to family, neighbours, local affiliations, countrymen, and ultimately to humanity in general. Without having to surrender any of these and other group affiliations, the citizen of the world's task is to 'draw the circles somehow towards the centre' so that they become members of a common community of concern and respect. This does not preclude paying special attention to those closest to us, but it does require that political deliberation presupposes the commonality that includes all of humanity.

Nussbaum has developed the educational implications of this account of world citizenship, initially in writing about American education (1996, 1997) and subsequently (though more briefly and implicitly) in work about women in developing countries (2003). In both cases she is sensitive to the relevance of context, accommodating students in the United States seeing themselves as defined by their more immediate affiliations. 'But they must also, and centrally learn to recognize humanity wherever they encounter it, undeterred by traits that are strange to them, and be eager to understand humanity in all its strange guises. They must learn enough about the different to recognize common aims, aspirations and values, and enough about these common ends to see how variously they are instantiated in the many cultures and their histories' (1997, p. 9). In teaching students that they share the world with citizens of other countries as well as their own, Nussbaum argues that we also learn about ourselves, developing the capacity to solve problems through international cooperation, and that we are enabled to 'recognize moral obligations to the rest of the world that are real and that otherwise would go unrecognised' (1997, p. 12).

Nussbaum's conception of liberal education for world citizenship embraces multiculturalism in that it would aim to introduce students to many groups' histories ands cultures (1997), developing an understanding that would 'recognize the worth of human life wherever it occurs and see ourselves as bound by common human abilities and problems to people who lie at a great distance from us' (1997, p. 9). She suggests three capacities required to thus 'cultivate humanity': to be able to criticise one's own traditions; the ability to perceive oneself as bound not only to local loyalties but also to other human beings; and being able to exercise the 'narrative imagination', imagining how it would be to find oneself in very different situations from one's own. Liberal higher education, the subject of *Cultivating Humanity* (1997) also requires knowledge of the humanities and social sciences, and of science, adapted to different contexts. Such education should be available to all human beings, and some of it can begin during primary schooling.

For Nussbaum the world citizens' capacities are necessary for participation in democracy. They are also prerequisites for the pursuit of justice. All people with a basic capacity for reason, which can be enhanced by education, have the potential to exercise the capacities of the world citizen. Presumably taking into account the specific moral demands of education for world citizenship in the United States, Nussbaum (1997) emphasises that the narrative imagination fosters *compassion*. Compassion involves recognizing the pain of another human being (1997, pp. 90–91). It calls for realisation that one is also vulnerable to misfortune: another's suffering could be mine.

Reading from the developing world the sizable literature on multiculturalism and education emanating from the western world, one is puzzled by the amount of attention paid to dealing justly with difference in western classrooms compared with the near silence on the unjust consequences of those states' relations with the developing world and its children. Nussbaum is one of the few authors who has ventured into the minefield of discussing democratic relations between western citizens and women in developing countries. She emphasises the centrality of literacy to education in the developing world, including its role in enabling women, especially, to participate actively in citizenship and politics (2003, p. 337). But I am less certain of her views on education for world citizenship in poor countries than in rich ones. No doubt the development of the central capabilities (see, for example, Nussbaum, 2004, pp. 352–353), especially literacy, generally contributes to citizenship education, and potentially to globalisation-from-below. But I'm sure that Nussbaum would share my view that in education for world citizenship in developing contexts it's not *compassion* that we seek from the narrative imagination. Still, to the extent that people in developing countries have access to global communications, the narrative imagination, being able to criticise their own traditions, and awareness of connections with other communities, probably are relevant to formulating their aspirations. But until systemic lack of opportunities to participate in local and national democratic processes is addressed, cosmopolitan citizenship in these contexts remains a remote possibility. This is especially so in remote rural communities where it is not possible to be anywhere but local.

Education for world citizenship presents many more possibilities in developed countries and regions like Europe. Access to global communications in well-resourced schools opens numerous opportunities for the narrative imagination to flourish, to reason from the point of view of others, to foster compassion and draw the circles towards the centre. If we follow the implications of this discussion towards their conclusion, it could be argued that cosmopolitan justice requires that future citizens in wealthy countries be actively encouraged to develop a sense of their positive and negative duties of justice to less privileged members of the global community. This is a claim that probably needs more systematic development. But it does at least go some way to making the case that when it comes to citizenship education, cosmopolitan democracy will not be well served by regionalism.

REFERENCES

Delanty, G. (1995). *Inventing Europe: Idea, identity, reality*. London: Macmillan.

Delanty, G. (2000). *Citizenship in a global age: Society, culture, politics*. Buckingham: Open University Press.

Dryzek, J. (2000). *Deliberative democracy and beyond: Liberals, critics, contestations*. Oxford University Press.

Enslin, P. & Tjiattas, M. (2004). Cosmopolitan justice: Education and global citizenship. *Theoria: A Journal of Social and Political Theory, 104*, 150–169.

Held, D. (1995). *Democracy and the global order: From the modern state to cosmopolitan governance*. Cambridge: Polity Press.

Held, D. (1998). Democracy and globalization. In D. Archibugi, D. Held & M. Köhler (Eds.), *Re-imagining political community: Studies in cosmopolitan democracy* (pp. 11–27). Cambridge: Polity Press.

Held, D. (1999). The transformation of political community: Rethinking democracy in the context of globalization. In I. Shapiro & C. Hacker-Cordón (Eds.), *Democracy's edges* (pp. 84–111). Cambridge: Cambridge University Press.

Held, D. (2002). Culture and political community: National, global and cosmopolitan. In S. Vertovec & R. Cohen (Eds.), *Conceiving cosmopolitanism: Theory, context, and practice* (pp. 48–58). Oxford: Oxford University Press.

Held, D. (2003). From executive to cosmopolitan multilateralism. In D. Held & M. Koenig-Archibugi (Eds.), *Taming globalisation: Frontiers of governance* (pp. 160–186). Cambridge: Polity Press.

Kant, I. (1970). *Kant's political writings* (H. Reiss, ed.). Cambridge: Cambridge University Press

Moellendorf, D. (2002). *Cosmopolitan justice*. Boulder: Westview Press.

New Partnership for Africa's Development (NEPAD) (2001). *Strategic framework document*. Retrieved 26 October, 2004, from http://www.nepad.org/2005/files/documents/inbrief.pdf.

Nussbaum, M. (1996). Patriotism and cosmopolitanism. In J. Cohen (Ed.), *For love of country: Debating the limits of patriotism* (pp. 3–17). Boston: Beacon Press.

Nussbaum, M. (1997). *Cultivating humanity: A classical defense of reform in liberal education*. Cambridge MA: Harvard University Press.

Nussbaum, M. (2004). Women's education: A global challenge. *Signs, 29*(2), 325–355.

Pogge, T. (1989). *Realizing Rawls*. Ithaca: Cornell University Press.

Pogge, T. (1997). Creating supra-national institutions democratically: Reflections on the European Union's 'democratic deficit'. *Journal of Political Philosophy, 5*(2), 163–182.

Pogge, T. (2002). *World poverty and human rights*. Cambridge: Polity Press.

Pogge T. (2003). The influence of the global order on the prospects for genuine democracy in developing countries. In D. Archibugi (Ed.), *Debating cosmopolitics* (pp. 117–140). London: Verso.

Smith, A. & Print, M. (2003). Editorial. *Cambridge Journal of Education, 33*(1), Special Issue: Citizenship Education in Divided Societies, 3–14.

Penny Enslin
University of Glasgow

STAVROS MOUTSIOS

THE DECLINE OF DEMOCRATIC POLITICS IN 'KNOWLEDGE SOCIETIES' AND THE INITIATIVES FOR CITIZENSHIP EDUCATION

INTRODUCTION

The early 21st Century is a historical time in that participation in education systems is increasing greatly and access to information and knowledge is immensely wide. This is certainly the reality in the wealthy parts of the world, where, to draw from the empirical record, 75% of infants receive pre-school education, almost all children go to primary school, about 90% of them participate in lower secondary education, more than 70% go to upper secondary schools, 40% of young people are expected to get some kind of Bachelor's degree, and a considerable share of the adult population takes part in continuing education programmes (UNESCO, 2000; OECD, 2004).

The vast majority of this population is on a daily basis immersed in the written and audiovisual environment of the Media and a substantial proportion of them communicates interactively through the Internet: at the moment half of EU residents, on average, and around 70% of the people living in North America, Australia and New Zealand, are Internet users (Internet World Stats, 2006). Some of these countries, accounting for 22% of the world's population, spend 84% of global expenditure on 'Research and Development' (UNESCO, 2000).

These are the 'knowledge societies' of our era which have succeeded in creating a majority of literate, informed and educated citizens, a *sin qua non* condition for vibrant democracies. However, these are the same societies in which democracy has reached a state of decline (Touraine, 1997; Bauman 1999; Castells, 2004; Beck, 2005; Held 2006). In Europe, recurrent Eurobarometer surveys show that the majority of the EU citizens do not think that 'their voice counts' and a considerable number of them are 'not satisfied with the way democracy works' in their country. Most EU citizens state repeatedly that they distrust their governments, their parliaments, their political parties and the European institutions (see for example Eurobarometer, 2003 and 2006). Similarly, in North America more than half of citizens believe that their will is not expressed in the way they are governed (Gallup cited in Castells, 2005), and a number of studies speak about a lack of trust and participation in political institutions. One of these studies, indented to attract public attention in the USA, declares this from its start: 'American democracy is at

M.A. Peters, A. Britton and H. Blee (Eds.), Global Citizenship Education: Philosophy, Theory and Pedagogy, 503-517.

risk. ... Americans have turned away from politics and the public sphere in large numbers, leaving our civic life impoverished' (Macedo et al, 2005, p. 1).

Why is civic life impoverished at a time when information and knowledge generation as well as education, in its various forms and manifestations, are expanded and continue to expand more than ever before? The research industry on 'civic engagement' and citizenship education, developed over the last decade in North America and in Europe but also across other parts of the world (see for example Hahn, 1998; Torney-Purta et al, 1999, 2001; Nelson & Kerr 2006; Weerd 2005), is not asking this question despite the fact that the commissioning of this stream of research signifies a political concern to address it. Neither much of this research nor the mainstream debate on citizenship education are placed in the context of contemporary political developments while issues about the relationship between those developments and current modes of knowledge transmission and acquisition are hardly touched upon.

This chapter will try to address these issues but by definition it can be no more than an allusion to what needs to be a substantial analysis about education and the contemporary 'crisis of democracy'. The analysis concerns the advanced 'knowledge societies', with particular reference to Europe but not to a specific country. The paper will argue that the source of the crisis lies in the overall prioritisation of economic competition over democratic participation at both national and transnational levels. It will also argue that the ways that knowledge is selected, organised and distributed both in and out of educational institutions is weakening rather than strengthening democratic citizenship. The first section of the paper points to policies of de-democratisation occurring in national and transnational contexts; the second section discusses the impact of the current modes of information and knowledge production and diffusion on active citizenship; and the third section reflects on the relation between contemporary education reforms and the current debate and initiatives for citizenship education.

DE-DEMOCRATISING POLITICAL LIFE

Democracy has been historically a limited political reality. Born in Ancient Greece around 500 BC, it lasted for two to three centuries and then, with the decline of the Greek *polis*, it was lost in history for about one and a half millennia. During the early Renaissance democratic forms of governance were revived in many Italian cities which attempted to constitute themselves as self-ruled communes against the authority of the church and the monarchs. However, it was mainly the American and the French Revolution and later on the labour movements of industrialism which promoted democracy as the dominant type of political and social organisation in the West. Despite substantial differences between the two historical eras, what characterises the political project for democracy is the establishment of a public sphere of dialogue, deliberation and critique and the pursuit of equality, social justice and individual and collective autonomy (Castoriadis, 1999).

Certainly, it cannot be discussed here to what extent and in what forms this project has been realised. It needs to be kept in mind though that democracy in modernity has been 'representative', bounded by the nation-state and co-existent with capitalism. In the post-1989 era, and, particularly, with the accelerated globalising process of the 1990s, representative democracy has allegedly expanded in most countries. Today 64% of states in the world are classified as 'electoral democracies' (Freedom House 2006) and their expansion is a universally legitimate aim.

However, the time of the formal expansion of representative or liberal democracy is also the time of its recession. Globalisation de-democratises decision-making in both economic and political spheres. Important political decisions are taken today within international networks of power rather than by the weakened national institutions of representation. The 'ethnopolis' of representative democracy is not transforming to the envisioned 'cosmopolis' (Delanty, 2000; Beck, 2005; Held 2006) but to a transnational power structure comprising nation-states, international organisations, super-state unions, governmental and non-governmental institutions and private corporations which, through formal and informal networking, make policies about a wide variety of issues. Network decision-making structures are commonly legitimised by the perception that they are more efficient in dealing with complex common problems. States, as Koenig-Archibugi (2002) notes, are not always considered able to pursue their own some goals or to perform some functions, because they lack sufficient organisational, material or knowledge capacity or simply because they are not willing enough to do so. Transnational structures of decision making and supranational institutions are allegedly able to mobilise resources directed to the achievement of targets and to problem-solving. Their problem-solving approach and their instrumental efficiency displace democratic procedures and obfuscate citizenship, as their decision making is hardly accessible by citizens' participation.

Democratic citizenship has also been undermined by the economic restructuring initiated in the 1980s in the USA and the UK and spread around the world after 1990 (mainly through the IMF, World Bank, OECD and WTO) prioritising economic and managerial efficiency in all major aspects of public life. Privatisation of state companies in many countries along with the shift from relatively stable lifelong careers to flexible and individualised work patterns have fragmented organised labour and reduced the participation of trade unions in firms' operations. The introduction of market rules in the public sector, as a way of increasing its organisational efficiency, has removed citizens' involvement in its strategies and services. Market values and rules have penetrated the discourse and very often the operation of a great array of public institutions, from transportation and communication to post offices and hospitals. Citizens in many countries are renamed as customers of state services who are eligible to market accountability rather than to public responsibility. The welfare state, the cornerstone of the legitimacy of the modern nation state, has entered a process of restructuring by both conservative and social democratic governments, which revised long standing distributive policies in favour of weakened socio-economic safety nets (see Eriksen and Weigård, 2000).

More importantly, economic globalisation, in its tremendously asymmetrical character, has placed the competition for survival or dominance between firms, countries, and people at the heart of contemporary politics. As a result, politics has been largely reduced to economic growth and economic growth has become the main political problem. Political debate is considered relevant as long as it is occupied with the increase of productivity, competitiveness and economic performance whereas democratic concerns are hardly part of mainstream debate. Mainstream debate is almost fully occupied by a more or less single reform agenda which transcends state borders and ideological (Right/Left) boundaries. This agenda is comprised of a set of recommendations, benchmarks or objectives related to economic performance and has been/is being promoted as the new universal order to which, allegedly, 'there is no alternative'. The general consensus between most political parties on the absence of alternatives removes, on the one hand, the political ground for critique and contestation of ideas on the part of citizens, and it encourages their turning in on their private lives and their individual striving for survival or success; on the other hand, it feeds upon the electoral power of political forces which counter-suggest identity particularism as an alternative to political instrumentality. This second consequence is underlined by Chantal Mouffe (2006, pp. 70-71) who points that the recent '...success of right-wing populist parties is the consequence of the lack of a vibrant democratic debate in our post-democracies' and that the discourse of these parties 'is replacing the weakened left/right opposition between 'the people' and 'the establishment'. And she explains:

> In a context where the dominant discourse proclaims that there is no alternative to the current neo-liberal form of globalisation and that we should accept its dictats, it is not surprising that a growing number of people are listening to those who proclaim that alternatives do exist and that they will give back to the people the power to decide (Mouffe, 2006, p. 70).

Indeed, in many European countries a considerable number of citizens (see Norris, 2005) tend to vote for extreme right-wing parties which have managed to place their agendas into the mainstream political debate (e.g. France, Austria, Belgium, the Netherlands, Italy, Greece, Denmark, Poland). Their influence is feeding and is being fed by the resurgence of nationalist ideologies (culture, ethnicity or language-based), by xenophobia, prejudice and racism and by violent religious fundamentalism, which are spreading suspicion and hatred within and across societies and they are collapsing codes of political communication and interpersonal understanding.

As Alain Touraine (1997, p. 240) pointed out concisely: 'We live in a world that has been both globalised and fragmented, and in which democracy is under threat from, on the one hand, the reduction of societies to markets and, on the other, the different forms of totalitarian politics ... be they nationalist or theocratic'. A decade later, nobody could seriously argue that this condition has been reversed. On the contrary, it has been aggravated by the 9/11 attack and the subsequent 'war on terror' which has proliferated surveillance measures – not only in the USA but throughout the world – with little concern for democratic rights (see Peters, 2005). National legislation, transnational anti-terrorist treaties, electronic systems of surveillance, along with discourses of threat and an atmosphere of constant emergency are drastically undermining fundamental civic liberties. As Beck (2005, p. 13) argues, these policies may lead to the death of democracy, as, in order to ward off possible dangers, states are acting against their own citizens.

With economic competition dominating social and political life, managerial efficiency displacing public involvement, transnational policymaking replacing citizens' participation, identity defensiveness and fundamentalism exploding within and across countries and surveillance measures constraining citizens' rights, democracy as a political project, aimed at strengthening *liberté, égalité,* and *fraternité,* is in a process of recession. Instead of helping to overcome this process, contemporary regimes of information and knowledge generation and diffusion, constitute, as the next section argues, one of its expressions.

INFORMATION, KNOWLEDGE AND POLITICAL OPINION

It is common to say that a democratic society is one which creates democratic citizens, not only through formal education, but through the lifelong learning of active citizenship. This means primarily that society should have the institutions which allow all citizens to make decisions, so that they 'learn by doing' citizenship. A very important condition for citizens to make decisions is of course to be able to formulate opinions. Democratic citizenship is exercised when political opinion is clearly distinguished from professional expertise, as Socrates teaches us through his famous dialogue with Protagoras (Plato/Taylor, 2002); specialised knowledge is invoked to materialise political decisions already made by citizens. Globalisation, as noted above, creates institutions which are impermeable to citizens' participation. In addition, policymaking in contemporary 'knowledge societies' is subject to forces of information management and professional and scientific expertise which obscure political opinion.

To be sure, 'knowledge societies' are those in which the highly profitable economic activities are located less in manufacturing and the production of physical goods and more in information and knowledge production and reproduction (see Burton-Jones, 2003; Peters, 2003). They are societies which prioritise new knowledge generation as a source of higher productivity and competitiveness. They are also societies fully immersed in the sounds, images and messages transmitted daily by the media and this has profound consequences for the function of political life. Actually, what is considered political life is almost entirely framed by the media, their political relations, entrepreneurial plans and market strategies. The media have a central role in organising politics and governance through electoral campaigning, information management, public opinion polls, image making, and marketing of policy measures; thus transforming citizens into viewers/listeners and democracies into 'mediacracies' (Castells, 2000).

Certainly, the invention and spread of the new information and communication technologies, with their potential to circulate information, knowledge and ideas interactively, decentralises communication and gives opportunities for political involvement to citizens. This why so much hope was invested in the Internet when it first appeared, as the potential technological infrastructure of a new public sphere, and, thus, of the revival of democracy. The Internet may allow citizens to become more knowledgeable about public affairs. It can be used as an accessible tool for organising political action worldwide (e.g., by 'anti-globalisation' movements), it can promote horizontal communication between citizens, facilitate electronic voting for referenda and elections, and decentralise and democratise governance institutions (see for example Barney 2004).

However, interactive technologies alone are not a sufficient condition for the promotion of democracy. ICT, like every kind of technology, is deeply connected with existing political and socio-economic conditions. The very access to the Internet, first of all, mirrors existing patterns of social, economic, educational and regional disadvantage (see Norris, 2001). Moreover, its use as a tool of political communication may be subject to the will of political regimes. The Chinese government, for example, is well known for expanding Internet use for production and consumption purposes and, at the same time, effectively blocking millions of politically undesirable websites in harmonious cooperation with ICT corporations from the West (Levy, 2006).

Both in the West and elsewhere the Internet is being used mostly for work, purchases, entertainment and interpersonal communication and much less for participation in political life. As Pippa Norris (2001) showed, the Internet mainly facilitates the political activism of those already engaged in politics. As far as formal politics is concerned, governments publish official documents on the Internet but rarely do they involve citizens in consultation processes and, similarly, political parties' web-sites seldom offer the possibility of feedback to their potential supporters. Overall, as Norris notes, political organisations changed the channel of communication from the traditional media to the Internet rather the nature of this communication. Certainly, the Internet has contributed towards the creation of a network-like mode of governance where, potentially, state, private sector, and civil society agencies are enabled to interact. But, as another scholar notes (Barney, 2004, pp. 136-137), 'network governance' has been primarily used to replace traditional forms of democratic representation with new modes of 'public management', to re-organise the public sector on a business-like basis, and to allow the penetration of the private sector in the institutions of public governance.

Apparently then the enthusiastic predictions of recent years about the revival of democracy through the Internet have not come true. The same holds for all electronic media, whose introduction to everyday life has been traditionally accompanied by correlations between more informed listeners/viewers/users and more participating citizens. However, as another researcher reminds us, such correlations do not stand up to scrutiny of the historical record of the 20th century:

> Opportunities to become better informed have apparently expanded historically, as the informational context of politics has grown richer and become better endowed with media and ready access to political communication. Yet none of the major developments in communication in the 20th century produced any aggregate gain in citizen participation. Neither telephones, radio, nor television exerted a net positive effect on participation, despite the fact that they apparently reduced information costs and improved citizens' access to information (Bimber, 2000, p. 57).

Evidently, old, new and interactive media have not expanded citizens' participation. Nonetheless, citizens are overwhelmed on a daily basis by massive flows of information and specialist knowledge which make the construction of a coherent picture of social life and the formulation of personal opinion extremely difficult. In the words of Bard and Söderqvist (2002, p. 84): 'all these statistical investigations, all this quasi-scientific research, in other words, all this torrent of new information that is so readily available to us in our efforts to make the world a little more comprehensible is precisely the mental disorder for which it believes it is the cure'. Indeed, fragmented data and expert specialist technical knowledge diffused through the media obscure a comprehensive understanding and a general perception of social and political reality.

However, the production and media management of specialist knowledge express the dominant mode of policymaking in contemporary societies, rather than someone's attempt to cure others' mental confusion. Policymaking today is based heavily on specialist knowledge and this knowledge is now increasingly produced beyond a single nation's borders. It is produced by international research networks and sponsored by transnational institutions and governments and it is widely used to issue policy recommendations, consultation documents or 'progress reports'. The production and use of specialist knowledge is a crucial tool for decision making, as it provides scientific support for what has been diagnosed as problematic and it ensures the legitimation of the proposed measures. Opposing views may be easily displaced as non-informed, non-specialised or irrelevant – because, after all, experts always know better – and thus political interests and goals are obscured behind scientific data.

Experts, as members of research networks or appointed committees, dominate policymaking agendas. They are themselves fully immersed in their specialised knowledge areas, following contemporary knowledge organisation in research institutions and higher education. The recent move towards interdisciplinary research consortia (conceptualised famously by Gibbons et al, 1994, as 'mode 2 knowledge production') testifies to the capacity of markets, transnational institutions and governments to bring together experts to work on economically and politically profitable projects rather than for a tendency towards a new holistic perception of what is researched. Contemporary dominant knowledge is fragmented, instrumental and exchangeable, as Lyotard (1984) pointed more than two decades ago and as Bernstein remarked characteristically:

> There is a new concept both of knowledge and of its relation to those who create it, a truly secular concept. Knowledge should flow like money to wherever it can create advantage and profit. Indeed, knowledge is not just like money: it is money. Knowledge is divorced from persons, their commitments, their personal dedication, for these become impediments, restrictions on flow, and introduce deformations in the working of the market ... Knowledge, after nearly a thousand years, is divorced from inwardness and is literally dehumanized (Bernstein, 2000, p. 86).

This divorce between the knower and knowledge, due to its dehumanisation and instrumentalisation, at a historical moment when access to education is almost universal, is not irrelevant to this apparently paradoxical weakening of democracy in contemporary 'knowledge societies'. In order to serve the enhancement of democracy, information and knowledge production and dissemination should facilitate citizens in formulating political opinion and enabling them to engage in dialogue and critique and ultimately to participate in political life. Instead, dialogue and critique are absorbed by the media-dominated public space and its commercialised forms of information. Moreover, citizens are overwhelmed by expertise, transmitted fragmented knowledge areas and socialised into perceiving knowledge as a source of productivity and competitiveness. This perception is now dominating education policies across many countries.

EDUCATION POLICIES AND CITIZENSHIP EDUCATION

Democratic education is certainly not limited to citizenship education as a school subject. Recalling Aristotle, democratic education presupposes *public* educational institutions which provide the potential to *all* learners for personal enhancement and political participation (see Kazamias, 2004). To do so educational institutions should have in place those organisational and pedagogic arrangements which allow every individual to develop their ability to take part in public life and to shape it. In other words, democratic education is primarily about imparting the qualities necessary for (future or current) citizens to learn how to rule and be ruled. For this purpose, school curricula and educational programmes should prioritise content which contributes to the development of critical judgment and independent thinking rather than the acquisition of specialised skills. The European inheritance of *paideia*, of *bildung*, of *general education, or culture générale*, despite its association with elitist forms of education throughout much of history, gives the potential for the intellectual, ethical and civic development of human beings and therefore the enhancement of democracy. However, instead of exploring this potential, contemporary reforms prioritise the contribution of education to technological and economic growth and therefore the effective transmission and acquisition of 'useful', exchangeable knowledge. The ultimate goal is that the economy draws from the appropriate human capital and the individual in turn manages to survive or retain or upgrade his/her status under the conditions of continuous economic, technological and managerial restructuring.

As a consequence one can identify, over the last few years, a process of 'vocationalisation' of educational programmes in European countries. In higher education old differentiations between universities and non-universities are being abolished and a common system is arising in which both types of institutions function as competitors, seeking research funding and constructing modularised programmes of study, responsive to labour market needs. Higher education is no longer seen as a space of autonomous generation of theories and the conduct of independent research. It is considered rather as the engine of the new economy destined to attract and produce high-skilled human capital. Secondary education systems are also being brought closer to labour market needs through the upgrading of the status of vocational paths and through the vocationalisation of the curricula of 'academic' paths. The traditional boundaries between the two paths are being blurred under education reforms seeking to introduce more production-related content. For the same purpose there is an increasing emphasis on the formation of specific competences, not simply as part of curricula and syllabi, but actually as a central principle for organising the transmission and acquisition of educational knowledge (see Green et al, 1999).

The assumed requirements of the knowledge-based economy are now determining the kind of educational knowledge to be emphasised in both compulsory and post-compulsory education. Today this is increasingly defined at transnational levels. The *Programme for International Student Assessment*, the well-known PISA framework, sponsored by the OECD, exerts considerable influence on national curriculum policies by classifying countries on the basis of average student performance in selected subjects. This is a mode of policymaking based on data processing, which is used by states to re-focus schooling on measurable performance targets. A similar thrust can be identified in the mode of education policy adopted by the European Union, which through the so-called Open Method of Coordination (OMC) encourages state-members towards common goals (see e.g. EC, 2002) by means of indicators and benchmarks, targets, performance comparisons, monitoring, evaluation and diffusion of 'best practices'. Thus reforms across the EU are defining production-related skills and stressing selected curriculum areas (i.e. science, technology, ICT and entrepreneurial skills) in compulsory and post-compulsory education, so that the EU becomes 'the most competitive and dynamic knowledge-based economy in the world' (EC, 2002).

By placing their education systems in the service of economic growth modern states tend to displace the anthropocentric contents of the general *paideia* which are necessary for the formation of democratic citizenship. This is not to say that education systems are abandoning humanities and curriculum areas appropriate for collective identity formation. On the contrary, some education systems tend to re-emphasise the teaching, for instance, of history, language, religious education and geography and national culture (Moutsios, 2004). This is primarily the result of many governments' response to a perceived threat against national, religious or cultural identities, allegedly imposed by globalisation, cultural diversification and the increasing presence of 'aliens' within their national space. Curriculum reform towards this direction is prominent in recent years in countries where new nation-states have been created (e.g. the dominance of national languages in the Baltic countries' curricula), where the affirmation of national, ethnic, or religious identities is pursued (e.g. the recent upheaval in Greece against the removal of established national myths from history textbooks), where the presence of immigrants is conceived as a threat to cultural 'purity' or where national memory is considered weak (e.g. Denmark's 'cultural canon') or where populist parties, as remarked above, mobilise the public against mainstream politics. Thus, by re-emphasising identity formation subjects as a response to reactions against educational instrumentality, governments undermine further the development of democratic education, as these aspects of the curriculum tend to share an exclusionist approach.

This vicious circle is hardly perceived by the research and benchmarking industry on citizenship education in which non-governmental and intergovernmental institutions have been engaged recently (e.g. Torney-Purta et al, 1999, 2001; Nelson & Kerr 2006; Weerd, 2005). As noted above, this type of research does not take into account the international political environment or the current modes of information and knowledge transmission to which young people, and all citizens, are exposed. This is certainly the case in the most prominent example of this sort of research, the IEA civic education study (Torney-Purta et al, 1999, 2001), which provides masses of data but adds little to our understanding about the education of tomorrow's citizens in the countries concerned. The study neglects the modern transnational political context whereas the background information given for the national contexts (e.g. political history and status of civic education) is hardly used to inform the analysis of the data. This is mainly due to the fact that the analysis follows the example of popular comparative surveys (conducted again by IEA or by the OECD) which use tests and psychometric techniques to define low and high scores and to rank countries according to their performance in selected subjects.

Defining score levels and indicators is also the approach of research sponsored by the EU, which is apparently alarmed by the persisting crisis of trust in institutions of democratic governance, and identity-based conflicts, and thus it is trying to revive citizenship education in its member states. But what kind of citizenship education is being pursued? Taking the most prominent example of the EU's recent initiatives, it becomes evident that the main concern is to ensure 'social cohesion' in order to facilitate economic growth rather to regenerate the public sphere. This is actually the official objective of the EU (EC, 2002, p. 12) which informs the production of indicators for citizenship education. In a recent major project on such indicators, sponsored by the EU (see Weerd et al, 2005), it is underlined that the 'school of thought' adopted by the EU is not the one which advocates a 'civil society as public sphere', shaped by democratic deliberation and participation. It is the 'school', supported by Robert Putnam, which advocates 'associational life' (i.e. membership in voluntary associations, networks and activities) leading to social capital and the fostering of economic success. The authors of the EU-funded report state this objective clearly:

> Putnam's view is that associations breed social capital, and that social capital breeds success. This line of thinking is reflected in the goals that the European Union set for 2010 at the Lisbon European Council. In these goals, active citizenship is referred to as participation in all spheres of social and economic life, and is presented as an important element in becoming the most competitive market and dynamic knowledge-based economy in the world ... the description of active citizenship used in this study is by no means universal or value-free. It is clearly related to [these] political goals (Weerd, 2005, pp. 14–16).

European citizenship then is related to the accumulation on the part of individuals of social capital and the maintenance of social cohesion so that the EU achieves the Lisbon goals (i.e. to become the most competitive knowledge economy). In other words, learning citizenship for the EU is learning how to associate with others in order to work more effectively for its economic growth.

Apparently, this vision of citizenship is not promoted through debates and consultations in national and local contexts in Europe, but through sponsored research consortia and bureaucracies assigned to produce quantifiable input/output/outcome indicators and mechanisms of 'monitoring'. This way of defining educational knowledge is fully compatible with the new modes of curriculum control adopted by many countries since the early 1990s. Starting from the UK, the USA and some other countries, there has been a widespread move towards the objectives-based approach in the organisation of knowledge, through the specification of measurable expected outcomes (Moutsios 2000). The objectives or outcome-based approach in organising and controlling the curriculum is not of course novel. It dates back to the times when behaviourism triumphed in psychology and was in turn transferred to curriculum theory. It returned with force through deliberate policies in the 1990s, marginalising ongoing theoretical debates and experimentation in teaching, and imposing a perception of learning as a linear progression upwards or as Stenhouse (1975, p. 83) would put it as 'teaching people to jump higher by setting the bar higher'. Today, behaviourist approaches underpin national curriculum frameworks, projects commissioned to devise indicators and expected learning outcomes, the country rankings of PISA and the benchmarking strategies of the EU alike.

The behaviouristic objectives approach, as a mode of regulating educational practices, stands against the development of collective and individual autonomy in/through schooling. Objectives are criteria of performance which are directly linked with evaluation. Evaluation, as Foucault (1977) has shown, has multiple regulative effects (i.e. correcting, training, categorising, normalising) over the evaluated. In education it can impose hierarchical visibility in the way schools operate and perform as well as their public comparison and classification. Evaluation stresses outcomes but it can alter pedagogic practice, by refocusing it on the outcomes expected. Evaluation mechanisms (e.g. standardised tests, evaluation boards, performance indicators and comparative data, monitoring schemes and published reports) have been used intensively for more than a decade now across Europe, North America and Oceania in order to monitor performances and pedagogic practices. As a consequence the autonomy of institutions, educationists, teachers, and communities to reflect on the way knowledge should be organised, a fundamental aspect of democracy practiced in/through education, has vanished. Educational institutions, very often even those experimenting with alterative pedagogic practices, have to standardise their work and orientate it towards measurable performances. Whereas democratic enhancement in the way schools work requires the pursuit of autonomy, equality, collegiality and critical reflection, the outcomes-driven policy brings about competition, differentiation and conformity to standardised practices.

The outcomes-driven policy appears to be part of a general political move to break with bureaucratic modes of regulation which stifle personal initiative and creativity. Indeed, bureaucratic educational management, sustained by formal circulars and prescribed material, suppresses autonomy and constrains the development of democratic relations and practices in educational institutions. Bureaucratic education systems – as most of them continue to be – impose uniformity and routine by disallowing professional initiative and socialising students into hierarchical power relationships. With the introduction of 'public management' methods in educational institutions those constraints are supposedly removed: hierarchies are flattened, bureaucracies are diminished and thus schools can be flexible and can control their own strategies and practices. The 'educational restructuring' movement as it has been/ is being spread across countries, is, supposedly, enhancing institutional freedom as it delegates authority and financial resources to schools for their day-to-day needs; it gives parents decision-making powers in school management; it reinforces the role of the headteacher, and it encourages schools to promote themselves to the public (Moutsios, 2000). However, as we know now, despite the rhetoric about freedom of choice and parental participation, this wave of reforms has been introducing market principles into the discourse, policies and organisational practices of institutions and transforming students/parents/citizens into customers. In other words this entire 'managerial revolution', which, supposedly, sets educational institutions free from bureaucracy and makes them autonomous, flexible, and innovative places to work and learn, has been replacing one mode of organisational control with another; bureaucratic conformity has become managerial conformity. Educational control is now exercised, directly or indirectly, at both national and transnational levels through the definition of goals and means and through the spread of the practically undisputed ideology of educational instrumentality.

Although the analysis of this ideology and the reforms it induces in education systems across countries has been undertaken by well known contributors in recent years (e.g Whitty et al, 1998), it is, notably, missing in the contemporary research and debate on civic education. Citizenship education is heavily researched, measured, and debated away from the very context it is practiced: the education system. But it is even more remarkable that this increased policy activity around citizenship education takes place at a time when education reforms are removing or diminishing all those curricular, organisational and pedagogic arrangements which would contribute to the active learning of democratic citizenship, celebrated so much by the official rhetoric.

EPILOGUE

Notwithstanding popular discourses about the global spread of democratic values and the role of lifelong and ICT-based learning in advanced societies, democratic citizenship is in a historical stage of regression. The current version of globalisation has placed societies in a trajectory of relentless economic competition which supersedes any substantial development of democracy. Despite the widespread legitimacy and the accelerated expansion of electoral democracy in the world, core decisions are being taken by/within transnational networks of economic and political power which define citizens' reality but which are not open to their participation. However, with the decisive help of ICT, knowledge is accessible in an unprecedented extent, but it is fragmented, commercialised, instrumental, highly specialised and it obscures political opinion. Recent education reforms are reinforcing these modes of knowledge organisation, as education systems are being aligned to policies of economic competitiveness. Curriculum reform, on the one hand, emphasises the formation of skills related to the new economy, and, on the other, stresses the re-formation of allegedly threatened cultural identities. Citizenship curricula are being developed to transmit values considered necessary for individuals to build social capital in order to associate with each other in a well-functioning market society, rather than to reinvigorate democratic participation. Participation in educational decision making is displaced by management methods imported from the private sector along with evaluation mechanisms and outcomes-driven pedagogic modes which standardise teaching and learning policies and practices.

The main direction that contemporary knowledge selection, organisation and distribution in and out of educational institutions is taking is not pointing to a renaissance of democracy as a political regime of deliberation and critique amongst citizens who are enabled and entitled to make decisions about the orientation of their societies. On the contrary, education, in its formal and informal dimensions, is fully aligned to the prevalent project of our age which is to create and sustain economically powerful 'knowledge societies' rather than vibrant 'knowledge democracies'.

REFERENCES

Bard, A. & Söderqvist, J. (2002). *Netocracy: The new power elite and life after capitalism.* London: Pearson Education.

Barney, D. (2004). *The network society.* London: Polity.

Bauman, Z. (1999). *In search of politics.* London: Polity Press.

Beck, U. (2005). *Power in the global age: A new global political economy.* London: Polity.

Bernstein, B. (1996). *Pedagogy, symbolic control and identity: Theory, research, critique.* London: Taylor & Francis.

Bimber, B. (2001). Information and political engagement in America: the search for effects of information technology at the individual level. *Political Research Quarterly, 54*(1), 53–67.

Burton-Jones, A. (2003). Knowledge capitalism: The new learning economy. *Policy Futures in Education, 1*(1), 143–159.

Castells, M. (2000). *The rise of the network society.* 2nd edn. Oxford: Blackwell.

Castells, M. (2004). *The power of identity.* 2nd edn. Oxford: Blackwell.

Castells, M. (2005). Global governance and global politics. *Political Science & Politics, 38*(1). http://proquest.umi.com/pqdweb?did=808865261&sid=1&Fmt=3&clientId=29782& RQT=309&VName=PQD.

Castoriadis, C. (1999). *The ancient Greek democracy and its significance for us today.* Athens: Upsilon Books [in Greek].

Delanty, G. (2000). *Citizenship in a global age: Society, culture, politics.* London: Open University Press.

Eriksen, E. and Weigård, J. (2000). The end of citizenship? New roles challenging the political order. In McKinnon, C. & Hampsher-Monk, I. (Eds.), *The demands of citizenship.* London: Continuum.

Eurobarometer (2003). *Eurobarometer 59: Public opinion in the European Union.* http://europa.eu.int/comm/public_opinion/archives/eb/eb59/eb59_rapport_final_en.pdf.

European Commission (2006). *Eurobarometer 64: Public opinion in the European Union.* http://ec.europa.eu/public_opinion/archives/eb/eb64/eb64_en.pdf.

European Commission (2002). *Education and training in Europe: Diverse systems, shared goals for 2010.* Luxembourg: Office for Official Publications of the European Communities.

Foucault, M. (1977). *Discipline and punish: The birth of the prison.* London: Penguin Press.

Freedom House (2006). *Freedom in the world: Selected data from Freedom House's annual global survey of political rights and civil liberties.* www.freedomhouse.org

Gibbons, M., Limoges, C. Nowotny, H., Schwartzman, S., Scott, P. and Trow, M. (1994). *The new production of knowledge: The dynamics of science and research in contemporary societies.* London: SAGE Publications.

Green, A. Wolf, A. and Leney, T. (1999). *Convergence and divergence in European education and training systems.* London: Institute of Education.

Hahn, C. (1998). *Becoming political: Comparative perspectives on citizenship education.* New York: State University of New York Press.

Held, D. (2006). *Models of democracy.* 3rd edn. Stanford: Stanford University Press.

Hirst, P. and Thompson, G. (1996). *Globalisation in question: The international economy and possibilities of governance.* Cambridge: Polity.

Internet World Stats (2006). http://www.internetworldstats.com/.

Kazamias, A., (2004). Paideia and Politeia in Europe – A symposium on education and citizenship, ancient and modern. In Buk-Berge, E., Holm-Larsen, S., & Wiborg, S. (Eds.), *Education across borders: Comparative studies.* Oslo: Didakta Norsk Forlag.

Koenig-Archibugi, M. (2002). Mapping global governance. In D. Held and A. McGrew (Eds.), *Governing globalization: Power, authority and global governance*. Cambridge: Polity.

Levy, S. (2006). Google and the China syndrome: The businesses know that building censorship into their search engines violates their principles. *Newsweek*, 13-02-2006.

Lyotard, J-F. (1984). *The postmodern condition: A report on knowledge*. Manchester: Manchester University Press.

Macedo, S., Alex-Assenoh, Y., Berry, J.M, Brintnall, M., Campell, D.E., Fraga, L.R., Fung, A., Galston, W.A. Karpowittz, C. F., Levi, M., Levinson, M., Lipsitz, K. Niemi, R. G., Putnam, R.D., Rahn, W.M., Reich, R., Rodgers, R.R., Swanstrom, T. Walsh, K.C. (2005). *Democracy at risk: How political choices undermine citizen participation, and what we can do about it*. Washington: Brookings Institution Press.

Mouffe, Ch. (2005). *On the political*. London: Routledge.

Moutsios, S. (2000). Curriculum control in 'deregulated' and bureaucratic educational systems: The cases of England and Greece. In Peschar, J.L. and Van der Wal, M. (Eds.), *Education contested: Changing relations between state, market and civil society in modern European education*. Lisse: Swets & Zeitlinger.

Moutsios, S. (2004). The identity of the European Union and the European pedagogic identities, in Buk-Berge, E., Holm-Larsen, S., and Wiborg, S. (Eds.), *Education across borders: Comparative studies*. Oslo: Didakta Norsk Forlag.

Nelson, J. & Kerr, D. (2006). *Active citizenship in INCA countries: Definitions, policies, practices and outcomes*. London: QCA-NFER.

Norris, P. (2001). *Digital divide: Civic engagement, information poverty, and the internet worldwide*. Cambridge: Cambridge University Press.

Norris, P. (2005). *Radical right: Voters and parties in the electoral market*. Cambridge: Cambridge University press.

OECD (2004). *Education at a glance: OECD indicators 2004*. Paris: OECD.

Peters, M. (Ed.) (2005). *Education, globalization, and the state in the age of terrorism*. Boulder, CO: Paradigm Publishers.

Peters, M. (2003). Education policy in the age of knowledge capitalism. *Policy Futures in Education, 1*(2), 361−380.

Plato − translated by Taylor, C.C.W. (2002). *Protagoras*. Oxford: Oxford Classics Paperbacks.

Stenhouse, L. (1975). *An introduction to curriculum research and development*. Oxford: Heinemann Educational.

Touraine, A. (1997). *Can we live together? Equality and difference*. London: Polity Press.

Torney-Purta, J., Schwille, J. and Amadeo, J.-A. (1999). *Civic education across countries: Twenty-four national case studies from the IEA civic education project*. Amsterdam: The International Association for the Evaluation of Educational Achievement.

Torney-Purta, J., Lehmann, R., Oswald, H. and Schulz, W. (2001). *Citizenship and education in twenty-eight countries: Civic knowledge and engagement at age fourteen*. Amsterdam: The International Association for the Evaluation of Educational Achievement.

UNESCO (2000). *Facts and figures 2000*. Paris: UNESCO Institute for Statistics.

Weerd, de M., Gemmeke, M., Righter, J. and Rij van C. (2005). *Indicators for monitoring active citizenship and citizenship education − Final report*. Amsterdam: Regioplan/European Commission.

Whitty, G., Power, S. and Halpin, D. (1998). *Devolution and choice in education: The school, the state and the market*. Buckingham: Open University Press.

Stavros Moutsios

MUNA GOLMOHAMAD

GLOBAL CITIZENSHIP: FROM THEORY TO PRACTICE, UNLOCKING HEARTS AND MINDS

THEORETICAL DISCUSSIONS ABOUT GLOBAL CITIZENSHIP: ISSUES OF
DIVERSITY WITH SOME CONSIDERATIONS FOR EDUCATION

Education has long been recognised as an instrument for social change, or social progress, as well as economic necessity. How significant, then, to promote global, or world, citizenship education by imagining a worldwide community where individuals can have meaningful democratic membership. A noteworthy challenge for global citizenship is to find a mutually common conception in a global climate of multi-national corporative barons and fragile eco-systems. Globalisation has its critics and rightly so if it contributes to further exploitation and continued inequalities. Global citizenship can make a valuable contribution if a key aim would be to explore a moral framework or ethical aspect, with the view to work toward an agreeable shared conception. One approach, which I presume may be helpful for education, is to promote the study of human relationships within and between different contexts, past, present and future. The intention would also be to extend the notion beyond interpersonal relationships to systemic and inter-institutional relationships in different contexts. This approach can be inclusive of a number of disciplines: philosophy, history, religion, culture and other traditions to name a few.

> A perspective of life that monetizes human relationships can only result in social fragmentation in a battlefield crowded with individuals, corporations, nations and blocks of nations and in an absolute inability to promote social justice. (Gushiken, n.d.)

The aim suggested here for global citizenship is to conceive of human relationship beyond monetization and reclaim a positive conceptualisation of global relationships. This chapter looks to discuss the way in which it may be possible to conceive of global citizenship in a learning environment that promotes and encourages a process of learning orientated to integration of individuals and societies without compromising differences.

World Citizenship, also known as International or Global Citizenship, can embody a theme of integration. I will use the terms global, international and world interchangeably in this chapter as the claim in this chapter is that they all suggest an expansive notion.

M.A. Peters, A. Britton and H. Blee (Eds.), Global Citizenship Education: Philosophy, Theory and Pedagogy, 519–533.

'Fostering world citizenship is a practical strategy for promoting sustainable development' (Baha'i International Community, 1993). This has never been timelier. A common assumption about mention of sustainable development is the valuable relationship between human beings and their natural environment, the fragility of the earth's eco-system under the care or abuse of humanity. Recently some attention has been given to the fragility of human ecology. Here, human ecology is intended to suggest the need to consider the need to highlight social injustices and the fragility of the human ecology in developing countries. In fact, to perhaps even reconsider the definition of humanity when such iniquitous conditions are allowed to persist.

The interest in Citizenship Education has been gathering momentum worldwide. World Citizenship, as many will know from the literature, is not a new concept although the political dynamics may be different now to Ancient times. Nevertheless, there are common themes found echoing beliefs shared by: the ancients, world religions, cultures; which can still resonate with conceptions of Global Citizenship Education in the twenty-first century. Renewed interest in values education, character education, virtues education and citizenship education, for example, seem to support this.

> The most important subsequent crystallization of the idea of a 'cosmopolis' is found in the basic philosophy of Zeno, founder of the Stoics, which, according to Plutarch, declares that all inhabitants of this world of ours should not live differentiated by their respective rules of justice in separate cities and communities, but ... should consider all men to be of one community and one polity. (O'Byrne, 2003)

Concerns about living differentiated lives, segregated from others, exist today just as the Stoics feared in ancient times. We are increasingly experiencing uncertain times and perpetuating a culture of fear, harnessing a cult mentality (Stein, 2001, cited in Richardson & Blades, 2006, p. 14). These fears of the unknown, of the strange and what is different have the potential to become translated into new conflicts if education cannot give space and lend support to learn from diverse perspectives. Citizenship education, certainly in Britain, is fast being seen as vital to reinforcing community cohesion. To a large extent, citizenship education remains localised in its outlook in as much as its main concern is to promote a conception of national identity: national citizenship and integration at national level. Many authors generally agree that citizenship has been largely understood within the bounds of nation state. Citizenship is, essentially, a modern concept becoming more established with modernity and the emergence of the nation state. The emergence of increasing reference to global citizenship suggests that previously imposed boundaries are becoming understood as less rigid, allowing for movement from local to global contexts and vice versa.

Ironically, separate communities and differences in an increasingly diverse, or multi-cultural, society is a growing concern in Britain. So much so that it could be said that a culture of fear is emerging. This condition is becoming more prevalent elsewhere too.

Fear of national disintegration lies at the heart of many recent public debates about American citizenship education. (Glazer, 1996, cited in Richardson & Blades, 2006, p. 19)

Recent debates about citizenship education and diversity may, likewise, suggest concern and fear of some for 'national disintegration'. Of course, citizenship education, whether national or international, has the potential to be unifying or divisive, depending on how it is conceived and how policies are implemented. We only need to look at examples from history to learn the consequences of citizenship education failing. Another concern is the danger of imposing forced boundaries, physical or otherwise, and the risk of creating homogeneity. The imposition of a dominant culture may be what is lurking behind fears of where possible extremes of the debate on 'Britishness' may lead.

Multiculturalism for some has negative connotations and it is interesting to see and hear the term 'diversity' recognised as part of the rhetoric of citizenship. Identity is also a loaded term and an aspect in the canon of citizenship, which carries significant influence. Identity and diversity are key to conceptualising global citizenship.

Identity must be seen as essentially contested and above all multi-layered. One of the greatest challenges facing democratic education is to accommodate diversity. (Tulby, 1995; Tourraine, 1998, 2000; Culhoun, 1999; cited by Delanty, 2000)

In Britain, for example, it is increasingly apparent that it is ethnically more diversely represented than before. For some, such changes in the face of Britain have been perceived as a cause for social angst: a burden on the economy, although economic theory and some studies may suggest otherwise:

...according to longitudinal data for individual workers in the UK – the British Household Panel Survey (BHPS) – average job security has actually improved since 1993... This result suggests that immigrants in the UK have largely been complements to rather than substitutes for native workers ... it appears that immigration has not eroded job security. (Giddens *et al*, 2006, p. 71)

Another claim is an increase in 'enclaves' of separate communities.[1] For others, however, it provides an enriching opportunity for language, cultural experiences and commerce. The expansion of the European Community, more trans-national exchanges for study and work and increasing numbers of immigrants has meant that cross cultural encounters are becoming more frequent and widespread across the European continent and in most places around the world.

There is a natural spillover of effects into education and these are also translated into the experiences gained in schools. How institutions, and I include schools here, approach the matter of diversity is extremely important. The consequences, undoubtedly, will determine future social contexts. Citizenship Education has become increasingly recognised as vital to curriculum development. For Britain, more specifically the National Curriculum for England and Wales, citizenship education has been identified as valuable for promoting community cohesion. Recognising its importance, the Department for Education and Skills in Britain set up the Diversity and Citizenship Review Group, in May 2006, and commissioned a research review on 'Diversity and Citizenship in the Curriculum'. In January 2007, the Diversity and Citizenship Review produced its findings (DFES, 2006) and made a key recommendation that schools in England and Wales, teaching Citizenship in secondary education should have a fourth strand introduced into the curriculum, giving emphasis to encourage an understanding of shared values. In addition to the existing three strands: Social and Moral Development, Community Involvement and Political Literacy a fourth would, thus, be included – Identity and Diversity. In response to the review's findings and recommendations, Britain's Secretary of State for Education, Alan Johnson, has said schools should, 'play a leading role in creating community cohesion' (quoted in BBC, 2007, 25 January). In the *Guardian*, a national broadsheet newspaper, he has been quoted to say:

> The values our children learn will shape the country Britain becomes. We are a nation built from and by people from other countries. We should celebrate our history and how it has created today's diversity, recognising the role played by immigrants in our success. (*Guardian*, January 26, 2007)

These recent developments and public recognition of government ministers is hugely significant to furthering the discourse. Although the value of recognition for diversity is immense there are still challenges to be faced. Not least, is the challenge to understand how to create a cohesive environment, with which citizens can identify; embracing shared values while holding onto their own uniqueness.

Identity, one aspect of citizenship, like the notion of unity and diversity has similar complex concerns. Identity is shaped by many factors: language, religion, culture or politics, to name some. The danger is, as Delanty puts it, 'citizenship has become refracted by the prism of identity' (Delanty, 2000). Perhaps troubling the canon is precisely what is needed to challenge, re-evaluate notions about citizenship and generate discussion about how to accommodate diversity. Educationalists are in a suitable position to provide the skills and space to review, what is deemed a predominantly western, canon of citizenship. In the twenty-first century a global conception of citizenship that is integrative, appreciative of differences but inclusive at the same time, can help alleviate potential conflicts caused by identity politics. The increasing influence, and transformative powers, of globalisation have led many to see this as creating an opportunity to, 'reconsider the meaning of citizenship' (Williams, 2003, p. 209) Reconceptualising global citizenship with reference to identity is something that is possible. Elsewhere, I have argued that Global/World Citizenship identity can be conceived in terms of a developmental construction of the self, conceptualised as integrated with others. (Golmohamad, 2004, p. 131)

Part of my contention is that education for global/international citizenship is at its best when it provides an environment that encourages listening to and engagement with varied perspectives, thereby enabling better understanding and respect for differences in a plural society. Another is that global, or international, citizenship has a transformative influence for challenging inequality and promoting justice by virtue of the fact that all are, a priori, citizens of the world, members of a single polity. The increasing argument for observing respect for human rights is a clear example, a definite beginning. This presents a moral imperative for citizens to be informed and act responsibly as stakeholders for the interests of the world as members who influence the delicate balance of the fragility of humanity.

Issues concerning diversity, unity and identity are certainly crucial and relevant to Global Citizenship. Generally speaking, there has been a gradual acceptance of the notion of 'global' in terms of the environment. In terms of Citizenship, however, the emphasis continues to be predominantly focused on local interest. Here, within the context of the global landscape, 'local interest' may refer to a national context. One such example would be the issue of Sudan's Dafur conflict and crimes against humanity. Immediately, such 'local' conflicts transfer themselves to the global arena, making a significant impact on the conscience of the rest of the world. There has been a gradual understanding and acceptance of the slogan, 'think global and act local' with respect to the environment, for example. It is, therefore, increasingly acknowledged that it is in the local interest to think globally. Continuing with global themes of concern, then, it follows that there has been a growing intolerance to injustices to humanity. Perhaps this is precisely because the single global polity of humanity transcends national boundaries. Consequently an international event or conflict affects us locally as an intolerable act because value is given to human life. There are all too numerous examples in our recent history of times when human response to human crises has been demonstrated with compelling force. The suggestion, here, is that implicit to Global Citizenship is a positive identification with a common humanity. Perhaps this is an issue, which education for global citizenship needs to bring the forefront of 'reconsidering the meaning of citizenship', reinforcing the notion to which Melissa Williams (2003) refers as a 'community of shared fate'. As citizens of the world we then have an invested moral interest to and, 'motivation to ameliorate that fate. This is enough to give some purchase to the idea of having respect for ones citizens, as a notion that is not simply equivalent to respect for persons' (Haydon, 2006).

Likewise, citizenship education, or education for global citizenship for that matter, is, I would argue, about cultivating an integrative attitude as much as it is about learning about the systemic mechanisms that safeguard society. Community cohesion, in a global sense, is multifarious, dynamic and complex. Above all it is multi-layered, at the centre of which lies the individual. The layers are best described as concentric circles with a graduation extending from the individual at the centre to a wider community. This describes a fluid movement of a reciprocal relationship. (Nussbaum, 1997) This cosmopolitan view resonates with ancient philosophy and some world religions. If attitudes can be encouraged to think in an expansive way, then individual responsibility for action and accommodating diversity in a community is, hopefully, more informed and accepting of difference. An integrative attitude, then, is one where, over time, the individual no longer projects their own aspirations or prejudices on others but, rather, can see, 'segregation first and foremost starts in the mind'.[1] If this is acknowledged then, '...the question is whether there is an easy way to get neighbours who may think the same, but not know it, to stop treating each other differently' (ibid). It is more than just good behaviour towards others. An integrative attitude toward others suggests greater empathy with others and a form of altruism (Danesh, 1997).

Developing a mindset implies the need for education, which is crucial to the project of reconsidering the meaning of citizenship and integration. An expansive vision offered with education for global citizenship incorporates a process that, over time, can help unlock closed attitudes and feelings towards others. It's only when individuals are allowed to encounter differences that they can then consider what distinguishes unity and diversity.

Education for Global Citizenship enables individual citizens to acquire skills and encounter experiences that: promote, explore, examine, synthesise and evaluate meaning about individual lives and societal contexts, trans-nationally and cross-culturally. Global Citizenship, therefore, provides a space to critically engage with others and the world. Provided that there is a suitable learning environment appropriated, students can successfully consult and learn what is distinct and what is common between them and the rest of the world. Such experiences are valuable to individual and collective learning. This approach allows for students to encounter social, cultural, religious and political differences in a supportive and safe environment. Furthermore, it provides for students to learn more explicitly about how to philosophically and practically engage with questions of value. Students need to be able to question, examine and evaluate what democracy is, what justice means, for example.

> ... human beings are value makers and value choosers, and that questions of value and ethics are, to a greater or lesser extent, relevant to all our experiences and interactions.' (Hatcher, 2002, p. 7)

As value makers and choosers, we ought to be able to consider and so be provided with opportunities to reflect upon questions of value. Likewise it seems relevant and important to reflect upon the narrative heritage: socio-historical, religious, political or otherwise to present the various perspectives of values. In this way citizens are able to make informed judgements. William Dustin (1997) presents a general model for constructing meaning in order to be able to conceptualise future European citizenship. His model incorporates both hermeneutic and homeostatic dimensions. It offers a valuable insight to considering how to interpret citizenship from a cultural history and construct meaning for possible alternative futures of world citizenship for individuals and communities.

It seems reasonable to suggest, therefore, that citizens be able to gauge how to interpret from particular cultural histories and heritages and imagine how to construct future narratives. This is where subjects such as history, religious studies, cultures or civilisation studies, for example, are important in light of their position to the world, contextualising different narratives of the world and studying their relationships. Collectively, what is passed on, from past and present generations, is valuable to form an overview of how 'neighbours' may think and strive to find a way to bridge across differences.

Another way to consider this is to be reminded of the Buddhist parable, the Indian legend of the blind men and the elephant. Each blind man is asked to describe what he considers to be the elephant as they are each presented with a part of the animal. But their individual descriptions only reveal a partial reality. Each, in turn, disputes with the other what is understood to be the elephant. It is not until they relinquish attachment to the particular perspective as the truth that they can extrapolate the reality of the elephant in full. Together, the particular perspectives allow a fuller image and a more comprehensive understanding to emerge. This is one approach to understanding others and appreciating different perspectives in the hope to achieve some synthesis of meaning.

The value of Unity in Diversity is that differences are not a means to segregation from one's neighbour. Rather, unity in diversity is about human sustainability, engaging with a process to promote social justice.

> Balancing unity and diversity is an on-going challenge for multi-cultural nation-states. Citizenship education can help to accomplish this goal .... Unity may be achieved at the expense of diversity. Unity without diversity results in hegemony and oppression, and diversity without unity leads to Balkanization and the fracturing of the commonwealth that alone secures human rights, equality and justice. (Banks, 2004)

How can education for global citizenship take on this challenge? This is a question that will be addressed in the next section.

EDUCATION FOR GLOBAL CITIZENSHIP

Martha Nussbaum (1997) sees education's primary role as preparing citizens for a democracy. She describes three core capacities essential for the cultivation of humanity, 'a classical ideal of the world citizen' and one, which she subscribes to of a liberal education: critical self-examination, the ideal of a world citizen, and the development of the narrative imagination.

'Self examination' follows the Socratic principle of living an 'examined life', where citizens or individuals do not accept blindly beliefs or ideas handed down to them. In order to cultivate their humanity citizens, therefore, need to, 'see themselves not simply as citizens of some local region or group but also, and above all, as human beings bound to all other human beings by ties of recognition and concern' (1997, p. 10). Global Citizenship need not remain in the abstract domain of our imagination. Nussbaum illustrates the narrative imagination as:

> the ability to think what it might be like to be in the shoes of a person different from oneself, to be an intelligent reader of that person's story, and to understand the emotions and wishes and desires that someone so placed might have. (1997, p. 11)

525

What I have tried to suggest is that education for global citizenship is about developing a mindset or attitude; about learning how to understand and engage with others in mutual respect. But it is not only concerned with toleration of difference. It also needs to provide an openness to encourage working collaboratively and cooperatively for a common good, a collective interest, based on egalitarian principles, which individuals inevitably stand to gain from. This aims to describe a consultative, participatory democracy from the grass roots. Effectively, to reconsider the meaning of citizenship also requires, by implication, reconsidering the role of the individual and society.

> ... citizens in a democratic society work for the betterment of the whole society, and not just for the rights of their particular racial, social, or cultural group... becoming citizen is a process. Education must play an important role in facilitating the development of civic consciousness and agency within students .... (Gonçalves e Silva, 2004)

It is against the backdrop of working for the *betterment of the whole society*, developing *civic consciousness* where education for global citizenship has an important role. The role of education for global citizenship, then, can be described as having a twofold purpose. First, is to cultivate an integrative mindset, offering encounters with diverse people and settings where possible. The second purpose is to channel knowledge and experience gained to some purposeful contribution, encouraging choices of vocations or careers and acts of service where it is possible to work for the betterment of the whole society.

> If we want to train human beings to participate in the construction of a better world it is important to emphasise the service aspect...People are resources. Development requires participation. People can take charge of their own development with proper education... Human beings have a noble, spiritual aspect. The role of education and development is to bring out those potentialities. (Dr Arbab Correa, representative of the Baha'i Development Foundation for the Application and Teaching of the Sciences (FUNDAEC))

Examples of young people taking a year out before starting a degree course at university, to travel, learn from new experiences and people and offer service, may be considered one appropriate response to this challenge. Another may be to provide an opportunity, offering a diverse group of people the experience to interact, explore: questions of value, global issues, physical encounters with varied environments, stimuli and discuss how they may creatively engage with such concerns to constructing a better sustainable environment, in its widest sense, for the whole of society.

This last proposition for an enriched programme of study, to experience diverse perspectives as well as think and act as global citizens, leads me to discuss The College for International Citizenship. This is a formidable project, which commenced in 2004, a unique collaboration of higher education institutions and local government in Birmingham, England. The college is designed to bring together international students to experience and engage in an interactive academic programme aimed at introducing international issues affecting global society. This is effectively done with the objective to hopefully equip students with essential and appropriate knowledge, skills and commitment to become active citizens of the world. As active international citizens, students are engaged in multiple ways, developing identifications with multiple associations and attachments. In this way, they are encouraged to think of interpersonal development, both within and beyond the course; as well as learn from the varied perspectives from around the world through interaction with their peers. All this is future directed, extending to how each may view what they gain from their experience at the college to implement concrete personal projects in their own national contexts. Thus, helping with national and international development with an integrative understanding. Ultimately, the programme of study works towards the gradual realisation of enabling world citizens to become valuable resources for constructing a better world through local engagement but with an integrative attitude with global consideration.

Students are involved in an intensive ten-week programme, graduating upon completion of the full course requirements. Repeatedly, students represent a wide spectrum of ages, nationalities, cultures, beliefs and personal experiences. In fact one could precede each of the previous terms with the prefix 'inter' and it would be an accurate description without exaggeration. Already, before beginning, the introduction to the course by its nature and representation the experience is distinct. For some, to have arrived is, itself quite an achievement. Whether it is because of little funds and need for sponsorship, or to satisfy visiting visa requirements students so far have managed to travel from many distant countries: Ethiopia, South Africa, Japan, India, Armenia, Turkey, Tibetan refugees in India, and Cameroon to name a few. Along with some British students there have also been other countries represented by British refugees and asylum seekers resident in Britain, but too numerous to list. Nevertheless, the point here is the emphasis given to the intake of students, which is to give an international experience and the representation of students certainly supports this motive. Tutors, too, are drawn from international backgrounds and experiences.

Pedagogically, the course is designed to provide interactive engagement, through discussions, group activities, 'with students fundamentally involved in the academic process' (College for International Citizenship, n.d.). They are provided with a rich local experience, learning more about the systemic structures and diversity of the local community of Birmingham and Britain, through formal and informal learning, making interesting comparisons with their own contexts. Another valuable and indispensable pedagogical tool is the use of a personal reflective journal, which is referred to during the course by each of the tutors with relevant dedicated questions to reflect upon. This provides an individualised dimension in addition to the content of the course delivered, through personal reflection, with feedback and further dialogue and conversation between each tutor and student.

There is more than one form of assessment for the course. The assessments are formally referred to as 'in-service learning' and a 'community development project plan', which relates to the students own community. These additional components of the course further enrich the student experience, contributing to local and national communities informed by expansive concerns. Student participation in the in-service learning is located in a Birmingham organisation in either the public or private sector. In-service learning is arranged as a 'work-based learning opportunity', which 'runs parallel to the core course'. As a piece of research, this task is carried out in pairs, not necessarily with the student's choice of partner. The research is a short-term arrangement: appropriated with the aid of interviews and/or questionnaires, spending a total of three hours in the organisation, examining its organisation and operation in view of international issues. This extends learning outside the classroom and gives concrete experiences of field work, related to, individual interests where possible, and particularly to aspects of study relating to the academic content of the course. For example, students may consider how conflict may be handled within the environment of the placement and the effectiveness of the strategies and policies in place. It does provide a service for both the student, who is familiarised with the policy and practice of the placement, and the host service provider, as students are required to complete a report of the experience. The report is written objectively and, upon approval, a copy of the report is provided for the host service provider and the experience shared with other students by way of formal presentation in the final 'transition' week of the course.

Briefly, the outline of the course is dedicated to the following subject areas:
- Leadership Skills
- Citizenship
- Political Systems
- Rights and Responsibilities
- International Trade and Economic Systems
- Education and National Development
- Environmental Change and Sustainability
- Peace, Violence and Conflict
- Local Influence to Global Citizenship
- Transition Week

My involvement focuses on two of the ten weeks from the core curriculum, namely: 'Citizenship' and 'Education and National Development'. For the purpose of this chapter I will focus on one of the modules taught, Citizenship. The delivery of a module on citizenship inevitably is best served by incorporating a multi-disciplinary approach and is sympathetic to a Socratic method. Questions of value are pertinent to individual citizens as 'value makers' and 'value choosers' and to realise the relationship citizens have to themselves and others, not to mention the state and world community; the subject is introduced by way of posing a question. The question is to ask who and what is meaningful to each student, in relation to them. The point is to engage students to take on the first capacity as described by Nussbaum, to self examine. The first task I present is one, which relates to attachment theory. Without describing the theories for attachment, suffice to say that this approach provides an invaluable tool, from a developmental perspective, to introduce the notion that encounters with others, from early on, help us to develop our orientation in the world. Thereby, our points of reference and values have evolved through others, initially with our parents or carers from early childhood through to our peers in adolescence and later our varied encounters in adulthood. What is important is to examine how we have accepted those values and what we identify as fundamental for citizens to flourish in a world community.

With this in mind, each student is presented with a diagram of three concentric circles. They are each asked to locate themselves at the centre and position others in proximity of distance to themselves depending on the relationship. The same exercise is carried out in the same way, this time positioning the values they hold to in proximity to themselves. This exercise provides a good point for discussion. The students exchange and compare their notes, often finding there are common areas by way of persons and/or values important to them. Usually, there is, identifiably, a common pattern of growth. Our strongest attachments are formed with those who we love and who we have experienced the most, usually. Over time, our circles of associations are extended with others and our concerns likewise may also increase. We often respond or react more significantly to those who are closest to us, or the values we identify strongly with. Comparing diagrams often reveals there are fundamental values, which can be agreed upon, values such as honesty, integrity are often mentioned. Perhaps this appears obvious and ones which cannot be argued against. But this is a positive beginning nonetheless, to discover some obvious truths of what we hold important. Effectively, what is agreed upon is how the self is an integral socio-moral construction of multiplicity, of people and values.

Students are challenged to work in groups and design a visual interpretation of how citizenship should be represented. This requires skills of communication, understanding and interpretation. Given the intercultural differences students, interestingly, rise to the challenge and are able to arrive with agreement on what they see as ideal citizenship. Some examples have depicted organic representations, using a diagram of a tree, or pineapple for example. While others have been very structured by way of illustrating a wall with foundations and bricks as representations of aspects identified by their group as important to conceiving citizenship. These are presented to the rest of the group and each presentation is evaluated through constructive enquiries and examination. Interestingly the use of metaphoric interpretations demands skill and thought to consider the implications for envisaging world citizenship. Here, the second capacity Nussbaum identifies, the ideal of world citizenship, is applied. Looking to the conceptualisation made by students for the ideal, it is interesting how discussions prove insightful. As in the example of a wall, for example, it needs to be secure with strong foundations and so on. Interestingly, a pineapple, if cultivated in the right environment with appropriate conditions and care can be propagated and so can flourish giving further fruit and making a sustainable crop. These illustrations remain as reference points for the remainder of the week and as the week progress the conceptions are revisited and reviewed.

Individual narratives are also shared and particular contextual representations of citizenship are presented and discussed. This occasion can be paralleled with development of the narrative imagination. It certainly develops mutual respect between students. Alternative narratives about contemporary issues from the media are also studied and discussed in light of the implications for citizenship.

Students are directed to consider past philosophical traditions and alternative models for citizenship. One such alternative draws from a psychological approach to understanding relationships. In this way, they are then encouraged to pursue what makes a healthy relationship and how healthy relationships flourish. There is similarity to be drawn from Dustin's model where alternative futures are sought from interpretations made with reference to individuals and the community.

Danesh's approach is a valuable resource. His thesis applies not only as an account for examining how interpersonal relationships develop, but also how systems of power, individuals and society, likewise, may flourish applying the same account. Although it is not possible to give a detailed account for the purposes of this chapter, it is important to stress how Danesh advocates an integrative model as desirable for healthy relationships of different kinds. An integrative model orientates towards growth and provides an encouraging environment. It promotes a worldview where individuals learn to accept difference but work through common human powers and main human concerns, as Danesh describes, to increase understanding and unity through those shared concerns. It is democratic developmental model incorporating a consultative approach to decision making. Each person in the relationship, whether experiencing the relationship in a personal, professional or institutional capacity, is valued equally and engages in a mutual common ground of interest.

Through the study of how relationships form and the processes involved in sustaining those relationships, an alternative approach to understanding how individuals may discover a mutual interest for the classical view of world citizenship as cultivating humanity emerges.[2]

CONCLUSION

Looking extensively at these various ways of interpreting citizenship helps to examine contemporary issues such as: population migration, immigration, and the balkanization of states, citizenship as status, values and beliefs, identity, participation, rights and duties (Delanty, 2000). Students are engaging in multifarious ways and able to critically evaluate, drawing conclusions and interpreting new ways to reconsider citizenship, giving consideration to their individual roles to help realise it.

The weeks' work is theoretically demanding but very engaging, as is commented upon from the feedback received and the enthusiasm expressed. The practical engagement is important to mention again, always orientating to finding meaning and possible alternative future conceptualisation of a subject that offers so much, cutting across many aspects if not all aspects of the curriculum.

Nussbaum describes world citizenship requiring:

… the would be world citizen to become a sensitive and empathic interpreter …

She continues that

… Education at all ages should cultivate the capacity for such interpreting.
(1997, p. 63)

A very pertinent quote from Ross Poole, cited by Hatcher, describes very vividly
what is carried out when we embark on the weeks' study of global citizenship.

… We are like archeologists trying to discover the plan of a city hidden
beneath the rubble of history. Our good is the pre-established unity of our
life; our task is to find out what it is and to live it ….

Alternatively, Poole describes another image if we are not disposed to the idea of
excavating like archeologists. This describes the life more:

… like artists attempting to bring into existence something which has never
existed before. When we find our good it will not be a discovery, but a
creation. (Poole, 1991, pp. 149–150, cited in Hatcher 1998, p. xvi)

If individuals are able to identify with a global concept then they are more ready to
take on the responsibilities that come with the territory, considering the
consequences and value of individual effort.

Current global concerns for the environment, poverty, conflict, and social
disaffectedness have raised awareness and citizenship education can allow citizens
to believe that they have a part to play in offering, what Paulo Freire describes as
'critical hope'. Global Citizenship cannot be bound by *jus de sanguis* (that
nationality is the same as one's natural parents) or *jus de soli* (that nationality is
determined by place of birth) as national citizenship has been traditionally and
legally defined. Neither can it be a status conferred to an individual by a particular
state. It has to be conceived of as a right, a moral imperative, to belong to a global
polity and a world community, alongside having local and national affiliations, as
we are all citizens in a community of shared fate.

What is recognisably distinct about the College for International Citizenship
experience is that, during the course of the ten weeks, veils of ignorance are
removed. Such veils are usually positioned in our imagination because of some
previous mistaken preconceived judgments passed on. Strangely wonderful is the
time when an Armenian and Turkish student, adversaries under any other
circumstances, grew to become good friends. These encounters provide individual
citizens with the opportunity to discover what they hold common with others and
how to value the distinct differences with mutual respect.

Our course of study travels a great territory. I have sympathy for the notion, and
use the example presented by Poole, of excavating for a good life and discovering
the hidden cities from history. But in so doing, along the way, I do feel that
additionally, and most significantly, many hidden cities are discovered in the hearts
and minds of students. Collaboratively, we find the hidden strengths and qualities

531

to encourage in each other, which contribute to forging longstanding friendships. I can attest to this as students still correspond with each other. They are living proof of lives transformed. Some have changed the course of their careers as a result. Others have furthered their education by going on to university to pursue an academic course. Others still have initiated local projects that have made a significant difference to the community.

Finally, what I hope this chapter has shown is that Global Citizenship Education can be successfully experienced in a learning environment. Sympathetic to the complex dynamics but not insurmountable, education for global citizenship offers an enriching study. It provides personal encounters with varied interactions. The example of the College for International Citizenship demonstrates active international understanding with local engagement. Significant to its success is the appreciation of the value of the individual and what potential can be discovered if allowed to creatively explore, examine and synthesise new meanings. It's the openness to new encounters, incorporating creative and multi-disciplinary approaches which ensures that understanding is achieved through mutual appreciation and respect for differences. All this is with the aim to find a common ground of unity. In the hope that education will cultivate capacities, thus providing an overview of a reality discovered through shared perspectives; world citizens who can become 'sympathetic, empathic interpreters' with integrative attitudes to themselves and others. As world citizens, thus, it's hoped that such examples will help balance the challenge of unity in diversity with conscious citizens working for the betterment of the whole society not forgetting to give emphasis to the aspect of service.

NOTES

[1] Trevor Phillips, head of the Commission for Racial Equality, recently argued that the nation is becoming more divided by race and religion, with young people being brought up in enclaves. See this BBC news story, by Dominic Casciani, 22 September 2005, for details: http://news.bbc. co.uk/1/hi/uk/4270010.stm

[2] For a more detailed description of Danesh's thesis look to publications by Danesh and the earlier mentioned article published by Golmohamad on the notion of the integrated self.

REFERENCES

Banks, J. (Ed.) (2004). *Diversity and citizenship education: Global perspectives*. San Francisco: Jossey-Bass.

Baha'i International Community (1993). *World citizenship: A global ethic for sustainable development*. A statement by the Bahá'í International Community to the 4th Pacific Islands Leaders Conference, based on a concept paper by the same name presented to the 1st session of the United Nations Commission on Sustainable Development, 14 June 1993 Retrieved 25 September, 2007, from http://www.bic-un.bahai.org/93-0624.htm.

BBC (2007, 22 January) Schools 'must teach Britishness'. Retrieved 25 September, 2007, from http://news.bbc.co.uk/1/hi/education/6294643.stm.

College for International Citizenship (n.d.). *What is the CIC?* Retrieved 25 September, 2007, from http://www.cfic.org.uk/main.php?section=4.

Danesh, H. (1997). *Psychology of spirituality*. Victoria, Canada: Paradigm Publishing.

Delanty, G. (2000). *Citizenship in a global age*. Milton Keynes: Open University Press.

DFES (2006). *Diversity and citizenship: Curriculum review*. London: DFES.

Dustin, W. (1999). *Towards an ethic of citizenship: Creating a culture of democracy for the twenty-first century*. Excel Press.

Giddens, A., Diamond, P. & Liddle, R. (Eds.) (2006). *Global Europe, social Europe*. Cambridge: Polity Press.

Golmohamad, M. (2004). World citizenship, identity and the notion of an integrated self. *Studies in Philosophy and Education, 23*, 131–148.

Gonçalves e Silva, P.B. (2004). Citizenship education in Brazil: The contributions of Indian Peoples and Blacks in the struggle for citizenship. In J.A. Banks (Ed.), *Diversity and citizenship education: Global perspectives* (pp. 185–217). San Francisco: Jossey-Bass.

Gushiken, L. (n.d.). *Challenges of the construction of a new morality*. Retrieved 25 September, 2007, from http://bahai-library.org/talks/construction.html.

Haydon, G. (2006). Respect of persons and for cultures as a basis for national and global citizenship. *Journal of Moral Education, 35*(4), 457–471.

Hatcher, W (2002). *Love, power and justice: The dynamics of authentic morality*. Baha'i Publishing Trust, US.

Nussbaum (1997). *Cultivating humanity*. Cambridge, MA: Harvard University Press.

O'Byrne (2003). *The dimensions of global citizenship: Political identity beyond the nation-state*. London: Frank Cass.

Richardson, G.H & Blades, D.W (Eds.) (2006). *Troubling the canon of citizenship education*. New York: Peter Lang.

Williams, M (2003). Citizenship as identity, citizenship as shared fate, and the functions of multicultural education. In K. McDonough & W. Feinberg (Eds.), *Citizenship and education in liberal-democratic societies: Teaching for cosmopolitan values and collective identities*. Oxford: Oxford University Press.

Muna Golmohamad
University of London, UK

Printed in the United Kingdom
by Lightning Source UK Ltd.
126974UK00001B/7-24/A

9 789087 903732